# LANGUAGE AND THE CREATIVE MIND

# LANGUAGE
# AND THE
# CREATIVE MIND

*edited by*

MIKE BORKENT, BARBARA DANCYGIER,
and JENNIFER HINNELL

CSLI
PUBLICATIONS
Center for the Study of
Language and Information
Stanford, California

Center for the Study of Language and Information
Leland Stanford Junior University
Printed in the United States
17 16 15 14 13 1 2 3 4 5

ISBN 978-1-57586-671-0 (cloth : alk. paper) –
ISBN 978-1-57586-670-3 (pbk. : alk. paper)
ISBN 978-1-57586-672-7 (electronic)

∞ The acid-free paper used in this book meets the minimum requirements of the American National Standard for Information Sciences—Permanence of Paper for Printed Library Materials, ANSI Z39.48-1984.

CSLI was founded in 1983 by researchers from Stanford University, SRI International, and Xerox PARC to further the research and development of integrated theories of language, information, and computation. CSLI headquarters and CSLI Publications are located on the campus of Stanford University.

CSLI Publications reports new developments in the study of language, information, and computation. Please visit our web site at
http://cslipublications.stanford.edu/
for comments on this and other titles, as well as for changes and corrections by the author and publisher.

# Contents

# Acknowledgments

In organizing the 11th biennial CSDL conference in Vancouver in 2012, and in editing this volume, we have sought to promote new directions and further connections across cognitive linguistic research. The results presented at the conference and in this volume could not have been accomplished without the support and participation of many.

We would like to thank the participants of the conference for making it a vibrant and exciting event. We had high hopes that the theme would generate interesting discussions, and all of the participants helped to make the dialogue productive and informative. Our thanks to the authors for taking up the task of further developing and sharing their stimulating research in this volume, including working very hard to meet our goal of publishing in 2013. We are grateful as well to our reviewers for their generosity in helping further refine the quality of this volume. We are also grateful to Emma Pease and the other staff at CSLI Publications at Stanford for the editing assistance as well as their ongoing support of the CSDL series.

Finally, we would like to express our thanks and indebtedness to our families, friends and colleagues, whose generous patience and support allowed us to organize the conference and to develop this volume.

# Contributors

MIKE BORKENT: Department of English, University of British Columbia, Vancouver, BC, V6T 1Z1, Canada.
mborkent@gmail.com

BROOKE O. BREAUX: Department of Psychology, University of Louisiana at Lafayette, Lafayette, Louisiana, 70504, USA.
bfo1493@louisiana.edu

DANIEL CASASANTO: Department of Psychology, University of Chicago, Chicago, IL, 60637, USA.
casasanto@alum.mit.edu

KENNY K. N. CHOW: School of Design, The Hong Kong Polytechnic University, Hong Kong, China.
sdknchow@polyu.edu.hk

NATHANIEL CLARK: Department of Psychology, UC Santa Cruz, Santa Cruz, CA, 94536, USA.
nbclark@ucsc.edu

BARBARA DANCYGIER: Department of English, University of British Columbia, Vancouver, BC, V6T 1Z1, Canada.
barbara.dancygier@ubc.ca

MARK DEGGAN: Co-ordinated Arts Program, University of British Columbia, Vancouver, BC, V6T 1Z2, Canada.
mark.deggan@ubc.ca

DAVID DELIEMA: Department of Education, University of California Los Angeles, Los Angeles, CA, 90095, USA.
david.deliema@gmail.com

PATRICK J. DUFFLEY: Département de langues, linguistique et traduction, Université Laval, Québec, G1V 0A6, Canada.
patrick.duffley@lli.ulaval.ca

LAUREL FAIS: Department of Psychology, University of British Columbia, Vancouver, BC, V6T 1Z4, Canada.
lfais@psych.ubc.ca

MARLENE JOHANSSON FALCK: Department of Language Studies, Umeå Universitet, Umeå, SE-901 87, Sweden.
marlene.johansson.falck@engelska.umu.se

MICHELE FEIST: Department of English, University of Louisiana at Lafayette, Lafayette, LA, 70504, USA.
feist@louisiana.edu

SEIKO FUJII: Department of Language and Information Sciences, The University of Tokyo, Tokyo, 153-8902, Japan.
sfujii@boz.c.u-tokyo.ac.jp

CHRISTINA GALEANO: Department of Linguistics, Simon Fraser University, Burnaby, BC, V5A 1S6, Canada.
cgaleano@sfu.ca

D. FOX HARRELL: Comparative Media Studies Program & Computer Science and Artificial Intelligence Laboratory, Massachusetts Institute of Technology, Cambridge, MA, 02139, USA.
fox.harrell@mit.edu

JENNIFER HINNELL: Department of Linguistics, University of Alberta, Edmonton, Alberta, T6G 2E7, Canada.
hinnell@ualberta.ca

JISUP HONG: International Computer Science Institute, Berkeley, CA, 94704, USA.
jhong@icsi.berkeley.edu

MITSUKO NARITA IZUTSU: Department of English Language and Culture, Fuji Women's University, Sapporo, 001-0016, Japan.
mizutsu@fujijoshi.ac.jp

KATSUNOBU IZUTSU: Hokkaido University of Education, Asahikawa, 070-0825, Japan.
idutsu@gmail.com

TAKESHI KOGUMA: Faculty of Education and Culture, University of Miyazaki, Miyazaki, 8892192, Japan.
kogumat@gmail.com

SILVA LADEWIG: Department of Cultural and Social Studies, European University Viadrina, Frankfurt (Oder), 15320, Germany.
mail@silvaladewig.de

RONALD W. LANGACKER: Department of Linguistics, University of California, San Diego, La Jolla, CA, 92093-0108, USA.
rlangacker@ucsd.edu

TEENIE MATLOCK: Cognitive and Information Sciences Department, University of California, Merced, Merced, CA, 95343, USA.
tmatlock@ucmerced.edu

WILLIAM H. MCKELLIN: Department of Anthropology, University of British Columbia, Vancouver, BC, V6T1Z1, Canada.
mcke@mail.ubc.ca

IRENE MITTELBERG: Human Technology Centre, RWTH Aachen University, Aix-la-Chapelle, 52070, Germany.
mittelberg@humtec.rwth-aachen.de

CAROL LYNN MODER: Department of English, Oklahoma State University, Stillwater, OK, 74078, USA.
carol.moder@okstate.edu

CORNELIA MÜLLER: Department of Cultural Studies, European University Viadrina, Frankfurt (Oder), 15230, Germany.
cmueller@europa-uni.de

MARCUS PERLMAN: Department of Cognitive and Information Sciences, University of California, Merced, Merced, CA, 95343, USA.
mperlman@ucmerced.edu

PAULA RADETZKY: Kamusi Project International, Renens, CH-1020, Switzerland.
paula.radetzky@gmail.com

RENA SHARON: School of Music, University of British Columbia, Vancouver, BC, V6T 1Z2, Canada.
nareana@mail.ubc.ca

FRANCIS F. STEEN: Department of Communication Studies, University of California, Los Angeles, Los Angeles, CA, 90095, USA.
steen@commstds.ucla.edu

PETER STOCKWELL: School of English, University of Nottingham, Nottingham, NG7 2RD, United Kingdom.
peter.stockwell@nottingham.ac.uk

EVE SWEETSER: Department of Linguistics, University of California, Berkeley, Berkeley, CA, 94720-2650, USA.
sweetser@berkeley.edu

VERA TOBIN: Department of Cognitive Science, Case Western Reserve University, Cleveland, OH, 44106, USA.
vera.tobin@case.edu

MARK TURNER: Department of Cognitive Science, Case Western Reserve University, Cleveland, OH, 44016, USA.
mark.turner@case.edu

ERIC VATIKIOTIS-BATESON: Department of Linguistics and Cognitive Systems Program, University of British Columbia, Vancouver, BC, V6T 1Z4, Canada.
Eric.Vatikiotis-Bateson@ubc.ca

BODO WINTER: Cognitive and Information Sciences, University of California, Merced, Merced, CA, 95340, USA.
bodo@bodowinter.com

# 'Language and the Creative Mind': New Directions in Cognitive Linguistics

MIKE BORKENT, BARBARA DANCYGIER, AND JENNIFER HINNELL

This volume appears as the next installment in the CSLI series of edited volumes on cognitive and functional linguistics, *Conceptual Structure, Discourse and Language* (CSDL). The name of the series reflects the theme of the first conference, held in 1994 at the University of California, San Diego, and the title of the first volume, edited by Adele Goldberg (1996). It is now also the name of the North American organization of cognitive and functional linguists—one of the national affiliate organizations of the International Cognitive Linguistics Association. In this volume, we present selected papers from the 11th biennial CSDL conference, held in Vancouver, Canada, on May 17–20, 2012.

Over the years, the conferences have reflected various emerging themes and research methods, following the developments in cognitive grammar, construction grammar, frame semantics, metaphor theory, blending theory, the rise of experimental methods, the study of situated cognition, embodiment, gesture, and many other research interests. For the most part, the work presented in the volumes has focused on the analysis of language and its cognitive underpinnings, but the study of cultural artifacts and the role of the human body began to figure more and more prominently in the selections presented in subsequent volumes.

In the time that has passed since the first conference in 1994, cognitive linguistics has developed not only in its theoretical sophistication, but also in its range of disciplinary and interdisciplinary interests. While focusing on the mechanisms of meaning emergence in linguistic contexts, the discipline

*Language and the Creative Mind.*
Mike Borkent, Barbara Dancygier, and Jennifer Hinnell (eds).

has demonstrated to researchers in other areas of study that its methodology is suitable to other arenas in which meaning construction is the focus. In a sense, it has become clear that the cognitive pathways of meaning construction described in the context of language use might be, to a large degree, the same pathways that our minds follow in processing visual artifacts, performative events, literary texts, and so on.

The explanatory and descriptive power of cognitive linguistic theories has helped promote new developments in linguistics and in other disciplines. There seem to be several ways in which the explanatory potential has been explored in various contexts. Most conspicuously, the close interaction between the study of language and the study of co-speech gesture has opened the door to a more structured view of linguistic communication as more appropriately described in terms of 'multimodal communication' (e.g. Forceville and Urios-Aparisi 2009; Müller et al. 2013). Also, researchers in stylistics, poetics, and semiotics (closely related disciplines, though many scholars insist on the importance of their dividing lines) have been looking for cognitive explanations of the extraordinary variety of meanings that emerge in the processing of literary texts (e.g. Stockwell 2009). Finally, disciplines interested in various forms of art (visual art, music, dance, and theatre) have found inspiration in the refreshed understanding of the connection between formal choices (embodied, visual, or auditory) and the potential for meaningful and emotionally fulfilling engagement of the listeners or viewers (e.g. Veale, Feyaerts, and Forceville 2013).

All of these areas of meaning emergence reflect the flexibility of the human mind, the body, and language; they capture the innovative and creative ways of expressing meaning. This seems to be the new power of the theories of language and cognition that the CSDL participants, presenters and authors have tapped into over the years.

For the 11$^{th}$ conference in Vancouver we thus chose a new theme: 'Language and the Creative Mind'. We wanted to see what an open invitation to reach beyond the traditional limits of cognitive linguistic enquiry would bring to the attention of both linguists and the representatives of the very-tentatively-related disciplines. The response we received through the papers that were presented at the conference and submitted to this volume helped us see the newly emerging understanding of the concept of 'creativity'. Rather than confirm the unpredictable, open-ended, and inscrutable nature of what creativity is often taken to represent, the facts presented suggest that new communicative forms and new meanings emerge in the innovative but fully cohesive manipulation of embodied concepts, along the paths established by familiar and predictable forms.

The analogy we can rely on here is that of the distinction between literal and figurative language. The distinction was a cornerstone of traditional work in linguistics. Meanings, it was claimed, are classical categories neatly packaged into convenient forms called words, and combined into more complex structures via rules. But since the emergence of metaphor theory and frame semantics, it has become clear that new meanings arise through trimming, expanding, projecting, or otherwise manipulating complex meaning structures in ways that serve new communicative needs. In their study of the nature of figurative language, Dancygier and Sweetser (2014) argue that figurative meanings emerge as a result of the manipulation of pre-existing frames, at appropriate levels of conceptual schematicity. We can talk about a number of such manipulation mechanisms (metaphor, simile, blending, irony, etc.), but we should also include the role some grammatical constructions play in the emergence of figurative meanings, as well as explain the influence of conceptual viewpoint on the nature of the manipulation. These observations refer primarily to the use of lexical and grammatical forms of language use, but there is no reason, in principle, that such considerations should not be extended to other areas of meaning emergence. In the course of the conference and in preparing this volume we have found various types of evidence supporting these ideas. However, as papers in this volume also demonstrate, cross-modal communication further complicates our understanding of creativity.

The papers gathered here have been grouped to reflect various aspects of the interaction between the body, language and cognition; they also represent various communicative modalities. The first section, *Creativity versus Conventionality*, brings together papers exploring various contexts in which forms of figurative thought are studied in connection to the emergence of more conventional forms of expression. Casasanto's paper begins the exploration, examining the role that language plays in the development of different kinds of metaphorical mappings, and reveals important processes that lead to the emerging mental models being either language-specific or universal. Feist and Breaux look at experimental data to argue that language users retain psychologically real connections between polysemous (literal versus metaphorical) uses of prepositions in English. In a similar vein, Duffley looks at constraints on creativity in idiomatic expressions, using a corpus to examine instances where speakers stretch the commonly understood bounds of the idiom. The examples analyzed show clearly that creativity can easily build on conventionality, as long as the idiom preserves some 'cognitive reality' of a scene; the meanings of idioms may be 'dormant', but can be easily awakened. A case for mappings of yet another kind—namely between mathematical concepts and spatial thinking—is made in Winter and Matlock, who find that mathematics uses conceptual structure from physical experiences (a theme we will come back to) in performing simple arithmetic. These papers all examine 'creativity' in the domain of metaphors in language use and reveal complex relations between areas of usage.

The next section, *Constructions and Frames*, offers several papers interested more centrally in formal aspects of linguistic expression—developing their explanations in frameworks such as cognitive grammar, construction grammar, or frame semantics. Langacker continues his work on nominal expressions by offering a detailed analysis of indefinite grounding and complex quantifiers: the semantic import of the 'a' in 'a little'. Isutzu and Isutzu examine grammaticalization pathways—precisely, what kind of process accounts for the final particle development in typologically different languages (English and Japanese). In an analysis drawing from both Cognitive Grammar and Mental Spaces Theory, Hong examines the grammaticalization process of the Korean connective *–taka*, and suggests constraints under which *–taka* can be used, while uncovering affective implications of the concepts of predictiveness and alternativity. Another analysis examining the constraints of linguistic constructions under a variety of criteria is Izutsu and Koguma's typology of voice constructions (benefactive and adversative) in Japanese, Korean, and Ainu. Lastly, in a frame semantic account of separation verbs (cutting/breaking) with regard to both physical situations and spatial terms, Fujii, Radetzky, and Sweetser suggest, on the basis of crosslinguistic data, that both lexical and constructional meanings emerge in the context of manipulation of multiple frames—a claim which proposes a different approach to both types of meaning. In sum, the types of processes identified in this section are not just familiar examples of grammaticalization or lexical patterns; rather, they reveal crucial components of the meaning processes involved.

In the section on *Creativity and Discourse,* readers will find analyses of a range of discourse forms—literary, political, scientific, and rhetorical. The studies provide examples of analyses that bring out both the specificity of each genre and the general mechanisms involved. Stockwell offers a creative reading of Ben Jonson's 'To Celia', suggesting that a combination of stylistic and cognitive methods yields the most fulsome analysis of literature. In applying Leonard Talmy's concept of fictive motion to larger scale literary constructions (rather than sentence or clause levels more often the purview of linguists), Deggan demonstrates that linguistic and conceptual tools can open new and promising avenues in literary investigations. Similarly, examinations of American public discourse demonstrate the explanatory power of cognitive linguistic analyses when applied to discourse-level phenomena. Matlock uncovers important features of political discourse, while Moder shows how the *think of it as* spacebuilder uses its constructional and metaphoric features to structure specific forms of discourse of science. McKellin extends the study of discourse beyond the English-speaking world in his examination of the cognitive allegories used by the Managalase of Papua New Guinea to negotiate, create, and manipulate social and political relationships. He shows how cognitive linguistic tools can help clarify the strategies employed by speakers in some of the most daunting forms of discourse. As we've seen in the papers in the first few sections, linguists have much to offer in the understanding of figurative meaning. Linguists, though, as this section suggests, can also learn much from examining various types of discourse—literary, political, scientific, or allegorical.

Many of the processes involved in these first three sections of the volume can also extend to other modalities. It is now commonly understood that the experience of the human body supports a range of conceptualizations and linguistic expressions, both literal and figurative. But it is also important to note how figurative conceptualizations and visual perceptions either prompt the body into action or use the body to support the conceptualizations. The penultimate section, *Viewpoint, Language, and the Body*, brings together several papers showing the ways in which language connects to viewpoint allocation and embodied action. This includes a study of gesture, but also discussions on the role of viewpoint research within cognitive linguistics and a look at the potential and importance of multimodal approaches to language and cognition. For example, in teaching an appropriate body posture in dance, an instructor may use an unrealistic conceptualization of a situation as a means to prompt appropriate posture or motion (Müller and Ladewig). Such studies suggest that the mind-body engagement is a feedback loop, rather than a unidirectional path. At the same time, the body can be prompted into spontaneous unusual posture and gesture by an attempt to linguistically describe a visual image (Mittelberg). As these examples suggest, multimodal contexts reveal the interactive quality of language, vision, and body motion, in ways that lead to new conceptualizations. The interaction between modalities is a subject that invites a number of new questions regarding language and embodied cognition.

The studies in this section also show that the now familiar trio of 'body, mind, and language' has more recently been complicated by another broad concept—viewpoint. As was suggested in the papers published in Dancygier and Sweetser (2012), 'viewpoint' phenomena direct the choices of linguistic expressions in ways much more complex than a representation of spatial viewpoint. The papers in the section devoted to viewpoint develop the idea further, suggesting that the concept may provide a clear and unambiguous way to connect language, gesture, and other forms of embodiment. Sweetser's paper gives a broad theoretical overview of instances when different communicative modalities represent different viewpoints, even if both (or all) are related to the speaker's experience of the event. Tobin looks at presuppositions as 'curse of knowledge' phenomena and uses Mental Spaces Theory to show how perspective-taking participates in such construals. DeLiema and Steen show the importance of looking at viewpointed gestures as evidence of dynamic processes of learning and conceptualization. On another methodological note, Steen and Turner make the case for a massive multimodal data source as the basis of multi-faceted, and more exhaustive, linguistic analysis. These papers clearly show how cognition relies on multiple communicative modalities and what a rich direction for further research such studies represent.

Finally, the section on *Sound, Image, and Communicative Modalities* presents analyses focusing on the role of visual and aural/oral forms, including music and vocal performance, in reflecting conceptualization processes. Sharon, Fais, and Vatikiotis-Bateson report on research that shows that bodily movement and gesture may be crucial elements of a singer's artistic expression. They consider the genre of Art Song (poetic lyrics and music) as an example of an inherently multimodal artistic genre, which has long resisted embracing the embodied movement as the third modality. Galeano takes the question in a different direction, asking about the correlations between musical structure and syntax, in descriptive terms and in avenues of acquisition. The correlation between sound and embodied behaviour is also centre-stage in Clark, Perlman, and Johansson Falck's paper, analyzing correlations between spatial verticality and pitch. Their discussion of 'vocal iconicity' and 'vocal gesture' opens new avenues in the study of embodied performance. Finally, embodiment becomes the central concept in the study by Chow and Harrell, looking at technological innovation as a mechanism which prompts alignment between bodies and material objects through the very design of these objects. The section thus shows again how multimodal interaction of embodied modalities lies at the core of meaning emergence.

The above examples show just some of the many avenues of interaction among concepts from cognitive disciplines and subdisciplines. But the overall message of the volume seems to be that the next stage in the study of language and cognition will need to focus on the types of networks that emerge across various modalities. Further, creativity can possibly be talked about not just in terms of the innovative use of pre-existing concepts, but in specific cross-modal and multimodal combinations. The nature of the interactions between the body, the mind, and language may be the area of study that needs to continue to develop for us to better understand the role of each of these fundamental components of communication.

Together, the papers collected here show new directions in the study of perceptual and conceptual connections between language and other communicative forms. They also open the discipline of cognitive linguistics to an engagement with more centrally creative domains of meaning emergence. This volume offers a substantial testament to the profitability of ongoing expansions of embodied cognitive approaches to interdisciplinary questions of communication, modalities, and creativity.

## References

Dancygier, Barbara, and Eve Sweetser. 2014. *Figurative Language*. New York: Cambridge University Press.

Dancygier, Barbara, and Eve Sweetser (eds). 2012. *Viewpoint in Language: A Multimodal Perspective*. New York: Cambridge University Press.

Forceville, Charles J., and Eduardo Urios-Aparisi. 2009. *Multimodal Metaphor*. Berlin/New York: Mouton de Gruyter.

Goldberg, Adele. 1996. *Conceptual Structure, Discourse and Language*. Stanford: CSLI.

Müller, Cornelia, Alan Cienki, Ellen Fricke, Silva Ladewig, David McNeill, and Jana Bressem (eds.). 2013. Body–Language–Communication: An International Handbook on Multimodality in Human Interaction. Volume 1. Berlin/New York: Mouton de Gruyter.

Stockwell, Peter. 2009. *Texture: A Cognitive Aesthetics of Reading*. Edinburgh: Edinburgh University Press.

Veale, Tony, Kurt Feyaerts, and Charles Forceville (eds). 2013. *Creativity and the Agile Mind: A Multi-Disciplinary Study of a Multi-Faceted Phenomenon*. Berlin: Mouton de Gruyter.

# Part I

# Creativity versus Conventionality

# 1

# Development of Metaphorical Thinking: The Role of Language

DANIEL CASASANTO

## 1 Introduction

People often talk using linguistic metaphors, and think using *mental metaphors:* mappings between concrete, perceptible domains like space, force, and motion and relatively abstract, imperceptible domains like intimacy, value, and time.[1] When speakers use expressions like a *close* friendship, a *high* price, or a *long* vacation, they activate mental representations of space —the same sort of representations that enable them to perceive spatial relations among objects and to interact with the physical environment. The claim that metaphors are ways of thinking, not just ways of talking, first advanced on the basis of patterns in language (Lakoff and Johnson 1980), is

[1] The term 'conceptual metaphor' (Lakoff and Johnson 1980; 1999) is often used ambiguously, even by metaphor theorists: Sometimes the term refers to expressions in language, other times to hypothetical nonlinguistic mental representations, and still other times to pairings of linguistic and nonlinguistic mappings. These ambiguities complicate discussions of the relationship between metaphorical language and metaphorical thinking. I will distinguish the linguistic and nonlinguistic components of 'conceptual metaphors' by using the terms *linguistic metaphor* to refer to expressions in language and *mental metaphor* to refer to the implicit associations between nonlinguistic source and target domains, which are hypothesized to underlie linguistic metaphors (Casasanto 2008a). Unlike simple associations, mental metaphors consist of a system of mappings, often between two analog continuums (e.g. space and time). Mental metaphors can exist in the absence of any corresponding linguistic metaphor (see Casasanto 2009).

*Language and the Creative Mind.*
Mike Borkent, Barbara Dancygier, and Jennifer Hinnell (eds).

now supported by a growing body of data from behavioral experiments (see Casasanto and Bottini 2013a for a review).

Where do our mental metaphors come from, and what role might language play in their development? Three answers to these questions have been proposed:

i. Mental metaphors are innate. Cross-domain mappings are the result of co-opting neural machinery that evolved for perception and action to support more abstract thinking (Pinker 1997). They are 'unlearned' (Walker et al. 2010: 21).
ii. Mental metaphors are learned via direct experience interacting with the physical world (Lakoff and Johnson 1999).
iii. Mental metaphors are learned via experience with language: Using linguistic metaphors invites speakers to construct cross-domain mappings that were not present in their pre-linguistic thought (Gentner 2001).

According to the first two proposals, language plays no role in the development of mental metaphors. On the third, language is necessary for the development of mental metaphors. Each of these three proposals could potentially explain the origins of some mental metaphors. However, in this chapter, I will argue that none of these proposals can explain how some of the most common metaphors in adults' language and thought develop, but that a complete picture begins to emerge when elements from all three proposals are combined. In some cases, it appears that (i.) *innate predispositions* may cause children (ii.) *to learn particular cross-domain correspondences as they interact with the physical world*, resulting in pre-linguistic mental metaphors that are (iii.) *subsequently shaped by experience using language*, or by other aspects of culture.

Which cross-domain mappings are found in infants' minds, how do they get there, and how might they change when children learn language? Cross-linguistic variation provides theoretical traction on questions about the origins of mental metaphors—questions that appear intractable when the mind is viewed through the lens of a single language. Experiments testing the linguistic relativity of mental representations of duration and musical pitch reveal a two-stage developmental process by which pre-linguistic mental metaphors (which may be universal) are shaped by linguistic experience, throughout our lifetimes.

## 2 Are Mental Metaphors Exaptations?

Ultimately, the origins of our mental metaphors may lie in the recycling of evolutionarily ancient neural systems for new uses: a process Steven Jay Gould and Elizabeth Vrba (1982) dubbed *exaptation*. Steven Pinker proposed the following sketch of how the neural substrates of perception and action could have been exapted to support abstract thought:

> Suppose ancestral circuits for reasoning about space and force were copied, the copies' connections to the eyes and muscles were severed, and references to the physical world were bleached out. The circuits could serve as a scaffolding whose slots are filled with symbols for more abstract concerns like states, possessions, ideas, and desires.
>
> (Pinker 2007: 355)

On Pinker's proposal, linguistic metaphors are 'vestigial cognitive organs' (1997: 356) that reveal evolutionary or historical connections between metaphorical source and target domains, but not active metaphorical mappings (Gentner (2001) calls this the *cognitive archaeology view*). In the years since this proposal was made, however, an abundance of experimental evidence has suggested that source-target mappings are not merely vestigial. On the contrary, source domain representations are activated highly automatically when people process target domains, and their activation has causal powers: changing how people think and feel (e.g. Casasanto 2009; Casasanto and Dijkstra 2010; Thibodeau and Boroditsky 2011). The view that source-target mappings are merely vestigial is untenable. Even if source-target links have been forged over phylogenetic time, there is clear evidence that they are activated in real time as we talk and think.

Are some source-target mappings innate? Several of the cross-domain correspondences that are reflected in adults' linguistic metaphors have been observed in infants (Walker et al. 2010; Lourenco and Longo 2011). Does that mean that these mappings are unlearned? Not necessarily—it just means they were not learned initially via language. Most of the observed mappings (e.g. between distance and duration, height and pitch, size and power) have observable correlates in the physical and social world; therefore, they could be learned from regularities in infants' physical and social experiences (see §3, below). Rather than positing that source-target mappings are innate, some researchers suggest that infants are innately predisposed to learn patterns of covariation between certain domains (e.g., core knowledge of social dominance guides infants to learn the relationship between physical size and power that gives rise to the mental metaphor Powerful is Big (Thomsen and Carey, in press)).

There is no clear evidence that any cross-domain mappings are innate (i.e. unlearned), but it seems plausible that some may be: a mapping like Powerful is Big that seem relevant for survival could be part of our mind's standard equipment. Importantly, evidence for innate mappings would still be compatible with the two-stage developmental process described here. An innate starting point for mental metaphors would not preclude a role for language in their later development – nor would their innateness imply that the same mental metaphors should be used universally by all adults.

## 3 Mental Metaphors from Correlations in Experience?

In the literatures on Conceptual Metaphor Theory (Lakoff and Johnson 1999) and embodied cognition, it is widely assumed that mental metaphors are not innate. Rather, they are learned on the basis of the unavoidable conflation of two types of bodily experiences: interoceptive experiences in target domains, and perceptuo-motor experiences in source domains. For example, the metaphor Affection is Warmth arises in children's minds as a consequence of feeling the physical warmth of their caretakers' bodies as they are held and comforted. According to some metaphor theorists, children initially conflate source and target (e.g. conceptually fusing warmth and affection) and later differentiate them (Johnson 1999; Lakoff and Johnson 1999).

This *theory of conflation* is often invoked, and resonates with ideas of Piaget's (1927/1969), but it has never been tested experimentally (for a detailed critique see Casasanto (2013); also Srinivasan and Carey (2010)). Just as there is no evidence that any mental metaphors are innate, there is no evidence that they are learned initially via exposure to covariation between source and target domains in the natural world during early childhood. It is clear that some source-target mappings are present in pre-linguistic infants, but to date, there are simply no data that can help us determine whether these mappings are innate or whether they are learned as infants track regularities in the physical and social environment.[2]

Abstracting away from the details of the theory of conflation, the proposal that many mental metaphors could be learned as children track patterns of correlation in their physical and social experience is appealing. To the extent that these correlations in experience are universal (based on universal aspects of the body and the world) this proposal can potentially help to explain how some mental metaphors have become enshrined in so many of the world's languages, without having to posit that the hundreds of ubiquitous mappings metaphor theorists have identified are all innate. This proposal could ultimately explain the *initial origins* of many of our basic mental metaphors.

For the present discussion about the role of language in the development of mental metaphors, however, it is not necessary to know whether the

---

[2] If infants were to show a cross-domain mapping reliably that did not correspond to any observable regularities in the physical or social environment, this would argue in favor of an innate basis for that mapping—though not necessarily for any other mappings.

pre-linguistic mappings that have been observed in infants are innate or learned. In either case, linguistic experience could determine how people subsequently *use* the mappings that were initially established pre-linguistically, when they talk and think.

## 4 Mental Metaphors from Linguistic Metaphors?

Cognitive psychologists have suggested that perhaps exposure to linguistic metaphors causes people to create mental metaphors, by inviting language users to build analogical bridges that they probably would not have constructed otherwise. For the most part, this idea has been tested for nominal metaphors like 'my lawyer is a shark' (e.g. Gentner et al. 2001): expressions that pass the grammar-school test of metaphoricity insomuch as most people will agree that they are not literally true. Such metaphors encourage a process Gentner (1983) and colleagues have called *structure mapping*, by which relations that obtain in the source domain are imported into the target domain via analogy, allowing inferences that come 'for free' in the source domain to be made about the target domain, as well. This language-mediated process can lead people to discover previously unnoticed parallels between the source and target.

Beyond nominal metaphors, the idea that language encourages us to discover cross-domain relationships has also been applied to the more frequent, 'invisible' metaphors that are the focus of most research on conceptual metaphor theory. The parade case of an invisible metaphor is the mapping between space and time. Outside of the cognitive science community, many people would deny the metaphoricity of expressions like 'my favorite scene is *coming up next*' or 'that was a *long* meeting.' Is language responsible for the construction of mental metaphors linking space and time? Lera Boroditsky (2001:20) suggested that it may be:

> Using spatial metaphors to describe time encourages structural alignment between the two domains and may cause relational structure to be imported from space to time. The mechanism for this type of metaphoric structuring may be the same as that used in analogical inference (Gentner, Bowdle, and Wolff 2001; Gentner and Wolff 1997). Language-encouraged mappings between space and time come to be stored in the domain of time. Hence, when spatiotemporal metaphors differ, so may people's ideas of time.

It is certain that temporal concepts like 'Wednesday' are learned through exposure to language and culture, and it seems possible that higher-order spatio-temporal thoughts like 'moving Wednesday's meeting *forward*' could be dependent on language, as well.

Yet, there are reasons to question whether language plays any role in the initial construction of more basic space-time mappings. For example, infants are sensitive to correspondences between spatial and temporal extent (Srinivasan and Carey 2010; Lourenco and Longo 2011). Some space-time mappings are established initially prior to any linguistic experience.

## 5 Analogical versus Correlational Metaphors

There appear to be (at least) two categories of mental metaphors, which can be distinguished according to the ways in which they are born and the ways that they die (or don't die). I will refer to these as *analogical metaphors* and *correlational metaphors*.[3] It is important to distinguish them for the present discussion because language plays very different roles in the development and online activation of these different kinds of mental metaphors.

**The birth of correlational metaphors.** As discussed above, it is easy to posit that some mental metaphors arise from correlations in direct bodily experience. Space-time mappings, for succession as well as extent, could be learned from observation of spatial changes over time. Affection and warmth co-occur in our experience; so do happiness and upright posture, intimacy and physical closeness, knowing and seeing, etc. As Lakoff and Johnson (1999) argue, it is impossible *not* to experience the co-occurrence of these source and target domains. No language required.

**The birth of analogical metaphors.** This is not the case, however, for lawyers and sharks. Have you *ever* seen a lawyer and a shark together? Inevitable co-occurrence cannot be what causes us to construct mappings between source and target for metaphors like 'my job is a jail' (assuming you are not a prison guard), 'my surgeon is a butcher,' or 'this book is a roller-coaster ride.' Someone had to construct these mappings via a creative act of analogy initially, but subsequently most of us construct these mappings because language invites us to do so.

**The death of analogical metaphors.** According to a body of experimental work by Gentner and colleagues, the way people process nominal metaphors depends critically on their novelty. The first time you ever heard someone say, 'my lawyer is a shark,' it is likely that you understood it via a process like Gentner's (1983) structure mapping. Creating a new mapping requires activating representations in both the source and target domains.

---

[3] This distinction overlaps with the distinction Grady (1999) proposed between metaphors based on *correlation* and *resemblance*. One point of departure lies in the difference between *analogy* vs. *resemblance*. Analogy is, essentially, relatedness without resemblance. Furthermore, the distinction proposed here is largely motivated by consideration of one body of experimental research supporting the *career of metaphor hypothesis* (Gentner et al. 2001) and a newer body of experimental research challenging its generality (Casasanto and Bottini 2013a).

Only then can relevant features of the source be transferred to the target (e.g. fierce, powerful, remorseless), and irrelevant features abstracted away (e.g. has multiple rows of teeth, breathes through gills).

Over time, this mapping process becomes unnecessary. As analogical metaphors become conventionalized, the source domain words essentially become polysemous. For instance 'a fierce, powerful, remorseless person' becomes one of the conventional meanings of 'shark.' Gentner and colleagues (2001) call the process by which novel metaphors become polysemies *the career of metaphor*. As evidence for this process, they note that novel metaphors generate congruity effects, measurable with reaction times: People process language more efficiently when, for a given target domain, the speaker uses the same source domain consistently throughout a discourse rather than switching source domains. These congruity effects disappear, however, for highly frequent metaphors, which have become fully conventionalized.

What is important for the present discussion is that, for the kind of metaphors that appear to result from language-mediated structure mapping, source-target mappings are *only* activated when they are novel.

**The death (or eternal life) of correlational metaphors.** The career of metaphor hypothesis does not appear to hold for correlational metaphors. It appears that these metaphors never die (or, for the sake of source-domain consistency, never retire). Space-time metaphors provide a compelling illustration of this point. It is difficult to estimate how frequently people use words like 'long' and 'short,' 'ahead' and 'behind,' etc. to refer to time. But people talk about time a lot: 'Time' is the most frequent noun in the English language (Boroditsky and Gaby 2011). And when we talk about time, it is hard to avoid using spatial metaphors (Clark 1973). It is safe to assume that verbal space-time metaphors are very frequent, and they are completely conventionalized -- probably far more frequent and conventionalized than the 'conventional' metaphors studied in the career of metaphor literature.

And yet there is a great deal of evidence that people activate source-target mappings when they process temporal language (Boroditsky 2000; 2001; Boroditsky and Ramscar 2002; Santiago et al. 2007; Torralbo et al. 2006; Ulrich and Maienborn 2010; Weger and Pratt 2008), and even when they process temporal stimuli without using language (Casasanto 2008b; Casasanto and Boroditsky 2008; Merritt, Casasanto, and Brannon 2010). Despite the frequency and conventionality of linguistic space-time metaphors, mental metaphors linking space and time are alive and well. The same seems to be true for mental metaphors linking distance and similarity (Casasanto 2008a), height and emotional valence (Meier and Robinson 2004), and size and power (Schubert 2005), to name a few examples.

**Summary of analogical vs. correlational metaphors.** The distinction between correlational and analogical metaphors is supported by a double-dissociation in the way they are born and the way they die (or don't die). For analogical metaphors, source-target mappings appear to be created by a process of structure mapping that is typically initiated by exposure to metaphors in language. There is often no opportunity to learn these mappings from correlations in direct experience, since many sources and targets (e.g. lawyers and sharks) may never be experienced together (see also Grady 1999). Analogical source-target mappings are active when the metaphors are novel, but not after they become conventional: Analogical metaphors retire.

For correlational metaphors, source-target mappings could in principle be learned as children observe covariation between source and target domains, without any linguistic input. Some mappings appear to be detectable in pre-linguistic infants (see below). Even for highly frequent, totally conventional metaphors (e.g. Temporal Extent is Spatial Extent), source-target mappings continue to be activated automatically when people process the target domains: Correlational metaphors may never retire.

What are the implications of the correlational / analogical distinction for the role of language in the development of mental metaphors? The parade cases of primary metaphor (e.g. Similarity is Closeness; see Casasanto 2008a) appear to be correlational, not analogical: They could in principle arise pre-linguistically, and they do not appear to retire. On this analysis, correlational metaphors do not depend on language – at least not for their *initial* development.

## 6 Hierarchical Mental Metaphors Theory

This analysis creates a problem. Analogical metaphors are based on linguistic experience, so it is easy to see how people who are exposed to different linguistic metaphors would develop correspondingly different mental metaphors, as a consequence (e.g. see suggestion from Boroditsky 2001, above). By contrast, correlational metaphors are based on regularities in the physical world that people should experience universally, so the resulting mental metaphors should be universal. I have argued that at least some space-time metaphors (for example) are correlational, and yet there is now a great deal of evidence that they are *not* universal (Boroditsky 2001; Casasanto 2008b; Fuhrman and Boroditsky 2010; Núñez and Sweetser 2006; Ouellet et al. 2010; Tversky, Kugelmass, and Winter 1991). How can correlational mental metaphors be grounded in universal experiences, yet also differ in people's minds according to the metaphors in their languages?

This problem dissolves if we posit that mental metaphors are constructed hierarchically. According to Hierarchical Mental Metaphors Theory (HMMT; Casasanto and Bottini 2013b), correlational mental metaphors develop in two stages, the second of which may extend throughout the lifetime. The mental metaphors that adults typically use are specific instances of more general families of mappings. These families may be evident in behavior from infancy, and reflect regularities in humans' experiences of the physical and social world, many of which may be universal. As children are exposed to peculiar aspects of their languages, cultures, or even their own bodies, certain mappings from a given source-target family become strengthened through repeated use, which weakens 'sibling' mappings as a consequence. The result is that people tend to think in language-specific, culture-specific, or body-specific mental metaphors: Relativity emerges from universals.

Two sets of studies illustrate the process by which language-specific mental metaphors arise from (presumably) universal mappings between space and time and between space and pitch.

## 7 Mental Metaphors for Duration and Musical Pitch

English speakers tend to express duration in terms of spatial extent (e.g. a *long* time, like a *long* rope). This uni-dimensional mapping has been assumed to be universal: a consequence of the unidirectional flight of time's arrow, and of universal aspects of our bodily interactions with the environment (Clark 1973). Indeed, it is difficult to avoid using uni-dimensional spatial metaphors when talking about the durations of events in English. Try replacing the word 'long' in the phrase 'a *long* meeting' with a synonym. Words like lengthy, extended, protracted, or drawn out would suffice, all of which express time in terms of linear extent. In contrast with English speakers, Greek speakers tend to express duration in terms of volume or amount (e.g. a *lot of* time (*tr. poli* ora), like a *lot of* water (*tr. poli* nero)). Greek speakers *can* express duration in terms of extent, just as English speakers can make use of volume or amount, but volume metaphors are more frequent and productive in Greek, whereas extent metaphors are more frequent and productive in English (Casasanto et al. 2004; Casasanto 2008b).

Does the tendency to talk about duration in terms of 1-dimensional or 3-dimensional space influence the way people tend to think about it? To find out, in one set of experiments English and Greek speakers were given non-linguistic psychophysical tests of their ability to estimate duration (Casasanto et al. 2004; Casasanto 2008b). Participants were asked to reproduce the durations of stimuli they saw on a computer screen (i.e. lines gradually extending across the screen or containers gradually filling up) while ignoring the spatial extent of the lines (distance interference) or the fullness of the containers (volume interference). English speakers had difficulty screening out interference from spatial distance when estimating duration: Lines that traveled a longer distance were mistakenly judged to take a longer time than lines that traveled a shorter distance. But their time estimates were relatively unaffected by irrelevant volume information. Greek speakers showed the opposite pattern: They had more difficulty screening out interference from volume, so fuller containers were judged to remain on the screen for more time than emptier containers, but their judgments were relatively unaffected by the spatial extent of lines. The pattern of distance and volume interference in these nonlinguistic psychophysical tasks reflects the relative prevalence of distance and volume metaphors for duration in English and Greek.

The cross-linguistic comparison between Greek and English speakers shows a correlation between temporal language and temporal thinking. Can language play a causal role in shaping nonlinguistic time representations? To test whether using volume metaphors in language can change the way people think about duration, the experimenters trained English speakers to use Greek-like metaphors for time (Casasanto 2008b). After about 20 minutes of exposure to these new metaphors, the effect of irrelevant volume information on English speakers' nonlinguistic duration estimates was statistically indistinguishable from the effect found in native Greek speakers. Together, these data show that people who use different temporal metaphors in their native languages conceptualize time the way they talk about it, even when they are not using language. Furthermore, linguistic experience can play a causal role in shaping mental representations of time. Producing or understanding spatio-temporal language like a Greek speaker, even for a few minutes, can cause English speakers to think about time differently, using a different kind of spatial scaffolding.

The psychophysical paradigm used to establish differences in temporal thinking between English and Greek speakers has been extended to probe cross-linguistic differences in people's mental representations of musical pitch. Pitch may be less abstract than time insomuch as it can be perceived directly with the ears. Yet, pitch may still be relatively abstract compared to space, and to the objects and actions we localize in space, which can often be perceived multimodally via some combination of sound, sight, touch, and smell.

Like English, Dutch describes pitches as 'high' (hoog) or 'low' (laag), but this is not the only possible spatial metaphor for pitch. In Farsi, high pitches are 'thin' (nāzok) and low pitches are 'thick' (koloft). Dutch and Farsi speakers' performance on non-linguistic pitch reproduction tasks reflects these linguistic differences (Dolscheid, Shayan, Majid, and Casasanto

2013). Participants were asked to reproduce the pitch of tones that they heard in the presence of irrelevant spatial information: lines that varied in their height (height interference task) or their thickness (thickness interference task). Dutch speakers' pitch estimates showed stronger cross-dimensional interference from spatial height, and Farsi speakers' from the thickness of visually presented stimuli. This effect was not explained by differences in accuracy, or in musical training. When trained to talk about pitches using Farsi-like metaphors (e.g. a tuba sounds thicker than a flute) for 20-30 minutes, Dutch speakers' performance on the non-linguistic thickness interference task became indistinguishable from native Farsi speakers'. Experience using one kind of spatial metaphor or another in language can have a causal influence on non-linguistic pitch representations.

What role is spatial language playing in shaping non-linguistic representations of time and pitch? Is language creating cross-domain associations, or is linguistic experience modifying pre-linguistic mental metaphors? Pre-linguistic infants intuit a link between more duration and more spatial extent (Srinivasan and Carey 2010), and also between more duration and more size (Lourenco and Longo 2011). Thus, both the distance-duration mapping that is most prevalent in English and the volume-duration mapping that is most prevalent in Greek may be present pre-linguistically. Likewise, infants as young as four months old are sensitive to the height-pitch ound in Dutch-speaking adults (but not in Farsi-speaking adults), and also to the thickness-pitch mapping found in Farsi-speaking adults (but not in Dutch-speaking adults; Dolscheid, Hunnius, Casasanto, and Majid 2012). There is no need, therefore, to posit that using linguistic metaphors causes people to construct these mappings *de novo*.

Together, these infant and adult data support a developmental story with two chapters, as posited by HMMT. First, children represent duration via a family of spatial mappings, which includes mappings from both spatial length and volume. Likewise, they represent pitch via mappings from both height and thickness. These initial mappings may be universal, based either on innate cross-domain correspondences (Walker et al. 2010) or on early-learned correlations between source and target domains in children's experience with the physical world (Lakoff and Johnson 1999). The distance-duration and volume-duration mappings could be learned by observing that more time passes as objects travel farther distances and as quantities accumulate in 3-dimensional space. Height-pitch mappings could be learned from seeing (or feeling) the larynx rise and fall as people produce higher and lower pitches with their voices. Thickness-pitch mappings could be learned from observing the natural correlation between the size of an object or animal and the sound that it makes (imagine the sound made by banging on a soda can vs. an oil drum).

Later, linguistic experience modifies these pre-linguistic source-target mappings. Suppose each time we use a linguistic metaphor like 'a long meeting' or 'a high soprano' we activate the corresponding mental metaphor. Repeatedly activating one source-target mapping instead of another (e.g. height-pitch instead of thickness-pitch) should strengthen the activated mapping and, as a consequence, weaken the competing mapping via competitive learning (Casasanto 2008b; Dolscheid et al. 2013). This process of strengthening one spatial mapping during language use, at the expense of the alternative spatial mapping, may explain how universal space-time and space-pitch mappings in infants become language-specific mappings in adults.

The hierarchical structuring of correlational mental metaphors may help to explain how source-target mappings can be important for our representations of target domains but also surprisingly flexible. For example, according to HMMT, Dutch speakers could be trained to think like Farsi speakers so quickly because they did not have to *learn* the thickness-pitch mapping during their 20-30 minutes of using Farsi-like linguistic metaphors. Rather, this linguistic training strengthened the association between thickness and pitch that was present in participants' minds from infancy (as indicated by data from Dutch 4-month olds), but which had been weakened as a consequence of their frequent use of height-pitch metaphors in language.

One prediction of HMMT is that specific source-target mappings should be easy to activate via linguistic training so long as they are members of one of the families of source-target mappings encoded in our minds (over phylogenetic or ontogenetic time) on the basis of observable source-target correspondences in the world. Mappings that are not members of a pre-linguistically established family (and that do not reflect correlations in our experience) should be relatively hard to activate via training, because these mappings would need to be created, not just strengthened.

In a test of this prediction, Dutch speakers were trained to used a thickness-pitch mapping that is the reverse of the mapping found in Farsi, and in the natural world: thin=low and thick=high. These 'reverse-Farsi' trained participants received the same amount of training as the participants trained to use the Farsi-like mapping. Whereas Farsi-like training had a significant effect on participants' nonlinguistic pitch representations, reverse-Farsi training had no effect (Dolscheid et al. 2013). Thus, brief linguistic experience caused participants to use the thickness-pitch mapping that reflects correlations between thickness and pitch in the world (and is evident in pre-linguistic infants). Yet, the same amount of linguistic experience was not effective at instilling the opposite thickness-pitch mapping, which has no obvious experiential correlates, and is therefore not predicted to be among the pre-linguistically established space-pitch mappings.

## 8 Conclusions

Language plays different roles in the development of different kinds of metaphorical mappings. Language appears to play a causal role in establishing analogical metaphors (e.g. Lawyers are Sharks), which are only processed via active source-target mappings when they are novel (Gentner et al. 2001). By contrast, language may not play any role in initially establishing correlational metaphors (e.g. Time is Space), some of which have been detected in pre-linguistic infants, and which persist as active source-target mappings in adults despite being highly conventional and very frequent.

Correlational metaphors are grounded in patterns of body-world interaction that may be universal. Yet, there is cross-linguistic variation in the way some target domains are metaphorized in language, and there is corresponding variation in the mental metaphors that members of different language communities tend to use. Any apparent tension between the *universality* of correlational mappings and their *linguistic relativity* can be resolved, however, by positing that adults' mental metaphors are constructed hierarchically. The specific mappings we tend to use (e.g. Duration is Spatial Extent for English speakers; Duration is Volume for Greek speakers), which are conditioned by language, are members of a superordinate family of source-target mappings (e.g. More Time is More Space). These superordinate mappings are conditioned by relationships between source and target domains in our experience of the natural world. Specific mappings that are absent from one's native language (and from one's habitual thought) can be activated quickly with exposure to new linguistic metaphors so long as the 'new' mappings are members of a pre-linguistically established family of mappings. As such, our mental metaphors are language-specific at one level of analysis but may be universal at another.

## References

Boroditsky, L. 2000. Metaphoric structuring: Understanding time through spatial metaphors. *Cognition* 75(1): 1–28.

Boroditsky, L. 2001. Does language shape thought? English and Mandarin speakers' conceptions of time. *Cognitive Psychology* 43: 1–22.

Boroditsky, L. and A. Gaby. 2010. Remembrances of Times East: Absolute Spatial Representations of Time in an Australian Aboriginal Community. *Psychological Science* 21(11): 1635–1639.

Boroditsky, L., and M. Ramscar 2002. The roles of body and mind in abstract thought. *Psychological Science* 13(2): 185–189.

Casasanto, D. 2008a. Similarity and proximity: when does close in space mean close in mind? *Memory and Cognition* 36: 1047–1056.

Casasanto, D. 2008b. Who's afraid of the Big Bad Whorf? Cross-linguistic differences in temporal language and thought. *Language Learning* 58(1): 63–79.

Casasanto, D. 2009. Embodiment of abstract concepts: good and bad in right- and left-handers. *Journal of Experimental Psychology: General* 138: 351–367.

Casasanto, D. 2013. Experiential Origins of Mental Metaphors: Language, Culture, and the Body. *Metaphorical Thought in Social Life,* eds. M. Landau, M.D. Robinson, and B. Meier. Washington, DC: American Psychological Association Books.

Casasanto, D., and L. Boroditsky. 2008. Time in the mind: Using space to think about time. *Cognition* 106: 579–593.

Casasanto, D., L. Boroditsky, W. Phillips, J. Greene, S. Goswami, S. Bocanegra-Thiel, I. Santiago-Diaz, O. Fotakopoulu, R. Pita and D. Gil. 2004. How deep are effects of language on thought? Time estimation in speakers of English, Indonesian, Greek, and Spanish. *Proceedings of the 26th Annual Conference of the Cognitive Science Society,* eds. K. Forbus, D. Gentner, and T. Regier, 186–191. Chicago, IL.

Casasanto, D. and R. Bottini, 2013a. Spatial language and abstract concepts. *Wiley Interdisciplinary Reviews*. In press.

Casasanto, D. and R. Bottini. 2013b. Mirror reading can reverse the flow of time. *Journal of Experimental Psychology: General*. DOI: 10.1037/a0033297.

Casasanto, D. and K. Dijkstra. 2010. Motor action and emotional memory. *Cognition* 115: 179–185.

Clark, H. H. 1973. Space, time, semantics and the child. *Cognitive Development and the acquisition of language,* ed. T. E. Moore, 27–63. New York, NY: Academic Press.

Dolscheid, S., S. Hunnius, D. Casasanto, and A. Majid. 2012. The sound of thickness: Prelinguistic infants' associations of space and pitch. *CogSci 2012: Proceedings of the 34th Annual Meeting of the Cognitive Science Society,* eds. N. Miyake, D. Peebles, and R. P. Cooper, 306–311. Austin, TX: Cognitive Science Society.

Dolscheid, S., S. Shayan, A. Majid, and D. Casasanto. 2013. The thickness of musical pitch: psychophysical Evidence for Linguistic Relativity. *Psychological Science*. 24(5) 613–621.

Fuhrman, O., and L. Boroditsky. 2010. Cross-cultural differences in mental representations of time: evidence from an implicit non-linguistic task. *Cognitive Science* 34: 1430–1451.

Gentner, D. 1983. Structure-mapping: a theoretical framework for analogy, *Cognitive Science* 7: 155–170.

Gentner, D. 2001. Spatial metaphors in temporal reasoning. *Spatial schemas and abstract thought*, ed. M. Gattis, 203–222. Cambridge: MIT Press.

Gentner, D., B. Bowdle, P. Wolff, and C. Boronat. 2001. Metaphor is like analogy. *The analogical mind: Perspectives from cognitive science,* eds. D. Gentner, K.J. Holyoak and B.N. Kokinov, 199–253. Cambridge: MIT Press.

Gentner, D., and P. Wolff. 1997. Alignment in the processing of metaphor. *Journal of memory and language* 37(3): 331–355.

Gould, S. and E. Vrba 1982. Exaptation—a missing term in the science of form. *Paleobiology* 8: 4–15.

Grady, J. 1999. A typology of motivation for conceptual metaphor: correlation vs. resemblance. *Metaphor in Cognitive Linguistics,* eds. G. Steen and R. Gibbs, 79–100. Philadelphia: John Benjamins.

Johnson, C. 1999. Metaphor vs. conflation in the acquisition of polysemy: The case of *see*. *Cultural, psychological, and typological issues in cognitive linguistics,* eds. H. Massako, C. Sinha, and S. Wilcox, 155–170. Amsterdam: John Benjamins.

Lakoff, G., and M. Johnson. 1980. *Metaphors we live by*. Chicago: Chicago University Press.

Lakoff, G., and M. Johnson. 1999. *Philosophy in the flesh: the embodied mind and its challenge to western thought*. Chicago, IL: University of Chicago Press.

Lourenco, S. F., and M. R. Longo. 2011. Origins and the development of generalized magnitude representation. *Space, time, and number in the brain: searching for the foundations of mathematical thought, eds*. S. Dehaene and E. Brannon, 225–244. Amsterdam: Elsevier.

Meier, B. P., and M. D. Robinson. 2004. Why the Sunny Side Is Up Associations Between Affect and Vertical Position. *Psychological Science* 15(4): 243–247.

Merritt, D. J., D. Casasanto, and E. M. Brannon. 2010. Do monkeys think in metaphors? Representations of space and time in monkeys and humans. *Cognition* 117(2): 191–202.

Núñez, R. and E. Sweetser. 2006. With the future behind them: Convergent evidence from Aymara language and gesture in the crosslinguistic comparison of spatial construals of time. *Cognitive Science* 30: 401–450.

Ouellet, M., J. Santiago, Z. Israeli, and S. Gabay. 2010. Is the future the right time? *Experimental Psychology* 57: 308–314.

Piaget, J. 1927/1969. *The child's conception of time*. New York, NY: Ballantine Books.

Pinker, S. 1997. *How the mind works*. New York, NY: Norton.

Santiago, J., J. Lupáñez, E. Pérez, and M. J. Funes. 2007. Time (also) flies from left to right. *Psychonomic Bulletin and Review* 14(3): 512–516.

Schubert, T. 2005. Your highness: Vertical positions as perceptual symbols of power. *Journal of Personality and Social Psychology* 89: 1–21.

Srinivasan, M., and S. Carey. 2010. The long and the short of it: on the nature and origin of functional overlap between representations of space and time. *Cognition* 116: 217–241.

Thibodeau, P. H. and L. Boroditsky. 2011. Metaphors we think with: The role of metaphor in reasoning. *PLoS One* 6(2).

Thomsen, L. and S. Carey. In Press. Core Cognition of Social Relations. *Navigating the Social World: What Infants, Children, and Other Species Can Teach Us*, eds. M. Banaji and S. Gelman. Oxford: Oxford University Press.

Torralbo, A., J. Santiago, and J. Lupiáñez. 2006. Flexible conceptual projection of time onto spatial frames of reference. *Cognitive Science* 30(4): 745–757.

Tversky, B., S. Kugelmass, and A. Winter. 1991. Cross-cultural and developmental trends in graphic productions. *Cognitive Psychology* 23(4): 515–557.

Ulrich, R., and C. Maienborn. 2010. Left–right coding of past and future in language: The mental timeline during sentence processing. *Cognition* 117(2): 126–138.

Walker, P., J. G. Bremner, U. Mason, J. Spring, K. Mattock, A. Slater, and P. Johnson. 2010. Preverbal infants' sensitivity to synaesthetic cross-modality correspondences. *Psychological Science* 21: 21–25.

Weger, U. W. and J. Pratt. 2008. Time flies like an arrow: Space–time compatibility effects suggest the use of a mental timeline. *Psychonomic Bulletin and Review* 15(2): 426–430.

# 2

# Conventional but Not Dead: The Role of Metaphorically-Based Connections in the On-Line Processing of Prepositional Meaning

MICHELE I. FEIST AND BROOKE O. BREAUX

## 1 Introduction

English prepositions are notoriously polysemous, evidencing uses that are clearly spatial (as in (1) and (2)) in addition to uses that are clearly abstract (as in (3) and (4)).

(1) The apple is *in* the bowl.
(2) The book is *on* the table.
(3) John is *in* love.
(4) Sue is *on* vacation.

There have been many explanations proposed for the polysemy demonstrated by Examples (1)–(4). Dominant in the field of Cognitive Linguistics is the idea that this polysemy may be explained via metaphoric connections, with spatial uses serving as the source for more abstract uses (Cuyckens and Zawada 2001; Lakoff 1987; Lakoff and Johnson 1980). Notably, these metaphoric connections are assumed by several network models of the lexical semantics of prepositions (e.g. Lakoff 1987; Tyler and Evans 2003). The grounding of abstract uses of prepositions in concrete ones implies that connections between the various uses are directional at the level of pro-

*Language and the Creative Mind.*
Mike Borkent, Barbara Dancygier, and Jennifer Hinnell (eds).

cessing, with the processing of concrete uses influencing the processing of abstract ones but not vice versa (cf. Boroditsky 2000; Casasanto and Boroditsky 2008; Gentner 2001; Grady 1999). However, these models, along with the connections between senses that they propose, remain untested at the level of processing.

One challenge to analyses of the lexical semantics of prepositions based on the proposals of Conceptual Metaphor Theory is that some researchers have concluded that highly conventionalized linguistic metaphors—such as those that center around the abstract meanings of prepositions—no longer share a conceptual connection with their metaphoric source (cf. McGlone 2001) while others discount the role of metaphor altogether, arguing that concrete and abstract uses of a single word are the result of thematic parallels or similarities in conceptual structure that exist between the two concepts (cf. Jackendoff and Aaron 1991; Murphy 1996; Murphy 1997). Thus, one important issue that arises regarding the multitude of uses associated with prepositions is the question of whether—and how—the spatial and abstract uses may be connected in the minds of speakers.

Although both the network models themselves and the proposed directional connections between uses of a single preposition remain untested at the level of processing, evidence that speakers have access to directional connections from spatial to abstract meanings has been found between the domains of TIME and SPACE, connected via the conceptual metaphor TIME IS SPACE (Boroditsky and Ramscar 2002; Casasanto and Boroditsky 2008). Based on the proposals of Conceptual Metaphor Theory, Boroditsky and her colleagues reasoned that if people's understanding of the abstract domain of TIME is structured by their understanding of the concrete domain of SPACE, then the activation of relevant spatial information should have a predictable influence on the processing of temporal information. Consistent with the proposals of Conceptual Metaphor Theory, these studies have found influences of the processing of spatial information on subsequent processing of temporal information, but not vice versa.

The current study shares a similar motivation with investigations of the processing consequences of the conceptual metaphor TIME IS SPACE, with its primary aim being to expand the finding by testing connections thought to be associated with a wide variety of conceptual metaphors. In particular, we are interested in testing for connections—those that are all too often simply assumed to exist—between the concrete and abstract senses of a single polysemous lexical item. Thus, we ask in this study whether there is evidence for psychologically real connections between concrete and abstract uses of individual lexical items, using the prepositions *in* and *on* as our test case. Furthermore, should there be evidence of connections, we ask whether the connections are directional, as suggested by Conceptual Metaphor Theory. If this is the case, we should see that the processing of spatial uses facilitates the subsequent processing of abstract uses, while the processing of spatial uses is unaffected by prior processing of abstract ones.

One source of evidence regarding connections within the conceptual system is the phenomenon of priming, by which access to a concept facilitates access to other concepts that are closely connected to it. If the connections posited by Conceptual Metaphor Theory are psychologically real, we should find evidence of priming between spatial and abstract uses, in general, and the directional facilitation of processing, in particular, when concrete uses precede abstract uses. However, one critical issue is that even though *in* and *on* are associated with both concrete and abstract meanings, these different meanings are accessed via the same lexical item instead of two different lexical items. Since accessing the same lexical item can result in a type of surface-level priming called repetition priming, which could potentially mask the deeper, meaning-based type of effects we are interested in testing, the lexical item itself was not considered a viable probe to determine whether concrete uses may prime abstract uses. To resolve this issue, in the experiments to follow we will use spatial images as points of access to the spatial meanings of the prepositions and prepositional phrases as points of access to the abstract meanings.

## 2 Experiment 1: Will Spatial Uses of *in* and *on* Prime Abstract Uses?

As a first test of the connections between abstract and spatial uses of *in* and *on*, we ask whether processing a spatial use of a preposition will facilitate subsequent processing of an abstract use, in line with the predictions of Conceptual Metaphor Theory. Participants were presented with an alternating series of images and phrases and were asked to decide whether each stimulus was natural/expected or unnatural/unexpected. If processing of abstract uses of prepositions is facilitated by prior processing of spatial uses, we should observe faster responses to natural/expected *in* and *on* phrases when they follow *in* and *on* images, respectively, than when they follow projective (*left-right* or *front-back*) images.

### 2.1 Method

#### 2.1.1 Participants

Twenty students at the University of Louisiana at Lafayette participated in exchange for course credit. All reported being native speakers of English.

### 2.1.2 Materials

Forty-eight prime-target pairs were created, with spatial images serving as the primes and prepositional phrases serving as the targets. There were four different categories of spatial images (*on* images, *in* images, *left-right* images, and *front-back* images) and two different categories of prepositional phrases (*in* phrases and *on* phrases), allowing each type of phrase to be preceded by either a related image (i.e. one depicting a spatial use of the preposition used in the phrase) or an unrelated image (i.e. one depicting a spatial use of a different preposition).

#### 2.1.2.1 Spatial Images

Forty-eight photographic images, each depicting two objects, served as access points for the spatial uses of the prepositions. The images were equally divided amongst four target spatial relations: *in, on, left-right,* and *front-back*. Half of the images were designed to be natural/expected, such as a photograph of a flower in a vase, and half of the images were designed to be unnatural/unexpected, such as a photograph of a banana in a shoe (see Figure 1). Prior to use, we conducted a series of norming studies, verifying that all images were easy for our participant population to classify as either natural/expected or unnatural/unexpected. In addition, we wanted to ensure that the intended spatial relation in the *in* and *on* images was salient to observers who were asked only to view and describe the photographs. The images selected for inclusion in the experiment were all correctly classified, with an overall mean accuracy rate of 96%, and highly rated on a 7-point scale as either natural/expected (close to 7) or unnatural/unexpected (close to 1), with an overall mean rating of 6.40 for natural/expected images and an overall mean rating of 1.66 for unnatural/unexpected images. In addition, the intended spatial relation was mentioned in descriptions of the selected *in* and *on* images at a mean rate of 85%.

FIGURE 1. Example *in* Images from Experiment 1.

#### 2.1.2.2 Abstract Phrases

Twenty-four *in* phrases and twenty-four *on* phrases served as access points to abstract meanings of the prepositions. Each phrase consisted of one target preposition (*in* or *on*) followed by an abstract noun. Half of the phrases were collected using a search of the Corpus of Contemporary American English (Davies 2008-) and were considered attested preposition-noun collocations, ranging in frequency from 11,405 instances (*in love*) to 2,544 instances (*in sight*) for those phrases headed by *in* and 3,083 instances (*on time*) to 553 instances (*on strike*) for those headed by *on*. These natural/expected phrases served as experimental stimuli. The remaining phrases were designed to be unnatural/unexpected and ranged in frequency from 4 instances (*in basis*) to 666 instances (*in work*) for those phrases headed by *in* and 7 instances (*on century*) to 116 instances (*on industry*) for those headed by *on*. These phrases served as fillers. As with the spatial images, prior to use we verified via a series of norming studies that the phrases were easy to classify as either natural/expected or unnatural/unexpected. The phrases selected for inclusion in the experiment were all correctly classified, with an overall mean accuracy rate of 91%, and highly rated on a 7-point scale as either natural/expected (close to 7) or unnatural/unexpected (closer to 1), with an overall mean rating of 6.65 for natural/expected phrases and an overall mean rating of 2.95 for unnatural/unexpected phrases.[1]

### 2.2 Procedure

Participants were presented with an alternating series of images and phrases in a randomized order on a computer screen (see Figure 2). They were asked to press the *Y* key (yes) or the *N* key (no) on their keyboard as quickly and as accurately as possible to indicate whether each image and each phrase seemed natural and expected without any additional information. They were instructed to use the index finger of their dominant hand to make all of their responses and to rest their finger on the *H* key between trials, allowing them to easily reach both the *Y* and *N* keys from a neutral location.

---

[1] To confirm that these phrases were 'abstract,' we searched the MRC Psycholinguistic Database (http://websites.psychology.uwa.edu.au/school/MRCDatabase/uwa_mrc.htm) for concreteness ratings for each of the 48 nouns participating in the abstract phrases. The concreteness ratings in the MRC Psycholinguistic Database draw on three sets of norms and range from 100 (least concrete) to 700 (most concrete) with a mean of 438 and a standard deviation of 120. Concreteness ratings were found for all but seven of our nouns, and an analysis of these concreteness ratings showed that these nouns were significantly lower in concreteness ($M$ = 352.17, $SD$ = 42.25) than the overall mean from the database, $z(40) = -4.58, p < .001$.

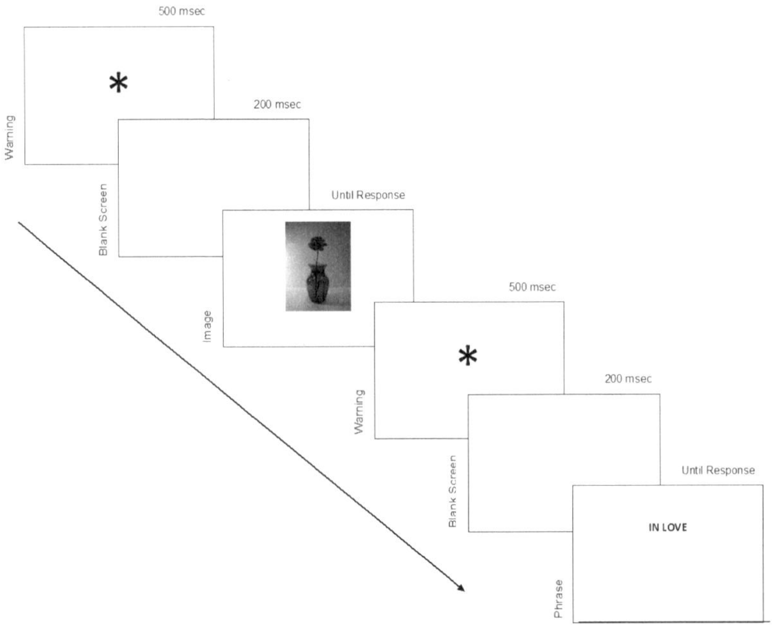


FIGURE 2. Schematic of a Single Trial.
Each screen shot is labeled by both a descriptive title (presented vertically on the left side of each screen shot) and a time stamp indicating the amount of time each was presented to participants (presented horizontally on the top of each screen shot).

Half of the experimental trials were designed to result in a matched 'yes-yes' response sequence (i.e. a natural/expected image followed by a natural/expected phrase) and the other half a mismatched 'no-yes' response sequence (i.e. an unnatural/unexpected image followed by a natural/expected phrase). Furthermore, half of each type of image-phrase sequence involved topological images ('related trials') and the other half, projective images ('unrelated trials'). Finally, half of the experimental trials involved *in* phrases and the other half involved *on* phrases (see Table 1). The remaining trials, involving unnatural/unexpected phrases, served as fillers.

TABLE 1. Related and Unrelated Pair Types in Experiment 1

| | Prime image | Target phrase |
|---|---|---|
| Related | *in* | *in* |
| | *on* | *on* |
| Unrelated | projective | *in* |
| | projective | *on* |

## 2.3 Results

Because our interest was in whether responses to abstract uses of *in* and *on* would be speeded following processing of spatial uses, we wanted to ensure that both the spatial images and the abstract phrases were processed by our participants. Thus, any response time associated with prime-target pairs in which a participant responded incorrectly to either the prime or the target was eliminated from further analysis. This resulted in the exclusion of 7.1% of the response times associated with natural/expected *in* phrases and 6.7% of the response times associated with natural/expected *on* phrases. An additional 1.3% of the response times associated with natural/expected *on* phrases fell four or more standard deviations above the mean response time and were also excluded from further analysis. Finally, because previous research has demonstrated substantial differences between abstract uses of *in* and *on* (e.g. Breaux and Feist 2010), *in* phrase response times were analyzed separately from *on* phrase response times.

### 2.3.1 IN Phrase Results

We observed a significant interaction of relatedness and response type, $F(1, 16) = 7.19$, $p = .016$, whereby participants responded faster to natural/expected *in* phrases when they were preceded by natural/expected *in* images ($M = 1089$ msec, $SD = 274$ msec) than when they were preceded by unnatural/unexpected *in* images ($M = 1381$ msec, $SD = 515$ msec), $F(1, 16) = 9.30$, $p = .008$; however, there was no significant difference in the amount of time that it took participants to respond to natural/expected *in* phrases when they were preceded by natural/expected ($M = 1250$ msec, $SD = 523$ msec) or by unnatural/unexpected projective images ($M = 1116$ msec, $SD = 208$ msec), $F(1, 16) = 0.49$, $p = .692$ (see Figure 3). There were no other significant effects or interactions.

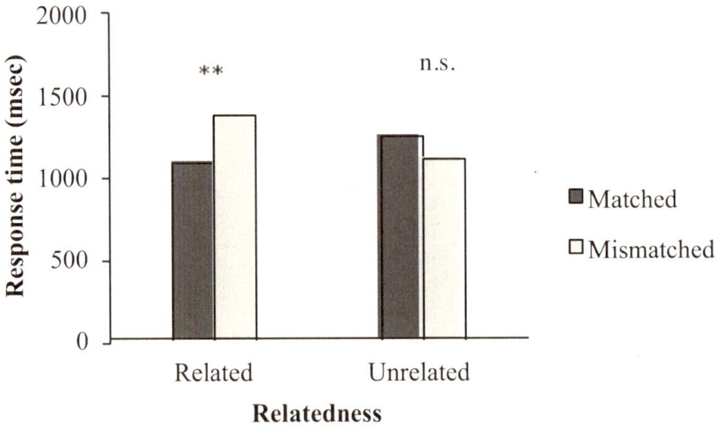


FIGURE 3. Response Times to *in* Phrases as a Function of Relatedness (related, unrelated) and Response Type (matched, mismatched) for the Prime-Target Pair; ** $p < .01$. n.s. $p > .05$.

### 2.3.2 ON Phrase Results

We observed an effect of response type whereby participants were significantly faster to decide that an *on* phrase was natural/expected when the preceding image was also natural/expected ($M$ = 1103 msec, $SD$ = 242 msec) than when the preceding image was unnatural/unexpected ($M$ = 1244 msec, $SD$ = 308 msec), $F(1, 16) = 11.46$, $p = .004$. This general finding would tend to support the idea that a processing cost was associated with switching the type of response required for both the prime and target to be correctly categorized. Notably, there were no significant effects or interactions involving relatedness, indicating that the processing of *on* images did not differentially affect access to abstract uses of *on*.

## 2.4 Discussion

We asked in Experiment 1 whether accessing a spatial meaning of a preposition would facilitate subsequent access to an abstract use, which would be indicative of a connection between the two whereby the abstract use is grounded in a spatial one, as argued for in Conceptual Metaphor Theory. The general logic underlying this experiment was that if the abstract meanings of prepositions are grounded in their spatial meanings and if these grounded connections influence how people process the abstract meanings, then the processing of a spatial prepositional meaning should facilitate processing of an abstract meaning of the same preposition, whereas processing a spatial prepositional meaning that is unrelated should not. The key factor is relatedness, whereby an effect or interaction involving relatedness would provide evidence supporting Conceptual Metaphor Theory. We observed such a connection for *in* whereby participants were faster to verify that a phrase was natural/expected if it was preceded by an image depicting a spatial *in* relation that was likewise natural/expected than if it was preceded by an unnatural/unexpected *in* image. When the preceding image depicted a projective spatial relation, no effect involving image naturalness was observed.

In contrast, the data collected in response to abstract *on* phrases revealed no evidence of a grounded connection between spatial and abstract uses of *on*. Indeed, the only factor found to influence response times for natural/expected *on* phrases was the natural/expected status of the preceding images, with faster responses following natural/expected images than following unnatural/unexpected images. Although this pattern of responses suggests that a processing cost was associated with switching the type of response required for both the prime and target to be correctly categorized, it fails to support the hypothesis of a grounded connection between spatial and abstract uses of *on*.

Thus, the results of Experiment 1 suggest that metaphorical connections may influence the processing of abstract uses of *in* but not *on*. In Experiment 2, we turn to the question of whether the processing of abstract uses may influence subsequent processing of spatial uses. If the connections between spatial and abstract uses are directional (cf. Boroditsky 2000; Casasanto and Boroditsky 2008; Gentner 2001; Grady 1999), response times to natural/expected spatial images should be unaffected by the preposition involved in the preceding abstract phrase. Alternatively, evidence that the response times to natural/expected images are affected by the preposition involved in the preceding abstract phrase could point toward a nonmetaphorical connection between the uses.

## 3 Experiment 2: Will Abstract Uses of *in* and *on* Prime Spatial Uses?

We designed Experiment 2 to ask whether there are connections between spatial and abstract uses of prepositions whereby accessing an abstract use would facilitate subsequent access to a spatial use. Such connections, while indicative of a relation between the various uses of a preposition, are contrary to the grounding assumption of Conceptual Metaphor Theory (cf. Lakoff 1987; Lakoff and Johnson 1980). Participants were presented with an alternating series of phrases and images and were asked to decide whether each stimulus was natural/expected or unnatural/unexpected. If processing of spatial uses of prepositions is facilitated by prior processing of abstract uses, we should observe (a) faster responses to natural/expected *in* and *on* images than to natural/expected projective (*left-right* or *front-back*) images when these images are preceded by natural/expected *in* and *on* phrases, indicative of a possible connection between the abstract and spatial uses of *in* and *on*, and (b) no difference in response times to the two types of images when these interleaved prepositional phrases are absent, indicative that the connections found cannot be attributed to ease of processing differences between the two types of images.

## 3.1 Method

### 3.1.1 Participants

Forty-one UL Lafayette students (nineteen in the control condition; twenty-two in the priming condition) participated in exchange for course credit. All but one participant reported being native speakers of English; data from the nonnative speaker were removed from further analysis. Data from three additional participants were eliminated due to low overall accuracy (< 75%), leaving seventeen participants in the control condition and twenty participants in the priming condition.

### 3.1.2 Materials

The materials for this experiment were the same as those used in Experiment 1.

## 3.2 Procedure

Participants were randomly assigned to either the priming condition or the control condition. In the control condition, participants were presented with topological (i.e. *in* and *on*) and projective (i.e. *left-right* and *front-back*) images in a randomized order on a computer screen; in the priming condition, the images were interleaved with abstract prepositional phrases. Half of the experimental trials in the priming condition were designed to result in a matched 'yes-yes' response sequence (i.e. a natural/expected phrase followed by a natural/expected image), and the other half a mismatched 'no-yes' response sequence (i.e. an unnatural/unexpected phrase followed by a natural/expected image); furthermore, half of each type of phrase-image sequence involved topological images ('related trials') and the other half, projective images ('unrelated trials'; see Table 2). In both conditions, trials involving unnatural/unexpected images served as fillers.

TABLE 2. Related and Unrelated Pair Types in Experiment 2

| | Prime phrase | Target image |
|---|---|---|
| Related | *in* | *in* |
| | *on* | *on* |
| Unrelated | *in* | projective |
| | *on* | projective |

### 3.3 Results

As in Experiment 1, any response time associated with a prime-target pair in which the participant responded incorrectly to either the prime or the target was eliminated from further analysis, resulting in the exclusion of 20.4% of the response times associated with natural/expected images preceded by *in* phrases and 3.3% of the response times associated with natural/expected images preceded by *on* phrases.[2] An additional 1% of the response times associated with natural/expected images preceded by *in* phrases were also excluded from further analysis because they fell four or more standard deviations above the mean response time. In the control condition, any response time associated with an incorrect response was eliminated from further analysis, resulting in the exclusion of 4.2% of the response times associated with natural/expected *in* images and their natural/expected projective counterparts (i.e. those projective images that were preceded by *in* phrases in the priming experiment) and 1.5% of the response times associated with natural/expected *on* images and their natural/expected projective counterparts. An additional 1.5% of the response times associated with natural/expected *in* images and their natural/expected projective counterparts and 0.5% of the response times associated with natural/expected *on* images and their natural/expected projective counterparts were also excluded from further analysis because they fell four or more standard deviations above the mean response time. Due to differences in procedure, response times were analyzed separately for the priming and control conditions. Finally, as in Experiment 1, results for *in* were analyzed separately from results for *on*.

[2] Because an exceptionally high percentage of response times associated with *in* images was eliminated from further analysis, we took a closer look at the accuracy data, which revealed that participants had difficulty correctly classifying unnatural/unexpected *in* phrases (accounting for the removal of 11% of the *in* pair data set). This difficulty is in line with prior observations that novel *in* phrases tend to be viewed as more interpretable than novel *on* phrases (cf. Breaux and Feist 2010).

### 3.3.1 IN Pair Results

We observed an effect of relatedness in the priming condition, $F(1, 16) = 18.93$, $p = .001$, whereby participants responded to the images in related pairs (i.e. topological images) significantly faster ($M$ = 1503 msec, $SD$ = 369 msec) than to the images in unrelated pairs (i.e. projective images; $M$ = 1804 msec, $SD$ = 396 msec). A similar effect was found in the control condition, $F(1,16) = 5.58$, $p = .031$, whereby participants responded to topological images (i.e. those that were part of related pairs in the priming condition) significantly faster ($M$ = 659 msec, $SD$ = 323 msec) than to projective images (i.e. those that were part of unrelated pairs in the priming condition; $M$ = 794 msec, $SD$ = 326 msec) (see Figure 4). This pattern of results suggests that the observed effect of relatedness in the priming condition may reflect processing differences between the *in* images and the projective images rather than being indicative of a connection between the abstract and spatial uses of *in*.

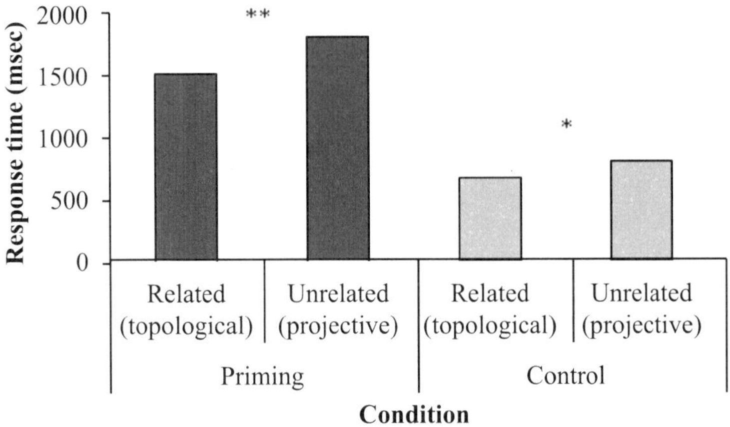


FIGURE 4. Response Times to Topological and Projective Images in the Priming and Control Conditions; ** $p < .01$. *$p < .05$.

### 3.3.2 ON Pair Results

As with the *in* pair results, we observed an effect of relatedness in the priming condition, $F(1, 18) = 9.11$, $p = .007$, whereby participants responded to the images in related pairs (i.e. topological images) significantly faster ($M$ = 1414 msec, $SD$ = 332 msec) than to the images in unrelated pairs ($M$ = 1605 msec, $SD$ = 351 msec). However, in contrast to the results for *in*, a similar effect was not observed in the control condition, $F(1,16) = 0.00$, $p = .987$, suggesting that the observed effect of relatedness in the priming condition does not reflect processing differences between the *on* images and the projective images but, rather, is indicative of a connection between the abstract and spatial uses of *on* (see Figure 5).

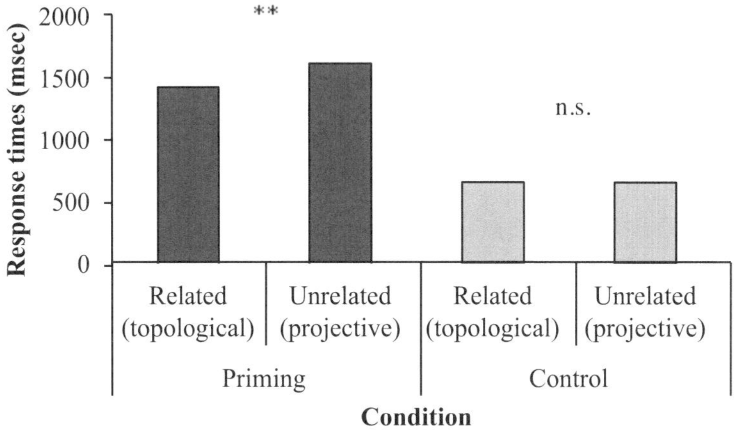


FIGURE 5. Response Times to Topological and Projective Images in the Priming and Control Conditions; ** $p < .01$. n.s. $p > .05$.

In addition to the effect of relatedness, we observed an effect of response type in the priming condition, whereby participants were significantly faster to decide that *on* images and projective images were natural/expected when they were preceded by natural/expected *on* phrases ($M$ = 1403 msec, $SD$ = 363 msec) than by unnatural/unexpected *on* phrases ($M$ = 1621 msec, $SD$ = 311 msec), $F(1, 18) = 10.81$, $p = .004$. This pattern of response times is the same as that observed for *on* phrases in Experiment 1 and suggests that there is a processing cost associated with switching response type across prime-target pairs.

### 3.4 Discussion

We asked in Experiment 2 whether accessing an abstract use of a preposition would facilitate subsequent access to a spatial meaning, indicative of a connection between the two that is distinct from those argued for in Conceptual Metaphor Theory. To find out, we asked participants to assess the naturalness of spatial images that were presented either in isolation or in a priming context whereby *in* and *on* phrases served as primes. The general logic underlying this experiment was that an asymmetry in response times such that topological images were responded to more quickly than projective images could be indicative of a connection between the abstract and spatial uses of these prepositions, provided that we could rule out the simpler explanation of an asymmetry involving ease of access across the two types of depicted relation.

Experiment 2 revealed an asymmetry in the time it took participants to respond to *in* images and projective images that was present regardless of whether they were preceded by the processing of *in* phrases. This pattern of results suggests that differences in the accessibility of the images themselves may account for the noted response time difference. In contrast, the asymmetry between *on* images and projective images was only observed when the images were preceded by *on* phrases, suggesting a connection between the abstract and spatial meanings of *on* whereby accessing an abstract use facilitated subsequent access to the spatial meaning.

## 4 General Discussion

The aim of the current study was to test for the existence of psychologically real connections between concrete and abstract uses of individual lexical items. We used the prepositions *in* and *on* as our test case and across two experiments found evidence that accessing one class of uses, either spatial or abstract, was facilitated by immediately prior access to the other class of uses, suggesting that there are psychologically real connections between concrete and abstract uses of these prepositions. However, the results also suggest that the finding of psychologically real connections must be qualified. First, we observed that the connections were not bidirectional, with the processing of spatial and abstract uses each influencing the processing of the other. Rather, the connections we observed were unidirectional, suggesting asymmetric relations between spatial and abstract prepositional meanings. Second, and more importantly, we observed that the directionality of the connections differed considerably depending on which preposition was being tested.

We turn first to the results for *in*. The results from Experiment 1 provide evidence of connections between spatial and abstract uses whereby access to spatial uses of *in* facilitated subsequent access to abstract uses of *in*. However, in Experiment 2 we observed no priming effect in which access to abstract uses facilitated subsequent access to spatial uses. This pattern of results is consistent with the grounding assumption of Conceptual Metaphor Theory (cf. Lakoff 1987; Lakoff and Johnson 1980), which states that abstract meanings grow from, and remain grounded in, concrete ones.

In sharp contrast to the results for *in*, we found no evidence of connections between spatial and abstract uses of *on* in Experiment 1, suggesting that accessing spatial uses of *on* may not facilitate subsequent access to abstract meanings. However, we did find evidence in Experiment 2 of connections between abstract and spatial uses of *on*, with access to spatial uses facilitated by access to abstract uses. Thus, while our evidence suggests that there are psychologically real connections between concrete and abstract uses of *on*, these connections are inconsistent with the direction of influence implicated by grounded metaphorical connections.

The difference we observed in the directionality of the connections between prepositional uses echoes differences between *in* and *on* in their combinatorial possibilities, particularly with regard to uses beyond the concrete spatial. Previous work has noted that *in* is more frequent, occurs in more contexts, and participates more freely in novel combinations than does *on* (Breaux and Feist 2010; Navarro i Ferrando 1998). We believe that these cross-preposition differences may be related to the differences we observed in the directionality of connections that are accessed during on-line processing. Strong connections from spatial to abstract uses may indicate that a metaphor is 'live,' leading to greater ease of combination, as has been observed for the preposition *in*. On the other hand, a more restricted ease of combination, as observed in earlier studies, and a strong connection from abstract uses to spatial ones, as observed for *on* in the current set of studies, may be hallmarks of a metaphor that is no longer productive. As a result, the connections that exist between different uses of a single lexical item may serve as clues not to the impetus of the different senses, but rather, to the current state of the lexical item as a vibrant, extendable entity.

While a difference in degree of metaphorical activity between the two prepositions is compatible with the patterns in our data, it leaves unexplored the possibility that, just as the two prepositions are not equivalent to each other, the individual senses of the prepositions may differ amongst themselves. As a case in point, many analyses of prepositional polysemy have proposed that individual abstract senses are linked to different concrete uses of the prepositions (e.g. Lakoff 1987; Tyler and Evans 2003).[3] Thus, it may be that some concrete uses of *on* are more metaphorically active than others (and likewise for *in*), suggesting that our results may stem from the cumulative effects of the degree of metaphorical activity associated with each of the concrete senses of *in* and *on*, rather than from differences between the two prepositions *per se*. Discriminating between these possibilities will involve more fine-grained studies along the lines of the studies presented here; we leave these follow-up studies to future research.

The current study is incompatible with an account of prepositional polysemy based in thematic parallels or similarities in conceptual structure that exist between concepts (cf. Jackendoff and Aaron 1991; Murphy 1996;

---

[3] We thank an anonymous reviewer for raising this point.

Murphy 1997), as such an account cannot explain the directionality observed in the priming results for both *in* and *on*. In choosing between accounts with a strong metaphorical component, however, the opposed directionalities observed in the connections for *in* and *on* similarly preclude a single account of polysemy which may apply to all polysemous terms. Rather, our results suggest that a clear understanding of the nature of the connections between uses of polysemous lexical items will require more fine-grained lexical semantic and psycholinguistic research, undertaken one lexical item at a time.

## References

Boroditsky, L. 2000. Metaphoric structuring: Understanding time through spatial metaphors. *Cognition* 75: 1–28.

Boroditsky, L. and M. Ramscar. 2002. The roles of body and mind in abstract thought. *Psychological Science* 13: 185–88.

Breaux, B. O. and M. I. Feist. 2010. Extending beyond space. *Proceedings of the 32nd Annual Conference of the Cognitive Science Society*, ed. by S. Ohlsson and R. Catrambone, 1601–06. Austin, TX: Cognitive Science Society.

Casasanto, D. and L. Boroditsky. 2008. Time in the mind: Using space to think about time. *Cognition* 106: 579–93.

Cuyckens, H. and B. E. Zawada. 2001. Introduction. *Polysemy in Cognitive Linguistics: Selected papers from the International Cognitive Linguistics Conference, Amsterdam, 1997*, ed. by H. Cuyckens and B.E. Zawada, ix–xxvii. Amsterdam: John Benjamins.

Davies, M. 2008–. The Corpus of Contemporary American English: 450 million words, 1990–present.

Gentner, D. 2001. Spatial metaphors in temporal reasoning. *Spatial Schemas in Abstract Thought*, ed. by M. Gattis, 203–22. Cambridge, MA: MIT Press.

Grady, J. E. 1999. A typology of motion for conceptual metaphor: Correlation vs. resemblance. *Metaphor in Cognitive Linguistics: Selected papers from the Fifth International Cognitive Linguistics Conference in Amsterdam, July 1997*, ed. by R.W. Gibbs and G. J. Steen, 79–100. Amsterdam/Philadelphia: John Benjamins.

Jackendoff, R. and D. Aaron. 1991. More Than Cool Reason: A Field Guide to Poetic Metaphor. [Review of the book *More Than Cool Reason: A Field Guide to Poetic Metaphor*, by G. Lakoff and M. Turner]. *Language* 67: 320–28.

Lakoff, G. 1987. *Women, fire, and dangerous things: What Categories Reveal About the Mind*. Chicago: University of Chicago Press.

Lakoff, G. and M. Johnson. 1980. *Metaphors We Live By*. Chicago: University of Chicago Press.

McGlone, M. S. 2001. Concepts as metaphors. *Understanding Figurative Language: From Metaphors to Idioms,* edited by S. Glucksberg, 90–108. New York: Oxford University Press.

Murphy, G. L. 1996. On metaphoric representation. *Cognition* 60: 173–204.

_____. 1997. Reasons to doubt the present evidence for metaphoric representation. *Cognition* 62: 99–108.

Navarro i Ferrando, I. 1998. A cognitive semantics analysis of the lexical units AT, ON and IN, in English. Doctoral dissertation, University Jaume I.

Tyler, A. and V. Evans. 2003. *The Semantics of English Prepositions*. Cambridge: Cambridge University Press.

# 3

# Creativity and the Sensorimotor Grounding of Mathematics

BODO WINTER AND TEENIE MATLOCK

## 1 Introduction

Hearing the word 'mathematics' often conjures up images of boring high school lectures and arduous problem sets. To many of us, mathematics seems like an overly abstract and seemingly untouchable subject matter, removed from any connection to the real world, and at the same time rigid and unwieldy. The mathematician Zagier (2012: 16) writes that 'most people cannot begin to imagine how mathematics and pleasure can be related at all', and he says that some people are even 'filled with dread at the mere thought of mathematics' (ibid., 12).

In this paper, we highlight the many ways in which math and creativity are connected. We argue that the inability to see the more creative aspects is part of what makes math seem so dreary to many. And we take an embodied stance on creativity in math, arguing that much of what can be called creative in this subject area arises from spatial mental imagery and the sensorimotor grounding of mathematical concepts. We discuss numerous experiments on mathematical metaphors such as MORE IS UP, MORE IS RIGHT and MORE IS BIGGER. Together, these studies support the existence of connections between our sense of number and our sense of space. Alongside these experimental studies, we discuss how the interplay between mathematics and the arts provides evidence for the spatial nature of creativity in mathematics.

*Language and the Creative Mind.*
Mike Borkent, Barbara Dancygier, and Jennifer Hinnell (eds).

## 2 Mathematics, Art and Space

Many people are unaware of the intricate connections mathematics has with the arts. Sometimes mathematics is reflected in art, and sometimes art leads to the discovery of new mathematics. In this section, we discuss examples of this interplay between these seemingly different fields, and we point out that a common theme that connects mathematics and the arts is their involvement in space and spatial creativity. After that, we discuss experimental evidence supporting a mental connection between math and space.

One example of the link between creativity and mathematics is seen in Renaissance art. During this epoch, artists became increasingly interested in representing the real world in spatially accurate perspectives. To do so, artists had to develop principles that would enable the projection of three-dimensional space onto the two-dimensional space of a canvas. This, in turn, led to the development of an entirely new branch of mathematics: projective geometry. Kline (1967: 230) says that 'The works of the Renaissance artists are hung in art museums. They could, with as much justification, be hung in science museums.' Thus, projective geometry is a branch of mathematics that can arguably be seen as stemming from creative exploration.

Another example of the intricate connections between space, art and mathematics is 'hyperbolic crocheting'. Hyperbolic spaces are an essential part of Non-Euclidian geometry, but Bellos (2010: 383) rightly calls hyperbolic geometry 'an utterly counter-intuitive type of geometry'. In fact, it has been claimed that it is impossible to build a stable real-world model of hyperbolic spaces that could be used to demonstrate how these spaces look like (cf. discussion in Henderson and Taimiða 2001). Because of this, it was hard to come up with a consistent mental image of how a hyperbolic space might look like, making the topic elusive and literally difficult to grasp. But then, the Latvian mathematician Daina Taimiða stumbled upon a way of constructing these spaces *while crocheting*. She discovered that hyperbolic spaces can be created following certain stitching patterns, an idea that was later formalized in Henderson and Taimiða (2001). This example demonstrates how something that was previously unimaginable and abstract has been made concrete and tangible through the creative exercise of crocheting.

A final example of the development of new mathematics through art is origami, which recently has underwent a resurgence of interest due to the development of computational origami (e.g. Demaine and O'Rourke 2007), a field that has great prospects of producing efficient engineering and design structures that use minimal space when folded, but that can serve numerous useful functions when expanded. Computational origami builds on a set of axioms that were discovered by Humiaki Huzita, a Japanese-Italian mathematician and origami artist. Again, we can see that a form of art (origami) drove the development and discovery of new mathematics.

Across these different examples it is clear that arts and mathematics are linked through their common involvement with space. Other examples of this connection include the mathematical art of M.C. Escher, the mathematics of tessellation in Arab mosaics, fractal art, and the aesthetically pleasing visuospatial proofs of the Pythagorean theorem (see Nelsen 1993).

It could be argued that art and mathematics cross-foster each other only when both already share the common denominator of space. However, this common denominator sometimes needs to be cognitively created afresh, which is a creative act. A case in point is the number *i* (the square root of negative one). For most of its history, *i* has been elusive and its status as a number was controversial. Lakoff and Núñez (2000 Ch.VI: 3), Mazur (2003) and Fauconnier and Turner (2001) argue that the concept of the number *i* becomes graspable once one mentally projects *i* and its multiples onto a number plane. Mazur (2003) argues that the creative act of coming up with the spatial image of *i* being located on a number plane played a pivotal role in the cultural acceptance of this concept. Moreover, the spatial view of this number unlocks new mathematics (such as polar coordinate geometry), which can then be applied to *i*.

To conclude this section, it seems that the history of mathematics, as well as the history of arts, support the idea that spatial mental imagery plays a role in leading to novel and ultimately creative insights in mathematics.

## 3 Embodied Mathematics and Experiments

Lakoff and Núñez (2000) use Conceptual Metaphor Theory (Lakoff and Johnson 1980; Gibbs 1994) to analyze mathematical ideas (see also Núñez 2005, 2007). They propose that mathematics can be seen as a system of metaphorical mappings such as ARITHMETIC IS OBJECT COLLECTION or ARITHMETIC IS MOTION ALONG A PATH. Alongside this research, mathematicians have also discussed how some of the seemingly abstract axioms at the foundation of mathematics (e.g. negative times negative yields positive) are grounded in concrete physical principles (Kline 1967: 371).

Alongside this more theoretical perspective, psychologists, cognitive scientists and neuroscientists have explored experimentally whether there are mental connections between space and mathematics. Dehaene, Bossini, and Giraux (1993) demonstrated that Western Europeans seem to think of numbers as being aligned on a left-to-right going number line. These researchers found that when participants saw relatively larger numbers on a screen (say, 8 instead of 2), they were faster to press a button with their right hand than with their left hand. This is interpreted as showing that if the response is consistent with a horizontal mental number line, responses are sped up. This general finding has been replicated in more than 100 experiments (see review in Wood et al. 2008), and it can be taken to suggest a mapping that can be called MORE IS RIGHT.

Other studies support a vertical mapping, in line with the metaphor MORE IS UP (cf. Lakoff 1987: 276–277). For example, Hartmann, Grabherr and Mast (2012) found that participants generated 'higher' numbers when their bodies were moved upwards, and 'lower' numbers when their bodies were moved downwards. In a similar vein, Winter and Matlock (2013) found that when participants were asked to call out numbers while they moved their head rhythmically upwards and downwards, they generated larger numbers when looking upwards. Sell and Kaschak (2012) found that when participants read sentences that contained quantity information such as the words 'more' or 'less', they were quicker to respond with an upwards oriented response button to larger implied quantities, and with a downwards oriented response button to smaller implied quantities.

Another mapping that has gained experimental support is MORE IS BIGGER, or QUANTITY IS SIZE. For example, when participants were shown relatively 'large' numbers (numerically speaking), they were quicker to respond if the number was presented in larger font (Henik and Tzelgov 1982). Hurewitz, Gelman, and Schnitzer (2006) found participants to systematically overestimate the quantity of dots if these covered more area. These results show that the mental concepts of size and numerical quantity are interacting with each other, in line with a metaphorical mapping of physical extent to numerical quantity.

While these studies provide evidence for conceptual mappings such as MORE IS RIGHT, MORE IS UP or MORE IS BIGGER, there is abundant evidence for mental connections between space and numbers in the field of neuroscience. Many neuroscientific studies on this topic have shown that the parietal cortex becomes activated when participants process numbers or quantities (Hubbard et al. 2005; Pinel et al. 2004). This brain area is not only implicated in the processing of number and quantity, it is also implicated in the processing of space, therefore, indicating that the mental connection between space and numbers is mirrored by a neurological connection as well.

Compared to the high-level interactions between the arts, mathematics and space discussed in Section 2, the experimental results discussed in this section are located at a much lower level, focusing on simple things such as mental arithmetic or numerical representation. The connection between abstract mathematics and simple numerical representations still needs to be made. However, initial evidence already supports the idea that the two levels are connected, and that spatial thinking in abstract mathematics builds on spatial thinking about basic numbers and simple mathematical operations. For example, when mathematics student explain abstract proofs from calculus, they tend to make co-speech gestures (see e.g. Marghetis and Núñez 2013), many of which are in line with the basic numerical representations that are discussed in the experimental studies mentioned above.

## 4 MORE IS BIGGER in Mental Arithmetic

Both for abstract mathematical concepts and the mental representation of numbers, spatial thinking has been claimed to play a heavy role. But, currently there is not much experimental evidence to support that idea that the spatial concepts discussed above play a role in *doing* math. In this section, we discuss a survey-based study that explores the role of the conceptual metaphor MORE IS BIGGER in performing simple arithmetic problems. The study seeks evidence for the activation of size-based concepts while computing routine addition and subtraction. A total of 203 University of California, Merced, undergraduates took part in the study and received extra credit in an undergraduate social sciences course. All participants were native speakers of English. Each received a two-page study, of which the first page contained the following instructions, with the second page as shown in Figure 1.

> On the next page, you will see a simple math equation above a box. Inside the box, you will see '=' preceded by the operator symbol '+' or '-'. Your job is to fill in the blanks by drawing circles to match the numerical values in the math equation above the box. For example, for the number '6', you would draw 6 circles. Please draw your circles as quickly as possible. You can turn the page now.

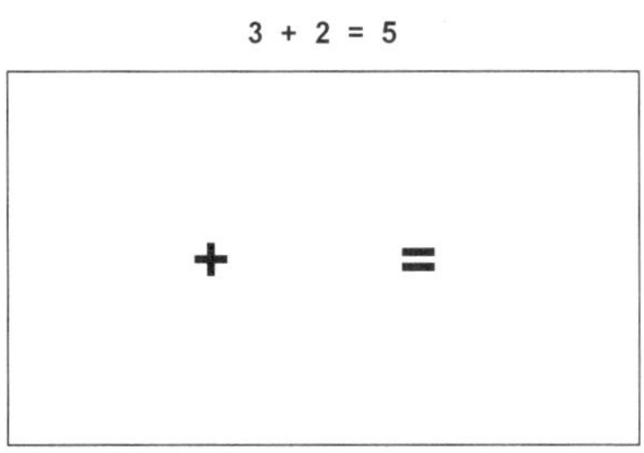


FIGURE 1. Example stimulus (addition condition) from the drawing experiment.

There were two conditions. Each participant was either in an addition condition (they saw either 3+2=5 or 2+2=4), or in a subtraction condition (they saw either 7-2=5 or 6-2=4). We predicted that addition should tacitly trigger the numerical concept 'more' because it represents an increase in quantity, and subtraction should trigger the concept 'less' because it represents a decrease in quantity. If these concepts are indeed mentally related to conceptions of size, differences in the *physical* size of the circles should arise. In other words, it should be the case that participants draw slightly larger outcome circles for addition than for subtraction.

We measured the rectangular area covered by circle groups by multiplying the largest horizontal extent of the group of circles with the largest vertical extent. Participants drew circle groups in clusters (127 participants) or horizontally lines (76). However, the interpretation of the results that we report below did not differ between cluster-drawers and line-drawers, thus we only report analyses that combined these two drawing strategies[1]. The results are displayed in Figure 2.

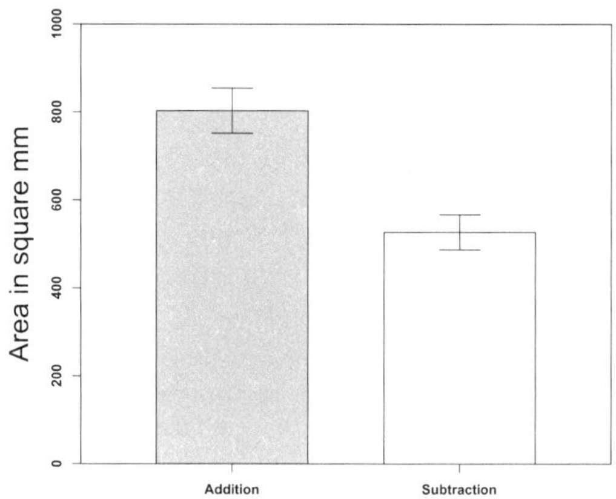


FIGURE 2. Overall circle area in addition and subtraction condition. Error bars represent standard errors.

Participants in our study drew circle groups about 3.04 square centimeter larger in the addition condition (*M*=5.27) than participants in the subtraction condition (*M*=8.31) (t(191.784)=4.25, p<0.001). This is in line with the idea that people naturally think about an increase in quantity, and concomitantly, about an increase in physical size when they are doing addition. So, even though the circle size is an irrelevant dimension with respect to solving this task (critically, we never asked people to pay attention to the size of the circles), we observed differences in area that are consistent with

[1] Only 12 participants drew circles arranged as vertical lines. Because these were too few to be analyzed separately, we excluded these 12 data points (6% of the overall data) from the analysis. All other items (215) were considered for the analysis. The four distances were measured by a research assistant. To assure reliability of measurements, the first author recoded 10% of the items. The two measurements correlated well with each other (r=0.89) and the average deviation between coders was low (~1.11 mm).

the idea that MORE IS BIGGER plays a role in mental arithmetic. These findings are also consistent with the idea that people use metaphors such as ARITHMETIC IS OBJECT COLLECTION (Lakoff and Núñez 2000) to reason about operations such as addition and subtraction.

It is worth noting that we only discovered an effect of size, and not an overall dislocation of the group of circles. For example, if participants were thinking about arithmetic in terms of motion along a path in this experiment, we would have expected the group of circles to be dislocated rightwards with addition (consistent with the metaphor MORE IS RIGHT) and leftwards with subtraction. However, this is not what we found. Apparently participants were more likely to respond in a way that is consistent with MORE IS BIGGER in this task. There are several reasons why this could be the case. First, MORE IS RIGHT is not expressed in English, but MORE IS BIGGER is. When we talk about numbers, we either use the language of size ('this is a huge sum') or the language of verticality ('this is a high number'), but we do not say 'this number is more towards the right' to say that a number is larger, except for maybe some really special circumstances (e.g. when talking about visually represented sequences). However, if language entrenchment were the only factor, we would also expect to find the circles to be physically higher in the addition condition because of the prevalence of talking about numbers in terms of verticality. This is not what we found.

Another reason why participants were more likely to draw larger outcome circles after addition rather than higher outcome circles might have to do with the fact that circles can be more readily interpreted as object collections, such as a pile of gumballs or pile of popcorn. When the quantity of such collections is varied, the overall size of the collection is expected to change, but not the horizontal or vertical dislocation of the collection. Thus, the task that we employed might be more readily interpreted in line with ARITHMETIC IS OBJECT COLLECTION and the consistent metaphor MORE IS BIGGER, than with ARITHMETIC IS MOTION ALONG A PATH. Which metaphors structure our thinking about arithmetic probably relies to some extent on the nature of the stimuli used and the nature of the task.

We have to admit, however, that there is an important alternative explanation for the data presented above. It could potentially be the case that we observed smaller circles after subtraction simply because with our subtraction items, the first number in the sequence was necessarily larger (**7**-2=5, **6**-2=4) than with addition (**3**+2=5, **2**+2=4). Maybe participants were drawing smaller outcome circles because these seemed smaller compared to 6 or 7. To disentangle our current hypothesis from this alternative explanation, future work needs to test zero addition and subtraction such as 5+0=5 and 5-5=0.

## 5 Implications and Conclusions

We discovered that when people drew circles to depict numbers in arithmetic problems, they drew larger circle groups for addition than for subtraction. Overall, these results lend support to the idea that mathematics imports conceptual structure from physical experiences, in line with such metaphorical mappings as MORE IS BIGGER. From this perspective, mathematics is in fact not that abstract, but instead deeply connected to concrete notions such as physical size.

Language reflects this as well: We use the language of physical size to talk about numerical quantities, such as when we say, 'This is a huge sum' or 'This is a large number'. And it seems to be the case that a number of quantity terms can be historically traced back to words that describe size or physical extent, for example, the word 'more' goes back to the Proto-Indo-European root **me-* 'big', and 'quantity' goes back to the Latin word *quantitatem* 'relative greatness or extent' (Harper 2012). So, our experiment (section 4) and other experiments on mathematical cognition (section 3) mesh nicely with these observations from synchronic and diachronic linguistics. There seems to be a lot of converging evidence that suggests that math is in fact not that abstract.

What are the implications of this embodied perspective of mathematics? In this section, we will discuss how this approach can be helpful in teaching mathematics, and how it can be used to get more people to become interested in this subject. Many people see mathematics as dreary or daunting. Some people actively try to steer away from this subject, and some of these people can even be classified as 'innumerates', as mathematical illiterates (Paulos 1988). Some people even have innate or neurological mathematical disorders, such as dyscalculia. Yet, in our everyday lives, we constantly need to add and subtract quantities, for example, when checking whether we have enough money to buy doughnuts and coffee at the diner, or when planning dinner parties. Moreover, much of our everyday work life requires us to perform simple calculations with numbers and quantities. How might embodied mathematics be helpful here?

If people really do think about numbers in terms of space, then we should try to foster these thought patterns. Bryant and Squire (2001: 175) mention that many developmental psychologists viewed the connection between space and numbers 'in a negative way'. They say that space for these psychologists 'is part of the problem in children's mathematics, not part of the solution' (cf. discussion in Walsh 2003). An embodied perspective would argue that the way we teach mathematics should be in line with our 'natural mappings'. Learning and teaching should be consistent with our natural tendencies to construe the world, and it should follow the natural way in which the human mind develops (Egan 1997). Thus, if we acquire spatial metaphors of numbers such as MORE IS UP and MORE IS BIGGER through embodied interaction with the world early on in our lives, we should embed these metaphors in teaching rather than trying to avoid them.

Some strands of mathematical education are already in line with this idea. For example, many mathematical textbooks for kindergarteners and first graders are colorful and full of concrete physical examples, and a lot of them reinforce such important concepts as the number line (consider the Number Line Frog that appears in many American textbooks). However, it seems that once children proceed to middle school and high school mathematics, a lot of this concrete approach is given up, even though, as Lakoff and Núñez (2000) argue, much of 'higher' mathematics seems to also rely on spatial mental imagery and other embodied concepts. It seems that this abstract way of teaching mathematics might unduly limit the creative exploration of this subject matter.

Middle school and high school mathematics teaching is typically fairly disembodied. However, in recent years, there is a growing interesting in actively pushing a more embodied perspective in mathematics education (see also Núñez, Edwards, and Matos 1999; Núñez 2007). For example, the Mathematical Imagery Trainer (Howison et al. 2011; Euson and Abrahamson 2005) uses movements in line with MORE IS UP to teach fractions and proportional progression (2:3 – 4:6 – 6:9). And, Cress, Fischer, Moeller, Sauter and Nuerk (2010) used a digital dance mat to teach relative numerical magnitudes. And, more and more teaching tools that promote numeracy in patients with dyscalculia start emphasizing space to increasing extents (Wilson et al. 2006).

We offer some ideas here. First, the involvement of mathematics in art and the involvement of art in mathematics (discussed in section 2) could be used as another avenue in making mathematics more interesting and more graspable. Adults and children who cannot or do not want to realize the beauty of math themselves might be motivated if confronted with some of the many examples that highlight the more creative aspects of mathematics. Zagier (2012: 16) points out that the 'mathematics that everyone learns in school is almost always just a collection of recipes for everyday use or, at best, in science.' Some of the most creative, interesting and aesthetically pleasing aspects of mathematics are never discussed in school mathematics. Even though some examples discussed in section 2 might not be immediately relevant for specific applications (e.g. leading towards calculus or linear algebra, topics important in engineering), they might be useful in keeping students interested in mathematics and making it seem like a topic that is less removed and abstract than is generally believed.

Second, given that we already have evidence for MORE IS BIGGER, MORE IS UP and MORE IS RIGHT, metaphor research needs to address such questions as: What are the specific advantages conferred by these different metaphors? Does structuring number space in one way as opposed to another help in certain situations? Do different people have different propensities to think about numbers in one way or another? And, under which conditions does which metaphor become salient? We also need to investigate further how these relatively low-level metaphors relate to more abstract and high-level mathematics such as calculus and linear algebra. Addressing these questions will be crucial for developing more advanced and more targeted embodied teaching tools.

Zagier (2012: 12) contrasts mathematics from other fields by pointing out that while other sciences 'are clearly characterized according to the objects they study: heavenly bodies, living things, human relationships', mathematics studies many different objects, some of which seem – at first sight – fairly abstract. For example, entities such as 'sets', 'equations' or 'imaginary numbers' appear to have no straightforward connection to the real world. However, when there is a lack of concrete physical objects, education can create these objects, sometimes in a physical form, such as in hyperbolic crocheting, and sometimes in a mental form, such as in the 'imaginary number line' of *i*. In this paper, we have argued that creating such mental objects can aid mathematical thinking, and more generally, we have argued that an embodied approach will prove useful for teaching mathematics.

## References

Bellos, A. 2010. *Alex's Adventures in Numberland*. London: Bloomsbury.

Bryant, P., and S. Squire. 2001 Children's mathematics: lost and found in space. In M. Gattis (Ed.), *Spatial Schemas and Abstract Thought* (pp. 175–201). Cambridge: MIT Press.

Cress, U., U. Fischer, K. Moeller, C. Sauter, and H.-C. Nuerk. 2010. The use of a digital dance mat for training kindergarten children in a magnitude comparison task. *Proceedings of the 9th International Conference of the Learning Sciences* (pp. 105–112). Chicago, IL. Online.

Dehaene, S., S. Bossini, and P. Giraux. 1993. The mental representation of parity and number magnitude. *Journal of Experimental Psychology: General*, 122, 371–396.

Demaine, E., and J. O'Rourke. 2007. *Geometric Folding Algorithms: Linkages, Origami, Polyhedra*. Cambridge: Cambridge University Press.

Egan, K. 1997. *The educated mind: How cognitive tools shape our understanding*. Chicago: University of Chicago Press.

Euson, K. C., and D. Abrahamson. 2005. Understanding ratio and proportion as an example of the Apprehending Zone and Conceptual-Phase problem-solving models. In J. Campbell (Ed.), *Handbook of mathematical cognition* (pp. 213–234). New York: Psychology Press.

Fauconnier, G., and M. B. Turner. 1998. Conceptual Integration Networks. *Cognitive Science*, 22:2, 133–187.

Gibbs, R. W. 1994. *The poetics of mind*. Cambridge, UK: Cambridge University Press.

Harper, D. 2012. Online Etymology Dictionary. [http://www.etymonline.com/]

Hartmann, M., L. Grabherr, and F. W. Mast. 2012. Moving along the mental number line: Interactions between whole-body motion and numerical cognition. *Journal of Experimental Psychology: Human Perception and Performance*, 38:6, 1416-1427.

Henderson, D. W. and D. Taimiða. 2001. Crocheting the Hyperbolic Plane. *Mathematical Intelligencer* 23: 17–28.

Henik, A., and J. Tzelgov. 1982. Is three greater than five: The relation between physical and semantic size in comparison tasks. *Memory and Cognition*, 10, 389–395.

Howison, M., D. Trninic, D. Reinholz, and D. Abrahamson. 2011. The Mathematical Imagery Trainer: from embodied interaction to conceptual learning. In G. Fitzpatrick and C. Gutwin (Eds.), *Proceedings of the ACM CHI Conference on Human Factors in Computing Systems*. New York: ACM. Online.

Hurewitz, F., R. Gelman, and B. Schnitzer. 2006. Sometimes area counts more than number. *Proceedings of the National Academy of Sciences*, U.S.A., 103, 599–604.

Hubbard, E. M., M. Piazza, P. Pinel, and S. Dehaene. 2005. Interactions between number and space in parietal cortex. *Nature Reviews*, 6, 435–448.

Kline, M. 1967. *Mathematics for the Nonmathematician*. Toronto, Canada: General Publishing Company.

Knops, A., A. Viarouge, and S. Dehaene. 2009. Dynamic representations underlying symbolic and nonsymbolic calculation: Evidence from the operational momentum effect. *Attention, Perception, and Psychophysics*, 71, 803–821.

Lakoff, G. 1987. *Women, Fire, and Dangerous Things*. Chicago: The University of Chicago Press.

Lakoff, G., and M. Johnson. 1980. *Metaphors we live by*. Chicago: The University of Chicago Press.

Lakoff, G., and R. E. Núñez. 2000. *Where Mathematics Comes from*. New York: Basic Books.

Marghetis, T., and R. E. Núñez. 2013. The Motion Behind the Symbols: A Vital Role for Dynamism in the Conceptualization of Limits and Continuity in Expert Mathematics. *Topics in Cognitive Science*, 1–18.

Mazur, B. 2003. *Imagining numbers*. New York: Farrar Straus Giroux.

Núñez, R. E. 2005. Creating Mathematical Infinities: The Beauty of Transfinite Cardinals. *Journal of Pragmatics*, 37, 1717–1741.

Núñez R. E. 2007. The Cognitive Science of Mathematics: Why is it relevant for Mathematics Education? In R. Lesh, E. Hamilton, and J. Kaput (Eds.), *Foundations for the Future in Mathematics Education* (pp. 127–154). Mahwah, NJ: Lawrence Erlbaum Associates.

Núñez, R. E., L. Edwards, and J.-F. Matos. 1999. Embodied Cognition as Grounding for Situatedness and Context in Mathematics Education. *Educational Studies in Mathematics*, 39 (1–3), 45–66.

Paulos, J. A. 1988. *Innumeracy: Mathematical Illiteracy and its Consequences*. New York: Vintage Books.

Pinel, P., M. Piazza, D. Le Bihan, and S. Dehaene. 2004. Distributed and overlapping cerebral representations of number, size, and luminance during comparative judgements. *Neuron*, 41, 1–20.

Nelsen, R. B. 1993. *Proofs Without Words: Exercises in Visual Thinking*. Washington: The Mathematical Association of America.

Sell, A. J., and M. P. Kaschak. 2012. The comprehension of sentences involving quantity information affects responses on the up-down axis. *Psychonomical Bulletin and Review*, 19, 708–714.

Walsh, V. 2003. A theory of magnitude: common cortical metrics of time, space and quantity. *TRENDS in Cognitive Sciences*, 7, 483–488.

Wilson, A. J., S. Dehaene, P. Pinel, S. K. Revkin, L. Cohen, and D. Cohen. 2006. Principles underlying the design of 'The Number Race', an adaptive computer game for remediation of dyscalculia. *Behavioral and Brain Functions*, 2:19. [online publication]

Winter, B., and T. Matlock. 2013. More is up… and right: Random number generation along two axes. In M. Knauff, M. Pauen, N. Sebanz, and I. Wachsmuth (Eds.), *Proceedings of the 35th Annual Conference of the Cognitive Science Society*. Austin, TX: Cognitive Science Society.

Wood, G., H.-C. Nuerk, K. Willmes, and M. H. Fischer. 2008. On the cognitive link between space and number: a meta-analysis of the SNARC effect. *Psychological Science Quarterly*, 50, 489–525.

Zagier, D. 2012. The beauty of numbers. *MaxPlanckResearch* 1, 12–17.

4

# How Creativity Strains Conventionality in the Use of Idiomatic Expressions

PATRICK J. DUFFLEY

## 1 Introduction

The most recent full-length study of idiomatic creativity (Langlotz 2006) rightfully views this phenomenon as a form of 'intelligent human behaviour that is based on general cognitive principles and processes.' These allow speakers to 'manipulate an idiom as a cognitive micro-model – a mental network that can be evoked to organise and communicate the abstract conceptual relationships in a target conceptualisation figuratively' (289–290). Based on Geeraerts' (1995) prismatic model of idiomatic meaning, Langlotz shows how in many cases the scene evoked by the literal meaning of the idiom is 'not deactivated or absent,' but works as a 'metaphorical standard of comparison in relation to which the idiomatic meaning is itself concretised' (108). Thus for example the literal meaning of the idiom *to take the bull by the horns* gives rise to the implicatures that the problem tackled was difficult to face and required effort and determination. Such idioms are consequently not impenetrable semantic units, but rather have a motivated and analyzable semantic structure that makes them open to variation and creativity, which can play on the literal scene (as in *to walk a narrow tightrope*), on the idiomatic meaning (as in *to walk a financial tightrope*), or on the correlation between the two (as in the description of the plot

*Language and the Creative Mind.*
Mike Borkent, Barbara Dancygier, and Jennifer Hinnell (eds).

of an Italian mafia movie which uses the expression *to kill Bertoli before he can spill the pasta*), as demonstrated by Langlotz (2006: 206–215).

However, according to Langlotz (2006: 193–194), in order for an idiom to be open to creative variation, the association between the literal and idiomatic scenes must be motivated and analyzable on the basis of entrenched conceptual patterns. Some idioms are claimed to be opaque and to resist conscious manipulation, such as for example *to kick the bucket*, in which the two-place transitive scene evoked by the literal meaning is nonisomorphic with respect to the one-place intransitive idiomatic meaning 'to die', and in which there is consequently no referent in the idiomatic scene corresponding to the direct object *bucket*. Invariability has also been claimed for *to kick the bucket* by a considerable number of other authors, making this idiom a sort of *exemplum classicum* of the category of invariable idiom. Newmeyer (1972: 297), for instance, states that *pail* could not be substituted for *bucket* when this sequence is used in its idiomatic meaning. Similarly, Gibbs et al. (1989) claim that *punt the bucket* cannot convey the meaning 'to die' since speakers are unable to semantically decompose *kick the bucket*. Fernando (1996: 48) describes this idiom as 'unlikely to tolerate any additions, even innovative ones.' Glucksberg (2001: 81–82) holds that it is 'difficult to imagine a context in which someone would say *kick the pail* instead of *kick the bucket*, as one cannot discern any communicative intent that would prompt a speaker to make this substitution.' Evans (2009: 241–243) uses *kick the bucket* as an example of a lexical concept whose corresponding form is restricted to the terms *kick*, *the*, and *bucket*, the only variation possible being the subject and tense-aspect-modality of the verb *kick*.

The goal of this paper will be to show that cognitive isomorphism and transparency are not absolute conditions for the variability of idiomatic expressions and that speaker creativity is not hampered by the referential opacity of idiomatic expressions whose literal scene is analyzable. More specifically the 'opaque' idioms *kick the bucket* and *shoot the breeze* (cf. Langlotz 2006: 129, 236) will be demonstrated to manifest all of Langlotz's basic forms of idiom variation, viz. constructional adaptations, literal-scene manipulation, topic indication and topic-related literal-scene manipulation.[1] Additional creative variations will also be attested and their production linked to the poetic function of language identified by Jakobson (1960) and the language-user maxim of 'extravagance' proposed by Haspelmath (1999). The data for this study has been collected from the Internet, which Wierzbicka (2009: 102) sees as holding 'great potential for the study of the semantics of phraseology.'

---

[1] I have omitted Langlotz's fifth category of ambiguation and punning, as it can be conflated with the category of topic-related literal-scene manipulation in my opinion.

## 2 Constructional Adaptation

Langlotz's first category of variation, constructional adaptation, includes things like aspectual variation, passivization and pluralization, which are associated with fitting the idiom to the literal scene to which it refers. As regards *kick the bucket*, Langlotz (2006: 221) agrees with Glucksberg (1993: 20) that this idiom does not appear in the progressive. This is claimed to be due to the semantic discrepancy between the transitional nature of dying and the momentary nature of kicking, with which the progressive can only be used if one wishes to describe a repetition of this punctual action. A google search for *is kicking the bucket* retrieved over 300 occurrences of this sequence, however, most of which referred to particular singular processes of dying. The first occurrence, given in (1) below, refers to the death throes of a pet fish. A good number of progressives were also found that referred to electronic devices which had begun to show signs of malfunction, as in (2).

(1) My Male Betta is Kicking the Bucket
(http://www.acquariumadvice.com)

(2) My Xbox is Kicking the Bucket
(http://www.tribalboyz.net)

Passivization is another constructional manipulation that is claimed to be excluded for *kick the bucket* by a number of authors (cf. Newmeyer 1974; Moon 1998: 208; Glucksberg 2001: 84; Langlotz 2006: 251; Wulff 2008: 2; Makkai 2011: 221). Langlotz attributes this to the intransitivity of the idiomatic scene and its consequent nonisomorphism with respect to the transitive action of kicking the bucket. Glucksberg puts the absence of the passive form down to pragmatic considerations, claiming that it makes no sense to place focus on the bucket, which, because it lacks a referent in the idiomatic scene, does not lend itself to topicalization. Glucksberg neglects to take into account however the depersonalizing function of the passive, which is attested in uses such as (3) and (4) below:

(3) LOL, Ian Shuttleworth wrote a joint biography of her [Emma Thompson] and Kenneth Branagh in 1995! I.e. when (he was under the impression that) they were still married. So it was really the last minute for that particular biography even if no buckets were kicked.
(http://www.forums.emma-thompson.org)

(4) no buckets were kicked, no coffins were nicked, no trolls expired, no babies were sired.
(http://community.tasteofhome.com)

Here the negative determiner *no* combines with the agentless passive to convey the absence of any deaths in the scenarios evoked by these sentences. The passive is also attested in another function which shows the influence of the transitivity of the idiom on the construal of the idiomatic meaning itself. In (5) and (6) below the meaning conveyed is that of the transitive 'kill' rather than the intransitive 'die':

(5) The Chaotic Combo is no more. Most of their buckets have been kicked. The City Council runs the town now, and they're too busy to care about Chris.

(http://doesi.deviantart.com)

(6) He [Christ] was so full of the Truth, that when His bucket was kicked, Truth is what came out.

(http://metroworshipcenter.blogspot.com)

This corresponds to the active construction with a possessive determiner illustrated in (7):

(7) He [Bin Laden] is better off dead and it's a shame we couldn't put him through the torture he caused all his victims before we kicked his bucket for him.

(http://www.rubbins-racin.com)

One sees here how the conceptual scaffolding provided by the literal meaning of the idiom allows possibilities that the paraphrase of the most commonly found idiomatic meaning does not. This provides interesting confirmation of Geeraerts' prismatic theory of idioms, as it constitutes evidence that the literal meaning of the idiom configures the view of the targeted scenario, with death being construed through a transitive image in the case of *kick the bucket*.

Passive forms are also attested with the idiom *shoot the breeze*:

(8) We jump back to the PTParty, where everyone seems to be having a great time. Drinks flow, the breeze is shot, the fat is chewed, and a rug is being well and truly cut by several of the folks in attendance, but we're not too interested in them right now. What we are interested in is a quiet secluded corner, where Twiggie sits on a beanbag looking out at the party.

(http://www.talkwrestlingonline.com)

In the above use the passive fulfils a depersonalizing function as it does in (3) and (4), the import of the passage being to provide a generic description of a stereotypical party, and so it is not consonant with the effect sought by the writer to identify who is shooting the breeze.

Langlotz (2006: 236) also claims that because of its opacity *shoot the breeze* does not allow any variation in the determiner introducing the noun, as it is unclear 'relative to which discursive referent, domain of knowledge or situational context this definiteness could be motivated.' The attestation of sequences such as *to kick the proverbial bucket* and *to shoot the proverbial breeze* shows however that the notion of definiteness does seem to characterize the nouns in these constructions. Moreover, both passive and active contexts show considerable variation in determiner usage. For the passive construction, the following were attested:

(9) Like most online groups, rides are posted, advice is given, breeze is shot, piss is taken and a bit of fun is had.
(http://www.kiwibiker.co.nz)

(10) Later, schlepping loads up to a gear cache, Daren, Matt and myself are sprawled out at el mirador, lounging and breaking under the damp overcast skies. Jake and Eva wander up the trail on their way to Campo Bridwell to cache gear. More breeze is shot. Later we meet up for a leisurely and friendly mate session at Campo Bridwell.
(http://patagonia.jaredspaulding.com)

(11) Most of the breeze was being shot by one sloppy looking 'veteran' driver who claimed to be not just 'supertrucker,' but 'superduper trucker'.
(http://www.layover.com)

In active constructions, other kinds of variation were discovered:

(12) We came back a couple of times to rent boards, pick up shirts, and just shoot a little breeze. Very cool place.
(http://www.yelp.ca)

(13) I'm just a little site in a big internet, and the fact you're taking the time to shoot some breeze with me says a lot. So again, thank you.
(http://kdm-racing.com)

(14) Having been told to dress in white, some took a stab at the possible theme by going in clockwork orangesque get up, others banked on the halloween proximity and dolled up nice and ghoullish, but everyone must have passed by the window on the way in where a ripley look a like and her crew were shooting their despondent breeze.
(http://www.metafilter.com)

Sentence (9) shows that the noun phrase is felt by some speakers to be sensitive to generic reference, while (10) and (11) exhibit the possibility of quantifying the noun *breeze*. Examples (12) and (13) involve yet other forms of quantification; (14) illustrates the possibility of introducing the noun by a possessive determiner.

The utterances attested with *kick the bucket* in (3) and (4) above also invalidate another of Langlotz's claims, namely that 'the compatibility constraint prevents this idiom from modifying or pluralizing the NP' (2006: 221). In fact, in the two contexts just cited only the plural seems possible, due to the need to negate the occurrence of whatever possible number of deaths might have taken place in the situations referred to. The plural form is also found outside of passive contexts; a search for the sequence *kicked their respective buckets* got over sixty hits, of which a typical example is given in (15):

(15) Dave Thomas and Frank Perdue have also kicked their respective buckets.

(http://boards.straightdope.com)

The plural corresponds here to a reference to a specific number of deaths.

## 3 Literal-Scene Manipulation

The second type of idiom variability identified by Langlotz is literal-scene manipulation. Here a modification of the idiom's literal meaning is used to imply some added information about the actual referent, as in *to walk a narrow tightrope* where the adjective expresses a greater degree of precariousness than the bare noun in the unmodified idiom. Although implied to be impossible in the literature, this type of variability is also found with both *kick the bucket* and *shoot the breeze*. In (16) and (17) below, a quality is attributed to the bucket in the literal scene in order to imply something about the person whose demise is envisaged in the idiomatic target scenario:

(16) When I was married to Prince, who stands to inherit a gazillion dollars when his parents kick their gold-plated bucket, I felt soothed by the cocoon of comfort that mega-wealth brings, yet also anaesthetized and dumbed-down by it.

(http://open.salon.com)

(17) Being naturally reluctant to kick his brimming bucket of life while still a lusty juvenile, Mr Bhosh was occupied in lamenting the injudiciousness of Providence.

(http://www.gutenberg.org)

The result is a fully consistent image on the literal level that is considerably richer than the standard image and consequently conveys a richer meaning on the idiomatic level. This type of variability was also found with *shoot the breeze* in cases such as (18)–(20):

(18) It had been a decent, barely decadent dinner. Held at the Monkey Bar in New York two weeks ago, GQ Tasty, a couple of forever-thirsty contributors, and one terrifyingly Machiavellian, high-powered Hollywood publicist sat down to shoot the warm April breeze over burgers, one lukewarm lobster thermidor and, for me, a perfectly cooked line-caught piece of striped bass.
(http://www.gq-magazine.co.uk)

(19) Friends can come too since Suzhou is equipped with private nooks where a group of 4–6 can just shoot the afternoon breeze.
(http://shootmeagainsir.wordpress.com)

(20) taking you to visit with and photograph the monks of ancient Angkor Wat we then shoot the sunset breeze at our favourite lake side rest spot.
(http://greentourscambodia.com)

Here the modifier of the noun characterizes the setting in which the chit-chat takes place. It would not appear to be the case therefore that literal-scene manipulation is 'highly restricted for opaque idioms' (Langlotz 2006: 210).

## 4 Topic Indication

Langlotz's third category of idiom variability is 'topic indication,' in which the element added to the idiom operates exclusively on the level of the idiomatic meaning, as in *to walk a financial tightrope*. This type is also attested with *kick the bucket*:

(21) Gadget was acting weird & looked like it was ready to kick its digital bucket.
(http://drfeelgoed.multiply.com)

Here *digital* operates on the figurative level to specify the type of demise as being that of an electronic device. Contrary to Langlotz's (2006: 211) claim that 'for topic indication to work, the idiomatic configuration must be potentially isomorphic,' there is no referent here that corresponds isomorphically to *bucket* in the idiomatic scene. Rather, the adjective *digital* characterizes something corresponding to the overall sense of the expression, namely the type of death referred to. Another case was found in which the adjective modifying *bucket* characterized the person who might die:

(22) Officials in Florida need to know who to contact if you are seriously hurt or kick your British bucket in an accident.
(http://www.britishflorida.com)

This would seem to exhaust the possibilities offered by the idiomatic scene for this expression, which involves both an act of dying and a being who dies.

Topic-indicating variations were also found with *shoot the breeze*. These generally referred to the subject of the small-talk, as in (23)–(24) below, or to the speaker's evaluation of it, as in (14) above with the adjective *despondent* and (25) below with *silly*:

(23) For my book *Brain Trust*, I chatted with Ian Stewart, mathematician, prolific puzzle author and very fun person to shoot the mathematical breeze with, who explains the following best card trick I've ever seen, invented by mathemagician Art Benjamin of Harvey Mudd College.
(http://www.britishflorida.com)

(24) So here we are, an expression of spiritual meaning, not a search for it. Sweet, huh? Let's meet on this Web site. Shoot the cosmic breeze. Compare notes.
(http://www.mightycompanions.org)

(25) so it came to pass that on my final Sunday I found myself at last at Henry's adobe hut deep down in the Tumbaco valley east of Quito, guzzling gutrot rum, shooting the silly breeze, and petting his mule Rocinante, the same hut where he blew his brains out with a pistol after falling in rash and unrequitable love ('woo the wench I shall') with a girl-woman almost young enough to be his granddaughter.
(http://spikejapan.wordpress.com)

## 5 Topic-Related Literal-Scene Manipulation

Lastly, Langlotz's fourth category of topic-related literal-scene manipulation is also attested with *kick the bucket*:

(26) All we know with certainty is that Titian died in 1576. (…) He may have been over, or under, 90 years old when he kicked the paint can.
(http://www.ft.com)

Here the literal scene of *kick the bucket* is adapted to the context of the death of a painter, with the substitution of *paint can* for *bucket* relating the literal meaning to the actual context of the target conceptualization. This topic-related literal-scene manipulation does not alter the idiomatic meaning, nor does it undo the structure of the literal scene; its effect is to tailor the literal scene to the topic, evoking not a generic death but rather one of a painter, and further implying that death put an end to Titian's painting career.

## 6 Poetic or 'Extravagant' Alteration

Above and beyond Langlotz's four categories of idiom variation, the expression *kick the bucket* was also attested in usage which corresponded to the poetic function of language identified by Roman Jakobson (1960) and the maxim of 'extravagance' ('talk in such a way as to be noticed') proposed by Haspelmath (1999). In effect, certain variants of this idiom seem to have to do with the esthetic quality and originality of the way the speaker expresses himself. This has been observed both on the level of form and of meaning. On the level of meaning, the fixed character of the idiom encourages some speakers to introduce variation for the sake of variety itself. Thus attestations were found of *pail* being substituted for *bucket*, and of *punt* and *flip* for *kick*:

(27) Hey everyone my phone kicked the pail last week and I lost everyone's everything.

(http://www.facebook.com)

(28) When Walter Cronkite punted the bucket recently, the title of 'Most Trusted Man in America' fell to – believe it or not – Jon Stewart.

(http://www.dallasobserver.com)

(29) Hermione Granger was dead. She had died, flipped the bucket, gone to the other side, seen the light, anything you want to call dying.

(http://www.fanfiction.net)

With *shoot the breeze*, three other nouns besides *breeze* and two other verbs besides *shoot* were attested:

(30) I'll be vlogging, blogging and logging all the happenings during the forum so feel free to tweet me @ThatGirl_Chloe and let's shoot the wind.

(http://techfluff.tv)

(31) How draining is it when you're generally quite chirpy, you think 'hey, I'll pop down to the pub, shoot some air with some chums, down some brews.'

(http://benigntumour.blogspot.com)

(32) Every woman likes to take care of her nails, especially when preparing for a special event or occasion, so why not take your bridesmaids out to the nail salon for some potential time together?

Your girls will be thanking you for being so thoughtful. You can even throw a spa party and shoot the zephyr to get rid of the wedding day stress. A girls' convention is all the time needed to heal stress, and what great way to de-stress than with a minute pampering?

(http://bestcarryonbagss.blogspot.ca)

(33) but I had a very good time, meeting up with a lot of you guys, exchanging ideas and just blowing the breeze with you all!

(http://www.wargamerau.com)

(34) Today was a total body push it – bleh. I upped all times on the machines to seven minutes (max allowed for this workout, too bad, so sad) and started getting through it. (…) And then... The Dreaded One! You know what? I did it! mmhmm. I think the IV helped. I did seven minutes on the stair climber at level five, which is something like 12,478 floors climbed or one lap on the stairs at a Friday Fun Run.

I stagger off that insult to all that is virtuous and wheeze the breeze with a trainer. He's checking on me, which I appreciate to no end. His biggest concern is burn out, he wants my suffering to last for decades not a few namby pamby months – that's for wimps!

(http://exerciseinfutility1.blogspot.ca)

Besides literal-scene manipulation, (34) above also shows the introduction of the poetic device of rhyme. Another form of sound-play was also found in which a word rhyming with *breeze* was substituted in order to produce a humorous effect based on the semantic relation between it and the adjective *icy* used in the previous context:

(35) Where do you go on icy adventures? Shoot the freeze on Talk!

(http://www.yelp.com)

On the level of form, three variants of *kick the bucket* were found in which the choice of lexical items was motivated not only by synonymy with the components of the standard expression but mainly by the desire to create alliteration, the first of which also contained a third semantic variant of *kick* not yet mentioned:

(36) Big Busted Bimbo Boots the Bucket
[blog post about the death of Anna Nicole Smith, American model, actress and TV personality who first gained popularity in Playboy Magazine]

(http://www.randompaul.blogspot.com)

(37) My 5-year-old Dell kicked the can a few weeks ago.
(http://www.copperykeenclaws.com)

(38) Thanks for the info. I didn't know Dolly [the cloned sheep] had punted the pail. I remember hearing a couple of years ago that she was showing signs of premature aging (...).
(http://forums.randi.org)

Example (38) also undermines the claim made by Gibbs et al. (1989) quoted above that *punt the pail* cannot convey the meaning 'to die.' Alliteration would also seem to be at work in the common, more vulgar variant of *shoot the breeze* employing the noun *shit*, which in its turn has spawned semantically-based variants with the nouns *crap* and *bull*.

## 7 Conclusions

As Fernando (1996: 2) has observed, 'idioms attract wordplay.' The very fact of having a more or less canonical form invites speakers to play around with the conventional phraseology in order to introduce effects of novelty and personal style. Another element that plays a role is the fact that an idiom is supposed to be more expressive than the literal expression to which it corresponds ('emotionally-charged' in the words of Brinton and Brinton 2010: 111); consequently, when the idiom starts to lose its novelty and expressive power, some speakers rejuvenate it by introducing creative variants of their own. As Haspelmath (1999: 1057) has noted, there is a tension in language users' behaviour between 'conformity' (talking like everyone else talks) and 'extravagance' (talking in such a way as to be noticed), and speakers sometimes 'want their utterance to be imaginative and vivid – they want to be little 'extravagant poets' in order to be noticed, at least occasionally.'

The uses that obey the maxim of extravagance represent the most striking example of the way in which creativity strains conventionality in the use of idioms. As in the field of art, speakers can take a conventional form and personalize it so as to create something new and striking out of what would otherwise be old and stale. Outside of the usage illustrated in (34) and (36)–(38), which exemplifies what Gibbs (1994: 265) has called 'the poetry of everyday speech,' we have also seen that an idiom which is thought to be opaque and nonisomorphic with respect to its target scene is amenable to the same types of variation as idioms which are transparent and isomorphic. This suggests that as long as an idiom's literal scene is analyzable it has a cognitive reality to which speakers can apply their imagination. Only idioms that are both nonanalyzable and nontransparent such as *by and large* (cf. Glucksberg 2001: 75) do not lend themselves very easily to creative variation.[2] Examination of more data would probably uncover further forms of creativity that the study of the two idioms considered in this paper has not brought to light. There are indeed more things in heaven and earth than are dreamt of in our philology.

## References

Brinton, L. J. and D. M. Brinton. 2010. *The Linguistic Structure of Modern English*. 2nd ed. Amsterdam: John Benjamins.

Evans, V. 2009. *How Words Mean. Lexical Concepts, Cognitive Models and Meaning Construction*. Oxford: Oxford University Press.

Fernando, C. 1996. *Idioms and Idiomaticity*. Oxford: Oxford University Press.

Geeraerts, D. 1995. Specialization and Reinterpretation in Idioms. *Idioms: Structural and Psychological Perspectives*, eds. M. Everaert, E. van der Linden, A. Schenk, and R. Schreuder, 57–73. Hillsdale, NJ: Lawrence Erlbaum.

Gibbs, R.W., N. Nayak, and C. Cutting. 1989. How to Kick the Bucket and not Decompose: Analyzability and Idiom Processing. *Journal of Memory and Language* 28: 576–593.

Gibbs, R. W. 1994. *The Poetics of Mind: Figurative Thought, Language, and Understanding*. Cambridge: Cambridge University Press.

Glucksberg, S. 1993. Idiom Meanings and Allusional Context. *Idioms: Processing, Structure, and Interpretation*, eds. C. Cacciari and P. Tabossi, 3–26. Hillsdale, NJ: Lawrence Erlbaum.

Glucksberg, S. 2001. *Understanding Figurative Language: From Metaphors to Idioms*. Oxford: Oxford University Press.

---

[2] Even here, one must agree however with Glucksberg (2001: 84) that an opaque noncompositional idiom can be varied productively 'if there are discernible relations between a modification and an idiom's original meaning and referents.' Two variants of *by and large* were indeed found on the Internet:

(a) It could have been broad and brash and an over-the-top cartoon. Instead, by and (not so) large, it feels like a kinder, gentler, warm and fuzzy *How to Succeed* which succeeds without giving in to temptations to schtick it up. (http://www.talkinbroadway.com)

(b) For India's sarkari health care by and large, or should that be by and small? is arguably one of the worst in the world. (http://blogs.timesofindia.com)

The whole sequence tends however to manifest the behaviour of a single word, as it can be suffixed by *-ly* (c), used as a pre-adjectival adverb (d), and written in hyphenated form (e):

(c) There is only one split among atheists that really matters, and because by and largely atheists are not formally organized, and atheism is largely a very loose mass phenomenon and not an organization, that essential split is often concealed by all sorts of things. (http://www.one-episcopalian-on-faith.com)

(d) Public pressure from a by and large thriving citizen sector continues, and there will be subsequent rounds of negotiation … (http://www.impacteconomy.com)

(e) With one noticeable patchy spot, a by-and-large fun (and funny) collection of Can Con shorts. (http://torontoist.com)

Haspelmath, M. 1999. Why is grammaticalization irreversible? *Linguistics* 37: 1043–68.

Jakobson, R. 1960. Closing Statements: Linguistics and Poetics. *Style in Language*, ed. T. A. Sebeok, 350–377. Cambridge, MA: MIT Press.

Langlotz, A. 2006. *Idiomatic Creativity*. Amsterdam: John Benjamins.

Makkai, A. 2011. On Redefining the Idiom. *Lacus Forum* 36: 215–27.

Moon, R. 1998. *Fixed Expressions and Idioms in English: a Corpus-based Approach*. Oxford: Clarendon Press.

Newmeyer, F. J. 1972. The Insertion of Idioms. *Papers from the Eighth Regional Meeting of the Chicago Linguistic Society*, eds. P. M. Peranteau, J. N. Levi, and G. C. Phares, 475–81. Chicago: Chicago Linguistic Society.

Newmeyer, F. J. 1974. The Regularity of Idiom Behavior. *Lingua* 34: 327–42.

Wierzbicka, A. 2009. Exploring English Phraseology with Two Tools: NSM Methodology and Google. *Journal of English Linguistics* 37: 101–29.

Wulff, S. 2008. *Rethinking Idiomaticity: A Usage-based Approach*. London/New York: Continuum.

# Part II

# Constructions and Frames

5

# The Indefinite Article in Complex Quantifiers

RONALD W. LANGACKER

## 1 Grounding and Quantification

The issue to be addressed is the status and meaning of the indefinite article in the core English quantifiers *a few*, *a little*, and *a lot of*. The description is part of a broader analysis of nominal expressions in Cognitive Grammar (Langacker 1991, 2004, 2008).

In this account, an expression's category is determined by its profile, the intersubjective focus of attention within the content evoked. A noun profiles a thing (abstractly defined), whereas verbs, adjectives, and prepositions designate relationships. The count/mass distinction—indicated by a circle vs. an ellipse—depends on whether the profiled entity is conceived as bounded. As shown in Figure 1(a), a plural is a special kind of mass noun.

A nominal (or 'noun phrase') incorporates grounding—a specification of the profiled referent's epistemic status. The key issue is whether the referent is identifiable at the current point in the discourse. Proper nouns (surveyed in Coates 2006) presuppose a unique referent identified to both interlocutors, so they stand alone as full, grounded nominals. These include both proper names (e.g. *Len Talmy*) and terms for abstract entities such as numbers (e.g. *seven*). Identification becomes an issue for nouns that specify types with multiple instances. Overt grounding is thus required: *a tree*; *that water*. A nominal is said to be definite or indefinite depending on whether the profiled instance is identified. As seen in Figure 1(b), this distinction is marked with a filled vs. an unfilled dot.

*Language and the Creative Mind*.
Mike Borkent, Barbara Dancygier, and Jennifer Hinnell (eds).

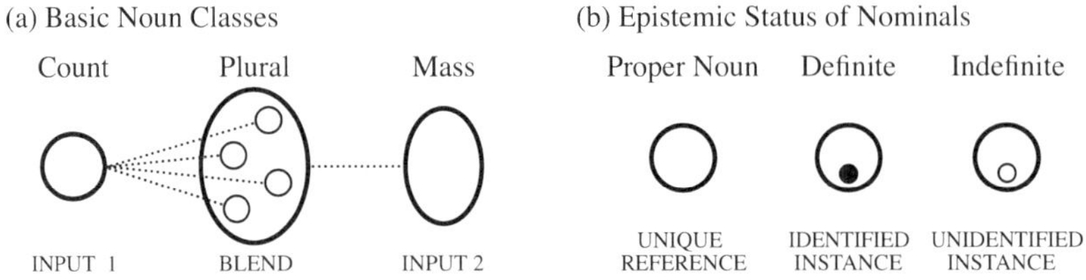


FIGURE 1

Definite grounding elements include demonstratives and the definite article. Our concern here is indefinite grounding, which for count nouns is effected by the indefinite article *a(n)*. For mass nouns the matter is far more complex. Because there is no supposition of bounding, the referent can be of any size and the delimitation of instances is arbitrary. The default for a mass is the absence of delimitation, in which case the referent is the maximal extension, i.e. the totality of its manifestations. Construed in this fashion, a mass noun's referent is unique, so it functions as a proper noun without explicit grounding: *She dislikes {apples / fruit}*. But any delimited portion of a mass constitutes a nonunique instance of its type. Delimitation is often implicit, a post hoc result of contextual interpretation: *She put {apples / fruit} in the bowl*. It is also imposed by various overt elements: definite determiners (*these apples*, *this fruit*, *the {apples / fruit}*; the indefinite article *sm* (unstressed *some*), the counterpart of *a* (*sm {apples / fruit}*); and quantifiers (*few apples*, *little fruit*).

The core system of English quantifiers comprises two basic groups distinguished by their semantic and grammatical properties: relative (*all*, *most*, *some*, *no*, *every*, *each*, *any*) and absolute (*many*, *few*, *much*, *little*, *several*, and the lower counting numbers). Semantically, relative quantifiers characterize the nominal referent in relation to the maximal extension of the type in question: the totality of its instances. They do not specify quantity in the narrow sense of invoking a scale of measurement. Rather, they indicate degrees of universality within the maximal extension (MX). As shown in Figure 2(a), for example, *most* profiles a mass that merely approximates universality within MX. By contrast, absolute quantifiers do invoke a scale and specify quantity independently of MX. The import of *many*, as seen in 2(b), is that the quantified mass extends along the scale beyond some tacit norm (n).

As for their grammatical differences, we observe in (1)(a)-(b) that absolute quantifiers have quasi-adjectival uses, occurring as clausal predicates or between a determiner and a head noun. By contrast, relative quantifiers do not occur as clausal predicates and are mutually exclusive with grounding elements, suggesting that they themselves serve this function. These gram-

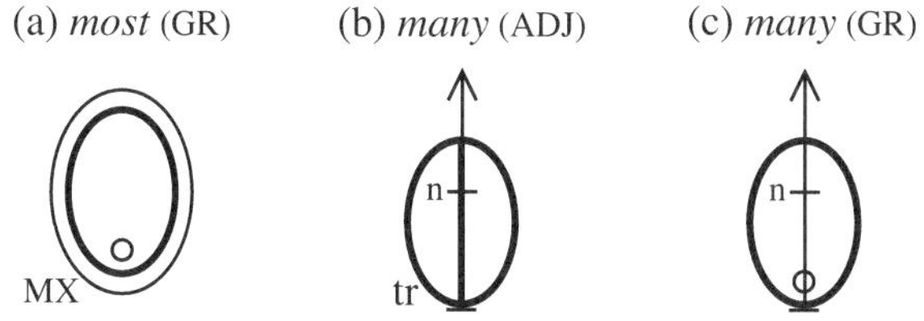


FIGURE 2

matical properties are reflected in certain features of Figure 2. In 2(a), the unfilled dot indicates the grounding function of *most,* whereby it designates an unidentified instance of some type. A general feature of grammaticized grounding elements is that they profile the grounded entity (in this case a mass) rather than the grounding relation (Langacker 2002). On the other hand, diagram (b) reflects the relational nature of adjectives. *Many* profiles the relationship wherein its main participant—the trajector (tr)—subtends a certain portion of the scale. It is comparable to *tall* except that its trajector is a mass instead of a vertically oriented object, and the scale measures quantity rather than height.

(1) (a) *Our problems are* **{many / few / several / three}**.
(b) *the* **{many / few / three}** *cars we own*; *the* **little** *wine I drank*
(c) **His friends are* **{all / most / some / no / every / each / any}**.
(d) **the* **all** *cars*; **these* **most** *people*; **an* **every** *boy*; **sm* **any** *wine*

Although the distinction between relative and absolute quantifiers is fairly clear, we cannot simply ascribe to them the functions of indefinite grounding vs. quantification (in the narrow sense). For one thing, these functions overlap. The central issue in nominal grounding, identification, is basically epistemic; to negotiate descriptions of the world, one needs to know what is being talked about. For referents that cannot be identified, relative quantifiers provide an alternate means of epistemic control by limiting a statement's scope to some proportion of MX. But while they do not specify absolute quantity, they clearly do have quantitative import: the instances delimited by *all*, *most*, *some*, and *no* are progressively smaller (less inclusive). Conversely, absolute quantifiers have epistemic import: a statement pertaining to *many* elements tells us more about the world than a statement pertaining to just *several*.

Not only that, but absolute quantifiers sometimes appear to function as grounding elements. While they can follow definite determiners, as in (1)(b), they more commonly occur initially: *many apples*, *few doctors*, *several complaints*, *six elephants*. This being the position of relative quantifiers and other grounding elements, the most straightforward analysis is to posit that absolute quantifiers assume grounding function in such expressions. If so, *many* has the semantic variant in Figure 2(c), where (like *most*) it profiles the quantified mass and construes it as an unidentified instance of some type. Moreover, this is hardly an idiosyncrasy of *many*, but an option available to any absolute quantifier. We must therefore recognize a general pattern of semantic alternation allowing absolute quantifiers to be construed as indefinite grounding elements.[1]

Like many semantic alternations, this one involves different profiles imposed on the same conceptual content: whereas the adjectival sense profiles the relationship between a mass and a scale of quantity, the grounding sense profiles just the quantified mass. Number terms have the same two variants—*those four elephants* (adjectival), *four elephants* (indefinite grounding)—as well as a third in which they function as proper names: *Four is greater than three*. These are sketched in Figure 3, where the quantity scale incorporates the discrete steps involved in counting. A number term profiles either (a) the relationship between a mass and the scale, (b) just the mass, or (c) just the portion of the scale which the mass subtends.

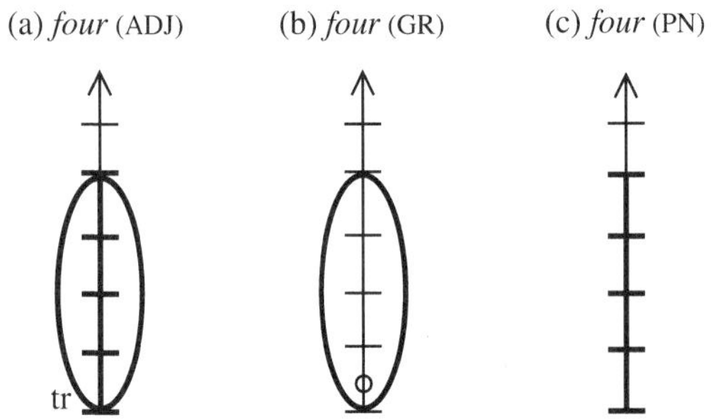


FIGURE 3

When they function as grounding elements, absolute quantifiers participate in the general pattern whereby such elements stand alone as full nominals (***Those*** *are valuable*; ***Four*** *have broken tusks*; ***Many*** *complained*). In the case of quantifiers, the resulting nominal can be incorporated in a higher-level nominal expression where an *of*-phrase defines the contextually relevant extension (as opposed to the maximal extension): *four of those elephants*; *most of his friends*; *many of the students*. Despite their important

[1] It makes little difference in Cognitive Grammar whether *many* itself has grounding import or inherits it from the pattern or from the construction as a whole. In this usage-based approach (Langacker 1999a: Ch. 4), general patterns are schematizations of particular expressions, hence immanent in them. Also, an element's meaning retains schematic features of the structures it appears in, which are part of its own characterization.

role in English quantification, these constructions do not affect the points at hand and will not be considered further.

## 2 Complex Quantifiers

Grounding is not a particular structural position or set of formal elements, but a semantic function that can be fulfilled in various ways. One way is periphrastically, through complex absolute quantifiers such as *a lot of* and *a dozen*. These form an open-ended set, grammaticized to various degrees, with no clear boundary between quantificational and nonquantificational meanings. As shown in (2), nouns in the $N_1$ slot indicate groups (e.g. *flock*), configurations (*bunch*), or containers (*box*). Some nouns are inherently quantificational: units of measurement (*pint*) and numerical expressions (*dozen*). Also included are the core quantifiers *a few*, *a little*, and *a lot of*.

(2) A periphrastic quantifying construction: *a* $N_1$ *(of)* $N_2$

(a) GROUP: *a {flock / herd / set / collection / host} of X*

(b) CONFIGURATION: *a {bunch / pile / stack / heap / pool} of X*

(c) CONTAINER: *a {box / barrel / bag / cup / can / keg} of X*

(d) MEASUREMENT UNIT: *a {pint / gallon / pound / ton / foot / yard} of X*

(e) NUMBER: *a {dozen / hundred / thousand / million / billion} X*

(f) EXTREME GRAMMATICIZATION: *a {few / little / lot of} X*

This construction reflects a still broader pattern in which a noun is modified by an *of*-phrase, e.g. *a descendant of Abraham Lincoln*. As seen in (3)(a), it is usually $N_1$ which functions as head in the sense that its referent is profiled by the nominal as a whole: *a descendant of Abraham Lincoln* refers to the descendant (not to Lincoln). But the periphrastic quantifiers have a number of special properties. For one thing, the prepositional object ($N_2$) is a mass expression which lacks explicit grounding. Also, *of* profiles a relationship of co-extension (as in *the state of California*), a special case of its general import of designating an intrinsic relation (Langacker 1999a: Ch. 3). Finally, the co-extensiveness symbolized by *of* is equated with a relation of co-extension inherent in the meaning of $N_1$ (Langacker 2009a: Ch. 3). A *flock*, for example, is co-extensive with the mass of creatures that constitute it.

(3) (a) [ [ *a* ***descendant*** $]_{NML}$ [ *of Abraham Lincoln* ] $]_{NML}$

(b) [ [ *a* ***flock*** $]_{NML}$ [ *of geese* ] $]_{NML}$

(c) [ [ *a flock* $]_{NML}$ [ *of* ***geese*** ] $]_{NML}$

Since $N_1$ and $N_2$ are co-extensive, the referent of the overall expression may be indeterminate: does *a flock of geese* refer to the flock or to the geese? Both options are evidently possible. As shown in (3)(b)-(c), either $N_1$ or $N_2$ can be the head in the sense that its referent is profiled by the full expression. It can further be argued that the semantic alternation does not affect grammatical constituency. Under either interpretation, the constituency is the same as in (3)(a), with a primary division into *a flock* and *of geese*.

Evidence for these points is provided in (4). In (a), *was* and *shaped like a V* indicate a singular subject; while in (b), *were* and *flapping their wings in unison* indicate a plural subject. Analogously, *three bags of mulch* refers to the filled bags in (c), since they *were sitting*, but to the mulch in (d), since it *was spread*. Examples (e) and (f) support the claim that the *of*-phrase forms a constituent even under the quantificational interpretation. If we force a break, *a flock of geese* can only be divided into *a flock* and *of geese*.

(4) (a) *A* ***flock*** *of geese was flying overhead, shaped like a V.*
(b) *A flock of* ***geese*** *were flying overhead, flapping their wings in unison.*
(c) *Three* ***bags*** *of mulch were sitting in the shed.*
(d) *Three bags of* ***mulch*** *was spread around the roses.*
(e) *She loves geese and ducks. She has* **a whole *flock*. *Of* geese**, *that is.*
(f) *She loves geese and ducks. *She has* **a whole *flock of*. Geese**, *that is.*

We must therefore posit a productive pattern of metonymic alternation, such that nominals of this sort can profile the referent of either $N_1$ or $N_2$. These options are shown in Figure 4, where the circle and ellipse respectively indicate the flock and the mass of geese (gg) it delimits. Their co-extensiveness, made explicit by the *of*-phrase, is represented by the double line connecting them. Observe that the overall referent, whether it be the flock or the geese, is an unidentified instance of its type. When *flock* is the head, this simply reflects its grounding by the indefinite article. When the profile shifts to the mass, the prior sequence (*a flock of*) assumes the semantic function of an absolute quantifier, which makes the referent indefinite: in terms of its functional organization, *a flock of geese* is analogous to *many geese*. And in accordance with the pattern noted previously—whereby initial absolute quantifiers are interpreted as grounding elements—the periphrastic *a flock of* also functions in this capacity.

Representing the same general construction as (3)(a), *a flock of geese* is expected to have the structure in (3)(b), with the compositional meaning in Figure 4(a). But in cases where $N_1$ and $N_2$ are co-extensive, the metonymic shift resulting in 4(b) is both natural and very frequent. The mass designated by $N_2$ is normally of greater interest by virtue of being what we actually use: with *a bunch of grapes*, we eat the grapes rather than the bunch; and if

(a) *a* ***flock*** *of geese* (b) *a flock of* ***geese***

FIGURE 4

we buy *a bag of mulch*, it is to put the mulch around the roses (not because we like the bag). This regular pattern of metonymic shift constitutes an augmentation of the basic construction. It is unproblematic in Cognitive Grammar, since there is no requirement that a composite expression inherit its profile from any particular component, nor that semantic function correlate with constituency.

As noted in (2), certain kinds of nouns tend to participate in this pattern, the key factor being co-extension. With terms for groups and configurations, $N_1$ and $N_2$ are co-extensive in the strong sense that they represent alternate ways of apprehending the same objective entity. Containers have a separate objective existence, but are effectively co-extensive with their content when it fills them. In all three cases the physical instantiation of $N_1$ is commonly less important than the delimitation it imposes on the mass. There is thus a tendency for $N_1$ to be reinterpreted as a unit of measurement. Even though such units are abstract, co-extensiveness is still a factor, as we mentally superimpose them on a mass (or conversely) by way of measuring it.

It is thus quite common for measurement terms to evolve historically from group, configuration, and container nouns. This is of course a matter of degree, and for many nouns the two senses co-exist. While *cup* still designates a physical object, *a cup of milk* may simply refer to a certain quantity of milk (irrespective of container). Since *gallon* no longer means 'pail', *a gallon of milk* can only specify quantity. Two periphrastic quantifiers, *a bunch of* and *a lot of*, have generalized and grammaticized to the point of encroaching on the core quantifier system at the expense of *many* and *much*. *Bunch* can still designate a configuration, profiled within the overall expression, as in (5)(a). But with *lot* the original group sense ('set of articles for sale') is no longer available for most speakers, so the only option is to profile the quantified mass ($N_2$), as seen in (5)(c)-(d).

(5) (a) *A* ***bunch*** *of grapes was sitting on the counter.*
(b) *A bunch of* ***grapes*** *were scattered all over the counter.*
(c) **A* ***lot*** *of grapes was sitting on the counter.*
(d) *A lot of* ***grapes*** *were scattered all over the counter.*

Figure 5 sketches the development of $N_1$ into a measurement noun. Initially it profiles a bounded physical entity, like a *barrel*, *bunch*, or *flock*, that is co-extensive with a mass it delimits. By nature such entities have the potential to serve a quantifying function. This potential starts to be realized when the noun is construed metonymically: instead of the physical entity per se, it comes to designate its volume, expanse, or extension. On this interpretation, for example, *a barrel of oil* is simply the volume of oil a barrel holds. Eventually the physical entity fades from the picture altogether. The noun then profiles a bounded segment on a scale of measurement, an increment of quantity. The profiled entity is still co-extensive with the quantified mass, but now the profile is specifically conceived as a segment of the scale.

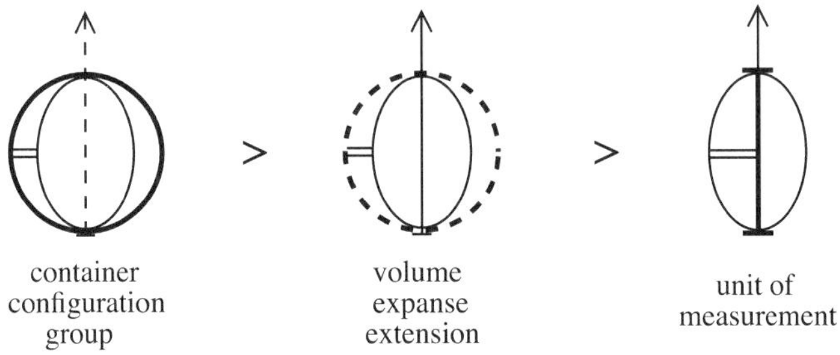


FIGURE 5

Nouns vary as to how far along this path they have moved and the extent to which earlier senses are still accessible. The noun *lot* has run the full course; for most speakers it is solely a unit of measurement. Being highly grammaticized, it is more schematic than other quantifying nouns: it does not measure any particular property (as do *gallon*, *acre*, and *ton*) and it occurs with either a plural mass (as does *many*) or a nonplural one (as does *much*). As shown in Figure 6(a), it merely specifies that the measured mass extends beyond some tacit norm.[2]

To be sure, *lot* has not grammaticized in isolation, but as part of the construction *a lot of X*. The import of *lot* itself thus has to be distinguished from the composite meaning of the overall expression. Figure 6(b) represents the composite meaning of *a lot of geese*. As expected, it is the same as for *a flock of geese* (Figure 4) except that the bounded entity serving to delimit the profiled mass is a unit of measurement (*lot*) rather than a group

[2] *Lot* is actually more schematic still, since the entity it measures need not be a mass. It also has adverbial uses, where (*inter alia*) it specifies the frequency of occurrences or the intensity of an experience: *She does that a lot*; *I like her a lot*.

(a) *lot* (b) *a lot of* ***geese***

FIGURE 6

(*flock*). But as we saw in (5)(c), with *lot* the only option is to profile the measured mass—unlike *flock*, *lot* cannot impose its profile on the composite whole. This is because it is only a unit of measurement, an abstract entity that is not per se conceived as having a real-world referent. So instead of a pattern of metonymic alternation (*a* ***flock*** *of geese* vs. *a flock of* ***geese***), we have only the shifted variant: *a lot of* ***geese***. The metonymic shift, made possible by co-extension in the case of nouns like *flock*, is made necessary by the meaning of *lot*.

## 3 Complex Core Quantifiers

Of the core absolute quantifiers, three stand out by being morphologically complex: *a few*, *a little*, and *a lot of*. To some extent these are still analyzable into component elements. While there is no doubt that *a lot of* is developing a monomorphemic version (*alotta*), its internal structure is still accessible and grammatically significant, as seen in (6).

(6) (a) *He has* ***a lot****, in fact* ***a whole collection****,* ***of antique autos****.*
(b) *Don't buy mulch—we have* ***{a lot / a whole lot / an awful lot / lots}****.*

What about *a few* and *a little*? Evidence that they are analyzable, and *a* meaningful, is the paradigmatic alternation in Table 1. In accordance with basic principles of linguistic analysis, the choice of *few* vs. *little* indicates whether the mass is plural or continuous, while the presence or absence of *a* is responsible for a positive vs. a negative construal.

| | Plural Mass | Continuous Mass |
|---|---|---|
| Positive | *a few* | *a little* |
| Negative | *few* | *little* |

TABLE 1. A paradigm of core quantifiers

*Few* and *little* are regarded as being negative in some way because they sanction negative polarity items (Klima 1964; Israel 2011), such as *any*. We see this in (7). Note first, in (a)-(d), that narrow-scope *any* requires a negative context. It thus co-occurs with *no*, but not with most other quantifiers. *Any* does however occur with *few* and *little*, which argues for their negativity. It is therefore rather striking that it fails to occur with *a few* or *a little*. These are evidently positive (or at least nonnegative), even though the quantities involved may well be the same.

(7) (a) ***No*** *guests consumed* ***any*** *wine.*
(b) **{**Three* / *Many* / *A lot of**}* *guests consumed* ***any*** *wine.*
(c) ***No*** *wine was consumed by* ***any*** *guests.*
(d) **{**Some* / *Much* / *A lot of**}* *wine was consumed by* ***any*** *guests.*
(e) ***Few*** *guests consumed* ***any*** *wine.*
(f) ***Little*** *wine was consumed by* ***any*** *guests.*
(g) ****A few*** *guests consumed* ***any*** *wine.*
(h) ****A little*** *wine was consumed by* ***any*** *guests.*

In what sense are *few* and *little* negative? I take a dynamic view of meaning and grammar, in which the conception of scales and quantities consists in mental operations of comparison and scanning (Langacker 1987, 2005). The very notion of a scale is based on such activity; its inherent directionality—naturally represented by an arrow—reflects the direction of scanning. I suggest that a scale consists in the summation of imagined comparison events, where the target of each serves as standard for the next, and where each registers a positive difference in value.

Based on a scale, at a higher level of conceptual organization, further operations give rise to scalar values and assessments of magnitude. Absolute quantifiers can thus be described dynamically in terms of scanning. In the case of the counting numbers, the operations responsible for the values are responsible for the scale itself: it is established by the counting sequence, where at each step an act of comparison registers the same minimal difference (a unit increment of value). In contrast, for *many*, *much*, *few*, and *little* the quantity scale is nondiscrete and values are computed, not with respect to the scalar origin, but to an implicit norm. Their adjectival senses are sketched in Figure 7(a)-(b): the value is reached by scanning either 'upward' or 'downward' from the norm, as indicated by a dashed-line arrow.[3]

[3] As is generally true for absolute quantifiers, each has a grounding sense as well, as shown for *many* in Figure 2. *Many* and *few* contrast with *much* and *little* in the nature of their trajector: a plural vs. a continuous mass. These need not be distinguished for present purposes.

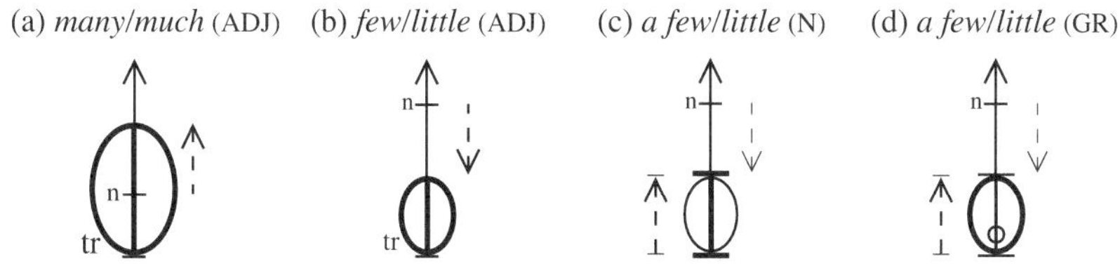


FIGURE 7

We can therefore say that *few* and *little* are negative because their essential import consists in downward mental scanning, running counter to the scale's inherent directionality. This is comparable to the negativity exhibited by adjectives like *unpleasant*, where the stem makes a scalar assessment and *un-* reverses its direction. *Many* and *much* are positive (or neutral) because the direction of scanning aligns with that of the scale. What about *a few* and *a little*? At first blush they seem problematic. On the one hand, they specify scalar values that are roughly the same as for *few* and *little*, i.e. the quantity is small or less than normal. But on the other hand, they are positive in the same way as *many* and *much* (e.g. they fail to sanction *any*). There is no real inconsistency, however, since *a few* and *a little* are complex: though based on negative forms, they are derived expressions with their own composite meanings.

Their positive import is evidently due to the indefinite article, which only occurs with nouns. It seems, then, that *few* and *little* receive a nominal construal in the context of these complex forms. When combined with *a*, they function as abstract units of measurement, comparable to *lot* in Figure 6 except that the quantity they indicate is less than the norm instead of greater. As shown in Figure 7(c), the profiled segment of the quantity scale is the one subtended by the trajector in the adjectival sense; it is reached by scanning downward from the norm. Superimposed on this basic conception, however, is a positive construal in which the quantity is assessed by scanning upward from the scalar origin. Reflecting the meaning of *a*, it represents a one-step departure from the origin: a single increment of value.

As abstract units of measurement, *a few* and *a little* are not conceived as having real-world referents, so expressions like *a few* ***beers*** or *a little* ***wine*** can only refer to the beers or the wine (not the quantity). Hence they participate in the general pattern wherein absolute quantifiers assume the function of grounding elements, as represented in Figure 7(d). But since *a few*, *a little*, and *a lot* necessarily undergo this metonymic shift, one might question whether the nominal variants in Figures 6(a) and 7(c) actually exist. There are indications that they do. First, their overt use as nouns is not at all impossible. Given a reason to say it, the following seems quite acceptable:

*A lot is more than a little*. The expression is directly analogous to *Four is greater than three*, cited earlier to illustrate the use of number terms as proper nouns (Figure 3(c)). Like number terms, *a few*, *a little*, and *a lot* have unique reference as the names of abstract measurement units.

A second point is that *a few* and *a little* conform to a broader pattern deriving measurement units from scalar values, being parallel to expressions like *a hundred*, *a thousand*, and *a million*. These alternate with expressions having the same numerical values but where *one* occurs in lieu of *a* (e.g. *one hundred*). Since *one* is primarily used in counting, *a* effectively marks their status as measurement units. In this guise they function as complex absolute quantifiers that directly precede the head noun: *a few days*, *a little time*, *a hundred years*. Lacking the preposition *of*, this construction represents a variant of the basic pattern for complex quantifiers. The difference reflects the origin of the quantifying noun. In the basic construction *a* $N_1$ *of* $N_2$, the source of $N_1$ is a group, configuration, or container noun, such as *lot*, *bunch*, or *barrel*; for these the notion of co-extensiveness, expressed by *of*, is inherent and fairly salient. By contrast, a main feature of the variant construction *a* $N_1$ $N_2$ is that $N_1$—*few*, *little*, or a number term—itself represents a scalar value. In this case the notion of co-extension, though still present (Figure 5), is less salient precisely because it does not involve a distinct, physically manifested entity (like a container).

Corroborating the count-noun status of $N_1$ is another constructional variant where it pluralizes: *{lots / hundreds / tons / loads / heaps / mountains / scads / oodles} of X*. Such expressions lend themselves to hyperbole (*mountains of laundry*), and $N_1$ is commonly nonliteral (*tons of fun*) or even nonexistent (**scad*, **oodle*). Both number terms and *lot* are used in this variant, so the question arises why *few* and *little* cannot be: **{fews / littles} of X*.[4] It may just be that the nominal value of *few/little* (Figure 7(c)) is too abstract and complex in origin to be seized upon for this purpose. Also, *few* and *little* by themselves have negative import, which is counter to the construction's hyperbolic spirit and its notion of unrestricted quantity.

## 4 The Indefinite Article

Our main concern is the nature and status of *a* in complex core quantifiers. It should now be clear that it remains a structurally significant element. But is it still a grounding element? Is it still to be identified as the indefinite article? What exactly does it mean?

---

[4] Number terms appear in the *a* $N_1$ $N_2$ construction, and *a lot of* is a core quantifier, so each patterns with *few/little* in a certain way.

We can first note that in quantifying expressions of the form *a* $N_1$ *(of)* $N_2$, *a*'s meaning pertains specifically to $N_1$—it does not ground $N_2$ or the nominal as a whole. This is quite evident with ungrammaticized expressions like *a flock of* ***geese*** or *a bag of* ***mulch***, as the indefinite article is semantically compatible with $N_1$ (a count noun) but not $N_2$ (a mass noun): *a {flock / bag / *geese / *mulch}*. At the opposite end of the spectrum, embedded in the grammaticized quantifiers *a few*, *a little*, and *a lot of*, its diminished accessibility argues against a major functional role in the full expression. There is no basis for supposing that *a* itself has taken on a meaning compatible with mass nouns, or that it functions individually to ground $N_2$ or the nominal overall.

In its basic use, the indefinite article occurs with a (common) count noun, which specifies a type conceived as having multiple instances. This multiplicity makes identifiability a central issue for nominal grounding. The definite and indefinite articles form a minimal system of opposing values in this regard: the choice of *the* vs. *a* indicates whether the referent is or is not uniquely identifiable at the current point in the discourse (Hawkins 1978; Langacker 1991: §3.1).

Along another axis, the indefinite article forms a minimal opposition with the number *one*. Now in a certain sense number is not an issue with count nouns, which (by the definition adopted here) are always singular. So while *a* does imply the quantity 'one', it does not oppose it to other numerical values; it is primarily a marker of indefiniteness, its quantitative import being secondary. It is also true, however, that a count noun stands in opposition to the corresponding plural, which implies some integral quantity greater than one. From this perspective the singularity of a count noun represents the minimal numerical value, the degenerate case where a plural mass collapses to just a single entity (thus losing its mass-like character). When conceived in relation to this broader range of options, the quantitative import of a count noun is indeed an issue. *One* is then used in lieu of *a*, as seen in (8). In terms of semantic function, *one* can thus be viewed as a quantitatively reinforced variant of the indefinite article. But as a counting number it belongs as well to the core system of absolute quantifiers. When it takes on grounding function, it instantiates the general pattern of absolute quantifiers being construed as indefinite grounding elements.

(8)(a) *We saw {**a** / just **one**} zebra.*

(b) *You should add {**a** / only **one**} cup of flour.*

(c) *She bought {**a** purse / **one** purse—the other was too expensive}.*

(d) *We need {**a** hundred copies / **one** hundred copies—not two hundred}.*

The indefinite article *a* and the counting number *one* are semantically quite similar but not identical. They both effect indefinite grounding and indicate the quantity 'one'. The difference lies in the relative salience of the grounding and quantifying functions: as a grounding element, the article has only secondary quantifying import; and as a quantifier, *one* assumes an indefinite grounding role only as a secondary development. Like other number terms (Figure 3), *one* can function adjectivally (*his one complaint*), as a grounding element (*one complaint*), and as a proper noun that names a numerical value (*One is less than two*). These are represented in Figure 8(a)-(c), and the indefinite article in 8(d). For the article the number scale is rendered with a dashed-line arrow to indicate that quantity remains in the background. Note the similarity of diagrams (b) and (d). When it assumes grounding function, *one* is equivalent to *a* except that quantity is foregrounded.

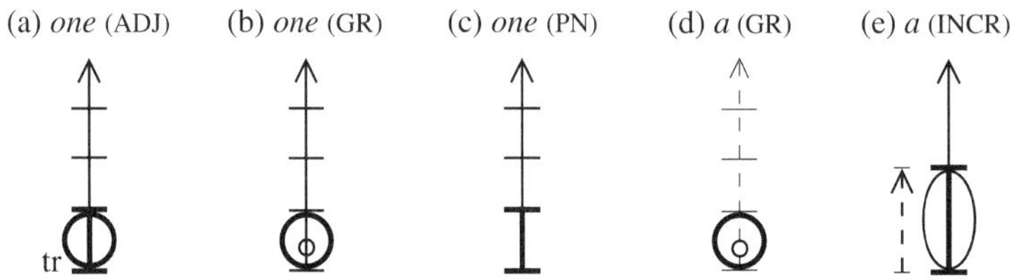


FIGURE 8

Figure 8(d) represents the indefinite article's basic meaning. In expressions like *a zebra*, it profiles a (single) unidentified instance of a count-noun type, which is specified by the following noun. The final matter to be addressed is whether the same meaning can be ascribed to the *a* that appears in *a lot*, *a few*, and *a little*.

We should not expect its semantic value to be precisely the same in this special context. An expression's meaning is shaped by the structures it occurs in and adapts to co-occurring elements (Langacker 2009b). And indeed, the indefinite article's full semantic potential cannot be realized when it combines with *lot*, *few*, or *little*, for they do not specify types with multiple instances. Instead, as shown in Figures 6(a) and 7(c), they designate vaguely delimited units of magnitude, extensions along a generalized scale of quantity. So to the extent that they are considered referential, their referents are unique—there is only one *lot*, *few*, or *little*, just as there is only one *seven*. Identification is therefore not an issue. It is possible to refer specifically to these abstract entities, as in (9)(a), but we see in (9)(b) that demonstratives are precluded, for without multiple instances their pointing function is vacuous. Also precluded are possessives, as in (c), since one person's *lot* or *little* is the same as another's. Likewise, we observe in (d)-(f) that questions concerning these quantities are formed with *how* instead of *which*. This indicates that, while *lot*, *few*, are *little* are rather vague, the specific values they subsume are not conceived as instances of a type.[5]

(9) (a) *A lot is more than a few.*

(b) **This lot is bigger than that lot.*

(c) **We each have a little money, but my little is less than your little.*

(d) A: *He has a lot of friends.* B: *How many?* (not **Which lot?*)

(e) A: *I bought a few postcards.* B: *How many?* (not **Which few?*)

(f) A: *They saved a little money.* B: *How much?* (not **Which little?*)

The *a* appearing in absolute quantifiers can thus be ascribed the meaning depicted in Figure 8(e). In this context it combines with a measure noun, which profiles some bounded extension on a scale of quantity. Being a vestigial grounding element, *a* itself profiles this abstract entity. The profiled measurement unit represents what is common to *lot*, *little*, *few*, *bunch*, *gallon*, *hundred*, etc. and is thus schematic in regard to quantity, whether the quantified mass is plural or continuous, and even the nature of the scale. There is no unfilled dot in 8(e) because a measurement unit is *sui generis*. This contravenes the indefinite article's basic meaning, in 8(d), where it presents an instance of a type as being unidentified. What, then, is left of this basic meaning? Since identification is not at issue, and the profiled entity is a measurement unit, quantification assumes center stage. What *a* conveys, I suggest, is merely the notion of a positive increment of value, represented by the dashed arrow in 8(e). In dynamic terms, it evokes a single, quantum-like step moving upward from the baseline of zero. This notion can be seen as immanent in the article's basic sense, since—starting from nothing—a single bounded entity (a count-noun referent) constitutes the first quantum step in building up the conception of a countable mass.

When *a* appears in a complex quantifier, with nothing more than this incremental sense, should it still be regarded as the 'indefinite article'? That depends on how we want to use the term: we can either reserve it for the basic, prototypical meaning, where it is directly motivated; or we can use it as a general term that also covers extensions from the prototype. The same

[5] Demonstratives do occur with *many*, *much*, *few*, and *little* (e.g. *that many*, *this much*, *that little?*). These are not cases of nominal grounding, but represent a distinct construction where *this* and *that* point to specific locations within a range of values on an adjectival scale (cf. *She's this tall*; *Is he really that unhappy?*).

issue arises with the label 'plural'. In its prototypical meaning, the plural morpheme designates a mass consisting of discrete elements, all instances of the same type, each of which is conventionally labeled by the count-noun stem on which the plural is formed. But many apparent plurals do not conform to this pattern: *shorts*, *binoculars*, *glasses*, *bleachers*, *catacombs*, *brains*, *guts*, *entrails*, *dregs*, *suds*, *vicissitudes*, etc. Either the complex entity they designate lacks discreteness (e.g. *guts*), or the constitutive elements are not equivalent to that designated by the stem (e.g. *glasses*), or the stem fails to occur individually (e.g. **dreg*, **sud*). All we can say in general for such cases is that the ending gives some vague indication of internal complexity. So long as the intent is clear, it makes no difference whether we refer to these as 'plurals' or reserve the term for the prototype.

We find departures from both the indefinite article and plural prototypes in absolute quantifiers where the quantifying noun is a unit of measurement. Identifiability is not at issue with measure nouns, so when $N_1$ is singular, *a* is limited to its incremental value (Figure 8(e)): *a {lot / bunch / ton / heap / gallon / pound} of X*. And when $N_1$ assumes plural form, as in *{lots / tons / heaps / mountains / scads / oodles} of X*, it only conforms to the generalized definition of plurality. Rather than consisting of discretely bounded units, the quantity it vaguely indicates is conceived as an amorphous multitude. The plural form suggests that the quantity is fairly large but has no specific quantitative import: the same pile of dirty clothes might be described as either *{lots / heaps / mountains} of laundry* or just *a {lot / heap / mountain} of laundry*. Conversely, if we start with *lots of laundry* and divide it into several piles, the content of single pile will not necessarily amount to *a lot*. Even precise measurement units lose their precision when pluralized—when we speak of *gallons of wine*, the volume indicated probably does not consist of an integral number of *gallon* units. We can make the quantity precise by adding a number term, e.g. *three gallons*. It is still not the case, however, that the component volumetric units are conceived as distinct, identifiable instances of a type.[6]

Since identification is not at issue, the *a* appearing in complex quantifiers is not a grounding element in the strictest sense. Its admittedly rather tenuous meaning—'positive increment of value'—is only a vestige of the indefinite article's grounding import. But it does make a semantic contribution. With typical measurement units, which themselves designate positive

[6] The notion of multiplicity that figures in both a canonical plural (like *zebras*) and a plural measurement unit (like *gallons*) is only one factor in the conception of distinct referents with the potential for individual identification. Identifiability is of course possible when a measurement term is construed metonymically: *The second gallon of wine tasted better than the first*. Here the two entities referred to are instances of *wine* (distinguished by their position in a temporal sequence), each quantified by the measurement unit *gallon*.

increments, *a* reinforces that notion. It also marks the distinction between a single increment and a larger, indefinite quantity involving multiplicity (*a gallon* vs. *gallons*). And in the special case of *few* and *little*, it overrides their negative nature by imposing the conception of a positive increment (*a few*, *a little*).

## References

Coates, R. 2006. Properhood. *Language* 82: 356–82.

Hawkins, J. 1978. *Definiteness and Indefiniteness: A Study in Reference and Grammaticality Prediction*. London: Croom Helm.

Israel, M. 2011. *The Grammar of Polarity: Pragmatics, Sensitivity, and the Logic of Scales*. (Cambridge Studies in Linguistics, 125.) Cambridge: Cambridge University Press.

Klima, E. S. 1964. Negation in English. *The Structure of Language: Readings in the Philosophy of Language*, eds. J. A. Fodor & J. J. Katz, 246-323. Englewood Cliffs, NJ: Prentice-Hall.

Langacker, R. W. 1987. *Foundations of Cognitive Grammar*, vol. 1, *Theoretical Prerequisites*. Stanford: Stanford University Press.

Langacker, R. W. 1991. *Foundations of Cognitive Grammar*, vol. 2, *Descriptive Application*. Stanford: Stanford University Press.

Langacker, R. W. 1999a. *Grammar and Conceptualization*. (Cognitive Linguistics Research, 14.) Berlin & New York: Mouton de Gruyter.

Langacker, R. W. 1999b. Virtual Reality. *Studies in the Linguistic Sciences* 29: 77–103.

Langacker, R. W. 2002. Deixis and Subjectivity. *Grounding: The Epistemic Footing of Deixis and Reference*, ed. F. Brisard, 1–28. (Cognitive Linguistics Research, 21.) Berlin & New York: Mouton de Gruyter.

Langacker, R. W. 2004. Remarks on Nominal Grounding. *Functions of Language* 11: 77–113.

Langacker, R. W. 2005. Dynamicity, Fictivity, and Scanning: The Imaginative Basis of Logic and Linguistic Meaning. *Grounding Cognition: The Role of Perception and Action in Memory, Language and Thinking*, eds. D. Pecher & R. A. Zwaan, 164–97. Cambridge: Cambridge University Press.

Langacker, R. W. 2008. *Cognitive Grammar: A Basic Introduction*. New York: Oxford University Press.

Langacker, R. W. 2009a. *Investigations in Cognitive Grammar*. (Cognitive Linguistics Research, 42.) Berlin & New York: Mouton de Gruyter.

Langacker, R. W. 2009b. Constructions and Constructional Meaning. *New Directions in Cognitive Linguistics*, eds. V. Evans & S. Pourcel, 225–67. (Human Cognitive Processing, 24.) Amsterdam & Philadelphia: John Benjamins.

# 6

# ‘Leap’ or ‘Continuum’?: Grammaticalization Pathways from Conjunctions to Sentence-Final Particles

MITSUKO NARITA IZUTSU AND KATSUNOBU IZUTSU[1]

## 1 Introduction

Most particles, either final or modal, historically developed from other linguistic resources, and even now new items are constantly recruited for this function. Of such linguistic resources, the present paper focuses on conjunctions to explore how the usage of coordinating and subordinating conjunctions in the final position leads to the development of final particles. Comparing sentence-final conjunctions in English and Japanese, we will investigate what kind of process accounts for the final particle development in the typologically different (i.e. head-initial or head-final) languages. In particular, we will extend our earlier analysis of sentence-final coordinating conjunctions (Izutsu and Izutsu, forthcoming) to subordinating ones, and provide an integrative account of their development into final particles. Mulder and Thompson claim that the final particle *but*, notably found in Australian English, developed as a result of moving along a ‘grammaticization continuum’ with ‘no “leap”’ from ‘initial *but*’ via ‘final hanging *but*’ to

[1] This research is supported by JSPS Grant-in-Aid for Scientific Research (C) (No. 23520517).

*Language and the Creative Mind*.
Mike Borkent, Barbara Dancygier, and Jennifer Hinnell (eds).

'final particle *but*' (Mulder and Thompson 2006, 2008; Mulder, Thompson, and Williams 2009). The comparison of sentence-final conjunctions in English and Japanese reveals that what in fact forms a continuum is not the development of English *but* but that of Japanese subordinating conjunctions into sentence-final particles.

Section 2 gives an overview of Mulder and Thompson's 'grammaticization continuum' account of final *but*. Section 3 summarizes our earlier study (Izutsu and Izutsu, forthcoming), which argues that the two types of final *buts* ('final hanging *but*' and 'final particle *but*') are analyzed as deriving from two different syntactic processes (TRUNCATION and BACKSHIFT) and hence that there is no 'grammaticization continuum' in the rise of the 'final particle *but*'. Section 4 looks at sentence-final conjunctions in Japanese, first observing that Japanese coordinating conjunctions also undergo the two distinct syntactic processes and then that subordinating conjunctions, via the process of truncation, are likely to develop into sentence-final particles. Section 5 makes cross-linguistic observations on sentence-final conjunctions, and argues that what forms a grammaticalization continuum is the development from Japanese subordinating conjunctions into sentence-final particles. Section 6 gives the concluding remarks of this paper.

## 2 Final *But*: 'Grammaticization Continuum'?

Australian English is well known for the use of the coordinating conjunction *but* in the final position, as referred to in the following 'Australian Word Map' comments:[2]

(1) a. In NSW, 'but' is appended to a sentence as a finish: I'm going to the shops, but.
b. Our 21-year-old neighbor in SE Queensland also uses 'but' to end and reinforce a sentence. e.g., 'Nice day but?' for 'It is a nice day'.
c. [Melbourne contributor] Asking for confirmation at the end of a sentence: 'Nice day, but'.
d. As in the recent conversation I had with my wife.
Self: 'She has long hair' wife: 'hasn't she but'
- the 'but' is acting as a strengthener of the sentence.

(http://www.abc.net.au/wordmap/,
also Mulder and Thompson 2008: 193)

Drawing on examples of *but* from various sources of data including the ones cited above, Mulder and Thompson (2006, 2008) postulate a 'gram-

[2] This usage is sometimes referred to as the adverbial usage of *but* and also observed in New Zealand, Irish and Scottish English and northern English dialects such as Geordie.

maticization continuum' from 'initial *but*' to 'final *but*', which is sketched as in (2). They argue that 'the behavior of *but* can be modeled as a continuum from a prosodic-unit-initial to a prosodic-unit-final discourse particle' (2008: 179). The final *but* is divided into three stages ('final 1/final hanging *but*', 'indeterminate', and 'final 2/final particle *but*'), analyzed respectively as having structures like '[X *but*]', '[X/Y *but*]', and '[Y *but*]'. Mulder and Thompson state that examples of the indeterminate stage are interpreted as either final 1 or final 2 *but*, arguing that 'it is out of this indeterminacy that the final 2 *but* emerges' (ibid., 195). This interpretation of data leads them to conclude that there is 'no "leap"' between the apparently different structures [X *but*] and [Y *but*] (ibid., 196).

(2)

| **initial *but*** | > | **Janus 1 *but*** | > | **Janus 2 *but*** |
|---|---|---|---|---|
| X [*but* Y] | | X [*but*,] Y | | [X *but*] |
| **final 1/final hanging *but*** | > | **indeterminate** | > | **final 2/final particle *but*** |
| [X *but*] | | [X/Y *but*] | | [Y *but*] |

(ibid., 195)

The indeterminacy of interpretation is illustrated with the utterance *my mum doesn't think so - but*, which Mulder and Thompson (ibid., 196) argue is interpretable either as 'my mum doesn't think so, but they are' (final 1 *but*) or 'but my mom doesn't think so'/'my mom doesn't think so though' (final 2 *but*). However, as we have argued elsewhere (Izutsu and Izutsu, forthcoming), this indeterminacy belongs to the observer(s) or addressee(s), not the speaker. As far as the speaker is supposed to intend one or the other interpretation, the interpretations are still different and thus considered to have two different syntactic sources.

## 3 Truncation and Backshift: Two Syntactic Processes of Final *But*

Although the grammaticization continuum proposed by Mulder and Thompson might at first sight be viable, the interpretive indeterminacy does not bridge a gap between final 1 and final 2 *but*s. Noticing that [X *but*] and [Y *but*] are heterogeneous structures, we have argued that the two types of final *but*s are analyzed as deriving from different syntactic processes: TRUNCATION and BACKSHIFT (Izutsu and Izutsu, forthcoming). [X *but*] (final 1 *but*) is analyzable as resulting from cutting [Y] off the underlying compound sentence structure [X *but* Y], while [Y *but*] (final 2 *but*) involves backshifting of *but* (i.e. using the conjunction after Y), as shown in (3):

(3) TRUNCATION: X, *but* ~~Y.~~ > X, *but*. (final 1/final hanging *but*)
BACKSHIFT: X, *but* Y. > X, Y *but*. (final 2/final particle *but*)

Since the truncation- and backshift-derived *but*s take different pathways to the final position, they exhibit some syntactic and prosodic differences: the possibilities of fronting and filler attachment and prosodic manifestations such as intonation and pause. The two types of *but*s also show different discourse-pragmatic meanings/functions. The truncation type of *but* (e.g. *You're right, but...*) expresses the meaning of hanging implication or suspension, while the backshift type of *but* (e.g. *Nice day, but*) adds affirmative, definitive, and reinforcing meanings to the clause that it is attached to, as we have seen in the 'Australian Word Map' comments in (1) above. Such discourse-pragmatic meanings of the backshift type are also pointed out in Richards (2005):

> **but** employed not as a conjunction (or disjunction) but shifted to the terminal position in a sentence, where it can play a number of roles.
>
> 1. it can be a terminator, a spoken full stop: 'It's a big job but'.
> 2. it can seek agreement, in the manner of 'isn'it?' (or *n'est ce pas*): 'It's a hot day, but?'
> 3. it can perform its usual function in an unusual place in the sentence: 'But I didn't do it' can become 'I didn't do it but'.
> 4. it can be little more than an unconsciously employed verbal tic.
>
> (As a linguist would put it: 'It's an interesting bit of syntax but'.)
>
> (Richards 2005: 35)

These differences indicate that truncation- and backshift-derived final *but*s are completely different in nature. Although they might look alike in that both of them occupy the sentence-final position, the backshifted *but* has some syntactic, prosodic, and discourse-pragmatic characteristics of sentence-final particles (SFPs), but the truncation type does not. In other words, the backshift type of *but* can be regarded as an example of 'final-particalization' (Mulder, Thompson, and Williams 2009: 340), and has become a 'fully developed' final particle (Mulder and Thompson 2008: 192), while the truncation type of *but* has not achieved such a status.

# 4 Sentence-final Conjunctions in Japanese: their Grammaticalization into Sentence-final Particles

## 4.1 Japanese Final-coordinating Conjunctions

We have also shown that a structural distinction similar to that between the truncation and backshift types of *but*s is also observed with Japanese coordinating conjunctions.[3] A Japanese coordinating conjunction (co.) generally

[3] See Izutsu and Izutsu (forthcoming) for the details of the discussion given in this section.

occurs between clauses as in [X, co. Y].[4] Like the truncation type of *but*, some Japanese coordinating conjunctions allow leaving the following clause (Y) unsaid or cut off; hence, the structure [X co.] results. On the other hand, like the backshifted *but*, some Japanese coordinating conjunctions can be placed in the sentence-final position, thus yielding the structure [(X,) Y co.].

In (4a) there is an example of the truncation type of *demo*, which corresponds to English final hanging *but*. The second clause is cut off, but its continuation is still suggested as shown in the parenthesis (*yapparihosii* 'I want one'), hence, a sense of hanging implication. On the other hand, (4b) is an example of the backshift type, where the final *demo* is shifted backward to the final position. Note that the *demo* can also be placed between the two sentences with the meaning of opposition between them ('I want one, but it's expensive').

(4) a. *Tasikani takai-yo,* ***demo*** *... (yappari hosii).*[5] [Truncation *demo*]
surely expensive-FP but still want
'It's expensive, but ... (I still want one)'.

b. *Tasikani hosii-yo. Sore-tte takai-yo,* ***demo***. [Backshift *demo*]
surely want-FP that-TOP expensive-FP but
'I want one. It's expensive, though'.

(Izutsu and Izutsu, forthcoming)

Like English *but*, these two types of Japanese final coordinating conjunctions differ in some syntactic and prosodic behaviors: the possibility of fronting, the compatibility with interjectory particles, and prosodic manifestations such as intonation and pause.

As Japanese coordinating conjunctions are backshifted to the final position, they come to serve some new discourse-pragmatic functions, which are largely classified into two types: (a) fine-tuning function and (b) emphatic/emotive function. The sentence-final position is often regarded as a place for a speaker to make a slight adjustment or modification of his/her utterance. For example, in (5), a dialogue version of (4b), *demo* is shifted backward to delay the antagonistic tone of the message that would be more

---

[4] One might argue that Japanese has no connectives that correspond to coordinating conjunctions in English and other languages. However, we hold that morphologically independent connectives such as *demo* 'but', *sikasi* 'but', and *sosite* 'and' can be naturally regarded as coordinating conjunctions in Japanese. See Yoda (2010) for a similar line of argument.

[5] The following abbreviations are used in the glosses: COP copula, CP connective particle, FN formal noun, FOC focus particle, FP final particle, HON honorific, PAST past tense, PERF perfect, SUB subordinating conjunction, TOP topic.

strongly communicated by initial *demo*. The backshifted conjunction helps the speaker to avoid immediate confrontation with the interlocutor:

(5) A: *Kono hon hosii-na.*
this book want-FP
'I want this book'.

B: *Sore-tte takai-yo,* ***demo***. (cf. ***Demo*** *sore-tte takai-yo.*)
that-TOP expensive- FP but
'It's expensive, though'. (ibid.)

On the other hand, the backshifted *demo* can also bear some emphatic/emotive meaning as in (6). The final syllable is often lengthened as in *demoo*, which suggests a strong tone of irritation:

(6) A: *Kono hon kat-tahoogaii-yo!*
this book buy-had:better-FP
'You should buy this book'.

B: *Dakara takai-n-dat-tebaa,* ***demoo!***
so expensive-FN-COP-FP but
'I'm telling you it is expensive!' (ibid.)

The emphatic and emotive meanings of final coordinating conjunctions are more conventionalized in some dialects of Japanese. The Osaka dialect, for instance, has developed another type of backshifted *but* (*sikasi*), as illustrated in (7). While *sikasi* does not normally occupy the final position in Common Japanese, it has a backshifted use in the Osaka dialect. The backshifted *sikasi* has nearly lost the original sense of opposition, and it is more like an intensifier or strengthener. An online dictionary/encyclopedia in Japanese gives the following explanation for the usage of *sikasi* in the Osaka dialect: '[*s*]*ikasi* "but" means "nevertheless/however" in the sentence-initial position; in the sentence-final position it serves as an intensifier, having a meaning more like "really"'(http://www.weblio.jp/content/しかし, our translation).

(7) a. *Okoru-de* ***sikasi***.
get:angry-FP but
'I'm gonna get angry, really'.

b. *Unagi buattu! Tee hurue-te kireeni tore-n-gana* ***sikasi***.
eel thick hand shiver -CP properly can:take-not- FP but
'The eel is thick! My hands are shivering, so I can't photograph it properly'.
(http://blog.livedoor.jp/h8739/archives/cat_10007870.html)

The Hokkaido and Hiroshima dialects of Japanese have a comparable backshifted use of 'and', as in (8). In the Hokkaido dialect, the conjunction *sosite* 'and' has some unique usages including a backshifted use, which can hardly be observed in Common Japanese (Izutsu and Izutsu 2010). The Hiroshima dialect also has developed a backshifted use of *hoide/hoite* 'and', a dialectal variant of *sosite* (Fujiwara 1993). As with *sikasi*, the backshifted *sosite* and *hoide/hoite* also express something different from their original sequential meaning. *Sosite* in (8a) expresses the speaker's surprise at the genuine German cuisine served in a restaurant, and the one in (8b) represents the speaker's irritation at being interrupted. (9a) and (9b) both function as rhetorical questions for blaming the addressee with irritation or surprise:

(8) a. (Informed that a restaurant serves good sausages at reasonable prices)
*Zawaakurauto-toka tuitekuru-wake* ***sosite****?*
sauerkraut-etc. come:with-FN and
'And does it come with sauerkraut as well?'

b. (Interrupted by a child while doing some work)
*Iyaa hontoni bundan bundan-de sigoto-ga susuma-nai.*
shit really interruption interruption-with work-NOM continue-not
*Kore sima-tte-ki-te* ***sosite****.*
this put:aside-CP-come-CP and
'Shit! I can't continue my work because of your interruption! Go and put this aside, anyway!'
(Izutsu and Izutsu 2010: 79)

(9) a. *Omae dare-nimukatte kabati tare-toru-n-nara-****hoidee****.*
you who-toward complaint flow-PERF-FN-COP-and
'Who are you complaining to?'
(qb5.2ch.net/test/read.cgi/sakud/1095421468/)

b. *Nantyuu kotoo yuu-n-nara-****hoitee****.*
what:sort:of thing say-FN-COP-and
'What a stupid thing you say!'
(Fujiwara 1993: 182)

Some of these backshifted conjunctions have been more or less grammaticalized into final particles, obtaining some new emphatic and emotional meanings while losing the original connective meanings ('conflict/opposition' for *sikasi* or 'sequence/addition' for *sosite* and *hoide/hoite*). The loss or bleaching of the original meanings deprives them of their functions as coordinating conjunctions. Accordingly, some such backshifted conjunctions can no longer be sentence-initial elements. Notice that *sikasi* in (7), *sosite* in (8), and *hoide/hoite* in (9) are awkward in the initial position. The conjunction *sikasi* 'but', for example, is quite natural in the final position as in (7b), but it is semantically anomalous in the initial position as in (10). The propositional content of the first sentence is causally, not concessively, related to that of the second sentence: the eel is thick, so I cannot photograph it properly for excitement.

(10) ??*Unagi buattu!* ***Sikasi****, tee hurue-te kireeni tore-n-gana.*
eel thick but hand shiver-CP properly can:take-not-FP
'The eel is thick! But I can't photograph it properly with my shivering hands'. (cf. 7b)
(Izutsu and Izutsu, forthcoming)

This shift in meaning and function can be regarded as analogous to the development of final *but* in Australian English. The fact that some backshifted conjunctions cannot be used in the initial position is one of the indications of their grammaticalization into final particles, i.e. 'final-particalization'. *Hoide/hoite* in the Hiroshima dialect shows a further development as a final particle; it is morpho-phonologically combined with the preceding copula *-nara* 'be' (i.e. *nara-**hoidee*** and *nara-**hoitee*** as in (9) above), and therefore can be viewed as 'one larger sentence-final particle' (Fujiwara 1993: 183).

As with 'final 1/final hanging *but*', Japanese also allows truncating a coordinate sentence, as seen in (4a) above. To the best of our knowledge, there are no sentence-final particles in Japanese that originate from the truncation type of final coordinating conjunction (cf. Fujiwara 1982, 1985, 1986; Konoshima 1966). The truncation type ends with non-terminal intonation, has a prosodic pause before it, and allows the continuation of an interjectory particle (Izutsu and Izutsu, forthcoming), all of which suggest that this type of final coordinating conjunction has sentence-initial, not final, characteristics, and therefore they are not likely to develop the usage of sentence-final particles.

## 4.2 Japanese Final-subordinating Conjunctions

It is a noticeable fact that Japanese has a further type of truncation, which can lead to the development of sentence-final particles. A rich variety of Japanese sentence-final particles have developed from subordinating, not coordinating, conjunctions by the process of truncation. Japanese unmarked complex sentences have the structure of [X-sub., Y], where the subordinate clause (X) generally precedes the main clause (Y). A subordinating conjunction like *-kedo* '(al)though' in (11a) is attached to the end of the subordinate clause. Notice that Japanese subordinate clauses often allow the following main clauses to be left unsaid, yielding the structure [X-sub.] as in (11b):

(11) a. *Wakaru-**kedo**,* *murida-yo.*
know-though impossible-FP
'Although I know (what you mean), it's impossible'.

b. *Wakaru-**kedo*** … .
'I know (what you mean) …'.

This clause structure is often called 'suspended clause' (Ohori 1995, 2000) or '*iisasi bun*' (Shirakawa 2009, among others) and can also be considered to represent a kind of 'insubordination' (Evans 2007), which is attested in a wide variety of languages.

There are some other examples of suspended (or insubordinated) clauses. (12a) is another example of concessive clause, (12b) and (12c) are examples of conditional clause, (12d) is an example of sequential clause, and (12e) is an example of causal clause:

(12) a. *Iki-takat-ta-**noni*** … .
go-want:to-PAST-though
'Though I wanted to go …'.

b. *Kore yat-temi-**tara** … ?*
this do-try:to-if
'What if you do this?'

c. *Kure-**ba** … ?*
come-if
'(What) if you come?'

d. *Okane-mo nai-**si*** … .
money-FOC not-and(SUB)
'I don't have money, and …'.

e. *Ima ukagai-masu-**kara/node*** … .
now go-HON-because
'I'm going to come [hear you] now …'.

These suspended clauses leave some implication hanging and are generally intended to invite inferences. This is clearly stated by Ohori (2000: 478), who argues that Japanese SCCs (suspended clause constructions) 'embody particular procedures for interpretation, namely preference for inference-intensive readings'. Itani (1992: 266) makes a similar observation: '[l]ike English rising intonation at the end of an utterance, Japanese utterances ending with *kedo/kara/node* ('but/because/because') might indicate that the utterance has not quite been finished and there is more to say. This way, the speaker can show her reserved attitude …'.

However, as conventionalization proceeds, some suspended or insubordinated clauses have lost the meaning of hanging implications or invited inferences and come to acquire some new discourse-pragmatic meanings, as exemplified in (13):

(13) a. *Uzai-n-desu-**kedo**!*
irritating-FN-COP-though
'You are irritating!'

b. *Kitinto yatteru-**kara**!*
appropriately be:doing-because
'I'm doing it appropriately!'

c. *Kitinto yatteru-**noni**!*
appropriately be:doing-though
'I'm doing it appropriately!'

d. *Maji iya-da-**si**.*
truly dislike-COP-and(SUB)
'I really don't like it'. (McGloin and Konishi 2010: 568)

e. *Wakatteru-yo Moo ii-**ttara**!*
understand-FP already enough-if:saying
'I understand. Enough already!' (Shinzato 2007: 184)

f. *Wakatteru-yo. Moo ii-**tteba**!*
understand-FP already enough-if:saying
'I understand. Enough already!'

The concessive conjunction in (13a) emphasizes the speaker's feeling of irritation or disgust, which is in clear contrast with (11b). The main difference is that the sound of *-kedo* in (11b) can sometimes fade out toward the end, while each syllable of *-kedo* in (13a) is more articulated, which somewhat reflects the increment of emotion. The causal subordinating conjunction *-kara* in (13b) and the concessive subordinating conjunction *-noni* in (13c) similarly convey the speaker's negative attitude toward uninvited or impertinent advice from the interlocutor, such as 'Don't be lazy!' or 'You're wasting your time!' (13b) is more directed toward the interlocutor, while (13c) sounds more like muttering or grumbling. The sequential conjunction *-si* in (13d) expresses the speaker's strong feeling of dislike, which McGloin and Konishi (2010: 566) characterize as 'adding emotional emphasis'. Apart from this function, they also identify the two other functions of the sentence-final *-si*: 'displaying the speaker's negative sentiment' and 'adding a complaining/teasing tone' (ibid., 567–570). This development of -*si* into a sentence-final particle is still an on-going process and is typically found in young people's speech. The conditional markers *-ttara* in (13e) and *-tteba* in (13f) should be regarded as complex subordinating conjunctions (Shinzato 2007, 2011). While *-ttara* is a contracted form of *-to ittara(-ba)*, which consists of the quotative particle *-to*, the verb *iu* 'say', and the perfect auxiliary *-ta*, and the subordinating conjunction *-ba* 'if', *-tteba* is a contracted form of *-to ie-ba*, which consists of the quotative particle *-to*, the verb *iu* 'say' and the subordinating conjunction *-ba* 'if'. Shinzato (2007, 2011) refers to these two subordinating conjunctions as 'quotative conditionals', and demonstrates that they were originally used to indicate the conditional/temporal relation between clauses. However, some free-standing *-ttara* and *-tteba* clauses have led to the development of the subordinating conjunctions into sentence-final particles with new discourse-pragmatic meanings. As sentence-final particles, *-ttara* in (13e) and *-tteba* in (13f) both acquire the illocutionary force to strengthen assertion (Shinzato 2007: 184). This functional shift from a hanging implication to an emphatic/emotive meaning suggests the grammaticalization into final particles.

The final-particalization of subordinating conjunctions is also common in many dialects of Japanese (Fujiwara 1986). The sentences in (14) represent only a few such cases. (14a) is from the Aichi dialect, and (14b) from the Fukuoka dialect: *-de* and *-ken* are originally causal subordinating conjunctions and have developed into final particles. (14c) is from the Kagoshima dialect and (14d) from the Kumamoto dialect: *-ga* and *-batten* have both developed from concessive subordinating conjunctions into final particles. Fujiwara (1986: 132) mentions that *-ga* in (14c) has an assertive tone similar to the genuine final particle *-yo*:

(14) a. *Itte-mina wakaran-**de**.* [Aichi dialect]
go-see don't know-because
'I'll never know unless I go'.

b. *Sukancha-**ken**.* [Fukuoka dialect]
dislike-because
'I don't like (him/her)!

c. *Koya nago emosan-**ga**.* [Kagoshima dialect]
this long have:not:seen-though
'Oh! I haven't seen you for a long time!'

d. *Nakatta-desu-**batten**.*[6] [Kumamoto dialect]
there:was:nothing-HON-though
'There was nothing'. (Fujiwara 1986)

[6] *-batten* is assumed to be a contracted form of *-batote*, the complex subordinating conjunction which consists of the connective particle *-ba*, the quotative particle *-to*, and the connective particle *-te* (Kyusyuu Hoogen Kenkyukai 2009: 81).

Some such forms are so conventionalized as final particles that they are no longer felt as subordinating conjunctions. For example, the final particle *-ga* in the Kagoshima dialect can even be used in incomplete clauses such as *Ja-ga ja-ga*, which means 'right, right'. Here, *-ga* is attached to the dialectal form of the copula *-da*.

Taking *-de* for an example, Fujiwara characterizes this process of final-particalization as quoted below:

> The connective particle *-de* is grammaticalized into a sentence-final particle. ... The sentence *Atokara iku-**de*** (I'll come later) could be regarded as a hanging implication form of *Atokara iku-**de**, mattore-yo* 'Because I'll come later, please wait'. The connective particle *-de* comes to acquire a function of *uttae* (appeal) in the sentence-final position.
>
> (Fujiwara 1986: 85, our translation)

The emergence of such a new discourse-pragmatic function, or more generally the pragmatic strengthening of speaker involvement (Traugott 1988), makes subordinating conjunctions more like sentence-final particles.

# 5 Cross-linguistic Observations on Final Conjunctions

## 5.1 Patterns of Final Conjunctions

We have seen that the so-called 'final-particalization' can occur with English and Japanese coordinating conjunctions as well as Japanese subordinating conjunctions, but their pathways to final particles are different. The patterns of final conjunctions in English and Japanese are summarized in Table 1. The alphabets in the table correspond to those of the sentences in (15). We have seen that English and Japanese final conjunctions share two discourse-pragmatic meanings: hanging implications/invited inferences and emphatic/emotive meanings. The meaning of hanging implication emerges by means of truncation, whether they are coordinating or subordinating conjunctions, as seen in (15a), (15c), (15e), and (15g). This process occurs both in English and Japanese regardless of their typological differences. Japanese final subordinating conjunctions such as (15g) can proceed one step further in the grammaticalization path to acquire emphatic/emotive meanings and behave like sentence-final particles as in (15h). However, the other three truncation types, (15a), (15c), and (15e), do not undergo such a development. This is due to the difficulty of reanalyzing the conjunctions as the final elements of the preceding clauses; since truncation operates across the two separate clauses, the conjunctions as part of one clause are not likely to be unified with the other as sentence-final particles.

For coordinating conjunctions, the emphatic/emotive meanings characteristic of sentence-final particles arise by means of backshift both in English and Japanese as in (15b) and (15f). Backshift can motivate final-particalization because a backshifted coordinating conjunction is still a part of the immediately preceding clause, which would follow the conjunction in an unmarked coordinate structure. Such final coordinating conjunctions have retrospective functions either to clarify an underspecified inter-clausal relation or to elaborate the discourse-pragmatic significance of the preceding clause.

TABLE 1. The patterns of final conjunctions in English and Japanese

| | | hanging implication/ invited inference | | emphatic/emotive meaning (final-particalization) |
|---|---|---|---|---|
| English (SVO) | coordinating conj. | (a) √ [truncation] | | (b) √ [backshift] |
| | subordinating conj. | (c) √ [truncation] | | (d) N/A |
| Japanese (SOV) | coordinating conj. | (e) √ [truncation] | | (f) √ [backshift] |
| | subordinating conj. | (g) √ [truncation] | ===> | (h) √ [truncation] |

(15) a. *Excuse me, **but**....* b. *Nice day **but**!*
c. *I know what you mean, **though**....* d. N/A
e. *Tasikani hosiiyo, **demo**....* f. *Okorude **sikasi**!*
g. *Wakaru-**kedo**....* h. *Uzain-desu-**kedo**!*

The two languages differ in the behavior of subordinating conjunctions as shown in (15d) and (15h). In English, subordinating conjunctions cannot express emphatic/emotive meanings in the final position. Since a subordinating conjunction is syntactically fixed in the clause-initial position (e.g., *I don't really enjoy sports, **although** I sometimes watch games*), it is virtually impossible to backshift the subordinating conjunction of a postposed subordinate clause for expressing emphasis or emotion (e.g., **I don't really enjoy sports; I sometimes watch games **although***).[7] On the other hand, the truncation of a complex sentence is possible as in (15c). Since it operates across

[7] Some people might argue that English allows the backshifting of the subordinating conjunction *though* (*I don't really enjoy sports. I sometimes watch games, **though***). However, *though* was originally an adverb, and its usage as a subordinating conjunction is a later development (Kellner 1956: §101, Mitchell 1985: §3401). We assume that the final *though* is motivated by its original adverbial function, not by the backshifting of its homophonous subordinating conjunction. On the other hand, *although* did not develop the adverbial usage and is therefore restricted to the clause-initial position.

two separate clauses, it is impossible to incorporate the conjunction as part of the first clause for reinforcement or emotional appeal. The resulting structure only entails hanging implications or invites some inferences.

On the other hand, some Japanese subordinating conjunctions have increasingly encoded speaker involvement via the process of truncation. Truncation-derived final subordinating conjunctions start with the meaning of hanging implication typical of suspended (or insubordinated) clauses as in (15g). As subordinating conjunctions frequently appear in suspended constructions and occupy the final position of utterances, they are gradually adapted to a function typical of the sentence-final position in Japanese, hence acquiring a new emphatic/emotive meaning. The sentence-final position in Japanese is a place generally occupied by genuine final particles (*shuujoshi*), which mark the completion of sentences and/or express a speaker's (inter)subjective attitudes.

## 5.2 Re-examination of a Grammaticalization Continuum

As we have seen in Section 2, Mulder and Thompson argue that 'the behavior of *but* can be modeled as a grammaticization continuum' (2008: 179), which is roughly described as initial *but* > final hanging *but* > final particle *but,* i.e. a shift from (a) to (b) in Table 1. However, we have argued elsewhere (Izutsu and Izutsu, forthcoming) that there IS a leap in the shift from initial *but* to final *but*, showing that 'final hanging *but*' and 'final particle *but*' arise from two different syntactic processes: TRUNCATION and BACKSHIFT. In the present paper, the examination of final conjunctions in English and Japanese reveals that a grammaticalization continuum is rather found in the development of Japanese subordinating conjunctions into sentence-final particles. In other words, it is the development from (g) to (h), not from (a) to (b) in Table 1, that really forms a grammaticalization continuum. As we have mentioned, such a development of final particles is more frequently observed in dialects of Japanese.

The grammaticalization from adverbial subordinating conjunctions into sentence-final particles in Japanese is quite a natural consequence of truncation processes and is viewed as a case of frequently occurring language phenomena. Japanese complex sentences have the unmarked structure [X-sub., Y], which often allows the main clause [Y] to be left unstated or cut off, yielding the structure [X-sub.]. This process has recently been known as 'insubordination' (Evans 2007) and reported to be prevalent across languages. Such insubordinated clause structures lend themselves to the emergence of sentence-final particles especially in head-final languages such as Korean (Sohn 1996; Rhee 2012), Manchu (Tsumagari 2000), Ryukyuan

(Nishioka and Nakahara 2000) and others, where adverbial subordinating conjunctions are attached to the end of subordinate clauses.

Insubordination also plays a role in the development of sentence-final particles from other types of subordinating conjunctions (complementizers) or nominal heads modified by subordinate clauses. In Japanese, for example, formal nouns following subordinate clauses such as *-no*, *-koto*, *-mono* (Fujii 2000) and *-wake* (Suzuki 1998) and the quotative particle (complementizer) *-to/tte* (Okamoto 1995) have also developed into sentence-final particles. The developmental process of such final particles is the same as the one discussed in 4.2; truncation yields a sentence structure ending with these elements, and the fixation in the final position assigns them the function of sentence-final particles. In other words, the development from (g) to (h) in Table 1 is grounded on quite a reasonable motivation for language change, while the development from (a) to (b) or from (e) to (f), which Mulder and Thompson (2008) claim to form a 'grammaticization continuum', is not. In fact, the structures of (a) and (e) on the one hand and those of (b) and (f) on the other derive from two different processes (truncation and backshift), and therefore (a) and (b) (and similarly (e) and (f)) cannot be regarded as forming a grammaticalization continuum.

## 6 Conclusion

There are two possible processes responsible for the rise of sentence-final conjunctions (TRUNCATION and BACKSHIFT). We have shown that truncation is operative on sentences with coordinating and subordinating conjunctions in English and Japanese and is involved in generating hanging implications or inferences, whereas backshift is responsible for the development of sentence-final coordinating conjunctions such as the final particle usage of *but* in Australian English as well as *sosite/hoide(hoite)* 'and' and *sikasi* 'but' in some dialects of Japanese. In the truncation type, Japanese subordinating conjunctions can, but English ones cannot, develop into sentence-final particles. Therefore, this development should be viewed as being sensitive to the language type: head- or verb-final languages. It is presumably motivated by suspended (or insubordinated) structures resulting from truncation as well as some discourse-pragmatic functions of sentence-final position.

We have also seen that Mulder and Thompson's claim that there is 'no "leap"' between the apparently different structures [X *but*] and [Y *but*] (2008: 196) is in fact untenable and argued that what instead forms a grammaticalization continuum is the development of Japanese subordinating conjunctions into sentence-final particles. In a head-final language like Japanese, subordinate clauses that stand alone and assume the meaning of hanging implication can be regarded as independent clauses with the subordinating conjunctions in the final position. The conjunctions then can develop their emphatic/emotive functions and be gradually seen as sentence-final elements corresponding to genuine final particles.

## References


Evans, N. 2007. Insubordination and its Uses. *Finiteness: Theoretical and Empirical Foundations*, ed. I. Nikolaeva, 366–431. Oxford: Oxford University Press.

Fujii, S. 2000. Incipient Decategorization of MONO and Grammaticalization of Speaker Attitude in Japanese Discourse. *Pragmatic Markers and Propositional Attitude*, ed. G. Andersen and T. Fretheim, 85–118. Amsterdam: John Benjamins.

Fujiwara, Y. 1982. *Hoogen Bunmatsushi 'Bunmatsujoshi' no Kenkyuu (Joo)*. Tokyo: Shunyoodoo.

Fujiwara, Y. 1985. *Hoogen Bunmatsushi 'Bunmatsujoshi' no Kenkyuu (Chuu)*. Tokyo: Shunyoodoo.

Fujiwara, Y. 1986. *Hoogen Bunmatsushi 'Bunmatsujoshi' no Kenkyuu (Ge)*. Tokyo: Shunyoodoo.

Fujiwara, Y. 1993. *Gengo Ruikeiron to Bunmatsushi*. Tokyo: Miyai.

Itani, R. 1992. Japanese Conjunction *kedo* ('but') in Utterance-final Use: A Relevance-based Analysis. *English Linguistics* 9: 265–283.

Izutsu, M. N., and K. Izutsu. 2010. 'Okashiisho Soshite': Hokkaidoo Hoogen no Hanashi Kotoba de Mochiirareru *sosite* no Imi/kinooteki Hoogen Tokusei. *Proceedings of the 25th Congress of the Japanese Association of Sociolinguistics Science*, 78–81.

Izutsu, M. N., and K. Izutsu. fc. Truncation and Backshift: Two Pathways to Sentence-Final Coordinating Conjunctions. *Journal of Historical Pragmatics* 15.1.

Kellner, L. 1956. *Historical Outlines of English Syntax*. Tokyo: Kenkyusha.

Kies, D. 1994. Adverbial *but*. *The Twentieth LACUS FORUM 1994*, 315–332. Lake Bluff, IL: Jupiter Press.

Konoshima, M. 1966. *Kokugo Joshi no Kenkyuu: Joshishi no Sobyoo*. Tokyo: Oofuusha.

Kyusyuu Hoogen Kenkyukai (ed.). 2009. *Kore ga Kyuusyuu Hoogen no Sokojikara!* Tokyo: Taisyukan.

McGloin, N. H. and Y. Konishi. 2010. From Connective Particle to Sentence-final Particle: A Usage-based Analysis of *shi* 'and' in Japanese. *Language Sciences*: 563–578.

Mitchell, B. 1985. *Old English Syntax, vol. II*. Oxford: Oxford University Press.

Mulder, J., and S. A. Thompson. 2006. The Grammaticization of *but* as a Final Particle in English Conversation. *Selected Papers from the 2005 Conference of the Australian Linguistic Society*, ed. K. Allan, 1–18.

Mulder, J., and S. A. Thompson. 2008. The Grammaticization of *but* as a Final Particle in English Conversation. *Crosslinguistic Studies of Clause Combining: The Multifunctionality of Conjunctions*, ed. R. Laury, 179–204. Amsterdam: John Benjamins,

Mulder, J., S. A. Thompson, and C. P. Williams. 2009. Final *but* in Australian English Conversation. *Comparative Studies in Australian and New Zealand English: Grammar and Beyond*, ed. P. Peters, P. Collins, and A Smith, 339-359. Amsterdam: John Benjamins.

Nishioka, S. and J. Nakahara. 2000. *Okinawago no Nyumon*. Tokyo: Hakusuisha.

Ohori, T. 1995. Remarks on Suspended Clauses: A Contribution to Japanese Phraseology. *Essays in Semantics and Pragmatics: In Honor of Charles J. Fillmore*, ed. M. Shibatani and S. Thompson, 201–218. Amsterdam: John Benjamins.

Ohori, T. 2000. Framing Effects in Japanese Non-final Clauses: Toward an Optimal Grammar-Pragmatics Interface. *BLS* 23: 471–480.

Okamoto, S. 1995. Pragmaticization of Meaning in some Sentence-final Particles in Japanese. *Essays in Semantics and Pragmatics: In Honor of Charles J. Fillmore*, ed. M. Shibatani and S. Thompson, 219–246. Amsterdam: John Benjamins.

Rhee, S. 2012. Context-induced Reinterpretation and (Inter)subjectification: the Case of Grammaticalization of Sentence-final Particles. *Languages Sciences* 34: 284–300.

Richards, K., and The Macquarie Dictionary. 2005. *Word Map: What Words are Used Where in Australia*, Sydney: ABC Books.

Shinzato, R. 2007. (Inter)subjectification, Japanese Syntax and Syntactic Scope Increase. *Journal of Historical Pragmatics* 8:2: 171–206.

Shinzato, R. 2011. Two Types of Conditionals in Japanese: A Case of *tara/teba* and *ttara/tteba*. A Paper Presented in the 12th International Pragmatics Conference, University of Manchester, July 5.

Shirakawa, H. 2009. *'Iisashibun' no Kenkyu*. Tokyo: Kuroshio.

Sohn, S-O. 1996. On the Development of Sentence-final Particles in Korean. *Japanese/Korean Linguistics*, vol. 5, ed. N. Akatsuka, S. Iwasaki, and S. Strauss, 219–234. Stanford: CSLI/Stanford University.

Suzuki, R. 1998. From a Lexical Noun to a Pragmatic Particle: *wake*. *Studies in Japanese Grammaticalization: Cognitive and Discourse Perspectives*, ed. T. Ohori, 67–92, Tokyo: Kurosio.

Traugott, E. C. 1988. Pragmatic Strenghening and Grammatlicalization. *BLS* 14: 406–416.

Tsumagari, T. 2000. Mansyuugo Dooshigobi *-ci* no Bunmatsu Yooho to *-cina* nitsuite. *Altai Hakpo* 10: 139–150.

Yoda, Y. 2010. Sore wa Hontooni Tooikoozo? *Nihongo Nihonbunka Kenkyuu* 20: 65–75.

7

# Negative Affect Conditionality in Korean *-taka*

JISUP HONG

## 1 Introduction

Korean *-taka*, which is considered an 'interruptive' or 'transferentive' connective (Choi 1961; Lee 1993), typically refers to a scenario in which the initial clause event has been discontinued in favor of the main clause event, as in (1). However, the connective also has a predictive conditional use, shown in (2), which is peculiar in requiring that both the protasis and apodosis be deemed undesirable by the speaker. Thus, predictive conditionality with positive affect cannot be expressed with *-taka*.

(1) chelswu-ka hakkyo-ey ka-taka cip-ey tolao-ass-ta
Chelswu-NM school-LOC go-CN home-LOC return-PS-IN
'Chelswu was on his way to school, when he returned home'.

(2) a. wuntong manhi ha-taka tachi-n-ta
exercise a.lot do-CN injure-PR-IN
'If you exercise a lot, you're going to get injured'
b. #wuntong manhi ha-taka kenkang hayci-n-ta
exercise a.lot do-CN health become-PR-IN
'If you exercise a lot, you're going to become healthy'.

Akatsuka and Sohn (1994) have proposed that the interruptive and conditional uses of *-taka* represent an ongoing process of grammaticalization, in which *-taka*'s interruptive sense, pertaining to external situations, has

*Language and the Creative Mind*.
Mike Borkent, Barbara Dancygier, and Jennifer Hinnell (eds).

developed a more internal or evaluative sense through subjectification (Traugott 1989, Traugott and Dasher 2002). The question remains, however, as to what interruption has to do with conditionality, and why specifically negative affect conditionality?

This paper takes up these questions and presents a cognitive-functional analysis of *-taka*'s polysemy in terms of Cognitive Grammar (Langacker [1991] 2002) and Mental Spaces Theory (Fauconnier 1985). As shown in (3)–(4), *-taka* also has nonconditional uses that convey aspectual relations besides interruption. Building on Sanders et al.'s (2009) Basic Communicative Spaces Network, and its differentiation of volitional and non-volitional content domains, and Dancygier and Sweetser's (2005) approach to conditional constructions, the present analysis models the semantics of conditional *-taka* as a conceptual blend. The structure of the inputs to the blend are then able to explain the requirement of negative affect.

(3) sewul-ey sal-taka paywuca-lul manna-ss-ta
Seoul-LOC live-CN spouse-AC meet-PS-IN
'He met his spouse when he was living in Seoul'.

(4) nemeci-taka heli-lul tachi-ess-ta
fall-CN waist-AC injure-PS-IN
'He injured his back when he fell'.

In the following section, I present an analysis of *-taka*'s prototypical uses for expressing aspectual relations. This serves as the basis for the analysis of the predictive conditional use and its negative affect requirement. The paper then concludes with discussion on the utility of polysemy analysis for uncovering which conceptual mechanisms are exploited by a construction or family of constructions.

## 2 Event-structural Analysis of *-taka*

In terms of Cognitive Grammar's process model of verb semantics, *-taka* can be modeled as establishing temporal and participant structural relations between its connected processes. Given a construction *P1-taka P2*, processes P1 and P2 are aligned temporally such that P2 starts within the bounds of P1, represented in Figure 1 by the dashed vertical line. The grayed out portion of the temporal profile indicates the portion that would not be scanned if P1 is construed as interrupted. The dotted line connecting the circles in Figure 1 represents an identity relation such that they are understood as being the same entity.

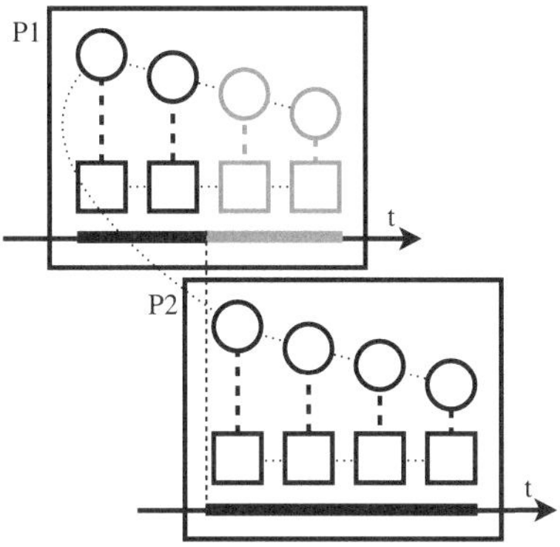


FIGURE 1. Event structure of *P1-taka P2*

In addition to event structure, -*taka*'s analysis also requires a subjective component. In their analysis of Dutch causal connectives Pander Maat and Sanders (2001) show that *daarom*, *dus*, and *daardoor* differ in terms of subjectivity (Langacker 1990). While *daarom* locates causality in the volitionality of an explicit Subject of Consciousness (SoC), the causal relation for epistemic domain uses of *dus* stems from the reasoning process of an implicit SoC—the speaker. When the causal relation does not involve any SoC, *daardoor* is used. These three patterns are illustrated in (5) below (Sanders et al. 2009: 21):

(5) a. Het was een warme dag. Daarom ging Jan zwemmen.
'It was a hot day. That's why Jan went swimming'.
b. Het licht bij de buren is uit. Dus ze zijn niet thuis.
'The neighbors' lights are out. So they are not at home'.
c. De zon scheen. Daardoor steeg de temperatuur.
'The sun is shining. As a result the temperature rose'.

In cases where the main clause of -*taka* involves a volitional, explicit subject of consciousness (SoC), the discontinuation of P1 in favor of P2, and the reason for doing so, are attributed to that SoC. Thus, in (1), an interruptive use of -*taka*, the decision to discontinue the trip to school is attributed to Chulswu, the explicit SoC. This volitional component is shown schematically in Figure 2. Given an in-progress initial clause process P1, the SoC decides to discontinue P1 and initiate P2. Implicit in the decision is an evaluation of P2 as more desirable than P1. This is analogous to the use of *daarom* in (5a), where Jan, the explicit SoC, decides to go swimming because it is warm.

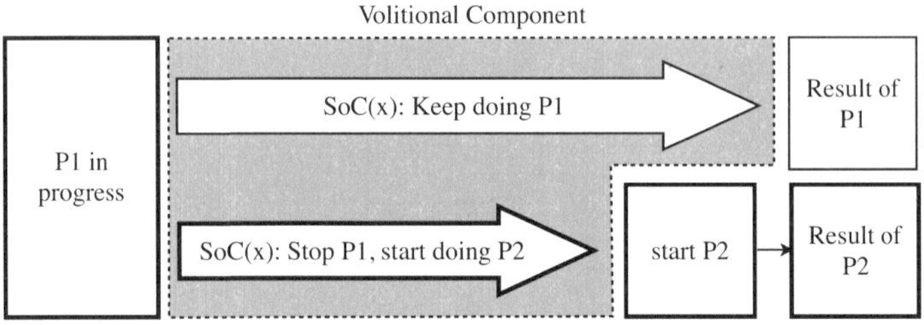


FIGURE 2. Volitional component of *P1-taka P2*

In terms of the Basic Communicative Spaces Network (BCSN) described by Sanders et al. (2009), *daarom* expresses causal relations in a content-volitional space. The content-volitional space is characterized by an explicit SoC, in contrast to epistemic and speech act spaces in which the SoC is implicit, and the content-nonvolitional space in which there is no SoC. Thus, cases like (1) represent content-volitional uses of *-taka*, for which a mental spaces configuration is shown in Figure 3. Volitionality in P2 and the mentioning of an explicit SoC in the speech act space result in the creation of a content-volitional space in which *-taka* is interpreted.

The present model also accounts for cases where *-taka* does not express interruption. When involuntary processes occur in the main clause, as in (3), *-taka* expresses concurrence. Here, the main clause describes a serendipitous event rather than a planned-out meeting. According to the present model, examples like (3) constitute content-nonvolitional uses of *-taka*. Figure 4 shows the corresponding mental space configuration in terms of the BCSN. In this case, since there is no volitionality involved in P2, *-taka* is interpreted in a content-nonvolitional space. As with interruptive uses, the temporal and participant structural relations are interpreted according to the model depicted in Figure 1.

The crucial difference between (1) and (3) is that because there is no SoC connected to the content-nonvolitional space, *-taka*'s volitional component is rendered irrelevant. As shown in Figure 5, without volitional interference, it is possible for P1 to continue to completion. Thus, all that *-taka* specifies is that P2, in this case meeting his spouse, occurs sometime inside the temporal bounds of P1—living in Seoul.

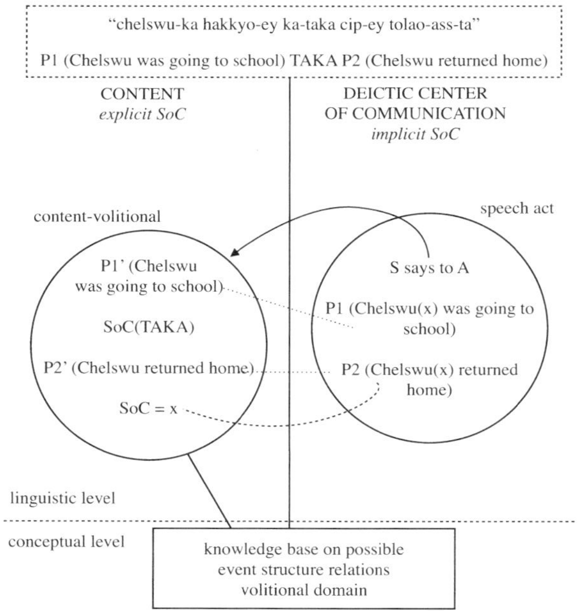


FIGURE 3. Content-volitional use of *–taka* in (1)

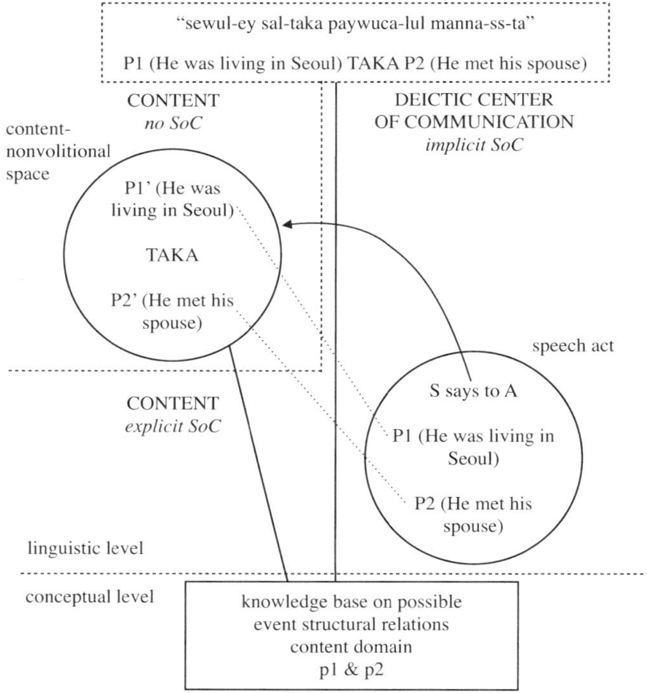


FIGURE 4. Content-nonvolitional use of *–taka* in (3)

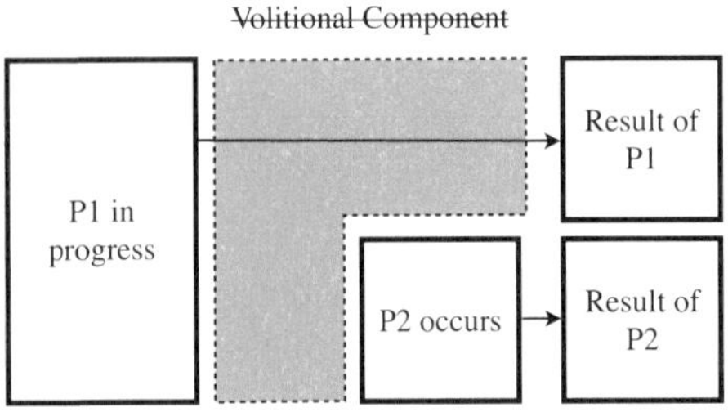


FIGURE 5. *P1-taka P2* in a nonvolitional space

An important feature of the model is that *-taka* is not inherently interruptive. In content-volitional uses of *-taka*, interruption of P1 follows from the volitionality of an explicit SoC. Content-nonvolitional uses not involving an SoC do not entail interruption, which explains why *-taka* can express concurrence. In such cases, the participant identity constraint and temporal alignment are all that are entailed, and the remaining details are determined by the speaker's understanding of possible event structure relations. The model thus predicts content-nonvolitional uses of *-taka* to permit a level of flexibility with regard to the circumstantial relationship between its conjuncts. In (6), for example, the injury is understood as occurring sometime toward the end of the fall, and the fall is in no way interrupted by the injury. Example (7) is also nonvolitional, but in this case, interruption of the dream is entailed by waking up, regardless of volitionality.

(6) nemeci-taka heli-lul tachi-ess-ta
fall-CN waist-AC injure-PS-IN
'He injured his back when he fell'.

(7) kkwum-ul kkwu-taka kkay-ss-ta
dream-AC dream-CN awake-PS-IN
'I woke up in the middle of a dream'.

While nonvolitional uses of *-taka* are predicted to be more flexible than the volitional use, due to the latter being subject to the added constraints of the volitional component, the two constraints specified by the event structural component by themselves yield a number of predictions about the kinds of process combinations *-taka* accommodates. For instance, it is necessary for the processes to have a participant slot that can be filled by the same entity. Thus, in cases like (8), where there is no participant slot in P2 that can accommodate an entity from P1, the clauses cannot be joined by *-taka*. In contrast, *-taka* can be used in (9), where *chi-ta* 'to strike,' used transitively, makes Chelswu the profiled participant in P2 as well. While this difference makes it possible to use *-taka* in (9), it also renders it a content-volitional, and hence interruptive use.

(8) *chelswu-ka hakkyo-ey ka-taka penkay-ka chi-ess-ta
Chelswu-NM school-LOC go-CN lightning-NM strike-PS-IN
'*Lightning struck while Chelswu was going to school'.

(9) chelswu-ka hakkyo-ey ka-taka kong-ul chi-ess-ta
Chelswu-NM school-LOC go-CN ball-AC strike-PS-IN
'Chelswu struck a ball while he was on his way to school'.

The content-volitional vs. content-nonvolitional distinction enables the model to make clearer predictions about what aspectual properties *-taka* requires for its conjuncts. Content-volitional *-taka* does not permit stative conjuncts, which follows from the initial clause process having to be one that can be volitionally discontinued. Thus, actively maintained states in the initial clause are predicted to be possible. While in (10), the subject cannot volitionally stop the stomachache, he can choose to discontinue waiting out the pain, as in (11)[1].

(10) *pay aphu-taka pyengwen-ey ka-ss-ta
stomach hurt-CN hospital-LOC go-PS-IN
'*I went to the hospital after my stomach hurt for a while'.

(11) pay aphu-n kes cham-taka pyengwen-ey ka-ss-ta
stomach hurt-NMZ thing endure-CN hospital-LOC go-PS-IN
'I went to the hospital after trying to wait out my stomachache'.

For content-nonvolitional uses of *-taka*, where the volitional component is not relevant, all four stative/active clause combinations are possible with respect to the two conjuncts. The event-structural relations applied to differing process types, however, yields different interpretations. With two imperfective processes, as in (12), *-taka* constructions tend to convey a transition from one state to another. In such cases, both the initial and main clause processes are construed with starting temporal bounds. Thus, (12) conveys that sometime after the stomachache started, it went away.

(12) payka aphu-taka koaynchanh-ta
stomach hurt-CN ok-IN
'My stomach was hurting and now it feels okay'.

Since content-nonvolitional *-taka* does not stipulate a discontinuation for P1, the model predicts the change of state vs. concurrence interpretation to depend on knowledge of the particular processes involved. While in (12),

---

[1] Example (10) is acceptable if understood to mean what is explicit in (11).

the stomach feeling okay entails that the stomach no longer be hurting, in (13), the stomachache is understood as continuing beyond the start of the headache.

(13) payka aphu-taka meli-to aphu-ta
stomach hurt-CN head-also hurt-IN
'My stomach was hurting and now my head hurts too'.

When content-nonvolitional *-taka* connects a nonstative initial clause to a stative main clause, the model predicts the *-taka* construction to allow for P2 processes which can be construed with a starting temporal bound, which is aligned to a point inside the temporal bounds of P1, with no discontinuation of P1 required. Thus in (14) the person's stomach began hurting on his way to see the doctor. It cannot mean that the trip to the doctor was discontinued.

(14) uysa-lul po-le-ka-taka payka aph-ass-ta
doctor-AC see-PURP-go-CN stomach hurt-PS-IN
'As I was going to see the doctor, my stomach started to hurt'.

The final combination to consider is a stative predicate followed by a nonstative one. The model predicts this to be a possible configuration for content-nonvolitional *-taka*, since the requirements of the volitional component do not apply. This is confirmed by (15), which is characterized by the same temporal alignment of P2 relative to P1, with discontinuation contingent on the particular processes involved.

(15) payka aphu-taka kicel hay-ss-ta
stomach hurt-CN faint do-PS-IN
'He fainted while he had a stomachache'.

Not any stative process, however, can be construed as having a starting temporal bound in its scope. Consequently, the model predicts that permanent states of affairs will not be compatible with *-taka* in either clause position. This is supported by the examples below.

(16) *ttokttokha-taka sihem-ey tteleci-ess-ta
smart-CN exam-LOC fall-PS-IN
'*He was smart, but then failed the exam'.

(17) *sihem kongpwuha-taka ttokttokhay-ss-ta
exam study-CN smart-PS-IN
'*As he studied for the exam, he became smart'.

Table 1 summarizes the possibility of various stative-nonstative process combinations for *-taka*. For content-volitional *-taka*, neither conjunct may

TABLE 1. Stative and nonstative conjunct combinations allowed by *-taka*

| | content-volitional | content-nonvolitional |
|---|---|---|
| STATIVE-taka STATIVE | N | Y |
| STATIVE-taka NONSTATIVE | N | Y |
| NONSTATIVE-taka STATIVE | N | Y |
| NONSTATIVE-taka NONSTATIVE | Y | Y |

be stative. For content-nonvolitional *-taka*, either conjunct may be stative. Thus, the present model of *-taka* in terms of both a volitional component and an event-structural component allows for a more precise account of *-taka*'s behavior with respect to the aspectual types of its conjuncts, not only in terms of combinations that are permitted, but also in terms of the resulting meaning variations.

In this section, I have proposed a conceptual model for *-taka* constructions in terms of volitionality and event structure and shown it to be effective in accounting for its aspectual variants. In the following sections, I extend the model to account for *-taka*'s predictive conditional use, and explain why it is constrained to predictions of undesirable outcomes.

## 3 Predictive Conditional *-taka*

Although predictive conditional *-taka* is quite common in terms of usage, a unified analysis relating it to the other uses of *-taka* has been elusive. Akatsuka and Sohn (1994) have pointed out that in using conditional *-taka* the speaker evaluates both conjuncts to be undesirable. For instance, in (2a), the speaker shows negative affect toward getting an injury and also toward exercising a lot. Use of the construction assumes that the addressee also recognizes P2, e.g. getting injured, to be undesirable, but allows for affective disagreement with respect to P1, e.g. exercising a lot. Conditional *-taka* is often used in cases where the addressee is engaged in the P1 activity at the time of speech. As described earlier, and shown in (2b), the construction does not allow for a positive, beneficial outcome in the apodosis. The following example demonstrates the subjective nature of this constraint—i.e. the requirement is that the speaker and the addressee agree as to the undesirability of the outcome. Example (18) is only acceptable if both the speaker and addressee consider weight loss as undesirable.

(18) yachey-man mek-taka sal ppaci-n-ta
vegetables-only eat-CN flesh sink-PR-IN
'If you only eat vegetables, you are going to lose weight'.

Another characteristic of conditional *-taka* constructions is that they consist of nonvolitional main clauses. It is difficult, if not impossible, to use conditional *-taka* with an agentive main clause. The context for (19)–(20) is one in which the addressee is playing with knives and the speaker is trying to

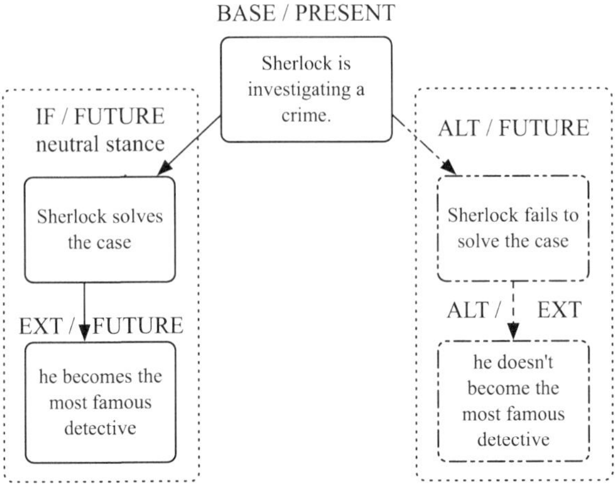


FIGURE 6. Predictive conditional with alternative spaces

issue a warning. While (19), where killing someone is an unintended consequence, can be expressed with *-taka*, (20), with an agentive main clause, cannot.

(19) khal kaciko nol-taka cwuk-nun-ta
knife with play-CN die-PR-IN
'If you play with knives (like that), you will die'.

(20) *khal kaciko nol-taka nwuku-lul cwuk-i-n-ta
knife with play-CN someone-AC die-CAUS-PR-IN
'*If you play with knives (like that), you will kill someone'.

In the examples above, *-taka* is used to make conditional predictions about possible future outcomes. According to Dancygier and Sweetser (2005), predictive conditionals construct alternative spaces in addition to conditional future spaces. In the alternative space, the protasis is negated such that the apodosis does not occur. An example space configuration is shown in Figure 6 for the *if* predictive conditional in (21).

(21) If Sherlock solves the case, he will become the most famous detective ever.

In the conditional future space, Sherlock solves the crime and becomes the most famous detective ever. There is also, however, an alternative space in which Sherlock fails to solve the crime, and does not become the most famous detective ever. Dancygier and Sweetser (2005: 46) point out that the building of alternative spaces is contingent on the epistemic stance of the construction toward the protasis. *If* predictive conditionals are neutral in epistemic stance toward their protases, resulting in the construction of alternative spaces, as shown in Figure 6. In contrast, *when* predictive conditionals have positive epistemic stance toward their protases, and consequently do not yield alternative spaces.

It is also possible for conditional spaces to be built up in the absence of explicitly conditional forms such as *if* and *when*. This is the case for *and*- and *or*-conditionals, where instead predictive verb forms supply the relevant space building parameters (Dancygier and Sweetser 2005: 237–239). Thus, (22) results in a space configuration similar to Figure 6, describing the same predictive scenario, except for the switch from a third to second person subject. This shift highlights a property of *and*-conditionals that distinguishes them from *if*-conditionals, which is that *and*-conditionals specifically involve the interests of the speaker and addressee (Dancygier and Sweetser 2005: 241). Thus, while 3rd person subjects are not specifically banned, *and*-conditionals are rarely used outside of specific pragmatic contexts.

(22) Solve that case, and you will become the most famous detective ever.

Similar to English *if* predictive conditionals, I propose that -*taka*'s conditionality stems from the construction of predicted future and alternative spaces. Like English *and*-conditionals, however, rather than being a part of -*taka*'s conventional semantics, conditional space construction is signaled by predictive verb forms in the main clause. The nonvolitional main clause of conditional -*taka* constructions results in the predictive future space being a content-nonvolitional space. For content-nonvolitional uses of -*taka*, the main clause process is an unintended event that occurs in the middle of the initial clause event. For instance, in (2a), in the predicted future space, the subject—in this case the addressee—exercises a lot and gets injured. As was the case for (22), neutrality of epistemic stance toward the predictive space results in the construction of an alternative space. In the alternative space, the SoC stops exercising and does not become injured. The predicted future and alternative spaces are depicted in Figure 7.

As one might expect, Korean conditional -*taka* is also similar to English *and*-conditionals in dispreferring 3rd person subjects. Example (23), which is a 3rd person version of (2a), does not yield a conditional interpretation, and instead constitutes a content-nonvolitional use of -*taka*.

(23) chelswu-ka wuntong manhi ha-taka tachi-keyss-ta
Chelswu-NM exercise a.lot do-CN injure-MD-IN
'Chelswu may get injured while exercising a lot'.

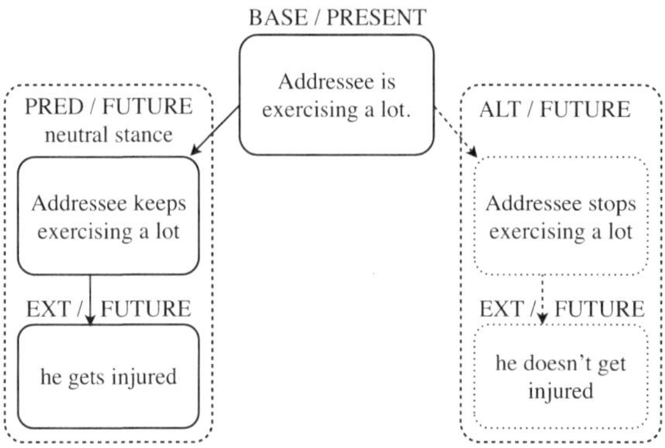


FIGURE 7. Predicted future and alternative spaces for (2a)

The modal marker *-keyss*, which in 1st person contexts signals a volitional commitment, in 3rd person contexts, conveys a conjecture about the future. Example (23) constitutes instead a nonconditional prediction that Chelswu will probably get injured. As for English *and*-conditionals, however, given the right pragmatic context, a conditional reading of (23) may be possible—for example, if it is uttered in the context of a passionate discussion between the speaker and the addressee about how they should do something about Chelswu's over-exercising.

## 4 Negative Affect Conditionality

Another important aspect of this analysis of conditional *-taka* is the volitionality of the SoC in the alternative space. Since the explicit SoC in the alternative space decides to discontinue the P1 process, as shown in Figure 7, the alternative space is a content-volitional space in which *-taka*'s volitional component must be taken into account. But whose volitionality is it that is represented in the alternative space? As pointed out for example (2a), repeated below, negative affect toward the protasis belongs to the speaker rather than to the addressee.

(2) a. wuntong manhi ha-taka tachi-n-ta
exercise a.lot do-CN injure-PR-IN
'If you exercise a lot, you're going to get injured'.

However, it is the addressee, rather than the speaker, that stops exercising in the alternative space.

Mental Spaces Theory is able to account for the kind of mixed consciousness evident in the alternative spaces of *-taka* conditionals through conceptual blends. Sanders et al. (2009: 40–41) show, in their analysis of Dutch epistemic causal *dus* in free indirect speech contexts, that the narrator's consciousness can be identified with that of an explicit SoC, creating a blended subjectivity. For example, in (24), the conclusion that the neighbors are not at home seems to belong to both Jan and to the narrator, with the narrator taking on Jan's perspective. This is accounted for through a blended epistemic space in which Jan's and the narrator's consciousness are merged.

(24) Jan ziet dat het licht bij de buren uit is. Dus ze zijn niet thuis.
P (Jan saw the lights at the neighbors' house were out.)
DUS Q (they were not at home.)

Similarly, I propose that the alternative spaces of conditional *-taka* constructions is a blended space in which the explicit SoC—the addressee in the case of (2a)—and the speaker's implicit SoC are combined, such that the explicit SoC acts according to the volitionality of the speaker. Thus, in the alternative space of Figure 7, the explicit subject, the addressee, acting out the speaker's will, stops exercising. This type of blended subjectivity was proposed in Lakoff's (1996) mental spaces approach to examples like (25), which involve a two-part conceptualization of self—the Subject, taken to be the locus of experience, and the Self, which represents the body.

(25) If I were you, I would hate myself.

In (25), the protasis sets up a counterfactual blended space in which the Subject of the speaker is combined with the Self of the addressee, and in which the blended subject-addressee hates himself. Similarly, the alternative future space for (2a), as depicted in Figure 8, is a blended space in which the Subject of the speaker is combined with the Self of the addressee. In the extension of that space, the blended speaker-addressee stops exercising a lot—according to the desires of the speaker—which results in the alternate outcome in which the addressee does not get injured. Figure 8 shows the mental spaces configuration for (2a) in terms of the Basic Communicative Spaces Network.

In Figure 8, the predictive future space is a content-nonvolitional space without an SoC whose volitionality is connected with the interpretation of *-taka*. Thus, in the predictive future space, *-taka*'s volitional component becomes irrelevant and only the event-structural relations apply. For content nonvolitional uses of *-taka,* discontinuation of the initial clause process oc-

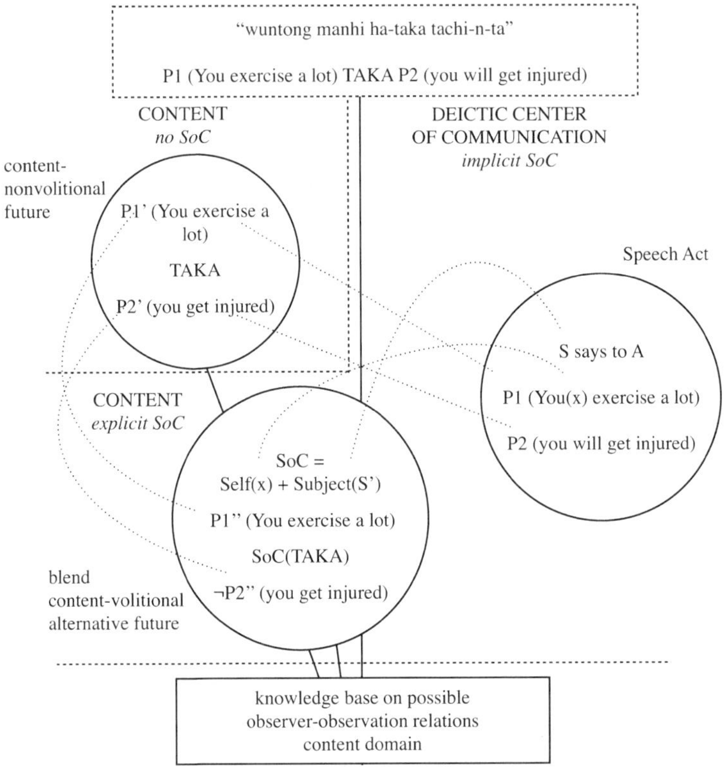


FIGURE 8. BCSN mental space configuration for (2a)

curs only if necessitated by the main clause process. In this case, exercising a lot continues until injury occurs, which would preclude further exercising. The alternative, volitional construal possible with *-taka* allows for the construction of an alternative space, a content-volitional space in which *-taka* is construed in connection with an explicit SoC. For content-volitional *-taka*, the volitional component specifies that the explicit SoC volitionally discontinues the initial clause process and starts doing something else. That other process is not specified in conditional *-taka*'s alternative space. However, the volitional discontinuation of the initial clause process in favor of another is sufficient to establish that in the alternative space, the specified nonvolitional main clause process—in this case getting injured—does not occur. As shown in Figure 8, the SoC in the content-volitional space is a blend of the Subject of the speaker and the Self of the addressee such that in the blended space, the explicit SoC—the addressee—acts volitionally according to the speaker's desires and stops exercising. Note that *-taka* in a content-volitional space requires volitional discontinuation of the P1 process, whereas *-taka* in a content-nonvolitional space does not.

Thus, in addition to explaining how an aspectual connective like *-taka* can take on conditional meaning, the present model is also able to explain why the construction cannot be used to predict desirable outcomes. The reason for this is that the predictive conditional use only occurs when the main clause is nonvolitional. Because of this, it is the content-volitional alternative space that always aligns with the volitionality of the speaker. Since the alternative space, rather than the non-alternative, predicted future space, is always affectively aligned with the speaker's desires, the non-alternative, nonvolitional predicted outcome must always be one that is undesirable to the speaker.

The BCSN mental spaces configuration for (2b), which attempts to predict a desirable outcome using conditional *-taka*, is shown in Figure 9. In the predicted future content-nonvolitional space, the addressee continues exercising a lot and becomes healthy. Becoming healthy does not require exercising to be discontinued, but note that content-nonvolitional uses of *-taka* do not require the P1 process to be interrupted. In the content-volitional alternative space, the blended SoC, comprised of the Self of the addressee and the Subject of the speaker, chooses to discontinue exercising a lot and consequently does not become healthy. As was the case for (2a), the discontinuation is volitional, according to the desires of the speaker. The discontinuation of exercise, however, results in an outcome contrary to the desire of the speaker, assuming that the speaker desires the well-being of the addressee and would thus presumably be in favor of the addressee's becoming healthy. What results is a pragmatic contradiction akin to saying, 'If I were you, I would stop exercising a lot so that I don't become healthy'.

Thus, because conditional *-taka*'s alternative space is always where the speaker's volitionality is represented, it is also the space in which outcomes desirable to the speaker are expected to obtain through the willful discontinuation of the initial clause process. Example (2b) specifies an outcome desirable to the speaker in the main clause, and hence in the predicted future space. This is, however, incompatible with the conditional *-taka* construction, because conditional *-taka* always represents the speaker's volitionality in the alternative space rather than in the predicted future space. This asymmetry was in turn because conditional *-taka* is only possible where the main clause is nonvolitional. Consequently, the non-alternative space, i.e. the predicted future space, always contains an outcome undesirable to the speaker, which, because it occurs in a content-nonvolitional space, arises unintentionally. The net effect is *-taka*'s negative affect conditionality.

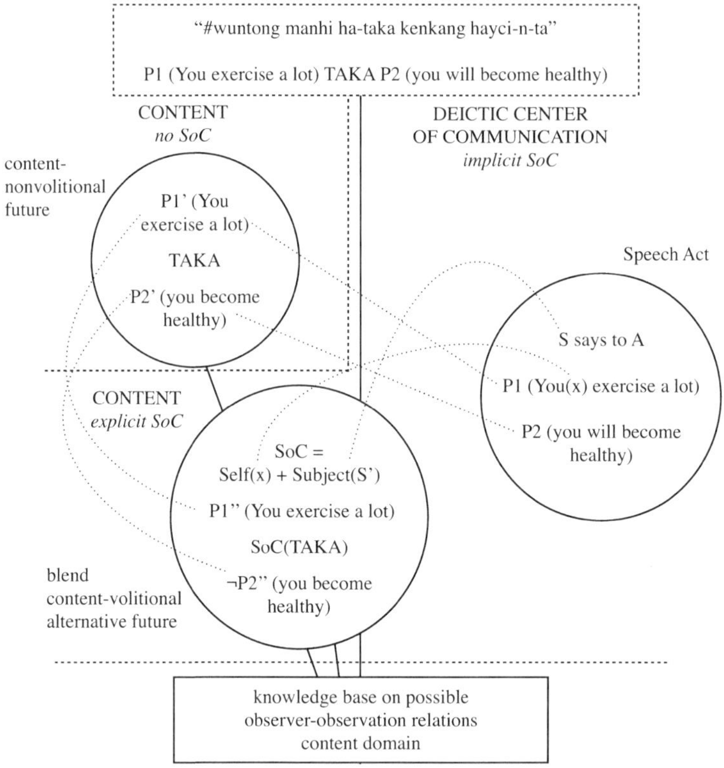


FIGURE 9. Mental spaces configuration for unacceptable example (2b)

## 5 Conclusion

In this paper I have given an analysis of Korean *-taka* connective constructions in terms of a model that situates the verbal semantics of Cognitive Grammar (Langacker [1991] 2002) within Sanders et al.'s (2009) mental spaces based communicative model. Crucial to this analysis was the articulation of a volitional component for *-taka*, in addition to event-structural constraints, which takes effect for content-volitional uses of *-taka* to yield interruptive semantics. For content-nonvolitional uses of *-taka*, the volitional component produces no effect, and the construction is able to convey a range of aspectual relations, provided they are consistent with the remaining temporal and participant structural constraints. Adopting Dancygier and Sweetser's (2005) alternativity approach to conditional constructions, the negative affect requirement on predictive conditional uses of *-taka* was proposed as resulting from -*taka*'s volitional component always being represented in the alternative space.

A notable feature of the present analysis is its reliance on details of -*taka*'s various senses to decompose its semantics along the lines of a range of underlying conceptual mechanisms. The analysis built on this approach was able to predict when the connective has or does not have interruptive semantics, and explain how this relates to predictive conditionality, as well as why in this particular case those predictions must be affectively negative.

## References


Akatsuka, N. and S. Sohn. 1994. Negative conditionality: The case of Japanese -*tewa* and Korean -*taka*. *Japanese/Korean Linguistics* 4: 203–220.

Choi, H.-P. 1961. *Wuli malpon (A grammar of our language)*. Seoul: Cengumsa.

Dancygier, B. and E. Sweetser. 2005. *Mental Spaces in Grammar*. Cambridge University Press.

Fauconnier, G. 1985. *Mental Spaces*. MIT Press.

Lakoff, G. 1996. Sorry, I'm not myself today: The metaphor system for conceptualizing the self. *Spaces, Worlds, and Grammar*, eds. G. Fauconnier and E. Sweetser, 91–123. University of Chicago Press.

Langacker, R. W. 1990. Subjectification. *Cognitive Linguistics* 1(1): 5–38.

Langacker, R. W. [1991] 2002. *Concept, Image, and Symbol: The Cognitive Basis of Grammar*. Berlin: Walter de Gruyter, 2nd edn.

Lee, K. 1993. *A Korean grammar on semantic-pragmatic principles*. Seoul: Hanguk Munhwasa.

Pander Maat, H. and T. Sanders. 2001. Subjectivity in causal connectives: An empirical study of language in use. *Cognitive Linguistics* 12(3): 247–273.

Sanders, T., J. Sanders, and E. Sweetser. 2009. Causality, cognition and communication: A mental space analysis of subjectivity in causal connectives. *Causal Categories in Discourse and Cognition*, eds. T. Sanders and E. Sweetser, 19–60. Berlin: Walter de Gruyter.

Traugott, E. C. 1989. On the rise of epistemic meanings in English: an example of subjectification in semantic change. *Language* 65(1): 31–55.

Traugott, E. C. and R. B. Dasher. 2002. *Regularity in semantic change*. Cambridge University Press.

8

# Favorable and Unfavorable Effects: A Typology of Benefactive and Adversative Constructions in Japanese, Korean, and Ainu

KATSUNOBU IZUTSU AND TAKESHI KOGUMA*

## 1 Introduction

Voice has long been a given grammatical category in language studies. Passive and middle as well as active voice are generally assumed to have morphosyntactic manifestations in a great majority of languages of the world; inverse and antipassive are accordingly supposed to be minor subcategories. Nevertheless, the morphosyntactic counterparts of the same voice in different languages often serve as neither functional nor conceptual counterparts. In fact, we often find English passive sentences hard to translate into natural Japanese passives: e.g., *An early reply would be appreciated* can hardly be expressed with passive forms in Japanese.

Grammatical voice could be metaphorically viewed as a distinction between the speaking voices of active and passive participants in the event designated. Thus it represents a distinction between what is recounted from the viewpoint of the active participant and what is told from that of the passive participant. As far as Japanese, Korean, and Ainu are concerned, such distinctions are far more concerned with a contrast between agent and recip-

*This study is partially supported by the Ministry of Education, Science, Sports, and Culture, Grant-in-Aid for Scientific Research (C), 23520482, 2011–2013.

*Language and the Creative Mind*.
Mike Borkent, Barbara Dancygier, and Jennifer Hinnell (eds).

ient rather than between agent and patient, and further with a difference among speaker, addressee, and others.

We find many more functional and conceptual counterparts of voice phenomena in benefactive and adversative (or malefactive) expressions. While Japanese has developed some benefactive and adversative constructions, the neighboring languages Korean and Ainu are generally viewed as underutilizing such constructions. Each language does however have some constructions like these. The present study makes a conceptual analysis of all those constructions and presents a typological perspective on them.

First, after outlining the well-attested benefactive and adversative constructions in Japanese, Korean, and Ainu in Section 2, we will argue in Section 3 that those languages have at least three more clausal patterns that can be counted as comparable benefactive or adversative constructions. Section 4 will propose a possible typological perspective on the constructions by recapitulating their differences and similarities in linguistic realization of agent/recipient, directionality of (un)favorable effect, and person restriction.

## 2 Benefactive and Adversative Constructions in Japanese, Korean, and Ainu

### 2.1 The 'give' and 'get' Benefactives

It is well known that some Japanese, Korean, and Ainu verbs with the sense 'give' are used to form certain benefactive constructions as illustrated in (1) (Teramura 1982; Shibatani 1990, 1994a, 1996; Nakagawa 1995; Tamura 1996; Smith 2010; Radetzky and Smith 2010, inter alia). Although their constructional meanings hardly manifest themselves in the English translations, the speaker obviously assumes a recipient (someone who is listened to) to receive a benefit or favorable effect from an agent (another one who listens). While the Japanese and Korean constructions in question allow any of the first, second, and third persons to be the agent and recipient, the Ainu one only tolerates a first-person recipient as will be discussed in Section 4.

(1) a. *kii-te-ageta*[*yatta*]. (JAPANESE)
listen-and-gave[gave]
'I listened (to you[him])' or 'You[He] listened (to her)'.

b. *kii-te-kureta*. (JAPANESE)
listen-and-gave
'He[You] listened to me' or 'He listened to you[her]'.

c. *deur-eo* *jueossda.* (KOREAN)
listen-and gave
'I listened (to you[him])', 'You listened (to me[him])', or 'He listened (to me[you/her])'.

d. *i=nu* *wa* *i=kor(par)e.* (AINU)
me[us]=hear and me[us]=give
'(Please) listen to me[us]'; *'He[She/They] listened to me[us])'.

Unlike Korean and Ainu, Japanese distinguishes between the benefactive situations with the first-person agent and that with the first-person recipient. The speaker is accordingly required to use *kureru* for the first-person recipient and *yaru* or *ageru* for the first-person agent, as manifested by the different interpretations in (1a-b).

Moreover, the *kureru* benefactive sentences exhibit a notably different behavior. In Smith's (2010) '*kureru* agentless benefactive sentences', the recipient of benefit (beneficiary) 'is always the speaker' and 'cannot be overtly stated in a sentence', as in (2). Japanese has another benefactive construction with the verb *morau* 'get/receive' as exemplified in (3). It differs in that the subject refers to the recipient rather than the agent of benefit.

(2) **ame* *ga* *watasi* *ni/* *no* *tame* *ni* *yande-kure-ta.*
rain NOM 1s DAT/ GEN sake DAT stop-give-PST
'It stopped raining (and I am thankful for that)'. (Smith 2010: 88)

(3) *kii-te-moratta.*
listen-and-got
'I[You/He] had myself[yourself/himself] listened to'.

## 2.2 The Adversative Passive and its Comparables

The Japanese adversative passive, instantiated in (4), amounts to a negative counterpart of the *morau* benefactive construction (Teramura 1982, Tsuboi 2010, among others). The recipient receives adversity or an unfavorable rather than favorable effect. Interestingly, Japanese sentences with *yaru*, *kureru*, and *morau* can also serve as adversative (or malefactive) constructions as illustrated in (5). Radetzky and Smith (2010: 113 n.9) note that such uses are 'highly constrained and marked (e.g., indicating sarcasm or, as a derived function of that, when challenging someone...)', as in (5b). However, *yaru* 'is more frequently used than the other two verbs in malefactive situations', especially when the agent is the speaker, as in (5a).

(4) (*katteni* *CD-o* *motidas-are-te)* *kik-areta.*
without:permission CD-ACC take:out-PASS-and listen-PASS:PAST
'I [You/He] had a CD (taken out and) heard (without permission)'.

(5) a. *Taroo-o izimete-yar-ta.*
Taroo-ACC pick.on-give-PST
'I picked on Taroo (he was asking for it, he deserved it [in the nasty sense])'.

b. *wasurute moraw-tewa komar-u.*
forget receive-if have.difficulty-NONPST
'It'll be bad (for me) if you forget'.
(Radetzky and Smith 2010: 114)

Hwang et al. (1988) note that Korean lacks equivalents to the Japanese V-*te morau* construction and adversative passive, where the recipient is coded in the subject. In contrast, Radetzky and Smith (2010) cite Lee (1974), reporting that Korean has a benefactive passive with *pat* 'receive' like (6a) and a malefactive passive with *tangha* 'be subject to' as in (6b) or *mac* 'encounter' as in (6c). In fact, those benefactive and malefactive passives are not verbal constructions comparable to the Japanese V-*te morau* construction and adversative passive. They are types of sentences with nominalization in which the verbs for 'receive/confront/encounter' take verbal-noun complements, as in English sentences like *The teacher enjoyed/earned/gained the esteem of students*, *The prisoner got/had/took a beating*, and *The woman got/suffered cold treatment*. However, they can also be treated as being comparable to the Japanese (adversative) passive in constructional terms, as will be argued in 2.3.

(6) a. *ku sensayng-un haksayng-tul-eykey conkyeng-pat-nun-ta.*
the teacher-TOP student-PL-AGT respect-PASS-PRES-DECL
'The teacher is respected by students'.
(Lee 1974: 151; cited from Radetzky and Smith 2010: 112)

b. *pholo-ka henpieng-eykey kwutha-tangha-ess-ta.*
P.O.W.-SUB M.P.-AGT beat-PASS-PST-DECL
'The prisoner of war was beaten (was subject to a beating) by an M.P'.
(Lee 1974: 151; cited from Radetzky and Smith 2010: 113)

c. *ce yeca-ka namphyen-eykey sopak-mac-ess-ta.*
that woman-SUB husband-AGT abandon-PASS-PST-DECL
'That woman was abandoned by her husband'.
(Lee 1974: 151; cited from Radetzky and Smith 2010: 113)

## 2.3 Two Types of Constructions for Benefactive and Adversative Event Conceptions

As shown by the above examples, Japanese, Korean, and Ainu can have two major types of linguistic realization of benefactive and adversative event conceptions. One is the agent-subject construction like the 'give' benefactives/adversatives illustrated in (1) and (5a) above. The other is the recipient-subject construction like the 'get' benefactives/adversatives exemplified in (3) and (4). Teramura (1982) refers to the paradigmatic relationships among a set of Japanese sentence patterns in (7), presenting a general view of their constructional and conceptual parallelism as in Table 1.

(7) a. *Kyaku-ga kita* (*Sonnim-i wassda*) (neutral, objective)
guest-NOM came guest-NOM came
'(I/We) had some guests'.

b. *Kyaku-ni ko-rareta* (*Sonnim-i wa-seo*
guest-DAT come-PASS:PAST guest-NOM come-and
*nancheohaessda*) (ill effect, damage)
was:troublesome
'(I/We) were embarrassed that we had some guests'.

c. *Kyaku-ga ki-te-kureta* (*Sonnim-i wa jueossda*) (benefit)
guest-NOM come-and-gave guest-NOM come gave
'(I/We) were glad that we had some guests'.

d. *Kyaku-ni ki-te-moratta* (*Sonnim-i wa jueossda*) (benefit)
guest-DAT come-and-got guest-NOM come gave
'(I/We) were glad that we had some guests'.

(Teramura 2001[1988]: 294)[1]

Teramura's view on Japanese benefactive and adversative in Table 1 can be further generalized into a cross-linguistic view as in Table 2 on the basis of our distinction between agent- and recipient-subject constructions and that between benefactive and adversative constructions. Sentences (1a-d), (3), (4), (5a-b), (6a-c), and (7b-d) instantiate an agent-subject benefactive, recipient-subject benefactive, recipient-subject adversative, or agent-subject adversative construction.

TABLE 1. Japanese benefactive/adversative (Teramura 2001[1988]: 294; our translation)

| case marking | benefit | damage |
|---|---|---|
| agent = *ga*-marked NP | *kyaku-ga ki-te-kureru* | |
| recipient = *ga*-marked NP (agent = *ni*-marked NP) | (*watasi-ga*) *kyaku-ni ki-te-morau* | (*watasi-ga*) *kyaku-ni ko-rareru* |

[1] Korean translations in parenthesis are the original; English gloss and translation are ours.

TABLE 2. Cross-linguistic view of benefactive/adversative constructions

| | BENEFACTIVE | ADVERSATIVE |
|---|---|---|
| agent-subject | (1), (7c) | (5a) |
| recipient-subject | (3), (6a), (7d) | (4), (5b), (6b-c), (7b) |

The benefactive and adversative constructions in Japanese, Korean, and Ainu can all be schematically described as having one of the structures in (8). The benefactive or adversative event is comparably encoded in a 'verb complex' (VC) in Talmy's (1991) terms. The verb complex is realized as 'conjunctive compound' in Shibatani's (2003: 263) terms or so-called light verb construction (a basic verb with a verbal-noun complement). In the agent-subject benefactive/adversative constructions, the agent of the event is designated in the subject NP as in (8a) and (8c). In the recipient-subject benefactive/adversative constructions, contrastively, it is designated in the NP suffixed by an oblique-case particle (obl.) as in (8b) and (8d).

(8) a. $NP_{(agent)}$ VC (AGENT-SUBJECT BENEFACTIVE)
b. $NP_{(recipient)}$ $NP_{(agent)}$-obl. VC (RECIPIENT-SUBJECT BENEFACTIVE)
c. $NP_{(agent)}$ VC (AGENT-SUBJECT ADVERSATIVE)
d. $NP_{(recipient)}$ $NP_{(agent)}$-obl. VC (RECIPIENT-SUBJECT ADVERSATIVE)

While the agent NP can be marked with the ablative (*-kara*) or agentive (*-niyotte*) as well as dative (*-ni*) particle in ordinary (non-adversative) passives like (9a-b), it must be marked with the dative rather than ablative or agentive particle in benefactive/adversative constructions as shown in (10). This formal limitation of the oblique-marked NP to the dative endorses the constructional status of the recipient-subject benefactives/adversatives.

(9) a. *kare-wa minna-**ni/kara/**$^{??}$**niyotte** sinrais-are-teiru.*
he-TOP everyone-DAT/ABL/AGT trust-PASS-PROG:PRES
'He is trusted by everyone'.

b. *kare-wa resukyuutai-**ni/**$^{??}$**kara/niyotte** sukuidas-are-ta.*
he-TOP rescue:team-DAT/ABL/AGT save-PASS-PAST
'He was saved by a rescue team'.

(10) a. *Kyaku-**ni/**$^{??}$**kara/**$^{??}$**niyotte** ko-rareta.*
guest-DAT/ABL/AGT come-PASS:PAST
'(I/We) were embarrassed that we had some guests'.

b. *Kyaku-**ni/**$^{??}$**kara/**$^{??}$**niyotte** ki-te-moratta.*
guest-DAT/ABL/AGT come-and-got
'(I/We) were glad that we had some guests'.

# 3 Other Benefactive and Adversative Constructions

## 3.1 Korean Double-accusative Construction

Korean seemingly lacks equivalents to the Japanese V-*te morau* construction and adversative passive, where the recipient is coded in the subject (Hwang et al. 1988). On the other hand, the so-called possessor raising or double-accusative construction, illustrated in (11), could be viewed as a Korean functional counterpart of the V-*te morau* construction and adversative passive, in which the 'raised' object, not the subject, refers to the recipient of the relevant favorable or unfavorable effect (cf. Shibatani 1994b).

(11) a. *Inho-ka Yumi-lul aphu-n son-ul cap-ass-ta.*
-NOM -ACC aching hand-ACC held
'Inho held Yumi by the aching hand'. (Kim 1989: 452)

b. *Chelswu-ka Yenghi-lul elkul-ul ttwulecikey po-ass-ta.*
Chelswu-NOM Yenghi-ACC face-ACC hard see-PAST-DECL
'Chelswu looked at Yenghi's face hard [enough to make a hole in it]'. (Vermeulen 2005: 158)

c. *Vampire-ka John-ul phi-lul ppal-ass-ta.*
Vampire-NOM John-ACC blood-ACC suck-PAST-DECL
'A vampire sucked John's blood'. (Cho 2003: 345)

d. *hyelkwan-i makhi-n hwanca-lul hyelkwan-ul ttwul-*
blood:vessel-NOM clogged patient-ACC blood:vessel-ACC bore-
*e-cwu-ki....*
and-give-ing
'To unclog the blood vessel of the patient who is suffering from clogged blood vessel ...'.
(Bak 2004: 34; our gloss and translation)

Although notions like 'inalienability', 'entailment', and 'affectedness' somehow condition the acceptable uses, an unfavorable effect (as in (11a-c)) or favorable effect (as in (11d)) on the first object entity (the recipient) seems to best characterize the constructional meaning.[2] In (11a), 'Yumi' is

---

[2] Yeon (2010) points out that the sentences in (i) 'are grammatical only when Mary is actually carrying/wearing the PS's [possessees]' and that (ib) 'is ungrammatical if John tore Mary's clothes but they were hanging in the closet'.

(i) a. *Kyengchal-i Mary-lul kapang-ul cap-ass-ta.*
Police-NOM -ACC bag-ACC catch-PAST-DECL
Lit. The police caught Mary in her bag.

the recipient or victim of the adversative event 'touching the aching hand'. In (11b-c), 'John' and 'Yenghi' serve as the recipients or victims of the adversative events 'looking' and 'sucking'. In (11d), 'the patient' amounts to the recipient or beneficiary of the benefactive event 'unclogging'.

### 3.2 Ainu *enci/unci*-passives

Ainu also lacks structural equivalents to the Japanese V-*te morau* construction and adversative passive, in which the recipient is coded in the subject. In some dialects, however, it has developed special pronominal prefixes (*enci=*, *unci=*), which are confined to passive constructions with a first person patient (Asai 1969; Izutsu 2004; inter alia). Such passive sentences can be largely characterized as denoting benefactive or adversative events, in which the recipient of the favorable or unfavorable effect is the first-person entity, as illustrated in (12c).

(12) a. *tankur* *en=kikkik.*
that:man 1.SG.OBJ =hit
'That man hit me'.

b. *tankur* *orowa* *en=kikkik=an.*
that:man from 1.SG.OBJ=hit=PASS

c. *tankur* *orowa* ***enci=****kikkik.*
that:man from 1.SG.PASS=hit
'I got hit by that man'.

d. *ku=kor* *topenpe* *opittano* ***enci=****ere* *okera* *a* *wa.*
1.SG.SBJ=have sweets all 1.SG.PASS=have:eat finish PERF FP
'I had all my sweets eaten'.
(Asai 1969: 796; our gloss, translation, and emphasis)

---

b. *John-i* *Mary-lul* *os-ul* *ccic-ess-ta.*
-NOM -ACC clothes-ACC tear-PAST-DECL
Lit. John tore Mary's clothes to the effect of affecting Mary.

c. *John-i* *Mary-lul* *shinpal-ul* *palp-ass-ta.*
Nom -ACC shoe-ACC step.on-PAST-DECL
Lit. John stepped on Mary on the shoe.

Moreover, Yeon argues that the 'affectedness' as well as 'contiguity' plays a role in the acceptability difference between the (iia) and (iib). As he notes, Mary is affected by the dog's biting in (iib) whereas she 'seems not to be affected' by John's eating/biting her apple in (iia).

(ii) a. **John-i* *Mary-lul* *sakwa-lul* *mek/mul-ess-ta.*
NOM ACC apple-ACC eat/bite-PAST-DECL
*Lit. John ate/bit Mary's apple to the effect of affecting Mary.

b. ?*Kay-ka* *Mary-lul* *sakwa-lul* *mul-ess-ta.*
dog-NOM ACC apple-ACC bite-PAST-DECL
'?The dog bit Mary in the apple'.

According to Asai (1969: 796), transitive events like the one designated in (12a) can also be expressed by ordinary passives (marked with the suffix *=an* or the prefix *an=*) as in (12b), while there is still another passive form (marked with the prefix *enci=*) that can be used to depict events with a first-person patient as in (12c). He further points out that this special passive form can convey some benefit or adversity as in (12d).

A brief consultation of Sunazawa (1983), an autobiography written in Ainu alongside Japanese glosses, reveals that the first-person passive prefixes *enci=* (singular) and *unci=* (plural) are both analyzable as denoting either benefactive or adversative events as in (13). The favorable or unfavorable effect is often specified by expressions like *ku=ekiroroan* 'I was happy' as in (13a-b), *ku=etoranne* 'I hated' as in (13d) and *inunukaski* 'pitiable' as in (13f), or implied by sentences like *Kindaici tono nispa ku=nukar* 'We got to see Mr. Kindaichi' as in (13c) and *ku=hese ka eaykap* 'I could hardly breathe' as in (13e).

(13) a. *icen poronno* ***enci=****kore kusu ku=ekiroroan.*<br>
money much 1.SG.PASS=give because 1.SG.SBJ=be:pleased:with<br>
'I was happy I got a lot of money'. (Sunazawa 1983: 84)

b. *orwa kespa an kor* ***enci=****tak pakno*<br>
then every:year be when 1.SG.PASS=invite as:that<br>
*ku=ekiroroan pe isam.*<br>
1.SG.SBJ=be:pleased:with thing be:absent<br>
'I was invited every year, and there was nothing as pleasing as that'. (Sunazawa 1983:182)

c. *orowa ku=yupo orowa* ***unci=****askeuk,*<br>
then 1.SG.SBJ=brother from 1.PL.PASS=invite<br>
*paye=as, Kindaici tono nispa ku=nukar.*<br>
go.PL=1.PL.EXCL.SBJ Kindaichi lord mister 1.SG.SBJ=see<br>
'Thus we were called by our brother, went there, and got to see Mr. Kindaichi'. (Sunazawa 1983: 184–185)

d. *sonno* ***enci=****eukoitak kuni ku=etoranne kusu ....*<br>
really 1.SG.PASS=speak:ill:of should 1.SG.SBJ=hate because<br>
'Because I really hated being spoken ill of ...'. (Sunazawa 1983: 86)

e. *... ney ta ku=mokor rusuy yakka* ***enci=****mososo*<br>
there at 1.SG.SBJ=sleep want:to though 1.SG.PASS=awake<br>
*kor sonno ku=hese ka eaykap pakno ku=yaynu.*<br>
when really 1.SG.SBJ=breathe either cannot as:that 1.SG.SBJ=think<br>
'I was awaken, though really sleepy, at that time and I felt I could hardly breathe'. (Sunazawa 1983:99)

f. *wen menoko orowa wenno* **unci=ye,** *Sueko inunukaski, ....*
bad woman from badly 1.PL.PASS=say Sueko pitiable
'We were basely slandered by a wicked woman and I pitied my daughter Sueko'. (Sunazawa 1983:118)
(our gloss, translation, and emphasis)

### 3.3 Japanese Inverse Construction

The Japanese 'inverse form' (Shibatani 2003, 2006) counts as another adversative construction.[3] According to Givón's (1994: 9) definition, inverse voice indicates that '[t]he patient is more topical than the agent but the agent retains considerable topicality', which stands in some contrast with passive voice in which '[t]he patient is more topical than the agent, and the agent is extremely non-topical ('suppressed', 'demoted')'. Shibatani (2006: 247) remarks that while the 'direct form' describes an action that 'originates in an agent higher in discourse relevance than the patient', the inverse form denotes 'situations where the action originates with an agent low in discourse relevance relative to the patientive terminal'. Therefore, the Japanese inverse form is primarily regarded as being 'obligatory when a motion is directed toward the speaker's sphere' as manifested in (14).

(14) a. *Boku-wa Ken-ni syootaizyoo-o okut-ta.* (Direct)
I-TOP Ken-to invitation-ACC send-PAST
'I sent an invitation to Ken'.

b. **Ken-ga boku-ni syootaizyoo-o okut-ta.* (Direct)
Ken-NOM I-to invitation-ACC send-PAST
'Ken sent an invitation to me'.

c. *Ken-ga boku-ni syootaizyoo-o okut-te ki-ta.* (Inverse)
Ken-NOM I-to invitation-ACC send-CONJ come-PAST
'Ken sent an invitation to me'. (Shibatani 2003: 278–279)

However, inverse forms often take on connotations of some unfavorable effect: (14c) implies that the speaker does not want to be invited, feeling the invitation to be an embarrassment or bother.[4] The presence and absence of similar connotations account for the major difference between the (a) and (b) sentences in (15) and (16). Unlike the direct form employed in (15a) and (16a) (*sawat-ta*), the inverse form used in (15b) and (16b) (*sawat-te-ki-ta*) is apt to convey that the speaker or the possessor of the object referent experiences an unfavorable effect like discomfort, unpleasantness, or displeasure.

---

[3] Shibatani (2006: 265 n.15) views the inverse marker (INV) as a grammaticalized form of the verb *kuru* 'come'.
[4] The speaker will opt for the *kureru*-benefactive if he/she feels the invitation to be pleasant.

(15) a. (*kizi-o tasikame-yootosi-te*) *Yumi-ga Ai-no kooto-o/ni*<br>
fabric-ACC examine-try:to-and Yumi-NOM Ai-GEN coat-ACC/DAT<br>
*sawat-ta.*<br>
touch-PAST<br>
'Yumi touched Ai's coat (to examine its texture)'.

b. (*kizi-o tasikame-yootosi-te*) *Yumi-ga Ai-no kooto-o/ni*<br>
fabric-ACC examine-try:to-and Yumi-NOM Ai-GEN coat-ACC/DAT<br>
*sawat-te-ki-ta.*<br>
touch-and-INV-PAST<br>
'Yumi touched Ai's coat (to examine its texture)'.

(16) a. *biyoosi-wa mazu kami-o/ni sawat-ta.*<br>
beautician-TOP first hair-ACC/DAT touch-PAST<br>
'First the beauty artist touched (my) hair'.

b. *sono misiranu otoko-wa kami-o/ni sawat-te-ki-ta.*<br>
that strange man-TOP hair-ACC/DAT touch-and-INV-PAST<br>
'That strange man touched (my) hair'.

# 4 A Typology of Benefactive/Adversative Constructions

## 4.1 Person Restriction and Directionality of (Un)favorable Effect

Section 2 reviewed the bona fide benefactive and adversative constructions in Japanese, Korean, and Ainu, and Section 3 outlined three other constructions that can be regarded as comparable constructions.[5] They can be summarized as in Table 3 and (17) on the basis of the distinction between agent- and recipient-subject constructions, and between benefactive and adversative constructions.

An effective taxonomy or typology of the benefactive/adversative constructions is only possible if the directionality of the relevant action is taken into consideration. Teramura (1982) emphasizes that basic Japanese verbs of giving and receiving are subject to person restrictions on their subject entities. He ingeniously describes such restrictions as in Figure 1 by specifying the directionality of transfer (the arrow) with relation to the subject referent (the circle) in the events that *yaru* 'give', *kureru* 'give', and *morau* 'receive' denote. The broken line demarcates the spheres of speaker, addressee, and third party, and the arrowhead points to the recipient's sphere.

[5] Those sections can also be seen as showing that a number of constructions in the three languages behave more like 'underspecified affectedness' constructions (Radetzky and Smith 2010: 114) which they say are 'European' traits. We owe this point to an anonymous reviewer.

TABLE 3. Benefactive and adversative constructions in Japanese, Korean, and Ainu

| | **Japanese** | | **Korean** | | **Ainu** | |
|---|---|---|---|---|---|---|
| | BENEFACTIVE | ADVERSATIVE | BENEFACTIVE | ADVERSATIVE | BENEFACTIVE | ADVERSATIVE |
| agent-subject | V-*te-yaru* [*ageru/kureru*] | V-*te-yaru*, V-*te-kuru* | V-*a*[*(y)eo*] *juda*, ACC ACC V | ACC ACC V | V *wa kor(par)e* | – |
| recipient-subject | V-*te-morau* | V-*(r)areru* | VN *badda* | VN *danghada* [*majda*] | *enci/unci*=V | *enci/unci*=V |

(17) AGENT-SUBJECT BENEFACTIVE: (Japanese) V-*te-yaru*[*ageru/kureru*]; (Korean) V-*a*[*(y)eo*] *juda*, ACC ACC V; (Ainu) V *wa kor(par)e*

RECIPIENT-SUBJECT BENEFACTIVE: (Japanese) V-*te-morau*; (Korean) VN *badda*; (Ainu) *enci/unci*=V

AGENT-SUBJECT ADVERSATIVE: (Japanese) V-*te-yaru*, V-*te-kuru*[6]; (Korean) ACC ACC V

RECIPIENT-SUBJECT ADVERSATIVE: (Japanese) V-*(r)areru*; (Korean) VN *danghada*[*majda*]; (Ainu) *enci/unci*=V

---

[6] V-*te-kureru* in a sarcasm sense and V-*yagaru* as in (i) can also be included in this category.

(i) a. *tondemonai-koto-o* *si-te-kureta-yo*.
outrageous-thing-ACC do-and-gave-FP
'[You] have done something outrageous'.

b. *kyaku-ga* *ki-yagat-ta*.
guest-NOM come-YAGARU-PAST
'(Much to my/our indignation) some guests came'.

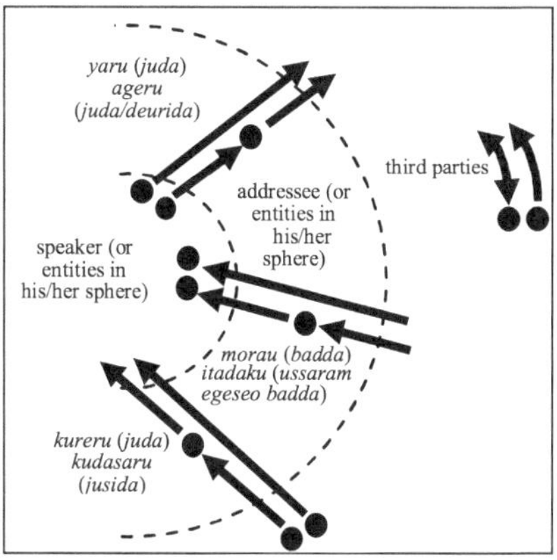


FIGURE 1. Japanese verbs of giving and receiving
(Teramura 2001[1988]: 154, our translation)

Teramura's graphic helps in gaining an overall perspective on similar person restrictions and directionalities observed in the benefactive and adversative constructions as in Figures 2 and 3, respectively. In both Japanese and Korean, the benefactives are applicable to the agent and recipient of any person. Their remarkable difference lies in the fact that Japanese makes a notable distinction between two types of verbs of giving *yaru/ageru* vs. *kureru* in accordance with the person of the subject referent. Korean employs almost exclusively one verb of giving *juda*.[7]

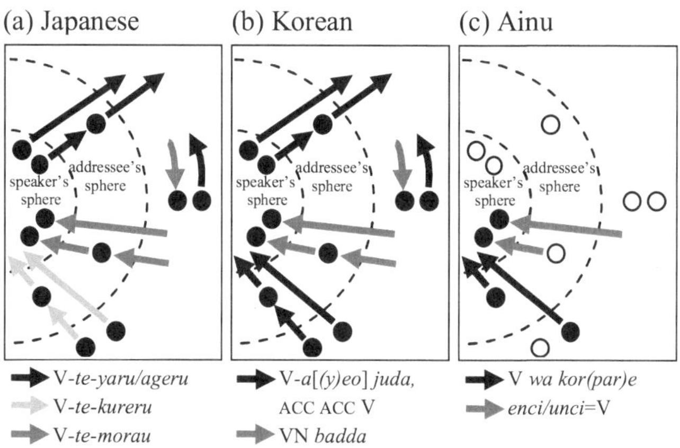


FIGURE 2. Directional distributions of Japanese, Korean,
and Ainu benefactive constructions

---

7 Although Korean has *dalda* besides *juda*, it is only used in imperative forms: *dalla* or *dao*.

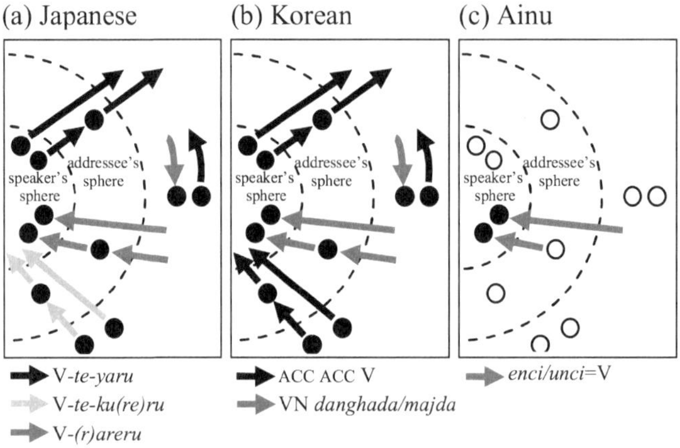


FIGURE 3. Directional distributions of Japanese, Korean, and Ainu adversative constructions

In contrast, Ainu has strong person restrictions on its benefactive constructions. The recipient is limited to the first-person entity as illustrated in (18). No examples with a second- or third-person recipient are attested in our text data. Moreover, a great majority of instances are in the imperative like (18a).

(18) a. *neno iki wa en=kore hani.* (Tamura 1996: 335)
like:that do:so and 1.SG.OBJ=give FP
'Please do it that way'.

b. *e=ek wa un=kore kusu.* (Tamura 1996: 335)
2.SG=come and 1.PL.EXCL.OBJ=give because
'Because you came for us'.

c. *ku=mipi usa totto hok wa en=kore,*
1.SG.SBJ=clothes etc. mom buy and 1.SG.OBJ=give
*ku=ekiroroan.* (Sunazawa 1983: 65)
1.SG.SBJ=be:pleased:with
'I was happy Mom bought me clothes'.
(our gloss, translation, and emphasis)

In the adversative constructions, the three languages differ much more markedly in restriction on person and directionality, as seen in Figure 3. Here again, Japanese is unique in that it distinguishes two agent-subject constructions on the basis of whether or not the recipient entity belongs to the speaker/addressee's sphere. Korean has developed both agent- and recipient-subject constructions, whereas Ainu only possesses a recipient-subject construction whose subject entity is limited to the first person.

Both Japanese and Korean have full-fledged benefactive and adversative constructions where any person (first through third) can be the agent and recipient, but they differ in that the relevant recipient is typically encoded (very frequently) by the subject in Japanese and (though less frequently) by the object as well as the subject in Korean. In contrast, the Ainu counterparts have very limited applicability in person; the recipient must be the first person. Those differences in person restriction and directionality are analyzable as reflecting the degree of 'de-subjectification' (Nakamura 2004, 2009; Machida 2011), whereby expressions originally for the speaker's experiences are extended to non-speakers' experiences.

## 4.2 Verb-colored and Satellite-colored Languages

As summarized in Table 3 above, Japanese benefactive and adversative constructions are formed with verbs of giving/receiving or the auxiliary verb *-(r)areru* and a verb that precedes them. Korean comparable constructions are comprised of a verb of giving preceded by a connective form of verb, of light verbs for 'receive/confront/encounter' with a verbal noun complement, or of a verb with two accusative-marked NPs. In Ainu, though the benefactive/adversative constructions can have a verb of giving, personal prefixes like *en/un/i=* or *enci/unci=* play a major role in instantiations of each benefactive/adversative construction.

While it might be somewhat controversial, the Korean accusative marker and Ainu personal affix can be viewed as 'satellites' rather than 'verbs' in Talmy's (1985, 1991) terms. The Japanese auxiliary verb can be equated with 'verb' in his terms. On these presumptions, the benefactive and adversative event conceptions can be described as having two possible paths to realization: verb and satellite. In a nutshell, the benefactive and adversative constructions can be either a verb-centered or satellite-centered structure. As long as the verb-satellite distinction among major elements of benefactive/adversative constructions is valid, we can come up with an interesting typology by analogy with Talmy's typology of 'verb-framed' and 'satellite-framed languages' (1991: 486). He presupposes that 'there is a fundamental and recurrent category of complex event that is prone to conceptual conflation and representation by a single clause' (482). He calls such an event complex 'macro-event', analyzing it as consisting of 'framing' and 'supporting events' related by an 'S-relation' (484). He argues that the world's languages generally divide into a two-category typology on the basis of the characteristic pattern in which the schematic core of the framing event, 'core-schema' (483), is mapped on syntactic structure. Languages that characteristically map the core schema into the verb are said to be 'verb-framed languages', while languages that characteristically map it onto the satellite are said to be 'satellite-framed languages' (486).

Benefactive/adversative event conceptions, which unfold in tandem with the framing and supporting events, can be termed 'coloring' events in that they serve to color or tinge the framing event with a happy or unhappy feeling. The core element of such event conceptions is identifiable as the transfer of a favorable or unfavorable effect. Languages that characteristically map the core element into the verb may be termed verb-colored languages. A typical example is Japanese. On the other hand, languages that characteristically map the core element of benefactive/adversative conception onto the satellite may be termed satellite-colored languages; Ainu can be classed as such a language. Korean seems to be located somewhere between the two language types, probably closer to Japanese, because the double-accusative construction alone has a satellite-centered structure.

It is an intriguing question whether the difference between the verb- and satellite-colored languages correlates with Talmy's (1991) typological distinction between verb-framed and satellite-framed languages. As shown in the middle column of Table 4, Talmy classifies Romances, Semitics, Japanese, Tamil, Polynesians, most Bantus, Most Mayans, Nez Perce, and Caddo as verb-framed languages, and most Indo-Europeans minus Romances, Finno-Ugrics, Chinese, Ojibwa, and Warlpiri as satellite-framed languages. He does not mention either Korean or Ainu, and our analysis of benefactive and adversative constructions has not yet been applied to most of the languages that he refers to. The possibility of such a typological correlation will be a subject sufficiently worthy of further investigation.

TABLE 4. Verb/Satellite-framed and -colored languages

| | **V/S-framed** | **V/S-colored** |
|---|---|---|
| Japanese | V-framed | V-colored |
| Korean | ? | less V-colored |
| Ainu | ? | S-colored |
| Romances | V-framed | ? |
| Semitics | V-framed | ? |
| Tamil | V-framed | ? |
| Polynesians | V-framed | ? |
| most Bantus | V-framed | ? |
| most Mayans | V-framed | ? |
| Nez Perce | V-framed | ? |
| Caddo | V-framed | ? |
| most Indo-Europeans | S-framed | ? |
| Finno-Ugrics | S-framed | ? |
| Chinese | S-framed | ? |
| Ojibwa | S-framed | ? |
| Warlpiri | S-framed | ? |

## 5 Conclusion

The present article demonstrated that Japanese, Korean, and Ainu have two types of benefactive and adversative constructions: agent-subject and recipient-subject constructions. Korean is more likely to encode the recipient in the object as in the double-accusative and V-*a*[(*y*)*eo*] *juda* constructions. In contrast, Japanese is likely to express the recipient in the subject or to leave it unexpressed when it is the speaker.

We further demonstrated that each construction differs from one another in the degree of (de)subjectification and person restrictions. Japanese and Korean benefactive and adversative constructions allow any person to be the agent and recipient, whereas Ainu counterparts require the recipient to be the first person. Moreover, Japanese tends to distinguish between the constructions in which the recipient is an entity in the speaker's or addressee's sphere and those in which the agent is such an entity.

We proposed a possible typological distinction between verb-colored and satellite-colored languages by analogy with Talmy's distinction between verb-framed and satellite-framed languages. Although it is premature to discuss the possibility of a correlation between the two typological distinctions, we believe that such a line of research will help to shed new light on the cognitive bases of benefactive and adversative event conceptions and their linguistic organizations.

## References

Asai, T. 1969. Ainugo no Bunpo: Ainugo Ishikari Hogen Bunpo no Gairyaku. *Ainu Minzokushi*, 771–800. Tokyo: Daiichi Hoki.

Bak, J. 2004. *Optional Case Marking of the Possessor in Korean: a Study of Double Accusative Marking of Possessor/Possessee in Korean Based on Corpus Study and Optimality Computation*. MA thesis. University of Manitoba.

Cho, S. 2003. A Conditioning Factor in Possessor Agreement Constructions. *Japanese/Korean Linguistics* 11: 343351.

Givón, T. 1994. The Pragmatics of De-transitive Voice: Functional and Typological Aspects of Inversion. *Voice and Inversion*, ed. T. Givón, 3–44. Amsterdam: John Benjamins.

Hwang, C, G. Lee, S. Chang, and G. Lee. 1988. *Hanlreo Daejo Bunseog*. Seoul: Myeongji Chulpansa.

Izutsu, K. 2004. A Cognitive Grammar Approach to Ainu. *The Ainu Language: A Linguistic Introduction*, ed. K. Izutsu, 1-44. Hokkaido University of Education.

Kim, Y. 1989. Inalienable Possession as a Semantic Relationship Underlying Predication: the Case of Multiple-Accusative Constructions. *Harvard Studies in Korean Linguistics III*: 445–467. Cambridge, MA: Harvard University.

Lee, C. 1974. *Abstract Syntax and Korean with Reference to English*. Seoul: Pan Korean Book Corp.

Machida, A. 2011. Nihongo Rareru Kobun no Keishiki to Imi. *Imi to Keishiki no Hazama*, ed. Y. Oba and S. Okada, 163–177. Tokyo: Eihosha.

Nakagawa, H. 1995. *Ainugo Chitose Hougen Jiten*. Tokyo: Sofukan.

Nakamura, Y. 2004. Shukansei no Gengogaku: Shukansei to Bunpo Kouzou-Koubun. *Ninchi Bunpouron II*, ed. Y. Nakamura, 3–51. Tokyo: Taishukan.

Nakamura, Y. 2009. Ninchi Moodo no Shatei. *Uchi to Soto no Gengogaku*, ed. A. Tsubomoto, N. Hayase, and N. Wada, 353–393. Tokyo: Kaitakusha.

Radetzky, P. and T. Smith. 2010. An Areal and Cross-linguistic Study of Benefactive and Malefactive Constructions. Zúñiga and Kittilä (eds.), 97–120.

Shibatani, M. 1990. *The Languages of Japan*. Cambridge: Cambridge UP.

Shibatani, M. 1994a. Benefactive Constructions: A Japanese-Korean Comparative Perspective. *Japanese/Korean Linguistics* 4: 39–74. Stanford: CSLI.

Shibatani, M. 1994b. An Integrational Approach to Possessor Raising, Ethical Datives, and Adversative Passives. *Proceedings of the Twentieth Annual Meeting of the Berkeley Linguistics Society: General Session Dedicated to the Contributions of Charles J. Fillmore*: 461–486.

Shibatani, M. 1996. Applicatives and Benefactives: A Cognitive Account. *Grammatical Constructions: Their Form and Meaning*, ed. M. Shbatani and S. A. Thompson, 157–194. Oxford: Clarendon Press.

Shibatani, M. 2003. Directional Verbs in Japanese. *Motion, Direction, and Location in Languages: In Honor of Zygmunt Frajzyngier*, ed. E. Shay and U. Seibert, 259–286. Amsterdam: John Benjamins.

Shibatani, M. 2006. On the Conceptual Framework for Voice Phenomena. *Linguistics* 44: 217–269.

Smith, T. Y. 2010. Cross-linguistic Categorization of Benefactives by Event Structure. Zúñiga and Kittilä (eds.), 71–95.

Sunazawa, K. 1983. *Watashi no Ichidai no Omoide: Kusukup Oruspe*. Sapporo: Miyama Shobo.

Talmy, L. 1985. Lexicalization Patterns: Semantic Structure in Lexical Forms. *Language Typology and Syntactic Description, vol. 3: Grammatical Categories and the Lexicon*, ed. T. Shopen, 57–149. Cambridge University Press.

Talmy, L. 1991. Path to Realization: a Typology of Event Conflation. *Proceedings of the Annual Meeting of the Berkeley Linguistics Society* 17: 480–519.

Tamura, S. 1996. *Ainugo Saru Hougen Jiten*. Tokyo: Sofukan.

Teramura, H. 1982. *Nihongo no Shintakusu to Imi I*. Tokyo: Kuroshio.

Teramura, H. 2001 [1988]. *Ilboneo eui Gumun gwa Euimi I*. Seoul: Hankuk University of Foreign Studies. (Korean translation of Teramura 1982)

Tsuboi, E. 2010. Malefactivity in Japanese. Zúñiga and Kittilä (eds.), 419–435.

Vermeulen, R. 2005. *The Syntax of External Possession: Its Basis in Theta-theory*. PhD dissertation. University College London.

Yeon, J. 2010. Constraints on Double-Accusative External Possession Constructions in Korean: A Cognitive Approach. *Selected Papers from the 2nd European Conference on Korean Linguistics*. ed. J. Yeon and J. Kiaer, 188–201. München: Lincom.

Zúñiga, F. and S. Kittilä (eds.). 2010. *Benefactives and Malefactives: Typological Perspectives and Case Studies*. Amsterdam: John Benjamins.

9

# A Multi-Frame Analysis of Separation Verbs

SEIKO FUJII, PAULA RADETZKY, AND EVE SWEETSER

## 1 Introduction

Verbs referring to cutting and breaking, often generally labeled verbs of SEPARATION, have been of interest to linguists as a laboratory for the study of crosslinguistic semantic universals and differences. Like spatial terms, separation verbs label perceptible physical situations, which could suggest possibilities for shared construal crosslinguistically by speakers with the same perceptual abilities—and also like spatial terms, separation verb systems manifest major differences across languages. In this paper, we examine Japanese cutting and breaking verbs in contrast with those of English and French, and argue that the ranges of meanings suggest the need for a frame-semantic approach—and, in particular, a frame-clustering or multi-frame analysis. We also propose the addition of some semantic parameters to those already noted by linguists as relevant to crosslinguistic comparison in this semantic domain.

In a ground-breaking study at the Max Planck Institute at Nijmegen, researchers showed sixty video clips to speakers of twenty-eight languages from a wide range of linguistic families, geographical areas, and lexical typologies (Majid et al. 2007; Majid, Boster, and Bowerman 2008). The clips show scenes of both more and less canonical events of separation, such as cutting a cloth with scissors or tearing it with a stick; or chopping a carrot into chunks with a cleaver, cutting it along its length, or using one's hand to karate-chop it apart. A number of parameters emerged as most fre-

*Language and the Creative Mind.*
Mike Borkent, Barbara Dancygier, and Jennifer Hinnell (eds).

quently relevant to linguistic distinctions. The first is the contrast between OPEN and CUT / BREAK / TEAR. It seems that there is a very general salience to the distinction between separating parts of a complex object built to be separated (taking the lid off a jar or the cap from a pen, opening a book) and disrupting the integrity of an object which is not structured for such functionally-intended separation. Secondly, the contrast between CLEAN and MESSY SEPARATION emerged as important. This correlates fairly well in English with the CUT vs. BREAK / TEAR division. A third parameter was TEAR vs. BREAK—that is, many languages distinguish separation or loss of integrity of flexible objects, such as fabric, from the loss of integrity of rigid objects, such as wood or carrots. And a fourth important parameter was the distinction between IMPACT and BENDING as a cause of the loss of integrity: Speakers might differently label a video clip of someone karate-chopping a carrot in two, as opposed to a video of a person bending a stick or carrot with two hands until it broke.

We would analyze these four parameters of separation verbs as aspects of varying *frames* of separation. Frame-semantic models were developed by Fillmore to treat lexical semantics in terms of structured Gestalt 'chunks' of human knowledge which categorize experience (Fillmore 1982; Fillmore 1985; Fillmore and Atkins 1992; Fillmore and Atkins 1994; Fillmore, Johnson, and Petruck 2003; Fillmore and Baker 2010; see also the FrameNet Project at framenet.icsi.berkeley.edu). There are multiple aspects to each of these separation frames—different force-dynamic routines involved in impact, forceful bending, pulling to rip, smashing with a hammer, or cutting with a knife; different sounds emanating from ripping fabric or paper as opposed to a breaking carrot or stick; different resulting visual patterns of separation; and so on. When these parameters correlate, a category emerges—for example, with a flexible 2-D object such as paper or fabric, use of a blade for separation (CUTTING) tends to result in a CLEAN SEPARATION, and it has its own muscular routine and sound effects; all of these contrast with the muscular routines, sounds, and MESSY SEPARATION that are likely to result from the forcible pulling of a flexible 2-D object with two hands (TEARING). This frame-semantic analysis is what we will be developing in the rest of this paper, as we show that languages differ in what frames they cluster into a single verb.

Our goal here is to complement the MPI study's results with a more detailed examination of a few languages. A crosslinguistic experimental approach has all the major advantages of its broad database; language-specific studies, on the other hand, have the advantage of depth, since they can examine distribution within corpora and tease out differences in meaning and grammatical use between semantically similar forms. English and Japanese will be the primary focus of this paper, although Bouveret and Sweetser's work on French and English will also be incorporated as background (Bouveret and Sweetser 2009a,b). English, French, and Japanese are quite distinct in their semantic typologies. English, for example, incorporates manner readily into lexical verb meanings such as *run, walk, skip,* and *jump,* but expresses path as a satellite, such as *into the room* (and is thus a 'satellite-framed' language in the sense of Talmy 1985; Slobin 1996; Talmy 2000: 213-288; and Slobin 2006, among others). French, on the other hand, normally expresses path in the verbal stem (*entrer* 'enter', *sortir* 'go out') and manner in an added modifier phrase (and is thus a 'verb-framed' language). Japanese uses manner adverbs, as well as other strategies such as serial and compound verbs and ideophones, which will not be discussed here. Since Japanese verb semantics is typologically so different from English, the comparison of the two systems is both of interest in and of itself, and also because it fills in the details of the broader typological picture.

In this paper, we focus on the concrete uses of separation verbs, although their metaphoric extensions also exhibit intriguing crosslinguistic differences, which we are investigating in ongoing research (e.g. Fujii, radetzky, and Sweetser 2013). Our analyses are based on data drawn from internet searches and corpora: the British National Corpus and the Japanese Web as Corpus (JpWaC), both accessed via WordSketch, and the Balanced Corpus of Contemporary Written Japanese (National Institute for Japanese Language and Linguistics 2008/2010). The authors' native-speaker intuitions about English and Japanese are of course used in evaluating this data.

## 2 New Parameters and the Internal Structure of Lexical Meaning

### 2.1 LOSS OF FUNCTIONALITY

Our first observation is that LOSS OF FUNCTIONALITY is a very important parameter in Japanese, English, and French, and this parameter needs to be added to the MPI list. The MPI video clips, for the most part, do not involve functional objects; only one plate and one teapot figure among the BREAK scenarios, and there are no actual garments among the TEAR and CUT scenarios, only pieces of cloth and string. (There are, however, various undamaged functional objects in their OPEN scenarios.) Yet, for a functional object, LOSS OF INTEGRITY very frequently causes LOSS OF FUNCTIONALITY. The Japanese transitive-intransitive pair *kowasu* / *kowareru,* often translated as 'break', is basically about functional destruction (which often involves damage to physical integrity). The primacy of functional destruction was evidenced in a pilot experiment, where we elicited responses from six native speakers of Japanese using the MPI video clips: *Kowasu* / *kowareru* were not produced for even a single one of the scenarios. By contrast, English *break* is primarily about loss of physical integrity, but frequently includes loss of functionality, and can in some cases (unlike, say, *cut* or *split* or *smash*) be extended to refer to just loss of functionality, such as a *broken* computer or cell phone—which need not be physically damaged to become nonfunctional. French *casser* (unlike other breaking verbs such as *briser* and *rompre*) is similar to English *break* in this usage (Bouveret and Sweetser 2009). In Japanese, as we see in (1), physical breaking of cookies can be described with *kowasu* if the cookies are understood to have lost functional value (e.g., are no longer a nice gift); (2) shows that a flood destroying (but not "breaking") rice paddies can also be described with *kowasu*.

(1) *watasi wa ... kukkii o* ***kowasite*** *simai masita*
I TOP ... cookie OBJ KOWASU.and REGRET POLITE.PST
'I ... unfortunately **broke** the cookies [on the way home].'
http://ameblo.jp/panda-sablee/entry-10899270028.html

(2) ... *ie ya hatake, tanbo o* ***kowasita*** *yoo desu*
... house and field paddy OBJ KOWASU.PST seem POLITE
'... it seems [the river] **destroyed** houses, fields, rice paddies.'
http://blog.ap.teacup.com/hinobudo/118.html

This comparison of *break* and *kowasu* shows us that similar frames may be involved in the meaning of two verbs, but that the distribution of the verbs may differ importantly, depending on which frame is more central to the verb's meaning. In English, *break* is most centrally about physical loss of integrity of a rigid object, and only by extension refers to functional loss without physical damage. One can *break* a cookie in half to share it; the cookie does not thereby lose functionality—indeed, it is not only just as edible as it was, but (within the food-sharing context) more useful than before. *Kowasu* cannot refer to such an action, since the cookie gains rather than loses functionality (see (11) in section 3.1), and the most central frame for *kowasu* is that of functional destruction (although, as mentioned above, functional destruction often involves physical damage as its cause).

## 2.2 FORCEFUL BENDING and BREAKAGE

The issue of centrality of frames to lexical meaning arises again with the Japanese verb *oru*. Although it is frequently translatable into English as 'break', this verb crucially involves FORCEFUL BENDING. (We use FORCEFUL BENDING to refer to a specific image-schema in which exerting pressure on both ends of an entity makes its ends approach each other, leading to bending.) BENDING is recognized by the MPI researchers as being salient, since it competes with IMPACT as a likely cause of breakage of a rigid object. However, unlike in Japanese, there is no verb in English or French where the most central frame refers to FORCEFUL BENDING, and where frames of SEPARATION or BREAKAGE are involved only secondarily. *Break* and *snap* are both potentially usable for forcefully bending a stick and breaking it, but they are centrally about breakage and need not involve bending, while *twist, bend*, and *fold* do not lexically indicate breakage. *Oru* most centrally refers to bending something over on itself, whether a 1-D or a 2-D entity—so it can translate into English as 'fold' or 'bend', as well as 'break' (see *origami*, referring to the practice of folding paper). In the case of a rigid and brittle entity, such as a stick, carrot, or long bone, the frame of FORCEFUL BENDING of an object over on itself naturally correlates with a particular result, namely breakage of the object in two; on the other hand, with a flexible entity, such as paper or cloth, bending will not result in breakage. The examples below are instances of *oru,* all of which involve forceful bending; of these, (3)–(4) do not involve breakage and (5)–(6) do. Note, especially for (4), that minimal force is involved in causing the bending. Our image schema of FORCEFUL BENDING does not specify the degree of force.

| (3) | *purasutikku-ban* | *o* | *(kanetu site)* | ***otta*** |
|---|---|---|---|---|
| | plastic-board | OBJ | heat.and | ORU.PST |

'[I] **folded** the plastic board (by heating it).'

| (4) | *napukin* | *o* | | ***otta*** |
|---|---|---|---|---|
| | napkin | OBJ | | ORU.PST |

'[I] **folded** the napkin.'

| (5) | *purasutikku-ban* | *o* | *(pakin-to)* | ***otta*** |
|---|---|---|---|---|
| | plastic-board | OBJ | with.a.snap | ORU.PST |

'[I] **broke** the plastic board (with a snap).'

| (6) | *koeda* | *o* | | ***otta*** |
|---|---|---|---|---|
| | twig | OBJ | | ORU.PST |

'[I] **broke** the twig.'

Attested example (7) shows the 'fold' sense exemplified in (4), while (8) shows the ambiguity of *oru*—the person is instructed first to score the plastic sheet, then *fold* it and *break* it so that it is removed from the whole.

| (7) | *kooto* | *no* | *poketto* | *ni* | *kositu* | *suru* | *hankati* | *o* | ***oru*** | … |
|---|---|---|---|---|---|---|---|---|---|---|
| | coat | GEN | pocket | DAT | stick | DO | handkerchief | OBJ | ORU | … |

'… **fold** a handkerchief that will stay securely in your suit pocket'

http://otakanp3.doorblog.jp/archives/20383444.html

(8)

| *sukoya* | *o* | *tukatte* | *puraban* | *o* |
|---|---|---|---|---|
| machinist's.square | OBJ | use.and | plastic.board | OBJ |

| *kegaite,* | ***ori**-tori* | *masu* |
|---|---|---|
| score.and | ORU-remove | POLITE |

'Use a machinist's square to score the plastic sheet, and **fold / break**-remove [it].'

http://blogs.dion.ne.jp/kaine/archives/cat_235821-1.html

We predictably find that English *break* is used for bones *(broken femur)* and, by metonymy, for associated body parts *(broken leg),* since separation caused either by impact or forceful bending may result in breakage, and English *break* is neutral with regard to the parameter of IMPACT VS. FORCEFUL BENDING. Both the unfortunate separation and the attendant loss of functionality are perfectly appropriate for the use of *break,* while alternative verbs, such as *bend* or *fold,* simply do not have the requisite meaning of separation. In Japanese, *oru* is the primary verb used for the breakage of long bones, even though it is ambiguous in the case of a bendable limb, so that *yubi o oru* can mean either 'bend [one's] finger' or 'break (a bone in) [one's] finger', as in (9) and (10); the ambiguity exists for *asi* 'leg', as well.

(9)

| *yubi* | *o* | ***otte*** | *kazoeru* |
|---|---|---|---|
| finger | OBJ | ORU.and | count |

'count by **folding** [one's] fingers **over**'

(10)

| *koronde* | *yubi* | *o* | ***otta*** |
|---|---|---|---|
| fall.and | finger | OBJ | ORU.PST |

'[He] fell and **broke** [his] finger.'

### 2.3 Two Additional Parameters

In breaking down the different classes of separation, as well as dividing CLEAN VS. MESSY SEPARATION, we also see it as necessary to posit two more parameters: (a) OVERALL VS. PARTIAL LOSS OF INTEGRITY, and within PARTIAL LOSS OF INTEGRITY, the parameter of (b) FOCUS ON DETACHMENT OF PIECES VS. FOCUS ON DEGREE OF AFFECTEDNESS OF THE WHOLE.

English *shred* and *smash* necessarily involve OVERALL LOSS OF INTEGRITY of the object (unlike *break* and *tear*). *Chip* refers to the detachment of a small piece which is not a part. In other words, it involves PARTIAL LOSS OF INTEGRITY and, within that, a FOCUS ON DETACHMENT OF PIECES. It does not specify the extent to which it is seen as damaging or affecting the whole. *Tear* and *rip* are neutral about OVERALL VS. PARTIAL LOSS OF INTEGRITY: You can tear an entire sheet of paper to bits (OVERALL LOSS OF INTEGRITY), tear off (detach) a piece of paper from the corner of a sheet (PARTIAL LOSS OF INTEGRITY), or tear the paper slightly at one edge (without detaching anything; PARTIAL LOSS OF INTEGRITY). Within PARTIAL LOSS OF INTEGRITY, *tear* and *rip* are also neutral about FOCUS ON DETACHMENT VS. FOCUS ON DEGREE OF AFFECTEDNESS OF THE WHOLE; even a small tear or rip in a shirt *may* (though need not) be seen as affecting its overall functionality—the tear might downgrade the shirt from professional wear to house-cleaning garb.

In contrast, Japanese *tigiru* 'tear' demands full DETACHMENT (at least prototypically into small piece(s)), without a FOCUS ON THE DEGREE OF AFFECTEDNESS OF THE WHOLE. In addition, there is a resulting INCREASE IN FUNCTIONALITY of those pieces (see next section). *Yaburu* 'tear, rip' is like *tear* and *rip* in that it is neutral regarding OVERALL VS. PARTIAL LOSS OF INTEGRITY and FOCUS ON DETACHMENT VS. FOCUS ON DEGREE OF AFFECTEDNESS OF THE WHOLE. It also does not specify the increase or decrease in FUNCTIONALITY of the resultant pieces. Although *yaburu* can be used in neutral scenarios as well, *tigiru* and *yaburu* may also involve the kind of manner distinction shown in English *tear* vs. *rip,* where the former can easily refer to separation done carefully and creating intended results (e.g., tearing along fold-lines to create smaller slips of paper), while the latter is more typically used if the action is careless or damaging to the entire object. These examples show how the new parameters interact with others, including, in particular, parameters such as INTENTIONALITY and FUNCTIONALITY, which will be discussed further in the next section.

## 3 Human Purposes and Intentions: FUNCTIONALLY USEFUL DIVISION versus ACCIDENTAL SEPARATION

### 3.1 FUNCTIONAL DIVISION

Since the MPI clips do not focus on the functionality of the objects undergoing separation, frames such as DIVISION—purposeful separation in order to make separate use of pieces (perhaps for DISTRIBUTION)—were not evoked. The DIVISION frame often involves a result that is *more functional* than the original whole, in the local context. Many English separation verbs seem neutral with respect to the parameter of FUNCTIONALLY USEFUL DIVISION, although verbs such as *shatter* (which focuses on division into small, indistinguishable fragments) would require quite a bit of contextualization to imagine as relevant to subsequent division, while *slice* often denotes not just cutting, but division of larger food items for distribution to consumers. We noted earlier that in English you can *break a cookie in two* to share it; you can also *cut a cake into pieces*, or *cut paper into small slips* (all examples of DIVISION FOR DISTRIBUTION)—or *cut / split firewood* into useful pieces for the fireplace, or *tear off a piece of bread* which is now the right size for eating.

As in English, some common Japanese separation verbs seem neutral with respect to the parameter of FUNCTIONALLY USEFUL DIVISION vs. ACCIDENTAL SEPARATION; but, of course, verbs that specify functional destruction (like *kowasu*) cannot be used in the DIVISION frame, as seen in (11). Examples (12)–(16) show the use of *waru* 'break a rigid object into pieces', *kiru* 'cut', and *tigiru* 'tear', all in contexts where the separation is functionally useful division.

(11) # *kukkii* *o* *hutatu* *ni* ***kowasita***
cookie OBJ two DAT KOWASU.PST
'[She] **broke** the cookie in two.'

(12) *kukkii* *o* *hutatu* *ni* ***watta***
cookie OBJ two DAT WARU.PST
'[She] **broke** the cookie in two.'

(13) *maki* *o* ***watta***
firewood OBJ WARU.PST
'[She] **split** the firewood.'

(14) *keeki* *o* ***kitta***
cake OBJ KIRU.PST
'[She] **cut** the cake.'

(15) *pan* *o* *(hito-kuti)* ***tigitta***
bread OBJ one-mouth TIGIRU.PST
'[She] **tore off** (a morsel of) bread.'

(16) … *aratte* ***tigitte*** *zaru* *de* *arai* … *masita*
… wash.and TIGIRU.and sieve INST wash … POLITE.PST
'… [I] washed [the lettuce leaves], **tore** [them], and washed [the pieces] in a sieve….'
http://www.ozmall.co.jp/bbs/3-124795-snew.aspx

Further evidence of this kind of FUNCTIONALLY USEFUL DIVISION usage is found in the fact that, in a more metaphoric domain, *waru* conventionally refers to mathematical division.

### 3.2 Human Intentionality and Agentivity

In addition to not focusing on the usefulness of the objects or the resulting pieces, the MPI scenarios illustrate only INTENTIONAL and AGENTIVE events of caused separation, without including UNINTENTIONAL or ACCIDENTAL ones. For example, the video clips include a person smashing a plate with a hammer, but not a dish being accidentally knocked off the table and breaking; and there are some deliberate cloth-ripping scenarios but none of a person catching her shirt on a nail and ripping it. There is a clip where the tearing agent is not observable—it looks as if the cloth is spontaneously ripping without any cause. But, in fact, intransitive separation verbs cross-linguistically do not ordinarily refer specifically to this odd kind of event. Instead, attested intransitive forms refer to actually-experienced scenarios of agent-deprofiled causal events, such as an accidental action by a volitional agent who does not intend the breakage *(The cup broke when Sue accidentally knocked it off the table)*, or a causal event not necessarily involving a volitional agent *(The electric wire broke during the storm)*. This is a pervasively relevant factor—most crucially for BREAK and TEAR verbs, less so for CUT verbs, whose meaning includes an instrument and thus an inferable agent. In English, *The cup broke* does not typically mean it spontaneously came apart, but it does indicate that we are not focusing on causation by an agent.

In Japanese, the parameter of AGENTIVE INTENTIONALITY VS. UNINTENTIONALITY (ACCIDENTAL) largely correlates with whether a transitive or intransitive verb form is used to describe a separation event. Take, for example, the transitive-intransitive verb pair *tigiru* 'tear' / *tigireru*. The transitives in (15)–(16) above are used to express a volitional and purposive action; the agent is intentionally tearing off a morsel of bread, or ripping lettuce into pieces, to make it more functional for eating. This, however, is not true of its intransitive counterpart, *tigireru,* in (17) below, where the result (an avulsion) was certainly not desired, nor was there a volitional causer.

| (17) | *ziko* | *de* | *yubi* | *ga* | ***tigireta*** |
|---|---|---|---|---|---|
| | accident | CAUSE | finger | SUBJ | TIGIRERU.PST |

'[Her] finger **tore off** in an accident.'

| (18) # | *ziko* | *de* | *yubi* | *o* | ***tigitta*** |
|---|---|---|---|---|---|
| | accident | CAUSE | finger | OBJ | TIGIRU.PST |

'[She] **tore** [her] finger **off** in an accident.'

(19) She **tore** her finger **off** in a construction accident.

English, as seen in (19), allows accidental events to be encoded in the same way as agentive, intentional events (i.e. with transitive verbs), with concomitant instantiation of experiencers as subjects—the same way that volitional agents are encoded in English. Japanese, by contrast, cannot express the same accidental event with the transitive construction (see (18)), but must use the intransitive, as in (17).

The same pattern can be seen in the Japanese transitive-intransitive pair *mogu* / *mogeru*. *Mogu* 'pull off, pick' involves an intentional pulling or turning motion which detaches a protruding object from an attachment-point—such as the fruit on a branch in (20). (This is similar to English *pick*, which is intentional and even purposive, in the case of harvesting.)

| (20) | *kaki* | *no* | *mi* | *o* | ***moida*** |
|---|---|---|---|---|---|
| | persimmon | GEN | fruit | OBJ | MOGU.PST |

'[I] **picked** the persimmon.'

The frame for *mogu*'s intransitive counterpart, however, contains no agent, and thus *mogeru* means 'fall off, come off'.

| (21) | *Pinokio* | *no* | *hana* | *ga* | ***mogeta*** |
|---|---|---|---|---|---|
| | Pinocchio | GEN | nose | SUBJ | MOGERU.PST |

'Pinocchio's nose **came off**.'

| (22) | *sutikku-gata* | *kuriinaa* | *no* | *kubi* | *ga,* | *kazin* | *no* |
|---|---|---|---|---|---|---|---|
| | stick-shape | cleaner | GEN | neck | SUBJ | family.member | GEN |

| *siyoo* | *tyuu* | *ni* | ***mogeta.*** | *marude* | *kamakiri* |
|---|---|---|---|---|---|
| use | while | DAT | MOGERU.PST | just.like | mantis |

| *no* | *kubi* | *to* | *dootai* | *ga* | ***tigireta*** | *yoo* | ... |
|---|---|---|---|---|---|---|---|
| GEN | neck | and | body | SUBJ | TIGIRERU.PST | seem | ... |

'The head [lit., 'neck'] of the ... stick vacuum cleaner **came off** when a family member was using it. As if a praying mantis's head had **come apart from** its body....'

http://durianjp.com/2006/11/post-564.html

*Mogeru* is nonagentive (i.e., there is no volitional causer), but it cannot be a spontaneous occurrence, either—which supports our observation above that intransitive verbs do not encode spontaneous separation. Rather, with *mogeru,* there must be an external and/or abnormal force that is causing the separation. For example, in the natural course of events, a piece of fruit ripens on a branch and then falls off spontaneously when it becomes overripe. This is not *mogeru*. However, if a bird flies into the fruit and the impact causes it to come off, *mogeru* can be used. Or, in the unnatural event of Pinocchio's nose growing so much that it falls off, *mogeru* can be used. Because this type of separation is 'unnatural' (or forcible), the event is usually viewed as negative or unfortunate. Compositional semantics would not predict this difference between intransitive *mogeru* and transitive *mogu,* which is purposive and usually viewed as fortunate. Also, *mogeru*'s bias towards an external or unnatural causal force is not present in all Japanese intransitives; for example, intransitive *kireru* 'cut' may refer to separation due to an internal weakness in the object—as we shall see below.

A notable point here is that we cannot fully predict the semantics of a Japanese intransitive verb from the semantics of the corresponding transitive plus the change in agent profiling or deprofiling. This is not only true of *tigiru* / *tigireru* and *mogu* / *mogeru,* but also of *kiru* 'cut' / *kireru*. We shall see this in section 5, where we touch on the issue of the ways in which specific semantics attaches to sublexical constructions.

## 4 Why Multi-Frame?

As a summary, we list here the major frames involved in the verbs we have been analyzing in this paper. Each verb is seen as a combination of frames, some of which are shared with other verbs. (Since we are looking specifically at separation verbs, of course SEPARATION is relevant to all of them.) Note that many of these verbs are neutral with respect to parameters such as LOSS OF FUNCTIONALITY or FUNCTIONAL DIVISION; also, for Japanese verbs, intransitive *-eru* verbs do not involve AGENTIVE INTENTIONALITY, although their transitive counterparts do.

Synopsis of Verbs and Frame Parameters

| | |
|---|---|
| KOWASU | LOSS OF FUNCTIONALITY<br>secondarily, potential PHYSICAL SEPARATION |
| ORU | FORCEFUL BENDING double of 1-D or 2-D object<br>may result in PHYSICAL SEPARATION |
| WARU | PHYSICAL SEPARATION by IMPACT of 2-D or 3-D rigid object |
| KIRU | CLEAN PHYSICAL SEPARATION<br>normally by BLADE INSTRUMENT used by agent |
| KIRERU | CLEAN PHYSICAL SEPARATION |
| TIGIRU | (usually MESSY) PHYSICAL SEPARATION of flexible object by PULLING<br>FOCUS ON DETACHMENT OF PIECES<br>INCREASE IN FUNCTIONALITY |
| TIGIRERU | like TIGIRU, but ACCIDENTAL or UNINTENTIONAL |

| | |
|---|---|
| MOGU | PHYSICAL SEPARATION of a protrusion by PULLING |
| MOGERU | ACCIDENTAL PHYSICAL SEPARATION of a protrusion |

| | |
|---|---|
| BREAK | PHYSICAL SEPARATION of a rigid object, by IMPACT, secondarily, potential LOSS OF FUNCTIONALITY |
| CUT | CLEAN PHYSICAL SEPARATION by BLADE INSTRUMENT (normally by agent) |
| TEAR | (usually MESSY) PHYSICAL SEPARATION of flexible 2-D or 3-D object by PULLING |
| SLICE | CLEAN PHYSICAL SEPARATION by BLADE INSTRUMENT also often involves FUNCTIONAL DIVISION |

As we suggested above, the frames involved in separation events are not randomly distributed; rather, they cluster together in ways that affect likely lexical meanings. For example, INTENTIONALITY clusters with DIVISION and INCREASE IN FUNCTIONALITY, since it is not typically the case that accidental separation creates new functional objects, or divides an object into pieces suitable for distribution among users. Similarly, IMPACT and PULLING and FORCEFUL BENDING correlate with MESSY SEPARATION and LOSS OF FUNCTIONALITY, while instrumental BLADE USE by an agent correlates with CLEAN SEPARATION. This is not to say that these correlations are inevitable; making flint arrowheads, when done by an expert, might be an example of impact that results in clean separation and a new functional object.

One reason why this clustering is important is that it affects data analysis. If one's data involves only (or almost only) examples where clean separation correlates with blade use, then these two frames will emerge from the data as a single parameter. As a result, one will not see the differences between English *cut*, which obligatorily involves a sharp blade-like instrument and therefore generally involves clean separation, and Japanese *kiru*, which only *canonically* involves a blade-like instrument but still must involve precise separation:

| | | | | | | |
|---|---|---|---|---|---|---|
| (23) | *kono* | *sinbun kizi* | *dare* | *ga* | ***kitta*** | *no?* |
| | this | news article | who | SUB | KIRU.PST | PART |

'Who **cut out / precisely tore out** this newspaper article?'

*Kiru* has a readily-accessible and frequently-used intransitive counterpart, while *cut* is almost exclusively a transitive verb in English (either the instrument or the agent *cuts* the theme). This is precisely because *kiru* does not have the same central focus on the blade (and therefore not the same focus on the agent) as *cut*.

Looking at any given verb as representing a multi-frame cluster allows us not only to notice correlations in parameters, but also to notice and study the internal structure of the cluster: for example, the centrality of one frame as opposed to another.

## 5 Constructions

Construction Grammar models hold that form-meaning pairings are present at every level of the grammar (Fillmore, Kay, and O'Connor 1988; Goldberg 1995; Michaelis and Lambrecht 1996; Kay and Fillmore 1999; Fried and Östman 2004; Goldberg 2006). Not only words and grammatical morphemes, but also larger constructions, need to be understood as carrying meaning: Fillmore, Kay, and O'Connor demonstrate this for the English *The Xer the Yer* construction, and Goldberg shows this for the English ditransitive. We argue that constructions, as well as lexical meanings, are important to the semantic expression of separation events.

The MPI study chose to focus attention on (1) specifically the lexical verbs (rather than longer phrases) chosen by speakers to label clips, and (2) the first choices that speakers made to label a given clip. This was likely a wise choice, given the amount of data being analyzed. However, in building a finer-grained semantic analysis, it is important to know what range of verbs are plausible labels for an event, not only which the first choice was in an experimental context. The same event can be labeled by more and less general verbs *(break* vs. *smash*, *shatter, crack);* the semantic relations between these verbs are part of a grammarian's data. Also, focusing solely on lexical verbs can be misleading, since sometimes the larger phrase is the only thing that determines a separation reading. For example, *He pulled the branch off the tree* (a possible label for one of the MPI clips in English) only marks separation in the particle *off; pull* is not a verb of separation. Since separation is about path (that is, moving the pieces apart, and the change from integrity and adjacency to nonintegrity and potential nonadjacency), it makes sense to include the full phrasal verb—particularly for manner-type languages, where path is often indicated outside the verb.

At the sub-lexical constructional level, different grammatical forms from the same verbal paradigm may have quite distinct semantic distributions, involving different (although related) frame clusters or 'frame landscapes.' We mentioned in section 2.1 that there are examples of English *break* which do not involve SEPARATION but only LOSS OF FUNCTION. The distribution of such examples, however, is strongly focused on the past participle *broken,* and less on intransitive and transitive *break*. *Broken cell phone* and *broken computer* (meaning a physically whole but nonfunctioning device) are pervasive on the internet, whereas there seems to be a generational gap between those who can say *I broke my computer / my Word program,* and those who cannot.

In Japanese, we can similarly contrast the transitive form *kiru* with the intransitive form *kireru* (see, as well, our discussions of *tigiru / tigireru* and *mogu / mogeru* in section 3.2). *Kiru* centrally includes a blade instrument as well as an agent—and hence is normally translated as 'cut', as in (24). Likewise, *kireru* can in some uses refer to an event involving an unmentioned agent and/or blade-like instrument. However, it frequently also refers to accidental, non-agentively-caused events—for example, a sandal strap coming apart, an electrical wire snapping in strong wind, or a shoelace breaking, as in (25).

| (24) | *kutu-himo* | *o* | *(hasami* | *de)* | ***kitta*** |
|---|---|---|---|---|---|
| | shoe-string | OBJ | scissors | INST | KIRU.PST |

'[I] **cut** the shoelace (with a pair of scissors).'

| (25) | *kutu-himo* | *ga* | | | ***kireta*** |
|---|---|---|---|---|---|
| | shoe-string | SUBJ | | | KIRERU.PST |

'The shoelace **broke / snapped**.'

As can be seen, good translations of these instances of *kireru* would not be 'cut', but rather 'snap' or 'break (under tension)'. Finer-grained analyses of individual languages, of the relationship between multiple sub-lexical meanings, of lexical polysemy, and of constructional meaning are needed to make these contrasts clear.

## 6 Conclusions

Our first conclusion from this study is that we should enrich the semantic models of separation verbs. In particular, we need to revise some frames (from BENDING to the force-dynamically more specific FORCEFUL BENDING) and also add some semantic frames to our analysis of these verbs, including LOSS OF FUNCTIONALITY, FUNCTIONAL DIVISION, INTENTIONAL CAUSATION, PARTIAL LOSS OF INTEGRITY, and OVERALL LOSS OF INTEGRITY. It seems likely that some of these frames failed to emerge from the responses to the MPI video stimuli because of the sorts of scenarios presented.

At a more general level, we have argued here that clusters of frames, and relationships between frames within a cluster, are crucial to semantic typology. The fact that *oru* means something like 'forcefully bend double on itself' easily explains why it also evokes the frame of BREAKING in the case of rigid objects; but that does not mean that it is semantically identical to the use of *break* in *She broke the stick*, which primarily profiles the BREAK frame and only implies forceful bending in many plausible scenarios.

Similarly, *kowasu* and *break* share significant semantic territory, but *kowasu* most centrally refers to FUNCTIONAL DESTRUCTION and only secondarily to BREAKING, while the semantics of *break* reverses the priority of these two frames. Verb semantics differ (crosslinguistically as well as within a language) not only in what range or combinations of frames can be evoked in a verb's polysemy network, but also in which frames are at the core of a multi-frame combination (FUNCTIONAL DESTRUCTION for *kowasu*, LOSS OF INTEGRITY for *break*).

We have also pointed out the importance of close examination of the relationship between lexical meaning and grammatical constructions; in fact, we feel that doing close corpus analyses of verb semantics in different languages naturally pushes the analyst towards a more 'radical' version of Construction Grammar, in the sense that it brings added awareness of the local nature of form-meaning mappings (Croft 2001, 2009). The unpredictable differences in semantic range between transitive *break* and participial *broken*, or between the transitive-intransitive pairs *kiru* 'cut' / *kireru, tigiru* 'tear' / *tigireru,* and *mogu* 'pick' / *mogeru*, show that construction-specific aspects of meaning occur at all levels of the grammar, even in the case of grammatically compositional forms. This interaction of verbal semantics with constructional semantics is both language-specific and verb-specific: Japanese transitive separation verb constructions almost always require a volitional subject, while English ones do not have such a restriction, and therefore the different semantic ranges of the two languages' transitive constructions interact with the possible meanings of verb forms. Corpus work brings up parameters and contexts that one would not have thought of otherwise, which can then be tested against native-speaker intuitions and in experimental settings.

It is not surprising that a corpus-based project should, in the end, point out some of the advantages of a close analysis of corpus data. Corpus-based and broader comparative approaches go hand in hand and should continue to be in dialogue in future semantic analyses of this and other domains.

## References

Bouveret, M. and E. Sweetser. 2009a. Multi-Frame Semantics, Metaphoric Extensions, and Grammar. *Proceedings of the Thirty-Fifth Annual Meeting of the Berkeley Linguistics Society.*

_____. 2009b. "Mapping Between Frames and Constructions: French and English Verbs of Breaking." Paper presented at the Third International Conference of AFLiCo (the French Cognitive Linguistics Association), Université Paris-X, Nanterre, 27–29 May 2009.

Croft, W. 2001. *Radical Construction Grammar: Syntactic Theory in Typological Perspective*. Oxford: Oxford University Press.

_____. 2009. Connecting Frames and Constructions: A Case Study of *Eat* and *Feed*. *Constructions and Frames* 11: 7–8.

Fillmore, C. 1982. Frame Semantics. *Linguistics in the Morning Calm*, ed. Linguistic Society of Korea, 111–138. Seoul: Hanshin.

_____. 1985. Frames and the Semantics of Understanding. *Quaderni di Semantica* 6: 222–53.

Fillmore, C. and B. Atkins. 1992. Toward a Frame-Based Lexicon: The Semantics of RISK and Its Neighbors. *Frames, Fields, and Contrasts: New Essays in Semantic and Lexical Organization*, eds. A. Lehrer and E. Kittay, 75–102. Hillsdale, NJ: Lawrence Erlbaum Associates.

_____. 1994. Starting Where the Dictionaries Stop: The Challenge for Computational Lexicography. *Computational Approaches to the Lexicon*, eds. B. Atkins and A. Zampolli, 349–393. Oxford: Oxford University Press.

Fillmore, C. and C. Baker. 2010. A Frames Approach to Semantic Analysis. *The Oxford Handbook of Linguistic Analysis*, eds. B. Heine and H. Narrog, 313–340. Oxford: Oxford University Press.

Fillmore, C., C. Johnson, and M. Petruck. 2003. Background to FrameNet. *International Journal of Lexicography* 16: 235–250.

Fillmore, C., P. Kay, and M. C. O'Connor. 1988. Regularity and Idiomaticity in Grammatical Constructions: The Case of *Let Alone*. *Language* 64: 501–538.

Fried, M. and J. Östman, eds. 2004. *Construction Grammar in a Cross-Language Perspective*. Amsterdam: John Benjamins.

Fujii, S., P. Radetzky, and E. Sweetser. 2013. "SPLITTING, CUTTING, and BREAKING Talk in Japanese." Paper presented at the 12th International Cognitive Linguistics Conference, University of Alberta, Edmonton, Alberta, 23–28 June 2013.

Goldberg, A. 1995. *Constructions: A Construction Grammar Approach to Argument Structure*. Chicago: University of Chicago Press.

_____. 2006. *Constructions at Work: The Nature of Generalization in Language*. Oxford: Oxford University Press.

Kay, P. and C. Fillmore. 1999. Grammatical Constructions and Linguistic Generalizations: The *What's X Doing Y?* Construction. *Language* 75: 1–33.

Majid, A., M. Bowerman, M. van Staden, and J. Boster. 2007. The Semantic Categories of Cutting and Breaking Events: A Crosslinguistic Perspective. *Cognitive Linguistics* 18: 133–52.

_____. J. Boster, and M. Bowerman. 2008. The Crosslinguistic Categorization of Everyday Events: A Study of Cutting and Breaking. *Cognition* 108: 235–50.

Michaelis, L. and K. Lambrecht. 1996. Toward a Construction-Based Theory of Language Function: The Case of Nominal Extraposition. *Language* 72: 215–247.

Slobin, D. 1996. Two Ways to Travel: Verbs of Motion in English and Spanish. *Grammatical Constructions, Their Forms and Meaning,* eds. M. Shibatani and S. Thompson, 195-219. Oxford: Oxford University Press.

_____. 2006. What Makes Manner of Motion Salient? Explorations in Linguistic Typology, Discourse, and Cognition. *Space in Languages: Linguistic Systems and Cognitive Categories,* eds. M. Hickmann and S. Robert, 59-81. Amsterdam: John Benjamins.

Talmy, L. 1985. Lexicalization Patterns: Semantic Structure in Lexical Forms. *Language Typology and Syntactic Description 3: Grammatical Categories and the Lexicon*, ed. T. Shopen, 57–149. Cambridge: Cambridge University Press.

_____. 2000. *Toward a Cognitive Semantics, vol. 2: Typology and Process in Concept Structuring*. Cambridge, MA: MIT Press.

# Part III

# Creativity and Discourse

# 10

# Creative Reading, World, and Style in Ben Jonson's 'To Celia'

PETER STOCKWELL

## 1 Jonson and the Literary World

The reputation of the English writer Ben Jonson largely rests on his status as a playwright, a late contemporary of Shakespeare and one who exerted a strong influence on Restoration drama. However, in his time and immediately after his death, Jonson was at least as celebrated for his production of masques (multimedia variety-shows featuring spectacular entertainments) and for his poetic writing. Other writers, describing themselves as the 'Sons of Ben' followed his dramatic principles, and the self-styled 'Tribe of Ben' included the poets Carew, Herrick, Lovelace and Suckling. In 1616 he was given an annual pension by King James I, an act that often leads to him being styled as the first formal poet laureate (though in fact by title that was first awarded to Dryden just over half a century later). Jonson's poetry remained popular largely through two collections, *Epigrams* and *The Forest*, which both appeared in a 1616 folio edition of his *Works*, though the *Epigrams* had also been collected four years earlier. Throughout the rise of his dramatic reputation, its decline in the 18th and 19th centuries, and rise again in the 20th and 21st centuries, Jonson's lyric poems have remained consistently admired. Among these is the following perennially popular lyric:

*Language and the Creative Mind.*
Mike Borkent, Barbara Dancygier, and Jennifer Hinnell (eds).

*Song: To Celia*

Drink to me, only, with thine eyes,
  And I will pledge with mine;
Or leave a kiss but in the cup,
  And I'll not look for wine.

The thirst, that from the soul doth rise,
  Doth ask a drink divine:
But might I of Jove's *nectar* sup,
  I would not change for thine.

I sent thee, late, a rosie wreath,
  Not so much honouring thee,
As giving it a hope, that there
  It could not withered be,

But thou thereon did'st only breathe,
  And sent'st it back to me:
Since when it grows, and smells, I swear,
  Not of itself, but thee.

(Jonson 1984: 102–3)

In this chapter, I will consider the popularity of this poem, and explore what is overwhelmingly its most common reading: a beautifully balanced poem of unrequited love. I will demonstrate how this reading can be generated from the text, drawing on the cognitive poetic framework of *text world theory*. However, I will also consider the positioning of the poem within the historicist paradigm of literary scholarship, and finally present a very rare and eccentric reading of the text, in an analysis that draws more on traditional *stylistics*. The point of the discussion is not so much to offer a simple literary-critical treatment of this Ben Jonson poem, but mainly to suggest that a cognitive approach to literature that neglects the central importance of the stylistic dimension can only ever be partial.

The 'cognitive turn' (Steen 1994), originally affecting literary studies mainly from within European stylistics and north American rhetoric and linguistics departments, has become a 'cognitive revolution' (Richardson and Steen 2002) that has touched most areas of the arts and humanities. In the rush to new projects and insights, however, there is a danger that the systematic application of cognitive linguistics and cognitive psychology is neglected in favour of a looser, more fanciful or less rigorous critical theory (as I have argued elsewhere, see Stockwell 2012). There is some evidence of this even in the best work in cognition and literature: work which is otherwise admirable by, for example, Scarry (2001), Hogan (2003), Gottschall

(2005), and in the collection edited by Jaén and Simon (2012). It is almost unfair to pick these examples out, because a cognitive framing of cultural literary studies is increasingly pervasive. However, it is my belief that this significant advance both in the content and the methodology of literary studies risks becoming a transient critical theory unless we retain a grounding in systematic stylistic analysis at the core of cognitive poetics. This chapter, then, stands as a corrective to cognitive approaches to literary studies that are insufficiently rooted in textuality and texture. In order to demonstrate the argument, I outline the most common, natural readings of the poem, and offer a cognitive analysis that operates mainly at the conceptual level. I select *text world theory* (see below) as the model for analysis, partly because it also offers a grounding of the exploration in a close stylistic account. The chapter ends with this account, and aims to show that a range of readings (even eccentric ones of the sort preferred by literary critics) can be encompassed by the approach.

## 2 Reading 'To Celia': A Text World Account

The most common reading of the Jonson poem is that it is a lyric, written by a man pretending to address a woman with whom he is in love, but being rejected. This is by far the overwhelming response of natural (that is, non-academic) readers as a simple online search for the poem and commentary on it will demonstrate. Most people do not seem to regard the poem as an actual letter of correspondence, but see it as being in the conventional tradition of a public declaration of feeling as a piece of artifice. Those academic readers who offer a reading of the meaning of the poem (largely older treatments such as Empson 1930, van Deusen 1957, Press 1958, and Nichols 1969) focus on its beauty and its simple lyricism. Interestingly for my later discussion, their model of Jonson as a lyricist of unequalled clarity causes these critics much consternation over the possibility that some parts of the poem are obscure or ambiguous. The two lines

> But might I of Jove's *nectar* sup,
> I would not change for thine

seem, in their opinions, to disrupt the tone of the poem, and in fact to say the opposite of what might usually be intended in a love lyric. Rather than accepting the ambiguity or exploring it further, these critics tend to try to resolve it as a manuscript mistake (perhaps 'for' is an error for 'fro' as a contraction of 'from'), or as an etymological note ('change' is meant in the sense of 'exchange'), or as a poetic contraction to preserve the metre ('I would not change [it] for thine'). However, these resolutions are problematic. As Dutton (1984: 23) points out in his introduction to *Epigrams and The*

*Forest*, 'Jonson was meticulous about his punctuation, the first significant English author so to be', and the poet himself saw the 1616 folio through the press personally. It seems on this occasion it is appropriate to trust the version of the text we have as above. I will return to this issue later on.

The most recent treatments of Jonson's work (see, e.g. Evans 1994, Sanders 2010, and Donaldson 2011) are centrally concerned not so much with interpretation of individual texts as with the cultural significance of the plays and poems in their historical context. The view of poems like 'To Celia' as masterful and influential lyrics is taken as given. It is a view shared by my own students. In an undergraduate class (held, pointedly, on St Valentine's day, February 14th), the consensus of the discussion was similarly that the poem was a clever and well-balanced example of a love-lyric, in the tradition if not the form of Shakespeare's sonnets. These readers did not notice that there was an apparent discrepancy in the two lines quoted just above. Instead, their only departure from regarding the poem as a simple love-lyric was to suggest that – in fact like many of Shakespeare's sonnets – the poem was as much about the poet's projection of his own poetic cleverness as about his genuine feelings. This sense that the artifice of the poem, its status as an art object, is foregrounded will be pursued in my analysis that follows.

The sense of balance, proportion, and poise (words all used by both my own students and by many online readers) can be accounted for within the terms of *text world theory* (Werth 1999; Gavins 2007a). This is a cognitive poetic model of discourse based on tracking the reader's mental representation of the text currently being read. The framework has a fractal structure, with reader and author occupying a *discourse world* at the top level, and co-creating a *text world* in the reader's mind. This is a working representation of the projected reality articulated not just by the semantics of the text but also conditioned by the reader's experience, culture, memories and other dispositions. Further *sub-worlds* or *world-switches* can be embedded within the matrix text world in order to designate alternations based on flashbacks or flashforwards, metaphors, negations, speculations and hypotheses, direct speech and thought, and modalised states-of-affairs. Text world theory – like the related approaches of possible worlds semantics (Ryan 1992; Semino 1997), schema poetics (Cook 1994; Cockcroft 2002) and conceptual integration (Fauconnier and Turner 2003) – can capture structural organisation and matters of fictionality very well, but it also has the advantage of being able to account rather neatly for some complex effects. For example, the foregrounding property of negation as a sort of positive absence is smartly captured in the notion of a negational world switch: a sub-world in which the item being negated is present for conceptualisation (see Stockwell 2011a). The experienced 'truthfulness' of a metaphor which is patently false is similarly captured in the notion of a metaphorical world switch (where the metaphorical properties hold), embedded in a matrix text world (where they simultaneously don't).

Text world theory is a model from cognitive science that has been used particularly in the context of literary reading both by its originators (see also Werth 1994, 1995a, 1995b; Gavins 2005, 2007b, 2010) and by subsequent researchers in cognitive poetics (Bridgeman 1998; Hidalgo Downing 2000; McIntyre 2006; Stockwell 2009; Giovanelli 2013). It is especially powerful in accounting for literary works which prominently feature fictional projections of imagination, anticipation or another form of alternativity, or the embedding of different voices, perspectives and beliefs. The framework can be used to explore not only these ontological and epistemological matters, but also the subjective and personal experience of readers engaging with imaginary worlds and fictional characters—in other words, matters of aesthetics. Furthermore, since the difference between what is and what should be is a modalised world switch, text world theory is showing that it can also address questions of literary, readerly and character ethics.

The Jonson poem 'To Celia' begins with an directive imperative ('Drink to me'), which of course strongly implicates an addressee. The poem continues consistently with this second-person 'thou' address. This is not an example of what Herman (1994) calls doubly-deictic 'you' (or even, here, doubly deictic 'thou')—in which a postmodernist, experimental or metafictional narrative plays with the conflation of second-person address to both a text world character and a discourse world reader. In text world terms, a reader can be discomforted by a constant and unstable toggling between themselves as a discourse world addressee and their sense of a text world character who is actually being addressed by both a discourse world author and a text world narrator: this sensation is what Gibbons (2012) calls 'bistable oscillation'. Herman (2002: 345) outlines a set of different functions of second-person address, from the *generalized you* and *fictional reference* within the text world right up to *doubly deictic you* as described above. In between these two poles lie what he calls *fictionalized* (or 'horizontal') address and *apostrophic* (or 'vertical') address. The former is when a text world character addresses another character within the same world, and the latter is when a text world character seems to address the reader at a higher world level.

The title 'Song: To Celia' appears to be a discourse world address from the authorial 'Ben Jonson' to a third named person, so the second-person imperative in the first line marks a switch into the text world in which the poetic lover sets out his desires: the address is switched to the direct co-participant 'thou' within that text world. This appears straightforwardly a horizontal address in Herman's terms. However, and though this form is conventionalised in love-lyrics, it is clear that many readers feel that they are 'overhearing' a private, intimate exchange. Though the poem is not addressed to the reader in the discourse world, the strength of the second-person address in this genre begins to approach the function of apostrophic or even doubly-deictic address.

What is odd at this point in the discussion is that all of my student readers (the majority of whom were women) identified more closely with the feelings of the presumed male speaker rather than with the directly-addressed 'thou', Celia. If they had to take a 'side', they took the part of the poetic voice, feeling sympathy for the spurned lover and feeling that Celia remained distant, other, and aloof. At first there seems to be a contradiction here, with readers making a trans-world identification with the poetic speaker, who is an enactor (a world-switched counterpart) of the discourse world author 'Ben Jonson', rather than with the text world addressee 'thou'/Celia. This identification is made in spite of the potential for an apostrophic address, and in spite of the correlation of gender with most of my readers.

We can resolve this apparent oddity, however, in two ways. Firstly, I have distinguished elsewhere (Stockwell 2009, 2011b) between empathy and sympathy in literary reading in terms of text world distance across world boundaries. Briefly, the most intense, empathetic 'feeling with' a character occurs when there is a direct connection across a single text world edge; whereas the less intense, sympathetic 'feeling for' a character tends to occur in text world situations which feature some sort of deflection of readerly perspective, such as mediation through another narrating character, or across several world-switches of memory or speculation. In 'To Celia', the poetic voice coming directly out of the text world is a strong enactor of the authorial voice 'Jonson', who occupies the same discourse world level as the reader, whereas the woman ('thou') in the text world remains silent, remote and displaced, and disembodied and rarefied ('eyes', 'kiss', 'breathe', 'smells'). It is not even certain whether the entitled 'Celia' is a real discourse world person or another imagined text world figment.

Secondly, the poem sets up a rich world texture that draws the reader's attention inwards, towards the deictic centre of the speaking poetic voice. It is this complex but highly balanced structure of switched worlds that accounts for the sense in the poem of balance, proportion and poise, as I believe and will demonstrate now. The timeline of the poem begins with speculation in the near-future across the first half of the poem (the first eight lines), and ends with a flashback to an earlier point ('I sent thee') which gradually returns to the present moment by the end of the second half of the poem (also over eight lines). The poem thus accomplishes a pleasing circular completion from immediate present imperative back to the present moment.

Within this temporal structure, the first half of the poem consists of four embedded worlds, each articulated by a pair of lines. The intial text world is established with two function-advancers ('Drink to me' and 'I will pledge'), both of which gesture towards a near-future moment but do so with a degree of certainty. Indeed, the combination of the imperative, the 'And' conjunction, and the future aspect—together with the promissory meaning of 'pledge'—strongly suggests a certain and definite promise or contract being established. The next two lines set up a parallel, alternative world switch triggered by 'Or', in which the syntactic structure (imperative; 'And'; future aspect promise) is repeated to the same effect. This parallel world remains closely linked to the matrix text world, not only in its echoic syntax but also in the semantic echo in which the definite reference to 'the cup' does not seem odd, since it has already associatively been evoked in 'Drink to me' in the initial world.

The third pair of lines continues with this echoic domain ('The thirst'). It is only by this point (it became apparent from my students' discussion) that the extended metaphor which has actually been running since the opening line is first noticed prominently. 'The thirst' is concretised spatially ('doth rise') and then personified ('Doth ask'), and this metaphorical world switch seems to be the catalyst for a sensitisation that notices retrospectively that there was a metaphor at work in 'Drink... with thine eyes' that blends eyes and mouth sensually, and then in the concretisation and temporal extension of 'leave a kiss'. The overall effect is too delicate and complex for easy logical denotative resolution, and seems instead to be an associative blend in which eyes and mouth, the thirst for wine and sensual desire, and body and soul are ill-definedly but positively present.

The final pair of lines in the first half of the poem introduce a modal world switch ('But might I') with a corresponding conditional within that same world and a further embedded negational world ('would not'). The negational world contains an ellipted 'for thine' which means 'for your wine'. The complete two lines, disentangled for their embedded worlds structure, goes something like: 'But if I had the opportunity to sup the most transcendent, divine wine, even then I would not take that opportunity in place of your wine'. The final ellipsis occludes the fact that her 'wine' is a further world-switched metaphor – but the inputs to this metaphorical meaning are composed of all of the ill-defined echoic and associative semantic domain that has been established over the first six lines: her 'wine' is her body and her soul and her as yet unrealised love. The complexity defies instant logical understanding, leaving a sensation that is more subliminal or associative: a sense of poise and apposite neatness that is ambient (for more on this notion, see Deggan, this volume, and for a different angle, Stockwell 2013). These are the lines which caused earlier literary critics such confusion, but a simple text world sketch shows the intricacies of their workings. It is important to note that I am not claiming the text world analysis here is a conscious reading; on the contrary, the analysis shows a complexity beyond the possibility of instant delineation. I am accounting for the subliminal effect which is more experiential than logical.

The emotional crescendo reached here has been attained by four anticipatory world switches of various types which have been mutually and complicatedly embedded. Though Jonson's original text is continuous, there is a mid-point pause or stanza break in almost all the many musical versions and most anthologies of the poem over the last four centuries. The second half of the poem does indeed feel different in quality from the first half. The world structure seems less complex and more consistent. It begins with a temporal world-switch to the narrative past ('I sent thee, late, a rosie wreath') and the narrative continues as the woman breathes on it, sends it back, and then it thrives and stands as a (perhaps delusional) love-token for him. However, this apparent simple narrative trajectory is disrupted by some artful sleight-of-pen. A fleeting negational world switch follows ('Not so much honouring thee'), and then the discourse returns to the matrix world in the narrative past in which the wreath receives a hope that in the woman's company it will not wither. But wait just a minute – we seem to have slipped from a factual narrative recount into a fantastical wish-world in which an inanimate wreath has hopeful feelings, in which a woman's presence prevents flowers from withering, and whose breath has such a restorative power and intensity that a dead wreath can grow again miraculously and transfer her scent to overpower the roses! In fact, we have ended up in this world of delusional absurdity because that fleeting negational world in fact referenced the prosaic reality in which the wreath's function simply was to honour her. In leaving that world we have been seduced into going along with the poet's delusion. The fleeting negational world is partly responsible for this, since the natural assumption of a fleeting world is of a return to the previous matrix world; instead, here, the formulation 'Not so much... as...' effects a further deflection into a world in which personified wreaths have emotions. The continuous syntax over the last 8 lines of the poem are also partly responsible for the reader's distraction: there is no pause in which as reader you can orientate yourself and realise you have been taken in.

However, most readers seem perfectly happy to be in the poetic persona's world by the end of the poem, feeling empathy for his unrequited situation, and identifying strongly with him rather than the addressed 'thee'. The complex world switching of the first half and the apparent consistency of the second half, the repeated ABCBABCB rhyme with its constant alternating return to the B rhyme ending, and the associative semantic consistency of the metaphorical threads throughout the poem, can all be readily interpreted as a finely balanced and consistently poised articulation. The artfulness of the poem lies in encouraging the reader to adopt an empathetic position in which—by apparently rational and reasonable calm argument—reason has been abandoned in favour of a satisfyingly intense if unreciprocated experience of love. The text world analysis points to a balance of the actual and the anticipatory.

## 3 'To Celia': Adding a Stylistic Account

The foregoing text world theory account requires a reasonably close attention to textuality, in order to identify the most likely points at which readers might create worlds and switches. The centrality of textuality is one of the reasons why I like text world theory as an analytical framework in cognitive poetics. However, if we rest at the conceptual-structural level and even though we can gain insight into some complexity, we still miss out, I believe, on features of the literary work that a closer stylistic analysis can bring to critical awareness.

A great deal of the literary criticism that deals directly with the text of the poem itself rather than its broad cultural significance is even then concerned merely with identifying historical and allusive elements in the text. Speculation as to the identity of 'Celia', for example suggests that she was the poet and friend of Jonson's, the daughter of Sir Robert Sidney the Earl of Leicester, Lady Mary Wroth, who lived at Penshurst Place, a great country house and the subject of one of Jonson's other most famous poems. On discovering this it might not be too fanciful to note the phonological echo of 'Mary Wroth' in 'rosie wreath', especially since the '-ie' ending on what might more normally be 'rose wreath' seems marked and not only for the sake of the metrics and the child-like or endearing diminutive.

The poem itself is a *cento* (from the Latin for 'patch' or 'patchwork'): it is a part-assembly of lines translated from the letters of Philostratus, a Greek philosopher and teacher of the 3rd century AD, who had settled in Rome, where he was then known as 'the Athenian'. The translation by Benner and Fobes (1989) renders Philostratus' words as: 'Drink to me with thine eyes only. Or, if thou wilt, putting the cup to thy lips, fill it with kisses, and so bestow it upon me' (*Letter 24*) and 'I sent thee a rosy wreath, not so much honouring thee (though this is also in my thoughts) as bestowing favour upon the roses, that so they might not be withered' (*Letter 30*). It is clear that this translation (with the middle- to early-modern English 'thine/thou/thy' and 'rosy') has been influenced by Jonson's now more famous text, but the nature of the original sampling is evident. The object of Jonson's original source was first noted in print by poet and naturalist John Dovaston (1815). Kenner (1964) suggests that if it took two centuries for the source to be identified then Jonson must have meant his readers to treat the poem as original, but of course there are flaws in this argument. It may be that the sampling was so obvious to contemporaries that it was not worth mentioning – in a print essay or reproduced conversation – as being worthy of note. And of course there is a suggestion in 20$^{th}$ century attitudes that a sort of plagiarism has occurred here, when in fact there is nothing of the sort: centos were evidence of the poet's erudition and artfulness, and offered an authoritative echo of classical wisdom. Jonson is 'not so much honouring' the classical tradition as drawing on its ethos and the breath of antiquity in order to preserve his poem against withering for future ages.

A brief stylistic observation is likely to note that different styles are in evidence in the poem, and these slight alterations align with the world-structure set out above. Overall, whenever desire or anticipation are being presented especially in the alternating words switches in the first half, the tone is relatively poetic, allusive, heavily metaphorical and self-conscious. By contrast, when worlds that are close to the speaker's actuality are in focus, the tone is more prosaic and narrativised across the second half. The first half consists of two promises of the form *DO X AND I WILL DO Y*, but the tone in which these are realised is neither legalistic nor threatening, in the mainstream reading of the love-lyric, but are instead aimed at drawing the addressed woman into the desire world offered by the writer. Nevertheless, the contractual flavour of *X THEN Y* seems to me to persist, even at a rather delicate level. This impression might be reinforced by the four-line propositional conceit that 'The thirst' is not simply based in the body but is a transcendent desire of the spirit, which then requires a divine drink, and this allows the writer to suggest that the woman's love is greater even than that divinity. The classical god Jove (Jupiter) is invoked partly so that hubris with the Christian God is not an issue. Jove was also particularly associated with wine and the grape harvest, so 'Jove's *nectar*' is denotatively simply *wine*, but of course nectar is also the drink of the gods which gave them immortality (from the Greek and previous Indo-European *nek-tar* – death-overcoming). For modern readers, 'nectar' also primes a sense of flowers, which makes the introduction of the 'rosie wreath' a couple of lines later more cohesive, though the botanical usage of 'nectar' was only just beginning in Jonson's period (the *OED* records 1609 as the first use in print in this sense).

The second, narrativised half of the poem presents, not so much the rather abstract desire-worlds of the first half, but rather what in the stylistic choices looks more practical: an object is sent, and then returned. The enjambed syntax iconically echoes the ongoing trajectory of the dispatched love-token. The distance between speaker and woman is also reinforced by this part of the text, and their separation is sketched by the spatial deictic difference between 'there' / 'thereon' and 'back to me'; this is also aligned with the temporal deictic shift from past tense for her ('sent', 'did'st breathe', 'sent'st') and present tense once the focus has shifted back to him ('Since when... grows... smells... swear'). This practicality of presentation masks the fact, of course, that the content of what is being presented at this point is a magical, miraculous or deluded impossibility. In fact, the strategy of a plain stylistic delivery of incredible content is a common generic pattern from religious parable to science fiction, and here it is part of the persuasive and empathy-generating aspect of the poem.

The poem cleverly and artfully blends body and spirit, sensual and transcendent desire, and of course the binaries of addressee/speaker, woman/man, over there / over here in consistently aligned ways throughout the text. Though, as I have observed, there is a rational structure to much of the poem (*X THEN Y* either as promise or as narrative sequence), this is realised with a poetic and metaphorical diction, and an incredible content. Much of the sense of the poem's cohesion and coherence lies in the echoic domains such as nectar-roses, drink-thirst, kiss-cup, as already mentioned, and in the central image of something not changing, immediately followed by the circular token of the wreath. There are other echoic connections across the poem. These connections are by their nature at such a level of subliminal delicacy that a stylistician can only raise them to the level of awareness and invite agreement, or not, as to whether they figured in your own initial impression. There are, for example, a great deal of 'th' sounds all the way through the poem: they are more densely occurring than in any other comparable stretch of English, and they are not restricted to the word 'the' (compare the last two paragraphs above of this chapter for a quick illustration). They reach their highest density in the line 'But thou thereon did'st only breathe'. It might not be fanciful to suggest that the alignment of these sound-patterns with the meaning of the poem generates an iconic association of 'th' with the sensual domain, one focused on the mouth, and particularly the tongue and lips foregrounded in its articulation. Primed or sensitised in this way, it is at least possible that 'sent'st' can be read or heard as 'sensed'. In fact, the senses (eyes/look, thirst/drink, breathe, sent'st/sensed and smells) are a particularly foregrounded feature across the poem.

So far, these simple stylistic observations are perfectly in line with the popular sense of the poem as an artful love-lyric, with the sense of empathy for the writer, and with the sense that the most appropriate schema for understanding the situation is one of hopeless but romantic unrequited love. However, it is entirely possible to produce an eccentric reading of the poem that is still consistent with stylistic evidence. In fact, it is difficult to cast aside the suggestion, throughout a detailed stylistic perusal, that a more sinister or troubling schema can reasonably be framed around the poem. This first suggested itself to me in the semantic scope of the restrictiveness of the word 'only' in the first line, and particularly because of the punctuation that separates it from the clause of which it is a part. There are several ways of reading the scope of 'only' in the first line:

> Drink to me metaphorically (that is, not with your mouth but simply with your eyes)
> Do nothing else except drink to me with your eyes
> Drink exclusively to me
> Drink to me with your eyes and with nothing else

The first two of these seem to me to underlie the most common reading of the poem. The first foregrounds the poetic-ness of the poem's metaphorical patterns that are to follow, and the second is a marker of insistence that will be read in the context of the rest of the poem as ardour. However, the final two glosses are also possible: in the first, 'only' restricts the scope of the imperative command, and in the second 'only' restricts the scope of the woman to her eyes alone. Both of these glosses suggest a relationship in which domination and passivity is more key. In fact, it is possible, thus primed, to find corresponding suggestions of a more sinister and unhealthy sort of relationship throughout the poem. The promissory syntactic structure of the first four lines now raises the formerly unrealised threatening flavour to a level of consciousness. The persuasive world-structure and syntax comes across as coercive, seductive and manipulative. The woman is silent throughout: she is to make a toast not by speaking but only with her eyes; she does not 'kiss' but rather passively leaves a kiss; she is reduced and disembodied down to her senses; her only action would be a definite and unambiguous rejection, but the writer frames it in a fantastical world that turns it into a token for himself.

There are sinister intimations of death throughout the poem. Thirst is literally life-threatening as well as metaphorically lustful. The phrase 'the soul doth rise' occurs, cunningly embedded in another clause. Jove is a figure not of romantic love but of violence, domination, and rape. A wreath can be funereal as well as celebratory. This last association might even be primed up by the insertion of 'late' in exactly the same appositional position as 'only' in the first line – and the parellelism is further reinforced by the sense that the poem falls into two halves and these are the first lines of each stanza. 'Late', in the common love-lyric reading, means *lately, recently*, but of course it also means 'dead', and had acquired this common usage a couple of centuries before Jonson. The word can attach semantically to the immediately preceding 'thee', with the suggestion that she has already died and is then sent a wreath. Alternatively, of course, the word can also be used in the sense of 'I sent thee a wreath too late to have its desired effect'. Finally, there is a marked contrast – certainly for a modern reader, at least – between the high-blown metaphor and allusion of most of the poem and the prosaic, colloquial and rather earthy 'it... smells, I swear'. There is, especially, in the unwanted intimacy of this, an element (isn't there?) of the obsessive, the stalker, the delusional misfit distracted by his own unreal fantasies, convincing himself of his own rightness by the appeal to a misogynistic tradition of literary seduction. 'I swear' binds up the religious oath with the manly curse, and smacks of protesting too strongly.

In this reading, the distraction in the second half of the poem (through the negational and metaphorical non-return of the world switch effected by 'Not so much honouring thee, As...') represents a trick played on the reader. You are drawn into the writer's fantasy world, accepting the conceit of non-withering roses in the woman's breath. The final line, with its self-reflexive tone, its negation and its implication of the woman ('Not of itself, but thee') leaves a sinister and unresolved sense for this more suspicious reader. The writer ends the poem not by returning the reader to the matrix text world of the first line, but to a point internal to his own worldview. The empathetic reader will have been absorbed into this perspective and will thus feel pity; the resistant reader might well recoil from this closeness and leave troubled and discomforted.

## 4 Stylistics for Creative Reading

It has to be said that the second of my readings here cannot be found 'in the wild'. The vast majority (even perhaps all) of the responses that I could find in an extensive scholarly and popular search share a view of the poem as an artful love-lyric. There are several conclusions that can be drawn from this.

Firstly, it seems clear to me that an historical view of the poem from a cultural studies perspective is interesting in both a generally significant sense and in a local, trivial sense, but any such treatment of the poem is inadequate without a stylistic dimension. It is not only the meaning (the readerly interpretation) of the poem that rests on understanding its stylistic patterns; the significance of the work in terms of its influence, generic position and place in literary history are also matters that can further be serviced by stylistic discipline.

Secondly, it is also apparent not only on this evidence but on similar arguments (see Gavins and Stockwell (2012), and contrastively Burke (2005)) that our collective excitement about the new opportunities being offered by a cognitive approach to literature should not blind us to the root empirical and evidential basis of textuality on which all cognitive poetics is and must be founded. To be blunt about it: where cognitive literary studies merely recapitulates the broad vacuity of cultural studies, it fails in its intellectual purpose. Where cognitive literary studies retains a cognitive stylistic grounding, then it is at its most successful.

Thirdly, however, it is clear that the scope of stylistics has been greatly and positively expanded by the cognitive turn in arts and humanities that it has most enthusiastically adopted. Stylisticians amongst literary scholars have been the first and most committed researchers in cognitive poetics. Detailed and principled stylistic analysis is not an add-on nor an optional ornamental extra to literary scholarship, but an essential element of basic training.

Fourthly, my discussion of the Jonson poem above demonstrates a feature of the practice of stylistics that shows it can be creative, productive and innovative at the interpretative level, as well as having a considerable explanatory and descriptive power at the analytical level. The sinister reading is eccentric in the sense that it does not largely feature in humanity's collective response to the poem over four centuries, but it is not impossible, implausible or even wilfully contrary or transgressive, since it can be demonstrated to have a grounding in stylistic patterns within a systematically disciplinary interpretative frame.

Lastly, it is not only this sort of eccentricity or strikingly contrary interpretation that stands as a form of creative reading. It should be apparent particularly from the earlier text world analysis of the poem that most of the delicate senses, the subliminal echoes, and the seductive readerly iconicity and aesthetics of Jonson's 'To Celia' require associations, connections, and enrichment from a reader's wider mental and embodied life. All reading involves space-filling and absorption in this sense. The poem's texture sets these patterns up, but it is readers who model, create and engage in the literary experience.

## References

Benner, A. R. and F. H. Fobes (eds). 1989. *Alciphron, Aelian, and Philostratus: The Letters*. New York: Loeb Classical Library.

Bridgeman, T. 1998. *Negotiating the New in the French Novel: Building Contexts for Fictional Worlds*. London: Routledge.

Burke, M. 2005. How Cognition Can Augment Stylistic Analysis. *The European Journal of English Studies* 9 (2): 185-96.

Cockcroft, R. 2002. *Renaissance Rhetoric: Reconsidered Passion – The Interpretation of Affect in Early Modern Writing*. London: Palgrave.

Cook, G. 1994. *Discourse and Literature*. Oxford: Oxford University Press.

van Deusen, M. 1957. Criticism and Ben Jonson's 'To Celia'. *EC* 7: 97–9.

Donaldson, I. 2011. *Ben Jonson: A Life*. Oxford: Oxford University Press.

Dovaston, J. F. M. 1815. Letter in *The Monthly Magazine* 39 (March): 123–4.

Dutton, R. (ed.) 1984. *Ben Jonson: Epigrams and The Forest*. Manchester: Carcanet Press.

Empson, W. 1930. *Seven Types of Ambiguity*. London: Chatto and Windus.

Evans, C. R. 1994. *Jonson and the Contexts of his Time*. Bucknell University Press.

Fauconnier, G. and M. Turner. 2003. *The Way We Think: Conceptual Blending and the Mind's Hidden Complexities*. New York: Basic Books.

Gavins, J. 2005. (Re)thinking Modality: A Text–World Perspective. *Journal of Literary Semantics* 34 (2): 79–93.

Gavins, J. 2007a. *Text World Theory: An Introduction*. Edinburgh: Edinburgh University Press.

Gavins, J. 2007b. 'And Everyone and I Stopped Breathing': Familiarity and Ambiguity in the Text-World of 'The Day Lady Died'. *Contemporary Stylistics*, eds M. Lambrou and P. Stockwell, 133–43. London: Continuum.

Gavins, J. 2010. 'Appeased by the Certitude': The Quiet Disintegration of the Paranoid Mind in *The Mustache*. *Language and Style*, eds B. Busse and D. McIntyre, 402–18. Basingstoke: Palgrave MacMillan

Gavins, J. and P. Stockwell. 2012. About the Heart, Where it Hurt Exactly, and How Often. *Language and Literature* 21 (1): 33–50.

Gibbons, A. 2012. *Multimodality, Cognition, and Experimental Literature*. London: Routledge.

Giovanelli, M. 2013. *Text World Theory and Keats' Poetry*. London: Bloomsbury.

Gottschall, J. 2005. *The Literary Animal: Evolution and the Nature of Narrative*. Evanston: Northwestern University Press

Herman, D. 1994 Textual 'You' and Double Deixis in Edna O'Brien's *A Pagan Place*. *Style* 28 (3): 378–410.

Herman, D. 2002. *Storylogic: Problems and Possibilities of Narrative*. Lincoln: University of Nebraska Press.

Hidalgo Downing, L. 2000. *Negation, Text Worlds, and Discourse: The Pragmatics of Fiction*. Stamford: Ablex.

Hogan, P.C. 2003. *Cognitive Science, Literature, and the Arts: A Guide for Humanists*. New York: Routledge.

Jaén, I. and J. J. Simon (eds). 2012. *Cognitive Literary Studies: Current Themes and New Directions*. Austin: University of Texas Press.

Jonson, B. 1984. *Epigrams and The Forest*, ed. R. Dutton. Manchester: Carcanet Press.

Kenner, H. 1964. *Seventeenth Century Poetry: The Schools of Donne and Jonson*. London: Harcourt.

McIntyre, D. 2006. *Point of View in Plays*. Amsterdam: John Benjamins.

Nichols, J. G. 1969. *The Poetry of Ben Jonson*. London: Routledge and Kegan Paul.

Press, J. 1958. *The Chequer'd Shade: Reflections on Obscurity in Poetry. Oxford: Oxford University Press.*

Richardson, A. and F. F. Steen (eds). 2002. 'Literature and the Cognitive Revolution.' Special Issue of *Poetics Today* 23.

Ryan, M-L. 1992. *Possible Worlds, Artificial Intelligence and Narrative Theory*. New York: John Wiley.

Sanders, J. (ed.) 2010. *Ben Jonson in Context*. Cambridge: Cambridge University Press.

Scarry, E. 2001. *Dreaming by the Book*. Princeton: Princeton University Press.

Semino, E. 1997. *Language and World Creation in Poems and other Texts*. London: Longman.

Steen, G. 1994. *Understanding Metaphor*. London: Longman.

Stockwell, P. 2009. *Texture: A Cognitive Aesthetics of Reading*. Edinburgh: Edinburgh University Press.

Stockwell, P. 2011a. Ethics and Imagination in Literary Reading. *Discourse and Creativity*, ed. R. Jones, 35–51. London: Pearson.

Stockwell, P. 2011b. Authenticity and Creativity in Reading Lamentation. *Creativity in Language*, eds J. Swann, R. Pope and R. Carter, 203–16. Basingstoke: Palgrave.

Stockwell, P. 2012. The Artful Science of Literature. *Sichuan Journal of Foreign Language and Literature* (original in Chinese, translated by J. Ma).

Stockwell, P. 2013. Atmosphere and Tone. *The Handbook of Stylistics*, eds P. Stockwell and S. Whiteley, Cambridge: Cambridge University Press.

Werth, P. 1999. *Text Worlds*. London: Pearson.

Werth, P. 1994. Extended Metaphor: A Text World Account. *Language and Literature* 3 (2): 79–103.

Werth, P. 1995a. How to Build a World (in a Lot Less than Six Days and Using Only What's in Your Head). *New Essays on Deixis: Discourse, Narrative, Literature, ed.* K. Green, 49–80. Amsterdam: Rodopi.

Werth, P. 1995b. 'World Enough and Time': Deictic Space and the Interpretation of Prose. *Twentieth Century Fiction: From Text to Context,* ed. P. Verdonk and J. J. Weber, 181–205. London: Routledge.

11

# What is Literary 'Atmosphere'? The Role of Fictive Motion in Understanding Ambience in Fiction

MARK DEGGAN

## 1 Introduction

This paper demonstrates how Leonard Talmy's influential conceptualization of fictive motion can be applied to larger scale literary constructions than are evident at the sentence or single-image level of figural discourse. To recall Talmy's definition, fictive motion describes mental and linguistic instances in which motion is ascribed to states and entities where no motion is incurred (2000, Chapter 2). Such instances usually feature the use of motion verbs to describe metaphorical movement in a static scene, as where a wilderness trail might be described as climbing a mountain. The formation introduced by this paper, *scenic motion*, also draws from cognitive linguistic framings of motion figures in language, but rather than focusing upon the metaphorical movement of an object against a ground, addresses the ascription of dynamic states to the physical or ambient qualities of a particular surroundings:

> The reticence of that misty landscape fled my gaze.
> The eeriness of the college buildings drew her in.

As seen of the second example, scenic motion extends fictivity to the 'atmospheric' grounds or settings of description. Many people are sensitive to how ambient aural and visual effects increase the level of dramatic tension

*Language and the Creative Mind.*
Mike Borkent, Barbara Dancygier, and Jennifer Hinnell (eds).

in film, or carry obvious metaphorical impacts: crashing waves as an analogy to the inner turmoil of a character, the slow gyration of sunlit leaves as a moment of respite from worldly pressures. Such projections can be more abstract than sensory. The French writer, Pierre Loti, described a valley in the Sinai as 'an enchanted place suddenly opening before one like a set change between high mountain ranges' (2006: 83).[1] Here it is not the valley suspended between mountain flanks that is of interest, but the fluidity of one's feelings for that *décor*.

Reflecting upon instances in which qualities of agency or motion are assigned to literary settings or environments, we are better able to describe the figurative projections by which textually described environments communicate significance in narrative fiction. In order to show how the atmospheric effects mobilized in literary texts carry dramatic and thematic force, examples will be drawn from Marguerite Duras's complex novella, *L'amant*, translated into English as *The Lover*.[2] Before turning to the literary material, a theoretical groundwork for scenic motion will be set out, as well as an indication of how the analysis of such figures may be of use to both literary and language-centred scholars. First, it is necessary to locate these initial reflections on scenic motion in relation to ecological approaches to art.

In recent years, attempts have been made to theorize the mood and ambience of complex environments in artistic works. For the German ecological philosopher, Gernot Böhme, the aesthetic 'atmospheres' given of texts feature 'the intertwinement of representational spaces with the spaces of bodily presence' (2002: 7). The motion figures addressed in this paper will also be seen to blend psychosomatic interior states with aesthetically meaningful sensory environments. While fictionalized mental spaces comprise the sorts of cognitive-sensory ecologies environmental theorists and literary critics have begun to notice, they may also be seen to underwrite metaphorical constructions at the environmental level. It is because such ecologies are both aesthetically and thematically dynamic that they are open to analysis through Talmy's description of fictive motion. 'Scenic motion' therefore offers not only a cognitive linguistic model for instances in which the ambi-

---

[1] The 1896 original reads: '*un lieu enchante [...] s'ouvre tout a coup, comme un décor qui change, entre deux haut portants de montagne*'.

[2] *The Lover* (1986; 1984 French original) is a lightly fictionalized and self-narrating recollection of the author as a colonial teenager growing up poor in French Indochina, and scandalously taking on, until her departure for the metropole, a wealthy Chinese lover. Duras's novella charts, in lyrical and often expressionistic prose, the personal, familial, and often self-centred social 'passions' and hypocrisies set in motion by the scenario. It simultaneously evokes two temporal spaces, that of the early 1930s in and around Saigon, and the narrator's reflections upon them in Paris of the mid 1980s. Neither of these settings achieves prominence, but together comprise a performative textual and thematic arena for the story's developments.

ent aspects of fictional settings are made thematically rich through being described via fictive motion figures, but an ecologically nuanced description of such constructions at the scenic or setting level of discourse. *Scenic* thus infers the atmospheric ecologies by which ambient fictional locations take on and maintain the performative qualities noted by Böhme.

## 2 Talmy and Fictive Motion

The designation for language's ability to rehearse the movements linking cognitive awarenesses of conceptual and sensory phenomena has undergone continuous development. In the contemporary era we tend to look to Leonard Talmy's 'virtual motion' (1983), Ronald Langacker's 'Abstract Motion' (1986), and Yo Matsumoto's 'Subjective Motion' (1996), as precursors to the more widely disseminated model of 'Fictive Motion' employed here (Talmy 1996, 2000). This latter model responds to what Talmy calls our 'cognitive bias towards dynamism', and the kinds of conceptual transferences by which dynamism is seen to play out in language and thought (1996: 213). The key qualification concerns what Talmy understands as 'linguistic instances that depict motion with no physical occurrence' (211). Of the instances cited below, only the last belongs to Talmy:

> The scenery rushed past.
> The cliff wall climbed over the trees.
> This road goes from Modesto to Fresno. (103)

In each of these samples, a focalized ground (the scenery, a road) is set in motion as a figure within some larger context. This process may be illustrated by considering the affective fallouts attending physical features which are already part of metaphorical constructions, such as a 'cliff wall' rearing up before one's eyes. There is a further aspect to the ascription of movement to stable objects and geographical features. This concerns the degree to which the act of perception or vision is made kinetic for the individual. As Matsumoto shows, in producing the figural effects that fictive motion intends, and where such processes are cognized in the mind of a particular individual, we find a marked 'subjective' aspect. It is one thing for an individual to note that a cliff is given to rise over a forest, where neither is in movement, but another to say the scenery rushes past where actual or factive motion is occurring—even if such motion is assigned to the wrong half of the figure-ground relation.

The important point, then, is not that motion, fictive or factive, inflects the affective states of viewers, but that such sensitivity extends to both the sensory *and* ideational categories at play, with relation to the force dynamics felt to animate them in relation to one's surroundings. As Langacker puts it, in expressions where motion is only mentally inferred, 'cognitive operations inherent in the conception of spatial motion are applied to static scenes as a way of mentally accessing them'. Further, it is '[t]hrough subjectification [that] the dynamicity inherent in the apprehension of events is transferred to the conception of static scenes' (529–30). To return to the notion of an immobile cliff wall *rising* over one, while it is clear that it is perception that is in motion and not the viewed object, one can still feel and communicate a sense of vertigo at following the line of the cliff face upwards. To cite a related example, looking from a train that is motionless while a different train sets off can trigger all the automatic physiological adjustments by which individuals accommodate actual movement. In this manner, responses to fictive motion rehearse the categories of factive motions with regard to both objects and environments.

A distinction arises here. An assertion such as *the road ran to the horizon* provides two possible actions. As Teenie Matlock has shown, it is not just 'actual' versus 'perceived' motion we need to consider, but the transitive and intransitive aspects of that motion (2004b: 234). A road may be figuratively doing the 'running', but there is a partly transitive function at work in that we construe movement for the road's running by visually, and so physically, following its path. Either the road is claimed to be in motion where no motion obtains, or the viewer's perception *moves* along that path. We must therefore distinguish between movements enacted physically, as where *my eyes followed the road as it ran to the horizon*, and those that are virtual and thus intransitive as *in the mist the road slipped away*, in which neither the road nor the viewer's gaze need be in motion. Here of course, the distinction may be elided in experience since one can both follow an actual visual path, say up the face of a cliff, while simultaneously imagining the cliff soaring over oneself. In short, regardless of whether the physical act of looking is being activated or not, real affects can be produced from 'soaring' cliffs just as one tends, say, to adjust for movement when approaching an escalator that is not in motion.[3]

Aside from the figural and affective richness of motion figures, the question of what is being set in motion needs to be understood in relation to the modal and aspectual conditions of the language in which such usages are couched. Perfective or imperfective verb forms play a role in this. It is one thing to comprehend that the cliff rose to an impressive height, for the perfective tense indicates that it rises no more, and another to comprehend it 'rising'. A statement's larger aspectual context is no less important. Just as

---

[3] Compare Matlock: 'narrative understanding experiments suggested that even though sentences with abstract motion describe no motion, people appear to simulate motion when interpreting them' (2010: 247)

Wordsworth's craggy mountain 'upreared its head' over the young poet in *The Prelude* (I: 378), powerful affects may yet be generated from perfective narrations through the activation of the conceptual structures by which mentally simulated motions unfold. As Matlock says, the work of comprehending simulated motion, 'like real motion or perceived motion, takes time to complete' (2004b: 239).

Qualifying words such as adverbs and adjectives can also alter the affective potential of fictive motion figures. Two examples should suffice, the first following from Wordsworth's *Prelude*, wherein the mountain's 'grim Shape' not only 'towered up between me and the stars' but 'strode after me' (379–80, 383), the second invented:

> The gloom of the forest pressed down upon her.

In the first, the *grimness* of the peak's shape intensifies the seeming movement of the mountain as the young poet's perspectives upon it are changed along with his viewing position. In the second, however, we find scenic motion created out of interior reflection alone. There the haunting quality of a forest gloom is imagined as having the status of an actant, hence the ascription of a scenic motion figure to the setting description: the gloomy atmosphere may be actual, but where it is imagined as *pressing* upon the human individual, the subjectively felt ambient qualities of the forest scene are sensed despite their merely fictive status vis-à-vis the subject. Similarly, where we find a road, cliff, or 'gloom' set in motion at a cognitive level, we need to see to what extent the storyworld is destabilized by the imputation of a more affectively wrought state to such motions.

> The road *lurched* sickeningly from Modesto to Fresno.
> The uneven scenery rushed *giddily* past.

In these statements we find a kind of textual force dynamics at work by which fictive or factive motions generate affective fall-outs according to the descriptors accorded them. Where motion figures are called in to sensorially substantiate shifts between topographical descriptions and the topological forms through which they are cognized (an island sinking 'miserably' out of sight beneath the horizon), we need to watch how it is not just adverbs and adjectives that complicate the abstract transitions by which factive motions occur, but the 'feel' of a descriptively nuanced scene.

More generally, fictive motion figures enhance or alter comprehension of novelistic settings. Where fictional scenes exhibit strong ambient effects in relation to their settings, as does the London weather in a Sherlock Holmes story, scenic constructions tend to destabilize the ground of the narrative—the foggy streets *swirling* before one's eyes, the windy, hazy towpath *moving faster* than the river. In such cases, scenic motion replicates the projection of psychological states onto particular settings rather as scenery moves about on the performance stage or trees appear to slip sideways when seen against blowing snow. The point is not that such effects have a cognitive or sensory effect on those experiencing them, but that they might take part in more complex metaphorical constructions: those trees departing like the lost souls in an accident one cannot otherwise recall, the towpath as the accelerating drudgery of despair.

While the physical aspect of atmospheres—sounds, smells, chromatic changes—have some relation to Talmy's account of the 'palpability' of entities, motion figures will not be addressed here as the motor-sensory aspects of 'ception', but aesthetically active ecologies of world and self. Where Talmy writes how in 'viewing a scene, one's experience is that one does not "see" such an entity explicitly but rather "senses" its implicit presence' (2000: 146), it remains to be understood how atmospheres intend communicative aesthetic structures in which ambient states underwrite the affective and thematic content of literary texts.[4] For the balance of this paper, Talmy's amalgamation of 'sensory stimulation, mental imagery, and currently experienced thought and affect' (139) will thus be applied to the totalized hypothetical environment we might term 'fictive atmosphere'.[5]

## 3 Atmospheres, Aesthetics, and Space

As seen of Böhme's statements concerning human sensitivity to ambience, atmospheres describe perceived qualities of space as quasi-objective states.[6] Atmospheres have entered ecologically aimed critical discourse as a way of abbreviating the complex nexus of individuals with the ambient qualities of their surroundings. In the present paper, atmospheres imply an analyzable aesthetic frame for the spatial and sensory settings of fictional texts. Aside from providing a means of capturing the just-tangible interface of humans with natural processes, the analysis of literary atmospheres allows us to

---

[4] The quoted line reflects Talmy's discussion of the semi-abstract gradient of 'palpability', though space disallows me from reviewing the tangible aspects of motion figures within the motor-sensory aspects of 'ception'. Atmospheres concern the connective processes by which fully abstract, and so interior subjective states and notifications emerge into the synaesthetic sensory realm of the semiabstract (2000: 153ff.). See note 6 below.

[5] Talmy locates fictive motion and its degree of concreteness or palpability within 'a single continuous cognitive domain, that of "ception"'(102), thus amalgamating the joint processes of conception and perception—that is to say, their joint sensory and ideational dynamics.

[6] The word itself fits the tropical ambience of Duras's Indochinese works. Despite the term's modern origins, atmosphere's etymological roots extend backwards from the Latin, *atmosphæra*, to the surrounding 'vaporous sphere' of the Greek term, *ἀτμό-ς + σφαῖρα*.

comprehend scenic-level representations of the co-presence (ecology) of subjects and objects.[7]

Given the range of effects that may be felt and discussed as personal impressions or moods, atmospheres respond to the synaesthetic qualities of natural description. Fictive motion may be a cognitively defined description of the connectivities between cognitive processing and motion events in the world, but the term is not nuanced enough on its own to map mental events across the changing atmospheric and sensory phenomena of the world. As Böhme writes, such connections are fundamentally ecological:

> In perceiving an atmosphere I sense what sort of environment I find myself in. The perception thus has two sides to it: on the one hand, there is the environment which radiates a certain quality of mood, on the other hand—me, participating in this mood through my very situatedness and thereby becoming aware where I now am... To put it the other way round, atmospheres are the very forms in which things and environments present themselves. (1995: §96)[8]

Ecological, yes, but as Böhme goes on, the affective and aesthetic ambiences around which our responses are organized are undividedly embodied in a way that is rarely stated in aesthetic thought.

> The space of bodily presence is essential to my bodily existence, since to be bodily present means to find oneself within an environment. [...] bodily presence is conceived as a state of being placed among things, and the order existing between things is understood as the order of their simultaneity, that is, of their reciprocal presence. (2002: 1)

The sense of an environmental or surrounding co-presence is noted by *The Oxford English Dictionary* entry on atmosphere:

> 4 a. fig. Surrounding mental or moral element, environment. Also, prevailing psychological climate; pervading tone or mood; characteristic mental or moral environment; fascinating or beguiling associations or effects.
> 4 b. spec. Applied to the background sounds that evoke a particular mood, impression, setting, etc., in a broadcast programme, etc.

How do we get from the dictionary definition of atmosphere to literary expressions of ambience as these impact fictional centres of consciousness? One route involves conceptual integration theory since, according to both models, an emergent structure can be seen to arise from the synaesthetic blending of a physical location's ambient qualities with the mental contents

---

[7] For an atmospheric view of ecological criticism, (or *ecocriticism*), see the articles of Rigby or Chandler (both 2011).

[8] As translated by Cameron Shingleton at http://www.cshingleton.com/2010/04/by-way-of-introduction-gernot-bohme.html.

of fictional subjects. For Eve Sweetser, exploring the interactions between 'sound and sense' in a fin de siècle verse play, not only is there 'a crucial relationship between the form space in language and the meaning space expressed by it', but where 'form-meaning blends' generate supplemental comprehensions, a 'new space' of understanding (2006: 32–3).[9] As Sweetser goes on to show, the ambient aural qualities of spoken poetry alter or enhance the discursive meaning of statements so made. Although no mention is made of performative ambience, Sweetser's laying out of the issues accords with the qualities of an aural atmosphere in the sense given by Böhme. Sweetser understands verse drama as forming a 'classic' case of conceptual integration 'where relationships in one space (poetic linguistic form) are construed as mapping onto, and dynamically building up, relationships in another distinct space (poetic linguistic meaning)' (34). In her reading, the meanings of the lines spoken in performance are enhanced by the less formalized 'meaning affordances' given of rhymed verse lines. For Sweetser, a new form/content crux is constructed by the speaking of poetic dialogue on stage, and what we might think of as the 'emergent' thematic excess produced through what Böhme has called the 'reciprocal presence' of selves and surroundings (2002: 1). By linking the insights of conceptual integration theory to those of Böhme's work on atmospherics, we can adapt Sweetser's account of the understandings generated by spoken verse to literary motion figures at the scenic level. In both cases, meanings are generated where relationships in one ambient space (a linguistically and poetically construed physical environment) are construed as mapping onto, and dynamically building up, relationships in another distinct spatial construct, in this case, a performative atmosphere). Where Sweetser saw performance impacting the comprehension of spoken verse in terms of linguistic forms being altered by their ambient effects, I want to underline the processes by which literary atmospheres give rise not only to emergent meaning spaces, but ones in which ambient settings are fictively *performative* in themselves.

Sweetser's article is also helpful in a more tactile way, and this has to do with her acknowledgment (albeit through different terms) that theatrical practices construct *atmospheres* by which meanings are altered according to the kinds of (here auditory) settings through which they are effected. Although textual 'meaning connections are possible in any poetic form, there are special affordances of form–meaning blending which arise from the superimposition of dialogue onto verse' (36). As a result of the blending of otherwise unnoticeable connections through audible rhyme, the playwright

[9] Here Sweetser is invoking the introductory model of conceptual integration theory proposed by Turner and Fauconnier (1995, 1996, 2002). Her essay concerns Edmund Rostand's French language verse play, *Cyrano de Bergerac* (1897).

was is to have 'put his meter and rhyme directly into his audience's consciousness, and even into his plot interactions' (47), so making dramatic and affective events out of the ambient qualities of spoken verse. Moreover, just as Sweetser notes how one of the play's protagonists understands herself to be winning a verbal argument because her then adversary is protesting 'more softly' (49), I would add that other ambient and therefore psychosomatic or synaesthetic qualities hold communicative weight. Such instances are readily assimilable to metaphorical constructions: the sound of the axes at the close of Anton Chekhov's play, *The Cherry Orchard*, the mists and endless shadows obscuring the polar-bound monster at the end of Mary Shelley's Frankenstein. In such works, atmospheric phenomena communicate sensory and thematic impacts to readers and audiences.

Duras's novella can now be brought constructively into the discussion. This is especially marked where ascriptions of motion to its Indochinese settings are used to communicate subjective states within the narrating protagonist. Early in *The Lover* we are invited to watch the landscape passing from a Mekong River ferry while integrating that view with the affectively valued fictive projections provided by the text. We are given the image of the narrator as a girl prior to her descent into the spiral of negative individuation, a potential we find rehearsed in the atmospheres and fictive and actual motions of the overall scene. At this stage of *The Lover* the ambient and psychosomatic aspects of the actual setting blend with the cognitive, sensory, and affective aspects of the girl's experience. Her responses can be overt or subtle. Faced with the vitality of rivers that 'flow as fast as if the earth sloped downwards', the girl fears being 'swept out to sea' (10–11). Elsewhere, 'a barely discernible distress suddenly seizes her, a weariness, the light over the river dims' (34). The blending of places and affects in the latter passage, especially, provides a dynamic means of integrating both sides of the mind/world equation, and as we see below, the central thematic and psychonarrational implications of the text.[10] In the next section, the dynamism ascribable to the blending process will be extended to Duras's settings in a more direct manner. First, it is important to sense the degree to which tropes of place communicate subjective force in the novella.

*The Lover* is conceived around the narrator's search for a comprehension that, while ultimately ineffable, allows the narrator to enter the affectively charged presence of that understanding. While the joining of interior

[10] More complexly, these descriptions are performative to the degree that they include not just the dynamics involved in simultaneously narrating the past as an intradiegetic totality while commenting upon it from the present (for instance through the projected 'image' of the girl shared by the narrator and her younger self), but those aspects of the scene that neither the girl nor the retrospective narrator can conceive, let alone control (10).

states and exterior description gives rise to atmospherically hued emergent spaces, these constructs often seem no more than geographically apt 'nowhere' spaces. Describing where one goes when one writes, the narrator displaces any actual location.

> That's the place where later on, once the present is left behind, I must stay, to the exclusion of everywhere else. The hours I spend in the apartment show it in a new light. It's a place that's intolerable [...]. On the other bank of the river. As soon as you've crossed to the other side. (75)

Literary works are full of fictional settings involving 'other side' settings. To cite a well-worn example, Joseph Conrad's *Heart of Darkness* (1899) posits a revised understanding of the Belgian Congo less through direct statements than the author's stylistics. By giving his African setting a strong atmospheric flavor, Conrad is able to suggest a different set of rules and metaphysical constraints than might be supposed of an actual fin de siècle colonial outpost. Duras, in turn, sets out 'the frightful loneliness of serving in outposts upcountry, stranded amid checkered stretches of rice, fear, madness, fever, and oblivion' (1986: 91), and plays on this charged setting as a means of creating dramatic tensions between interiority *and* the equally subjectivized ambience that comes of facing 'oblivion'. In other words, tension is generated between the novella's atmospheric treatment of a particular landscape form and 'the meaning space expressed by it'. For Duras's narrator, writing brings her to the 'area on whose brink silence begins'. Such silence is not merely a facet of a specific location, but becomes the psychosomatically charged scenic ground by which Duras 'locates' the waste of a life lived in the wake of trauma. The 'area' she means might be an interior setting, but she turns it into an atmospheric occurrence with powerful thematic impacts.

> What happens there is silence, the slow travail of my whole life [...]. I've never written, though I thought I wrote, never loved, though I thought I loved, never done anything but wait outside the closed door. (1986: 25)

It is to comprehend the modes by which that effaced area is inaugurated within the text that Leonard Talmy's model of fictive motion has been called in to negotiate the dynamics by which the uncoded 'contents' of trauma are vitalized within *The Lover*.

## 4 Mobile Dislocations: Place, Self, Mood

This section addresses the moods Duras raises in her text via the affective fallouts of fictive motion figures. In the first place, the feeling of dislocation suffered by the novella's narrative centre is not fantastic or imagined, but inflected by the figurative interiorization of the narrative's presumably actual settings:

> You always went home with the feeling of having experienced a sort of empty nightmare of having spent a few hours as the guest of strangers with other guests who were strangers too, of having lived through a space of time without any consequences and without any cause, human or other. It was like having crossed a third frontier, having been on a train, having waited… (65)

This sort of disorienting or unassimilable narrative environment is difficult to categorize save as an emergent figurative space. Before turning to a passage in which motion figures produce moods from light, colour, touch, and so on, we might consider Böhme's model of participation with place through mood.

> The space of moods is physical expanse, in so far as it involves me affectively. The space of moods is atmospheric space, that is, a certain mental or emotive tone permeating a particular environment, and it is also the atmosphere spreading spatially around me, in which I participate through my mood [...] it is at the same time the extension, or better, the expanse of my presence itself. The space of moods is the space which, in a sense, attunes my mood, but at the same time it is the extendedness of my mood itself (2002: 5).

Duras often raises physical phenomena in a manner similar to Böhme's notion of ecological participation. In the following passage, the protagonist's mood becomes inflected by the night-time atmosphere:

> I can't really remember the days. The blue [of night] was more distant than the sky, beyond all depths, covering the bounds of the world [*recouvrait le fond du monde*]. The sky, for me, was the stretch of **pure brilliance crossing** [*qui traverse*] **the blue**, that cold coalescence beyond all colour. […] **The light fell from the sky** in cataracts of pure transparency, in torrents of silence and immobility. The air was blue, you could hold it in your hand. **The sky was the continual throbbing of the brilliance of the light**. **The night lit up everything**, all the country on either bank of the river as far as the eye could see. (Duras 81–82)

The lines in bold indicate the ascription of movement to phenomena that is to some degree already kinetic. Since light does travel from its source, including the cool glow of the nocturnal dome, it is not unwarranted to consider light that 'fell from the sky', or the blueness given of atmospheric reflection. To this category of movement we might also add the 'throbbing' transparent blues, or the light 'crossing the blue' of the sky. Duras's description maps the participation of the narrator in a particular ambient setting. In this way the sky is not the cause of her mood, but an effect. It may be atmospheric in the most basic etymological sense, but the night sky is not here agentive despite being seen to *traverse* the ground of its own colour. These usages are *imagistic* in the impressionistic sense that their sensory effects ('you could hold it in your hand') are both visually fleeting and extended over time. Duras makes more direct use of images in the novella, not all of which are described: 'I often think of the image only I can see now, of which I've never spoken' (3). Elsewhere the image stands for a scenic comprehension that is not quite a picture but a mobile state incorporating fictive motion figures such as an image following one about:

> So, I'm fifteen and a half.
> It's on a ferry crossing the Mekong River.
> The image lasts all the way across. (5)

The notion of a particular impression accompanying an unfolding narrative event is not untypical of the novella's reliance upon figural usages incorporating movement. Just as the narrator claims that '[t]he story of my life doesn't exist. [...] There are great spaces where you pretend there used to be someone, but it's not true, there was no one' (8), we find the author effacing narrative 'spaces' through fictive movement figures. Like the narrator's younger self, the novel's physical spaces are often viewed as negative presences—'detached, removed from all the rest' (10). Böhme tells us that an environment presents a 'certain quality of mood' (1995: §96), but in Duras's more mobile renderings, such moods animate a dislocated *ecology* of 'no one' and no where. Many of Duras's descriptions of her narrator's atmospheric surroundings are accompanied by dynamic topologies, the 'great region of waters soon to disappear into the caves of ocean', or 'the surrounding flatness **stretching** as far as the eye can see' (11 my emphasis). Böhme might set out an ambient setting in terms of 'bodily presence', but his account does not, like Duras's, poetically dynamize that ambience through fictive motion events.

Theatrical practice offers another means of linking Böhme's atmospheric 'space of moods' (2002: 5) to the performative settings Duras utilizes. *Scenography* concerns the theatrical manipulation of the performance space's scenic apparatus, and thus defines the art of communicating through manipulations of the dynamic sensorium by which performance spaces are constituted and made performative. Scenography embraces the same outcomes and processes I see of scenic motion, while providing a more overt factive dynamics to the kinds of sensory or ambient tropes that performances and textual descriptions engage. Both consciously construct ambient effects with powerful subconscious or unconscious effects on the receiving individual, and both are in this sense *dynamic*. Like the fictive motion seen of 'a cliff soaring skywards', a backcloth suddenly and continuously lifted to a great height from the stage can induce vertigo. The motion of the cloth is both actual and symbolic—the physically moving cloth being dynamically and simultaneously transformed into the 'soaring' rockface. In both cases, the textual description and the scenographic action on stage, the locus of action, the 'scene', is rendered affectively and conceptually active. Scenographic examples are common in Duras's text. The 'light [that] fell from the sky' (81) and the 'image' which 'lasts all the way across' the traversal of a river (5) are theatrically actualizable effects. While such scenic actions are a part of the 'staging', they remain tropes for larger thematic contents. The 'pure' light from the night sky is ultimately debased by the less innocent noise of animals (82), while the unreality of the girl's self-image extends dangerously beyond her ability to negotiate the beginnings of her destructive affair with an older man. Fictive motion tropes are thus utilized wherever the author wishes to place her narrator in the Böhme-like *space of moods* that comes of crossing to the 'other side' of experience, or to perform the affective fallouts of being 'swept out to sea'.

## 5 'Scenic Motion' and the Dissolution of the Image

As seen above, fictive motion signifies a cognitive linguistic description of the process by which ideation maps itself through mobile categories of 'language and visual perception' (Talmy 2000: 100). When applied to literary texts, fictive motion events indicate more than the dynamic bias of human cognition, but heightened confluences of emotional, narrative, and thematic significance. The goals of this essay can be restated around this observation. In aesthetic discourse, fictive motion offers a lens onto the textual and cognitive processes by which language upholds the sorts of thematic projections at which fiction excels. Fictive motion is yet only one part of the process we might notice. Remembering that the retrospective focalizing centre of Duras's *The Lover* is an older woman reflecting upon a past seduction by an older man in the charged colonial setting of French Indochina, motion figures help the author to project her younger self's social and ethical quandaries onto the places she moves through. At one stage, the aural ambience underscoring the couple's first intimacy situates the forbidden lovers within a space that is as exotic as it is disjunctive. Here we need to note the degree to which the conditions of the setting unlatches the pair from their location in space and time, shunting them into the ambient noise and seemingly amoral darkness of Saigon's Chinese quarter:

> The noise of the city is very loud, in recollection it's like the soundtrack of a film turned up too high, deafening. I remember clearly, the room is dark, we don't speak, it's surrounded by the continuous din of the city, caught up in the city, swept along with it. (40)

In Böhme's model, there is both the mood given of environments and the self 'participating in this mood through [one's] very situatedness'. In the case of Duras, at the moment that the protagonist is seen to separate herself from accepted colonial mores through engaging in an interracial affair, the physical setting she occupies becomes isolated within the 'continuous din' and darkness of the scene. The deictic centre of the scene, its here and now, is confined to 'the room' at the heart of a disjunctive urban scene. In being 'caught up' and 'swept along' by the nocturnal ambience, the setting is fictively placed in motion as though carried upon the surrounding noise and absence of light. In this manner, Duras uses a now scenic motion construction to communicate the girl's own lack of control.

It is helpful to break down the process by which the scene's mobile ground is underwritten by the novel's use of ambient effects in relation to the 'static' focal position of the girl. First, the city noise heard in the room is 'deafening'. Instead of being defined as an island in the 'dark', the room is rather located vis-à-vis sound. By being 'surrounded by the continuous din' or 'soundtrack' of the city, the noise of the room sets out an *atmosphere*. It is this atmosphere, and not the place, that provides the locative ground of the scene. Second, the figure given of the scene is the narrator, whose 'recollection' this is ('I remember clearly'). While the deictic centre of these reflections is placed *within* the ambient qualities of the scene, the room itself is described as being 'surrounded' by sound such that it is carried away by that ambience. In short, it is the atmospheric ground of the scene, and not the narrator, that is imagined to be in motion.

This ungrounding of the scene reflects the social positioning of the girl and the man. Their actions separate them from their expected societal roles, casting them off just as the room is figuratively cast off. By being imagined in motion, the presumed stability of the colonial city is also unmoored, subsumed by the centreless aural atmosphere created for the scene. Because no landmarks are given by which to measure the room's trajectory, the presumptive ground of motion—the aural atmosphere of 'the city'—becomes equally fluid. The fact that noise is by nature kinetic does not alleviate the difficulty of a room and its human occupants being swept away by sound. The scene as a whole has been dynamized via the fictive motion events playing upon it. The key issue is not whether we find fictive motion to be more metaphorical or sensory (see Jiménez Martínez-Losa 2007), nor the extent to which its usage is cognitively motivated through being processed synaesthetically (Matlock 2004a), but that the place of the lovers' intimacy has been scenographically set in motion like a wheeled platform upon a darkened stage. Because the fictive motion figures engaged by Duras encompass both figures and grounds, the term, scenic motion, is appropriate.

There is a temporal aspect to these negotiations, in which we do well to recall Matlock's work on how the temporal aspects of motion figures give rise to thematic effects (2004b: 239). Duras likewise uses time to intensify her protagonist's responses. Later, for instance, the outline of a ship carrying loved ones is described as being '**swallowed** up in the curve of the earth [...] on a slow day you **could see** it slowly sink' (111, my emphasis). Like the scene of intimacy being carried away, this description rehearses, in time, the narrator's sense of slowly entering a ground or situation outside of her full comprehension. By constantly employing time and motion figures, Duras suggests that no landmark is capable of conceptually anchoring the experiences of the narrator's younger self—her lack of control and selfhood are no more stable than the dehumanizing flux of the colonial situation.

There are other ways of formulating the displacements of fictive motion in the novella. One of these is the process of *voiding* wherein deictic centre components become 'indeterminate'—'temporarily shift to null during a scene description' (Zubin and Hewitt 1995: 141). Voiding becomes a frame by which significance may be drawn from the inversion of figure/ground relations. Here, a voided content comes to act as a landmark for a given scene. In this reading, impossible spaces such as the locationless ambience of the city take on deictic attributes as the ground of narrative change, the space wherein the city is figuratively swept-away upon its own aural excess. For Duras, the focalizing centre defined by the girl is *voided* along with the room, hence her attention to the 'great spaces where you pretend there used to be someone' (8). This reading is substantiated in other ways. Most tellingly, by making the places occupied by the girl atmospheric, and then by representing those atmospheres via motion figures, the girl and the colonial spaces through which she moves are literally 'debased'. The result is that the novella's atmospheric modulations become a field of interior actuality parallel to the more prosaic exterior actions of the girl and her lover.

Scenic motions can also enable extended metaphor. *The Lover*'s opening sequence foregrounds the mobility of both the subject and sea plain:

> In the misty sun of the river [...] the banks have faded away, **the river seems to reach to the horizon**. It flows quietly, without a sound, like the blood in the body. No wind but that in the water. [...] its moving waters sweep through [...]. Everything flows towards the Pacific, no time for anything to sink, all is swept along by the deep and headlong storm of the inner current, suspended on the surface of the river's strength. (21–2, my emphasis)

While the surface movements in the passage are inaugurated through a fictive motion figure (marked in bold), the 'everything' that is flowing is described as being 'suspended on the surface' of the apparently bankless river.

This immobility is an instance of Talmy's parallel frame of fictive stationariness whereby a moving entity such as a ship's bow wave is reimagined as being still (e.g. 2000: 101, 171). As with the otherwise motionless room swept away by the noise of the city, Duras utilizes the immobility of the river's 'surface' to highlight the superficial stability of the narrative's personal and colonial milieu, including the psychological normativities attending them. In the cited passage, both stillness and apparent motion lie 'suspended on the surface' while the surface itself is given to flow. Equally, the girl is immobilized *and* adrift in the midst of her affective responses to the river scene, descriptions linking her 'barely discernible distress' to the 'slight deafness or fog' of the river (34).

More can be said about this setting. Spread across the landscape, the river becomes less a trajector than a scene atmospherically sustained by 'muddy light' or the 'misty sun'. The river 'flows quietly' or 'its moving waters sweep', yet where its banks have 'faded away' the river subsumes the plain such that it 'seems to reach the horizon'. The girl's physical self partakes of this conflation of movements. Almost as though she were accommodating her riverine landscape to Böhme's environmentally conceived 'space of bodily presence' (2002: 7), Duras raises the 'blood in [the] body' and the 'wind' in the water as constituents of the 'storm of the inner current' (1986: 21–2)., Like the flotsam, too, the girl is 'suspended on the surface of the river's strength', that is, upon the mobile surface of the waters. By giving the ground or landmark its own trajectory along with analogues of human vitality (flowing without sound, or 'like blood'), Duras's scenic motion figure suggests that both the narrator's younger self and her ecological connectivities are creatures of forces and affects beyond conscious control. Accordingly, the self and its surroundings form a psychosomatically hued forum for thematically apt figurative mappings. This last observation can be extended: where narrative significance follows from the employment of scenic motion tropes, the figurative language used suggests more than the partly subliminal relations of the human individual to places. Just as the novella's largely retrospective narrating voice moves through past and the present temporal planes and linguistic tenses (sometimes in the same paragraph), the text's complex negotiations of narrative consciousness are expressed through evoking fictive motion events alongside interior states.

A single line allows us to see how sensory phenomena is fictively mobilized in the text as an ecologically apt mapping of subjective moods onto the atmospheric conditions of the storyworld. We have already encountered Duras's description of the 'blue' nocturnal light of the region. Following this passage, we learn how such nights were 'different' enough to set 'the country dogs baying at mystery', whereupon the dogs 'answered one another from village to village, until the time and space of the night were utterly consumed' (82). This effacement of the night's deictic coordinates suggests that the girl once again finds herself in the midst of a foundationless sensory plane in which a 'magical' atmosphere is fictively erased or 'consumed' along with the terms by which human consciousness navigates its worldly or moral habitats. In this way, scenic motion events can be used to stitch or sever individuals from meaningful connections to environments. Sensitivity to one's ecological involvements infers awareness of where one stands in a given scenario. With *The Lover*, Duras uses such sensitivity as a staging post in a process of human disorientation.[11]

## 6 Conclusion

Through Duras's use of ambient or *scenic* motion figures, the otherwise unrepresentable psychosomatic circumstances of *The Lover* become open to a more effective nexus of issues concerning the structures and stylistics of language, cognition, and literary and ecologically directed criticism. As a closing model of the *scenic motion* form attuned to the literary revelation of consciousness, one last passage illustrates how it is not just rivers or rooms that are opened to the processes of literary poiesis, but the cognitive orientations extending through the mind, body, and affects. Here the body is raised as a dynamic presence *stretching* or *launching* itself beyond view, and thus into the performative realms of the ambient, that is to say, towards the scenography of fear or 'pleasure':

> Less and less clearly can he make out the limits of this body, it's not like other bodies, it's not finished, in the room it keeps growing, it's still without set form, continually coming into being, not only there where it's visible but elsewhere too, stretching beyond sight [s'étend au-delà de la vue], toward risk, toward death, it's nimble, it launches [il part] itself wholly unto pleasure. (99)

Fictive motion thus offers an analytic tool for comprehending the complex tropes of fictional poiesis while doing justice to both language-based and literary investigations. Unlike Talmy's efforts to exclude 'linguistic' or 'nonspatial' metaphor from his study, atmospheric investigations into the synaesthetic aspects of ambience allow us to track the literary and figurative potential of fictive motion constructions where applied to settings. Likewise, *scenic motion* generates a cross-disciplinary scenographic frame by which to focus attention upon the ecological fallouts of setting constructions

[11] Space does not allow me to reconceive my terms in relation to the fictional means by which Duras's narrator strips her protagonist of any clear perspective onto the past; indeed, of the metaphorical mappings and projections by which conceptual processing is said to proceed (e.g. see Lakoff and Turner 1989).

in fictional narratives. Awareness of the embodied and ecological aspects of places allows a fuller analysis of the figural usages by which settings communicate thematic and affective content through representations of the interactive collusion of world with embodied consciousness.

## References

Böhme, Gernot. 1995. *Atmosphäre. Essays zur neuen Ästhetik*. Frankfurt am Main: Suhrkamp.

_____. 2002. The Space of Bodily Presence and Space as a Medium of Representation. *Transforming Spaces: The Topological Turn in Technology Studies*. Eds. Mikael Hård, Andreas Lösch, Dirk Verdicchio. [Online publication of the international conference held in Darmstadt, Germany, 22-24.03.2002]. Web. 14.09.2011.

Chandler, Timothy. 2011. Reading Atmospheres: The Ecocritical Potential of Gernot Böhme's Aesthetic Theory of Nature. *Interdisciplinary Studies in Literature and Environment* 18.3 (Summer): 553–68.

Duras, Marguerite. 1986. *The Lover*. B. Bray, trans. New York, HarperCollins.

Fauconnier, G. and M. Turner. 1996. Blending as a Central Process of Grammar. *Conceptual Structure, Discourse and Language,* ed. A. Goldberg. Stanford, CA: CSLI. 113–30.

_____. 1998. Conceptual Integration Networks. *Cognitive Science* 22.2: 133–88.

_____. 2002. *The Way We Think*. New York: Basic Books.

Goddard, Cliff. 1998. *Semantic Analysis: A Practical Introduction*. New York: Oxford University Press.

Jiménez Martínez-Losa, Noelia. 2007. Towards a typology of fictive motion events: Review of existing proposals and presentation of new perspectives. *Interlingüística* 17: 562–569.

Lakoff, G. and M. Turner. 1989. *More than cool reason*. Chicago: University of Chicago Press.

Langacker, Ronald W. 1987. *Foundations of Cognitive Grammar. Vol I: Theoretical Prerequisites*, Stanford, Stanford University Press.

_____. 2008. *Cognitive Grammar: An Introduction*. Oxford: Oxford UP.

Loti, Pierre. 2006. *Le désert*. Lausanne: Payot.

Matlock, Teenie. 2004a. Fictive Motion as Cognitive Simulation. *Memory and Cognition* 32.8: 1389–1400.

_____. 2004b. Conceptual Motivation of Fictive Motion. *Studies in Linguistic Motivation*, eds. G. Radden and K. Panther. New York: Mouton de Gruyter. 221–248.

_____. 2010. Abstract Motion Is No Longer Abstract. *Language and Cognition* 2.2: 243–60.

Matsumoto, Yo. 1996a. How abstract is subjective motion? A comparison of coverage path expressions and access path expressions. *Conceptual Structure, Discourse & Language*, ed. A. Goldberg. Stanford: CSLI, 359–373.

_____. 1996b. Subjective motion in English and Japanese verbs. *Cognitive Linguistics* 7.2: 183–226.

Rigby, Kate. 2011. Gernot Böhme's Ecological Aesthetics of Atmosphere. *Ecocritical Theory: New European Perspectives*, ed. Axel Goodbody and Kate Rigby. Charlottesville: University of Virginia Press. 269–96.

Sweetser, Eve. 2006. Whose rhyme is whose reason? Sound and sense in *Cyrano de Bergerac*. *Language and Literature*. Vol. 15, No. 1: 29–54.

Talmy, Leonard. 2000. *Towards a Cognitive Semantics. Vol. 1*. Cambridge, MA: MIT Press.

_____. 1983. How language structures space. *Spatial Orientation: Theory, Research, and Application*, eds. H. Pick, L. Acredolo. New York, Plenum Press. 225-82.

Tsur, Reuven. 2003. *On the Shore of Nothingness: Space, Rhythm, and Semantic Structure in Religious Poetry and its Mystic-Secular Counterpart. A Study in Cognitive Poetics*. Exeter: Imprint Academic.

Turner, M. and G. Fauconnier. 1995. Conceptual Integration and Formal Expression. *Journal of Metaphor and Symbolic Activity* 10.3: 183–204.

Zubin, D., and L. Hewitt. 1995. The Deictic Center: A Theory of Deixis in Narrative. *Deixis in Narrative: A Cognitive Science Perspective*. Eds. Judith Duchan, Gail Bruder, and Lynne Hewit. Hillsdale NJ: Lawrence Erlbaum. 129–55.

# 12

# Motion Metaphors in Political Races

TEENIE MATLOCK

## 1 Introduction

In the 2012 United States presidential election, Democratic candidate Barack Obama framed many of his campaign ads with the word 'Forward.' This slogan, and others that implied motion, appeared on bumper stickers, lawn signs, billboards, websites, Facebook walls, and TV advertisements all across the United States. Obama's opponent, Republican candidate Mitt Romney, also used language that implied movement. Declarations such as 'Let's turn this country around' figured prominently in his campaign. And in news coverage prior to the election, journalists and commenters used language that implied motion. Statements such as 'Obama, Romney race to close election finish', 'Nearing the finish line, presidential candidates make a final push in battleground states' and 'Obama, Romney make a mad dash in a final bid for votes' were splashed across the front pages of newspapers and other media.

Why is motion language prevalent in political elections? What is the nature of the conceptual structure of such language, including language that was used by politicians, the media, and the general public in the last US Presidential election? What can we infer about the cognitive architecture that drives such framing? This chapter discusses motion metaphors in the context of elections. It considers why motion language is frequently used in political campaigns, and what it says about the creative power of metaphor. Analyzing the use and conceptual content of such metaphors is important to

*Language and the Creative Mind.*
Mike Borkent, Barbara Dancygier, and Jennifer Hinnell (eds).

gaining a coherent understanding of how framing can influence attitudes about the electability of candidates, and ultimately, who winds up in office.

## 2 Motion Metaphors

Motion metaphors are common in everyday communication. They pervade all languages, registers, and situations. We constantly hear, read, utter, write, or internally verbalize metaphorical statements such as *This week raced past*, *The road runs from Del Mar to San Diego*, *The young lovers came to a dead end*, and *He went from crying to laughing in less than a minute*. Each of these expressions contains motion language (e.g. *raced, runs, came, went*), but no actual motion is conveyed. With *This week raced past,* time is experienced as 'moving' past stationary observers (Clark 1973). With *The road runs from Del Mar to San Diego*, a freeway is construed as mental 'motion' or scanning along a path, or as linear extension through actual space (Matlock 2004; Talmy 2000). With *The young lovers came to a dead end*, a romantic relationship is conceptualized in terms of movement along a path (Gibbs and Nascimento 1996). With *He went from crying to laughing in less than a minute*, a person is construed as 'moving' from a state of sadness to one of happiness (Kövecses 2000). These metaphorical motion expressions differ from literal motion expressions such as *The car raced past*, *The athlete runs from Del Mar to San Diego*, *The cyclists came to a dead end,* and *He went from the school to the post office in less than a minute*, in which agents move along paths toward goals (see Talmy 1983).

How do we make sense of expressions that include motion language but express no physical movement? The answer rests in our ability to anchor our understanding of relatively abstract things, states, and situations, in our embodied experience with motion in the world (see Gibbs 1994, 2006; Johnson 1987; Lakoff and Johnson 1980, 1999). To grasp the meaning of nonliteral motion language, we draw on our direct experience with motion, as pedestrians, cyclists, runners, drivers, and passengers, and on our indirect experience with motion, as viewers of other entities in motion, including people, dogs, cars, planes, escalators, clouds, and cartoon characters.

Motion makes an excellent source domain because it is grounded in our everyday embodied experience (Gibbs 1994; Lakoff and Johnson 1980; Johnson 2007; Lakoff and Johnson 1999). It is no accident that motion serves as a source domain in virtually all cultures, and that it is the foundation of a number of metaphors in English, including TIME IS MOTION, CHANGE IS MOTION, LIFE IS A JOURNEY, FORM IS MOTION, and LOVE IS A JOURNEY. We are constantly in motion, observing motion, or reflecting on motion. As phenomenologist Maxine Sheets-Johnstone notes, 'We literally discover ourselves in motion' (Sheets-Johnstone 1999: 136). Critically, in processing motion metaphors, we dynamically simulate certain aspects of movement along a path toward a goal (see Feldman 2008; Gallese and Lakoff 2005; Gibbs and Matlock 2008; Matlock 2004; Narayanan 1999). The capacity to mentally reenact action is not limited to metaphorical construal. It is in fact an integral part of reasoning, both nonliteral and literal, about events, states, and situations (for discussion of simulation in everyday thought and action, see Barsalou 1999, 2008; Bergen 2012; Gibbs 2006; Glenberg and Gallese 2012; Zwaan 2004).

## 3 Motion Metaphors and Elections

A political election of any significance brings on a hailstorm of messages and images designed to capture attention and sway opinions. A single word alone can influence perceptions of an individual or issue. For example, in the 2008 US presidential election, 'maverick' was used to describe GOP candidate John McCain. The word was an appropriate way to frame Senator McCain because it portrayed independence and rebellion. It also resonated to the Tom Cruise character, Maverick, a feisty fighter pilot in the film 'Top Gun' (before going into politics, McCain was a Navy pilot in the Vietnam War).[1] Framing in this way (and others) is known to create bias, often in terms of gains and losses, which can ultimately influence people's opinions and actions (see Kahneman and Tversky 2000).

Framing can have a strong effect on attitudes toward political candidates and issues. It is known to influence how (or even whether) people will vote on election day (for discussion of framing in political language, see Chong and Druckman 2007; Druckman and Parkin 2005; Lakoff and Wehling 2012; Matlock 2012). Negative language can be an especially powerful framing device, but when it becomes excessive, it can backfire and lead to low voter turnout (see Ansolabhere and Iyengar 1997; Lau 1982). Recent cognitive science research reveals that slight variations in linguistic information can differentially influence how people think about social topics. In particular, metaphor can affect attitudes about immigration and minimum wage (Landau, Sullivan, and Greenberg 2009) as well as crime reduction (Thibodeau and Boroditsky 2011). Even subtle changes in grammatical form can bias opinions, for instance, opinions about the past actions of politicians, and whether or not they are electable (see Fausey and Matlock 2011).

[1] The word 'maverick' was coined in 1867 when American rancher Samuel Maverick refused to brand his livestock. It became a metonymy for animals that are not obviously part of the herd, and was extended to people who can be rebellious or out of step with the group.

Metaphor is often used in political framing. Extensive research by Berkeley linguist George Lakoff and colleagues shows that our beliefs and behaviors related to government and political leaders are grounded in basic cognitive systems, including our entrenched feelings about basic family values and morals (Lakoff 1996, 2008; Lakoff and Wehling 2012). Lakoff's groundbreaking research has done a superb job explaining how and why people develop and maintain particular belief states in the realm of politics. Conservatives often appeal to a conceptual system that portrays the government as an authoritarian father (i.e. political leader) that rules the family (i.e. citizens) with an iron fist. In this system of beliefs, limited guidance or support is offered, and any 'child' who errs is subject to strict punishment. In contrast, progressives naturally appeal to a system in which the government is a nurturing parent that provides its 'children' with guidance, support, and forgiveness (see Lakoff 1996).

Experimental semantics research has just begun to investigate the use and understanding of motion metaphors in politics, especially in the context of elections. In a recent *American Scientist* article, I discussed the role of metaphor in framing political messages, for instance, in campaign slogans and in coverage of election developments. I explained how the use and understanding of metaphorical motion language in this context is anchored in our conceptual understanding of actual motion, and more specifically, of races, including knowing that races have start points and endpoints as well as winners and losers (Matlock 2012). The ubiquity, coherence, and consistency of such language reflects the metaphor POLITICAL CAMPAIGNS ARE RACES. Here I discuss how this and other motion metaphors are used in the context of campaign races.

The conceptual structure of POLITICAL CAMPAIGNS ARE RACES shares conceptual structure with other motion metaphors that populate everyday language and thought.[2] In POLITICAL CAMPAIGNS ARE RACES, politicians are construed as racing along the campaign path toward a successful election outcome. On the path, they can move ahead or slip behind each other, as in 'Obama is racing ahead of Romney' or 'Obama is inching ahead of his opponent.' They can also pass or slip behind other entities, even their own past election results. For example, in the 2012 election, statistician Nate Silver predicted that 'President Obama has the chance to run ahead of his 2008 margins.' In this statement, Obama is racing against himself in two different

[2] Motion metaphors are part of EVENT STRUCTURE, a coherent collection of metaphors that share basic conceptual structure grounded in our everyday embodied experience with events and actions (Lakoff and Johnson 1999).

elections, in 2008 and in 2012.[3] In POLITICAL CAMPAIGNS ARE RACES, 'motion' can occur in various ways, for instance, quickly or slowly, and with or without much effort. One beautiful example of this occurred a few weeks before the 2012 election. *New Scientist* reported, 'Barring a political earthquake Barack Obama will be re-elected at a canter,' suggesting easy, leisurely movement. Another nice example appeared in the primary election, when the Democratic National Committee head declared, 'Mitt Romney is limping into New Hampshire' to emphasize his sudden 'iffy' status relative to Republican competitor Rick Santorum.[4]

Different directions of 'motion' can be emphasized in metaphors related to campaigns, and more generally, government leadership. In the 2012 campaign race, the Democrats framed many of their messages with motion in a forward direction. A nice example of this followed the 2012 Summer Olympics in London. When a victorious outcome was beginning to look rather bleak for the Democrats, Barack Obama told his constituents, 'This is not going to be a race like Usain Bolt, where we're like 40 yards ahead and we can just kind of start jogging 10 feet before the finish line,' making reference to the stunning Jamaican sprinter who won three gold medals. 'We're going to have to run through the tape.' And it didn't stop there. A few weeks later, Democrats mass-mailed a letter enclosed in an envelope that displayed the message, 'We're not going back. We're moving forward.' This example reflects a NATIONAL POLITICS AS MOVEMENT metaphor, whereby a nation is construed as traversing a path toward the future, with movement that can be altered (e.g. turned around, sped up, stalled). Using forward motion to frame their messages made good sense for the Democratic Party in 2012. It implied hope and new opportunities, and it conveyed a commitment to staying the course. It resonated to metaphorical statements associated with previous victorious elections, including those of President Bill Clinton, whose campaign featured Fleetwood Mac's song, which featured the lyrics, 'Don't stop thinking about tomorrow / Don't stop, it'll soon be here / It'll be better than before / Yesterday's gone / Yesterday's gone,' another instantiation of NATIONAL POLITICS AS MOVEMENT.

Republicans also framed their campaign messages in terms of movement in the 2012 Presidential race. Some of their statements stressed forward motion, but some emphasized NATIONAL POLITICS AS MOVEMENT. Many Republican messages emphasized the need to turn the nation around, or to go back to the good old days (e.g. when Ronald Reagan was Presi-

---

[3] Conceptual integration theory would elegantly account for this with multiple input spaces to represent Obama in different elections (see Fauconnier 1997; Fauconnier and Turner 1998).

[4] In this case, we also see difficulties in purposeful action are difficulties in movement (via impediments on the path toward a goal or via physical injury).

dent). In speeches leading up to Election Day, Republican candidate Mitt Romney implored, 'Let's turn this country around.' He also tweeted, 'With your help, we will turn out country around and get America back on the path to prosperity'. His running mate, Paul Ryan made consistent statements, such as, 'We know what needs to be done to turn the country around and offer the leadership to do it.' The popular media also appealed to NATIONAL POLITICS AS MOVEMENT, for instance, in headlines such as 'Romney is the turnaround expert US needs' and 'The Romney Turnaround'.

In the months preceding the November Election, a NATION AS VEHICLE metaphor also appeared in campaign talk. With this mapping, the nation is construed as a moving vehicle, for instance, a train, which can be damaged and derailed by opponents. In August 2012, Romney promised to 'cut the deficit and put America on track to a balanced budget.' Reactions to this promise were mixed. In May 2012, Rick Santorum, who had run against Romney in the primaries, asked his fellow Republicans to 'rally behind Mitt Romney and his vision to put our county back on track.' Around that same time, a headline in the *San Francisco Examiner* read, 'Romney is the wrong candidate to put America back on track.'

## 4 The Finish Line

Metaphor is the heart of creativity. By drawing on our familiar, embodied experiences we can understand what is unfamiliar, abstract, and novel (Gibbs 1994, 1997; Lakoff and Johnson 1980). Motion metaphors such as POLITICAL CAMPAIGNS ARE RACES influence how we view campaigns, feel about political candidates, and vote at the polls. Some motion expressions persist from election to election (e.g. 'political race', 'running mate', 'finish line'), but others are emphasized or deemphasized depending on factors such as the candidates' personalities, current economic health of the nation, and time to the Election. In the 2012 presidential election, promising to stay the course and continue moving forward worked well for incumbent candidate Barack Obama. Promising to turn the country around and go back to the good old days did not work well for competitor Mitt Romney.

Politicians, speechwriters, and news reporters all use motion language to frame political campaign messages, including language pertaining to horse races and sporting events (see Brettschneider 2008). Yet they seem to pay little attention to the detailed semantics of such language, the motivation behind its use, or the effect it has on voters. Investigating the creative powers of metaphor in framing campaign messages is useful because it can spawn or alter beliefs about who should and who should not be in office. Investigating how metaphors work in the head, across party lines, and over time is of great value to understanding the political mind. It is also important to understanding the dynamics and creative force of metaphor in everyday thought.

## Acknowledgments

Thanks goes to George Lakoff, Nathan Monroe, and Elisabeth Wehling for enlightening discussions related to this research. Special thanks goes to the editors of this volume, and the two anonymous reviewers who provided useful, informative comments on the manuscript.

## References

Ansolabehere, S. and S. Iyengar. 1997. *Going Negative: How Political Advertising Divides and Shrinks the American Electorate*. New York, NY: The Free Press.

Barsalou, L.W. 1999. Perceptual symbol systems. *Behavioral and Brain Sciences* 22: 577–660.

Barsalou, L.W. 2008. Grounded Cognition. *Annual Review of Psychology* 59: 617–645.

Bergen, B.K. *Louder than words: The new science of how the mind makes meaning*. New York: Basic Books.

Brettschneider, Frank. 2008. Horse Race Coverage. *The International Encyclopedia of Communication*. Wolfgang Donsbach, ed. Blackwell Reference Online. http://www.communicationencyclopedia.com/subscriber/tocnode?id=g9781405131995_chunk_g978140513199513_ss23-1

Chong, D. and J.N. Druckman. 2007. Framing Theory. *Annual Review of Political Science* 10: 103–126.

Clark, H. H. 1973. Space, Time, Semantics, and the Child, ed. T. E. Moore, *Cognitive Development and the Acquisition of Language*, 27–83. New York, NY: Academic Press.

Druckman, J.N. What's It All About? Framing in Political Science, *Perspectives on Framing*, ed. G. Keren, 279–301. New York, NY: Taylor and Francis.

Druckman, J.N., and M. Parki. 2005. The Impact of Media Bias: How Editorial Slant Affects Voters. *The Journal of Politics* 67: 1030–1049.

Fauconnier, G. 1997. *Mappings in Language and Thought*. Cambridge, UK.: Cambridge University Press.

Fauconnier, G., and M.B. Turner. 1998. Conceptual integration networks. *Cognitive Science* 22: 133–187.

Fausey, C.M. and T. Matlock. 2011. Can Grammar Win Elections? *Political Psychology* 32: 563–574.

Feldman, J. 2008. *From Molecule to Metaphor: A Neural Theory of Language*. MIT Press.

Gallese, V., and G. Lakoff. 2005. The Brain's Concepts: The Role of the Sensory–Motor System in Reason and Language. *Cognitive Neuropsychology 22*:455–479.

Gibbs, R.W. 1994. *The Poetics of Mind: Figurative Thought, Language, and Understanding*. New York, NY: Cambridge University Press.

Gibbs, R.W. 1997. How Language Reflects the Embodied Nature of Creative Cognition. *Creative thought*, eds. T. Ward, S. Smith, and J. Vaid, 351–373. Washington, D.C.: American Psychological Association.

Gibbs, R.W. 2006. *Embodiment and Cognitive Science*. New York: Cambridge University Press.

Gibbs, R.W., and T. Matlock. 2008. Metaphor, Imagination, and Simulation: Psycholinguistic Evidence. *Cambridge Handbook of Metaphor and Thought*, ed. R. Gibbs, 161–176. New York: Cambridge University Press.

Gibbs, R.W., and S. Nascimento, S. 1996. How We Talk When We Talk about Love: Metaphorical Concepts and Understanding Love Poetry. *Empirical approaches to literature and aesthetics,* eds. R. Kreuz and M. MacNealy. Norwood, NJ: Ablex.

Glenberg, A., and V. Gallese. 2012. Action-based Language: A Theory of Language Acquisition, Comprehension, and Production. *Cortex*, 48: 902–922.

Johnson, M. 1987. *The Body in the Mind: The Bodily Basis of Meaning, Imagination, and Reason*. Chicago, IL: The University of Chicago Press.

Johnson, M. 2007. *The Meaning of the Body: Aesthetics of Human Understanding*. Chicago, IL: The University of Chicago Press.

Kahneman, D., and A. Tverky. 2000. *Choices, Values, and Frames*. New York, NY: Cambridge University Press.

Kövecses, Z. 2000. *Metaphor and Emotion: Language, Culture, and Body in Human Feeling*. New York, NY: Cambridge University Press.

Lakoff, G. 1996. *Moral Politics: How Liberals and Conservatives Think*. Chicago, IL: The University of Chicago Press.

Lakoff, G. 2008. *The Political Mind: Why you can't Understand 21st-century American Politics with an 18th-Century Brain*. New York, NY: Penguin Press.

Lakoff, G., and M. Johnson. 1980. *Metaphors We Live By*. Chicago, IL: The University of Chicago Press.

Lakoff, G., and M. Johnson. 1999. *Philosophy in the Flesh*. Chicago, IL: The University of Chicago Press.

Lakoff, G., and E. Wehling. 2012. *The Little Blue Book: The Essential Guide to Thinking and Talking Democratic*. New York, NY: Free Press.

Landau, M.J., Sullivan, D., and J. Greenberg. 2009. Evidence that Self-Relevant Motives and Metaphoric Framing Interact to Influence Political and Social Attitudes. *Psychological Science* 20: 1421–1427.

Lau, R. R. 1982. Negativity in Political Perception. *Political Behavior* 4: 353–377.

Matlock, T. 2004. Fictive Motion as Cognitive Simulation. *Memory and Cognition* 32: 1389–1400.

Matlock, T. 2012. Framing Political Messages with Grammar and Metaphor-How Something is Said may be as Important as What is Said. *American Scientist* 100: 478–483.

Narayanan, S. 1999. Moving Right Along: A Computational Model of Metaphorical Reasoning about Events. In *Proceedings of the National Conference on Artificial Intelligence* (AAAI '99), 121–28.

Sheets-Johnstone, M. 1999. *The Primacy of Movement*. Amsterdam: John Benjamins.

Talmy, L. 1983. How Language Structures Space. *Spatial Orientation: Theory, Research, and Application*, eds. H. Pick and L. P. Acredolo, 225–282. New York, NY: Plenum Press.

Talmy, L. 2000. *Toward a Cognitive Semantics*. Cambridge, MA: MIT Press.

Zwaan, R.A. 2004. The Immersed Experiencer: Toward an Embodied Theory of Language Comprehension. *The psychology of learning and motivation, Volume 44*, ed. B.H. Ross, 35–62. New York: Academic Press.

13

# *Think of it as:* Spacebuilders and Grounding in Public Science Discourse

CAROL LYNN MODER

## 1 Introduction

In cognitive linguistics, early studies focused on metaphor as a cognitive process, rather than on a usage-based examination of metaphorical expressions (Lakoff and Johnson 1980, 1999). Given this focus, researchers gave scant attention to the form of metaphorical expressions and their relation to their discourse context. In Blending Theory, Fauconnier and Turner (2002) continue the focus on the cognitive aspects of metaphor—as one of several realizations of the mental process of blending—but they also grant a greater role to the linguistic form of the expression that cues the blend. Drawing from Fauconnier's concept of spacebuilders (Fauconnier 1994), Fauconnier and Turner posit that particular grammatical expressions cue the listener in constructing a blend. While Fauconnier and Turner illustrate the blending process with contextually authentic examples, they do not specifically consider situational discourse relations—the ways that speaker, hearer, setting, and genre might play a role in the mappings that a metaphorical expression might cue. The mental spaces approach outlined in Oakley and Coulson (2008) extends the theory to incorporate discourse-based factors. In their analysis of a political metaphor in a radio news program, they adapt Langacker's concept of grounding (1999), and illustrate how the situational knowledge of the speech event and its purposes and participants cue the ongoing mapping in the discourse. The work of Oakley and Coulson sug-

*Language and the Creative Mind.*
Mike Borkent, Barbara Dancygier, and Jennifer Hinnell (eds).

gests that a mental spaces model supplemented with a focus on discourse-based grounding best accounts for the novel use of metaphor in this genre.

In this paper, we employ such a discourse-based mental spaces approach to examine the use of metaphorical expressions in scientists' public discourse about new findings, focusing on expressions introduced by the spacebuilder *think of* __ *as* __. In the analysis, the study draws on prior work investigating the relations between metaphorical expressions and the grounding of discourse relations between speakers and hearers (Cameron 2003; Semino 2008; Moder 2008, 2010a, 2010b).

In a detailed analysis of the use of metaphors in science education, Cameron (2003) suggests that effective metaphors mediate conceptual alterity—differences in knowledge and understanding—between the teacher and the students. Cameron divides the metaphors used in her data into two kinds: conventionalized and deliberate. Conventionalized metaphors frequently occurred in the discourse with relatively fixed meanings shared by members of the speech community. Deliberate metaphors were those coined by a speaker for a particular purpose in a particular discourse context. Deliberate metaphors occurred as dynamic constructions intended to create learning opportunities, though in some cases the particular metaphors used were not effective owing to hearer confusion about which aspects of the source domain to map onto the target domain. In a similar vein, Semino (2008) suggests that scientific knowledge is constructed through social processes that require speakers and hearers to negotiate gaps between expert and general knowledge. The work of Cameron and Semino highlights the critical importance of considering the extent to which a speaker accommodates the listener's knowledge of both target domain knowledge and source domain knowledge in the use of a metaphorical expression.

The negotiation of knowledge gaps can be complicated by varying levels of metaphor entrenchment in the speaker and hearer's discourse communities. In science, it is common to distinguish explanatory metaphors used to teach scientific concepts from what Boyd has called theory constitutive metaphors (Boyd 1993). Explanatory metaphors vary in their conventionality; some metaphors are used commonly in instruction within a discipline, whereas others would be more like Cameron's dynamically constructed deliberate metaphors. Theory constitutive metaphors are an intrinsic part of the linguistic repertoire of a scientific community. Boyd suggests such metaphors are inextricably linked to the development and experimental testing of a particular theory. Indeed, he suggests that members of the theoretical community would have difficulty expressing key concepts and processes without using language that references the metaphor. An example of a theory constitutive metaphor cited by Boyd (1983) is the 'brain as computer', a metaphor inherent in terms like *processing, modules, working memory, accessing, retrieval, storage* and many others. Boyd and Kuhn (1979:1993) have both argued that change in scientific theory is brought about by concomitant shifts in the dominant scientific metaphor. In Kuhn's terms: 'theory change ... is accompanied by a change in some of the relevant metaphors and in the corresponding parts of the network of similarities through which terms attach to nature' (Kuhn [1979]1993: 539). Kuhn points out that such changes in the way terms attach to nature result from empirical evidence that puts pressure on the accepted relations, but he also notes that changes in the similarity network may or may not result in changes in the theory itself. The deep entrenchment of theory constitutive metaphors in the language and thinking of members of a scientific community and the long path to metaphor shift may pose problems for those who seek to communicate new findings to the general public. The conceptual alterity created by the inaccessibility to the general public of scientifically entrenched source-target mappings may lead to problematic mappings in discourse contexts.

The questions of discourse context, accessibility, and linguistic form are central to Moder's studies of metaphorical and non-metaphorical linguistic expressions in news magazine discourse (Moder 2008, 2010a, 2010b). These studies have highlighted the relevance of prior discourse activation and particular linguistic forms in cuing metaphorical mappings. Based on an analysis of expressions in which the form *like* precedes a noun phrase, Moder finds that differing forms of the constructions used in metaphorical expressions provide distinct cues to the hearer about the accessibility of the information in the prior discourse context; more accessible concepts are coded with linguistic forms that cue the listener to connect prior information to the source domain, whereas less accessible information is encoded with forms that cue the listener to open relationally linked spaces (Moder 2010b). Moder posits specifically that two common constructions used to express metaphorical mappings, *It's like NP* and NP *be a* NP, direct the listener in mapping the relevance of the utterance to the prior discourse. In the *It's like* NP construction, *like* functions as a spacebuilder, alerting the hearer to open a new space for extended relational links between two discourse entities, while the NP *be a* NP construction elaborates the discourse entity in support of the main discourse topic with the meanings of the metaphorical expressions explicitly elaborated in the discourse context preceding and following the expression (Moder 2008, 2010a).

In order to more fully elaborate the way the speaker's construal of the listener's knowledge informs the dynamic use of metaphor in discourse, it is critical to further examine spacebuilders and the mapping of metaphorical expressions in domains where the reduction of conceptual alterity is a primary goal. The public science domain is of particular interest because it involves participants with widely discrepant background knowledge of the target domain. The metaphorical expressions in this domain may encode mappings that are conventional to the scientist, but novel to the public audience or they may encode deliberate novel metaphors. The success with which the participants negotiate conceptual alterity is critical to the effectiveness of the metaphorical mappings in this domain.

## 2 Spacebuilders in Public Science Discourse

In this paper we focus on the mappings cued by an explicit spacebuilder often used to introduce metaphorical expressions in science discourse, *think of* __ as __.[1] In spoken American media discourse, the expression *think of* _ *as* _ links a set of possible constructions with varying elements preceding and following it. An examination of the spoken section of the Corpus of Contemporary American English (COCA) indicates that the overwhelmingly most frequent element filling the first slot is the pronoun *it*, suggesting that the fixed expression *think of it as* may serve as an anchor point for the construction network (Goldberg 2006). The slot following *think of it as* is filled most frequently with a Noun Phrase (75% of the exemplars), and of those Noun Phrases the vast majority are indefinite (85%). The *think of it as* _ expression occurs clause initially in about 20% of the exemplars. When it is preceded by a pronoun, *I* is most frequent, followed by *you*, we, and *they*.

This network of constructions can fulfill varying functions within a discourse context, including making explicit the way a discourse entity should be construed within a framing category (...you don't really think of Colorado as a fall destination. *You think of it as a winter destination. But it's really a great fall destination*). The framing category introduced by the expression often invites a metaphorical mapping; this was the case in 40% of the COCA spoken corpus exemplars. When the expression occurs clause initially, it is most likely to introduce a metaphor (78% of clause initial exemplars). The other forms of the construction that are more likely to introduce a metaphor than a non-metaphor are *you can think of it as* and *I like to think of it as*.[2]

The metaphorical expressions for the study were drawn from a researcher-collected corpus of American National Public Radio news maga-

[1] In keeping with a usage-based radical construction grammar approach (cf. Bybee 2010; Croft 2001), we do not further designate the elements in the slots of the construction prior to investigating the specific structure in context.

[2] First person plural and third person pronouns most frequently introduced a category typically associated with an entity, which was then called into question in the subsequent discourse (*We think **of it as** being hopeless. Well, that's often no longer the case.; They think of it as ratings or whatever, and it's not.)*

zine programs (1,000,000 words). Moder (2010b) has observed a number of distinctive properties concerning the use of metaphorical expressions in this genre. Of particular relevance to this study is that the news story is framed by an overview and then presented through edited segments of relatively spontaneous comments by newsmakers or interviewees, interspersed with linking comments and segues by a reporter or host, and closed with a summative comment. When an interviewee uses a metaphorical expression in the story, the host or the reporter may use the metaphor in the overview and/or in the conclusion to frame the story. Such metaphorical framing increases the salience of the metaphor for listener.

We selected segments in which a scientist discussed a recent finding, examining all instances of metaphorical expressions using the spacebuilder *think of __ as __*. Metaphorical expressions were categorized through larger corpus searches as either deliberate explanatory metaphors introduced by the scientist for discourse specific purposes or theory constitutive metaphors common to the scientific field. Examples of each of these two types of metaphorical expressions were then analyzed with respect to the linguistic form of the expression, the position of the spacebuilder in the discourse, the explicitness and position of the mapping of the inferences from source to target domain, and the accessibility of the information relevant to the mappings in the prior discourse context.

We begin with an examination of a deliberate explanatory metaphor and then discuss a problematic use of a theory constitutive metaphor.

## 3 Deliberate Metaphor

The spacebuilder *think of __ as __* occurred often in the science corpus to introduce a deliberate explanatory metaphor at the beginning of a scientist's extended explication of a new research finding. The examples of the three main constructions with which these metaphors were introduced are given in Table 1.

TABLE 1. Deliberate Metaphor Constructions

| | |
|---|---|
| *Think of __ as __* | *Think of it as a revolving door…* |
| *(And* or *So) you can think of __ as __* | *And you can think of it as very similar to how a thermostat works...*<br>*You can think of that continent as an amazing layer cake …* |
| *I like to think of __ as __* | *I like to think of it as a tame tornado...* |

Three of the constructions we described from the COCA spoken corpus feature in the science corpus. The first example in Table 1 shows *think of __* *as* __ initiating the utterance. The second group in Table 1 shows the construction with the second person pronoun *you* and the modal verb *can*. In a few instances, this construction may be preceded by a discourse marker, either *and* or *so,* both markers that signal continuity in the flow of the discourse (Schiffrin 1988). Both of these constructions explicitly cue an epistemic space (Dancygier and Sweetser 2005), in which the speaker is inviting the listener to follow his or her reasoning through the relational mapping between the target and source domain. The third construction in Table 1 uses the subject-verb phrase *I like* followed by an infinitive marker. The *I like* phrase creates a subjective epistemic mapping, highlighting the reasoning as conventional for the speaker. The expression invites the listener to share this conventional path of relational reasoning. All three constructions occurred in the science corpus primarily before metaphors.[3]

Table 1 gives three examples with the most common filler of the first slot, the pronoun *it*. The use of the pronoun *it* codes the discourse entity to which it refers as active and in focus at the time of the utterance (see Chafe 1994; Ariel 1988). Table 1 also shows one use of a definite noun phrase, *that continent*. Such definite phrases code an active discourse entity, but one slightly lower on the accessibility hierarchy (Ariel 1988).

The slot following *as* was typically filled with an indefinite noun phrase. The predominant use of indefinite noun phrases indicates that the entity in this slot is not already accessible in the discourse and is very likely new information. These indefinite noun phrases are typically modified in ways that help to introduce the relational mappings that will be made to the entity in the first slot. In some cases the second slot begins with a phrase that explicitly codes a relation of similarity *(very similar to),* cueing more process-oriented mapping relations between entities.

The deliberate metaphor we will examine in detail is presented in Example (1). In this example, the construction *you can think of* __ *as* __ occurs in a news story that reports the findings of a study conducted at Vanderbilt University on the brain mechanisms that cause impulsivity. The study linked specific deficits in the autoreceptors in the midbrain that act as dopamine sensors with impulsive behavior. In order to explain the function and processes of autoreceptors, Joshua Bucholtz, then a doctoral candidate in neuroscience who worked on the project, deliberately introduces the source domain of home-heating thermostats and then draws relations between this newly mentioned source domain and the already active target domain of autoreceptors. The form of the construction, '*And you can think*

---

[3] As discussed above, these constructions were frequently associated with the introduction of metaphors in the COCA spoken corpus, but in the science corpus the metaphorical association with these constructions was much stronger.

*of it as very similar to how a thermostat works'*, uses the pronoun *it* in the first slot, highlighting the immediate accessibility of the target entity.

Example (1) Autoreceptors as Thermostats

> Host: Everyone makes snap decisions from time to time, but now researchers think they may know why some people are more impulsive than others. NPR's Geoff Brumfiel reports that it may come down to **a kind of chemical thermostat in your brain.**
> BRUMFIEL: Josh Buckholtz is a researcher at Vanderbilt University... Researchers like Buckholtz think that the brains of impulsive people have too much dopamine. Dopamine is a chemical that our brain releases when it wants something....
> BRUMFIEL: Dopamine is produced by neurons in the midbrain. That's the lower-middle bit of the brain. It's then piped out to other regions, where it creates the drive to get the things you want. Normally, sensors in the midbrain, called autoreceptors, keep dopamine at the right level.
> BUCKHOLTZ: **And you can think of it as very similar to how a thermostat works.** In your house, you have a furnace that produces heat and sends it through pipes all over your house, and a thermostat that sends a signal to your furnace to stop producing heat, or to produce more heat if it's too cold.
> BRUMFIEL: The Vanderbilt researchers suspected that **the dopamine thermostats** of highly impulsive people are broken. To find out, they took 32 healthy volunteers—some impulsive, and some not. They scanned their heads and found that, on average, impulsive people had **fewer thermostats**. To test the idea still further, the team gave volunteers a drug that releases dopamine, and scanned their brains again. Sure enough, impulsive people released more dopamine.
>
> ME 7/30/10[4]

Although the expression appears at the beginning of the scientist's turn, the reporter appears to have edited the story to preserve the discourse continuity. The prior utterance introduces '*sensors in the midbrain, called autoreceptors*' as a key discourse entity, making this entity the likely referent of *it* for program listeners. In the slot following *as,* Buckholtz uses a clause that cues a similarly mapping between the active discourse entity, the autoreceptors, and the entity introduced in the *of* phrase, a thermostat.

---

4 All examples are taken from naturally occurring discourse from the corpus under study. Examples are transcribed using orthographic conventions to facilitate reading. Here the abbreviation ME 7/30/10 indicates that the example came from the National Public Radio program *Morning Edition* broadcast on July 30, 2010. TON in the later example refers to the program *Talk of the Nation*. The expression under discussion is presented in **bold face**.

An examination of the prior discourse context indicates that before the new source domain is introduced, several features related to the main discourse topic have been made accessible to listeners. These include impulsivity and its causes, as well as the importance of dopamine and its regulation by sensors in the midbrain. In this example, the source domain has also been previously activated. In the story overview, the host has introduced the general topic of impulsive behavior and the finding related to dopamine sensors: 'it may come down to **a kind of chemical thermostat in your brain'.** Here he previews the specific metaphor that the scientist will use later in the segment. It is notable that the host uses the metaphor in a noun form with the tuning device (Cameron and Deignan 2003) *kind of* to alert the hearer to the metaphorical mapping. Also briefly activated before the spacebuilding construction appears is the lexical item *piped*, which may relate to both the target and source domains.

Following the '*And you can think of it as very similar to how a thermostat works'* construction, the scientist explicitly mentions the elements of the new source domain that correspond to some of the active relations in the target domain. These elements include the house, the furnace producing heat and sending it through pipes all over your house, and the thermostat that sends a signal to the furnace to stop producing heat or to produce more heat. In the edited segment, the scientist does not go on to explicitly map the connections between source and target; it is the reporter in the subsequent turn who does this by first characterizing '*dopamine thermostats*' as '*broken*' in impulsive people and then stating that such people have '*fewer thermostats*'. The first characterization seems to create a more coherent relation in the context of heating thermostats, but the latter less plausible source domain description of the number of thermostats holds better for the findings of the study relating to autoreceptors.

The scientist's use of the source domain of the thermostat is categorized here as a deliberate metaphor for several reasons. First, as we have seen in Example (1), Buckholtz introduces the concept of the thermostat to highlight aspects of the working of dopamine autoreceptors. However, he himself does not present the source-target combination in the form of a noun-noun combination, as we might expect if the term were commonly used in the field.[5] It is first the host and then the reporter who use the terms *chemical thermostat* and *dopamine thermostat* to refer to the mapping. Comparison of the terms Buckholtz uses in this interview with the terms he used in the *Science* article on which the story is based provides further evidence that this metaphorical expression is not characteristic of the field. In writing for a community of fellow scientists, Buckholtz does not use the term ther-

---

[5] See Moder (2004) for a discussion of Noun-Noun metaphorical expressions

mostat at all. He and his co-authors use phrases such as *midbrain autoreceptor availability* and *diminished inhibitory autoreceptor control* (Buckholtz et al. 2010). Furthermore, a search through the *Science* archives for the word *thermostat* found a total of 526 articles in which the term appears. The uses in these articles overwhelmingly refer either to a piece of equipment or to a biological or environmental mechanism related specifically to temperature regulation. Only seven instances used the term *thermostat* to refer to a regulatory mechanism not related to temperature. Four of these referred to various regulatory processes (*molecular thermostat*, *transcriptional thermostat*, a thermostat in the pituitary that regulates hormones, and response regulators in bacteria). Three instances occurred in reviews citing language used in books written by scientists for a general audience (*rhetorical and political thermostat*, *belief systems as simple as thermostats*, and *a genetic thermostat for loneliness)*. The lack of any use of the term *thermostat* to refer to dopamine autoreceptors provides strong evidence that the mapping is not a theory constitutive metaphor inherent in the scientific discourse community.

Though the use of this mapping is demonstrably deliberate in this radio news story, other evidence suggests that it was not an entirely novel use for the speaker. Buckholtz is quoted as using this metaphor in a print source to illustrate the same finding. The metaphor appeared in an August 3, 2010 website posting taken from a Vanderbilt University news release (*Putting the brakes on impulsive behavior*). The consistency of the mapping in the posting with that in the radio story makes it likely that Buckholtz deliberately developed the metaphor in advance to present the autoreceptor findings to the general public. The use of the term *thermostat* may have been more readily available as a model because of its general use to refer to other regulatory mechanisms in science.

We have seen that *think of __ as __* is a spacebuilder that can function in the public science discourse of the radio news magazine genre as part of a construction that introduces a deliberate metaphor, one likely selected by the scientist to make underlying scientific concepts accessible to a general audience. This spacebuilding expression creates an epistemic space in which the listener can join the speaker in reasoning through a set of relational mappings between target domain features already activated in the prior discourse, connecting them to more familiar elements from a newly-introduced source domain. When the correspondences between these domains is explicitly mapped in the discourse, conceptual alterity is reduced and listener comprehension appears be facilitated.

## 4 Theory Constitutive Metaphor

We now consider the use of the spacebuilder *think of _ as_* to introduce a theory constitutive metaphor. The example we have chosen employs a deeply entrenched mapping of molecules and receptors using the metaphor of a lock and key. The first theoretical use of this metaphor is credited to the Nobel prize-winning German chemist Emil Fischer. In 1894, he published a landmark article in which he described the *lock and key* (*Schlüssel und Schloss)* concept for the interactions of an enzyme and substrate. In drawing this metaphorical relation, Fischer particularly noted the influence of geometric structure on the play of chemical affinities, suggesting that for some molecules only a unique key would result in an interlocking chemical process (Fischer 1894). This lock and key concept was later transferred to the interaction of various kinds of receptors and their ligands.

A search of the *Science* archives for the phrase *lock and key* found 136 articles, all of which used the phrase to describe chemical interactions of various kinds. Of interest is the extent to which more recent articles begin to question the validity of this metaphor in light of more recent knowledge in the relevant fields. A 1991 article is titled, 'Rusting of the Lock and Key Model for Protein-Ligand Binding' (Jorgensen 1991). A second article notes that recent findings that question the unique fit of a single substrate into a stable enzyme have 'wreaked havoc on the lock and key world view' (Uversky and Dunker 2008: 1340). In the specific domain of taste receptors—the topic of the example we will examine—a similar shift in the scientific acceptance of the lock and key metaphor has occurred (see Wellendorph, Johansen, and Brauner-Osborne 2009).

Given the deep entrenchment of the traditional lock and key metaphor in scientific theory and its more recent 'rusting' as a result of new research methods and new findings, a scientist who uses the metaphor in the public domain is on shifting ground. We now turn to a discussion of such a problematic use. The topic of the program from which Example (2) comes is a study co-authored by the interviewee Robert Margolskee, a molecular biologist at Monnell Chemical Senses Center. The findings, concerning two new ways that the body can detect sweetness, appeared in the *Proceedings of the National Academy of Sciences* in March 2011. It is important to note that the written paper did not refer to the lock and key metaphor and that its results would not be consistent with the simplistic lock and key model of taste (Yee et al. 2011).

Prior to the segment we will examine, Joe Palca, the host of the program *Talk of the Nation Science Friday,* has introduced the concept of flavor components and the question '*what goes on in your mouth that causes your brain to say sweet?*' He then introduces the study, the author and the main finding of new pathways for detecting sweetness. The segment is an interview, in which the host poses questions to which the scientist responds. Example (2) starts with Palca's first question, to which Margolskee responds by giving an overview of the study, highlighting that the process is '*more complicated than we thought*'. As he begins to explain the process, he uses the terms '*receptor proteins*' and '*sweet-responding taste cells*'. This explanation is meant to serve as background, characterizing what '*we knew about for a while*'. Had he continued, Margolskee would likely have then moved to his intended focus on explaining the new results. However, Palca intervenes with a question, presumably intended to mitigate conceptual alterity by contextualizing the terms used in relation to language more familiar to listeners. Margolskee responds, clarifying these terms. Palca then poses another background question, asking for an explanation of the relation between the chemical interaction and the perception of sweetness. Margolskee's response falls back on the entrenched, but problematic, theory constitutive metaphor: '*So you can think of the sweet receptor protein and the sugar or sweetener as kind of a lock and key...*'.

Example (2) Lock and Key

> PALCA: So what happens? I mean what's going on? We put something sweet in our mouth, and something responds to it. What is that?
> Dr. MARGOLSKEE: Well, we've learned that sweet is a bit more complicated than we thought it was based on work over the past several years. And so our recent work makes it more complicated.
> When you get a sweet substance, a sugar or something artificial like saccharine, it stimulates these receptor proteins on the very outer tips of the sweet-responding taste cells. And we knew about that for a while...
> PALCA: So these are the taste buds?
> Dr. MARGOLSKEE: These are taste cells right in the taste buds. So the taste bud contains about 50 or 100 taste cells, and maybe a quarter of them are responding to sweet stuff, and a different percentage of them will respond to salty and sour and bitter and something called umami, which is actually a Japanese word that has to do with delicious amino acids like monosodium glutamate.
> PALCA: Okay, and so this chemical interaction or biochemical interaction between the protein that makes the receptor on the surface of the taste bud, that's a chemical event. But something happens in the brain that makes this turn into a perception of an event or a sweetness event.
> Dr. MARGOLSKEE: Correct. **So you can think of the sweet receptor protein and the sugar or sweetener as kind of a lock and key**, and when they encounter each other, it opens the lock. The door opens up. It excites the sweet taste cell, and that sends a signal to the brain, to particular centers of the central nervous system that respond to sweet. TON 3/11/2011

The placement of this expression is similar to that which we observed for the deliberate metaphor in Example (1). The *you can think of __ as __* construction occurs at the beginning of the turn, preceded by the discourse marker *so*. Though the construction is similar in form to that in Example (1), it differs in that two definite Noun Phrases, *the sweet receptor protein* and *the sugar or sweetener*, appear in the first slot. Neither of these entities was in immediate focus in the prior discourse, though these entities had been activated earlier. Also different is that the second slot includes a tuning device *kind of* followed by two new discourse entities *lock* and *key*.

When the *think of __ as __* construction introduces the theory constitutive metaphor, a substantial amount of information about the target domain had been previously activated. However, unlike in Example (1), the prior discourse in Example (2) has not put into immediate focus the key entities of the target domain to which the new domain might map, nor has the *lock and key* source domain itself been previewed. Given the detailed and diffuse information activated, the listener would be unlikely to generate a scientifically sound mapping for the metaphor. The theory constitutive metaphor is recruited in order to reduce the conceptual alterity between listeners and the scientist about what had been thought of as basics of the science of taste, but the mapping of the metaphor is made problematic because it describes a model which the scientist's own research has called into question. A full mapping of the metaphor may elucidate prior models of taste perception, but it will paradoxically impede the explanation of the new findings. In order to negotiate this problem, the scientist bleaches the metaphor by restricting his explanation only to currently valid links between domains. For the non-scientist, the resulting mapping lacks the conceptual links the metaphor would best support. The most compelling aspects of the similarity network originally mapped by the lock and key model were the geometric correspondences of the molecules and the receptors and the specificity of the interaction between the receptor and the ligand. Neither of these relations is entirely consistent with current research.

The communicative difficulty of this quandary for the scientist is evidenced in the vagueness of the mapping he provides. Margolskee maps the sweet receptor protein and the sugar as a lock and key. Since the counterpart correspondence is not explicitly mapped, one might assume that these terms are to be linked in the order in which they are mentioned (receptor = lock, sugar = key), and indeed this is the usual mapping. However, greater ambiguity is introduced by the use of '*they*' and '*it*' in the following sentence ('*when they encounter each other, it opens the lock'*). Here it seems that it is the encounter of the two entities that opens the lock. The listener may well wonder whether the receptor is the lock and the sugar is the key or whether the interaction is the key. If the interaction is the key, then what is the lock?

Rather than clarifying this relation in the subsequent utterance, Margolskee shifts to the use of the term '*door*', which does nothing to clarify the continued ambiguity of the referent of *it* in the following sentence, which shifts away from the lock and key to less contested target domain language (*excites, sends signals*). Thus, the need to make use of only those elements of the entrenched theory constitutive metaphor that are not invalidated by current research impairs the effectiveness of the metaphor in increasing listener background knowledge and reducing alterity.

Immediately following the excerpt shown in Example (2), Margolskee transitions from this background information, calling what he has just described into question: '*we thought we knew how that worked, but it turns out it's more complicated*'. He then goes on to discuss the complexity of his findings mentioning '*extra pathways , extra mechanisms*' that '*respond to the metabolic state of the taste cell*'. The lock and key metaphor does not recur in descriptions of the results of the study, but it does recur later in the interview in response to a call-in question about miraculin.

Example (3) Lock and key reprise

> **Margolskee**:...Miraculin is a protein, and you find it in the miracle fruit. And there a number of other related proteins that can be found in special plants and berries, oftentimes in Africa. So in addition to miraculin, you have things called thaumatin, brazzein, monelin. Now, those other proteins, they're intensely sweet on their own. They don't need acid or sour stimuli, and we know how they work. They will bind tightly to the sweet receptor protein. **This is, again, this lock-and-key type of model.** Now, miraculin is a little bit special. It probably doesn't normally bind to the sweet receptor protein—or, at least, **it doesn't bind in a way that will open up the lock.** But at low pH, under acid conditions, either the miraculin adopts a particular conformation or the sweet receptor does, so that it's now perceived as sweet. So it's not that miraculin is working on the sour channel, the sour taste cells or the sour responding taste nerves, it's tricking the sweet taste cells and the sweet-responding taste nerves to say there's something sweet out there. TON 3/11/2011

The use of '*lock and key type model*' in this response suggests that Margolskee has not fully rejected either the theory or its associated metaphor. He appears to have modified the network of similarity to accommodate new findings without abandoning the model. As in Example (2), we see here that he uses lock and key very generally to refer to binding relations between a receptor protein and a stimulus, but the discussion of miraculin's changing conformation, like the results of his own study, whittle away at the more extended mapping the metaphor previously encoded. When a theory constitutive metaphor is thus bleached of the more obvious possible source-target mappings, its value in redressing the conceptual alterity between the scientist and the public is greatly reduced.

We have seen in this example that theory constitutive metaphors may be positioned and make use of constructions and space-builders in a way that is similar to the use of deliberate metaphors in this genre. However, the discourse context reveals subtle differences both in the form of the constructions and the explicitness of the metaphorical mapping in the discourse. The theory constitutive metaphors do not reference the main discourse entity in current focus, but instead provide background on other accessible entities in the target domain. The clearest formal indication of this is the use of definite noun phrases, rather than the pronoun *it,* in the first slot of the *think of __ as __* construction. A further difference is that the theory constitutive metaphors are not elaborated as clearly and extensively either in the prior or the subsequent discourse.

The conventionality of theory constitutive metaphors for the scientist creates the potential for mismatch with the conceptual frameworks of listeners unfamiliar with established mappings. In addition, paradigm shifts and new findings may bleach the empirically supportable mappings of the old metaphors in a way that makes the metaphorical expression less relationally effective for the listener.

## 5 Conclusions

We have discussed the use of the spacebuilder *think of __ as __* by scientists in public discourse about new findings. Within related constructions, this spacebuilder may introduce a source domain for deliberate metaphors in science, but may also introduce a theory constitutive metaphor. In the two examples we have discussed, the spacebuilder occurs in the construction *you can think of __ as*. The target domain of the metaphor fills the first slot. The source domain of the mapping is most typically introduced in the second slot with an indefinite Noun Phrase. The conceptual alterity between the scientist and the listener is addressed in the discourse context through the extensive activation of key information about the target domain prior to the use of the spacebuilder. The construction opens an epistemic space in which the listener can follow the speaker's reasoning through a set of relational mappings that link the source domain to the activated elements of the target domain and provides cues to the listener about the accessibility of the information to be mapped. The anchor construction, in which the first slot of the construction uses the pronoun *it,* cues a main discourse entity that is accessible and in focus. In the science corpus, this was most likely to introduce a deliberate metaphor. A definite noun phrase in the first slot introduces a less accessible discourse entity; this is more likely to occur with theory constitutive metaphors. In both deliberate and theory constitutive metaphor, the spacebuilding construction is followed in the discourse with relational correspondences between the elements of the source domain and the target domain. The explicitness with which these counterpart correspondences are established by the speaker may be affected by the speaker's sensitivity to differences in speaker/listener conceptual frameworks. In the case of deliberate metaphors, the scientist is typically aware of the need for clear and explicit mapping. This results in more explicit and more immediate activation in the prior discourse of elements of the target domain and in the following discourse of the correspondences between target and source domains. With theory constitutive metaphors the conventionality of metaphors for scientists may pose a barrier to listener understanding. Even more problematic is the use of a theory constitutive metaphor that is shifting to accommodate new findings.

The results of this study suggest that discourse accessibility and awareness of the need to mitigate conceptual alterity are the keys to unlocking effective science metaphors in public discourse.

## References

Ariel, M. 1988. Referring and Accessibility. *Journal of Linguistics* 24: 65–87.

Boyd, R. 1993. Metaphor and Theory Change: What is 'Metaphor' a Metaphor for? *Metaphor and Thought,* A. Ortony, ed., 481–532. Cambridge: Cambridge University Press.

Buckholtz, J. W., M. T. Treadway, R. L. Cowan, N. D. Woodward, R. Li, A. S. Ansari, R. M. Baldwin, A.N. Scwartzmann, E. S. Shelby, C. E. Smith, R. M. Kessler, and D. H. Zald. 2010. Dopaminergic Network Differences in Human Impulsivity. *Science* 329: 532.

Bybee, Joan. 2010. *Language, Usage and Cognition*. Cambridge: Cambridge University Press.

Cameron, L. 2003. *Metaphor in Educational Discourse*. London: Continuum.

Cameron, L. and A. Deignan. 2003. Combining Large and Small Corpora to Investigate Tuning Devices Around Metaphor in Spoken Discourse, *Metaphor and Symbol* 18: 149–160.

Chafe, W. 1994. *Discourse, Consciousness, and Time*. Chicago: University of Chicago Press.

Croft, W. 2001. *Radical Construction Grammar: syntactic theory in Typological Perspective*. Oxford; Oxford University Press.

Dancygier, B. and E. Sweetser. 2005. *Mental Spaces in Grammar: Conditional Constructions*. Cambridge: Cambridge University Press.

Fauconnier, G. 1994. *Mental Spaces: Aspects of Meaning Construction in Natural Language*. Cambridge: Cambridge University Press.

Fauconnier, G. and M. Turner. 2002. *The Way We Think*. New York: Basic Books.

Fischer, E. 1894. Synthesen in der Zuckergruppe II. *Berichte der Deutschen Chemischen Gesellschaft* 27: 3189–3232.

Goldberg, A. 2006. *Constructions at Work: The Nature of Generalization in Language*. Oxford: Oxford University Press.

Jorgensen, W. L. 1991 'Rusting of the Lock and Key Model for Protein–Ligand Binding' *Science* 254: 954–955.

Kuhn, T. S. 1979; 1993. Metaphor in Science. *Metaphor and Thought*, A. Ortony, ed., 533–542. Cambridge: Cambridge University Press.

Lakoff, G. and M. Johnson. 1980. *Metaphors We Live By*. Chicago: University of Chicago Press.

Lakoff, G. and M. Johnson. 1999. *Philosophy in the Flesh*. New York: Basic Books.

Langacker, R.W. 1999. *Grammar and Conceptualization*. Berlin: Mouton de Gruyter.

Moder, C. L. 2004. *Icebox moms* and *hockey dads*: Context and the mapping of N–N metaphorical expressions. *Language, Culture, and Mind*, Michel Achard and Suzanne Kemmer (eds), 109–121. Stanford: CSLI Publications.

Moder, C. L. 2008. *It's like making a soup*: Metaphors and Similes in Spoken News Discourse. *Language in the Context of Use: Cognitive Approaches to Language and Language Learning*, Andrea Tyler, Yiyoung Kim, and Mari Takada (eds), 301–320. Berlin: Mouton de Gruyter.

Moder, C. L. 2010a. Form, Discourse and Construction: American English *like* NP. *Meaning, Form and Body*, Faye Parrill, Vera Tobin, and Mark Turner (eds), 203–222. Stanford: CSLI Publications.

Moder, C. L. 2010b. Two puzzle pieces: Fitting Discourse Context and Constructions into Cognitive Metaphor Theory. *English Text Construction* 2: 294–320.

Oakley, T. and S. Coulson. 2008. Connecting the dots: Mental Spaces and metaphoric language in discourse. *Mental Spaces in Discourse and Interaction*, T. Oakley and A.. Hougaard (eds), 27–50. Amsterdam: John Benjamins.

Putting the brakes on impulsive behavior. http://www.futurity.org/health-medicine/putting-the-brakes-on-impulsive-behavior

Semino, E. 2008. *Metaphor in Discourse*. Cambridge: Cambridge University Press.

Schiffrin, D. 1988. *Discourse Markers*. Cambridge: Cambridge University Press.

Uversky, V.N. and A. K. Dunker. 2008. Controlled Chaos. Science 322: 1340–1341.

Wellendorph, P., L. D. Johansen, and H. Bräuner-Osborne. 2009. Molecular Pharmacology of Promiscuous Seven Transmembrane Receptors Sensing Organic Nutrients. *Molecular Pharmacology* 76: 453–465.

Yee, K.K., S.K. Sukumaran, R. Kotha, T.A. Gilbertson, and R.F. Margolskee, 2011. Glucose transporter and ATP-gated K+ ($K_{ATP}$) metabolic sensors are present in type 1 taste receptor 3 (T1r3)-expressing taste cells. *Proceedings of the National Academy of Sciences* 108: 5431–5436.

# 14

# Conceptual Blending in Allegorical Political Rhetoric: Creativity in Managalase (Papua New Guinea) Oral Tradition

WILLIAM H. MCKELLIN

## 1 Introduction

In this chapter I will examine the contribution of Cognitive Linguistics to our understanding of the emergent mappings of the cognitive allegories (Harris and Tolmie 2011) used by the Managalase of Papua New Guinea to negotiate, create, and manipulate social and political relationships. These allegories are both a means of negotiating important political relationships and occasions to demonstrate verbal artistry. Conceptual Integration and Blending Theory is developing from an approach that commonly focusses on the product, rather than the process of conceptual integration, into a theoretical model that attempts to elucidate the cognitive and social aspects of language processing (Hougaard 2005). This examination of Managalase allegories will explore the dynamic interaction of speakers and their audiences that produces creative conceptual and social blends.

Managalase political allegories, *ha'a*, are a genre of oral performance employed by politically experienced men and women with extensive knowledge of oral traditions and involvement in politics. They are an example of a ubiquitous process (Gibbs 2011) in which speakers employ met-

*Language and the Creative Mind*.
Mike Borkent, Barbara Dancygier, and Jennifer Hinnell (eds).

aphors in extended discourse. In performances of ha'a, Managalase draw upon conventional allegorical motifs to strategically arrange marriages, create political alliances through pig exchanges and feasting, and make subtle accusations about others. Performances of Managalase allegories may range from brief statements to elaborate narratives with complex, multiple motifs, and thematic constructions. They may occur as private interchanges between two parties, or public orations with large, responsive audiences. Even in the public arena of the village, these metaphorical negotiations shield the participants from explicit attributions of intent and public political commitments. In many ways, they are similar to the political 'trial balloons' from unnamed sources in North American politics. Ha'a's indirectness is designed to deceive a general audience.

Managalase refer to this indirect or hidden communication as 'suara kuaraman', likened to taking an alternate path through the forest that circumvents the more public route through a village. Ha'a initially seem to be simple stories that may be a bit out of context, but to the politically and rhetorically astute, these stories offer alternative paths for interpretation. As Fauconnier noted, 'Typically, a particular context or discourse creates a strong bias for following a particular accessing path, and other paths formally possible for the single sentence form are not even considered consciously. These paths can remain available, however' (Fauconnier 2006: 663). Speakers employ ha'a to purposely leave two, if not more paths available for a well-informed, knowing audience.

If the audience responds by recognizing a story as a particular kind of genre event (Steen 2011), an allegory, replying in kind engages them in negotiation. If in the end the negotiations fail, the narrative is dismissed as an inconsequential story, enabling the participants to save face, and give them utterable deniability.

I discovered this allegorical form of political rhetoric after spending about a year in Jinebuina Village, on the Managalase Plateau in Oro Province, Papua New Guinea. I had anticipated studying the same kinds of forceful rhetoric reported in the New Guinea Highlands, in which big-men paced up and down the central mall rallying their kinsmen and supporters and berating the recalcitrant to take part in multi-village feasts that would bring renown to the leader and his partners. After a year, all I had heard were the Village Counselor's pleas to cut the grass or work on the roads, interspersed with the occasional call for assistance in preparing for a feasting exchange.

Then one evening, as I sat on the veranda of my house, Evelyn, an older widow with two sons who were of marriageable age, started to speak to the village. For all to hear she said,

> When I was a young woman and visited peoples' houses, they would give me young fresh, green betelnut to chew. Now when I visit people they give me old hard orange betelnut. When I chew it, it makes my gums bleed.

After she spoke, Evelyn waited for responses from her audience. There were a few laughs, some calls for more betelnut, and chatter that led to a meeting between Evelyn and her fellow kinsmen. While I was able to follow her story, I had no idea of its meaning, so I asked her younger son, my assistant. He replied that he did not know either; her story, he said, was one of those 'trick' stories, ha'a, which are intended for older people. Her speech, I discovered, followed on the rumors I had heard earlier in the day while I was with her in her garden concerning her eldest, unmarried son and a young widow. Evelyn's ha'a led to a discussion in the privacy of her house, to consider if the elopement of her eldest son with the widow, was acceptable to his kinsmen, and if they would legitimate the union by contributing to his gift of bridewealth to the prospective wife's kinsmen, thereby establishing wife-giver/wife-receiver affinal relationships between the respective sets of kin.

This story introduced me to the intricate, hidden dimensions of suara kuaraman among the Managalase, which is similar to indirect forms of discourse found elsewhere in Papua New Guinea (Aufenanger 1962; Merlan and Rumsey 1991; Strathern 1975).

In the village, I found it entertaining to compose allegories, but nerve-wracking to be the intended audience, expected to reply on the spot to the speaker in a way that would not commit me to an interpretation whose consequences I did not fully appreciate. The real-time, online processing of allegories—their composition, responses, and interpretations in sensitive political settings—raises questions about the ways in which conventional motifs are instantiated, and interpreted by participants, during speeches before live audiences.

Ha'a enable participants to renegotiate or re-enforce the social and political relationships that serve as the social grounding of the discourse. Through these stories, Managalase speakers are able to creatively explore what is socially and politically possible. As Brandt observed:

> ...it is possible, and indeed common, for us to construct online fictions—not for their entertainment value, as one might think, but to create inferences about some real-world circumstance.
>
> (Brandt 2008: 112)

Ha'a provide us with an opportunity to examine two concepts in Cognitive Linguistics—grounding and intersubjectivity or shared intention. Negotiations and ha'a in particular are based on fluid and perspectivally distinct assessments of relationships. Ha'a also call into question the extent to which the nature of negotiations and Managalase language ideology support the assumption that participants must share intentions and mutual knowledge (Brandt and Brandt 2005; Croft 2009; Hougaard and Oakley 2008).

Conceptual Integration and Blending Theory provides theoretical tools to examine how speakers create these narratives with conventional motifs as they engage audiences in subtle and often lively performances. Discourse, interaction, and the social dimensions of language use have recently received attention with the goal of making the cognitive processing of language in social settings more transparent (Hougaard 2008) and offering a means of examining the ways that these conventional motifs are creatively deployed in social and political negotiations.

## 2 Mental Spaces, Conceptual Integration, and Blending

Mental Space Theory was developed to account for the dynamic, online processing of linguistic information (Fauconnier 1997) and has given rise to Conceptual Integration and Blending Theory (Fauconnier and Turner 1998; Fauconnier and Turner 2002). Conceptual Integration and Blending occurs as the result of the selective projections and mapping across Input spaces (referred to by numbers), under the guidance of a Generic spaces to create a new frame in the Blending space through the processes of composition, completion, and elaboration (Fauconnier and Turner 2002). In alternative theoretical formulations the numbered Inputs are replaced by Presentation and Representation spaces, while the Generic and Blending spaces are replaced by additional Grounding or Semiotic spaces and a variety of alternatives to the Blending space (Brandt and Brandt 2005; Oakley and Coulson 2008). In these more recent formulations, developed to examine language processing in social interaction, grounding is characterized as:

> [the] situational knowledge [that] contributes to the understanding and management of discourse. Grounding involves specifying (1) the discourse participants and their roles, (2) the rhetorical situation that serves as the immediate local context for the current communicative act, (3) the situational and (4) argumentative relevance of the mental spaces network.
>
> (Oakley and Coulson 2008: 30)

In many ways, this characterization of Grounding is very similar to Steen's concept of 'genre event' in which genres 'provide sociocultural, psychological, and formal (linguistic or multimodal) orientation as well as order to people in the complex universe of media and communication, even in the academe' (2011: 21).

Cognitive linguists have elaborated upon the original concepts of Mental Spaces Theory by recognizing additional processes such as frame shifting (Coulson 2001) and frame metonymy (Panther and Radden 1999), and expanding the types of mental spaces to include Narrative Spaces (Dancygier 2012). Narrative spaces are a particular form of mental space that are constructed and limited by the linguistic expressions of the text. They contribute to the emergence of the story as the links between narrative spaces establish coherence in story construction. Narrative spaces also present the narrators' viewpoint (Dancygier 2012).

## 3 Managalase Genres and Motifs

Managalase distinguish a number of genres of oral tradition. Each is associated with different expectations for composition and performance, and each implies different sources of knowledge as the basis for composition and comprehension. Many forms of oral tradition and verbal art are treated as part of an individual's property or estate, with rights of ownership to particular songs and stories. These forms of traditional knowledge are tied directly to the place to which they refer, and are shared among the people who also share the crops grown and game hunted at these sites.

This social division of authoritative knowledge forms the basis of Managalase epistemology and language ideology. From it, they derive their hesitancy to make claims about others' knowledge and intentions, a reticence they share with other groups in Papua New Guinea (Duranti 2010; McKellin 1984; McKellin 1990; Robbins and Rumsey 2008; Schieffelin 2008). These assumptions are somewhat at odds with our common suppositions that communication requires speakers and listeners to share intentions and knowledge.

Ha'a or 'allegory' is only one of a number of genres described as *suara kuaraman*, 'indirect speech'. In addition to ha'a, two forms of song, *ivitit* and *java*, employ indirect metaphorical allusions. *Ivitit*, a genre of personal song and dreams are among the forms of suara kuaraman, Dreams are also a form of indirect communication between the dreamer and a dead relative. These indirect forms of discourse hide or mask the intentions of the speaker, particularly in negotiations, and are the subject of *naham*, 'explication' or 'interpretation'.

Motifs are named, conventionalized patterns of communication that have prototypic interpretations. They are often identified metonymically by one of their elements, which evokes memories of the Presentation-Representation pairs and Blends from past performances. Some motifs, like the betelnut ha'a described earlier, are recognized throughout the Plateau, while others are based on more privileged knowledge such as the motifs used by particular clans, or figures based on songs like ivitit or stories associated with specific places, and only known to their owners and their kinsmen.

The ability to use ha'a as a rhetorical form, either as a speaker or member of the audience, is dependent on familiarity with a range of motifs and their previous publically recognized interpretations, awareness of the immediate social context and alternatives that a speaker or his or audience may be willing to entertain, and opportunities to develop performative competence. Consequently, access to and knowledge of a large repertoire of motifs demonstrates a speaker's broad network of social affiliations, knowledge of oral traditions, and familiarity with previous performances and interpretations of ha'a through extensive political activity. Members of the audience also must be able to demonstrate the same broad understanding of motifs that the speaker might use, and an awareness of social activities that might be the subject of the speech. Thus, a person's ability to develop the skill to compose clever allegories and interpret them is dependent upon the occasions when he or she can engage in important social exchanges and political negotiations. Given the constraints on learning particular motifs, speakers can restrict their audience to a targeted few by their selection of motifs.

Though ha'a are composed using conventional motifs, interpreting ha'a is not simple or straightforward. Every ha'a, particularly those used in negotiations, enables the speaker to offer alternative paths of interpretation and action. The various audience members must identify the real or hypothetical social actions and contexts that may precipitate a performance and use their own repertoire to identify a contextually appropriate motif and interpretation.

By restricting the audience and obscuring their goals, speakers are able to reduce potential jealousies among exchange partners and avoid the public loss of face if negotiations fail.

## 4 Motifs and Blending

Managalase ha'a operate at two different levels of granularity (Oakley and Crisp 2011), each of which offers the participants different alternative paths. At one level, ha'a is a genre event that offers the options of treating a performance either as an allegory or as an everyday narrative. Once the allegorical level is evoked metonymically by the presentation of an element from the motif-frame, the motif-frames offer additional alternative paths for composition, completion, and elaboration. An accomplished narrator forces audience members to evaluate and reevaluate several possible metonymically evoked motif-frames as the negotiation unfolds.

From the path established by the motif-frame, the audience members proceed to construct mappings and produce a blend or blends that conform to each of their social assumptions and expectations that serve as the ground for the interaction. They use their knowledge of the motif, its prior uses, current social information, and the changes in social relationships that might be implicated by the blend in their acceptance and rejection of possible projections. If the negotiations are successful, the blend created by the ha'a is instrumental in creating new or maintaining old social relationships. If the negotiations fail, the participants have the option of reassessing the genre event and reverting to the frame in which the narrative is an everyday story.

The multiple paths made available by motif-frames will be clearer with two examples. While a betelnut ha'a such as the one told by Evelyn may appear simple, it may be used to arrange a marriage or negotiate an exchange of pigs. In both cases, the stakes are considerable for the parties involved. One of my assistants was single when I first worked in Jinebuina. He said that he carefully examined betelnuts offered to him when he visited other villages, because the gift of a betelnut could also evoke the betelnut motif-frame. If he took and chewed a betelnut that had a design carved into the skin the act may have unwittingly committed him to marriage.

Another common motif is the *kua* 'dog' ha'a. Dogs, among the Managalase, are not man's best friend. While dogs play an essential role in tracking pigs or marsupials, once they find game, instead of leaving it for their masters, they may run off into the bush and eat it themselves. The Managalase phrase for stealing, *neze abenan*, literally translated is 'take to the bush', which describes theft as hiding something (or someone) away from the watchful eyes of others. Thus, dog ha'a are used to convey theft or loss. Dogs also have other undesirable characteristics that may be evoked by their mention: they are promiscuous and eat the scraps that even pigs reject.

I found this motif useful towards the end of my first stay in Jinebuina. When I first arrived in the village, I had two bush knives, which I marked by carving my initials into the handle. After living in the village for only a month, one of the knives went missing. I had forgotten about the knife until we were preparing to leave, almost two years later, when a man from another village whom I did not recognize came to visit. As he sat next to me on my veranda, I noticed that he was carrying a bush knife that had my initials carved in the handle. Accusing the man of theft risked the potentially dangerous loss of face for him and me. He may have unwittingly received the knife as a gift. So, as he walked down the steps of my house and headed up the village I said, 'There goes someone's dog and he is carrying something, I wonder what it is?' The man kept going, but the following day, I found my bush knife on the bench of my veranda. He was not publically accused of theft and I was not responsible for his loss of face.

The motif-frames evoked by presenting ha'a offer audience members a variety of elements to create projections and construct blends. Each audience member's assessment of their current and prospective relationship with the speaker contributes to selecting the path they take.

## 5 Blending in Allegorical Interactions

While ha'a can be brief statements, spoken in apparent privacy to mask the meaning from unintended audiences, or to enable a person to save face, they are also performed with audiences who participate in their telling and thereby demonstrate their own verbal artistry and political acumen. The interaction that follows is only a portion of a long saga of events that shaped the village of Jinebuina before, during, and after my first extended stay. It involves the delicate balancing of social and political affiliations between two major factions of the community that might be soothed by a feast that would reconcile the two sides. Negotiations for the feast were jeopardized by an elopement that could upstage the reconciliation and force a postponement of the feast. To complicate matters further, the elopement itself also threatened to realign the social relationships of the participants in the performance, by transforming clan mates, who should assist each other in exchange, into affines and exchange partners, separated by their obligations to support the 'prospective groom' by giving bridewealth to the bride's family.

Prior to my arrival, a fight had broken out among members of the Bun'ora clan over participation in the funerary rituals following the death of a clan mate. One set of Bun'ora brothers, led by Makai the Village Counsellor, held a mourning feast. Baho and his close kinsmen among Bun'ora were invited, but the message arrived too late for them to participate. When they did arrive, a fight broke out between Makai's close kin and Baho's cohort over the timing of the feast. During the melee, Baho hit one of Makai's brothers, seriously injuring him with a blow to the head with a heavy wooden broadsword. Makai's brother recovered after several weeks in the hospital but he carried a three-inch indentation in his forehead that served as a constant reminder of the fight.

Following the melee, the cluster of Bun'ora houses at the top of the village dispersed, and Baho and some of his other close kinsmen moved from Jinebuina to establish a new village at Kavan. Baho said that he would not return to live in Jinebuina or use his Bun'ora hunting land in the mountains nearby. Instead, Baho strengthened his ties to the Kuba'ora clan. Much to Makai's dismay, and in a blow to his prestige as a political leader, the fight divided the village of Jinebuina and the Bun'ora clansmates who should collaborate in exchanges.

For several years, rumors circulated in the village about an imminent feast in which Makai and his brothers would receive a pig from Baho in recompense for their injuries. Unfortunately, before the feast could take place, Makai died of dysentery and plans for the pig feast evaporated for a time. However, just before Baho's speech, rumors began to circulate again about the long awaited reconciliation feast.

There were four participants in the interchange: Baho, the first speaker, who presents the ha'a, Kivide, who responds first, followed by Nevil, and finally Dajahare, who provides the '*naham*' interpretation. Each had differing affiliations to the Bun'ora clan and therefore each man approached the interchange with different networks of social relationships that provide the ground for their interactions and narrative viewpoints. At the beginning of this performance, Baho and Nevil had a close relationship because they were also fellow members of the Kuba'ora clan. Kivide was most closely allied with Makai's faction of Bun'ora, and Dajahare was primarily identified with a third clan, but maintained some Bun'ora and Kuba'ora affiliations. Though Dajahare and Baho were kinsmen, Baho's marriage to Dajahare's sister made their predominant relationship that of affines or in-laws and exchange partners. This was the political landscape, the social ground, when Baho appeared one afternoon and stood in the village mall, in front of Nevil's house and told the story that follows.

Baho's story is ostensibly an account of hunting with dogs and looking for weaving cane. The audience members' initial task is to determine the genre of the story to evoke expectations that are appropriate for genre-level mental spaces.

Baho mentions several objects that could metonymically evoke a ha'a genre event and several different motif-frames: the dogs, the path, and the fallen tree that blocked it, as well as the cane for weaving. The Presentation space of Baho's ha'a is expressed by three structurally distinct portions of his story: Lines 1–5 establish Baho's viewpoint, recalling past events in Jinebuina, where he had lived and raised dogs until his departure for the new village at Kavan. In Line 6, Baho's viewpoint is altered as he changes to the present. Perhaps more significantly, he also builds a new epistemologically distinct narrative space that presents hypothetical events—the blockage of a path with a fallen tree, which he could not see before setting out to look for cane. Lines 11–12 indicate another change of viewpoint with a return to past tense when he states that he found an alternative to weaving with cane from his hunting territory so he returned to Kavan.

**Baho's Ha'a[1]**

1. Listen to me.
2. Before, I raised many dogs when I lived in Jinebuina.
3. I raised many dogs, went up into the mountains, caught game, brought it back, and ate it.
4. Then, a little while ago, we fought, (I) went down there (to Kavan) and my dogs died. I no longer go up to the mountains as a result. I no longer go up to the mountains.

[1] The Managalase text of this narrative is available on request.

5. I no longer go up to the mountains.
6. Now, because I was living down there, I couldn't see if a big wind came and blew a tree over.
7. So, I thought I might go and get some black cane (for weaving belts), prepare it and maybe catch some game or pull out some yellow cane (to weave a design in the belt).
8. So, I thought I would go up (to my usual place) look up and see the cane standing there.
9. I would climb up, get the cane, and prepare it.
10. I would go up, see the game, get some black and some yellow cane, prepare them, and return home, so I went up the path.
11. But, the path was blocked (by a fallen tree) so I stopped, thought I would prepare the black cane, get some game to eat and leave (without the yellow cane).
12. I went back (home), found (another kind of yellow cane), prepared it, used it in my weaving, and came up here.
13. I am finished.

Baho, an accomplished speaker, presented a wealth of potential figures to his audience that may have amalgamated several different motif-frames into a single complex narrative. The audience members must evaluate the potential paths to each motif-frame based on their individual viewpoints and their assessments of the social relationships that ground Baho's presentation, and the possible social relationships that might provide the ground for their responses. As the interaction proceeds, and a particular metonymically identified path is selected and elaborated upon, one figure is foregrounded while the other potential figures are backgrounded or ignored in the blending process.

As Baho finished, Kivide replied immediately, creating a new narrative space that introduced his own viewpoint as a member of Bun'ora and close kinsman of the Counsellor Makai. Kivide begins the sequence of responses by construing Baho's story as a dog ha'a, defining the narrative as a ha'a genre event, establishing a metonymic reference to the dog motif-frame, and initiating the projection to the representation of something lost—the conventional representation in the dog motif-frame. Kivide's construction however is limited. He does not suggest that he knows what is lost or where. Furthermore, in selecting his projections, Kivide also constrains the scope of the dog motif-frame by making no specific reference to the other attributes of dogs that the frame could evoke—promiscuity, which remains accessible in this case, and an indiscriminate appetite. Kivide also selects the dog from among the other possible metonymically evoked frames, which he ignores in his construction—the path that is blocked, the fallen tree, and the two types of cane.

By construing Baho's story as a ha'a, Kivide collaborates with Baho in what may be a negotiation, and invites the participation of his audience to further compose, complete, and elaborate the blend by supplying additional mappings.

**Kivide's response**

14. Baho told a story. Did you understand it?
15. Baho left something of his here.
16. You stole it so he has come up here to look for it and he has asked that whoever has seen it not wrap it up and put it away, but let him see it.
17. If something of yours dropped, we would bring it here, put it down and ask whom it belongs to and give it to him.
18. We should help him by bringing out (the thing that he has lost) and putting it here.
19. Now they should give it to him quickly.
20. If I was walking around and saw a small knife, spoon or something else that dropped and was lying there, I wouldn't take it and keep it. I would take it quickly to the owner and give it to him. Others might try to trick him.
21. If I (had something) that fell on the ground and the owners were looking for it I would tell them and give it to them. If they didn't know where it was I would get it quickly.
22. Listen to me. You heard that he was looking for something and has asked you to look for it.
23. He brought something here, put it down and someone took it; that is why he has come up here to ask us.
24. Whoever took it, don't wrap it up and put it away, but find it and give it to him quickly to finish this.
25. He is looking for something, he said.
26. I am finished.

Baho's decision to tell his ha'a in front of Nevil's house was a clear invitation for Nevil to respond. Nevil introduces a third narrative space with a new viewpoint. Nevil, a Kuba'ora kinsman of Baho's, makes reference to Baho's initial presentation of the dog, while also accepting the link to Kivide's blend that something or someone is lost. Nevil claims ownership of the missing dog, and in doing so, he accepts Kivide's construal of Baho's story as an allegory and as a dog ha'a. He contributes to the incomplete blend initiated by Kivide by identifying himself as the dog owner and stating that Baho's wife has told him that what they are looking for is down near Baho's house in Kavan. Thus, the projections constructed by Nevil begin to link to a specific dog and a specific object in the bush.

**Nevil's response:**

27. I haven't seen one of my dogs and am looking for it.
28. I was looking for it when Roti (Baho's wife) came here chasing it.
29. I was looking when Roti came up here to speak to me.
30. 'Your dog is staying down there (near Kavan)'.
31. 'Isn't that why you are looking around?'
32. That is what I heard and (why I have spoken).
33. Now, perhaps (the story) is finished.

Dajahare's *naham*, 'interpretation', at the end of the exchange, creates a fourth narrative space that articulates the blend, and links to Baho, Kivide, and Nevil's narrative space presentations of the dog ha'a. As a kinsman and/ or in-law to all of the participants, he establishes a fourth viewpoint of a person not directly involved in the social implications of the negotiations and responsible for taking concrete steps to transform the elopement into a socially legitimated marriage. He is the first to establish the link between the presentation of the dog to a missing boy (and girl) and to their elopement. He focusses exclusively on the dog motif (Line 37). The dog, he explains, is a boy whom Nevil fed—a son. Dajahare created this blend based not only on the dog as a thief (initially selected by Kivide), one who takes goods or food from its owner into the bush (*neze abenan*), but also on his knowledge of the people involved and the other elements of the dog motif-frame. He widens the scope of the dog motif-frame construction by including both the dog ha's reference to loss or theft that was initiated by Kivide, by introducing another prominent feature of the dog motif-frame—promiscuity—in his mention of elopement.

**Dajahare's explanation:**

34. Nevil told a story.
35. I will explain it.
36. I will explain.
37. A dog that he fed did something so he has told an allegory about it.
36. He thought about the story and then spoke.
38. A boy from here went down and got a wife and we didn't see what happened, so (Baho) came up here and told us the story we have just heard.
39. Baho came up here looking for the dog that he had fed game. He wants his brothers and cousins to chase it with him.
40. So, Nevil spoke, we heard him and I have explained what he was thinking when he spoke.
41. It was a dog of Nevil's: one that he had fed.

42. Nevil had raised the dog and they went around together.
43. He went around with it but the dog stayed down there with relatives when he came back.
44. That person went there: stayed with them and ate. They gave him food and game. Those people who are looking for him gave him food and game to eat.
45. The dog stayed and ate and thought, 'They will go'.
46. They went looking (for him) but the dog stayed there.
47. 'Your dog went down there and stayed with us', they said.
48. They thought, 'Who gave the dog scraps of food to eat? What did it smell?' They went looking and I stayed here looking and have now found it.
49. This (interchange) is finished now.

To this Baho responded simply and briefly.

**Baho's Response:**

50. I got what I was looking for.

In summary, the interchanges that followed from Baho's performance demonstrate that frame metonymy plays an important role in evoking potential figurative narrative frames and selecting the paths of coherence among the narrative spaces constructed by each of the participants. But, by focusing exclusively on the dog motif, Kivide and Nevil reject the potential metonymical evocation of additional motif-frames: the path, the fallen tree, that blocks it.

Dajahare also follows along the dog ha'a connections established among Baho, Kivide, and Nevil's narrative spaces. His selection from among the alternative motif-frames presented by Baho is driven by the social interests of Kivide and Nevil as evidenced by their selection of the dog motif. From their social and politically shaped viewpoints, the dog-motif and the elopement and marriage that it seems to address takes precedence over the alternative potential motif-frames. Treating this ha'a as the opening of marriage negotiations is consequential, because the elopement, if transformed into a marriage acceptable to Nevil and the boy' other kinsmen, as well as Baho and the girl's extended kin, the marriage will transform Baho's relationship to Nevil from that of fellow Kuba'ora clan mates into opposing sets of in-laws.

However, Dajahare had the option of reintroducing the motif-frames that the others ignored—the path and the fallen tree. Kivide's suppression of the middle section (Lines 6–11) that mentions the path blocked by the fallen tree is significant because he appears to ignore an important set of alternative motif-frames. Line 6 begins with Baho changing his viewpoint from past to present. More significantly, in Line 7, he begins with a frame builder *E'ero*, 'So', and prosodically marked information units (Chafe 1994; McKellin 1984) to create a hypothetical space in which the path and the fallen tree are mentioned. From my own viewpoint, as a member of the audience, and one treated as a kinsman of Makai, my sponsor in the village, it seemed peculiar that Kivide, Nevil, and Dajahare ignored the textual space building elements of the ha'a which could evoke the path and tree motif-frames and offer an alternate construal of Baho's ha'a that might have opened negotiations for a reconciliation feast between Baho and his alienated Bun'ora kin.

In Lines 4 and 5 Baho mentions that he no longer goes up to the mountains to hunt. This was actually the case. After the fight with Makai's faction, Baho could not return to the Bun'ora hunting territory that he shared with Maki and other Bun'ora men until they were reconciled. The mapping of 'path' to exchange is common in everyday conversation, and is frequently used to refer to routes connecting exchange partners, most significantly the 'paths' that women take from their natal village to that of their husband's on marriage. Likewise, the mapping between trees and people is frequent and profound, to the extent that people are named after special trees, *marura*. A fallen tree, a person—perhaps Makai, whose death halted the plans for the reconciliation feast exchange—blocked Baho's presentation, the path to the mountains. This was my speculation at the time, shared by a few who were also in the audience, but, since none of the participants explored these motif-frames, it is difficult to assess this alternative construction.

Because Kivide, Nevil, and Dajahare rejected the path motif-frame and the route to reconciliation, Baho was left in a difficult social and political position. He remained alienated from his Bun'ora kinsmen and, if the elopement did develop into a marriage, he would lack their support for the exchanges that he would now conduct with formerly close clan mate, and now in-law Nevil.

Thus, by presenting two sets of motif-frames, Baho evoked alternative frames for his developing social and political relationships. The ha'a enabled Baho to create and test the acceptability of four possible social outcomes. His audience could (1) recognize the story as allegorical and legitimate the elopement by transforming it into an exchange marriage, (2) treat the allegory as an attempt to reconcile the Bun'ora factions, (3) combine the outcomes of the first two possibilities, or (4) ignore the allegorical potential of the story and avoid all of the negotiations. The selection of the dog motif-frame by Kivide, Nevil, and Dajahare and the rejection of the tree and path motifs reflected their political viewpoints, which focused on the elopement and discounted the possible attempt at reconciliation.

In the end, the elopement was legitimated as a marriage, making Nevil and Baho in-laws, but the reconciliation between Baho to his Bun'ora kin failed to materialize. For Baho and Nevil, this marriage was a lost opportunity for each of them to expand their social and political alliances by arranging more strategic marriages. Baho was also denied the opportunity to consolidate his alliance with his Bun'ora brethren. Furthermore, the outcome created a new affinal relationship with Nevil that forced their fellow Kuba'ora kin to choose whom they would cooperate with in future exchanges and political alliances.

When I returned to Jinebuina four years later I found Baho and one of his former adversaries Aresa (Makai's brother) living in houses side-by-side. When asked about the apparent reconciliation, Aresa explained that after his brother, who was injured in the fight, died, he told Baho a ha'a based on the song about a place where they both had rights. When asked if this was in response to Baho's earlier allegory, Aresa cocked his head, grinned impishly, but said nothing. Perhaps the portion of Baho's ha'a that Kivide and the others ignored had not gone unnoticed. Baho was, finally, reconciled with his Bun'ora brethren.

## 6 Conclusion

Baho's ha'a provides an opportunity to demonstrate the usefulness of Cognitive Linguistics, particularly Conceptual Integration and Blending Theory, to examine the dynamic process of constructing and interpreting complex allegories used by Managalase to negotiate delicate social and political relationships. Blending Theory, and the Mental Space Theory on which it is founded, have proven well suited to capture the dynamic, ephemeral nature of the politically calculating oral performance by Baho and the improvised responses by his audience members. This approach helps to capture the complex flow of information—momentary inputs that create multiple mental and narrative spaces, and transitory emergent blends that are created during spontaneous verbal interaction. Blending in these speeches, unlike those in literature, are spontaneously heard, interpreted, responded to, and acted upon. The only remaining traces of the process are individuals' memories and the new social relationships they create.

These theoretical tools also help to elucidate the processes through which ha'a instantiate conventional allegorical motifs in particular social and political contexts. Speakers and members of the audience juggle multiple narrative and mental spaces while they selectively present, accept, and reject projections based on their information about current events, their understanding of social relationships, and the participants' assessments of the social and political consequences of the various alternative cognitive and social constructions. The theory's frame-based understanding of knowledge helps to articulate the relationship among particular narrative frames, blending processes, and more comprehensive and stable Managalase cultural models of kinship, reciprocity, marriage, and loss.

This excursion into allegorical negotiations is also an opportunity to reassess Conceptual Integration and Blending Theory's understanding of ground, intersubjectivity, and assumptions about shared intentions and common knowledge among speakers and audience members. We have seen that in Managalase ha'a such as Baho's, the linguistic and social grounding of the interaction and of the object of negotiation is unstable. The genre of the story may remain in suspense while the social relations and roles of the participants are also under negotiation.

Managalase would also agree with Croft's (2009) contention that we cannot read each other's minds. Based on Managalase epistemology and a language ideology that are rooted in an embodied notion of knowledge, Managalase would hesitate to assume that shared intentions and knowledge are the basis for communication, particularly in negotiations. Managalase would embrace the notion that each individual assumes unique epistemological and narrative viewpoint. The nature of negotiations assumes a difference of assumptions, values, and viewpoints among the participants. The goal of interactions using ha'a, like most negotiations, is to produce sufficient joint attention and coordination of intentions to create new social relationships for social and political action.

In performances of ha'a, speakers and their audience are attempting to negotiate and reframe the problematic, fluid social relationships that also serve as the context or ground for further social interactions. The parties' divergent interests in these negotiations highlight the need to distinguish the positions and assumptions of each of the participants. For this reason, it is difficult to meld their diverse viewpoints into a single common Ground or Semiotic space (Brandt and Brandt 2005; Oakley and Coulson 2008; Oakley and Hougaard 2008). Depending on the acceptability of the proffered relationship, Managalase speakers and their audience may not even agree on the genre of the story.

An alternative approach is to consider performances of ha'a and the construction of blends produced as a result, as boundary objects (Star and Griesemer 1989) or mediating artifacts (Engeström 2001) in social activities. Just as museum specimens and medical records can serve as a focal point that brings together specialists with different disciplinary lenses to work together, ha'a's metonymically evoked motif-frames, with their under-determined, partial structures provides a basis for collaborative, coordinated joint ventures that enable participants' to retain their distinct narrative and epistemological viewpoints. Rather than conceptualizing these blends as emanating from or based on shared intentions or common knowledge, the blends of these oral performances are the fleeting focal points shared by the participants who see future relationships though the same translucent mediating artifact from parallactic angles against different complex social and political backgrounds. In performances of these allegories, the goal is not simply to produce interesting blends, but to create new social and political realities, and new grounds for interaction.

## References

Aufenanger, H. 1962. Sayings with a Hidden Meaning (Central Highlands, New Guinea). *Anthropos* 57. 325–35.

Brandt, Line and Per Aage Brandt. 2005. Making Sense of a Blend: A Cognitive–Semiotic Approach to Metaphor. *Annual Review of Cognitive Linguistics* 3. 216–49.

Chafe, Wallace L. 1994. *Discourse, Consciousness, and Time: The Flow and Displacement of Conscious Experience in Speaking and Writing*. Chicago: University of Chicago Press.

Croft, W. 2009. Toward a Social Cognitive Linguistics. *New Directions in Cognitive Linguistics*, ed. by V. Evans and S. Pourcel, 395–420. Amsterdam: John Benjamins.

Dancygier, B. 2012. *The Language of Stories: A Cognitive Approach*. Cambridge: Cambridge University Press.

Duranti, Alessandro. 2010. Husserl, Intersubjectivity and Anthropology. *Anthropological Theory* 10. 16–35.

Engeström, Yrjo. 2001. Expansive Learning at Work: Toward an Activity Theoretical Reconceptualization. *Journal of Education and Work* 14. 133–56.

Fauconnier, Gilles. 1997. *Mappings in Thought and Language*.

_____. 2006. Pragmatics and Cognitive Linguistics. In L. Horn and G. Ward (eds), *The Handbook of Pragmatics*. Oxford: Blackwell.

Fauconnier, Gilles and Mark Turner. 1998. Conceptual Integration Networks. *Cognitive Science* 22. 133–87.

_____. 2002. *The Way We Think: Conceptual Blending and the Mind's Hidden Complexities*. New York: Basic Books.

Gibbs, Raymond W. 2011. The Allegorical Impulse. *Metaphor and Symbol* 26. 121–30.

Harris, Randy Allen and Sarah Tolmie. 2011. Cognitive Allegory: An Introduction. *Metaphor and Symbol* 26. 109–20.

Hougaard, Anders. 2005. Conceptual Disintegration and Blending in Interactional Sequences: A Discussion of New Phenomena, Processes Vs. Products, and Methodology. *Journal of Pragmatics* 37. 1653–85.

Hougaard, Anders and Todd Oakley. 2008. Introduction: Mental Spaces and Discourse Analysis. *Mental Spaces in Discourse and Interaction*, ed. by T. Oakley and A. Hougaard. Amsterdam: John Benjamins.

McKellin, William H. 1984. Putting Down Roots: Information in the Language Managalase Exchange. Dangerous Words: Language and Politics in the Pacific. New York: New York University Press.

_____. 1990. Allegory and Inference: Intentional Ambiguity in Managalase Negotiations. *Disentangling: Conflict Discourse in Pacific Societies*, ed. by K. Watson Gegeo and G. White, 335–72. Stanford: Stanford University Press.

Merlan, Francesca and Alan Rumsey. 1991. *Ku Waru: Language and Segmentary Politics in the Western Nebilyer Valley, Papua New Guinea*. Cambridge: Cambridge University Press.

Oakley, T. and S. Coulson. 2008. Connecting the Dots: Mental Spaces and Metaphoric Language in Discourse. *Mental Spaces in Discourse and Interaction*, ed. by T. Oakley and A. Hougaard, 33–57. Amsterdan and Philadelphia: John Benjamins.

Oakley, Todd and Peter Crisp. 2011. Honeymoons and Pilgrimages: Conceptual Integration and Allegory in Old and New Media. *Metaphor and Symbol* 26. 152–59.

Oakley, Todd and Anders Hougaard. 2008. *Mental Spaces in Discourse and Interaction*. Amsterdam: John Benjamins Pub. Co.

Panther, Klaus-Uwe and Günter Radden. 1999. *Metonymy in Language and Thought*. Amsterdam: John Benjamins.

Robbins, Joel and Alan Rumsey. 2008. Introduction: Cultural and Linguistic Anthropology and the Opacity of Other Minds. *Anthropological Quarterly* 81. 407–20.

Schieffelin, Bambi B. 2008. Speaking Only Your Own Mind: Reflections on Talk, Gossip and Intentionality in Bosavi (Png). *Anthropological Quarterly* 81. 431–41.

Star, Susan Leigh and James R. Griesemer. 1989. Institutional Ecology, 'Translations' and Boundary Objects: Amateurs and Professionals in Berkeley's Museum of Vertebrate Zoology, 1907–39. *Social Studies of Science* 19. 387–420.

Steen, G.J. 2011. Genre between the Humanities and the Sciences. Bi-Directionality in the Cognitive Sciences: Avenues, Challenges, and Limitations, ed. by M. Callies, W.R. Keller and A. Lohöfer, 21–42. Amsterdam: John Benjamins.

Strathern, Andrew. 1975. Veiled Speech in Mt. Hagen. *Political Language and Oratory in Traditional Society*, ed. by M. Bloch, 185–204. London: Academic Press.

# Part IV

## Viewpoint, Language, and the Body

15

# Creativity Across Modalities in Viewpoint Construction

EVE SWEETSER

## 1 Introduction

It is no news to embodied cognitive science researchers that perception and cognition—even imagined perception—are not just embodied but *view-pointed*. We have no God's-eye perception and cognition.[1] But so far, these researchers have dealt primarily with the question of single viewpoints, not with the ways in which multiple viewpoints live in single minds and bodies. I shall here discuss ways in which language and co-speech gesture are creatively used to represent viewpoints—even complex combinations of viewpoints which no single described person is thought of as experiencing, although the narrator of the description, and the reader or listener, get to experience them all. To give one very simple example, imagine that a speaker moves one hand in fast curves through the air, as she says *We were just careening down the mountain road*—and simultaneously manifests on her face the expression of terror that she felt as a passenger in the careening car. Her hand gesture gives more the visual viewpoint that a spectator might have had of the car's overall path, while her face gives the emotional viewpoint of her past frightened passenger self.

[1] See Dancygier and Sweetser (2012) and Bergen (2012) for relevant reviews of some of this research on viewpoint, and Barsalou (2010), Bergen and Chang (2005) and Feldman (2006) for general reviews of embodied cognition and its relation to language.

*Language and the Creative Mind*.
Mike Borkent, Barbara Dancygier, and Jennifer Hinnell (eds).

As cognitive science now knows well, viewpoint is not just a pervasive feature of language and cognition, we might even call it an *invasive* one: we are not only constantly but *inevitably* aware of other people's viewpoints as well as our own. We have no non-viewpointed perception of the world: our bodies are always asymmetrically constrained in visual and manual access to the world, as well as in motion—the space in front of us is accessible in a way that the one behind us is not. And there's more to it, which has been much less examined than the single viewpoint. As soon as there's another person sharing space with me, my body tracks what they can see or reach, as well as what I can see or reach. This awareness doesn't necessarily mean that I participate actively in the other viewpoints which I am tracking—though I could. For example, I *could* quite vividly imagine your view of the sunset, and move to look over your shoulder to share your vantage point because my previous view wasn't good enough. But without any vivid imagining, I still can't help knowing in what general direction you're able to see. I also can't help what your body posture and face tell me about your emotional states; and even though I may have rather different emotional states of my own, I can't help inhabiting yours too, to some extent. This is why it's exhausting to spend a lot of time with someone who's in severe pain, or in serious emotional depression.

In everyday life experience, what this means is that my body fully represents, naturally and automatically, its own perceptual and emotional and cognitive experiences—and it also both absorbs and impinges on aspects of the experiences of people around me. To do all this, it uses my own neural hardware for embodying experience. The old *out of sight, out of mind* dictum has some truth to it: I will be less strongly affected by others' experiences if they are not physically enacting their experience in my presence.

But what does all this mean for linguistic representation of viewpoint? Or for that matter, for linguistic and gestural representation of viewpoint in oral narrative? The narrator has to use her single text, or her single body and voice, to represent all the aspects of viewpoint which are imagined to be distributed among characters in the narrative. In the imagined situation, as in life, differing viewpoints are distributed across many bodies—each body has viewpointed experience, impinged on by others but distinct. Nobody can simultaneously *be* the car passenger and the spectator watching the car's path from an outside vantage point. But in the representational form, one single text—or one single body—may be required to represent all of those.

Consider an American Sign Language narrative, described by Paul Dudis (2004a,b), which tells the story of an encounter between a hearing librarian and a Deaf library patron who has inadvertently been making noise in a library. The signing narrator's body represents the seated patron, while a V-hand point downwards towards his face represents the disapproving gaze of the standing librarian. But simultaneously the signer's face initially represents the librarian's disapproving expression, which is presumably located not on the patron's body but on the (unrepresented) body of the librarian at the other end of the gaze. The signer then switches facial expression to represent the discomfited look of the patron, as he becomes conscious of the librarian's disapproving attention. What might be surprising to some is the first combination: it might look to a naïve nonsigning observer as if the signer's body is representing someone with a disapproving facial expression (who is also being looked at), whereas in fact at that point it represents someone *being looked at by* a person with a disapproving facial expression. The signer has only one face—which has to represent the faces, in turn, of both participants in the described exchange, even while his hand continues to represent the visual view of the librarian, and his trunk continues to represent the seated library patron who is being looked at.

## 2 Embodied Viewpoint in Language

Language itself is as viewpointed as cognition; in this section of the paper, I will resume some of the basic observations about language and viewpoint (Sweetser [2012] gives more detail and references). Speakers cannot use basic linguistic forms such as pronouns and deictics without 'giving away' their choice of viewpoint. *This, that, here, there*, choice of tenses, and so on—all these tell you when and where objects and events are with respect to some Ego, some perceiver and observer. Your *here* is often my *there*, so speakers have to choose whose viewpoint to represent, as in English when someone accepts an invitation by saying *Sure, I'd love to* ***come*** *to your party*—the verb *come* is representing the addressee's (party-giver's) viewpoint. If the speaker were to subsequently turn to a housemate, however, she might say *Let's* ***go*** *to Chris' party on Saturday* and would be most unlikely to say *come* (*cf.* Fillmore 1997[1971]; Sweetser 2012).

Languages vary as to the ways in which some Ego's viewpoint is represented in standard spatial reference. Relative spatial reference systems refer to spatial relations in small, local space in terms of viewpointed body-based spatial relations such as back/front and left/right. So in English I might say *the paper is to the left of my computer on the desk*, even when I'm giving someone directions about how to find the paper, when neither of us is actually present in the office described. In an Absolute directional language (Levinson 1996, 2003) I would need to say instead something like *the paper is to the east of my computer on the desk*, which would describe the same situation, since I face south as I work in my campus office, so the east side of the computer is the left side from the computer-user's perspective. The difference is that the east/west distinction does not require the bodily position of an imagined viewer or computer user to be comprehensible: a global directional viewpoint is enough. But to understand what would be *the left of the computer*, I have to imagine a computer user in canonical orientation with respect to the computer, and compute that user's left and right.

Languages also vary in how they use spatial deictic forms to represent social rather than physical spatial viewpoint. Hanks (1990) cites Mayan speakers using distal ('that-there') deictic forms to refer to objects which were physically right next to them, but which belonged to (were socially connected to) someone else, and not available for the speaker's use; conversely, the same speakers used proximal 'this-here' forms to refer to more physically distant objects which were the speaker's own belongings or normally accessible for their use. Rubba (1996) reports similar usages by American English speakers in San Diego, where speakers (all interviewed in the same location on the UCSD campus) used distal forms to refer to neighborhoods that were culturally alien to them, and proximal ones to refer to neighborhoods where they felt comfortable. In these cases, linguistic forms associated with physical viewpoint are extended to refer to social viewpoint.

But viewpoint doesn't stop with the set of forms standardly labeled as deictic. Any choice of a linguistic form expresses viewpoint, inasmuch as it expresses some conceptualizer's *construal*, in Langacker's sense (1987, 1991). The same person might correctly be described as *Professor Jones*, or *Joe*, or *my cousin*, or *a guy from Berkeley*, or *Sue's father*, or *Daddy*, depending on who is describing and who is addressed. In choosing any one form, I have made a decision as to how to prompt construal from my particular addressees in that particular situation.

Most crucially, such choices are already intersubjective, in the sense of Verhagen (2005). I am likely to refer to my across-the-hall office neighbor as *Lev* among colleagues and graduate students, as well as in addressing him, but I might call him *Professor Michael* to an undergraduate student. This is presumably because I am adopting the description form which the undergraduate would use. (The undergraduate is not equally free to do likewise—that is, s/he would not as plausibly use Lev Michael's first name in talking about him to me, on the grounds that I would be likely to use it.) Similarly, it would be inappropriate to say *the book* (as opposed to *a book*) unless I think my addressee shares my cognitive ability to readily identify a book being referred to. In using a definite article, I am crucially manifesting my understanding of my addressee's cognitive relationship to the referent. So even when a linguistic expression only manifests one particular viewpoint (such as more or less formality in describing a faculty member, or the choice of *come* or *go* to describe attendance at a party), the choice of that expression often normally involves taking multiple viewpoints into account, not just the speaker's own most likely individual perspective.

## 3 Mixed Viewpoint in Language Use

Narratologists—in this respect well ahead of cognitive science research—have long been aware of multiple viewpoint representation in language, Genette (1980) being a major milestone for this aspect of narratology. What is termed Direct Speech and Thought is characterized by representation of what a single person would say or think—often, though not always, this corresponds to expression of one viewpoint. And in particular, we seem to expect a single utterance or sentence to express a coherent viewpoint; obviously the next utterance in the sequence could be a reply from another participant, but in general there seems to be an unspoken expectation that sentence boundaries, or speaker shifts, correspond to possible places for shifts in viewpoint. But of course that's not always so. Ann Banfield's (1982) 'unspeakable' sentences are literary examples of combinations of linguistic forms which can only be interpreted coherently in a context where they express embedded narratorial viewpoint. A sentence such as *Soon she would be telling Daddy all about it, the nasty tattle-tale!* expresses both the imagined narrator's description of the sentence's subject (third person form *she*, and the description *nasty tattle-tale*), as well as the described subject's own description of her parent (*Daddy*). The narrator would presumably not directly refer to this person as *Daddy*, but uses the form to represent the subject's usage and viewpoint. Without the support of a context involving multiple established viewpoints, these combinations of forms don't even make sense; in such a context, they powerfully represent the embedded structure.

I want to issue a caveat here; Direct Speech and Thought can express embedded viewpoints too. A character who is not the addressee's sibling could say *So I suppose you'll tell dear Daddy all about this*, intending *dear Daddy* to be a sarcastic quotation of the addressee's probable reference form for her parent. In that sense, these sentences are not unspeakable: one does not have to be a literary narrator to embed viewpoint, and thus produce an utterance with heterogeneous viewpoint markers. However, third-person narration in literary texts has been a major locus of exploration and creativity for authors trying to express both the narrator's and the characters' viewpoints, and hence a productive focus for research in narratology. Genette's work led the way in this area; Sanders and Redeker (1996) have offered a model of indirect narrative viewpoint in terms of Mental Spaces Theory, while Zunshine (2006) has examined historical development of strategies of viewpoint embedding in English literature.

A particularly thoroughly documented example is narratorial exploitation of the fact that imperfective verb forms evoke immersion in (internal experience of) an ongoing situation, while perfective forms evoke external viewpoint on a situation as a whole (Genette [1980]; Fleischman [1990]). Because this is so, narrators of third-person narratives (famously and innovatively, Flaubert's narratorial voice in *Madame Bovary*, but also of course Virginia Woolf and many more authors since) can combine a past-tense third-person narrative with imperfective verb forms, as ingredients in the Free Indirect Style, in what is now commonly called Free Indirect Speech and Thought (FIST). *Emma sat at the window; the snow fell* does not produce the same impression as an imperfective *Emma was sitting at the window; the snow was falling*. The impression given by the imperfective past is one where the narrator's viewpoint is still present (hence, past third-person references to the character and the character's present) but is 'immersed' in the local imagined experiential viewpoint of the character (hence the imperfective forms).

Similarly, Nikiforidou (2012) examines the 'impossible' and very ordinary combination of past tense with *now* in English literary texts, often used in FIST contexts and perhaps to be seen as a component of FIST.

(1) They now saw, tied to the fence, Ratliff's buckboard and team. (cited by Nikiforidou from Faulkner, *The Hamlet*)

The PAST + *now* construction is not restricted to literary texts: history books and journalistic settings also use it, with the same general effect of maintaining the narrator's distance from a past third-person setting, while still partially empathizing with the viewpoint of participants in that setting. Nikiforidou gives a formal analysis of this as a mental-space blend; it is also discussed in Dancygier (2012, Chapter 7) as part of a broader treatment of formal blends which create viewpoint blends. Similar blends of narratorial and character viewpoint have been analyzed as built up by connective uses in third-person text (Sanders, Sanders and Sweetser 2009, 2012).

We might note here the contrast between FIST usages and the English Narrative Present construction, which has been little studied because it seems to occur primarily in spoken language. Canonical usages in jokes are helpful data, however, as in (2).

(2) A Martian **walks** into Zabar's [a New York deli], and he **looks** around in **there** and **says**, 'I'll have one of those round things with holes in the center.' So they **give** him a bagel and he **takes** a bite of it. And **then** he **says**, 'Gee, this would go great with lox and cream cheese.'

This is apparently the inverse of PAST + *now*; it might be called the PRESENT + *then* construction. *Now* would be inappropriate as a replacement for *then* in this context—perhaps more obviously disruptive than *then* would be in (1). Notice also the use of distal *in there*; it could not readily be replaced by the proximal *in here*, which would express the viewpoint of 'present' participants in the scenario. The Narrative Present construction, like FIST, combines formal elements marking the narrator's viewpoint and the described participants' viewpoint—but chooses different elements to combine. And the resulting overall viewpoint is strikingly different from FIST. Though much further examination is needed to define the difference, the Narrative Present seems in part to negotiate a close, informal relationship between the narrator and the listeners, in a way that FIST does not.

Vandelanotte (2009, 2012) points to another interesting combination of linguistic forms, not previously recognized by narratologists, which he labels Distanced Indirect Speech and Thought. DIST combines pronoun and tense use appropriate to the actual speaker in the speech situation (in Example (3), notice the use of *you* and past tense) with content, descriptions and phrasing attributed to the quoted speaker (it is not the current speaker, but the past quoted speaker who is imagined to have used phrases such as *not going to be a bookkeeper long* or *going to do wonders*). Like Free Indirect Speech and Thought, DIST combines elements of two voices or viewpoints. But unlike the immersive effect of FIST, where the narrator (despite past tense and third person forms) aligns with the character's perspective, DIST produces a different, distancing effect in viewpoint.

(3) **You** was goin' to do wonders, **you** was! **You** wasn't going to be a bookkeeper long – oh no, not **you**. (cited by Vandelanotte [2012] from Elmer Rice, *The Adding Machine*)

Direct Speech equivalent: I'm going to do wonders, I am!...
FIST equivalent: He was going to do wonders, he was! ...

Dancygier (2012) offers a wide-ranging treatment of relationships between linguistic and narrative structures, including in particular the kinds of blending of viewpointed labels (pronouns, address forms), tense markers, and other forms to build multiple viewpoints in relation to each other. Her analysis of viewpoint embedding and compression (Chapter 7) offers blending analyses of several of the constructions discussed here. In other parts of the book she discusses topics such as the mixing of visual viewpoint in narrative—an issue which should have been brought into this paper if there had been space and time. One of her over-arching points, shared with Nikiforidou, Vandelanotte and Sanders, Sanders and Sweetser, is that to a significant extent we can pinpoint the individual contributions of forms to the composite viewpoints constructed by narratives. In (3), for example, we know that the use of *you* to refer to the present interlocutor is a link to the speaker's real interaction space, while the past tense forms indicate that the quoted speech was in the past, and the 'quoted' expressions relate to past speech of the current addressee. We can even say that the choice of *you* marks a clear decision *not* to identify with the speaker of those past quoted speech acts—to keep those referential systems distinct from the current frame of reference.

Despite these observations about compositionality in viewpoint constructions, linguists are very far from being able to predict, based on the semantics of particular elements such as tense markers or pronouns, the kinds of different overall viewpoint effects produced by particular combinations of those forms. But it is becoming increasingly evident that this is a major locus of creativity in writing. Not only is embedded viewpoint representation done by combining forms expressing the narrator's and the character's (or the speaker's and the described subject's) different viewpoints, but different kinds of embedded viewpoint can be built by choosing different combinations of formal elements.

## 4 Multiple Viewpoints in One Body: 'Impossible Gestures'

The next question, however, is whether gesture can—like language—simultaneously represent more than one viewpoint. And the answer is clearly yes. Parrill (2009) documents 'dual-viewpoint' gestures, where for example both an observer-viewpoint large-scale path and a character-viewpoint handshape or facial expression are represented simultaneously (see also Stec [2013] for a review of literature on gestural viewpoint). In a way, this is predictable, or at least expectable, since gesture has so many more degrees of simultaneity than speech. Only one sound at once can come out of a vocal tract; but co-speech gesture is more like signed language in this regard. The independence of the various gestural articulators (two hands, trunk posture, head and trunk orientations, facial expression, eye gaze, eyebrow position, etc.) seems even at first glance to offer rich opportunities for the same kinds of simultaneous multiple viewpoint representations which were observed in Dudis' (2004a,b, 2007) ASL examples. In another example, Dudis (2007) cites an ASL story-teller who is describing a fight over a card-game; the signer's body remains a card-player, with his left hand shaped to hold cards, while his right arm reaches up to mime hitting his own face—enacting the arm of another participant in the story who is hitting the card-player. This kind of *partitioning* of the body—which can assign one part of the body to represent parts of one scene-participant, and other parts to represent a different participant—has been described in detail in Dudis' work. The scene depicted in these cases is distributed over multiple imagined bodies—but enacted by a single body.

In analyses presented at the 2012 ISGS meeting in Lund, Stec and Sweetser discussed examples where videotaped narrators (English speakers, telling stories about autobiographical incidents) simultaneously manifest more than one physical viewpoint in their bodily gestures and postures. And by this we mean 'impossible gestures' on the order of Banfield's unspeakable sentences. As an example, let us take a story where the narrator is telling how when she was a college student, she helped a female friend with a class project by agreeing to go with the friend and apply for a marriage license at a town hall. The reason she was the one doing this was that her birth certificate says 'male' on it; it is accompanied by a stapled-on correction sheet saying 'female.' They wanted to find out how the town hall officials would respond to this. As she tells about the encounter, she enacts the town hall official and holds in her hands an imaginary birth certificate document, looking down at it skeptically (Figure 1).

FIGURE 1

So far, so good, she is enacting only one person's body. But she continues to hold the imagined document in her hands as she raises her head and voices her own past self's responses to the official—clearly at this point, her voice and face are enacting one participant's viewpoint while her hands are still enacting the other participant (Figure 2). This is an impossible gesture, if we were to imagine it as representing a single bodily viewpoint. The town hall official could not have played the part of the narrator's past self or made her utterances (and was apparently looking down at a document rather than at her interlocutor); the narrator's past self did not have the document in her hands. We thus have dual-viewpoint enactment here, with two character viewpoints enacted, rather like Dudis' ASL library narrative. And the reason appears to be the same obvious one adduced by Dudis: the narrator has only one body, and needs to express more than one body's behaviors.

FIGURE 2

Further, this narrator continues to keep her hands in 'document-holding' position as (in Figure 3) she turns her head and eye-gaze to her real-world interlocutor, who has asked her why she didn't just detach the stapled-on correction sheet before giving the document to the official; she responds that she didn't think of it. She then returns her gaze to the story world, which is 20 degrees or so to the right of the interaction line with her real interlocutor. This is rather a different phenomenon from the two-character gestures. Here, she 'holds onto' a story character's manual pose while enacting verbally (and with facial expression) her own current part in the Real Space conversation with her real-world interlocutor. Once again, this is not a possible single-viewpoint gesture/posture combination: the narrator is not holding a document in her hands, and the official is not turning to talk to the real-world interlocutor. In this case, the dual gestural structure represents narrative embedding, as do the linguistic strategies mentioned above (FIST, DIST, Narrative Present). With gestural embeddings of this kind, the retention of the story-character's viewpoint seems frequently to be a way of visi-bly holding the floor for return to the narrative, even while granting the temporary floor to an interruption by the story-listener. We have other such examples from other narrators; sometimes the narrator is not retaining a character's pose but simply keeps her hands up, ready for action, in the space currently reserved for the narrative gestures, while she turns away from that space and interacts with the real-world interlocutor.

FIGURE 3

We did note in our English story-tellers that seven of the ten subjects at some point briefly 'enlisted' the real-world interlocutor as a stand-in for a depicted interlocutor in a past recounted conversation. That is, the narrators enacted their Past Selves, and shook fingers at, or expostulated with, their real-world interlocutors directly, turning towards them and making eye contact. This blend would be impossible for ASL story-tellers, who are required to do what English story-tellers seem to do *most* of the time, namely disengage gaze from the interlocutor and turn 20 degrees or so away from the interlocutor to build a new space for the fictional interaction. Since gaze is a (perhaps the) primary cue distinguishing real from fictive interaction for ASL narrators, ASL narrators cannot 'off-load' representation of a fictive interlocutor onto the real interlocutor, while English narrators can and sometimes do.

As a footnote here, visual art would provide us with yet more objects for analysis of viewpoint blends. It is commonplace in painting to use a depicted character's gaze as a cue to guide the viewer's gaze. De Mey's (2006) work on van Eyck has documented this, as well as other aspects of van Eyck's uniquely sophisticated viewpoint depiction. The artist's Ghent Altarpiece, painted to hang in a particular chapel of Ghent Cathedral, replicates in the painted scene exactly the angle of light which would have been coming through the windows of that chapel. Every reflective surface depicted (every glass or metal object) and every shadow cast, is depicted as if the light came into the painted world from the windows of the chapel. This is most unusual, since paintings normally represent the light of the depicted scene completely without reference to any imagined real-world light setting in which the painting might be displayed. In this case, van Eyck could be seen as creating the impression for the viewer that s/he is in the same physical space as the depicted painted characters (the Virgin Mary and the Angel Gabriel, as well as others), since s/he shares their visual access to light.

This is only a start, and we have much more analysis to do. But it seems that oral storytellers use their bodies in space—in quite creative ways—to represent complex combinations of narrator and character viewpoints. And some of those combinations are quite analogous to the solutions found by ASL narrators, or by literary authors, to the same kinds of problems. Visual artists are finding creative solutions of different kinds.

## 5 Conclusions

Given how complex the representation of 'single' viewpoint can get, it is fascinating to go one step further and see the creativity involved in representation of multiple viewpoints in language and gesture, and even visual art. As artists and art critics have always known, creativity consists in finding new and elegant ways to use the resources of your chosen medium. And each of the media mentioned above has different resources.

Face-to-face interaction, in spoken or signed language, has all the resources of an inherently viewpointed body in space, to represent viewpoint phenomena. It also, as literary narratologists might not predict, has the viewpoint resources of language and can combine linguistic forms in ways that mark embedding or combining of viewpoints: in the ironic *Yeah, I'm just* ***so*** *annoying, insisting on transparent grading standards*, the speaker attributes the judgment *so annoying* to the imagined quoted speaker, but the *I* and the phrase *transparent grading standards* are clearly her own. We might initially think that the single body is a limitation on representing multiple bodies—or at least, we might think that it would be confusing to addressees to unpack the blends and realize that one fist represents part of an attacker, while the rest of the body represents the person being attacked. But clearly this is no problem for humans interpreting interaction—and why should it be, for people who can understand Free Indirect Style?

Written language lacks the face-to-face affordances—gestural and intonational—and has a long tradition of making up for this lack by various sophisticated narratorial techniques, including blending of linguistic forms from different viewpoints. Some blending 'recipes' are characteristic primarily of spoken language (the Narrative Present) while others (FIST, DIST) are more characteristic of particular genres of written language. Readers and listeners unpack these blends smoothly and comfortably, building the multiple points of view in relation to each other.

Current cognitive science has not fully assimilated the study of literature or gesture, let alone the study of visual art. So there are almost entirely different sets of scholars examining literary texts, oral narrative, co-speech gesture, signed language structure, speech processing in laboratory settings, and visual art. But since all of these phenomena are created and performed by humans, with deeply viewpointed perception and cognition, it seems important to consider them together. Some progress is happening in this area. Dancygier and Sweetser (2012) have brought together studies of written literary narratives, ASL narratives, and co-speech gesture. Turner (2006) brought studies of art together with cognitive science in a new way, while numerous scholars, notably Dancygier (2012), Hogan (2003a, 2003b) and Herman (2004, 2009), have been working to build more cognitively oriented theories of literary narrative. We can hope for more interdisciplinary connections in the future. But the full range of human creativity—and the ways in which creativity is similar or different across modalities—is waiting to be investigated.

## References

Banfield, Ann. 1982. *Unspeakable Sentences: Narration and Representation in the Language of Fiction*. Boston: Routledge and Kegan Paul.

Barsalou, Lawrence. 2010. Grounded cognition: past, present and future. *Topics in Cognitive Science* 2, 716–24.

Bergen, Benjamin. 2012. *Louder Than Words: The New Science of How the Mind Makes Meaning*. New York: Basic Books.

Bergen, Benjamin and Nancy Chang. 2005. Embodied construction grammar in simulation-based language understanding. In Jan-Ola Östman and Mirjam Fried (eds). *Construction Grammars: Cognitive Grounding and Theoretical Extensions*. 147–90. Amsterdam: John Benjamins.

Casasanto, Daniel. 2009. Embodiment of abstract concepts: Good and bad in right- and left-handers. *Journal of Experimental Psychology: General*. 138(3), 351–367.

Casasanto, Daniel and K. Jasmin. 2010. Good and bad in the hands of politicians: Spontaneous gestures during positive and negative speech. PLoS ONE 5(7), e11805.

Dancygier, Barbara. 2012. *The Language of Stories: A Cognitive Approach*. Cambridge: Cambridge University Press.

Dancygier, Barbara and Eve Sweetser (eds). 2012. *Viewpoint in Language: A Multimodal Perspective*. Cambridge: Cambridge University Press.

De Mey, Marc. 2006. Mastering ambiguity. In Mark Turner (ed. *The Artful Mind: Cognitive Science and the Riddle of Human Creativity*. 271–304. New York: Oxford University Press.

Dudis, Paul. 2004a. *Depiction of Events in ASL: Conceptual Integration of Temporal Components*. Ph.D. dissertation, University of California, Berkeley.

_____. 2004b. Body partitioning and real-space blends. *Cognitive Linguistics* 15:2, 223–38.

_____. 2007. Types of depiction in ASL. Ms., Gallaudet University.

Fauconnier, Gilles and Mark Turner. 2002. *The Way We Think: Conceptual Blending and the Mind's Hidden Complexities*. New York: Basic Books.

Feldman, Jerome. 2006. *From Molecule to Metaphor: A Neural Theory of Language*. Cambridge, MA: MIT Press.

Fillmore, Charles J. 1997 [1971]. *Lectures on Deixis*. Stanford CA: Center for the Study of Language and Information. (Originally published 1971 by the Indiana University Linguistics Club as *The Santa Cruz Lectures on Deixis*.)

Fleischman, Suzanne. 1990. *Tense and Narrativity: From Medieval Performance to Modern Fiction*. Austin: University of Texas Press.

Genette, Gérard. 1980. *Narrative Discourse: An essay in Method*. Ithaca: Cornell University Press.

Hanks, William F. 1990. *Referential Practice: Language and Lived Space in a Maya Community*. Chicago: University of Chicago Press.

Haviland, John. 2000. Pointing, gesture spaces and mental maps. In David McNeill (ed.). *Language and Gesture*. 13–46. Cambridge: Cambridge University Press.

Herman, David. 2009. *Basic Elements of Narrative*. Malden MA and Oxford: Wiley-Blackwell.

_____. 2004. *Story Logic: Problems and Possibilities of Narrative*. Lincoln: University of Nebraska Press.

Hogan, Patrick Colm. 2003a. *Cognitive Science, Literature and the Arts: A Guide for Humanists*. New York: Routledge.

_____. 2003b. *The Mind and its Stories: Narrative Universals and Human Emotion*. Cambridge: Cambridge University Press.

Kita, Sotaro (ed.) *Pointing: Where Language, Culture and Cognition Meet*. Mahwah NJ: Lawrence Erlbaum.

Langacker, Ronald W. 1987. *Foundations of Cognitive Grammar*. 2 vols. Stanford: Stanford University Press, vol. I.

_____. 1991. *Foundations of Cognitive Grammar*. 2 vols. Stanford: Stanford University Press, vol. II.

Levinson, Stephen C. 1996. Relativity in spatial conception and description. In John J. Gumperz and Stephen C. Levinson (eds). *Rethinking Linguistic Relativity*. 177–202. Cambridge: Cambridge University Press.

_____. 2003. *Space in Language and Cognition: Explorations in Cognitive Diversity*. Cambridge: Cambridge University Press.

Liddell, Scott. 1998. Grounded blends, gestures and conceptual shifts. *Cognitive Linguistics* 9:3, 283–314.

_____. 2003. *Grammar, Gesture and Meaning in American Sign Language*. New York: Cambridge University Press.

McNeill, David. 1992. *Hand and Mind: What Gestures Reveal About Thought*. Chicago: University of Chicago Press.

McNeill, David and Susan Duncan. 2000. Growth points in Thinking-for-Speaking. *Language and Gesture*. 141–161. Cambridge: Cambridge University Press.

Nikiforidou, Kiki. 2010. Viewpoint and construction grammar: the case of past + now. *Language and Literature* 19:3, 265–84.

_____. 2012. The constructional underpinnings of viewpoint blends: *The Past + now* in language and literature. In Dancygier and Sweetser (eds). *Viewpoint in Language: A Multimodal Perspective*. 177–197. Cambridge: Cambridge University Press.

Özyürek, Asli. 2002. Do speakers design their cospeech gestures for their addressees? The effects of addressee location on representational gestures. *Journal of Memory and Language* 46:4, 688–704.

Parrill, Fey. 2009. Dual viewpoint gestures. *Gesture* 9(3), 271–289.

_____. 2010. Viewpoint in speech-gesture integration: Linguistics structure, discourse structure, and event structure. *Language and Cognitive Processes*, 25(5), 650–668.

Parrill, Fey and Eve Sweetser. 2004. What we mean by meaning: conceptual integration in gesture analysis and transcription. *Gesture 4*, 197–219.

Rubba, Johanna. 1996. Alternate grounds in the interpretation of deictic expressions. In Gilles Fauconnier and Eve Sweetser (eds). *Spaces, Worlds and Grammar*. 227–61. Chicago: University of Chicago Press.

Sanders, José and Gisela Redeker. 1996. Perspective and representation in speech and thought in narrative discourse. In Gilles Fauconnier and Eve Sweetser (eds). *Spaces, Worlds and Grammar*. 290–317. Chicago: University of Chicago Press.

Sanders, José, Ted Sanders, and Eve Sweetser. 2009. Causality, cognition and communication: a mental space analysis of subjectivity in causal connectives. In Ted Sanders and Eve Sweetser (eds). *Causal Categories in Discourse and Cognition*. 19–59. Berlin: Mouton de Gruyter.

_____. 2012. Responsible subjects and discourse causality: How mental spaces and perspective help identifying subjectivity in Dutch backward causal connectives. *Journal of Pragmatics* 44, 191–213.

Stec, Kashmiri. 2013. Meaningful shifts: A review of viewpoint markers in gesture and sign language. *Gesture* 12(3), 327–360.

Stec, Kashmiri and Eve Sweetser. 2012. Significant breaks: Space and viewpoint transitions in gesture. Paper presented at the 2012 International Gesture Studies Conference, in Lund, Sweden.

Sweetser, Eve. 2012. Introduction: Viewpoint and perspective in language and gesture, from the Ground down. In Dancygier and Sweetser (eds). *Viewpoint in Language: A Multimodal Perspective*. 1–22. Cambridge: Cambridge University Press.

Sweetser, Eve and Marisa Sizemore. 2008. Personal and interpersonal gesture space: functional contrasts in language and gesture. In Andrea Tyler, Yiyoung Kim, and Mari Takada (eds). *Language in the Context of Use: Cognitive and Discourse Approaches to Language and Language Learning*. 25–51. Berlin: Mouton de Gruyter.

Turner, Mark (ed.) 2006. *The Artful Mind: Cognitive Science and the Riddle of Human Creativity*. New York: Oxford University Press.

Vandelanotte, Lieven. 2009. *Speech and Thought Representation in English*. Berlin/New York: Mouton de Gruyter.

_____. 2012. 'Wait till you got started': How to submerge another's discourse in your own. In Dancygier and Sweetser (eds). *Viewpoint in Language: A Multimodal Perspective*. 198–218. Cambridge: Cambridge University Press.

Verhagen, Arie. 2005. *Constructions of Intersubjectivity: Discourse, Syntax and Cognition*. Oxford: Oxford University Press.

Zunshine, Lisa. 2006. *Why We Read Fiction: Theory of Mind and the Novel*. Columbus, OH: Ohio State University Press.

# 16

# Multimodal Construction Grammar

FRANCIS STEEN AND MARK TURNER

## 1 Introduction: Massive Multimodal Data

When people meet, they invariably communicate in multiple modalities: the eyes, gestures, and tones of voice merge with the perceived affordances of the surroundings into an integrated and partially shared experience. Multimodal communication predates and contextualizes language, and extends into a series of social, artistic, and technological innovations, from dance to cave paintings, from theater to cinema, from town criers to television news. Over the past hundred thousand years, our species has grown from a few roving bands to some seven billion individuals, linked by densely tangled electronic networks. That adds up to a lot of multimodal communication, a rich treasure trove of data comparable in complexity to the information available to astrophysicists, zoologists, and geneticists. Yet the datasets scholars rely on for deciphering the hidden orders of human communication remain overwhelmingly textual. The relatively few and small corpora we have of multimodal communication often come from specialized circumstances, such as interviews conducted by experimenters in whiteroom lab settings. In this article, we explore ways to broaden the foundations of our study of human communication.

Methodologically, we need to check our hypotheses against data. In the face of small, biased, and narrow archives of data, language scientists have often relied on personal introspection to choose between hypotheses. Yet, it is well-recognized by now in cognitive linguistics that although personal intuition can be a source of hypotheses, it has weaknesses as a test of hy-

*Language and the Creative Mind.*
Mike Borkent, Barbara Dancygier, and Jennifer Hinnell (eds).

potheses. For example, as Dąbrowska (2010) shows, judgments made by linguists diverge from those made by the general population. She concludes that 'syntacticians should not rely on their own intuitions when testing their theories'.[1]

For all these reasons—the sparseness and the biases of the data, the relative lack of systematicity, the relative lack of multimodality, the unreliability of introspective data—there has been a push in linguistics to develop corpora and methods for investigating cognitive linguistic questions through big datasets, some of them multimodal.

We hope to assist in this project for a new scientific future by deploying the resources of The Distributed Little Red Hen Lab. Red Hen (for short) is a global enterprise whose goal is to create a massive systematic corpus of ecologically valid multimodal data, along with new tools and practices to analyze this data. We record audiovisual news broadcasts systematically, and supplement the resulting dataset with other audiovisual records. This is made possible by Section 108 of the U.S. Copyright Act, which authorizes libraries and archives to record and loan audiovisual news programs. We sketch here a path toward computer-assisted, statistically-assisted analyses of massive multimodal communicative data and provide some illustrations of Red Hen's current capabilities.[2]

## 2 The Data

Red Hen's core dataset consists of the NewsScape Library of International Television News, housed and maintained securely at the library of the University of California, Los Angeles. Other datasets are in development. NewsScape consists of roughly 200,000 hours of broadcast network news, in a variety of languages. These data reveal the quick cultural creativity and extraordinary cultural variation of network news. They include roughly a billion words of timestamped closed-captioned texts, and roughly a billion words of transcripts. Red Hen ingests another hundred hours or so of global network news daily. We have begun to capture several Scandinavian channels and two channels from Spain, and we are currently working on expansion to other languages.

Red Hen has developed code for putting transcripts, where they exist, into time-stamped registration with the closed-caption text and aligning both with the audiovisual stream. Red Hen is also extracting on-screen text

[1] Ewa Dąbrowska (2010). Naive v. expert intuitions: An empirical study of acceptability judgments. *The Linguistic Review* 27, 1-23, page 1.

[2] The supporting website for this article, which archives audiovisual materials, is on the system's citation server, at http://vrnewsscape.ucla.edu/mind/SteenTurnerMMCG.html.

with optical character recognition and exploring ways to deploy speech-to-text transcription for broadcasts that lack closed-captions. Funded by a four-year National Science Foundation grant, Red Hen employs graduate students in Statistics, Computer Science, Information Studies, Communication Studies, and Political Science at UCLA and the University of Illinois Urbana-Champaign (UIUC) to develop techniques for automatic story segmentation, topic hierarchies, named entity recognition, speaker identification, and geospatial tagging. Computer vision students work on person detection, face recognition, and the characterization of visual features in facial expressions, clothing, and pose. Landscapes, buildings, vehicles, objects, and symbols are also being tagged, to permit richer description of the affordances of the environment and their systematic use in visual communication. Scholars of audio analysis examine the collection for strong emotions, vocal characteristics, and patterns of music use. Information scholars are developing new and interactive forms of data visualization. Broadcast news presents a series of hard problems to multiple disciplines, calling for trans-disciplinary collaboration.

Red Hen data are highly multimodal, including speech, on-screen text, gesture (broadly defined), bodily stance, music, sound effects, graphics, and a range of other audiovisual expressions. Red Hen data are legendarily ecologically valid: human beings find TV news immersive throughout their lifespan, in all developed cultures and in all of the most-commonly studied languages. The data are broadcast daily to billions of people worldwide—for an impression, see the supporting website, which presents pictures of people in various environments attending to the news.

While the experience of watching the news is now ubiquitous, as a mode of human communication it remains a cultural novelty. The technologies and practices of multimodal news communication have undergone rapid developments over the past century—a blink of an eye compared to the history of language. They represent significant cognitive innovations: at no previous point in human history have people had the ability to assemble representations of events that to a high degree reproduce the human experience of vision and hearing. The technologically mediated communicative practices of television news present an opportunity and a challenge to our understanding of the human communicative system, inviting us to extend our study of linguistic phenomena into new multimodal forms of expression.

What do we think is happening when we watch the news? How do we make sense of the scene? Human beings have a rich experiential understanding of scenes of face-to-face 'communicative joint attention'. Joint attention is a human-scale scene in which some people are attending to something and know they are all attending to something and know also that they are engaged with each other in attending to it (Tomasello et al. 1995; Tobin 2008). In 'communicative joint attention' people are not only jointly attending but also communicating with each other about the focus of their attention, even if the communication is very sparse, consisting perhaps of only pointing. We use the term 'classic joint attention' to refer to perhaps the most fundamental scene of communicative joint attention, in which two or a few people in face-to-face presence are not only attending to something that is directly perceptible but are moreover communicating about it in a sustained way. (Thomas and Turner 2011, Part 3.) The multimodal patterns of managing classic joint attention have been closely studied in the tradition of Erving Goffman (1967), notably in Kendon (1990), for example.

Watching the news is not a scene of classic joint attention, but it tacitly builds upon that understanding. The many mental spaces needed to make sense of a scene of watching network news include classic joint attention, the broadcast viewer, everyone in the viewer's environment involved in jointly watching the broadcast, everyone outside the viewer's environment involved in watching the broadcast, the staff involved in crafting the communication, the crews that handle the technology, the technology itself, the items that are the focus of the news and to which our attention is directed, and so on and on and on. This diffuse mental network would be intractable to the viewer except that we can blend its many connected mental spaces into an anchoring scene of *blended joint attention*, much of whose structure is provided by the all-important input space of classic joint attention. In the blend, we are in a scene of human-scale classic joint attention. Some of the management and communication techniques available in classic joint attention project down easily to the blend, some do not, and the blend develops emergent techniques of its own, which it is our purpose to study.

We are not deluded by this blend; Contrary to the claims of Reeves and Nass (1996), it is not simply the case that we equate the media with reality. The blend integrates conceptual structure from multiple sources into a seamless and mentally manageable whole. We know, for example, that, in the full mental network, the anchor who addresses us as 'you' or who says 'I will show you that in a minute' and who is looking at 'us' does not actually know us or see us. In the vast mental network surrounding and anchored by the human-scale scene of blended joint attention, we know that there are hundreds of agents, and people we do not see, and technological manipulation, and so on. Our attention, however, is typically focused on the meanings made available through high levels of compression achieved inside the blend. Inside the blend, we are in a congenial scene structured by the concept of classic joint attention. Accordingly, many of the linguistic constructions and words and gestures developed for classic joint attention can be projected to the blend and used directly of the blend. We do not need to invent entirely new language or gestures in order to run and understand this scene of news broadcasts. To be sure, as we will see, new or extended communicative constructions can also emerge in this blend, but they are based on constructions we already know from our normal scenes of classic joint attention.

One of the basic research missions of Red Hen is to analyze such multimodal constructions.

## 3 What is a Construction?

Construction grammarians use the term 'construction' in a range of ways, but in all of them, a construction is a mental packet, consisting of a form-meaning pairing that speakers of a language know. Goldberg writes,

> A construction is defined to be a pairing of form with meaning/use such that some aspect of the form or some aspect of the meaning/use is not strictly predictable from the component parts or from other constructions already established to exist in the language. On this view, phrasal patterns, including the constructions of traditional grammarians, such as relative clauses, questions, locative inversion, etc. are given theoretical status. Morphemes are also constructions, according to the definition, since their form is not predictable from their meaning or use. Given this, it follows that the lexicon is not neatly delimited from the rest of grammar, although phrasal constructions differ from lexical items in their internal complexity. Both phrasal patterns and lexical items are stored in an extended 'constructicon'. (Goldberg 1996: 68.)

A construction might include various related elements for which traditional linguistics has various names—phonology, internal syntax, external syntax, semantics, pragmatics, and so on. Constructions can be more or less 'lexically filled'. For example, the 'Way' construction (Israel 1996) and the 'What's X doing Y?' construction (Kay and Fillmore 1999) require that the lexical item 'way' and the lexical items 'what' and 'doing' fill the right spots in instances of the constructions. Examples of the 'Way' construction include 'she found her way to the market' and 'he lied his way to the top'. Examples of the 'What's X doing Y?' construction include 'What are you doing talking to me?' and 'What's this coffee cup doing on my coffee table?'

The basic vocabulary we need to talk about research into multimodal constructions comes from the notion that to know a language is to know a *relational network of constructions and how they can be blended to create forms* that when expressed count for (many) other speakers of the language as belonging to the language. They count as expressions in the language because those other speakers are able to find in their own relational network of constructions some established constructions that blend to produce just those forms. By 'constructicon', we will mean this knowledge of constructions and how to blend them. Broadly, knowing a language is knowing such a relational network of constructions and how its constructions can be blended to produce forms that can be expressed. Accordingly, the two-year-old and the eighty-year-old from different geographical areas can both be thought to 'know' a single language even though what they know might be considerably different. We modify our knowledge of constructions and the way they blend as we develop.

Crucially, the constructicon is multimodal. We can sum up our project as the investigation through the powers of Red Hen of multimodal constructions and how they blend. In exploring the ways in which the idea of a construction in linguistics extends and generalizes to technologically mediated forms of multimodal communication, as they have been extended to interpersonal forms of multimodal communication, we remain open to the possibility of radical discontinuities and unprecedented innovations. Our point of departure is that network news relies heavily on a carefully orchestrated system of generating blended joint attention, creatively building on a series of constructions we recognize from the analysis of linguistic communication.

## 4 Linguistic Constructions

One way to use Red Hen is to study her texts. These include closed-captions, transcripts, and on-screen text. In this way, Red Hen offers a dataset for garden-variety linguistic inquiry. Red Hen is for this purpose similar to other corpora, such as the Corpus of Contemporary American, the British National Corpus, and the Russian National Corpus.

As an example of how Red Hen can help us study constructions, consider Turner's (1987) analysis in *Death is the Mother of Beauty* of conceptual connections and their integration. Its data consisted of expresses using kinship terms, such as 'mother'. The data were acquired by tracking down remembered examples, recording adventitious encounters with expressions in speech and writing, scouring concordances and historical dictionaries and lexicons, and otherwise making use of all of the back-of-the-envelope tricks of data acquisition that characterize much of traditional linguistics. The data were recorded on 3-inch-by-5-inch index cards and stored in index boxes until they could be typed into a flat file in an account on a Unix mainframe at the Lawrence Berkeley Laboratory. We now live in a different universe. A search of Red Hen finds thousands of such examples in seconds. The search produces ranges of nonliteral uses of kinship terms conforming to the analyses in *Death is the Mother of Beauty*, such as 'Ayn Rand is the mother of objectivism', 'Virginia is the mother of presidents', and, in a usage familiar from Saddam Hussein's famous phrase, 'the mother of all battles' (reportedly understood quite differently in Iraq and the United States), usages such as 'Virginia is the mother of all battleground states' (where, contextually, the battles are about US national elections) and 'She is the mother of all whistlers'. One finds memorable examples such as 'Pink is the mother of all colors'.

These examples can be studied or at least perused by the researcher one after another, in human time and at a human pace. But Red Hen is additionally ready to export all her hits to a comma-separated-value file, which can then be fed to a software package like R (see http://www.r-project.org), and subjected to statistical analysis.

The clausal construction involved in 'Death is the mother of beauty' is the 'X is the Y of Z' construction. This xyz construction has routine everyday uses, as in 'Paul is the father of Sally'. It has been analyzed by Turner and Fauconnier (Turner 1991, 1998; Fauconnier and Turner 2002). xyz contains the 'y-of' construction. A 'Y of' expression prompts us to perform the following operations:

(1) Call up an input space for the relational frame containing y (the element named by Y).
(2) Construct a blended space.
(3) Project from the element y selectively to create an element y' in the blend.
(4) Provide for a w in the input space that will bear an appropriate relationship to y.
(5) Project from that element w selectively to create an element w' in the blend.
(6) Project the y-w relationship selectively onto y'-w' in the blended space.
(7) Provide open-ended connectors from y' and w' in the blend. We expect these connectors to make connections at some point.
(8) Expect the open-ended connector from w' in the blend to connect to something picked out by the noun phrase that will follow 'of'.

In an xyz construction, we additionally call up a relational frame containing x and z (the elements named by X and Z), and attach the open-ended connector from y' to x and from w' to z. It is possible to compose y-of constructions. That is, what follows the 'of' in the first Y expression can be another Y expression, for as long as we like: 'The doctor of the sister of the boss of Hieronymous Bosch'.

Red Hen can of course be asked to search for examples of such constructions. One could, for example, check various hypotheses about frequency of patterns. In the Red Hen data, we find two standard patterns for y, as follows: (1) y belongs to a standard frame commonly applied to the x-z scene; y is a role connecting at least two things in that frame; x is the value of one of those roles and z is the value of the other. Examples are *archbishop* and *aunt*. (2) y is the anchor of an entrenched generic blending template used to blend together two conflicting frames. Examples are *ancestor, anchor, architect, author, backbone, bane, birthplace, blood, blueprint, bottleneck, capital, cradle,* etc., as in phrases like 'He is the architect of our business plan and that business plan is the backbone of our operation'. But, impressively, one also finds in Red Hen very many data calling for blends of strongly conflicting frames where there is no already-entrenched y-based blending template. Examples are 'The head of the C.D.C. told Congress MRSA is the cockroach of bacteria', 'Bakersfield is the Alaska of California', and 'These flame retardants are the asbestos of our time'.

Red Hen provides data for considering related constructions, of the sorts originally studied in (Turner, 1991), such as the $xy_{adjective}$ z form. When the y in an xyz conceptual pattern is a commonplace transformation of one thing into another, its form may be $xy_{adjective}z$, so 'Language is the fossil of poetry' may be expressed as 'Language is fossil poetry'. When the y-w conceptual relation is a part-whole frame relation, the form may be $xz_{adjective}y$, so 'Las Vegas is the Monte Carlo of America' may be expressed as 'Las Vegas is the American Monte Carlo'. Red Hen offers up great ranges of such constructions related to the xyz construction, such as 'Westerns are back in the TV saddle', 'She is gymnastics royalty', 'He is passing the ethical buck', and 'Iran could be this year's Japan'.

Investigations along these lines are in principle no different than investigations run on any text corpus, although for some purposes Red Hen may offer some advantages derived from content or ease of search. Red Hen to this extent takes her place alongside text corpora.

But because Red Hen is multimodal, we can instantly look for *visual* correlates of the xyz construction. Network news, to give viewers an idea of what some event is about, frequently position a photograph or footage of the new event next to a photograph or footage from some old, well-known event, and this presentation is not to be understood as indicating that the two represented scenes combine or connect in reality. For example, when Anders Behring Breivik exploded a car bomb in front of government offices in Oslo in 2011, several news channels showed his face alongside that of Timothy McVeigh, the 1995 Oklahoma City bomber, visually conveying the message that Breivik is the Timothy McVeigh of Norway.

## 5 'Errors'

As Hofstadter and Moser (1989: 185) observed, 'the study of speech errors and action slips can reveal a great deal about the hidden organization of the minds that produce them'. Because so much of the speech in news broadcasts is improvised, extemporaneous, and live, as opposed to written or edited or both, Red Hen's data may have advantages in containing linguistic 'errors' that might serve as windows on grammatical processes. For example, it is a natural hypothesis that when there are rival forms available for prompting for a meaning that the speaker wants to express, and moreover those forms are related in a way that makes it easy to produce a blend of both, 'errors' might result, as in 'This is my future wife-to-be' (Cohen 1987). But if we are right in our hypotheses about the production of such errors, then we should be able to predict their relative occurrence, probabilistically. We might have to listen for an impractical amount of time in order to acquire enough data to test our hypotheses, and of course these errors are likely to be edited out of written data or even unconsciously suppressed during human transcription. But Red Hen has the actual performances and increasingly has machine transcription and speech-to-text transcription that may preserve the errors; in addition, the audio recordings are instantly available for systematic verification.

Let's ask Red Hen to do it, as follows: There are many patterns related to the xyz construction. Let us return to mathematics and create an example of an xyz clause: 'This number theory problem is the Mt. Everest of mathematics'. The w, presumably something like *challenging mountains to be climbed,* is not mentioned. We have the following related patterns:

(1) xyz itself, 'This number theory problem is the Mt. Everest of mathematics'. w is not mentioned.
(2) x is y, 'This number theory problem is Mt. Everest'. Neither w nor z needs to be mentioned.
(3) x is the z-equivalent of y, 'This number theory problem is the mathematics equivalent of Mt. Everest'. (This is a case, for us, on the cusp: We could say equally easily, 'This number theory problem is the mathematical equivalent of Mt. Everest'.)
(4) x is the equivalent of y, 'This number theory problem is the equivalent of Mt. Everest'.
(5) x is the $z_{adjective}$-y, 'This number theory problem is the mathematical Mt. Everest'.

But 4 and 5 are very close. Since $z_{adjective}$-y is a noun whose head is y, it is easy to slide it into the noun-phrase position for y in 4. Do we get 'errors' where the speaker produces 'x is the equivalent of $z_{adjective}$-y', like 'This number theory problem is the equivalent of the mathematical Mt. Everest'? We asked Red Hen, and found just such an 'error', produced by a high-end car dealer who was engaged in an interview with a TV reporter as they walked amongst some spectacular antique cars that were to be auctioned at a legendary event the next day: 'That car is the equivalent of the automotive Mona Lisa'. (See the supporting website.) Any editor would have corrected that sentence before publication. The accepted alternatives are: 'That car is the Mona Lisa of automobiles' (pattern 1), 'That car is the Mona Lisa' (pattern 2), 'That car is the automobile/automotive equivalent of the Mona Lisa' (pattern 3), 'That car is the equivalent of the Mona Lisa' (pattern 4), and 'That car is the automotive Mona Lisa' (pattern 5). And yet, what would have been regarded as an error in written language may be much more acceptable in multimodal communication: the overdetermining 'equivalent' in this sentence provides an additional cue to the hearer to construct a blend, and the extra cue may be communicatively useful. Red Hen can accordingly be used to find and analyze not only familiar linguistic constructions but also context that might lead to the production of what are routinely regarded as errors, and, given the massive amount of data in Red Hen, to test predictions of statistical patterns of errors.

## 6 Co-Speech Gesture

The study of co-speech gesture has flourished in the last few decades, and Red Hen offers a great wealth of data because all of the text is tagged with thumbnails that one can click to see a recording of the actual performance of the utterance, including gesture. It is easy to think of indefinitely many investigations of co-speech gesture for Red Hen to run. For example, although the temporal adverb 'previously' is etymologically connected to movement along a path, it is probably not analyzable as such to most current speakers of English. How do they gesture when they say it? We asked Red Hen to find in a very limited date range examples of 'previously' at the end of a sentence. Red Hen found many, several of which have gestures, even when anchors, trained out of hand gesturing, use the word. Senator Kelly Ayotte on CBS Face the Nation for 2013-02-24, says, 'You had the Secretary of Education on previously', and nods her head laterally to her left when she says the word. (See the supporting website.) Red Hen hopes to help develop machine recognition of gesture and annotation of text for co-speech gestures. This machine recognition is built on training from clips that have been hand-tagged by human experts. Naturally, Red Hen data might be better or worse for specific purposes in gesture study. Those who prefer elicited data from controlled experimental conditions might have methodological concerns over using observational data, but, on the other hand, Red Hen data has the advantage of being completely free of the corruptions that come from demand characteristics of experimental data involving human beings or the strangeness of elicited conversation under lab scrutiny. Those who prefer to study spontaneous, untrained gesture may have qualms about studying the gestures of such trained performers as news anchors and reporters. But on the other hand, first, a great deal of Red Hen data consist of spontaneous, untrained performance by people who happened to be recorded in public places, many of whom were presumably unaware that they were being recorded; and second, perhaps there is much to be learned about communication by studying the performances of highly expert communicators, who, for all their training, often land in the position of extemporizing without a script or without even warning of the breaking news story.

We offer as an example of co-speech gesture that can be studied within Red Hen the performance of US Secretary of State Hillary Clinton while testifying before the Senate Foreign Relations Committee, chaired by Senator John Kerry, on Capitol Hill in Washington, DC, March 2, 2011. (See the supporting website.) Her testimony was recorded and broadcast by Russia Today, whose main news broadcast is systematically ingested by Red Hen. Of course, politicians use a vocabulary of prepared gestures (e.g. closed rather than open-finger) that is quite distinctive relative to everyday gestures, but then again, the study of prepared performance in gesture is interesting in its own right, and Red Hen has massive gestural data from nonpoliticians or, more generally, nonperformers. One research project using Red Hen would be to contrast the practiced performers with others. In a way, everyone is a practiced performer; The question is instead what they have practiced for.

The RT anchor frames the situation and introduces the topic to the viewer:

> Hillary Clinton says the US is losing an information war to foreign media outlets, including RT. This week the Secretary of State asked Congress for more cash to step up America's efforts to get its message across.

We begin by recognizing viewpoint: the situation defines Clinton in the role of a Secretary of State arguing for enhanced funding of her Department. Her public performance thus embodies an enduring institutional logic, one that is reflected in and reinforced by the details of the visual setting: the microphones, the panel of senators, the sheer presence of the media. This acknowledged role play does not vitiate the force of her arguments; rather, her performance has the force of the entire State Department, underlining how seriously the institution views the development of competing global television news outlets.

Against the backdrop of a silent and grim Clinton, the on-screen text flashes,

> CLINTON: US LOSING GLOBAL INFO
> WAR AS MULTI-POLAR REALITY BITES

The multimodal blend assembles these two sources of information—the facial expression and the on-screen text—into a single, integrated interpretation: Secretary Clinton is the embodiment of the State Department and the entire US, and she expresses, in a compressed form, the emotional meaning of a loss, coupled with an aggressive determination to attempt to face the facts and avoid further losses. The unfocused gaze and drawn mouth suggest sadness and resignation, while the clenched jaw hints of a determination to fight back. The human visual system interprets faces with extreme speed, and without needing to translate the features into verbally expressed concepts; Only a slowed-down analysis allows us to identify the elements of the crossmodal blend.

Yet Clinton's clenched performance is effortlessly contained by the triumphal ethical superiority of the RT reporter, who melodramatically proclaims,

> War declared. The US is now officially in an information battle with foreign media, which provide alternative views on world news -- views which often run in contrast to the coverage of events by the US mainstream media.

Before the Secretary's testimony begins, RT has already reconfigured the loss of US dominance as progress, a positive development facilitating multiperspective understanding.

Gesturally, Clinton opens by metaphorically taking hold of the entire concept in a precision grip, staring intently with wide-open eyes on her unseen interlocutor, declaring 'We are in an information war'. Casting her glance briefly aside, indicating thought, she angles her wrist and hand to point towards herself, saying, 'And we are losing that war; I'll be very blunt in my assessment', as she tilts her head slightly to the right, appearing less imposing or threatening, and bobs her head up and down with a slight smile, as if eagerly eliciting agreement.

In the space she creates with these simple gestures, Clinton situates herself as the US in the center of a symbolic space. With an open hand she swings her right arm in an upward sweeping gesture, opening up this space to the competition in the global war of information; Her gaze pointedly fixed straight ahead, she extends her arm fully to the side and down in an expansive movement, freezing her shoulder in the down position, saying, 'Al Jazeera is winning'. The gesture masterfully conveys at once an unspoken acknowledgment of the strength, significance, and enduring presence of the opponent and his unwelcome status; He is not granted the inclusive grace of even a glace, a brief moment of symbolic eye contact. After a brief, pregnant pause she raises her extended hand slightly, opening up the space further as she expands the list: 'The Chinese have opened up a global English-language and multi-language television network', nodding at each word to convey the brute fact of the audacity of the encroachment. Finally, 'The Russians have opened up an English-language network. I've seen it in a few countries, and it's quite instructive'. Closing her eyes for a moment in the cognitive equivalent of a black screen transition, she raises her arm and indicates a retreat by gesturing repeatedly towards herself: 'We're cutting back, the BBC is cutting back'. The Secretary herself is gesturally mapped as personifying the entire Anglo-American alliance, graphically under threat by other perspectives. This bodily language facilitates the rapid construction of the complex cognitive models that Clinton is compressing into a few minutes of testimony.

As viewers of RT, we watch all this nested within an outer frame: in an ironic twist, the Secretary is testifying that the US is losing an information war precisely to the channel in which we are watching her testimony. Watching RT, we become allies of alternative sources of information, positioning us on the disruptive but winning side in the information war.

## 7 Audiovisual Correlates of Linguistic Constructions

Cognitive linguists routinely study basic mental operations and phenomena that are not exclusive to language but that are deployed in language and leave their mark on its structure: mental space phenomena, conceptual integration, categorization, image-schematic structuring and transformation, fictive motion, force dynamics, viewpoint phenomena, scanning ... Since the news deploys other modalities than speech and text, it is an obvious project to look for the ways in which these basic mental operations and phenomena are deployed in those other modalities.

Many words in many languages prompt us to build conceptual integration networks containing relations of counterfactuality, such as 'safe', 'accident', 'dent', 'mistake', 'Good thing ...', 'Too bad, ...', and so on. The news presents counterfactuality so routinely that it is surprising that the stereotype of the news is that it presents 'what's happening'. The news has standard routines for audiovisual prompting of the counterfactual. One of the most straightforward of these standard routines is to show a visual prompt for the actual counterfactual scene. For example, a young woman who stars as a student in a based-on-a-true-story film about a high-school teacher who was fabulously successful in teaching mathematics to inner-city poor youth reports, 'I thought if only I had come to this school, if only I had him for a teacher, I would have learned math', and the TV news immediately shows a picture of a young woman dressed as a student standing with the legendary teacher, so we can map the speaker onto the student (see the supporting website). A woman at the beauty parlor says 'If only I had some shoes', and the TV news immediately shows a vast array of shoes (see the supporting website). It is easy for us to imagine the counterfactual, but not to *perceive* it. Television is using its standard technique in these cases of moving an operation that is normal to human imagination into actual human perception. The bizarre perceptual phenomenon does not seem bizarre to us at all because it is a familiar imaginative phenomenon.

Such data, in which the news visually presents a representation of the counterfactual scene or counterfactual elements needed for constructing the blend, are vast and often subtle and nuanced, falling into a variety of types. Consider the word 'detour', which prompts us to construct one space with one path A on which something travels and another space with another path B on which the same thing travels. When we blend these so as to take both paths but travel on A, then the counterfactual relationship between travel on A and travel on B is compressed to *absence of travel on B*. Language for expressing this blend includes 'direct', 'quick', and so on. If we blend the same inputs so as to take both paths but travel on B, then the counterfactual relationship between travel on A and travel on B is compressed to *absence of travel on A*. Language for expressing this blend includes 'detour', 'delay', and so on. Red Hen offers a specific case in which police traveling to an island took path B by inflatable boat, and during the period of the travel, scores of young people were murdered on an island not far from Oslo, Norway. In this presentation, the 'detour' causes a 'delay', used as an invitation to the audience to construct a network with a counterfactual connection between the two journeys. Without explicitly accusing the police, the news is designed to lead its viewers to contemplate the alternative scenario and to compare the two outcomes. The delta of this operation is additional deaths: taking the 'shortest route' would accordingly have 'saved lives'. All during the linguistic presentation, the news is showing a satellite image of the geographical area, with the diagrammatic trace of the possible and the actual travel by the police. The dynamic travel that in fact did not happen is shown first, followed by the route actually taken (see the supporting web site). The words 'Dette er den korteste veien til Utøya' ('this is the shortest route to Utøya') and 'politiet valgte å kjøre denne omveien' ('the police chose to take this detour') are accordingly paired with visual presentations for the blend that prompt for the activation of the different input spaces, the counterfactual relationship between them, and the compression to features like *absence, detour, delay*, and so on.

This depiction of the counterfactual exemplifies how the news uses the multimodality of the presentation to prompt for the understanding that we linguists usually analyze by inspecting the linguistic phenomena only. Red Hen would seem to be a natural dataset for such investigations. Presumably, for example, one could investigate gestural prompts for the construction of counterfactuality and blending to produce emergent structure.

Let us consider a specific grammatical construction for which there was originally an implicit hypothesis about its natural alignment with multimodal presentation. Nikiforidou (2010 and 2012) analyzes the role of blending in a construction she calls 'Past tense + proximal deictic', with emphasis on the cases where the proximal deictic is 'now'. This well-known construction is also broadly analyzed (Dancygier 2012, Chapter 7; Sweetser, this volume). The preferred patterns are 'was/were + now', as in 'It was now possible ...' and, for a noncopula verb, 'now + past tense', as in 'He now saw that ...'. Nikiforidou provides 'a detailed blueprint of the blending mappings cued by the [past + proximal deictic] pattern' (2012: 177). Essentially, the pattern calls for a blend of viewpoints, in which our overall understanding is stage-managed from the point of view of a narrator but some self or consciousness located in a previous time is contextually available and prominent, and the events experienced in that previous time are to be construed 'from the point of view of that consciousness, as that character's thoughts, speech or perceptions' (2010: 266). The blended viewpoint takes on elements of different perspectives and compresses a time relation. The mental space of the narrator's condition is still the mental space from which the narrated space is accessed and built up, but the experiential perspective comes from inside the narrated events. There is considerable emergent structure in the blend. In the blend, it is possible to have not only knowledge that is available only at a distance, but also the experience, perception, and realization available only up close.

In a study of the British National Corpus, Nikiforidou (2012) shows that this is a highly productive construction, even outside of literary genres. Presciently, Nikiforidou writes that the grammatical pattern has the 'effect of zooming in on the events' (180). Let us consider 'zooming in'. A human being can shift focus and attention and can locomote or lean forward or back in order to change the angle that objects subtend in the visual field, but, absent assisting technology, a human being cannot zoom in on or zoom out from an actual percept—that is, a human being cannot, without changing the location of the head, change the angle that objects subtend in the visual field. Yet, it is easy to 'zoom' in visual imagination, as anyone can demonstrate. In your mind's eye, picture some landmark near where you live—a familiar building, a bridge, a body of water, for example—or picture a person. Now, in visual imagination, zoom in. Now zoom out. Zooming seems to be a very common and easy manipulation in imagination. Perhaps imagination works this way because we do have the actual experience of an image in the visual field getting 'larger' as we move toward it or 'smaller' as we move away from it, and we can of course do time-scaling in imagination because of blending, so zooming in imagination is available as a product of blending over experience, but not projecting to the blend the movement of the viewer. Does the news adopt this mental functionality of the zooming imagination by using a photographic visual-field analogue of mental zooming? That is, does it move an operation from imagination into perception? Yes. For screens that result from camerawork, we have available a mental blend in which our eye is fused with the camera lens or with the through-the-lens viewfinder. Now, when the camera zooms—which it can do because it has a lens array that our eyes do not have—our vision, in the blend for the news, *zooms*. So the next question is: When we are in a news scene of narration and the narrator uses the *past* + *now* construction, does the camera zoom in on the self or consciousness that had the experiences?

Yes. Or rather, that is what we often find in Red Hen. There is a hitch in providing this *past* + *now* visual zoom, because the narrator speaks *at one time* about a consciousness *at a previous time*. That is a mismatch. The consciousness and its experiences are not available in the narrator's immediate environment, or indeed in any of the mental spaces we have for considering the production and broadcast of the narration. How do we deal with the mismatch? The news production team must provide some suitable prompt for that consciousness in the past, but it isn't with them. There are several ways to resolve the mismatch. The three most common appear to be: (1) have the person who is coreferential with the consciousness we are narrating reenact the events, with the appropriate setting and staging and so on, and film that scene; (2) find archival still photos of that person at the time and present them, perhaps, a Kens Burns effect, as the narrator uses the *past* + *now* construction; (3) find historical film footage containing the person and run that footage as the narrator uses the *past* + *now* construction. One can, of course, do all three. For all three of these expedients, one can zoom in on the images. Of course, narrators on the news usually just narrate, without using this extra production, but such zooming production is easy to find in Red Hen. Nikiforidou did not explicitly predict these data, but implicitly she did, and the data support her intuition of what is going on mentally.

Here are two examples (see the supporting website for the clips). In the first, the narrator is telling the story of Kim, who as an adult had to deal with her mother's continuing to invest in what Kim came to understand was a fraudulent business scam. While the narrator uses phrases like 'Kim now saw ...' and 'Kim now wondered ...', we see scenes of what must be a more recent Kim balancing a checkbook, shaking her head, doing sums, comparing documents, and so on. Kim is reenacting her consciousness and behavior from the past. The production team uses camera zoom and jump cut to get closer to the image of Kim's reenactment of her scenes of realization as the narrator uses the *past* + *now* construction.

Nikiforidou writes of the linguistic construction,

> In blending terms, ... resolution of (apparent) conflict is often achieved through the mechanism of compression, whereby elements that are conceptually separate in the input spaces are construed as one in the blended space. The construction at hand, I suggest, cues a particular kind of compression, namely compression of a time relation. The dynamic, continuously updated character of such blending networks renders them particularly suitable for representing meaning in a narrative, where formal clues may often give conflicting instructions even within the same sentence (as is the case with FIS [Free Indirect Speech]). (2012: 179)

We see in the news the audiovisual analogue of this blending prompt: in the news, we have input spaces in which the narrator and the production team have a viewpoint on the past and on the orchestration and arrangement of all the mental spaces involved in the network of the narrative, and we have a particular input space that has Kim and her experiences, and we are prompted to create a blended space that has projections from both the orchestrating viewpoints and Kim's viewpoint, creating there a great compression not only of viewpoint but also of time.

One of the most interesting and common uses of *past* + *now* occurs when the narrator and the narrated consciousness are coreferential. We find many such examples in Red Hen, such as a documentary on the Pentagon Papers, in which Daniel Ellsberg, who leaked the Pentagon Papers, is narrating in advanced age his exploits in the period 1967–1971 (see the supporting website). As he narrates, we see historical footage of several presidents discussing the Vietnam conflict publicly, along with historical footage of the war. But we also see, in montage, close-ups and zooms of Ellsberg at the time. Perhaps these scenes are acted, using an actor to play the young Ellsberg—the audience is not told. In montage, as the historical footage runs, we are treated to close-ups of fingers—which we are to take as belonging to Ellsberg—running over the typed words of pages of the Pentagon Papers. We see 'Ellsberg' opening volumes, closing them, shifting them, inspecting the documents, all in great close-up, and using various zooming techniques. Ellsberg the narrator is using the *past* + *now* construction: 'I now saw that [President Lyndon] Johnson was continuing a pattern of presidential lying'. We construct a viewpoint blend in which the viewpoint of the orchestration of the entire narrative is projected from the mental space with Ellsberg the narrator but the viewpoint on the experience of realizing what was happening is projected from the space of Ellsberg as he reads the Pentagon Papers for the first time. There is extraordinary emergent structure in this blend, including Ellsberg's ability to speak for his young self in a way that probably would not have been available to him at the time, and of course and enduring, manufactured, compressed character for 'Ellsberg' the man: young Ellsberg and old Ellsberg are of course extremely different things, but the analogies between them, including analogies of viewpoint, can be compressed to a characterological unity in the blend.

Just in passing, we acknowledge that it is possible to deploy not only *re-inforcing* or *supplementary* linguistic and audiovisual constructions but also *conflicting* constructions. This is a standard technique of humor and various forms of entertainment. It is also a technique of news broadcasts whose brand is based in an explicit and reliable political or ideological stamp. These shows routinely ridicule the opposition by providing footage of the opposition with accompanying audiovisual constructions designed to make them look stupid.

## 8 Novel Broadcast Constructions

Since new constructions arise by blending existing constructions and conceptual arrays, there is really never any construction that is truly 'novel'. Human cognition and expression is highly conservative, although what we focus on is often the emergent structure. Accordingly, when we discuss 'novel broadcast constructions', we do not mean to indicate that they are not based on antecedent constructions. On the contrary, everything new that human beings contrive is deeply based in established input spaces. Otherwise, it would be not novel but rather unintelligible.

The power of broadcast news to use so many modalities simultaneously, not as a combination but rather as a system that different disciplines have tried to approach as a linear sum, produces a wealth of partly-novel broadcast constructions. Consider, for example, the extraordinary work of news broadcasts to talk about the future, as in weather forecasts. What is required in this case is amazing compressions over not only time, space, causation, and agency, but also possibility. Some of the audiovisual prompts for these compressions are spectacular but look utterly natural. For example, in weather reports about impending meteorological reports such as hurricanes, one can find the usual linguistic expressions, such as 'likely', 'perhaps', 'threat', and so on, both in the speech of the weather forecaster and in the on-screen text. Graphics often accompany these verbal reports, and the graphics can be extremely sophisticated while striking viewers as entirely ordinary. It is common, for example, to display, using compression of time and space, the future of a hurricane. One sees representations on a map that we are to take as prompting for a conception of the path of the hurricane, and also the hurricane's size, but there is more: As the path moves into the future, there is an expanding width to the cone of incidence for the hurricane, not because the radius of the hurricane itself is expanding, but because our ignorance of the probable location of the hurricane is increasing. The conical graph on the map compresses not only time and space but also epistemic stance. We seem to have here a visual correlate of an evidential marker. (See website for an example.)

## 9 Conclusion

The multimodal dimensions of human communication present a rich field of discovery and insight that extends existing linguistic theories into other modalities, providing new opportunities for systematically testing and validating intuitions. The different modalities of a communicative act are not simply redundant, but provide new aspects of meaning that a multimodal analysis can uncover. Nor is the construction of meaning across modalities mechanically additive; rather, meanings emerge as crossmodal blends that rapidly synthesize selected features of the information into new wholes. To understand human communication, we must develop a new facility for understanding the grammar of multimodal meaning construction.

The Red Hen project aims to integrate a multimodal data collection of global television news with data enhancement, multimodal data mining, and cognitive analysis of multimodal communicative practices. Television news represents a uniquely available dataset of common communicative practices, with the additional attraction that it has been deliberately crafted by professional teams to grab attention, convey complex meanings in a rapid and compressed format, and persuade by implication. The way in which television succeeds in tapping into ancient interpretive structures in our cognitive system makes its detailed examination particularly revealing.

## References

Cohen, Gerald. 1987. *Syntactic Blends in English Parole*. Frankfurt, Bern, New York: Peter Lang.

Dąbrowska, Ewa, 2010. Naive v. expert intuitions: an empirical study of acceptability judgments, *The Linguistic Review* 27, 1–23. DOI 10.1515/tlir.2010.001.

Dancygier, Barbara. 2012. *The Language of Stories: A Cognitive Approach*. Cambridge: Cambridge University Press.

Dancygier, Barbara and Eve Sweetser (eds). 2012. *Viewpoint in Language: A Multimodal Perspective*. Cambridge UK: Cambridge University Press.

Fauconnier, Gilles and Mark Turner. 2002. *The Way We Think: Conceptual Blending and the Mind's Hidden Complexities*. New York: Basic Books.

Fillmore, C. J. 2006. Articulating Lexicon and Constructicon. Presentation at the Fourth International Conference on Construction Grammar, Tokyo, Japan.

Fillmore, Charles J., Russell R. Lee-Goldman, Russell Rhodes. 2011. The FrameNet Constructicon. In Boas, H.C. and Sag, I.A. (eds), *Sign-based Construction Grammar*. Stanford: CSLI Publications.

Goffman, Erving. 1967. *Interaction Ritual: Essays in Face-to-Face Behavior*. Chicago: Aldine

Goldberg, Adele. 1996. Construction Grammar. In Brown, E. K. and J. E. Miller (eds), *Concise Encyclopedia of Syntactic Theories*. New York: Pergamon.

Hofstadter, Douglas and David J. Moser. 1989. To Err is Human; To Study Error-making is Cognitive Science. *Michigan Quarterly Review*, Volume 28, number 2, 185–215.

Israel, Michael. 1996. The *Way* Constructions Grow. In Goldberg, Adele, editor, *Conceptual Structure, Discourse and Language*. Stanford: CSLI. 217–230.

Kay, Paul and Charles Fillmore. 1999. Grammatical Constructions and Linguistic Generalizations: The What's X Doing Y? Construction. *Language*, Vol. 75, No. 1, pages 1–33.

Kendon, Adam. 1990. *Conducting Interaction: Patterns of behavior in focused interactions*. Cambridge: Cambridge University Press.

Nass, Clifford and Byron Reeves (1996). *The Media Equation: How People Treat Computers, Television, and New Media Like Real People and Places*. New York: Cambridge University Press.

Nikiforidou, Kiki. 2012. The constructional underpinnings of viewpoint blends: The Past + now in language and literature. In: B. Dancygier and E. Sweetser (eds), *Viewpoint in Language: A Multimodal Perspective*. Cambridge: Cambridge University Press. 177–197.

Nikiforidou, Kiki. 2010. Viewpoint and construction grammar: The case of *past* + now. *Language and Literature* 19(2): 265–284.

Thomas, Francis-Noël and Mark Turner (2011). *Clear and Simple as the Truth: Writing Classic Prose*. Second Edition. Princeton: Princeton University Press.

Tobin, Vera. 2008. Literary Joint Attention: Social Cognition and the Puzzles of Modernism. (unpublished dissertation).

Tomasello, M. 1995. Joint Attention as Social Cognition. In Moore, C. and Dunham, P. (eds), *Joint Attention: Its Origins and Role in Development*. Mahwah, NJ: Lawrence Erlbaum Associates.

Turner, Mark. 1991. *Reading Minds: The Study of English in the Age of Cognitive Science*. Princeton, New Jersey: Princeton University Press.

Turner, Mark. 1998. Figure. In Cristina Cacciari, Ray Gibbs, Jr., Albert Katz, and Mark Turner, *Figurative Language and Thought*. New York: Oxford University Press, 1998.

Turner, Mark. 1987. *Death is the Mother of Beauty: Mind, Metaphor, Criticism*. Chicago: University of Chicago Press.

17

# Thinking with the Body: Conceptual Integration through Gesture in Multi-Viewpoint Model Construction

DAVID DELIEMA AND FRANCIS STEEN

## 1 Introduction

Educational researchers in the fields of science, technology, engineering, and math (STEM) have recently come to recognize the value of teaching students to construct, critique, revise, and apply models (Lehrer and Schauble 2006; Schwarz et al. 2009). A model represents an object, a phenomenon, or an idea (Gilbert 2000) through analogy: a mapping between the target to be modeled (e.g. the solar system) and the source materials that create the model (e.g. wire, styrofoam, tape). In school, national standards for math and science emphasize the benefits of creating and reasoning from models (National Research Council 2002; National Council of Teachers of Mathematics 2000) even while modeling activities remain on the fringe in many classrooms (Windschitl, Thompson, and Braaten 2008). In this article, we contribute to existing research on students' model-based reasoning with a fine-grained look at the interaction between two modeling resources: spatial reasoning and the body.

Students' capacities for spatial reasoning and embodied thinking are likely to impact how they engage in model-based reasoning. With respect to

*Language and the Creative Mind.*
Mike Borkent, Barbara Dancygier, and Jennifer Hinnell (eds).

the former construct, sophisticated spatial reasoning capacities are not only cross-cultural and diverse (O'Meara and Pérez Báez 2011) but also predictors of future participation in STEM fields (Wai, Lubinski, and Benbow 2009). Models, as spatial depictions of target systems, call on the spatial reasoning skills of the scientists and students who interact with them. From a complementary standpoint, recent empirical and theoretical research in embodied cognition (Gibbs 2005) underscores that spatial reasoning occurs less in a cognitive vacuum than in a body tethered to small and large visual features of the landscape. On challenging spatial reasoning tasks, for example, participants routinely externalize or offload their spatial thinking onto the hands and arms in gesture (Schwartz and Black 1996). Even more importantly, from an educational standpoint, actions of the body are increasingly becoming recognized as shapers of thought (Goldin-Meadow and Beilock 2010) and markers of learning (Gerofsky 2010). Taken together, these findings suggest that the nexus between gesture and spatial reasoning is rich with potential for educators concerned with cultivating students' model-based reasoning.

In the following, we explore how students negotiate the tension in their gestures between enacting different viewpoints and maintaining a coherent display of space and time in the model. For example, when modeling planetary orbit with gesture (Crowder 1996), students might spin in circles on both feet (depicting the planet from the *character viewpoint*) or they might stand still while using the finger to trace several circles in the air (depicting an *observer viewpoint* outline of the planet). As students transfer from one viewpoint to another for different components in the system, embodying at various points planets, suns, and moons at different scales and locations, students are still tasked with assembling a model that maintains some geographical and temporal consistency. In the space in front of and around the body, a student may gesture a fist-shaped planet located to the left, to the right, or in the center, moving speedily across or drifting lethargically. Because gestures occur in a topology of space and time, they present visible and tangible landscapes throughout which speakers can relate the locations and movements of model components. How students drift between different gestural viewpoints while still maintaining spatiotemporal continuity in the model—and what implications this has for learning outcomes—are our core concerns in this chapter.

We address the above research questions with a methodology in which students gesture in response to a sequence of verbal prompts, a protocol that elicits what we call *listening gestures*. The instruction to gesture in response to verbal prompts allows students to employ the body as a vehicle for organizing new information, while at the same time generating a powerful real-time display of the stages of comprehension for the researcher. In this way, our research design recruits gesture as a probe to investigate the learning process, analogous to a learning-aloud protocol (Clement and Steinberg 2002), but with a heightened spatiotemporal immediacy. We select for our analysis two students who responded very differently to this activity, each in her own way typical of the bi-modal distribution in our full study,[1] and each illuminating the microgenetic change in the learning process.

## 2 Inanimate Character and Observer Viewpoints

One of the modeling resources we examine in this paper, viewpoint, describes how students move their bodies *as* the component in the model or *as an observer* of the component in the model. Numerous studies of STEM environments have meaningfully documented how students' and teachers' adoption of multiple and flexible viewpoints impacts teaching and learning (de Freitas and Sinclair 2012; Crowder 1996; Enyedy et al. 2012; Gerofsky 2010; Hall 1996; Lindgren 2012; Nemirovsky and Monk 2000; Ochs et al. 1996; Warren et al. 2001; Wilensky and Reisman 2006). To further educational researchers' understanding of viewpoint, and to set the stage for its involvement in learning, we begin by reviewing research on gestural viewpoint from cognitive linguistics research on storytelling.

The spoken words of stories often sound out to the accompaniment of gestures, and these gestures often show the actions of story events from different viewpoints. For example, in telling the story of Babe Ruth's legendary Called Shot, a speaker might use his own body to show how Babe Ruth pointed toward the outfield bleachers. The speaker might then *step out* of Babe Ruth's body and trace an arc in the air showing the flight of the home run ball clearing the outfield fence. These two gestures instantiate from different viewpoints: character viewpoint (C-VPT) and observer viewpoint (O-VPT) (McNeill 1992; Parrill 2009). The character viewpoint refers to gestures that reenact the action of the story character such that the gesturer and the story character move their bodies in similar ways (McNeill 1992; Parrill 2009). In the C-VPT Called Shot example, the storyteller moves part of his own body in the same way Babe Ruth moved his body in the past; both bodies point toward a distant object. On the other hand, observer viewpoint gestures involve the body conforming to how an object or character appears when observed from a distance. In the O-VPT Called

[1] Our research team is still analyzing the data from the full study. We would like to acknowledge the support of the UCLA Office of the Vice Chancellor for Research and the Academic Senate Council on Research for Transdisciplinary Seed Grant A1118 and the National Science Foundation Grant 1028381. This material is also based upon work supported by the National Science Foundation Graduate Research Fellowship under Grant No. DGE-0707424.

Shot example, the storyteller uses part of his own body to display the trajectory of the baseball as seen from afar.

In a departure from the stories traditionally investigated in cognitive linguistics, we study STEM models in which the components lack human-like bodies, such as planets, computer data, or atoms. However, many of the character viewpoint definitions in the field take for granted an approximate one-to-one mapping between the bodies of the story characters and the body of the storyteller. Maws of cartoon dogs map onto the mouth of the storyteller and arms of superheroes onto human arms. Some definitions of C-VPT even exclude objects that cannot have viewpoints, such as baseballs, buildings, or clouds (Parrill 2009), classifying those gestures instead as metaphoric (McNeill 1992). Accordingly, the character viewpoint gesture, in its traditional sense, can be defined by the storyteller and the story character enacting actions with homologous articulators (e.g., if Sylvester the Cat runs in the cartoon on his feet, the gesturer telling the story about the cartoon simulates running also on his own feet); the storyteller uses his own 'articulator to represent a character's articulator' (Parrill 2012: 104). These prototypical targets are well studied, but we should be careful not to underestimate the creativity or fertility of the character and observer viewpoints, which extend beyond these natural mappings (Crowder 1996; Lindgren 2012; Ochs, Gonzalez, and Jacoby 1996).

In structuring gesture enactments metaphorically (Parrill and Sweetser 2004), speakers can depict inanimate components (such as electrons, computer data, or planets) from both character and observer viewpoints. In an education context, it is important to classify metaphorical gestures (McNeill 1992) along the dimension of viewpoint because the viewpoint dynamically structures how the model unfolds in space and time. As students need to reason carefully about spatiotemporal relations to understand new models, educational researchers should be attentive to how space and time interact with gestural viewpoint, even in the context of models of inanimate material. In this chapter, we attempt to track how inanimate C-VPTs and inanimate O-VPTs shape students' reasoning about spatial and temporal characteristics of models during a learning activity.

## 3 Spatiotemporal Topology

While the distinction between character and observer viewpoint addresses the mappings between the body of the speaker and the features of the target modeled, the spatiotemporal topology refers to the scale of the gestured components, the location throughout which those components move, and the structure of events in time. Students exploring a model need to develop an understanding not only of how the shape of their bodies map onto objects in the model, but also of how the objects are positioned or move relative to each other over time.

These spatial aspects of gesture have been extensively documented in the literature. Descriptions of spatial concepts are frequently accompanied by co-speech gestures (Alibali, Heath, and Myers 2001). For example, college students perform gestures while reasoning about spatial puzzles (Emmorey and Casey 2001) and mechanical models (Schwartz and Black 1996), and adults and children perform gestures while talking about solutions to the spatial Tower of Hanoi puzzle (Garber and Goldin-Meadow 2002). As problem solvers animate the components of spatial puzzles with gestures, they make visible the spatial characteristics of the model. That is, if the hand gesture revolves counter-clockwise, the puzzle piece to which the gesture refers is also understood to revolve counter-clockwise (Emmorey and Casey 2001). In addition, an observer viewpoint gesture can be presented as spatially close to the story action (*inside* or *proximal perspective)* or far away from the story action (*outside* or *distal perspective)* (Crowder 1996; Gerofsky 2010; McNeill 1992). This body of work suggests that a variety of spatiotemporal topologies play an integral role in co-speech gesture.

In this study, we focus on two constructs within the area of spatial reasoning: scale and topology. Scale refers to the depiction of the size of the component. ASL signers, for example, can represent the same component at different scales on subsequent turns. A signer might depict a motorcycle at the scale of the full human body in one turn and then depict the same motorcycle at the scale of a small object that fits in the palm of the hand on the next turn (Dudis 2004). The motorcycle shrinks in size from an object that a person can ride to something you can hold in your hand. Topology tracks how gestured elements create an organized geographical layout of objects, even if transient. While talking about family lineage, for example, Lao speakers make spatially consistent points toward empty space as if family tree diagrams were floating in front of their bodies. As a cognitive artifact, the body becomes 'a visuospatial representational resource' (Enfield 2001: 1). Environmentally coupled gestures (Goodwin 2007)—gestures that reference physical objects in the space around the body—are grounded in the given spatial layout of structures in the environment, yet uncoupled gestures must also conserve a spatial topology over some time window, however brief. A fascinating literature explores cultural variability in the spatial language and spatial thinking that occurs (in broad strokes) either relative to the speaker's body or relative to objects or geographical landmarks present in the environment (for an overview, see O'Meara and Pérez Báez 2011).

These constructs point to the need to track how students organize the scale of gestured representations and the spatial arrangement of those representations as they learn to model a new system. By examining how students establish and manipulate the spatiotemporal topology of the modeled system, in conjunction with their adoption of multiple viewpoints, we aim to illuminate a critical dimension of learning.

## 4 Integration Across Viewpoint and Space: A Case Study

In bringing together the constructs of gesture viewpoint (observer or character) and gesture space and time (spatiotemporal topology), we find a potential challenge to the process of conceptual integration. Modeling requires an understanding of both the repertoire of actions that components can take and the way those actions relate to other components (Lehrer and Schauble 2006). It is not enough to know that planets rotate; the student also needs to know *where* planets rotate and *around which* other planets. In the gesture stream, the student can both feel the action of the component and track how that action relates geographically to previous and future actions. The body provides the former feeling equipment and the empty area around the body provides the later location for organizing spatiotemporal landscapes.

The multi-viewpointed nature of cognition poses a challenge to learners: How do students dynamically transition between character and observer viewpoints while maintaining a sense of how events in one part of the system relate to events in other parts of the system? The switch from viewpoint to viewpoint in the model may demand re-presentations of scale and/or space. While research suggests that sensory metaphors are rife in human language and recruited in a loosely organized 'in-pieces' fashion (diSessa 1993), we know less about how students coordinate multimodal knowledge fragments into coherent wholes. The conceptual blending framework (Fauconnier and Turner 1998) presents a cognitive mechanism, but empirical approaches are needed to detail the process of conceptual integration during learning activities.

## 5 Method

The present case study was part of a larger study conducted at a West Coast university with college students (*N*=20) aged 18–22. Restrictions based on demographics were not used, but participants with extensive existing knowledge of the target concept, packet switching, were excluded from the study. The study used convenience sampling of undergraduates enrolled in an introductory communications course and followed IRB guidelines.

Student participants learned the concept of packet switching, the logic of a digital network at the heart of the Internet. In packet switching, individual pieces of data (packets) move according to network rules between different relay nodes (routers). A message is broken up into packets at the sending computer, tagged with information about its origin and destination, and sent through a web-like network toward the receiving computer (see Figure 1). Copies are made at each router and used in the case of failed transmissions; receipts are returned to confirm delivery. Students were taught the concept of unicasting, which involves a chain of packets directed toward one destination, and students were also taught the concept of multicasting, which involves packets proliferating throughout the network in response to requests from any number of destination computers. In the activity instructions, we instructed half of the sample (*n*=10) to listen to verbal

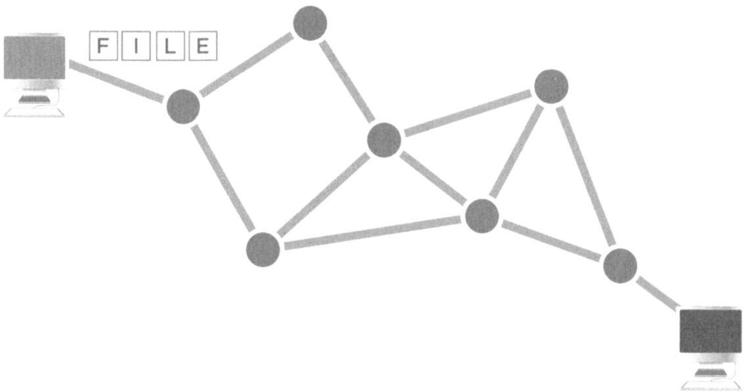


FIGURE 1. A packet-switching network, in which the message, FILE, is broken up into smaller packets—F, I, L, E—and routed through the network.

statements about the packet switching system and try to model the system with their bodies. As these gestures signify an interlocutor's words, we refer to them as listening gestures. The other half of the sample (*n*=10) listened to similar instructions but did not gesture. In this chapter, we report on only two students from the listening gesture condition.

The activity took place in one-on-one interactions between the student and the researcher. Students were instructed to stand up and model each sentence with gestures, and informed that the researcher would read the full 27-sentence narrative twice (study phase 1 and 2). Each verbal prompt described a single, goal-direction action. The listening gestures protocol was designed on analogy with the learning-aloud protocol (Clement and Steinberg 2002) to gain insight into the processes of learning through real-time monitoring. The protocol is particularly useful for investigating the role of spatiotemporal representations in concept development, contributing to the understanding of the multimodal dimensions of human cognition and communication (Steen and Turner, this volume). As a mandatory learning strategy, the protocol is disruptive, typically either facilitating or hindering learning and potentially useful for contrastive studies. The factors affecting the nature of the disruption were not investigated in the current study.

The study phase of the session was video recorded with a stationary camera placed in the corner of the room and focused on the participant. The narrative describing packet switching contained verbs typically used to describe human actions, such as *grab*, *travel*, and *cut*. These verbs metaphorically structure the actions of packets and routers through human actions, for example, as in the phrases, '...it chops up the email' and '...before throwing the packet toward the next router'. Each prompt was read with clear enunciation (on average 3 words per second) with a 4-second pause between each prompt. The experimenter produced no gestures and participants did not ask any questions during the reading. After the study phase, students walked across campus to an fMRI facility where they responded aloud to 45 open-ended questions about packet switching from inside the scanner (the fMRI part of the study will not be reported here). After walking back to the lab, the researcher asked the student to explain in words everything he/she remembered about the operation of packet switching, what we call the *explanation phase*. The explanation phase was meant to evoke a round of unprompted co-speech gestures. Finally, students were given a written post-test with open-ended questions about packet switching.

## 5.1 Measures

*Character versus observer viewpoint:* Real packets and routers on the Internet do not, of course, have hands, feet, and a head. However, we propose that the definition of an inanimate character viewpoint can build on Parrill's (2012) C-VPT definition: the speaker and the story character conduct an action with homologous body parts. In the inanimate context, the gesturer construes the inanimate component as having a human-like articulator. The storyteller can map his own body part onto a figurative but analogous hand, finger, body, or head of the inanimate component. That is, the gesturer can metaphorically construe routers as having *hand-*, *feet-*, or *head-like* articulators. Whenever the inanimate component is construed in the gesture as having a human-like articulator (e.g. a router has a *hand*) and the gesturer uses his/her own analogous articulator (e.g. his own hand) to enact an action of the component (e.g. throwing), we consider that the gesturer has adopted the character viewpoint of that component. Examples would include a packet with a hand that can *grasp*, a packet with a hand that can *scribble*, a router with a head that can *look*, or a packet with arms that allow it to *run*. Alternatively, an observer viewpoint (O-VPT) gesture would constitute representations that depict the shape or trajectory of a component. The hand plays the role of an outsider sketching descriptions of component entities. The target component, in this case, is not construed as having an homologous human articulator, but rather, the articulator of the gesturer forms the shape or trajectory of the component. Examples include a closed fist that represents a motionless packet, a flat hand that depicts the trajectory of a moving packet, or both hands tracing the square shape of a router.

*Spatiotemporal topology*: As the gesture-based simulation of the system unfolds, the gestural representations offer a visual landscape that details the locations and sizes of components in packet switching. The two dimensions of scale and location comprise a partial description of the spatiotemporal topology. Take the example of a gesture in which the fist represents a small packet moving from right to left across the body. The fist represents the size; the right to left (transverse) axis on which the packet moves represents direction of movement. Gestural models, in this way, provide a rich window onto the spatial organization of representations. As participants formulate listening gestures in response to words describing packet switching, they can interpret verbal spatial descriptions relative to either the past locations of gestured components or the present location of the body. In the former object-centered frame of reference, spatial features of sentences are encoded with respect to the direction of movement of components from previous gestures. In the later relative frame of reference, the body of the gesturer encodes the spatial meaning (O'Meara and Pérez Báez 2011). For example, object-centered spatial reasoning would map the word *left* onto the left part of the axis on which a gestured packet moved in the previous turn. Relative spatial reasoning would map the word *left* onto the left of the gesturer's body regardless of where the gestured packet just moved. Throughout this text, the terminology for spatial relations will use the body of the gesturer as the reference point (e.g. right refers to the right of the gesturer's body from the gesturer's viewpoint).

## 6 Results

In this section, we detail how two participants—Jen, the student pictured with light hair, and Beth, the student pictured with dark hair (names are pseudonyms)—gestured a subset of packet switching concepts during study phases one and two and during the explanation phase. What struck us was how these two students differed in their approaches to organizing representations in space. We selected Jen and Beth as prototypical members of two clusters that evenly divided the sample. Our research team is currently analyzing the results from the full sample.

### 6.1 Jen on Source and Destination Computers and Packet Trajectory

Row 1 of Figure 2 contains snapshots of Jen in study phase one creating her first listening gestures that model the start and destination of the packet journey (S1a, S1b) and the pathway the packet takes (S1c). Jen then gestures these concepts a second time in round two of the study phase (S2a, S2b, S2c) and a third time as co-speech gestures accompanying her own description in the explanation phase (E1a, E1b, E1c).

In round one, Jen gestures first in response to the prompt, 'the computer stamps each packet with a precise tag that tracks three things: the starting point of the journey, the destination of the journey ... ' (S1a, S1b), and then in response to the prompt, 'the packets rush out from the computer into the network' (S1c). With respect to the first prompt, Jen points in sequence toward the space to the left (S1a) and to the right (S1b) of her body, indicating the location of the source computer and the destination computer. For the second prompt, she traces with both fingers the trajectory of packets entering the network. In this turn, Jen starts at the center of her torso and traces a loop with each hand toward the sides of her body. Then, Jen returns her hands to the center of her torso and traces two more loops in the direction directly out in front of her body (S1c).

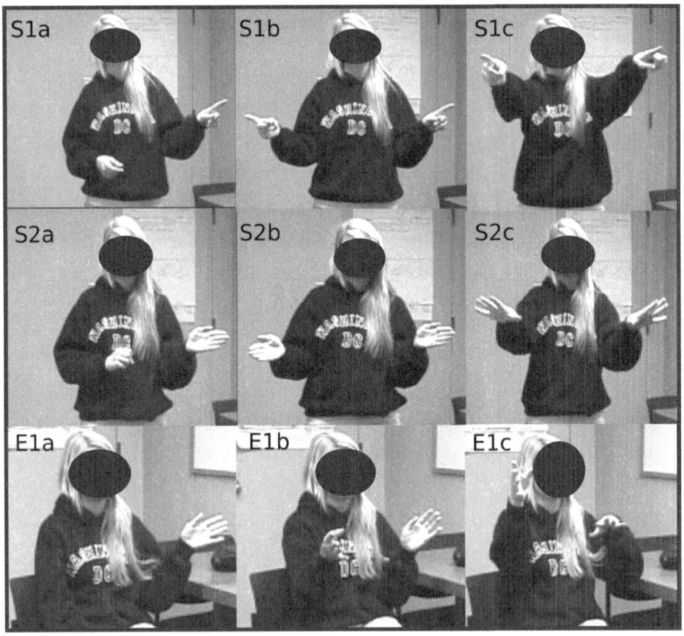


Figure 2. Jen gestures the source and destination locations and the packet trajectory.

These gestures generate a skillful display of the verbal description. The hands point to two empty spaces at opposite ends of the body to signify the start and end of the journey. Then, the hands dynamically trace the pathway that multiple packets take through the network, spreading out like arcs in a fountain. Without any training or any feedback, Jen maps the language onto her body, referring to locations and pathways from an observer viewpoint. In round two of the study phase, Jen constructs listening gestures for the same two concepts in response to the same two prompts. This time, the full hands stand in as the shape of the source (S2a) and destination (S2b) computers, and then instead of tracing a packet, Jen steps into the character viewpoint of the source computer and simulates the motion of throwing the packet into the network (S2c). All three gestures reappear when Jen, over an hour later, explains in her own words her understanding of packet switching (E1a, E1b, E1c). She again uses her hands to stand in as the source and destination computer (while saying 'it goes from a single source to another single source'), and then simulates a computer throwing a packet into the network (while saying, 'the packet ... is sent'). Agency is granted to the computer without which the packet would not enter the network. In round two and in the explanation phase, Jen shifts seamlessly from the viewpoint of an observer marking the location of two computers to the viewpoint of a character (the source computer) launching packets.

For each prompt, Jen creates a creative, original, and intelligible mapping of words onto her own body, using both character and observer viewpoints. As she gestures, she *simultaneously* builds up an organized spatiotemporal topology. That is, the source and destination computers always materialize in specific locations: the left of the body and the right of the body respectively (S1a, S1b, S2a, S2b, E1a, E1b). The packets also move along a constant sagittal axis starting at the center of the body and moving forward directly in front of the body (S1c, S2c, E1c), with a few exceptions to this rule in the explanation phase. Examined in this light, we notice that Jen creates a sequence of individual, disconnected spatiotemporal topologies. In the second prompt, the packet, upon entering the network, starts not at the location that Jen depicts the source computer in the previous prompt, but rather from a new location in the center of the body. In addition, instead of heading in the direction of the destination computer from the previous prompt, the packet moves on a new axis extending out in front of the body, headed toward an unknown destination. The pattern of placing source and destination computers to the left and right on the transverse axis and then sending packets from the center toward the front on the sagittal axis appears in study phase one and two and in the explanation phase.

In the transition from the first to the second prompt, then, Jen starts more or less afresh, rebuilding the spatial topology. She generates an intelligible representation of each prompt from a blank slate. The gestures are memorable, repeating again in the second round and in the explanation phase as they establish a fixed pattern. Importantly, the spatiotemporal topology is consistent *within* each of Jen's gestures for a single prompt. That is, the source and the destination appear in different locations and one after the other in time. Similarly, the packet moves in time from one place to another along a direct spatial route. It is *across* these prompts that the spatial topologies diverge. We have noted that in study phase round two and in the explanation phase, Jen transitions from an observer viewpoint showing two computer locations to a character viewpoint acting as the transmitting computer. In the former, the hands depict the computer shape; in the latter, the source computer has a *hand*, and Jen shows that hand throwing material toward the network. The viewpoint shift triggers a scale shift. That is, in the former, packets would be the size of small specks on the hand. In the later, the packet would be the size of a tennis ball. Looked at another way, the throw from the computer viewpoint in the second prompt takes up about as much space as does the full network in the previous prompt. In short, the viewpoint switch results in a scale switch that may be partly responsible for driving Jen to rewrite the model's spatial order.

### 6.2 Beth on Source and Destination Computers and Packet Trajectory

Figure 3 shows Beth in a parallel set of snapshots to Jen in Figure 2. While listening to the first of the two prompts in study phase round one, Beth places emblematic symbols for the number one (a single index finger, S1d) and the number 3 (three fingers, S1e) in two different locations (left of the body and right of the body, respectively), showing the start and destination of the packet journey. The number symbols mark that the tag on the packet tracks three items, two of which are the source and destination locations. In this way, the location of the gestured number symbol corresponds to the location of the computers while the number itself refers to the number of items the packet tag stores. In the second round of the study phase, Beth more simply points to the two computer locations (S2d, S2e). In the explanation phase, Beth curves her hands around what appear to be two small objects (E1d, E1e) to depict the source and destination computers (while saying, 'you have a computer over here and that's the starting place and you have a computer over here and that's the ending place'). In this way, Beth symbolizes the start and finish in three different ways: locations of emblematic numbers, locations revealed through deictic gestures, and locations of iconic objects around which the hand wraps. As in Jen's case, the spatiotemporal order of these symbols is constant within each prompt: the source

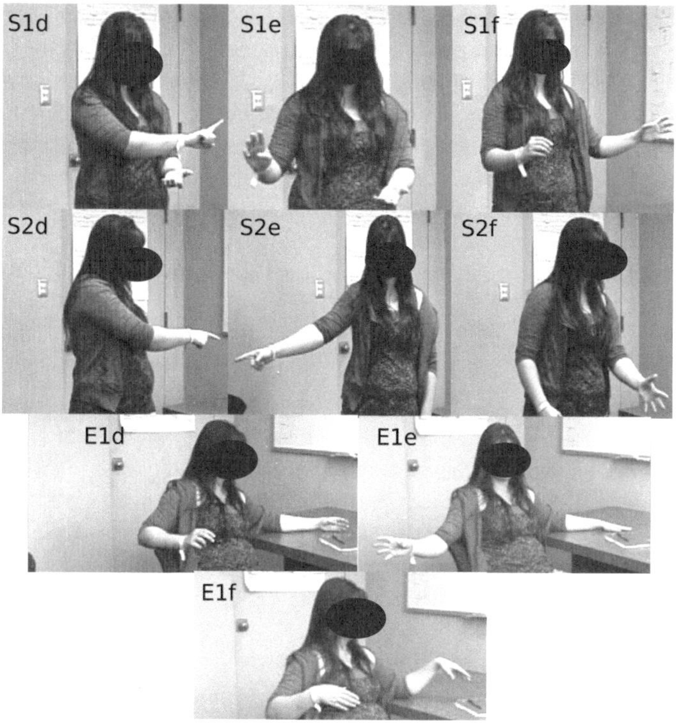


FIGURE 3. Beth gestures the source and destination locations and the packet trajectory.

computer always appears first and to the left while the destination computer appears second and to the right.

Jen and Beth differ, however, in the degree to which they spatiotemporally integrate adjacent prompts. Both in rounds one and two of the study phase, Beth uses her full left hand to depict an O-VPT shape of a packet and shows that packet departing (S1f, S2f) from the exact location of the source computer in her model of the prior prompt. In addition, she shows the packet moving in the direction of the prior location of the destination computer. Accordingly, the spatiotemporal organization of the model in the first prompt—source computer first and to the left, destination computer second and to the right—guides how Beth spatiotemporally organizes the second prompt—packets move from left to right. In the explanation phase, even when Beth adopts the viewpoint of the source computer, modeling the act of throwing the packet (E1f) into the network (while saying, '...those get sent out'), she starts the throw from the prior location of the source computer.

Beth's listening gestures modeling the second of the prompts are guided by the spatiotemporal topology that she created in the model of the previous prompt. She links the organization of time and space across prompts, in effect generating a single underlying spatiotemporal representation. The spatiotemporal order exists despite Beth using all three of emblematic, deictic, and iconic gestures and even switching from an observer viewpoint detailing packet shape to a character viewpoint symbolizing a computer throw. Furthermore, the spatiotemporal topology is conserved across both rounds of the study phase and even an hour later during the co-speech gestures of the explanation phase.

### 6.3 Multicasting on Two Pathways

In this section, we detail another example of Jen providing within-prompt spatiotemporal integration and of Beth providing both within-prompt and across-prompt integration. In this part of the study phase, the researcher reads aloud the following two prompts describing multicasting: 'When the packet reaches the router, it reveals its tag. In this case, two different destination computers need the packet: one located at the end of the left pathway leading away from the router, and one at the end of the right pathway leading away from the router.'

In responding to the first of these prompts, Jen simulates grabbing a small bit of material from the space in the center of her body, carries it in her right hand to the right, and then opens the hand. In response to the second prompt, Jen makes an emblematic gesture with two fingers to show the number two, and then presents an upward-facing, left-handed flat palm to the left of her body followed by an upward-facing, right-handed flat palm to the right of her body. The C-VPT action of grabbing and transferring the packet in the first prompt occurs along a transverse axis from center toward right space. The O-VPT depiction of the location of the destination occurs in space to the left of the body and to the right of the body. In this way, the spatial organization of the gestures is not conserved across prompts. Packets move from left to right on the transverse axis and then from the center out in front on the sagittal axis. In summary, for the second half of the prompt, instead of construing the words *left* and *right* from the packet viewpoint (an object-centered frame of reference), Jen depicts the words *left* and *right* with respect to her own forward-facing body (a relative frame of reference). Within each prompt, the gestural model is spatially organized; across prompts, the layouts diverge.

Beth, on the other hand, does organize the spatial layout of the model across prompts. In response to the first prompt, she traces an O-VPT trajectory of a packet moving from left space to center space, before modeling in center space the C-VPT packet prying open its own tag with both hands. For the second prompt, Beth indicates the left and right pathway toward the two destination computers relative to the existing axis and direction on which the packet just traveled (an object-centered frame of reference). That is, Beth traces two different pathways to the space to the right of her body, one extending slightly to the left and the other slightly to the right of the packet's earlier transverse trajectory. In this way, Beth presents a packet that never veers from the transverse axis on which it travels. The packet moves along the axis from left to center, headed toward destination computers to the right. Each new entity or event described in words appears in a logical spot on this axis, even when Beth moves from an O-VPT packet depiction to a C-VPT packet depiction and then back to an O-VPT pathway depiction. In round two of the study phase and in the explanation phase, Beth creates the same spatial topology. Furthermore, in round 2, she moves her full body into the space to the right, turns back toward center, and makes a pulling 'come here' motion, showing from a C-VPT the destination computers requesting the packet. The character viewpoint request gesture, then, is shifted over to the prior spatial location of the destination computer. This effectively laminates a relative spatial framework onto an object-centered framework. Instead of thinking about how destination computers *somewhere out there* would construe space, Beth moves her whole body into the location where destination computers had appeared in her past gesture layouts. Beth can then use her own relative space as synonymous with the computer's object-centered space.

## 6.4 Learning Comprehension

How does spatiotemporally constructed conceptual integration affect learning comprehension? As the results we present here are based on two participants, we have no basis for inferring causation or even correlation, yet this case study suggests the need for follow-up research. Jen, although near perfect in depicting the meaning of each individual prompt, disrupts the spatiotemporal topology in round one on 46 percent of her gestures and in round two on 30 percent of her gestures. Beth, on the other hand, disrupts the spatiotemporal topology in round one on 6 percent of her gestures and in round two on 3 percent of her gestures. That is, both students correctly interpret the actions described in each prompt, but Beth goes to greater lengths to fit those actions into a highly organized spatiotemporal topology. Beth's gestures are coherent with respect to the topology expressed in the previous gesture, creating a cumulative topology; her gestures provide evidence of the formation of a coherent and tacit underlying spatiotemporal representation.

On the post-test, Jen correctly describes many of the actions that take place in packet switching: packets receive tags, routers receive receipts, routers make copies. However, Jen struggles to draw correct inferences about questions that require stringing together multiple actions in the system. She is unable to determine how many copies would be made when packets pass through multiple routers in unicasts and in multicasts, where and when those copies are made, and how routers know where to send packets. The actions that comprise these topics are individually described in the prompts, but they must be systematically related to other prompts to reveal the answers. In the explanation phase, Jen leaves out almost every step of the multicasting process and conflates aspects of unicasting and multicasting. Beth, on the other hand, is able to recall individual actions in packet switching and draw inferences across actions. She correctly reasons about the number of copies made in unicasting and in multicasting and the locations where those copies are made. In the explanation phase, she correctly describes all of the aspects of unicasting and multicasting.

## 7 Discussion

Complex models must typically be taught by breaking them down into simpler components. Each component must be understood separately, a task that may require both creativity and dedication. Yet this is not sufficient: the whole must be constructed out of a series of specific relations between the parts. A genuine understanding emerges out of a dynamic integration of components that preserves their known causal relations. This secondary integration cannot be taken for granted.

In this study, using listening gestures as an investigative activity, we induce and uncover a contrastive dynamic in a two-stage process of conceptual integration. Each verbal prompt was carefully designed to generate an individual gesture event, defined as a single, goal-directed action. In describing our participants' gestures, we note how the adoption of a particular character or observer viewpoint generates a distinctive dynamic topology, in which each element in the prompt is modeled as a rich spatiotemporal process. In the first stage, event-based causal relations are modeled as bodily motions in space in ways that are highly metaphorical; for instance, copying an electrically encoded packet of information is modeled by a gestural metaphor of grasping a fist-sized object and moving it to an adjacent location. A complex conceptual integration network is required to project the relevant features of the spatiotemporal topology onto domain-specific content such as packets, routers, and cables from the target, resulting in a creative blend that constitutes a preliminary understanding of an action from a single prompt.

We see that in Jen's case, each individual model is created afresh, with no relation to the preceding. This modular strategy results in a basic understanding of the target model, along with limited abilities to generate new inferences and a failure to grasp the more complex behaviors of the system. In contrast, Beth adopts an integrative strategy that results in a richer understanding of the target model, associated with enhanced abilities to generate new inferences and a confident grasp of the more complex behaviors of the system.

What is Beth doing? Our analysis suggests she uses the movement of her body in space and time to build an integrated spatiotemporal model, a learning strategy we call *thinking with the body*. In response to each verbal prompt, she adopts a suitable character or observer viewpoint and generates a distinctive gesture to model a particular component of the target system in space and time. This spatiotemporal topology in turn orients and guides her subsequent gesture, which may adopt a different viewpoint, develop a new gestural metaphor, and generate a new and supplementary extension of the spatiotemporal model. By attending to her own creations as a context at each stage for her new creations, she cumulatively builds a model that encodes not only the individual components in an accurate manner, but also their internal relations (Figure 4).

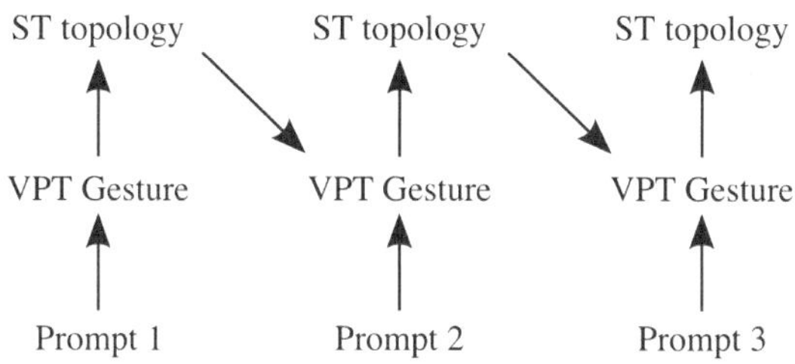


FIGURE 4. Thinking with the body involves a recursive process of spatiotemporal continuity linking gestural events across changing viewpoints.

What we have aimed to show in this chapter is that gestural acts, in generating complex patterns in space and time, provide a dynamic scaffolding for conceptual development. Despite the fact that the conceptual integration networks for individual gestural acts have been extensively studied, the application of gestural studies to the Learning Sciences requires that we examine the integration of multiple gestural acts into complex and dynamic representations. Through two contrasting case studies, we have shown how a succession of viewpointed gestural acts in a recursive manner can become incorporated into and simultaneously contribute to the elaboration of a cumulatively constructed spatiotemporal topology, possibly facilitating high-level modeling with an impressive power to generate new inferences.

## References

Alibali, M. W., D. C. Heath, and H. J. Myers. 2001. Effects of visibility between speaker and listener on gesture production: Some gestures are meant to be seen. *Journal of Memory & Language* 44: 169–188.

Clement, J. J. and M. S. Steinberg. 2002. Step-Wise Evolution of Mental Models of Electric Circuits: A "Learning-Aloud" Case Study. *The Journal of the Learning Sciences* 11(4): 389–452.

Crowder, E. M. 1996. Gestures at work in sense-making science talk. *The Journal of the Learning Sciences* 5(3): 173–208.

de Freitas, E. and N. Sinclair. 2012. Diagram, gesture, agency: theorizing embodiment in the mathematics classroom. *Educational Studies in Mathematics* 80: 133–152.

diSessa, A. A. 1993. Toward an epistemology of physics. *Cognition and Instruction* 10: 165–255.

Dudis, P. G. 2004. Body partitioning and real-space blends. *Cognitive Linguistics* 15(2): 223–238.

Emmorey, K. and S. Casey. 2001. Gesture, thought and spatial language. *Gesture* 1: 35–50.

Enfield, N. J. 2005. The body as a cognitive artifact in kinship representations: Hand gesture diagrams by speakers of Lao. *Current Anthropology* 41(6): 51–81.

Enyedy, N., J. A. Danish, G. Delacruz, and M. Kumar. 2012. Learning physics through play in an augmented reality environment. *International Journal of Computer Supported Collaborative Learning* 7(3): 347–378.

Fauconnier, G. and M. Turner 1998. Conceptual integration networks. *Cognitive Science* 22: 133–187.

Garber, P. and S. Goldin-Meadow 2002. Gesture offers insight into problem solving in adults and children. *Cognitive Science* 26: 817–831.

Gerofsky, S. 2010. Mathematical learning and gesture: Character viewpoint and observer viewpoint in students' gestured graphs of functions. *Gesture* 10(2–3): 321–343.

Gibbs R. W. Jr. 2006. *Embodiment and Cognitive Science*. New York: Cambridge University Press.

Gilbert, J. K. 2000. *Developing models in science education*. Dordrecht, The Netherlands: Kluwer.

Goldin-Meadow, S. and S. Beilock. 2010. Action's influence on thought: The case of gesture. *Perspect Psychol Sci* 5(6): 664–674.

Goodwin, C. 2007. Environmentally coupled gestures. *Gesture and the Dynamic Dimension of Language*, ed. S. D. Duncan, J. Cassell and E. T. Levy, 195–212. Amsterdam: John Benjamins.

Hall, R. 1996. Representation as shared activity: Situated cognition and Dewey's cartography of experience. *Journal of the Learning Sciences* 5(3): 209–238.

Lehrer, R. and L. Schauble. 2006. Cultivating model-based reasoning in science education. *The Cambridge handbook of the learning sciences*, ed. R. K. Sawyer, 371–388. New York: Cambridge University Press.

Lindgren, R. 2012. Generating a learning stance through perspective-taking in a virtual environment. *Computers in Human Behavior* 28(4): 1130–1139.

McNeill, D. 1992. *Hand and mind: what gestures reveal about thought*. Chicago: University of Chicago Press.

National Council of Teachers of Mathematics (NCTM). 2000. *Principles and Standards for School Mathematics*. Reston, VA.

National Research Council. 2002. Scientific research in education. *Committee on Scientific Principles for Educational Research*, ed. R. J. Shavelson and L. Towne, Washington, DC: National Academy Press.

Nemirovsky, R., C. Tierney, and T. Wright. 1998. Body motion and graphing. *Cognition and Instruction* 16(2): 119–172.

Ochs, E., P. Gonzalez, and S. Jacoby. 1996. When I come down, I'm in a domain state: Grammar and graphic representation in the interpretive activity of physics. *Interaction and grammar*, ed. E. Ochs, E. A. Schegloff, and S. Thompson, 328–369. Cambridge: Cambridge University Press.

O'Meara, C. and G. Pérez Báez. 2011. Spatial frames of reference in Mesoamerican languages. *Lang. Sci.* 33: 837–852.

Parrill, F. and E. Sweetser. 2004. What we mean by meaning: Conceptual integration in gesture analysis and transcription. *Gesture* 4(2): 197–219.

Parrill, F. 2009. Dual viewpoint gestures. *Gesture* 9(3): 271–289.

_____. 2012. Interactions between discourse status and viewpoint in co-speech gesture. *Viewpoint in Language: A Multimodal Perspective*, ed. B. Dancygier and E. Sweetser, 97–112. Cambridge: Cambridge University Press.

Schwartz, D. L. and J. B. Black, J. B. 1996. Shuttling between depictive models and abstract rules: Induction and fall-back. *Cognitive Science* 20: 457-497.

Schwarz, C. V., B. J. Reiser, E. A. Davis, L. Kenyon, A. Acher, D. Fortus. . . J. Krajcik. 2009. Developing a learning progression for scientific modeling: Making scientific modeling accessible and meaningful for learners. *Journal of research in science teaching* 46(6): 632–654.

Wai, J., D. Lubinski, and C. P. Benbow 2009. Spatial Ability for STEM Domains: Aligning Over 50 Years of Cumulative Psychological Knowledge Solidifies Its Importance. *Journal of Educational Psychology* 101(4): 817–835.

Warren, B., C. Ballenger, M. Ognonowski, A. S. Rosebery, and J. Hudicourt-Barnes. 2000. Rethinking diversity in learning science: the logic of everyday sense-making. *Journal of research in science teaching* 30(5): 529–552.

Wilensky, U. and K. Reisman. 2006. Thinking like a wolf, sheep, or a firefly: Learning biology through constructing and testing computational theories, An embodied modeling approach. *Cognition and Instruction* 24(2): 171–209.

Windschitl, M., J. Thompson, and M. Braaten. 2008. Beyond the scientific method: Model-based inquiry as a new paradigm of preference for school science investigations. *Science Education* 92(5): 941–967.

# 18

# Metaphors for Sensorimotor Experiences: Gestures as Embodied and Dynamic Conceptualizations of Balance in Dance Lessons[1]

CORNELIA MÜLLER AND SILVA H. LADEWIG

## 1 Introduction

When dancers explain body movements in teaching contexts they are faced with the complex and challenging task of 'translating' movement into language. The creative solutions for the specific and subjective sensorimotor experiences they find provide exciting insights for cognitive linguists into 'language and the creative mind', the topic of this book. Based on the analysis of two dance workshops on balance and posture in two different dance styles—ballet and Argentine tango—we will propose that gestures are subjective forms of embodied conceptualizations that are used by teachers and students to communicate differing sensorimotor experiences of balance in these two kinds of dance. In a nutshell this paper discusses the interplay of metaphor, embodiment, and gesture. It departs from other studies on metaphor and gesture in several regards.

[1] Research presented here was funded by the German Ministry for Education (BMBF) within the project 'Body Language of Dance and Movement'. The project was conducted in collaboration with Sabine Koch and Thomas Fuchs, both of Heidelberg University.

*Language and the Creative Mind.*
Mike Borkent, Barbara Dancygier, and Jennifer Hinnell (eds).

### 1.1 Languaging of Movement: Metaphors and Gestures in Pedagogical Contexts

By using rich data from pedagogical contexts we hope to open up novel perspectives on metaphor theory. So far metaphor theorists commonly build their assumptions on the nature of metaphor on data that does not involve pedagogical contexts (on the contrary, for analogy theorists this is a common source and goal of their work, see Holyoak and Thargard 1995). Dance lessons are of particular interest for metaphor scholars because they involve talking about body movements and the sensorimotor experiences that come with them and thus further our understanding of the role of experience in metaphoric meaning making.

### 1.2 Dynamic View on Metaphor

Our analysis and our theoretical reflections will underline the dynamic, temporal, and discursive character of metaphors observed in these pedagogical settings. We will reconstruct how metaphors emerge from the sensorimotor experiences of the dance teachers and how they are transformed by both teachers and students in a constant flow of communicative interaction. Taking a dynamic view on metaphors we will argue that rather than thinking of metaphors in terms of concepts or even categories, metaphoric meaning construction must be conceived of as a process, not a product (Cameron 1999, 2009; Fiumara 1995; Gibbs 1993; Müller 2008a).

Different expressive modalities are involved in this process: speech and gestures, and it would also appropriate to describe much of what we will be talking about as multimodal metaphors – metaphors whose source and target are expressed in different modalities (Müller and Cienki 2009; Forceville and Urios-Aparisi 2009). We particularly want to address the dynamic unfolding of metaphoric expressions in both speech and gestures that are used to express the subjective sensorimotor experiences of body movements in dance and that eventually structure the discourse about balance.

This focus on metaphors as dynamic and emergent from the interaction in discourses is in harmony with Lynne Cameron's discourse or systematic metaphors (Cameron 2011; Zanotto, Cameron and Cavalcanti 2008). Cameron's dynamic discourse metaphors are metaphors that coparticipants in an interaction find to talk about and to organize an important part of larger scale discourses. Examples from Cameron's work on reconciliation discourse between an IRA bomber and the daughter of a victim include: 'Being affected by terrorism is participating in a game of chance' (Cameron and Maslen 2010: 117), and 'Violent conflict is a game with rules and terrorists break the rules' (Cameron and Maslen 2010: 131). Cameron suggests that those systematic metaphors evolve from the discourse dynamics and take a lead role in finding paths of mutual understanding and of empathy (Cameron 2009, 2010a; see also Cameron's website for the empathy network[2]). In Cameron's model, systematic metaphors emerge from many single usages of metaphoric expressions, be they mono- or multimodal, words, gestures, or pictures. Notably, Cameron does not make any claims about the cognitive reality of those systematic metaphors and we will follow her path in that regard. On the other hand, the focus of this paper will be on the subjective embodied metaphoric conceptualizations that dancers find to describe and communicate their subjective experiences. Thus, we will address individual metaphoric understandings of sensorimotor experiences that are visible in the interactive reactions of the participants in the workshop.

In doing this, we are advocating a dynamic view on metaphor. We shift focus from metaphors as single units to metaphors as a dynamic category. Metaphors evolve, change and develop with the flow of discourse and they can be activated and waking in one context and not activated and sleeping at another moment in the conversation (Müller 2008a, b).

### 1.3 Metaphors for 'concrete' Sensorimotor Experiences

Metaphors are used to understand 'concrete' sensorimotor experiences. Our analysis provides new insights into the canonical concept of metaphors as understanding abstract notions in terms of concrete ones. Much of current metaphor analysis centers around cases in which a more concrete source domain or vehicle is used to understand a more abstract target domain or topic. Examples from Conceptual Metaphor Theory are LOVE IS A JOURNEY; UNDERSTANDING IS GRASPING; and CHANGE IS MOTION. In a Critical Discourse Analysis of a speech by US President Barack Obama, Teun Van Dijk mentions that: '(...) good and bad periods may be coherently referred to through various mutually coherent NATURE metaphors, such as rising tides with prosperous moments, still water with peace, and raging clouds and raging storms with difficult periods.' (Van Dijk 2012: 595, capitalization in the original). Also in the results from Cameron's discourse dynamics analysis of metaphors, vehicles tend to be more on the concrete side than the metaphoric topics (see the examples above).

In this article, we are interested in metaphors that people find to describe a very 'concrete' and highly subjective bodily experience—the sensorimotor experience of a balanced body. Finding and maintaining balance is a prerequisite for any kind of dance, and, despite the fact that in very fundamental sense it is also prerequisite of all our everyday movements, dancers need to develop a highly specific, enduring, and stable balance in the center of the body. This is a specialized body knowledge, which differs

---

[2] http://www.open.ac.uk/researchprojects/livingwithuncertainty

across different dance styles, and this is what we are interested in. Our analysis of how dancers communicate metaphorically about balance will take into consideration verbal as well as gestural expressions of metaphoricity; It will, however, target primarily the gestural part of the metaphoric expressions. Why? Because we want to advocate that gestures in and of themselves are embodied and dynamic conceptualizations of movement.

### 1.4 Gestures Display the Embodied Grounds of Metaphoric Meaning

Extending the notion of gestures from hand gestures to full-body gestures, we will argue that those different kinds of gestures come with different forms of embodiment. Because dance lessons are about body movement, they offer an interesting field of study, also for reflections of the notion of embodiment, so popular in contemporary cognitive sciences. Here, we will argue that gestures are a particular type of embodied conceptualization of perceived or conceived actions, objects or events. Gestures may show subtle subjective understandings that would go unnoticed without a close appreciation of the individual gestural forms people use (Müller 2009, 2010).

Thinking of gestures as embodied conceptualizations in and of themselves might sound somewhat tautological, but in the light of different possible forms of gestural depictions it appears noteworthy. At least this is the line of argument we will follow in this chapter. Offering a refined understanding of the embodiment that we observe when dancers talk and gesture about the body in motion, we will point out that their gestures are 'embodied' in importantly different senses: A full-body pantomime accompanying a teacher's explanation differs from a hand-gestured version of the same body movement. We will argue that these gestures constitute different forms of embodied conceptualizations and are different subjective experiential grounds for metaphoric expressions in speech and gesture.

### 1.5 Embodiment and Metaphor Theory

Lakoff and Johnson early on proposed that 'the essence of metaphor is understanding and experiencing one kind of thing in terms of another' (Lakoff and Johnson 1980: 5). However, research on conceptual metaphors has taken off mainly on the 'understanding' part of metaphor. Only some twenty years later did the role of experiential grounds of metaphors began to receive more focused interest. Grady's (1997) distinction of primary and secondary metaphors captures the difference between conceptual metaphors that are grounded immediately in sensorimotor experiences, such as in UNDERSTANDING IS GRASPING, ACTION IS MOTION, or CHANGE IS MOTION, and those that are complex metaphors built on various primary metaphors, such as A PURPOSEFUL LIFE IS A JOURNEY (Lakoff and Johnson 1999: 49–56;

Johnson 2007: 178–179). In a more recent account of primary metaphors Johnson describes the generalized nature of embodied experiences that lead to the emergence of the primary metaphor: PSYCHOLOGICAL PROXIMITY IS PHYSICAL CLOSENESS (Johnson 2007: 178).

> A primary metaphor is based on an experiential correlation between a particular sensorimotor domain and some domain pertaining to a subjective experience or judgement. For example, each of us has repeated experiences in which being intimate (emotionally and psychologically) with a person is correlated with being physically close to them. The repeated co-activation of neural patterns associated with the subjective experience of intimacy and the sensorimotor experience of being physically close establishes the cross-domain neural connections that define the primary metaphor Psychological Intimacy Is Physical Closeness. This neural co-activation becomes the basis for a conceptual mapping of entities, structures, and relations from the source domain (physical closeness) onto the target domain (psychological intimacy). We then metaphorically conceive of being emotionally intimate with someone as being physically close to them. This primary metaphorical conception gives rise to the ordinary ways we talk about relationships as in 'We used to *be so close*, but over the past few months we've been *drifting apar*t'.(....).
>
> (Johnson 2007: 178)

Lakoff and Johnson's assumptions go along with an understanding of embodiment in primary metaphors as a neural activity that provides a cross-domain mapping between source and target domain: 'imagery associated with the source domain entities can be activated and thereby associated with the target-domain entities neurally connected to them' (Lakoff and Johnson 1999: 56). Distinguishing three levels of embodiment—the neural level, the phenomenological level and the level of the cognitive unconscious (Lakoff and Johnson 1999: 102–104)—they support the cognitive science assumption that meaning is fundamentally embodied (Lakoff and Johnson 1999: 462).

A phenomenological take on embodiment has gained much currency in the cognitive sciences recently (Gallagher 2008; Gibbs 2005; Johnson 2007; Sheets-Johnstone 1999, to name just a few). Gibbs defines this new cognitive science understanding of embodiment as follows: 'Embodiment is more than physiological and/or brain activity, and is constituted by recurring patterns of kinesthetic, proprioceptive action that provide much of people's felt, subjective experience' (Gibbs 2005: 12).

Such a view of an 'embodied mind' (Gibbs 2005: 12) has not only become an influential theoretical framework for neuro-psychology (cf. Barsalou's Perceptual Systems Simulation Theory, Barsalou 2008) but also provides support for some of the cognitive linguistic claims about the embodied grounds of lexical meaning. In several brain imaging studies Pulvermüller and colleagues (Pulvermüller 2001; Moseley et al. 2012 may serve as examples) could show that the processing of action and object words activates the respective sensorimotor brain areas, such that, for instance, the mental processing of grasping involves an activation of the brain regions for the motor activity of grasping. Using a priming task setting, Wilson and Gibbs (2007) found that also for comprehension of metaphoric usages of the word 'grasp' such as in 'grasping a concept', the sensorimotor experience of a grasping movement facilitates understanding: 'For example, making a grasping movement before seeing *grasp the concept* facilitates people's access to their embodied, metaphorical understanding of concept, even if concepts are not things that people can physically grasp' (Wilson and Gibbs 2007: 723).

Such psychological and neurological findings provide strong support for the intimate connection between bodily experiences and word meaning in particular between sensorimotor experiences and metaphor. For metaphor theory in particular the rise of embodiment research has had important consequences. By putting embodiment at center stage, the experiential side of metaphor appropriately receives a comparable amount of scholarly interest as the understanding part of metaphor.

Now, can an analysis of speech, gesture and body movement offer any new insights into the relation between embodiment and metaphor? Obviously, it cannot give access to a neurological level of generalized sensorimotor experiences. What it can do, however, is to provide insights into the individual, subjective, and dynamic level of experience that characterizes any ad hoc uses of metaphors. While experimental settings address generalized experience, our studies address subjective experiences and the ad hoc construction of metaphoric meaning in the flow of an ongoing discourse. While cognitive linguistic notions such as conceptual metaphors, primary metaphors, image schemas (for instance Johnson 1987, 2007; Lakoff and Johnson 1999, for an overview see Croft and Cruse 2004; Evans and Green 2006) or a cognitive science understanding of word meaning more generally (as in Barsalou's and Pulvermüller's work) all address generalized sensorimotor experiences that give rise to or are activated when we process word meaning, this chapter is interested in the local, subjective, and interactive processes of experiencing and understanding the body in motion.

### 1.6 Gestures as Expressive Movements

Gestures *are* sensorimotor experiences (Kappelhoff and Müller 2011). They show that sensorimotor programs for grasping are active, when for instance someone is talking about grasping a concept and is performing a grasping movement at the same time (see Müller 2008a, b; Müller and Tag 2010).

But gestures are embodied in a further more fundamental sense: they are *felt experiences* in a phenomenological sense (Kappelhoff and Müller 2011; Sheets-Johnstone 1999). This means that whenever I perform a gesture this performance comes along with a feeling of movement and is immediately perceived as movement. In that sense we speak of gestures *as expressive movements* (Kappelhoff and Müller 2011). The notion of expressive movement was developed in the context of German Expression Theory/Psychology (Bühler 1933, Wundt 1920) and in Philosophical Anthropology (Plessner 1925/1982). Again this perspective on embodiment is in harmony with theoretical developments in cognitive science that follow the phenomenological tradition. The following quote from Gallagher (2008) may illustrate this facet of the embodiment discussion:

> On the embodied view of social cognition, the mind of the other person is not something that is hidden away and inaccessible. In perceiving the actions and expressive movements of the other person in the interactive contexts of the surrounding world, one already grasps their meaning; no inference to a hidden set of mental states (beliefs, desires, etc.) is necessary. When I see the other's action or gesture, I see (I immediately perceive) the meaning in the action or gesture; and when I am in a process of interacting with the other, my own actions and reactions help to constitute that meaning. (Gallagher 2008: 449)

Our analysis concerns a type of metaphoric gesture that must be regarded as subjective, embodied, and dynamic conceptualization. In the gestures we can see – that and how metaphors are embodied conceptualizations and we can see that metaphor construction is a process. The use of gestures with speech over the course of time reveals that this dynamic way of metaphoric meaning construction may structure entire workshops.

In summary, in this paper we will address subjective forms of experiences in the flow of interaction, and describe how people find metaphoric ways to talk, gesture, and to conceptualize the body in motion in dance lessons. In particular we will focus on how teachers and students go about finding, communicating, and depicting the bodily experiences of finding balance in classes for ballet and Argentine tango.

## 2 Why Dance Lessons? Data and Setting

An important motivation for choosing dance lessons as contexts was that we expected them to provide a rich context for studying the grounding of meaning in the experiences of bodily movement. Obviously, teaching dance movements brings embodied forms of communication center stage and this is why we chose this setting in the first place. Teachers search for metaphors for the particular sensorimotor experiences of balance they are concentrating on; they work with metaphors in speech and gesture until the students have successfully incorporated a particular movement pattern. Dance lessons therefore appear to be a perfect context for studying metaphoric gestures as embodied conceptualizations.

The study was conducted as part of an interdisciplinary project, 'Language of movement and dance', in which the languaging of body movement and dance was researched against three disciplinary backgrounds: Psychology and Movement Analysis (Sabine Koch, Heidelberg), Phenomenological Philosophy and Psychiatry (Thomas Fuchs, Heidelberg) and Cognitive Metaphor Theory and Gesture Studies (Cornelia Müller, Frankfurt (Oder)).[3]

The database for our study comes from a collection of dance lessons. We collected data from different types of dance such as ballet, Argentine tango, waltz and movement studies. In order to be able to compare the different dances, we asked the teachers to do workshops on balance, posture, walking and turning, and on sharing space. In addition, we asked them to do two free trainings. The data we are using for this chapter come from two workshops on balance and posture: one ballet workshop and one on Argentine tango. We recorded the lessons with two video cameras: one static camera recording the entire room (including the mirror), a flexible camera that followed the teacher. The teacher carried a portable microphone. Teacher and students were told that we were interested in a linguistic analysis of communication in dance lessons; they did not know that we were actually interested in gesture analysis. The workshops were structured as follows:

(1) Warming up

(2) Main part of the class (1): alternating sequences of the teacher explaining and the students practicing

(3) Short break with interview of the group: after an hour of rehearsing the group of students was asked for first impressions on how they were getting along with the lesson so far.

(4) Main part of the class (2): lesson continues.

(5) After the class: short interviews with students and teacher. Students were asked once again how they liked the lesson and what they liked

---

[3] A major aim of the project was to investigate the roles of role of body movements for the emergence of meaning based on phenomenological, psychological and cognitive-linguistic theories. Another one was an analysis of the relation between body memory, metaphor and movement (cf. Koch et al. 2012; Kolter et al. 2012). From an applied point of view the project has generated deeper understanding of communicating body movements and bodily experiences for the applied fields of dance or movement therapy and dance education. The project was funded by the German Ministry of Education (BMBF) in the program 'Translation functions of the humanities'. For further details see:
www.psychologie.uni-heidelberg.de/projekte/bewegung/index.shtml.

or disliked about it. The teacher was asked about her/his preparation of the lesson and also about her/his impressions of how the lesson had gone.

## 3 Methods: Linguistic Gesture Analysis and Identification of Waking Metaphors

In our analysis we combined two methodologies: A form-based linguistic approach of Gesture Analysis (Ladewig and Bressem, forthcoming; Müller 2010, 2013, submitted; Müller, Bressem and Ladewig 2013) and the cognitive linguistic Metaphor-Foregrounding-Analysis (Müller and Tag 2010). The linguistic method of gesture analysis takes gestural meaning as motivated. Therefore the 'meaning' of the form of a bodily movement is the ground upon which an analysis of gestural meaning rest and this is why we take form as starting point for the reconstruction of the meaning of gestures. A form-based approach is supported by a linguistic annotation system for gesture (Bressem, Ladewig and Müller 2013) which uses the ELAN Software for the annotation of the dynamics of emerging multimodal meaning Transcription of speech and gesture, as well as the form-based analyses of full body movements, hand gestures and speech are all carried out in ELAN (for more details on ELAN, see Wittenburg, Brugman, Russel et al. 2006, http://www.mpi.nl/tools).

### 3.1 Identifying Waking Metaphors

Our analysis addresses the discourse level and the level of metaphoric expressions. Although we believe that many of the metaphoric expressions we are interested in may reside in conceptual metaphors, we think that the semantic details of multimodal metaphoric expressions deserve more attention than they receive in many analyses of multimodal metaphors and/or metaphoric gestures. Our analysis of the dance lessons will hopefully convincingly show that taking this perspective puts us in a position to see how embodiment grounds meaning in a very concrete and mundane way.

When considering metaphor on the level of metaphoric expressions there are at least two different approaches to the analysis and identification of verbal metaphors in discourse that come to mind: The Metaphor Identification Procedure developed by the Pragglejaz group (Pragglejaz 2007 in metaphor and symbol), extended by Steen's metaphor group at the VU university Amsterdam (MIP-VU Steen 2010) on the one hand and Lynne Cameron's discourse dynamics approach (Cameron and Maslen 2010). Both takes on metaphor identification address the metaphoric potential of metaphoric expressions on the verbal level. In the case of MIP and MIP-VU, this goes along with the assumption that a proper identification procedure needs to follow a word by word analysis and a checking of potential metaphoricity for each word in a given sentence or utterance. The decision about metaphoricity of a word starts with an analysis of the context in which the word is used. In a second step a corpus based dictionary is consulted. If the respective lexical entry contains a more basic contemporary meaning than in the given context of use, and 'if it contrasts with the basic meaning, but can be understood in comparison with it' the word is identified as a metaphor (Pragglejaz 2006: 3).

In the case of Cameron's discourse dynamics approach (Cameron 2009, 2010a) potential metaphors on the level of verbal expressions are determined heuristically using a less strict version of the MIP (Cameron is a member of the Pragglejaz group, see also Cameron and Maslen 2010b) and grouped into larger scale discourse metaphors (Cameron, Low and Maslen 2010). Those groupings of metaphors help to identify the systematic metaphors that are relevant for structuring discourses even over longer time spans (Cameron 1999; Cameron and Maslen 2010a,b; Cameron, Low and Maslen 2010; Cameron 2010b).

Our take on the identification of metaphors relates to both approaches, though differs in important regards. It relates to both in that it also focuses on metaphoric expressions, rather than on conceptual metaphors in the first place. It differs from both in that it makes a distinction between sleeping and waking metaphors (Müller 2008a,b). Waking metaphors are metaphoric expressions which receive the speaker's and the listener's attention, sleeping ones do not. Waking metaphors are characterized by activated metaphoricity, for example metaphoric meaning is being actively foregrounded and is therefore considered in the focus of attention (Müller and Tag 2010). If, for instance, a verbal metaphoric expression is accompanied by a gesture which exhibits the source domain of the verbal metaphor, metaphoricity is foregrounded because it is expressed in two modalities at the same time. This type of foregrounding follows an iconic principle, but foregrounding can also be achieved by syntactic, semantic, and by interactive means (for more details see Müller and Tag 2010).

In the analysis we are presenting here, we concentrate uniquely on activated 'waking' metaphors. We document how they dynamically emerge and evolve over the course of the dance lesson – including the two interview settings and across teachers and students.

### 3.2 Visualizing the Dynamics of Metaphor

In order to visualize the dynamic processes involved in metaphoric meaning making, we applied a time line notation that documents activated metaphoricity in two modalities—speech and gesture (including full body movements)—in keynote (PowerPoint is equally possible) (cf. also Kolter et al. 2012). It was first developed for the annotation of multimodal metaphors in a collaborative project of linguists and film scholars (Kappelhoff and Müller 2011; see footnote for project website[4]).[5]

Metaphoric expressions are shown as boxes on a timeline and the size of these boxes corresponds roughly to the length of a verbal, gestural, or verbo-gestural metaphoric expression as identified in the ELAN Software. The upper arrow represents the flow of speech, the lower one the flow of body movements along a discourse. The graphic patterns of the boxes correspond to the different metaphoric meanings. In Figure 1 the arrows depict the source domain of a metaphor as up and down movement, the boxes with a waving pattern show the source domain of a waving movement, and the round spiral represents a spiral movement as the source domain, that was either performed downwards or upwards (for more detail, see Kappelhoff and Müller 2011; Kolter et al. 2012).

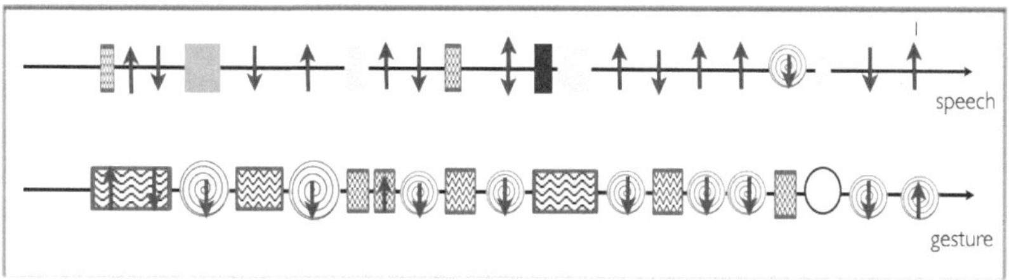


FIGURE 1. Timeline annotation in keynote.

To sum up, our analysis of metaphors in body movements, gestures and speech concerns only waking metaphors, for example metaphors that are activated through foregrounding activities. For the identification of metaphoricity in gesture the linguistic form-based method is applied. The analysis of metaphorically used gesture and speech concerns two larger methodological steps:

(1) ELAN annotation: transcribing speech, gesture and body movements, identifying metaphoric expressions in speech and gesture;

(2) Timeline annotation in keynote: documenting the sequencing of metaphors across modalities and over time and speakers.

---

4 http://www.languages-of-emotion.de/en/expressive-movement.html

5 Many thanks go to Sarah Greifenstein, Christina Schmitt, and Susanne Tag, who were vital forces in developing this schematic notation for the dynamics of waking metaphors. Müller and Tag (2010) developed an earlier version for the documentation of foregrounded metaphoricity. We adopted this notation for the dance project to a finegrained linguistic documentation of the emergence and movement of metaphoric meaning between two expressive modalities: full body movement, gesture and speech.

## 4 Metaphors for Balance in Classes of Ballet and Argentine Tango

It is not a simple task to communicate the ballet- or tango-specific experiences of balance. Very often teachers come to use metaphoric expressions to characterize and communicate them. We will give two examples of discourse metaphors for balance the teachers found and used spontaneously in their workshops on balance and posture. Notably, we asked them during the interview if they found the metaphors on the spot or whether they belonged to a 'repertoire' of their communicative teaching resources. Both teachers explained, that yes, they do have some metaphoric expressions that they repeatedly use but the ones found for balance did not belong to them or were variations of a metaphor they had used before.

We speak of discourse metaphors because instantiations of these metaphors in speech and gesture were used along the workshop by teachers and students—and even in the interviews after the lesson, participants used them to describe their experiences with working on finding balance. These metaphors appear to structure and organize the discourse about balance and they operate on a level of discourse which is comparable to Cameron's systematic metaphors (Cameron 2009, 2010a,b).

Teachers use metaphors that link their subjective bodily experience of balance in ballet or in tango to a target domain (finding balance). These subjective bodily experiences, this feeling of balance, is of course imprinted by the movement characteristics of the particular dance styles. The ideas of what is balance and how to achieve a characteristic posture differ strongly between dance styles. In ballet a stable, strong, and static center of the body is how balance is achieved. A rather static upper body with great strength is the anchor for the legs and arms to look and feel light and elegant. In Argentine tango finding balance also needs a strong center, but the idea of stability comes from a good connection to the ground. This good connection to the ground ensures balance and a smooth walking and turning. The center and the legs receive their stability by 'thinking into the ground'. While ballet is all about thinking 'up' and 'light', tango is all about thinking 'down' and 'heavy'.

The metaphors the two teachers find to describe their respective feelings of balance express this differing ideas of what balance is. The ballet teacher invents the metaphor of a horizontal silk thread pulling the navel towards the spine. The idea is that an erect hip position is a core element for an upright and stable upper body and the subtle and yet strong material silk corresponds to the idea of lightness and strength. The metaphor that emerges for balance in the ballet class can be formulated as follows: Finding balance is feeling a silk thread pulling the navel towards the spine (Figure 2).

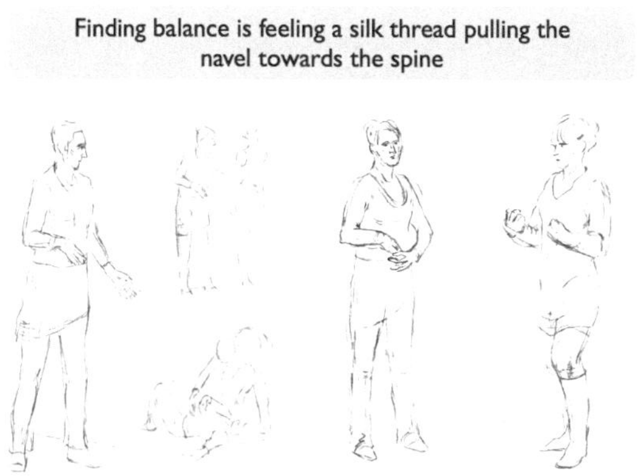


FIGURE 2. Balance in a ballet class: The silk thread metaphor in body, speech, and hand gesture.

The tango teacher's metaphor, on the contrary, works with an extremely heavy and bulky material: an iron anchor chain. These are very different metaphoric source domains to describe a sensorimotor experience of balance in the two dance styles. For the tango teacher, what is important, is that the students get the idea and the feeling of a heavy leg which behaves like an anchor chain pending in the water. This is how he conceptualizes balance, how he explains the students to become and remain balanced as they are moving over the dance floor. The heavy chain stabilizes the dancer like a heavy anchor chain stabilizes the ship. He notes that it is the weight of the chain which stabilizes the ship not a fixed anchor in the ground. This is the scenario the tango teacher uses to help the students to find the particular way of a balanced and anchored moving that is characteristic for Argentine tango. We can formulate the metaphor the tango teacher finds and which is used along the class in the following way (Figure 3): Argentine tango – Finding balance is feeling stable like a ship with a pending anchor chain. Notably, these cases of metaphor are mappings from a 'concrete' source domain to a 'concrete' target domain. The target domain or the topic is a 'concrete' sensorimotor experience and the source domains or vehicles are imaginary scenarios that probably none of the participants have ever experienced in real life. Nevertheless, the imagined scenarios are embodied scenes that apparently help finding a highly specific body movement (and posture): namely, to construct balance from an erected hip position (in ballet) or from a heavy leg (in Tango).

FIGURE 3. Balance in Argentine tango: The anchor chain metaphor in body, speech, and hand gesture.

Over the course of the lessons, the teachers, and successively also the students, verbalize and embody these scenarios in body movement and hand gestures and turn them into lived experiences. These embodied metaphoric scenarios pave the way to the particular experience of balance that the teachers are addressing and could also be accounted for as metaphoric blends. In the following section we will take a closer look at how different forms of embodiment in metaphoric gestures are used to achieve this goal.

## 5 Feeling and Depicting the Sensorimotor Experience of Balance: Metaphoric Gestures

Teachers of movement and dance often are faced with the challenge of communicating highly subjective experiences, and we have seen that the ballet and the tango teacher find different metaphors to express their respective dance specific experience of balance. Analyzing the temporal flow of the emerging metaphors it is clear that the teachers take time to work out an appropriate metaphoric conceptualization for that particular class. They both find the metaphor as they teach, and in both cases the metaphor is verbalized and gestured. We asked them later in the interviews whether they had prepared the metaphors for the class, and both assured that this was not the case.

## 5.1 Feeling the Body in Motion: Metaphoric Body Gestures

So, apparently, the metaphors emerged spontaneously during the class, as they were teaching. In both cases, the metaphors emerged, during a group exercise for balance. This means that the teacher's experience of balance becomes the topic, the target domain, and, at the same time, provides an experiential ground for the metaphor to emerge.

In the middle of explaining an exercise the ballet teacher comes up with a description of the movement feeling: 'the feeling is a silk thread' (*das Gefühl ist ein Seidenfaden*) and while saying this, she points to the navel with both hands, which is where the imagined silk thread is supposed to be hooked, and moves her hip backwards. We recall that the movement she wants her students to perform is to erect the hip. The silk thread pulls the navel towards the spine and the effect of it is an erect hip—a prerequisite for balance and an upright posture (Figure. 4). Interestingly enough, nobody can see her gestures, because they are all leaning against the mirror with their backs—all seeking to find this particular feeling for balance. The teacher is looking out of the window in a thoughtful manner and searches for a description while she is concentrating on the hip movement and the particular sensorimotor experience that comes with it.

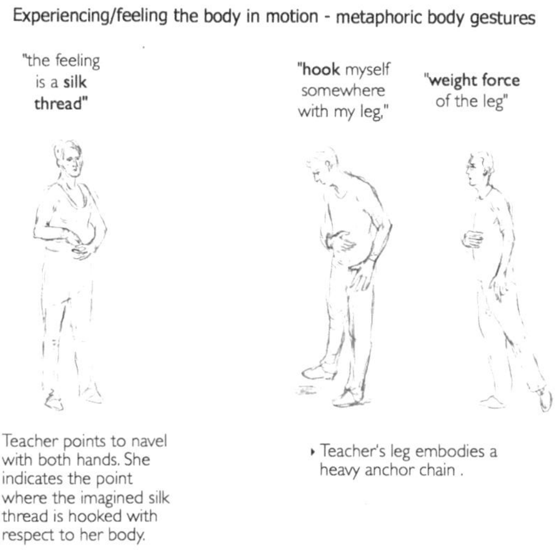


FIGURE 4. Teachers experience balance as specific body movement and find metaphoric body gestures.

We consider this full body movement (moving the hip backwards) as *metaphoric body gesture*. Such a full body movement targets the immediate sensorimotor experience in the body itself, the sensorimotor experience that is central for achieving and maintaining balance. She uses the metaphoric body gesture and verbalizes it to capture her subjective experience of the hip movement so that her students can work with it and find a similar kind of sensorimotor experience.

We have seen that the tango teacher finds a different type of metaphor to describe and evoke his subjective experience of balance in dancing Argentine tango, 'The anchor chain metaphor'. However, he also finds this metaphor as he is talking and teaching and searching for the best explanation to describe this sensorimotor experience of balance that he is targeting in his class. While he is showing the movement to two dancers he says: 'I hook myself somewhere with my leg' and put 'weight force on the (free) leg'. As he is describing this anchoring scenario his free leg becomes the heavy anchor chain, it represents the weight of an anchor chain pending in the water and is extended behind the body, just like an anchor chain drifting behind a ship (Figure 4). Again what we observe here is a metaphoric body gesture, which again targets the immediate sensorimotor experience of balance for tango dancing. What we observe here is that subjective experiences of balance give rise to what we term metaphoric body gestures. Both teachers find metaphoric body gestures for their particular experiences of balance, of sensorimotor experience. Both teachers find them ad hoc in the flow of communication and both find them because of a communicative need: they want to evoke a similar sensorimotor experience in the students of their class.

We consider metaphoric body gestures as a particular kind of embodied conceptualization, because they address the sensorimotor experience in situ, right in the location of the body that is at stake and because they are performed with the body parts that supposedly trigger those particular experiences of balance the teachers aim to evoke and inscribe in the bodies of their students.

## 5.2 Depicting the Body in Motion – Metaphoric Hand Gestures

Metaphoric hand gestures, in turn, are different kinds of embodied conceptualizations: they depict the bodily experience of balance addressed in the metaphor rather than enacting it. And again we find this type of gesture frequently used in both workshops.

In the ballet class, metaphoric hand gestures are used only by the students in the interview situations, whereas in the tango class the teacher uses them extremely often (Figure 5). At one moment during the workshop, he gives a series of verbo-gestural accounts of the qualities of this chain. He first says: 'The chain is quite heavy and slow (...)' and with his right hand he acts as if grasping and holding a chain or a big rope high up in the gesture space. He continues his explanation: 'because this super heavy chain', and moulds with two curled hands a long round and thick object, which extends in a wide vertical diagonal axis across his lower gesture space. In the last instance of this sequence he has moved the imagined chain slightly up to now grasp it at two ends (technically, he acts as if grasping an imagined chain). This metaphoric hand gesture comes with the following part of his utterance: 'move the heavy chain hanging in the water' (Figure 5).

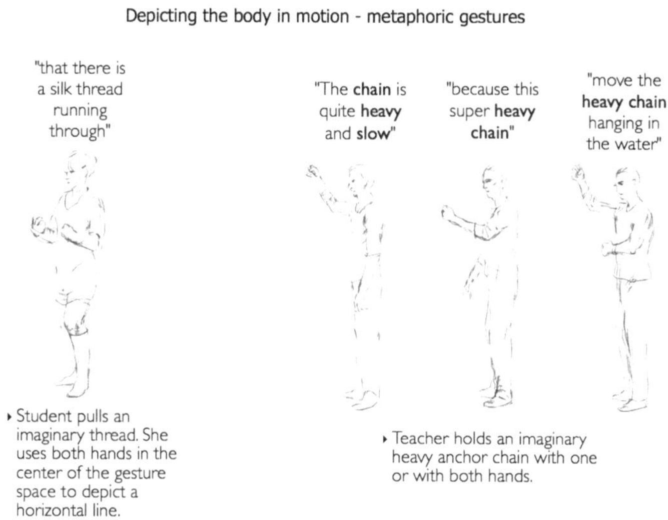


FIGURE 5. Depicting bodily experiences: the silk thread metaphor and the anchor chain metaphor in speech and hand gesture.

In the ballet class a student provides a minute account of this aspect of the training and in doing so she performs a very subtle gesture in front of her body, in which the two hands have a similar hand shape and move synchronously from the center of the body outwards. Her handshapes suggest that she holds the two ends of a delicate thread, fixed with her thumbs on her curled index fingers. With the horizontal outward movement she evokes the impression of extending an imagined thread between her hands. She performs this gesture while she is talking about 'a silk thread running through (the body horizontally)' (Figure 5).

This closer account of the forms of the four gestures shows that the gestures depict very clearly the different source domain objects: a silk thread and an anchor chain. Gestures operate on mundane experiences such as grasping or holding different sized objects to depict an important aspect of the scenario evoked by the source domain. Because they describe the specific sensorimotor experience of finding balance in ballet or in Argentine tango they come with a different type of experience than metaphoric body gestures. Metaphoric body gestures provide an imagination that directly addresses the experience of balance in the responsible body part. Metaphoric hand gestures, on the contrary, describe and depict important facets of the imaginary scenario that paves the way to finding balance, but they are not part of the actual experience of balance themselves. In that sense, metaphoric hand gestures are further away from the actual sensorimotor experience of balance; they are a different form of embodied conceptualization and are closer to linguistic forms of communication than metaphoric body gestures.

# 6 The Dynamics of Embodied Metaphoric Conceptualizations

Much of what we have said so far could only be tracked down because our analysis departs from the dynamics of the interaction and an analysis of the gesture's form. Our analysis brings together the meaning of the form with the context of use in which it is embedded and the sequential placement in the ongoing interaction (Bressem, Ladewig and Müller 2013; Ladewig and Bressem, forthcoming; Müller 2010, 2013; Müller, Bressem and Ladewig 2013). Because we consider all the single instances of metaphor uses within their larger scale orchestration we see that metaphoric gestures emerge and achieve their meaning (in the widest sense of the word) only in the concert of this dynamic arrangement across modalities, across speakers, and time. Metaphoric conceptualizations emerge in an intertwined process between different expressive modes, they emerge, unfold and change in an interactive process that reacts to the needs and moves of students as much as of those of the teachers, and they end up building characteristic interactive trajectories.

## 6.1 Metaphors Intertwine Across Modalities and Across Time

When we examine how and when metaphoric expressions in speech, gesture and body movement are used over the course of the workshop, we see that they are intertwined in different ways. Without going too much into those details here, we would like to point out that the particular temporal patterns vary between the two workshops: In the tango lesson the metaphor occurs at first only in the body movement (Figure 6, tango), whereas in the ballet class it is used verbally in the beginning (Figure 6, ballet). A moment after the first bodily enactment, the tango teacher uses the metaphor across all three modalities simultaneously (Figure 6, tango); the ballet teacher shows a more successive temporal pattern in the use of the different modalities (ver-

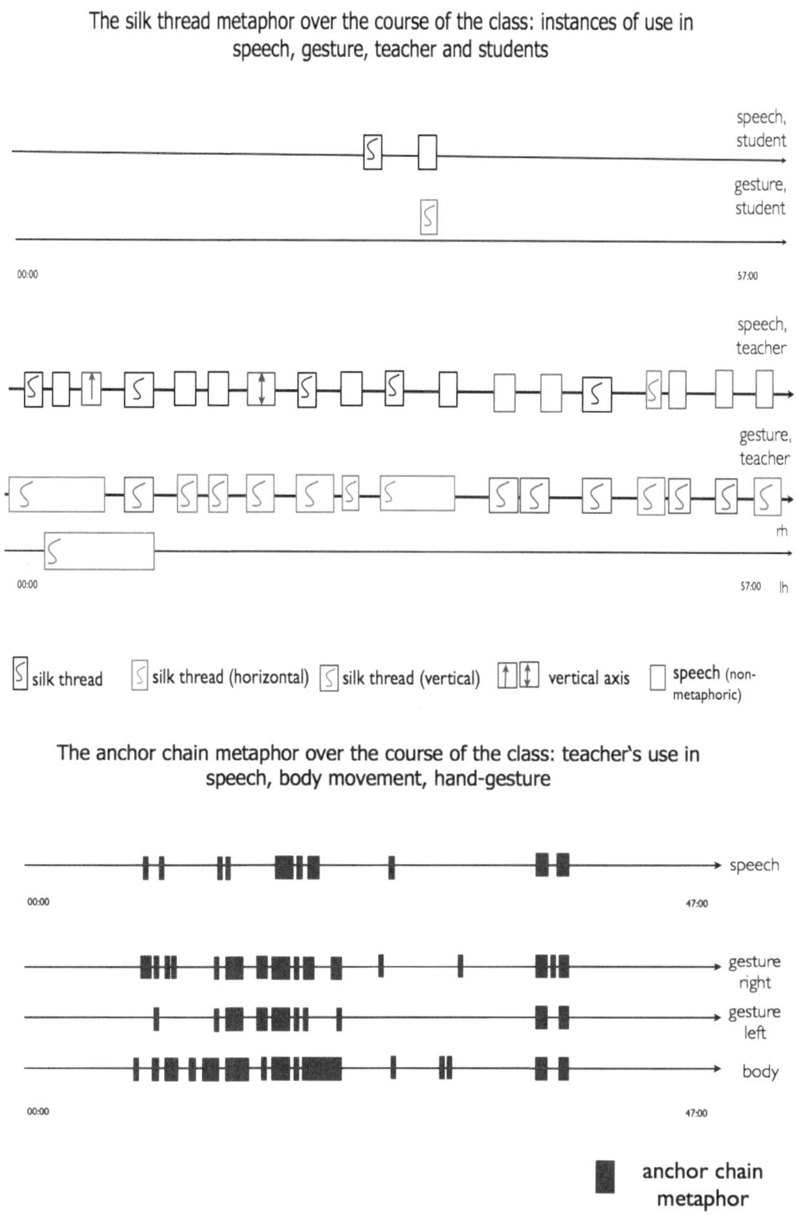


FIGURE 6. The silk thread metaphor and the anchor chain metaphor show different temporal patterns, intertwining across modalities, participants and time.

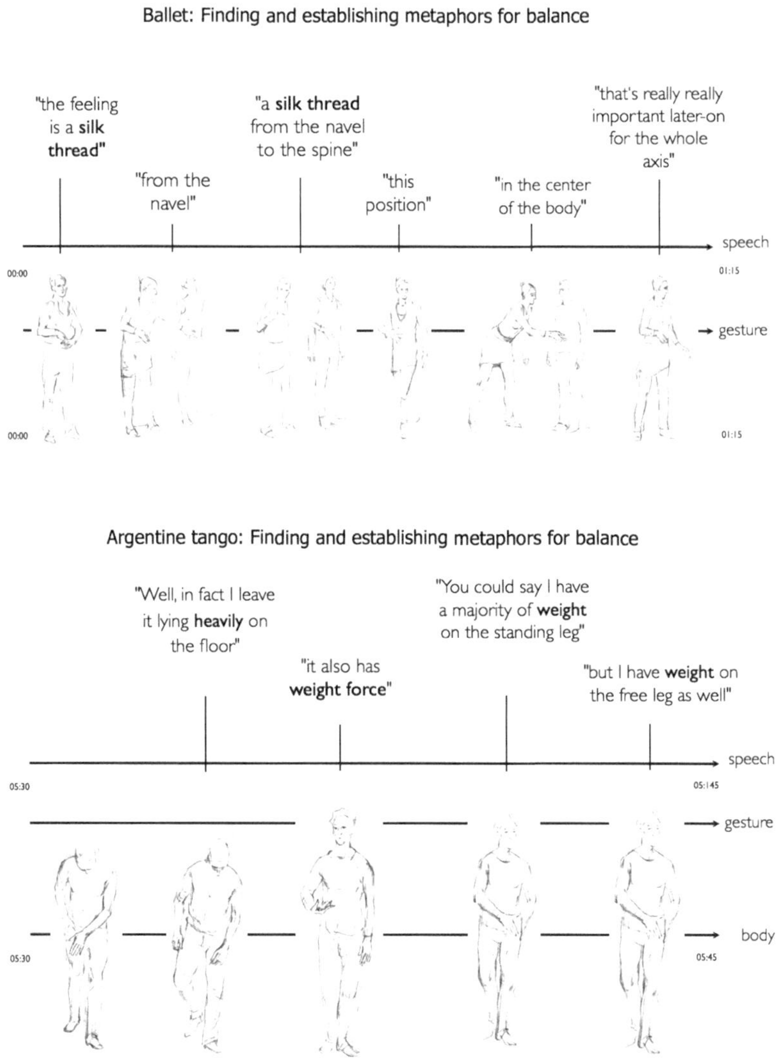


FIGURE 7. Finding and establishing metaphors for balance in ballet (above) and tango (below) as an unfolding orchestration between modalities.

balizing and then body gestures) and begins immediately to execute them interactively with a student (gesturing with the body of a student) (Figure 6, ballet). The schematic depictions in the keynote notation that are provided in Figure 6 show the first part of the ballet workshop (including the interaction between teacher and one student) and the entire course of the tango workshop, but for the tango class we have only notated the teachers uses of the anchor chain metaphor.

### 6.2 Finding Metaphor is a Process

Both teachers face a similar complex task of finding the appropriate expressive means to get students to feel something they have not felt before. They need to lead them to experience a highly specific form of movement and to make a sensorimotor experience that is new for them and that is fundamental to finding balance for dancing ballet or Argentine tango. Both teachers take time and need time to find and to establish the metaphor they conceive of as a suitable tool to work on finding this particular feeling for balance which characterizes their respective dance style. Figure 7 shows the unfolding of this process of finding an appropriate metaphor, which includes successions, simultaneities and alternations of metaphoric expressions in speech, body, and hand gesture for both teachers (Figure 7).

### 6.3 Interactive Trajectories of Metaphors for Balance

Teaching is a dynamic enterprise in many respects and as our analyses of the two workshops document, it is also a highly creative process. The classes we have observed and the work of the dance teachers we have analysed makes this very clear. On the one hand we have observed general patterns, which we have presented in some detail thus far; On the other hand, when we look at how the two teachers employ for instance the two different types of embodied conceptualizations—metaphoric body gestures and metaphoric hand gestures—we find significantly different trajectories for the two teachers and for their interaction with the students.

In the ballet class the teacher only uses the metaphoric body gesture (including pointing gestures that locate it), while the tango teacher uses both forms right from the beginning: the metaphoric body gesture and the metaphoric hand gesture (Figure 8). The ballet class is characterized by a rather linear trajectory from the teacher's bodily experience of balance to metaphoric body movement with metaphoric speech (including interactive gesturing with the body of the students), and the students depicting of that experience with metaphoric hand gestures. In the first phase of the ballet class, the teacher finds and establishes the verbal and body metaphor of the horizontal silk thread; In the second phase, she uses those two modes of expres-

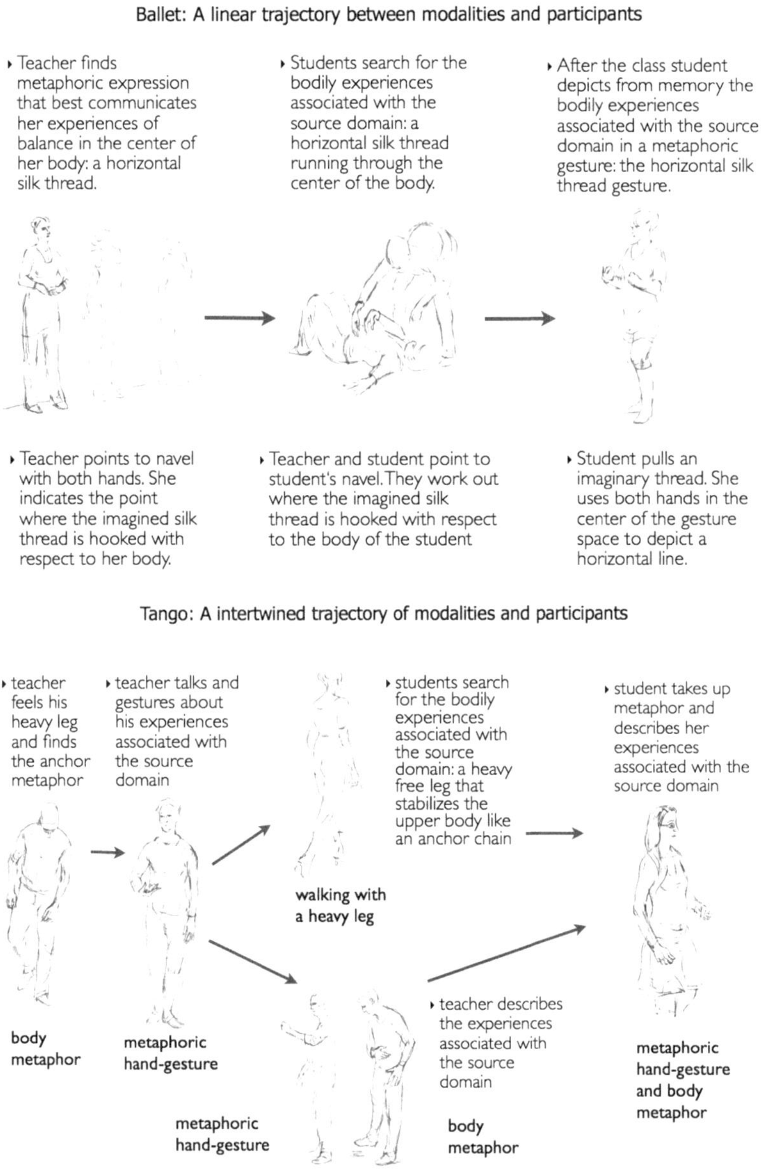


FIGURE 8. Different interactive trajectories of metaphors in speech, body, and hand gesture and between teacher and students. From the bodily experience of balance to metaphoric body gesture, metaphoric speech, and metaphoric gestures.

sion, to work with the students, on inscribing this type of movement and the sensorimotor experience that comes with it. Only in interviews during and after the ballet class, we find metaphoric hand gestures (used by the students). The metaphoric hand gestures are only used by the students to retrospectively characterize their experiences. The teacher never uses them. This means that the ballet teacher focuses in her workshop on experiencing the sensorimotor pattern which characterizes the grounding of balance in an erect position of the hip: the horizontal silk thread pulling the navel to the spine. It is either verbalized or embodied in a full body movement – a metaphoric body gesture – and then addresses the immediate sensorimotor experience associated with this movement of the hip.

The tango teacher, on the contrary, follows a different style (Figure 8). In his class the different modes of expressions are intertwined from the beginning: he uses all three forms of metaphoric expressions for finding balance right from the start and accordingly addresses the students both on the sensorimotor level associated with the feeling of a heavy leg (metaphoric body gesture of pending anchor chain) and on the level of describing this particular feeling gesturally (metaphoric hand gesture depicting anchor chain) and verbally (in multiple descriptions of the qualities of an anchor chain). Also we find both forms of gestures in the students as well. Apparently, they were ready to take both bodily types of explanations up immediately.

The two workshops therefore appear to be characterized by differing interactive trajectories of metaphor use across modalities, participants and time: over the ballet class the metaphor emerges and unfolds in rather linear fashion: finding—working—depicting; in the tango class the three communicative activities cluster from the onset producing an intertwined trajectory.

We therefore would like to point out that teaching balance in dance classes must be described as a temporal and sequential orchestration of cognitive and interactive processes: Cognitive semiotic processes responsible for the emergence of metaphoric meaning from and for sensorimotor experiences and interactive processes responsible for the moment by moment change of usage contexts. This is, in a nutshell, what we consider the dynamics of embodied metaphoric conceptualizations.

## 7 Conclusion

In talking about their experiences of balance dancers exhibit their subjective understandings in the ways they use their body as an instrument in communication. They show their particular understandings in the different kinds of gestures they use: a metaphoric body gesture documents that they have a local bodily understanding of the particular type of balance that is addressed; a metaphoric hand gesture documents that they can describe an important aspect of a scenario that supposedly leads to the desired experience of balance in the body, though it does not show how balance in the center feels.

The different gestural modes of representation, which underlie these two types of gestures, document this difference in embodiment (Müller 1998, 2009, 2010): when the hand gestures depict the silk thread or the iron chain, the hands act as if molding a thread or an iron chain. The embodied feeling is one of molding a stretched, long object. When a body part becomes an anchor chain, the body represents the respective object. In this body gesture the leg becomes a heavy anchor chain or the center of body becomes the hook of a horizontal thread pulling the navel towards the spine. The embodied feeling coming with this mode of representation relates immediately to the body part that is the metaphoric target.

We have argued that the hand gestures and the body gestures come with different types of embodied experiences and they show different experiential grounds for the metaphoric meaning that evolves and changes over the course of the dance lessons. The metaphorically-led understanding of balance in the two classes is therefore in a constant flow and adjustment. There is not one static moment in which a metaphor is activated, rather what we observe is a constant and joint shaping and reshaping of metaphoric meaning. The activation of metaphoricity is an interactive process of creating mutual understanding. Metaphors should not be reduced to the level of activating lexical categories or a particular type of lexical processing. We suggest that when metaphors are used in those types of pedagogical and interactive settings they function as a resource of constructing and activating subjective forms of embodied understanding. As expressive movements, metaphoric gestures import the subjective felt experiences of metaphoric meaning and display different facets of the embodied nature of metaphor. Gesture analysis therefore offers a more fine-grained understanding of embodiment in metaphor and may well challenge traditional language-based theories of metaphor.

Metaphors appear to serve as valuable means for understanding and experiencing concrete and highly specific sensorimotor experiences such as particular concepts of balance within different dance styles. What is striking is how other types of experiences are recruited as source domains or vehicles. Teachers work here with fully imaginary scenarios: silk threads running horizontally through the body or legs turning into heavy anchor chains are nothing that we can actually experience. But in our imagination we can. We can imagine a silk thread pulling our navel towards the spine and we can imagine a leg becoming a heavy chain stabilizing our walking and dancing. The source domain operates with the imagination of the dancers and the body movements turn the imagined worlds into lived and felt experiences. What we observe here in mundane contexts of dance lessons, the embodying and living of these imagined scenarios, is something that drama theory, theatre and film theory have dealt with for centuries (cf., Kappelhoff 2004 for a historical discussion of those concepts and a theoretical framework for film analysis).

We have seen that gestures as embodied metaphoric conceptualizations may exhibit subtle differences of individual subjective understandings as we go along in our ordinary conversations. We can only speculate that these gestures go along with a neurological activation of the respective brain areas. Findings from neuropsychology and psychology at least provide indirect experimental support for such an argument (Pulvermüller 1999; Moseley et al. 2012; Wilson and Gibbs 2007). What experimental settings rule out, obviously, are the subjective experiences people have outside of the laboratory. Yet this is what we are interested in and it is here where gesture analysis can offer new perspectives onto individual cognitive processes—insofar as we accept a consideration of gesture as embodied conceptualizations and as embodied forms of thought and understanding. Particularly in teaching dance, metaphors (in speech, gesture, and body) appear to be extremely useful means to communicate embodied experiences.

Looking at metaphors for sensorimotor experiences in dance contexts therefore appears to indicate that we need to revise the standard view of metaphor as a primary means of understanding something abstract in terms of something concrete. Putting gesture analysis center stage quite naturally reveals the temporal and discursive character of these metaphoric conceptualizations and it directs attention to the fact that there are different forms of embodiment in metaphor and gesture.

## Acknowledgments

We would like to thank Mathias Roloff for providing the drawings (http://www.mathiasroloff.de), Lena Hotze for her collaboration in the analysis and her support in finalizing this article, Jan Bakels, Sarah Greifenstein, Christina Schmitt for their input regarding the embodiment discussions, and Benjamin Marienfeld and Dorothea Böhme for sharing their knowledge in various forms of metaphor analysis. This analysis would not have been possible without the intensive theoretical and methodological work carried out in another project: We are grateful to Hermann Kappelhoff (FU Berlin) and the team of the project 'Multimodal metaphor and expressive movement': Dorothea Böhme, Franziska Boll, Sarah Greifenstein,

Stefan Rook, Thomas Scherer, Christina Schmitt, and Susanne Tag (http://www.languages-of-emotion.de/en/expressive-movement.html).

## References


Barsalou, Lawrence W. 2008. Grounded Cognition. In *The Annual Review of Psychology* 59: 617–645.

Bressem, Jana, Silva H. Ladewig and Cornelia Müller. 2013. Linguistic Annotation System for Gesture. In Müller, Cornelia, Alan Cienki, Ellen Fricke, Silva H. Ladewig, David McNeill and Sedinha Teßendorf (eds), *Body – Language – Communication: An International Handbook on Multimodality in Human Interaction*. (Handbooks of Linguistics and Communication Science 38.1). Berlin/ Boston: De Gruyter Mouton: 1094–1120.

Bühler, Karl. 1933. *Ausdruckstheorie. Das System an der Geschichte aufgezeigt*. Jena: Gustav Fischer.

Cameron, Lynne. 1999. Identifying and describing metaphors in spoken discourse data. In Cameron, Lynne and Graham Low (eds), *Researching and applying metaphor*. Cambridge: Cambridge University Press: 105–132.

Cameron, Lynne. 2009. The discourse dynamics approach to metaphor and metaphor-led discourse analysis. *Metaphor and Symbol*, 24(2): 63–89.

Cameron, Lynne. 2010a. The discourse dynamics framework for metaphor. In Cameron, Lynne and Robert Maslen (eds), *Metaphor Analysis: Research Practice in Applied Linguistics, Social Science and the Humanities*. London: Equinox: 77–94.

Cameron, Lynne. 2010b. Metaphors and discourse activity. In Cameron, Lynne and Robert Maslen (eds), *Metaphor Analysis: Research Practice in Applied Linguistics, Social Science and the Humanities*. London: Equinox: 77–94.

Cameron, Lynne. 2011. *Metaphor and reconciliation: The discourse dynamics of empathy in post-conflict conversations*. London: Routledge.

Cameron, Lynne: *Metaphor and the Dynamics of Empathy in Discourse*. URL: http://www.open.ac.uk/researchprojects/livingwithuncertainty/.

Cameron, Lynne, Graham Low and Robert Maslen. 2010. Identifying metaphor in discourse data. In Cameron, Lynn and Robert Maslen (eds), *Metaphor Analysis: Research Practice in Applied Linguistics, Social Science and the Humanities*. London: Equinox: 116–146.

Cameron, Lynne and Robert Maslen (eds). 2010a. *Metaphor Analysis: Research Practice in Applied Linguistics, Social Science and the Humanities*. London: Equinox.

Cameron, Lynne and Robert Maslen. 2010b. Identifying metaphor in discourse data. In Cameron, Lynn and Robert Maslen (eds), *Metaphor Analysis: Research Practice in Applied Linguistics, Social Science and the Humanities*. London: Equinox: 97–115.

Croft, William and Alan Cruse. 2004. *Cognitive Linguistics*. Cambridge: Cambridge University Press.

ELAN: *(Eudico Linguistic Annotator) was developed at the Max Planck Institute in Nijmnegen*. URL: http://www.mpi.nl/tools.

Evans, Vyvyan and Melanie C. Green. 2006. *Cognitive linguistics: An introduction*. Edinburgh: Edinburgh University Press.

Fiumara, Corradi. 1995. *The metaphoric process: Connections between language and life*. London/ New York: Routledge.

Forceville, Charles and Eduardo Urios-Aparisi. 2009. *Multimodal Metaphor*. Berlin/ New York: Mouton de Gruyter.

Gibbs, Raymond W. 1993. Process and products in making sense of tropes. In Ortony, Andrew (ed.), *Metaphor and thought*. Cambridge: Cambridge University Press: 252–276.

Gibbs, Raymond W. 2005. *Embodiment and Cognitive Science*. Cambridge: Cambridge University Press.

Gallagher, Shaun. 2008. Understanding Others: Embodied Social Cognition. In Calvo, Paco and Antoni Gomila (eds), *Handbook of cognitive science: An embodied approach*. Amsterdam: Elsevier.

Grady, Joseph E.,. 1997. *Foundations of meaning: Primary Metaphors and Primary Scenes*. Ph.D.diss., University of California, Berkeley.

Johnson, Mark. 1987. *The body in mind. The bodily basis of meaning, imagination, and reason*. Chicago/ London: University of Chicago Press.

Johnson, Mark. 2007. *The meaning of the body. Aesthetics of human understanding*. Chicago: Chicago University Press.

Kappelhoff, Hermann. 2004. Matrix der Gefühle. Das Kino, das Melodrama und das Theater der Empfindsamkeit. Berlin: Vorwerk.

Kappelhoff, Hermann and Cornelia Müller. 2011. Embodied meaning construction. Multimodal metaphor and expressive movement in speech, gesture, and in feature film. In *Metaphor and the Social World*, 1: 121–153.

Koch, Sabine, Thomas Fuchs and Cornelia Müller. 2010. *Körpersprache von Tanz und Bewegung. Bedeutungsemergenz, Versprachlichung und therapeutische Nutzung*. URL: http://www.psychologie.uni-heidelberg.de/projekte/bewegung/index.shtml.

Koch, Sabine, Thomas Fuchs, Michela Summa and Cornelia Müller. 2012. *Body Memory, Metaphor, and Movement*. Amsterdam: John Benjamins.

Kolter, Astrid, Silva H. Ladewig, Michela Summa, Sabine Koch, Cornelia Müller and Thomas Fuchs. 2012. Body memory and the emergence of metaphor in movement and speech. An interdisciplinary case study. In Koch, Sabine, Thomas Fuchs, Michela Summa and Cornelia Müller (eds), *Body Memory, Metaphor and Movement*. Amsterdam/ Philadelphia: John Benjamins: 201–226.

Ladewig, Silva H. and Jana Bressem (forthcoming). New insights into the medium hand – Discovering Structures in gestures based on the four parameters of sign language. *Semiotica*.

Lakoff, George and Mark Johnson. 1980. *Metaphors We Live By*. Chicago/ London: Chicago University Press.

Lakoff, George and Mark Johnson. 1999. *Philosophy in the flesh. The embodied mind and its challenge to Western thought*. New York: Basic Books.

Mandel, Mark. 1977. Iconic devices in American Sign Language. In Friedmann, Lynn A. (ed.), *On the Other Hand*. London: Academic Press: 57–107.

Mittelberg, Irene and Linda R. Waugh. 2009. Metonymy first, metaphor second: A cognitive-semiotic approach to multimodal figures of speech in co-speech gesture. In Forceville, Charles and Eduardo Urios-Aparisi (eds), *Multimodal Metaphor*. Berlin/ New York: Mouton de Gruyter: 329–356.

Moseley, Rachel, Francesca Carota, Olaf Hauk, Bettina Mohr and Friedemann Pulvermüller. 2012. A Role for the Motor System in Binding Abstract Emotional Meaning. *Cerebral Cortex* 22: 1634–1647.

Müller, Cornelia. 1998a. *Redebegleitende Gesten: Kulturgeschichte – Theorie – Sprachvergleich*. Berlin: Arno Spitz.

Müller, Cornelia. 1998b. Iconicity and gesture. In Cavé, Christian, Guaitella and Serge Santi (eds), *Oralité et gestualité: Communication multimodale, interaction*. Montréal/ Paris: L'Harmattan: 321–328.

Müller, Cornelia. 2008a. *Metaphors Dead and Alive, Sleeping and Waking. A Dynamic View*. Chicago: University of Chicago Press.

Müller, Cornelia. 2008b. What gestures reveal about the nature of metaphor. In Cienki, Alan and Cornelia Müller (eds), *Metaphor and Gesture*. Amsterdam: John Benjamins: 219–245.

Müller, Cornelia. 2009. Gesture and Language. In Malmkjaer, Kirsten (ed.), *The linguistic encyclopedia*. Abington/ New York: Routledge: 214–217.

Müller, Cornelia. 2010. Wie Gesten bedeuten. Eine kognitiv-linguistische und sequenzanalytische Perspektive. *Sprache und Gestik. Sonderheft der Zeitschrift Sprache und Literatur* 41(1): 37–68.

Müller, Cornelia. 2011. Reaction Paper. Are 'Deliberate' Metaphors really Deliberate. A Question of Human Consciousness and Action. *Metaphor in the Social World* 1: 61–66.

Müller, Cornelia. 2013. Gesture as a medium of expression: The linguistic potential of gestures. In Müller, Cornelia, Alan Cienki, Ellen Fricke, Silva H. Ladewig, David McNeill and Sedinha Teßendorf (eds), *Body – Language – Communication: An International Handbook on Multimodality in Human Interaction. (Handbooks of Linguistics and Communication Science 38.1)*. Berlin/ Boston: De Gruyter Mouton: 202–217.

Müller, Cornelia (submitted). How gestures mean. The construction of meaning in gestures with speech.

Müller, Cornelia, Jana Bressem and Silva H. Ladewig. 2013. Towards a grammar of gestures: A form-based view. In Müller, Cornelia, Alan Cienki, Ellen Fricke, Silva H. Ladewig, David McNeill and Sedinha Teßendorf (eds), *Body – Language – Communication: An International Handbook on Multimodality in Human Interaction. (Handbooks of Linguistics and Communication Science 38.1).* Berlin/ Boston: De Gruyter Mouton: 702–728.

Müller, Cornelia and Alan Cienki. 2009. Words, gesture and beyond: Forms of multimodal metaphor in the use of spoken language. In Forceville, Charles and Eduardo Urios-Aparisi (eds), *Multimodal Metaphor*. Berlin/ New York: Mouton de Gruyter: 329–356

Müller, Cornelia and Susanne Tag. 2010. Attention, foregrounding and embodied activation. Multimodal metaphors in spoken discourse. *Cognitive Semiotics* 6: 85–119

Niedenthal, Paula M., Lawrence W. Barsalou, Piotr Winkielman, Silvia Krauth-Gruber andFrançois Ric. 2005. Embodiment in Attitudes, Social Perception, and Emotion. *Personality and Social Psychology Review* 9(3): 184–211.

Plessner, Helmut. 1925/1982. Die Deutung des mimischen Ausdrucks. Ein Beitrag zur Lehre vom Bewußtsein des anderen Ichs. In Plessner, Helmut (ed.), *Gesammelte Schriften VII. Ausdruck und menschliche Natur*. Frankfurt am Main: Suhrkamp: 67–130.

Pragglejaz Group. 2007. MIP: A method for identifying metaphorically used words in discourse. *Metaphor and Symbol* 22: 1–39.

Pulvermüller, F. 1999. Words in the brain's language. Behavioral and Brain Sciences, 22: 253–336.

Sheets-Johnstone, Maxine. 1999. *The Primacy of Movement*. Amsterdam/ Philadelphia: John Benjamins.

Sowa, Timo and Ipke Wachsmuth. 2002. Interpretation of shape-related iconic gestures in virtual enviroments. In Sowa, Timo and Ipke Wachsmuth (eds), *Gesture and sign language in human-computer interaction*. Berlin: Springer: 21–33.

Sowa, Timo. 2006. *Understanding coverbal iconic gestures in object shape descriptions*. Berlin: Akademische Verlagsgesellschaft Aka GmbH.

Steen, Gerard J., Aletta G. Dorst, Berenike J. Herrmann, Anna A. Kaal, Tina Krennmayr and Trijntje Pasma. 2010. *A method for linguistic metaphor identification: From MIP to MIPVU*. Amsterdam: John Benjamins.

Streeck, Jürgen. 2008. Depicting by gesture. *Gesture* 8(3): 285–301.

Streeck, Jürgen. 2009. *Gesturecraft. Manufacturing shared understanding*. Amsterdam/ New York: John Benjamins.

Van Dijk, Teun A. 2012. Discourse and Knowledge, In James Paul Gee and Michael Handford (eds), Handbook of Discourse Analysis. London: Routledge: 587–603.

Wilcox, Sherman. 2007. Routes from gesture to language. In Pizzuto, Elena, Paola Pietrandrea and Simone Raffaele (eds), *Verbal and signed languages: Comparing structures, constructs and methodologies*. Berlin/ New York: Mouton de Gruyter: 107–131.

Wilson, Nicole L. and Raymond W. Gibbs. 2007. Real and Imagined Body Movement Primes Metaphor Comprehension. *Cognitive Science* 31: 721–731.

Wittenburg, Peter, Hennie Brugman, Albert Russel, Alex Klassmann and Han Sloetjes. 2006. ELAN: a Professional Framework for Multimodality Research. *Proceedings of LREC 2006, 5th International Conference on Language Resource and Evaluation*. URL: http://www.mpi.nl/people/wittenburg-peter/publications.

Wundt, Wilhelm. 1900–1920. *Völkerpsychologie: Eine Untersuchung der Entwicklungsgesetze von Sprache, Mythus und Sitte. Erster und Zweiter Band. Die Sprache*. Leipzig: Engelmann.

Zanotto, Mara S., Lynne Cameron and Marilda C. Cavalcanti. 2008. *Confronting Metaphor in Use. An applied linguistic approach*. Amsterdam/ Philadelphia: John Benjamins.

# 19

# Balancing Acts: Image Schemas and Force Dynamics as Experiential Essence in Pictures by Paul Klee and their Gestural Enactments

IRENE MITTELBERG

## 1 Movement and Balance in Artworks and Gesture

Our sense of balance is essential to functioning in the world. Entrenched through bodily interactions with the environment—such as moving on uneven grounds or being exposed to physical forces—it enables us to perceive (im)balance in various physical and cultural domains of experience. These include life balance, physical and emotional well-being, power relations, ecological systems, but also arguments, models, and mathematical equations (Johnson 1987: 74ff.). Balance is an integral part of what Gallagher (2005) subsumes under the notion of *body schema*, which posits tactile and sensorimotor capacities as central to the physical, social and cognitive being-in-the-world of a unified body and mind. The upright and stable posture of the torso or full body is a precondition for many basic physical activities: e.g. standing, sitting, walking, riding a bike, and performing coordinated manual actions such as eating, writing, drawing, or playing an instrument.

More artful bodily balancing acts comprise dance and certain kinds of acrobatic performances (examples of which are captured in the pictures discussed below). So naturally balance is also a constitutive aspect of aesthetics regarding both nature and culture (Arnheim 1974; Stebbing and

*Language and the Creative Mind.*
Mike Borkent, Barbara Dancygier, and Jennifer Hinnell (eds).

Heim 2011). It influences the way we experience topographic gestalts such as landscapes or architectural space, as well as works of fine art such as music, drawings, paintings, or sculptures. One is usually able to tell, for instance, whether a given statue or pictorial composition is well-balanced or not, regardless of its being highly referential or highly abstract. What is decisive here is a perceived (un)equal distribution of physical forces and weight (Johnson 1987). In ancient cultures, too, balance and proportion belong to the universal organizing principles of aesthetic composition (Conkey and Hastorf 1990). Recent neuroscience studies examining the role of edges, contrasts, lines, and contours in human object recognition indicate that balance, for example symmetry, in visual stimuli evokes neural activation in higher visual processing areas, leading to *what* and *where* paths in the brain (van der Helm and Treder 2009). In light of these observations, the goal of this paper is to offer multimodal evidence for the idea that the embodied image schema BALANCE, as originally proposed by cognitive linguists (e.g. Johnson 1987; Lakoff 1987; Lakoff and Johnson 1999; Talmy 1988), can be assumed to constitute, together with other basic schemas, the bodily and conceptual basis for the broad range of experiential domains and their metaphorical elaborations, in which balance is of central significance.[1]

Exploring the structuring functions of image schemas, it will be argued that depictions in both paintings and 'descriptive gestures, those forerunners of line drawing' (Arnheim 1969: 117), compel their interpreters to relate to the bodily postures and actions performed in front of them in ways that seem to be pre-structured by internalized patterns of cognitive, physical and cultural experience. In the moment of contemplation, one's own sense of balance may align and resonate, or not, with a pictorial composition due to sensorial responses feeding into embodied processes of association and meaning-making (Friedberg and Gallese 2007; Gibbs 2006). Movement and its significance for our understanding of ourselves, others, and cultural artifacts take center stage here (De Preester 2013; Foolen et al. 2012; Johnson 2007). Drawing on Krois' (2011: 273ff.) insights into the connection between embodiment and enactivism in the visual arts, the intent is to demonstrate how pragmatic links between physical action, social interaction and communicative behavior may create strong embodied correlations, which in turn have the capacity to dissolve the distinction between active movement and still images (Varela, Thompson and Rosch 1991). Among the art histo-

[1] See Johnson (1987: 75; italics in the original): '... the *meaning* of balance begins to emerge through our *acts* of balancing and through our *experience* of systemic processes and states within our bodies. I shall argue that the meaning of balance is tied to such experiences and, in particular, to the image-schematic structures that make those experiences and activities coherent and significant for us'.

rians and philosophers who, as Krois, integrate embodied cognition into their theory of the image, Bredekamp's (2010) conception of 'picture acts' succinctly captures the practical, cognitive and affective dimensions of what pictures do and what onlookers do with pictures (see also Brandt 2006). The participants of the present study do something with pictures in that they carefully observe and describe them multimodally, employing words, gestures, and their entire body, often fully reenacting the postures and actions of the figures portrayed in the pictures.

Due to limits of space, this paper cannot provide a comprehensive overview of the current discussions in the various scholarly fields that interlace here. Nor can the analyses offered below do justice to the noteworthy historical and theoretical aspects of the fine artworks at hand. Focusing on the idea of balance and related schemas, it will be suggested that by analyzing corporeal descriptions of visual art we may find further support for Krois' (2011: 218) thesis that images are not simply visual, but transmodal phenomena. The paper evolves as follows: after laying out the theoretical foundation, image-schema analyses of three artworks by Paul Klee are provided and related to video and motion data recordings of participants describing the same artworks inside a motion capture lab. Among the strategies used in the multimodal descriptions, aspects of balance, full-body enactments, and viewpoint are of particular interest. Overall, this paper aims to offer glimpses at 'felt qualities' of meaning (Johnson 2005: 31), hoping to shed light on people's cross-modal understanding of artworks, that is, 'exemplary cases of embodied, immanent meaning' (Johnson 2007: 234).[2]

## 2 Image Schemas and Force Dynamics in Gesture and Art

The guiding assumption of this paper is that image-schematic and force-dynamic structures may motivate not only the compositional structure of artworks, but also underpin cognitive, physical, emotional and communicative responses on the side of the beholder. Before delving into the analyses, a brief overview of previous work on images schemas and force gestalts in multimodal communication is provided.

### 2.1 Cross-modal Conceptualization through Image and Force Schemas

Embodied image and force schemas are central to experiential accounts of meaning. In light of Johnson's (1987: xiv) definition of image schemas as 'recurring, dynamic patterns of our perceptual interactions and motor programs that give coherence and structure to our experience', we can expect

[2] For cognitive approaches to visual art see also Brandt (2006); Bundgaard (2009); Krois et al. (2007); Lakoff (2006); Sonesson (2007); and Turner (2006).

gestures and artworks to provide additional evidence for their 'semiotic reality' (Danaher 1998: 190). The PATH schema is an example of a pervasive image schema, consisting of a beginning (SOURCE), a vector constituting a PATH, and an end point (GOAL). It gets instantiated, for instance, by traveling from A to B, walking up a winding staircase, a bridge connecting two river shores, or by the timeline of a project (Johnson 2007: 136).

In addition to recent work on image schemas in language (e.g. Hampe 2005), there is a growing literature on the functions such patterns perform in other semiotic systems and multimodal communication (e.g. Forceville and Jeulink 2011; Turner 2006). Gesture research, for instance, could show that communicative body posture and movements may indeed reflect a range of basic schemas such as PATH, OBJECT, CONTAINER, LINK, BALANCE, CYCLE, STRAIGHT, CENTER-PERIPHERY, and FORCE (e.g. Cienki 1998a/b, 2005, 2012; Ladewig 2011; Mittelberg 2006, 2010b; Zlatev 2005). Given the visuo-spatial mediality of gestures, spatial-relations schemas (Lakoff and Johnson 1999) are of particular interest for our purposes. Providing means to project conceptual structure into gesture space, they may underpin systematic, often metaphoric, uses of its different segments to reify discourse items or highlight relations between ideas, locations, or moments in time (e.g. LEFT/RIGHT; CENTER/PERIPHERY; FRONT/BACK UP/DOWN; e.g. Calbris 2003; Evola 2010; Mittelberg 2010b; Núñez and Sweetser 2006; Sweetser 1998).

Regardless of the medium in which they materialize, image schemas are assumed to be dynamic, multimodal conceptual gestalts that drive conceptualizations and construal operations, but do not necessarily get fully instantiated. In gesture, salient qualities of a posture, hand configuration or an ephemeral line drawing sketched in the air also tend to lend only minimal support to the evocation of the entire schemas. However, due to their own embodied experience with physical actions, tactile explorations of the world, and a broad range of semiotic processes, interlocutors are able to infer sensorimotor, haptic, pragmatic, as well as cognitive entailments.[3] These may trigger multimodal associations guided by, for instance, frames (Fillmore 1982), metonymy (Mittelberg 2006, 2013), and/or metaphor (e.g. Cienki and Müller 2008; Mittelberg and Waugh 2009; Müller 2008; Parrill and Sweetser 2004).

Force-dynamics also play an important role in structuring our physical and cognitive experience (Talmy 1988, 2000). Though we are not necessarily consciously aware that 'our bodies are clusters of forces and that *every* event of which we are a part consists, minimally, of forces in interaction'

---

[3] These observations align with Popova's (2005) suggestion to examine in more depth the cross-modal nature of image schemas; see also Johnson (2007: 136ff.).

(Johnson 1987: 42; italics in the original). Basic experiences include exerting force on objects or people, e.g. by pulling or pushing, and forces felt on one's own body such as GRAVITY, BLOCKAGE, or REPULSION. Through imitating actions using manual gestures or their entire bodies, speakers can easily (re)enact physical activities such as walking against the wind, carrying heavy items, or, as we will see below, staying balanced on a tightrope (Mittelberg 2010, 2013). Metaphorical extensions of force gestalts may not only mediate the feeling of social pressure and emotional burden, but also guide, as the present study exemplifies, our perception and interpretation of visual art (Johnson 1987, 2005).

## 2.2 The BALANCE Schema in Acts of Perception and Expression

The BALANCE schema situates itself at the juncture of image schemas and force dynamics. It belongs, as pointed out in the introduction to this paper, to the elementary structures that 'operate in our bodily movements, perceptual acts and orientational awareness' (Johnson 1987: 75). In its most basic sense, balancing is a bodily activity 'that requires an ordering of forces and weights relative to some point, axis or plane' (ibid., 98–9). In order to stand and walk without falling, humans need to learn how to balance themselves around their vertical axis and to sustain an upright posture. Anchored in the speaker's body, gestures are intimately linked to body balance and the related metaphorical projections, for example using both hands as though one were weighing ideas (McNeill 1992).

As for visual perception, Arnheim (1954) revealed a 'structural skeleton' (Figure 1 below) underlying the dynamic forces that allow us to sense (im)balance in arrangements of abstract figures and other elements in visual configurations. This hidden structure is assumed to support our grasp of the distribution of weight and force vectors within an image.

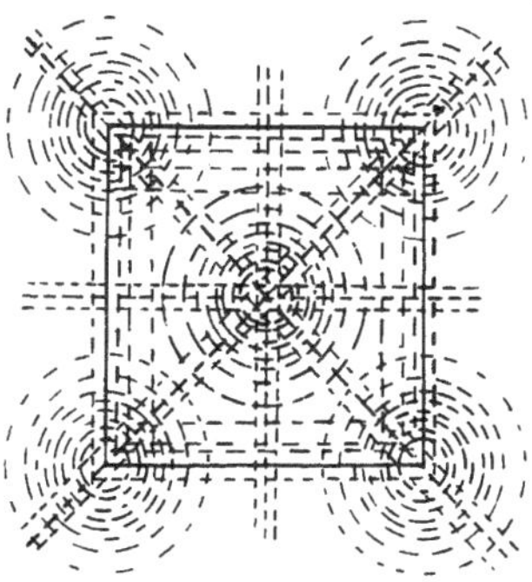

FIGURE 1. Balance pattern (Arnheim 1954: 13)

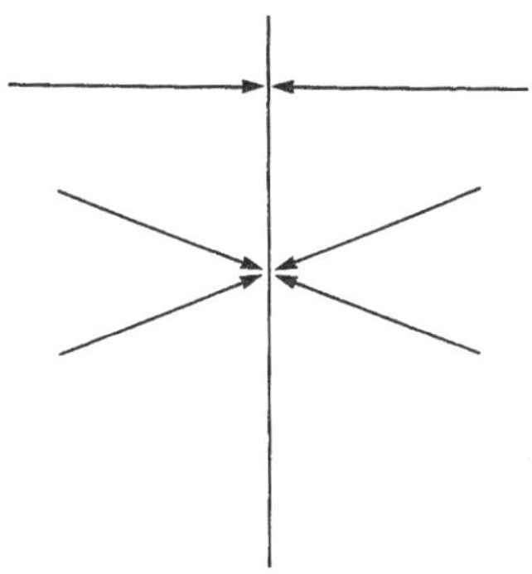

FIGURE 2. Axis balance (Johnson 1987: 86)

Based on analyses of masks, statues and paintings, Johnson concluded that the prototypical axis BALANCE schema (see Figure 2) functions as the primary schema, that is, the structural core of all its variants and elaborations. Crucial for our purposes is the insight that '[b]alance in visual perception already involves a metaphorical projection of schematic structure from the realm of *physical* and gravitational forces and weights to a domain of *visual* forces and weight in "visual space"' (99; italics in the original). By the same token, art appreciation involves active perception; balance or imbalance is something we may sense and not something residing within the picture itself (e.g. differences in weight emanating from particular colors).

According to Lakoff (2006: 154), 'image schemas [...] give form to art': our embodied, enacting mind imposes image schemas onto a visual scene or other kinds of multimodal streams of sensory information. In this way, orientational and spatial relations, as well as motor control schemas are assumed to link perceptual to conceptual structure, and form to meaning. As Krois (2011: 222f.) pointed out, image schemas can be considered as a specific kind of logic of visual images, contributing to their transmodal functions (see also Krois et al. 2007). These theoretical aspects will now be explored through analyzing specific instances of visual artworks and bodily performances.

## 3 Enacting Embodied Structure: BALANCE in Three Klee Pictures and their Multimodal Descriptions

At first sight, the visuo-spatial modalities of interest here appear quite different: carefully composed, static and silent two-dimensional paintings are related to spontaneously performed, ephemeral three-dimensional coverbal gestures. However, from a performance point of view, paintbrush strokes and line drawings are, just like gestural movements, manual practices of meaningful expression (Arnheim 1969; Taylor et al. 2012). Accordingly, they share a number of properties, especially regarding techniques of sign creation (Müller 1998) and the cognitively and culturally prestructured nature of picture and gesture spaces. Since semiotic representation tends to be partial, abstracting salient elements from a witnessed or imagined scene, or some other complex sensorial experience, is central to expression in both media. For bodily semiotics, metonymy has been shown to be a key principle in indexically anchored *ad hoc* expressions of both content and felt qualities of meaning (Johnson 2005; Mittelberg 2006, 2010a, 2013; Mittelberg and Waugh 2009). Abstraction and metonymy are intimately linked to viewpoint, a focus of the analyses presented in this section: subjective (selective) portrayals can be done from several different perspectives such as character or observer viewpoint (McNeill 1992). Speakers have been observed to shift viewpoints on a given scene or to signal several of them with different articulators simultaneously (e.g. hands, eye-gaze, torso; Stec 2013; Sweetser 2012).[4] According to the present view, the different modes and degrees of abstraction and iconicity in both gesture and visual art necessarily draw on (parts of) image schemas and force gestalts. These internalized structures may serve as schematic blueprints and trigger visceral impulses and imaginative elaborations when we construe, verbalize and physically (re)enact essential qualities of experience.[5]

For the present purpose, the focus will be on descriptive gestures, which may evoke not only concrete objects (such as pictures), but also mental imagery and conceptual structures. Importantly, the three Klee pictures were selected such as to allow a high degree of alignment between image and beholder: In all three pictures, human-like figures take center stage, trying to stay balanced in one way or another, while seemingly moving and/or being exposed to different kinds of physical forces. Likewise, the study participants occupy the center of their personal gesture spaces and engage their full bodies when describing and elaborating their perceptual experience of the artworks.

To closely study communicative performances involving natural, bodily media (e.g. spoken or signed discourse, gesture, head movements, body posture, dance, etc.) the use of technical media like audio and video recordings is a necessary prerequisite (see also Müller, this volume). In order to see to what extent co-speech gestures produced in mid-air are comparable to drawings captured on paper or canvas, the multimodal descriptions elicited for this study were not only filmed, but the speakers' hand motions were also tracked with a full-body optical motion capture system. Through visualizing otherwise invisible movement traces, this technology allows us to not only create three-dimensional images of gestural excursions through space, but to also map how they evolve through time.

Three American English native speakers (two females, one male) participated in the study. For 60 seconds at a time, each painting was projected on a screen in front of them, without disclosing the title. Afterwards, the participants were asked to describe each painting from memory to the interviewer, first focusing on formal aspects (such as composition, colors, figures,

---

[4] For recent work on viewpoint in sign, gesture, speech and written texts, see Dancygier and Sweetser (2012). For a comparative study of abstraction, metonymy and viewpoint in gesture and Cubist paintings, see Mittelberg (2006, 2011).

[5] In his account of a mental architecture for perception, Brandt (2006) proposes a neurosemantic economy of art perception combining aesthetic and pragmatic registers.

objects, etc.), then on semantic, emotional and aesthetic qualities. Each of the subsections below is dedicated to one of the pictures and will proceed from a brief description of the image to an analysis of the principal underlying image-schematic and force-schematic structures. Then, examples from the video and motion-capture data will highlight some of the most interesting multimodal strategies employed by the participants. As stated earlier, comprehensive interpretations of the pictures cannot be provided here. For the moment, we will focus on iconic and structural aspects; deeper strata of meaning will have to await ensuing work.

### 3.1 Angelus Novus (1920)

Among Paul Klee's (1879-1940) numerous portrayals of angels, the *Angelus Novus* (Figure 3) is probably the best known (Zentrum Paul Klee 2012). Also referred to as the *Angel of history*, the picture was in the possession of Walter Benjamin for several years. In the center of the pictorial space we see a figure combining features of a human being, a bird, an angel, and perhaps other creatures. The background does not show any particular elements, except that the beige color behind the figure turns into shades of orange and brown closer to the edges of the image. The transparent looking creature, identified by the title as an angel, is holding up its upper forelimbs vertically on both sides of the body. Its wings, which resemble human arms and hands, seem to help him stay in place, as if to counteract wind or resist some other physical forces seemingly acting on it. Its wide-open, sideward looking eyes seem to be attending to something with worry. While its eye-gaze appears to be directed to its left, neither the figure's head nor its body is turned that way. The feet do not seem to be set on the ground with equal stability: most of the body's weight is resting on the stronger looking left leg, while the right foot is placed slightly forward and outward.

An image-schema and force-dynamic analysis reveals the following underpinning structures. The figure situated in the CENTER of the image space is clearly the focus, with some shading applied in the PERIPHERY. By holding up both wings (RIGHT-LEFT), the body is kept in a state of BALANCE. Through holding its right foot steadily down on the ground and shifting most of its weight onto it (GRAVITY), the angel appears prepared to fend off something with its raised left wing (UP; BLOCKAGE) which appears bigger, stronger and thus more salient than its right counterpart. Its entire posture signals readiness to block anything that might come towards it (BLOCKAGE; TOWARDS/AWAY FROM). This could also metaphorically signal some sort of inner REPULSION. Its focused eye-gaze directed to the left further could also express ATTRACTION towards something out there, thus creating a vector or a HORIZONTAL axis leading into the off (SOURCE-PATH-GOAL). If we assumed that something was moving towards the angel, we could imagine a PATH, along which a moving person or entity was approaching the figure from a location outside the picture (SOURCE-PATH-GOAL). It could also be the case that the angel itself tries not to move along some other hidden axis or path. If the unevenly distributed darker shades represent smoke or flames, the immediate environment would make movement into any direction impossible.

FIGURE 3. P. Klee, *Angelus Novus* (1920)

FIGURE 4. Full-body enactment

One cannot help but wonder what the angel might be looking at. Benjamin's (1987) own reading of the image suggests that the angel is facing the past: the ruins of the First World War. This interpretation resonates with recent advances in cognitive science and gesture studies suggesting that in most Western cultures the past tends to be conceptualized as being located to the left of or behind the speaker (Calbris 1990).[6]

Overall, the gestural descriptions of this picture show a strong tendency for full-body enactments (see also Müller, this volume). Assuming character viewpoint (McNeill 1992; Sweetser 2012), the participant shown in Figure 4 (who cannot see the picture while describing it) mirrors the angel in an astonishingly close fashion by mimicking its posture, arm position, leg placement, and eye-gaze. For a moment, the speaker becomes the angel. When verbalizing her impression that the figure seemed to be in mid-

[6] But see Núñez and Sweetser's (2006) work on spatial metaphors for time in the Aymara culture; see also Kress and van Leeuwen (2006) for related observations regarding a spatial grammar of pictures.

movement, she actually adds movement to the scene by rotating her arms. Figure 5 shows a motion-capture data plot of these repeated circular hand and arm motions representing the angel's imagined wing movements.[7]

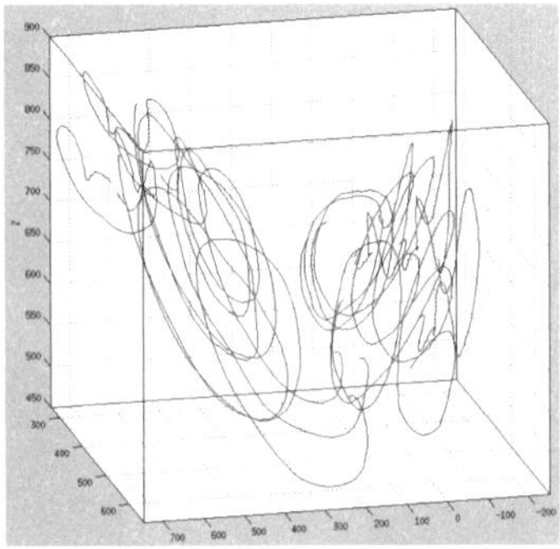

FIGURE 5. Motion-capture data plot of enacted wing movements (see Figures 3 and 4)

To summarize, not only the posture of the angel, but also the sensed movement of its body and limbs are physically enacted by the speaker. This active portrayal thus supports Krois' (2011: 218) understanding of pictures as transmodal phenomena (see introduction). In light of the prototypical balance schema put forth by Johnson (1987: 86; Figure 2, Section 2.2), it seems safe to say that this schema can be detected as underpinning the image of the angel, with a focus on the vertical axis running down through its upright head and body. Around this axis, weight and forces are quite equally distributed (e.g., the stronger left wing is balanced out by the right wing plus the right leg). Emanating from the angel's relatively large head, its eye-gaze maps onto the horizontally oriented vectors meeting at eye-level (Figure 2). At the same time, the upper and lower limbs as well as the lower body map onto the diagonal vectors shown in the same Figure. Arnheim's (1954) hidden skeleton of balance patterns (Figure 1) can also be made out in the image as so far as all lines and weights seem to coincide more or less with a feature of the structural skeleton. As a result, the angel's balancing act evokes in the viewer a sense of dynamic symmetry that can be readily

[7] Transcript of speech accompanying the gestural enactment shown in Figure 5: 'Oh, uh, it looks like it's kind of in mid-movement just cause it's... the one leg is a little... moved and the... feathers are sort of swept to one side... does it look like it's in the middle of... doing something.'

enacted. Through her corporeal posture and actions the perceptual experience becomes physical and real for the speaker.

### 3.2 Tightrope Walker (1923)

A tightrope walker's chief task is to stay balanced while gradually moving forward on a high wire suspended up in the air. While the *Tightrope Walker* (Figure 6) is not Klee's only work showing such acrobatic performances, it is one of the most intricate compositions of this nature.

FIGURE 6. P. Klee, *Tightrope Walker* (1923)

FIGURE 7. Video still: 'it looks stable'

This image of the *Tightrope Walker* combines a number of compatible underlying structures and relations. In this prototypical instance of a balancing act, set against the backdrop of a luminous cross structure, the tightrope runs parallel to the lower edge of the horizontal structure of the cross (HORIZONTAL; STRAIGHT), but it seems to be only virtually supported by it. The rope, however, clearly supports the figurine (SUPPORT). As such, the high wire represents the borderline between above and below (UP/DOWN). Almost at the center of the image (CENTER/PERIPHERY), the cross's vertical pole cuts the pictorial space into two panels (VERTICAL; SPLITTING), of which the right one is, especially in the image's lower regions, a little wider than the left one (RIGHT/LEFT). Holding on to a balancing pole with both hands held more than shoulder-width apart, the tightrope walker manages to BALANCE out the weight and physical forces pulling on his body and on the two ends of the pole (GRAVITY; SCALE). In the moment captured here, the figurine, traversing the image from left to right, has just passed the intersection of the cross-like structure. His walking PATH probably started at the small platform on the left-hand side (SOURCE) and is about to end only a few steps further down to the right (GOAL). From there, he would be able to leave the high wire by sliding down a rope leading towards the ground which is only hinted at by darker shades of brown. The platform on the left (SURFACE; SUPPORT), from which a rope ladder is hanging, also builds the entry/exit point of a network structure below the tightrope, consisting of vertical and diagonal lines and planes. Upon closer scrutiny, these lines and planes seem to be passing through a schematic head with a mouth, chin, nose and eyes. While these facial elements are slightly displaced, the head appears to contain (CONTAINMENT), despite its high degree of abstraction, (mental) SUBSTANCE and structures.

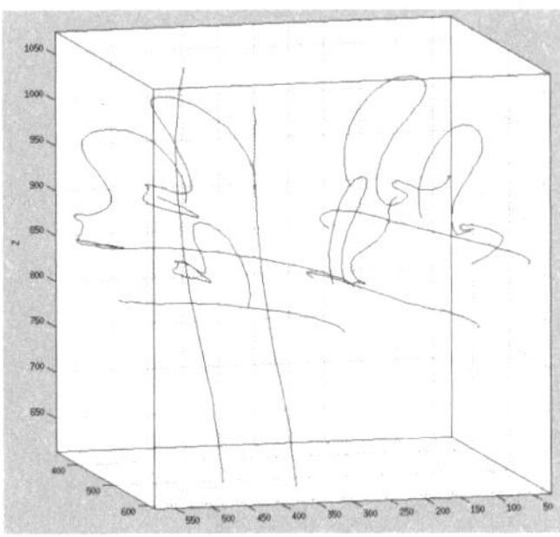

FIGURE 8. Motion-capture data plot: cross

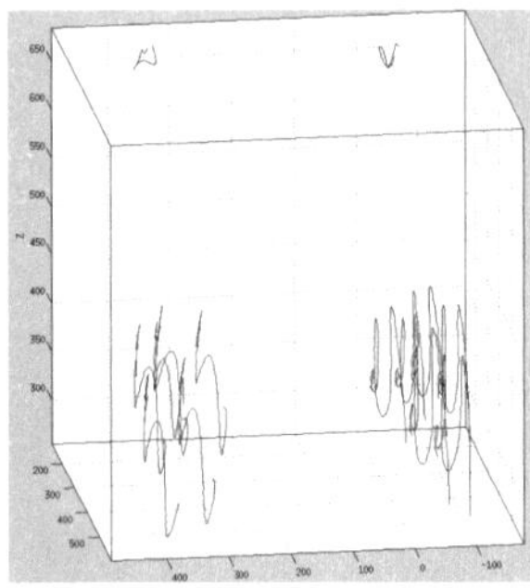

FIGURE 9. Motion-capture data plot: balancing

Regarding the descriptions of the *Tightrope Walker*, several multimodal portrayal strategies deserve particular attention. All three participants enacted the figure's posture and actions with their gestures or entire bodies. They also performed viewpoint shifts (Stec 2013) several times during their performances. We further see a tendency to describe the pictorial composition from an observer point of view, thus laying out the background as well as the distribution and relation of structures, elements, and colors. One participant adopted observer viewpoint when sketching the cross with thumb and index finger into the air and placing an imaginative figure on top of the rope, here functioning as a sort of virtual reference structure (Mittelberg 2008). Figure 8 above shows the movement traces of this gestural description (the figurine is the small loop-like shape on the left). In mid-sentence, the speaker shifts from observer to character viewpoint, from where she then imitates the figure's posture, leg position and the action of holding the balancing pole. Finally, her face serves as a projection surface when she imitates the figure's pointed face by seemingly extending her own nose.[8] The insight we can draw from this is that the adopted viewpoint has an influence not only on the construal of a scene, but also on what kind of metonymic modes are operationalized and what semiotic practices are chosen to deliver an effective multimodal performance (Mittelberg 2013).

Another participant directly commented on issues of balance, saying that the structures and objects hanging down from the rope would probably serve to keep everything in balance. In the moment captured in Figure 7, he pretends to be the figure up on the tightrope (character viewpoint), moving his hands up and down as though he were testing the stability of the situation (Figure 9 shows captured movement traces of his hands). Although it seems rather unlikely, the figure on the rope looks quite stable to him.[9] Through this mini-performance the original scenario is elaborated. By drawing on his own experience with (im)balance, the speaker instills movement and force dynamics into a static image. Hence, the image becomes alive.

What is crucial here is that, given the overall distribution of weight and forces, both the image and the tightrope walker seem perfectly balanced. A look at the following two schemas provided by Johnson (1987: 86) backs up this impression. The twin-pan balance schema (Figure 10) represents the situation of the tightrope walker up on the rope, with the balancing pole he

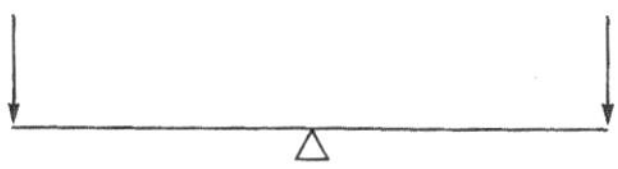

FIGURE 10. Twin-pan balance (Johnson 1987:86)

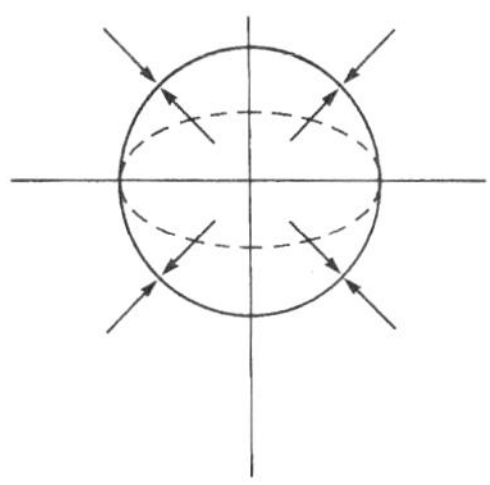

FIGURE 11. Equilibrium (Johnson 1987:86)

[8] Transcript of the verbal description (Fig. 8): 'Uhm, in the... background of the picture there is like a white cross... uhm, which is very different from the rest of the picture which is also... uhm, like tan except for the bottom where it could (...). It almost looks like it could be green. Uhm, and then, on top of that, it looks like... uhm... like a man or some sort of figurine is standing on it, and he's holding something and he... is looking to the side, so it almost looks like he's going like this, cause one leg looks, uhm... more stretched out than the other... and... his uhm, head is drawn and the face are like a teardrop, so... it's very... pointed... uhm...'

[9] Transcript for Figs. 7 and 9: 'It was walking on maybe some triangles and some more square objects and uhm, odd shapes drawn together until it kind gave you the idea that it was balancing somehow to... to form a kinda like teeter-tottering the line on the... uhm, objects building it up with the... the little person. It looks stable but realistically ... uhm no, I doubt it.'

is holding in his hands mapping onto the horizontal line. The equilibrium schema (Figure 11) can further be said to represent the entire scenario, including the cross in the background, the high wire, and the structures hanging down from it. These mappings are of course not exact, but allow us to understand variations on the theme BALANCE.

### 3.3 Dance of a Mourning Child (1922)

This last picture contrasts with the previous ones in several respects. As the title indicates, it features a child absorbed in a dance (Figure 12). What immediately catches the viewer's eye is the oversized head tilted to the side. Contrary to the figures studied so far, this one is positioned off-center, i.e. to the left side (CENTER/PERIPHERY; LEFT-RIGHT) and does not hold its head up straight (STRAIGHT; VERTICAL; UP/DOWN). The girl does not try to stay in control of its upright posture, as the *Angelus Novus* and the *Tightrope Walker*, but gives in to the head's tendency to draw sideward (GRAVITY). The CENTER of the image is left unoccupied except for a light color spot. At first sight, the distribution of weight might seem uneven in the overall pictorial composition as well as within the figure's body. The small body does not seem substantial enough to counterweigh the large head. However, with her fully extended arms pointing to her right side, and by holding some sort of line or balancing rope with both hands, the girl manages to create a BALANCED composure carried by the flow of the dance movement.

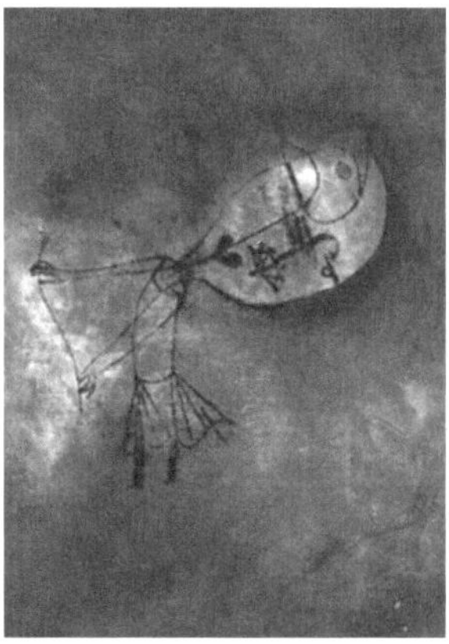

FIGURE 12. P. Klee, *Dance of a Mourning Child* (1922)

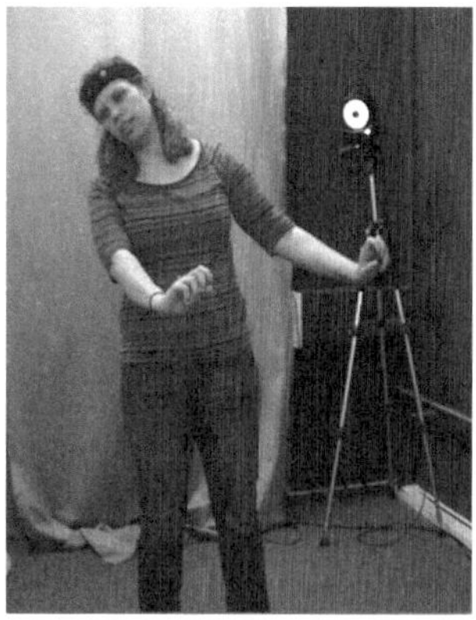

FIGURE 13. Enactment of child's posture

Due to the flowing skirt and the different shades of light and dark red, one can feel the different forces and the bodily movement captured in the picture. Several sets of parallel VERTICAL and DIAGONAL lines further create a sense of balanced geometry. The girl's head remains salient due to its size, lighter coloring, and clearly articulated lines, some of which are straight and parallel, the heart-shaped mouth, and the small umbrella hanging down from one eye. The heart functions as the anchor point of figure and image.

In their multimodal descriptions from memory, the participants referred to many of these pictorial details. Again, they showed a strong tendency to mirror the figure's full-body posture as well as the particular distribution of weight along the vertical axis. For example, the participant shown in Figure 13 enacts the figure's tilted head and extended arms, as well as its position of the legs and the eye-gaze directed downward. Keeping character viewpoint all through the sequence, she draws an icon of the heart-shaped mouth onto her own lips and two lines imitating the figure's eye slits onto her own eyes.[10] She then evokes the flowing skirt around her hips and upper legs by repeated manual up-and down movements. The motion-capture data plot provided in Figure 14 visualizes the semiotic practices employed: we can detect the set of traces evoking the flowing skirt in the lower regions of gesture space, the traces of outward going hands a little higher up in space, and the iconic forms depicting the mouth and eye slits in the upper segment. Crucially, each of these bimanually produced pairs of signs shows features of an internal symmetry; they are balanced in their own way.

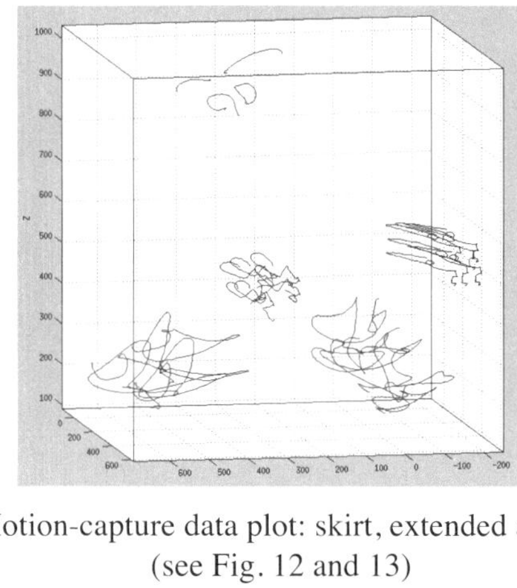

FIGURE 14. Motion-capture data plot: skirt, extended arms, mouth, eyes (see Fig. 12 and 13)

[10] Transcript of verbal description (Fig. 13): 'I thought it was a girl, because, uhm she looked like she was wearing some sort of short flowing skirt uhm, and... uh her head was turned to this side if I were mirroring what she was doing and her arms were like this. Uhm, and... uh.. her mouth was almost in the shape of a heart and... uhm, I kept trying to see if her eyes were open or closed, and it looked like they were just slits.'

When trying to match this picture with the various balance schemas proposed by Arnheim (1974) and Johnson (1987; see Sections 2.2, 3.1 and 3.2 above), it is not as obvious which one would be the most suitable. The balancing mechanisms at work here are not as straightforward as in the previous images, probably due to the imaginatively distorted proportions of the body parts. The axis balance schema (Figure 2) seems the most fitting, with the heart-shaped mouth at the intersection of the two straight lines. It is the movement of the body around its own axis that seems to contribute a decisive dimension to this particular balancing act.

This observation leads us to a core aspect of the recurrent patterns of the related experiences that make up the tissue of the BALANCE schema. According to Johnson (1987: 97), 'The balance schema (...) has three important properties: symmetry, transitivity, and reflexivity.' The latter property, reflexivity (A balances A), seems to be pertinent in connection to the pictures and corporeal enactments seen in this paper. Whereas Johnson (ibid.) points out that reflexivity is not experienced directly, since 'we are, after all, never in a position to balance something with itself', it seems justified to say that a body's equilibrium depends on a state of balance within itself, even if this internal structure consists of different body parts which can be said to build a bodily diagram with metonymic relations holding between the individual parts (Mittelberg 2008, 2013). Balancing oneself (e.g. when standing, walking, or dancing) seems an important facet of the experiential essence of human existence.

## 4 Synthesis and Concluding Remarks

Given the centrality of physical, emotional and aesthetic balance in people's lives, it perhaps does not come as a surprise that comparable patterns of experience could be detected in both Klee's pictures and their gestural descriptions and enactments. In his observations on 'The Body as Expression, and Speech', Merleau-Ponty (1962) puts into relief the deep interconnection of bodily perception, gestural expression and human understanding. He rightly points out that gestures may actually *create* meaningful semiotic material, instead of simply *referring* to something other than themselves; in certain moments, they basically *are* the world:

> It is through my body that I understand other people, just as it is through my body that I perceive 'things'. The meaning of a gesture thus 'understood' is not behind it, it is intermingled with the structure of the world outlined by the gesture.
>
> (Merleau-Ponty 1962: 216)

In this paper, the world to be perceived and understood presented itself in the form of artworks by Paul Klee. The iconic structures found in the pictures and their gestural descriptions have been assumed to be motivated, at least to some degree, by embodied image schemas, force dynamics, metonymy (e.g. abstraction), and metaphor. More specifically, clusters of image and force schemas played an important role regarding the images' composition, but also in how the participants portrayed the scenarios inside their gesture spaces. Besides sketching the compositional features and proportions from an observer's point of view, the participants' preferred multimodal story-telling technique proved to be full-body enactments adopting character viewpoint. With a very fine sense of the distribution of weights and physical forces in the pictures, the participants repeatedly turned themselves into living image icons (Peirce 1960) of Klee's human-like figures and their actions. In the process, they virtually transposed themselves in the position of these figures to enact, and at times elaborate, the depicted scenes from image-internal vantage points.

So when engaged in art perception, our bodily senses seem to be in touch with our creative and imaginative capacities, which allows us to see and feel balance in spaces and contexts we are not part of, but attentively observe. The focus of analysis was on gestures describing formal properties of the images and not (yet) on the metaphoric construal of mental states and emotions evoked in the viewers. Generally, our access and recall of pictorial compositions is assumed to rely on creative metaphorical elaboration:

> And it is by virtue of this metaphorically imposed structure that we can understand and reason about the relevant abstract entities. It is the projection of such structure that I am identifying as the 'creative' function of metaphor, for it is one of the chief ways we generate structure in our experience in a way that we can comprehend. The key to seeing how such creativity is possible is the recognition of a dimension of metaphorical projection based on image schemata, such as those of balance.
>
> (Johnson 1987: 98)

For creative expressions in visuo-spatial modalities, two metaphorical concepts seem to be fundamental: FORM IS MOTION and MOTION IS FORM (Lakoff and Turner 1989; Mittelberg 2010b). These metaphors, as well as the other embodied structures and forces laid out in this paper, seem to not only guide our experiences and comprehension of the world, but also gestural instances of *exbodiment* of inner images and inclinations (Mittelberg 2013). The present observations confirm that embodied schemas and action patterns play a central role in art appreciation; they also bring to light some of the ways in which subjective dimensions factor into the alignment of images, seen as 'transmodal phenomena' (Krois 2011: 218), and the body/mind of the beholder (Bredekamp 2010; see Taylor et al. 2012 for experimental work supporting this claim). Future research shall explore in more depth the relation of formal and emotional/aesthetic dimensions of full-body art appreciation and description. For now, let us turn to Paul Klee, whose remarks resonate well with the views brought together here:

> In the past we represented things we had seen on earth, things we liked seeing or might have liked to see. Today we reveal the relativity of visible things; thus expressing the belief that the visible is merely an isolated aspect in relation to the universe as a whole, and that other, invisible truths are the overriding factors. There is a striving to express the essential character of the accidental.
>
> (Klee 1968: 185)

It seems that embodied image schemas and action patterns help us see, feel and express 'the essential character of the accidental' in various connected ways. As the research strands discussed in this paper suggest, these patterns underpin both the creation and interpretation of expressions in different semiotic systems. For instance, tilting one's head over sidewards may evoke a sudden loss of balance. Such metonymic moments may profile a specific facet of the experiential gestalts that feed into how we understand a particular scenario through drawing on connected physical and semiotic experiences that cut across several modes of perception and expression.

## Acknowledgments

The author thanks Matthias Priesters for producing the motion-capture data plots and helpful comments on previous versions of this paper. Special thanks also to Kensy Cooperrider and Vito Evola for valuable feedback. This research was funded by the Excellence Initiative of the German Federal and State Governments.

## References

Arnheim, R. 1969. *Visual Thinking*. Berkeley: University of California Press.

Arnheim, R. 1974. *Art and Visual Perception: A Psychology of the Creative Eye*. Berkeley: University of California Press.

Benjamin, W. 1986. Theses on the Philosophy of History. *Critical Theory Since 1965,* ed. H. Adams and L. Searle, 680-685. Tallahassee, FL: Florida State University Press.

Brandt, P. A. 2006. Form and Meaning in Art. *The Artful Mind: Cognitive Science and the Riddle of Human Creativity,* ed. M. Turner, 171–188. Oxford/New York: Oxford University Press.

Bredekamp, H. 2010. *Theorie des Bildakts*. Berlin: Suhrkamp.

Bundgaard, P. F. 2009. Toward a Cognitive Semiotics of the Visual Artwork – Elements of a Grammar of Intuition. *Cognitive Semiotics* 5: 42–65.

Calbris, G. 1990. *The Semiotics of French Gestures*. Bloomington: Indiana University Press.

Calbris, G. 2003. From Cutting an Object to a Clear-cut Analysis: Gesture as the Representation of a Preconceptual Schema Linking Concrete Actions to Abstract Notions. *Gesture* 3: 19–46.

Cienki, A. 1998a. Metaphoric Gestures and Some of Their Relations to Verbal Metaphoric Expressions. *Discourse and Cognition: Bridging the Gap*, ed. J.-P. Koenig, 189–204. Stanford: Center for the Study of Language and Information.

Cienki, A. 1998b. STRAIGHT: An Image Schema and its Metaphorical Extensions. *Cognitive Linguistics*, 9: 107–149.

Cienki, A. 2005. Image Schemas and Gesture. *From Perception to Meaning: Image Schemas in Cognitive Linguistics*, ed. B. Hampe, 421–442. Berlin/New York: Mouton de Gruyter.

Cienki, A. 2010. Gesture and (Cognitive) Linguistic Theory. *Ways and Forms of Human Communication*, eds. R. Cabellero Rodriguez and M. J. P. Sanz Cuenza, 45–56. Ediciones de la Universidad de Castilla-La Mancha.

Cienki, A. and C. Müller, Eds. 2008. *Metaphor and Gesture*. Amsterdam/ Philadelphia: John Benjamins.

Cienki, A. and I. Mittelberg. 2013. Creativity in the Forms and Functions of Gestures with Speech. *Creativity and the Agile Mind: A Multi-Disciplinary Study of a Multi-Faceted Phenomenon*, eds. T. Veale, K. Feyaerts, C. Forceville, 231-252. Berlin/New York: Mouton de Gruyter.

Conkey, M. and C. Hastorf. 1990. *The Uses of Style in Archaeology*. Cambridge: Cambridge University Press.

Danaher, D. S. 1998. Peirce's Semiotic and Cognitive Metaphor Theory. *Semiotica* 119(1/2): 171–207.

Dancygier, B. and E. E. Sweetser, eds. 2012. *Viewpoint in Language: A Multimodal Perspective*. Cambridge, MA: Cambridge University Press.

De Preester, H., ed. 2013. *Moving Imagination*. Amsterdam/Philadelphia: John Benjamins.

Evola, V. 2010. Multimodal Cognitive Semiotics of Spiritual Experiences: Beliefs and Metaphors in Words, Gestures, and Drawings. *Form, Meaning, and Body*, eds. F. Parrill, V. Tobin and M. Turner, 41–60. Stanford: CSLI Publications.

Fillmore, C. J. 1982. Frame Semantics. *Linguistics in the Morning Calm. Selected Papers from SICOL* 1981. L. S. o. Korea. Seoul, Hanshin: 117–137.

Foolen, A., Lüdtke, U. M., Racine, T. P. and J. Zlatev, eds. 2012. *Moving Ourselves, Moving Others. Motion and Emotion in Intersubjectivity, Consciousness and Language*. Amsterdam/Philadelphia: John Benjamins.

Forceville, C. and M. Jeulink. 2011. The Flesh and Blood of Embodied Understanding: The Source-Path-Goal Schema in Animation Film. *Pragmatics and Cognition* 19 (1): 37–59.

Friedberg, D. and V. Gallese. 2007. Motion, Emotion and Empathy in Esthetic Experience. *Trends in Cognitive Sciences* II/5: 197–203.

Gallagher, S. 2005. *How the Body Shapes the Mind*. Oxford: Oxford University Press.

Gibbs, R.W. 2006. *Embodiment and Cognitive Science*. Cambridge: Cambridge University Press.

Hampe, B., ed. 2005. *From Perception to Meaning: Image Schemas in Cognitive Linguistics*. Berlin/New York: Mouton de Gruyter.

Jakobson, R. 1956. Two Aspects of Language and Two Types of Aphasic Disturbances, *On Language*. eds. L. Waugh and M. Monville-Burston: 115–133. Cambridge, MA/London: Harvard University Press.

Johnson, M. 1987. The *Body in the Mind: The Bodily Basis of Meaning, Imagination, and Reason*. Chicago: University of Chicago Press.

Johnson, M. 2005. The Philosophical Significance of Image Schemas. *From Perception to Meaning: Image Schemas in Cognitive Linguistics*, eds. B. Hampe, 15–33. Berlin/New York, Moutin de Gruyter.

Johnson, M. 2007. *The Meaning of the Body: Aesthetics of Human Understanding*. Chicago: Chicago University Press.

Klee, P. 1986. *Pedagogical Sketchbook*. London: Faber and Faber.

Kress, G. R. and T. van Leeuwen. 2006. *Reading Images: The Grammar of Visual Design*. 2nd edition. New York: Routledge.

Krois, J. M., Rosengren, M., Steidele, A. and D. Westerkamp, eds. 2007. *Embodiment in Cognition and Culture*. Amsterdam/Philadelphia: John Benjamins.

Krois, J. M. 2011. *Körperbilder und Bildschemata. Aufsätze zur Verkörperungstheorie ikonischer Formen*, ed. H. Bredekamp and M. Lauschke. Berlin: Akademie Verlag.

Ladewig, S. 2011. Putting the Cyclic Gesture on a Cognitive Basis. *CogniTextes* 6.

Lakoff, G. 1987. *Women, Fire, and Dangerous Things: What Categories Reveal About the Mind*. Chicago: University of Chicago.

Lakoff, G. 2006. The Neuroscience of Form in Art. *The Artful Mind: Cognitive Science and the Riddle of Human Creativity*, ed. M. Turner, 155–169. Oxford/New York: Oxford University Press.

Lakoff, G. and M. Johnson. 1999. *Philosophy In The Flesh: the Embodied Mind and its Challenge to Western Thought*. New York: Basic Books.

Lakoff, G. and M. Turner. 1989. *More than Cool Reason: A Field Guide to Poetic Metaphor*. Chicago: Chicago University Press.

McNeill, D. 1992. *Hand and Mind. What Gestures Reveal about Thought*. Chicago: Chicago University Press.

Merleau-Ponty, M. 1962. *Phenomenology of Perception*. New York: Humanities Press.

Mittelberg, I. 2006. *Metaphor and Metonymy in Language and Gesture: Discourse Evidence for Multimodal Models of Grammar*. Ph.D. Dissertation, Cornell University. Ann Arbor, MI: UMI.

Mittelberg, I. 2008. Peircean Semiotics Meets Conceptual Metaphor: Iconic Modes in Gestural Representations of Grammar. *Metaphor and Gesture*, ed. A. Cienki, and C. Müller, 115–154. Amsterdam/Philadelphia: John Benjamins.

Mittelberg, I. 2010a. Interne und externe Metonymie: Jakobsonsche Kontiguitätsbeziehungen in redebegleitenden Gesten. *Sprache und Literatur* 41(1): 112–143.

Mittelberg, I. 2010b. Geometric and Image-schematic Patterns in Gesture Space. *Language, Cognition, and Space: The State of the Art and New Directions*, eds. V. Evans and P. Chilton, 351–385. London: Equinox.

Mittelberg, I. 2011. Focus on Form: Reflections on the (Neuro)Aesthetics of Abstraction in Painting and Gesture. *Neuroästhetik. Perspektiven auf ein interdisziplinäres Forschungsgebiet,* ed. K. Herrmann, 110–120. Kassel: Kassel University Press.

Mittelberg, I. 2013. The Exbodied Mind: Cognitive-Semiotic Principles as Motivating Forces in Gesture. *Body – Language – Communication: An International Handbook on Multimodality in Human Interaction. Volume 1.*, eds. C. Müller, A. Cienki, E. Fricke, S. Ladewig, D. McNeill, and S. Tessendorf, 750–779. Berlin/New York: Mouton de Gruyter.

Mittelberg, I. and L. R. Waugh. 2009. Metonymy First, Metaphor Second: A Cognitive-semiotic Approach to Multimodal Figures of Thought in Co-speech Gesture. *Multimodal Metaphor*, eds. C. Forceville and E. Urios-Aparisi, 329–356. Berlin/New York: Mouton de Gruyter.

Müller, C. 1998. *Redebegleitende Gesten. Kulturgeschichte – Theorie – Sprachvergleich*. Berlin: Berlin Verlag.

Müller, C. 2008. *Metaphors Dead and Alive, Sleeping and Waking. A Dynamic View*. Chicago: University of Chicago Press.

Müller, C., this volume.

Núñez, R. and E. Sweetser. 2006. With the Future Behind Them: Convergent Evidence from Aymara Language and Gesture in the Crosslinguistic Comparison of Spatial Construals of Time. *Cognitive Science* 30: 401–450.

Oakley, T. 2005. Force-dynamic Dimensions of Rhetorical Effect. *From Perception to Meaning: Image Schemas in Cognitive Linguistics,* ed. B. Hampe, 443–473. Berlin/New York: Mouton de Gruyter.

Parrill, F. and E. Sweetser. 2004. What We Mean by Meaning. Conceptual Integration in Gesture Analysis and Transcription. *Gesture* 4 (2): 197–219.

Peirce, C. S. 1960. *Collected Papers of Charles Sanders Peirce (1931–1958). Vol. I.: Principles of Philosophy, Vol. II: Elements of Logic*, eds. C. Hartshorne and P. Weiss. Cambridge: The Belknap Press of Harvard University Press.

Popova, Y. 2005. Image Schemas and Verbal Synaesthesia. *From Perception to Meaning: Image Schemas in Cognitive Linguistics*, ed. B. Hampe, 397–419. Berlin/New York: Mouton de Gruyter.

Sonesson, G. 2007. The Extensions of Man Revisited: From Primary to Tertiary Embodiment. *Embodiment in Cognition and Culture*, eds. J. M. Krois, M. Rosengren, A. Steidele and D. Westerkamp, 27–53. Amsterdam/Philadelphia: John Benjamins.

Stebbing, P. D. and S. Heim. 2011. The Creative Quartet: Contrast, Rhythm, Balance and Proportion. Universal Principles of Organic and Aestehtic Creativity. *Neuroästhetik. Perspektiven auf ein interdisziplinäres Forschungsgebiet*, ed. K. Herrmann, 14–31. Kassel: Kassel University Press.

Stec, K. 2013. Meaningful Shifts: A Review of Viewpoint Markers in Co-Speech Gesture and Sign Language. *Gesture* 12 (3): 327–360.

Streeck, J. 2009. *Gesturecraft: The Manu-facture of Meaning*. Amsterdam/Philadelphia: John Benjamins.

Sweetser, E. E. 1998. Regular Metaphoricity in Gesture: Bodily-based Models of Speech Interaction. *Actes du 16e Congrès International des Linguistes*, Elsevier.

Sweetser, E. E. 2012. Viewpoint and Perspective in Language and Gesture, From the Ground Down. *Viewpoint in Language: A Multimodal Perspective*, eds. B. Dancygier and E. E. Sweetser, 1–24. Cambridge: Cambridge University Press.

Talmy, L. 1988. Force Dynamics in Language and Cognition. *Cognitive Science* 12: 49–100.

Talmy, L. 2000. *Towards a Cognitive Semantics*. Cambridge, MA: MIT Press.

Taylor, E. T., Witt, J. K., and P. J. Grimaldi. 2012. Uncovering the connection between artist and audience: Viewing painted brushstrokes evokes corresponding action representations in the observer. *Cognition* 125 (1): 26–36.

Turner, M. 2006. The Art of Compression. *The Artful Mind: Cognitive Science and the Riddle of Human Creativity*, ed. M. Turner, 93–113. Oxford/New York: Oxford University Press.

Turner, M., ed. 2006. *The Artful Mind: Cognitive Science and the Riddle of Human Creativity*. Oxford/New York: Oxford University Press.

Varela, F., E. Thompson and E. Rosch. 1992. *The Embodied Mind: Human Cognition and Experience*. Cambridge: MIT Press.

Winawer, J., Huk, A. C. and L. Boroditsky (2008). A Motion Aftereffect From Still Photographs Depicting Motion. *Psychological Science* 19 (3): 276–283.

Zentrum Paul Klee, ed. 2012. *Paul Klee – Die Engel*. Osfildern: Hatje Cantz Verlag.

Zlatev, J. 2005. What's in a Schema? Bodily Mimesis and the Grounding of Language. *From Perception to Meaning: Images Schemas in Cognitive Linguistics*, ed. B. Hampe, 313–342. Berlin/New York: Mouton de Gruyter.

20

# Where Do Cognitive Biases Fit Into Cognitive Linguistics? An Example from the 'Curse of Knowledge'

VERA TOBIN

## 1 Introduction

It is a truth widely acknowledged (e.g. Piaget 1932; Fillmore 1975; Baron-Cohen 1995) that human beings have a remarkable ability to think about and adopt the perspectives of others. However, despite these spectacular performances of perspective taking, our abilities in this arena are both limited and riddled with biases. These biases are studied extensively in cognitive psychology, social psychology, economics, and cognitive approaches to decision making. Cognitive linguistics, however, despite its longstanding interest in viewpoint and perspective, has given them much less direct or explicit attention. This paper suggests that some models of meaning construction in cognitive linguistics are in fact very well suited to addressing the contributions of cognitive bias, and presents one illustrative integrated account.

The 'curse of knowledge' is a pervasive cognitive bias that makes it very difficult for us to imagine, once we know something, what it is like not to know it (Camerer, Loewenstein, and Weber 1989; Birch and Bloom 2003). Here, I will argue that the curse of knowledge is an artifact of a more general cognitive shortcut that is implicated in features of 'correct' sentence interpretation such as presupposition projection, as well as in the phenomena that are traditionally described as curse-of-knowledge errors.

*Language and the Creative Mind*.
Mike Borkent, Barbara Dancygier, and Jennifer Hinnell (eds).

Linguistic forms that mark aspects of viewpoint may express aspects of a language user's own immediate perceptions and conceptions, but can of course also be deployed in service of much more complex representations. We can speak and think of other places and times; we can produce negation and counterfactual conditionals; we can represent the speech and thoughts of others (including imagined others); we can embed perspectives within other perspectives, layer them, or blend them in a host of fleeting or extended modes of discourse presentation.

Many models of meaning construction within cognitive linguistics (and elsewhere) describe that process in terms of mental representations. None of these models, to my knowledge, claims to model cognitive biases like the curse of knowledge, but mental spaces theory (Fauconnier 1985, 1997; Cutrer 1994) does have a theoretical apparatus that accounts for ways that structure tends to flow from one mental representation to another. This apparatus offers an elegant solution to a number of classic problems in semantics and pragmatics, none of which are normally understood to have anything to do with the egocentric biases implicated in drawing inferences or with our shortcomings in reasoning about other minds. But, it turns out, there are good reasons to think that at least some of them do, and that in particular the mental spaces account of presupposition captures something important about how that phenomenon reflects those biases.

## 2 Biases In and Of Perspective-taking

It is often the case that one person in an interaction knows more about some relevant subject than another person does. This state of affairs is known in strategic intelligence and economics as an 'information asymmetry'. Asymmetric information can be of significant tactical value. Confidence artists, hustlers, and investment bankers all make their livings by cashing in on such advantages.

The career of the gambler Alvin Thomas, better known as 'Titanic' Thompson, provides a parade of illustrations of the advantages a carefully cultivated asymmetry can confer (compiled in loving detail in Cook 2011): A professional-caliber golf player and the model for the character Sky Masterson in *Guys and Dolls*, Titanic Thompson's signature hustle was to beat a man playing right handed, then offer a double-or-nothing match in which he would play left handed—capitalizing on the fact that he was, unbeknownst to his opponent, actually a lefty. His greatest joy was rigging proposition wagers, bets on apparently random events about which he secretly had information his opponent did not: how many watermelons were stacked on a farm truck passing by (he had paid the farmer for a count that morning); whether he could hit a 500-yard golf drive (he could, when it was on the frozen Lake Michigan); whether he could cut a flower off its stem just by throwing playing cards (no trick, just practice).

More mundanely, workers generally know more about their own ability and motivation than prospective employers do. Most sellers are better informed about the true value of their products than buyers are, though a knowledgeable collector of Northern Soul records may well be better informed about the true value of a copy of Frank Wilson's 'Do I Love You' than the seller who found it in a box in the basement—and if so, that buyer can make a tidy profit by capitalizing on this information gap. The way things seem to work, in other words, and our usual assumption, is that knowing more gives you the upper hand. But it turns out that this is not quite right.

The economists Colin Camerer, George Loewenstein, and Martin Weber (1989) tested this premise by putting people into a number of situations where they should, theoretically, have been particularly well positioned to predict and take advantage of the judgments of their less-informed counterparts: they had a financial incentive to do so (which ought to provide motivation to think carefully) and they received feedback about the accuracy of their predictions (which should help them to correct for errors in their assessments). Yet, despite these marks in their favor, the better-informed participants consistently let their private information affect their behavior even when it was to their advantage not to do so.

Camerer, Lowenstein, and Weber coined the term 'the curse of knowledge' to describe this tendency. More recently, some cognitive and developmental psychologists (e.g. Birch and Bloom 2003; Keysar, Lin, and Barr 2003; Birch 2005) have suggested that young children's difficulty with false belief tasks, usually taken as evidence that they lack a 'theory of mind', are of a piece with curse-of-knowledge effects in adults. It may be that all of these difficulties reflect a single fundamental bias in social cognition that is more acute in younger children, who have less inhibitory control (Leslie and Polizzi 1998), but persists in some form for our entire lives.

In the realm of language, the curse of knowledge seems also to affect people's judgments of the decodability of their own utterances, and especially of the degree to which meaning is 'obviously' conveyed by linguistic and paralinguistic structure. For instance, utterances are often potentially ambiguous, but speakers have many tools to constrain that ambiguity for their interlocutors' benefit. However, while we do deploy those tools and believe that we are making ourselves clear by doing so, several studies (e.g. Newton 1994; Keysar and Bly 1995; Kelley and Jacoby 1996; Kraljic and Brennan 2005) suggest that our judgments in those moments are 'cursed'. We are systematically biased to think that we have been understood. Even speakers who have been warned that what they are about to say is ambiguous underestimate how ambiguous their own utterances will be and greatly overestimate the helpfulness of their attempts at disambiguation.

For instance, Keysar and Henley (2002) gave speakers syntactically ambiguous sentences and asked them to say them in such a way that another participant would understand them as unambiguous: e.g. 'Angela killed the man with the gun' said so as to convey the notion that Angela used the gun to kill the man, rather than that the man had the gun. Then the speakers were asked how they believed the listener would understand the sentence, and how confident they were in that assessment. The majority of speakers were both confident and wrong. Similarly, as illustrated in Figure 1, overhearers who were given privileged information about another speaker's intentions overestimated how transparent those intentions would be to a third party (Keysar 2000).

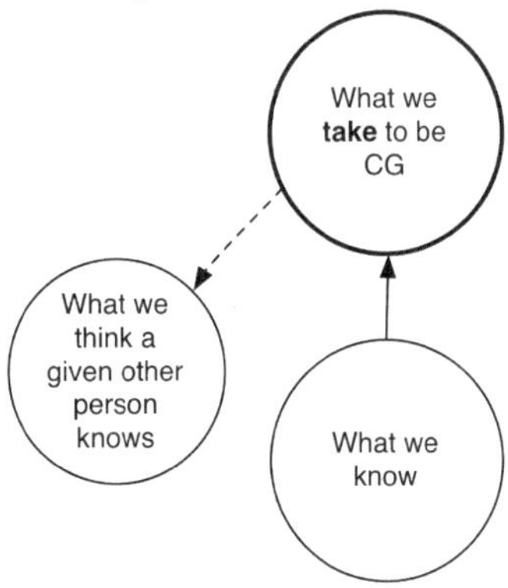


FIGURE 1. Over-projection and assessing the transparency of intentions

Results of this sort suggest that speakers don't just rely overmuch on their own mental states to guide their performance, though they certainly do that; they also actively over-project information from their own perspective to their assessment of what is in the common ground. This brings us to the question of how best to incorporate these patterns of over-projection into our accounts of linguistic viewpoint phenomena that are frequently discussed in terms of what speakers and hearers are assumed to know, believe, bring readily to mind, or be able to infer about the matter under discussion. The classic example is the case of presupposition.

## 3 Presupposition

### 3.1 Overview

Presupposition has historically enjoyed considerable attention from linguists and philosophers of language, as a topic of interest to larger debates about the interaction and division of labor between semantics and pragmatics. The modern philosophical study of presupposition began with Gottlob Frege's (1892) observations about some curious referential properties of proper names and temporal clauses. From there it served as a testing ground for truth-conditional accounts of the propositional status of definite descriptions (Russell 1905) and the relationships between sentences, statements, and speakers (e.g. Strawson 1952), and onward into a variety of theories that engage in one way or another with issues of contextual appropriateness. These latter approaches embrace positions from Karttunen's (1973: 6) suggestion that presuppositions are a matter of 'some ... conversational principle' regarding who 'can be assumed to share the speaker's beliefs', to van der Sandt's (1992) theory that presuppositions behave much like anaphora that need to be resolved with respect to their linguistic context, and Beaver's (1999: 3) claim that presuppositional phenomena are 'not naturally explained in terms of truth conditions but in terms of plausibility'.

Anyone sitting down to consider the phenomenon today can thus partake of well over a hundred years of prior theorizing and digging up of troublesome examples. Some of these investigations are of greater relevance to current trends in linguistic inquiry than others. As Levinson (1983: 167) remarked, 'there is more literature on presupposition than on almost any other topic in pragmatics ... and while much of this is of a technical and complex kind, a great deal is also obsolete'. In the thirty years since that writing, that body of scholarship has only grown larger, and its foundational works of course grow older every year.

Levinson was correct in his observation that 'Much that [once] seemed confusing and mysterious has become clearer now that some basic distinctions and frameworks have been established' (1983: 167–168). Nonetheless, there seems to be some room left at the table for new accounts of presupposition, particularly within the frameworks of dynamic semantics (e.g. Beaver 2001) and probabilistic processing models (e.g. Lassiter 2012)—and similarly, I would suggest, as an entryway for integrating research on reasoning under uncertainty with cognitive-linguistic models of meaning construction in discourse.

Broadly speaking, a presupposition is an inference or proposition whose truth is taken for granted in the utterance of a sentence. Presuppositions are usually tied to the use of particular lexical items or linguistic constructions, called presupposition triggers. So, for instance, consider the word *regret* in Example (1), as discussed in Fillmore (1985: 249):

(1) John regretted signing the letter.

Under the standard interpretation of this example, the sentence *entails* that John felt regret, but *presupposes* that he signed the letter, and this is because, as a factive verb, *regret* presupposes its complement.

Presuppositions typically survive negation, as seen in (2) and (3), both of which presuppose that Henrietta was late:

(2) Henrietta realized she was late.

(3) Henrietta didn't realize she was late.

... unless the negation is taken to reject the entire framing of the presupposition trigger, in what is sometimes called 'sentential' or 'metalinguistic' negation.

(4) John didn't *regret* signing the letter, because he didn't sign it in the first place!

(5) I didn't stop kicking my cat, because I never kicked her at all!

(6) The king of France isn't bald, because there is no king of France!

The circumstances in which presuppositions survive within complex sentences, as they do in (3) and in a number of other contexts where entailments do not, and those in which they evaporate, as they do in (4–6), have been the source of much puzzlement for linguists and philosophers. This 'projection problem'—the problem of how to describe and explain when presuppositions project from an embedded context and when they do not—has been a major focus of the research on presupposition since the 1970s, and it is at the heart of the mental spaces account of the mechanism Fauconnier (1985, 1997) calls 'presupposition float'.

### 3.2 Mental Spaces: Inheritance and Presupposition Float

The behavior of presuppositions in embedded contexts is one of the foundational puzzles motivating the original formulation of mental spaces theory. The argument—which to readers of this volume may by now seem hardly necessary to make—is that aspects of meaning that are difficult or impossible to handle under a purely formal or logical analysis prove much more tractable when considered as the outcome of cognitive processes of meaning construction, particularly 'the consequences of minds capable of setting up networks of mental spaces and optimizing the content within' (Oakley 2009: 168).

There are two points here of relevance to the issue of cognitive bias and linguistic perspective: *networks of mental spaces* and *optimizing the content within*. Unlike the possible worlds of truth-conditional semantics, mental spaces are partial and contingent. They are fundamentally cognitive rather than logical entities, constructed and revised in people's minds in response to linguistic and other prompts. In other words, mental spaces are a model of the representations that constitute the meanings we construct as we think and talk. These are linked together in networks that are built up dynamically in working memory and can be stored in episodic memory. One mental space leads to another, and mental spaces can inherit structure from other spaces.

In mental spaces theory as originally formulated, the formal principles that govern this inheritance find their place in the theory not on the basis of their psychological or neurological plausibility (though the theory as a whole certainly aspires to be cognitively plausible), but because of their parsimony and utility within the logical structure of the mental spaces framework. In other words, their proposed dynamics are justified by their efficiency in accounting for existing puzzles in semantics and pragmatics. They are certainly not presented first and foremost as accurate descriptions of how or when humans make mistakes. On the contrary, the arguments for their validity are grounded in how well they explain subtle and complicated *successful* navigations of complex semantic and pragmatic structure. They are plausible insofar as they get meaning construction 'right'. So how do they fit in with something like the curse of knowledge, which appears to be all about how people get things wrong?

As discussed in Section 3.1, a traditional defining feature of presuppositions has been that they can survive under negation or one of a variety of other embedding contexts, but it is tricky to predict when presuppositions of embedded clauses will give rise to presuppositions for an entire sentence, or of a multisentence piece of discourse.

For instance, the cleft construction in a sentence like *It was meeting his niece that changed Jack's mind* triggers the presupposition that something changed Jack's mind. This presupposition can project from a variety of embedded contexts, as seen in (7a–e).

(7) a. It wasn't meeting his niece that changed Jack's mind. (negation)

b. If it was meeting his niece that changed Jack's mind, he won't mind babysitting her. (antecedent of a conditional)

c. Was it meeting his niece that changed Jack's mind? (question)

d. Maybe/it's possible that it was meeting his niece that changed Jack's mind. (possibility modal)

e. Presumably/probably it was meeting his niece that changed Jack's mind. (evidential modal, probability adverb)

f. Maria thinks that it was meeting his niece that changed Jack's mind. (belief operator)

Such embedded presuppositions can be cancelled or blocked under the right circumstances, and it has proved difficult on a sentence-level analysis to provide categorical accounts of what those circumstances might be. For instance, consider a pair of examples like (8), discussed in Fauconnier (1997):

(8) a. If John has children, then John's children are bald.

b. If John is here, then John's children are in New York.

Despite their structural similarities, (8a) and (8b) do not behave the same way with respect to presupposition. The sentence as a whole in (8a) does not presuppose that John has children, while the sentence as a whole in (8b) certainly does. Why?

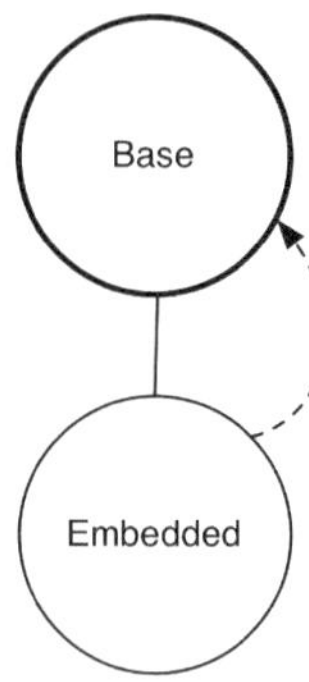


FIGURE 2. Presupposed structure 'floats up' to the base

The mental spaces account of this phenomenon is as follows: presupposed information propagates through a mental space network according to a general principle of *presupposition float:* Information grammatically introduced as presupposed relative to one mental space will 'float' to the next space and continue to propagate to the next higher space, unless structure already in that space either *entails* the presupposition or *is incompatible* with it. So (8a) sets up a space ('if...') that is hypothetical with respect to the base (i.e. the sentence as a whole), as well as an expansion space ('then...') that is subordinate to that hypothetical space. In the hypothetical space, the proposition that John has children is set up non-presuppositionally. In the expansion it is set up presuppositionally. And so when it 'floats' from the expansion up to the next higher space, it 'meets itself' and stops—and as a result it is not projected to the base and does not hold for the sentence as a whole. Because the antecedent in (8b) does not set up structure that entails that John has children, the presupposition in that case floats freely all the way up through the network, and the sentence as a whole does in fact presuppose that he does.

The focus in the Fauconnier account is on the circumstances under which presuppositions are blocked from propagating all the way to the base, because this is the crucial question for the projection problem. But the presupposition float principle also means that whatever we know, we by default ascribe to the speaker's reality and the conversational ground. This tendency obtains especially for that which we know *implicitly*; that's the special thing about presupposition, as we'll see in more detail in the next section. This projection of information within the mental space network begins to resemble the apparently erroneous projections associated with the curse of knowledge. In other words, the kinds of mistakes catalogued in the literature on egocentric biases predict that we will systematically project information from certain less general contexts to more general ones, and so—in the Mental Spaces account—do the patterns of sentence interpretation seen with embedded presupposition.

These examples demonstrate that there is at the very least a suggestive family resemblance here, but we have not yet shown that the patterns of projection from less general to more general in these two sets of phenomena are more than broadly congruent. To see most clearly how the habits of thought captured by the curse of knowledge are part and parcel of ordinary language processing at the semantics/pragmatics interface, we will want to consider the phenomenon of so-called 'presupposition accommodation' (Lewis 1979).[1]

### 3.3 Presupposition Accommodation

Most presupposing constructions can be used informatively; that is, they can carry presuppositions that are not already part of the common ground and yet still be felicitous. For example, if I say, 'I have to pick up a package for my sister' to someone who has no idea whether or not I had any siblings, my interlocutor can easily accommodate the presupposition triggered by *my sister* (namely, that there exists a person who fills this role), taking that information to be part of a newly expanded but still backgrounded shared set of contextual assumptions for the discourse.

Under the common ground account (as seen in Heim 1983, 1992, following Karttunen 1974 and Stalnaker 1970), presupposition is a precondi-

[1] Like almost everything to do with presupposition, the notion of 'accommodation' is not without its critics (see, for instance, Gauker 2008). However, the linguistic behavior itself—the fact that things that look like presuppositions can be used appropriately in contexts where the presupposed propositions are in fact discourse-new information—is generally accepted as a phenomenon in need of explanation.

tion for felicitous utterances, which imposes requirements on the context that must be satisfied. That 'context' of utterances consists of the common ground, defined as mutual knowledge or common beliefs among participants of a conversation. Under this account, (9) has as a requirement that the common ground includes the proposition that someone broke the vase; in other words, a speaker who asserts (9) does so assuming that this requirement has been satisfied.

(9) It was Margaret who broke the vase.

The utterance thus requires that it is taken for granted and not subject to (further) discussion that someone broke the vase. But, as Lewis (1979: 340) observes:

> It's not as easy as you might think to say something that will be unacceptable for lack of required presuppositions. Say something that requires a missing presupposition, and straightaway that presupposition springs into existence, making what you said acceptable after all. (Or at least, this is what happens if your conversational partners tacitly acquiesce.)

Indeed, it is not only possible but very common for presuppositions to be informative.

The particular subtlety of the way that an informative presupposition introduces new information into the discourse is that, by definition, it is not asserting the presupposed content but treating it as both already *known* and already part of the shared, implicit context. Thus presupposition accommodation also involves presupposition float, even when the presupposition is not syntactically embedded. While an explicit assertion obtains and can be disputed at the level of the speaker's reality (SR in Figure 3), presuppositions seem to do something more: 'floating' by default, unless they meet themselves or are contradicted, up to the common ground.

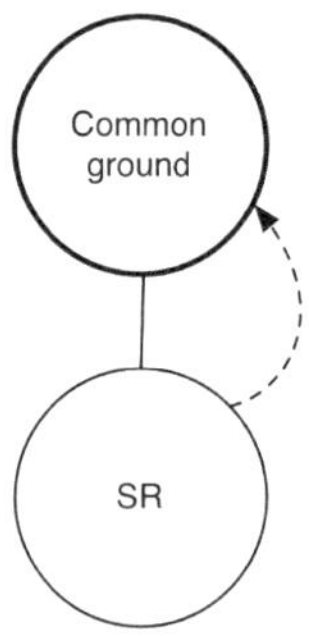


FIGURE 3. Accommodation, floating to common ground

So here we have the first ingredient of projection from embedded contexts into more general ones. The examples from the cognitive bias literature, however, don't stop there—they show that people habitually ascribe information from one limited or embedded perspective in reasoning about a separate limited perspective. In addition to presupposition float, mental spaces theory holds that structure is sometimes also automatically projected in the opposite direction, via a principle called *space optimization*: 'relevant structure not explicitly contradicted is inherited within the child-space' (Fauconnier 1997: 112). The utterance 'I wish that whiny brat Edward were your brother instead of mine', for instance, sets up a base space of the speaker's reality, and a subordinate 'wish' space that is counterfactual with respect to that base. In the base space, Edward is the speaker's brother. In the wish space, he is not. Many facts and inferences about Edward that obtain at the base level are blocked from being projected to the wish space. For example, in the base space, Edward and the speaker have the same parents, share half of their DNA, and so on. Those properties do not project to the wish space because they are incompatible with the counterfactual. But other features of Edward that are facts in the speaker's reality space are projected by default to the wish space, such as his (alleged) quality of being a whiny brat.

When space optimization works together with presupposition float, then, embedded or informative presuppositions can float up to the common ground and from there be projected into new child spaces via optimization, as illustrated in Figure 4. This result is exactly parallel to the 'cursed' information propagation pattern discussed in Section 2 and illustrated in Figure 1. In both cases, privileged information—information salient to the speaker that was not originally shared by her interlocutors—propagates through the network and is ascribed by default to all participants.

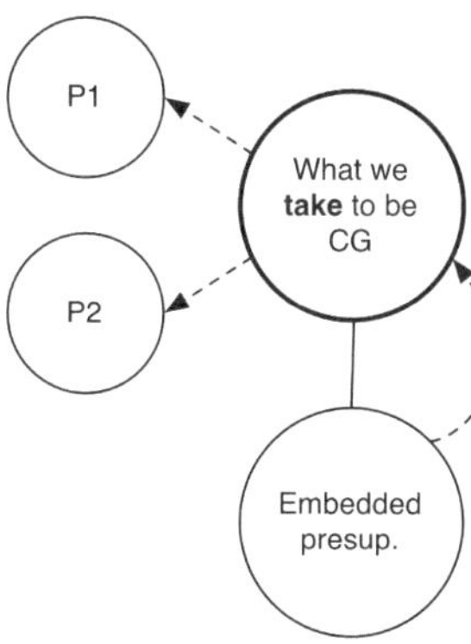


FIGURE 4. Projection through the network

This kind of accommodation projection is connected to the curse of knowledge in two ways: First, because presupposition accommodation always involves presupposition float, it makes embedded information available for profligate projection into our representations of other embedded perspectives in the network, just as we see with analogous privileged information in the wide array of studies on the curse of knowledge and the illusory transparency of intentions. Second, it is also necessary *because* of people's biased inclination to overestimate what of their knowledge is already in the common ground.

Recall from Section 2 that curse-of-knowledge effects are particularly well documented in the context of linguistic communication. Indeed, recent studies (Bromme, Jucks, and Runde 2005; Wu and Keysar 2007) suggest that the more information speakers share in a conversation overall, the more they overestimate their interlocutors' knowledge about new topics. This means that even if we started out with a state of affairs in which the rule for these expressions was that one was licensed only ever to use presupposing constructions to reference information that was already in the common ground, we would very quickly run into a great many cases where a speaker had mistakenly assumed that some referent was known and salient to her audience, or that her audience shared her background knowledge and beliefs about the topic at hand. Thus, even if no one were deliberately using presuppositions to introduce new information, the occasion would certainly, indeed frequently, arise.

If (as they do) hearers will accommodate such uses, it is a short step to conventionally using presuppositions informatively—if it is clear that hearers *can* accommodate these uses of presupposing constructions, why not for efficiency's sake bring uncontroversial information into the common ground as a presupposition (cf. Givón 1995)? From there, of course, a variety of rhetorically motivated, and even underhanded, possibilities arise for using presupposing constructions as a way of treating potentially controversial information as uncontroversial, less readily available for refutation, and more readily available for default projection across a network of embedded perspectives.

## 4 'Cursed' Projections

Studies of the curse of knowledge and related biases often treat them as a sort of lapse from ideal approaches to communication and understanding. The analysis in Keysar (2007), for instance, dwells on how these effects 'introduce a systematic reason for miscommunication' and suggests that our reliance on our own perspective in discourse means that we should consider misunderstandings not as 'a product of noise and random error' but an endemic product of our 'disregard for the perspective of the other'. With presupposition, however, the structures of default projection from the origo to other perspectives constitute a completely ordinary and even necessary component of meaning construction.

Cognitive linguists are used to thinking about the quirks of other general human cognitive abilities as being reflected in and constitutive of the organization of language. As, for instance, psychological models of memory and categorization have been central to models of both grammatical categories and lexical semantics in cognitive linguistics, so too can psychological models of heuristics and biases in reasoning under uncertainty help to explicate many of the processes that structure pragmatic inferencing and information packaging (Lambrecht 1994) for referring expressions and clausal structure.

This approach fits in well not only with the linguistic-theoretical structures of mental spaces theory, but also with two related bodies of recent research on how people think and behave when they interact with one another: the role of motor and perceptual simulation in both linguistic and non-linguistic understanding, and the pervasiveness of immediate, unconscious behavioral alignment in face-to-face interaction.[2]

Together, the research on simulation and the research on interactive alignment suggest that we go through the world continually, automatically, and *mutually* synching ourselves up with the people we encounter: We echo their actions and utterances directly (Garrod and Pickering 2009) and perceptually (Pecher and Zwaan 2005); we borrow their syntax (Du Bois 2007)—and they do the same with us. Even people with amnesia converge on shared terms for novel objects with their interlocutors over the course of a conversation (Duff et al. 2005). At the same time, we need to fill out these echoes rapidly and behind the scenes. Mapping information from our own perspective is a quick and efficient way of generating good approximations. The resulting frequent and persistent projection of perspectives is in keeping with both the kind of default interpretation we see across both standard curse of knowledge effects and the structural features of presupposition projection.

This phenomenon, incidentally, is one of the ways that stories can exploit the curse of knowledge to create clever misdirections and surprises.[3] Many twist endings hinge on a hidden coreferentiality—Jekyll and Hyde are

[2] For a fine overview of the former and its potential role in linguistic performance, see Bergen (2012); for the latter, see Louwerse et al. (2012).

[3] See Tobin (2009) for further discussion of the curse of knowledge and narrative surprises, and Dancygier (2004) for an interesting analysis of the prevalence of Jekyll-and-Hyde-like 'decompressions of identity' in narrative discourse generally.

the same man, the Planet of the Apes was Earth all along, Harry Lime was the 'third man' at his own funeral, Darth Vader was once Anakin Skywalker. To have a character say 'Mr. Hyde and Dr. Jekyll are two different people' may well serve only to alert the reader that things are far more likely to be the other way around. But a sentence like 'in case of the decease of Henry Jekyll... all his possessions were to pass into the hands of his friend and benefactor Edward Hyde', presupposes, rather than asserts, its deceptions. When a crucial bit of misinformation is delivered via something other than a discourse-foregrounded entailment, the mechanisms of 'project what you know' that govern presupposition are particularly likely to produce the desired result: a misleading, but ultimately aesthetically appealing, systematic overpopulation from embedded perspectives.

Research on egocentric biases and reasoning under uncertainty thus turns out to provide psychologically and neurologically grounded support for some of the technical details of mental spaces theory that were previously motivated primarily for their explanatory and descriptive utility in handling linguistic data. The case of presupposition provides a promising model for integrating biases into our understanding of 'correct' interpretive phenomena, and also for the converse: we can and should use our finely observed understanding of linguistic phenomena to tease apart the uses and limits of egocentrism and automatic alignment in social cognition.

## References

Baron-Cohen, S. (1995). *Mindblindness: An essay on autism and theory of mind.* Cambridge, Mass.: MIT Press.

Barsalou, L. W. (1999). Perceptual symbol systems. *Behavioral and Brain Sciences*, 22(4), 577–660.

Barsalou, L. W. (2010). Grounded cognition: Past, present, and future. *Topics in Cognitive Science*, 2(4), 716–724

Beaver, D. (1999). Presupposition accommodation: A plea for common sense. *Logic, Language and Computation*, 2, 21–44.

Beaver, D. I. (2001). *Presupposition and assertion in dynamic semantics.* Stanford: CSLI Publications .

Bergen, B. (2012). *Louder than words: The new science of how the mind makes meaning*. New York: Basic Books.

Bergen, B., and N. Chang, (2005). Embodied construction grammar in simulation-based language understanding. *Construction Grammars: Cognitive Grounding and Theoretical Extensions*, 147–190.

Birch, S. A. J. (2005). When knowledge is a curse: children's and adults' reasoning about mental states. *Current Directions in Psychological Science*, 14(1), 25–29.

Birch, S. A. J., and P. Bloom, (2003). Children are cursed: An asymmetric bias in mental-state attribution. *Psychological Science*, 14(3), 283–286.

Camerer, C., G. Loewenstein, and M. Weber (1989). The curse of knowledge in economic settings: An experimental analysis. *Journal of Political Economy*, 97(5), 1232–1254.

Cook, K. (2011). *Titanic Thompson: The man who bet on everything*. New York: Norton.

Cutrer, L. M. (1994). *Time and tense in narrative and in everyday language*. Thesis.

Dancygier, B. (2004). Identity and perspective: The Jekyll-and-Hyde effect in narrative discourse. In M. Achard and S. Kemmer (eds), *Language, culture, and mind* (pp. 363–76). Stanford, CA: CSLI Publications.

Dancygier, B., and E. Sweetser (2012). Viewpoint in language: A multimodal perspective. Cambridge, UK: Cambridge University Press.

Du Bois, J. W. (2007). The stance triangle. In R. Englebretson (ed.), *Stancetaking in discourse* (pp. 139–182). Amsterdam: Benjamins.

Duff, M. C., J. Hengst, D. Tranel, and N. J. Cohen (2005). Development of shared information in communication despite hippocampal amnesia. *Nature Neuroscience*, 9(1), 140–146.

Fauconnier, G. (1985). *Mental spaces: Aspects of meaning construction in natural language*. New York: Cambridge University Press.

Fauconnier, G. (1997). *Mappings in thought and language*. Cambridge, UK: Cambridge University Press.

Fillmore, C. J. (1985). Frames and the semantics of understanding. *Quaderni Di Semantica*, 6(2), 222–254.

Fillmore, C. J. (1975/1997). *Lectures on deixis*. Stanford, CA: CSLI Publications.

Frege, G. (1892/1952). On sense and reference. In P. T. Geach and M. Black (eds), *Translations from the philosophical writings of Gottlob Frege* (pp. 56–78). Oxford: Blackwell.

Garrod, S., and M. J. Pickering (2009). Joint action, interactive alignment, and dialog. *Topics in Cognitive Science*, 1(2), 292–304.

Gauker, C. (2008). Against accommodation: Heim, van der Sandt, and the presupposition projection problem. *Philosophical Perspectives*, 22(1), 171–205.

Gibbs, R. W. (2006). Metaphor interpretation as embodied simulation. *Mind and Language*, 21(3), 434.

Givón, T. (1995). *Functionalism and grammar*. Philadelphia: John Benjamins.

Heim, I. (1983). On the projection problem for presuppositions. In *Proceedings of WCCFL* (Vol. 2, pp. 114–125).

Heim, I. (1992). Presupposition projection and the semantics of attitude verbs. *Journal of Semantics*, 9(3), 183–221.

Karttunen, L. (1973). Presuppositions of compound sentences. *Linguistic Inquiry*, 4(2), 169–193.

Karttunen, L. (1974). Presupposition and linguistic context. *Theoretical Linguistics*, 1(1–3), 181–194.

Kelley, C. M., and L. L. Jacoby (1996). Adult egocentrism: Subjective experience versus analytic bases for judgment. *Journal of Memory and Language*. 157–175.

Keysar, B. (2000). The illusory transparency of intention: Does June understand what Mark means because he means it? *Discourse Processes*, 29(2), 161–172.

Keysar, B. (2007). Communication and miscommunication: The role of egocentric processes. *Intercultural Pragmatics*, 4(1), 71–84.

Keysar, B., and B. Bly (1995). Intuitions of the transparency of idioms: Can one keep a secret by spilling the beans? *Journal of Memory and Language*, 34(1), 89–109.

Keysar, B., and A. S. Henly (2002). Speakers' overestimation of their effectiveness. *Psychological Science*, 13(3), 207–212.

Keysar, B., S. Lin, and D. J. Barr (2003). Limits on theory of mind use in adults. *Cognition*, 89(1), 25–41.

Kraljic, T., and S. E. Brennan (2005). Prosodic disambiguation of syntactic structure: For the speaker or for the addressee? *Cognitive Psychology*, 50(2), 194–231.

Lakoff, G. J., and M. Johnson (1999). *Philosophy in the flesh: The embodied mind and its challenge to western thought*. New York: Basic Books.

Lambrecht, K. (1994). *Information structure and sentence form*. Cambridge: Cambridge University Press.

Langacker, R. W. (1993). Universals of construal. In *Proceedings of the Annual Meeting of the Berkeley Linguistics Society* (Vol. 19).

Lassiter, D. (2012). Presuppositions, provisos, and probability. *Semantics and Pragmatics*, 1–37.

Leslie, A. M., and P. Polizzi (1998). Inhibitory processing in the false belief task: Two conjectures. *Developmental Science*, 1(2), 247–253.

Levinson, S. C. (1983). *Pragmatics*. New York: Cambridge University Press.

Louwerse, M. M., R. Dale, E. G. Bard, and P. Jeuniaux (2012). Behavior matching in multimodal communication is synchronized. *Cognitive Science*, 36, 1404–26.

MacWhinney, B. (2005). The emergence of grammar from perspective. In D. Pecher and R. A. Zwaan (eds), *Grounding cognition* (pp. 198–223). Cambridge: Cambridge University Press.

Newton, E. L. (1990). *The rocky road from actions to intentions*. Thesis.

Oakley, T. (2009). Mental spaces. In F. Brisard, J. -O. Östman, and J. Verschueren (eds), *Grammar, meaning and pragmatics* (pp. 161–178). Amsterdam: John Benjamins Publishing.

Pecher, D., and R. A. Zwaan (2005). *Grounding cognition*. Cambridge: Cambridge University Press.

Piaget, J. (1932). *The moral judgment of the child*. London: K. Paul, Trench, Trubner and Co.

Russell, B. (1905). On denoting. *Mind*, 14(4), 479–493.

Stalnaker, R. C. (1970). Pragmatics. *Synthese*, 22, 272–289.

Strawson, P. F. (1952/2011). *Introduction to logical theory*. New York: Routledge.

Talmy, L. (1996). Fictive motion in language and 'ception'. *Language and Space*, 21, 1–276.

Tobin, V. (2009). Cognitive bias and the poetics of surprise. *Language and Literature*, 18(2), 155–172.

Van der Sandt, R. A. (1992). Presupposition projection as anaphora resolution. *Journal of Semantics*, 9(4), 333–377.

# Part V

## Sound, Image, and Communicative Modalities

# 21

# Wiggle Room: How Gestural Parameters Affect Singer and Audience Cognition in Art Song Performance

RENA SHARON, LAUREL FAIS, AND ERIC VATIKIOTIS-BATESON

'A language is a flash of the human spirit, the vehicle by which the soul of each culture comes into the material world.'

(Davis 2001)

'Does music convey anything at all beyond its play of sounds? ... Is there any common ground upon which to lay a foundation for a theory of meaning?'

(Almén and Pearsall 2006)

## 1 Introduction

Biological organisms naturally engage in coordinated behavior. Highly skilled behaviors such as spoken communication, singing, or playing a musical instrument exploit this truism to attain more intricately organized and more controlled coordination. So, for example, the basic tendency for two people walking side by side to fall into step with each other can be modified into a highly synchronized march or tango. The fluidity and beauty of such actions depends on sophisticated engagement by performers for whom the outcome has become a coveted goal. The highly skilled performance of a piece of music requires that substantial cognitive, neuromotor, and metabolic resources be marshaled and carefully integrated. The result is more impressive than casual coordination, and more fragile. For example, a minute

*Language and the Creative Mind.*
Mike Borkent, Barbara Dancygier, and Jennifer Hinnell (eds).

change in timing that would go unnoticed for two people walking in step can become a glaring performance error in music or song. What's more, once a behavior becomes a desired outcome, it becomes susceptible to aesthetic interpretation whereby one instance of a performance can be preferred to another. While this is useful in training, it also constrains the performance stylistically to be carried out in one way rather than another; in other words, a form emerges that, even if arbitrary from the perspective of any known causal factors, suppresses other forms as different and/or undesirable.

For the past several years, we have taken a multipronged approach, collaborating as musicians and scientists to understand how coordination within and between performers, including talkers, i.e., linguistic 'performers', contributes to the execution of over-learned expressive behaviors. From data capture in the laboratory to in-situ live performance environments, we have tracked initiatives in a new artistic modality with research in the related emergent properties of gesture and cognition. This jointly-written chapter focuses on the particularly rich domain of Art Song, in which a pianist and a singer must bring to life a work of art that consists of a poem and a piece of music written for that poem. The task for the Art Song duo is daunting because the audience may have no prior experience with the poem (and increasingly with poetry in general) and therefore has only fleeting access as the piece is performed.

To make matters even more complex, Art Song performance parameters have become defined in a way that challenges the final coordination link between performers and audience. We present results of our converging efforts as scientists and musician 1) to modify performance style to better connect with audiences, including expanding the range of the singer's body motions and introducing more tangible dramatic devices such as an actor representing the intended recipient of the song, and 2) to provide quantitative support for these modifications through analysis of the coordination between a singer's voice and body motion, and between the acoustics of the voice and the piano. Finally, we do not at present have the facilities to record the data for quantifying the coordination between musicians and audience; however, we exemplify how such an analysis could be done using our coordination analysis of the rock group, Queen, and a large audience of 72,000.

## 2 Art Song: An Introduction

When language is fused to music, it ignites the phenomenon of Song. The expressive vocalization of pitched tones joined to words is a human commonality of individual and collective story-telling, sustaining enduring cultural bonds across time and space. The ancient instinct to animate rituals, learning, celebrations and pastimes with chant and texted melody is woven into the entire world's communal structures, apparently impelled by an intriguingly ubiquitous sense that to fully express the complex and layered entirety of perception and emotion, language is inadequate. Wrapping textured tones around words seems to enhance the conveyance of how we feel about what we think—and what we think about how we feel.

A substratum of Song known in English by the term 'Art Song' (a.k.a. *Lieder, Mélodie, cancion*, etc.) comprises an immense and continuously expanding global collection—over 100,000 songs in 100+ languages—of poetry by 10,000 poets set to music by 12,000 composers. Performed in Western operatic vocal style joined to a diversity of world instruments, the voice and soundscapes generate an extraordinary symbiosis as word and music fuse into a hybrid conjunction of modalities. 'It has been suggested that music and language are at opposite poles of a communicative continuum, almost meeting in the middle somewhere near poetry' (Cross 2003: 8-9). Art Song draws that arc to closer coalescence. A soprano soaring to her vocal stratosphere creates an embodied metaphor of Hermann Hesse's images of untrammeled soul-flight and *life lived a thousandfold* ('Beim Schlafengehen', R. Strauss, 1948); a pianist and singer synchronously exhale the Symbolist evocation of '*l'extase langoureuse*' (P.Verlaine, C. Debussy, 1888); a fragile fragment of melody spins a suspended wonderment, as a young man soon to be extinguished by war is enraptured by the ephemeral beauty of a cherry tree in bloom ('*Loveliest of Trees*', A.E. Housman, 1887, set by G. Butterworth, I. Gurney, and by 39 other composers). When Art Song succeeds, its sound-forms can trigger a powerful cascade of multimodal synaesthetic and visceral cognition.

Art Song proposes specificities upon the abstract structures of Western classical music, for which meaning-making normatively relies largely upon conjecture and theoretical studies of harmonic and structural analysis. The compendium of ambiguities involved in discerning a composer's intent is a quandary residing at the enigmatic core of musical interpretation (see Cross 2005). In the Art Song mode, that debate is granted some temporary mediation. The relationship of text and sound introduces sets of analogs, or 'lexicons of correlates' aligning musical sounds with poetic imagery, events, and emotion at extreme degrees of discernable intent. The sounds become cyphers, evoking rare insights into the composer's embedded creative processes (Johnson 2003). In turn, the musical components condition and situate poetic ambiguities through the impact of melody, harmony, ambiance, rhythm, speed, sonar texture and gesture (Malin 2010). Effectively, Art Song is an interpretive thesis of the poetry, and a reciprocal translation in which two modalities merge into a hybrid third form.

At the interstice of conscious and subconscious perception, sung words are perhaps literally 'heart-felt' by performer and listener through the complex neurophysiology required for sound production and reception (Russo 2012). The pitched, vibrated, articulated words can trigger aspects of text comprehension to supplement normative verbal processing. When all conditions of communicative connection are met, the experience of a live operatic voice singing poetry directly to an audience is formidably intense.

Such attributes and utilities should make Art Song a consummately appealing genre. However, the genre is at imminent risk of *disappearing* as a performance modality. The Art Song recital is a genre that is increasingly isolated into a specialized audience sector, even in the European countries of its native origins. Current market assessments predict the disappearance of Art Song from the classical performance circuit within 30 years (Sharon 2011; Serinus 2012). With dimming career prospects, Art Song repertoire has begun to be marginalized in many university programs to the extent that a trained performer network may not exist within several generations, thus putting the repertoire at risk of devolving to a primarily archival existence of recordings and scores.

While there are many for whom the art form is a passion, informal surveys gathered over the past 10 years indicate that even among audiences with considerable fluency in classical music modalities, a large percentage describe disaffection for Art Song ranging from mild alienation to hostile antipathy (Sharon 2012). Rather than feeling united in a space of heightened communal understanding, listeners often express a sense of being 'left out of the enlightened and sophisticated inner circle'. Common complaints include feeling unengaged, citing incomprehensibility of text, expressive monotony, emotional distance. The listener is left to decide whether the disconnection is a personal 'shortcoming'—or an inherent deficit in the art form itself: 'I wondered whether this was perhaps an Emperor's New Clothes situation'. Either way, in that inhospitable equation Art Song is defeated.

## 3 The Cognitive Challenges of Art Song Recital

The tremendous evolution in popularity for the contemporary Opera genre poses a dynamical comparison to the Art Song recital. In packed houses around the world audiences are paying top ticket prices at multiple performances to experience highly-charged, epic, sung narratives unfolding within dramatic stage environments of convergent media stimuli. At the centre, a conductor waves arms to direct a fantastic collaborative mass of orchestra players, vocalists, chorus, and dancers through a panoramic audio-visual sensory immersion. Singers stride the expanse of the stage gesturing abundantly while singing at peak volume, range, and resonance. To facilitate comprehension of the libretto—since operatic vocalization tends to substantially obscure comprehension of verbal language—the digitized text, generally in the primary local language, is projected on monitors above the stage or on seatbacks so that the audience can follow the libretto while maintaining maximal stage connection.

In stark contrast, the Art Song recital environment is austerely minimalist. The 'set' usually consists of a grand piano, with perhaps a large standing vase of flowers and a small table with a glass of water. Sometimes an ornamental rug may be added to invoke a $19^{th}$ century Salon. A singer and a pianist in formal attire are the sole occupants of the stage. For the familiarized recital listener, the simplicity is intrinsic to the aesthetic of the form; a profound communion of poetry and sound. However, for the opera-lover who has come to hear a favourite tenor up close and personal, it can be an experience of sensory deficit and exigent meaning-making efforts beyond the customary scope of musical entertainment.

Operatic and Art Song recital singing employ essentially the same mechanisms of vocal production, but significant differences define their actualization.

### 3.1 Directness of Connection with the Audience

In the traditional operatic realm the audience members are observers of a separate, constructed reality in which the performers are immersed. While exceptions occur, in general no direct relationship between singer and audience exists even when a singer is alone on the stage and facing outward directly toward the hall. The singer sings either to other characters or to him/herself within an imagined reality. The audience's connection is empathically woven through communion with a character's plight as it unfolds in the narrative thread. When Puccini's Tosca sings her aria before flinging herself off a parapet, she sings as a character within her own world; the audience experiences her tragedy from the insulated distance of the spectator, across a gulf reinforced by the orchestra situated between domains.

The Art Song vocalist faces the audience directly. No props—nor even a music stand or microphone—establish any sort of intercession between the singer's body and the audience. The pianist, situated in profile at the piano, is only directly connected with the audience during bowing acknowledgments. Ideally, it is a setting designed for a deep and intimate engagement of a sweeping range of poetic eras and worldviews.

### 3.2 Gestural and Spatial Parameters

In the recital protocol, the robust gesture of operatic singing is supplanted by a set of proscribed movements.

#### 3.2.1 Placement on the Stage

In traditional practice, the Art Song singer stands at the bend of the piano in a relative stasis, rarely moving beyond an implied half-circle extending to a width and depth of about 4 to 10 feet from the axis point at the curve of the piano.

#### 3.2.2 Use of Gesture

In common practice the performer normally enacts minimal movement of hands, torso, legs, and feet. Until recently, performers were trained to keep hands cupped at the center of the body, or to have one hand holding the edge of the grand piano. Current practice often has the arms positioned at the sides of the body, with some latitude, depending upon the school of practice, for movement of the forearms and hands.

When a world-renowned baritone electrified a Vancouver audience at the beginning of the 21st century in a recital that claimed about 12 square feet of stage space and extensive complex gestural expressivity more commensurate with operatic parameters, he self-described his actions in a backstage question-and-answer session as 'renegade'. The extreme polarization of views following his performance articulated the conundrum: many professionals found his stagecraft objectionable, while the general audience manifested a prolonged ovation and reported an immediacy of emotional connection and comprehension. That polarity is at the core of the question of the future of Art Song: can artistic integrities be sustained in an array of adaptive practices for the 21st century audience?

A profound philosophical rationale for the quiet body aesthetic is the notional shift of awareness from the *body as medium* to the *body as conduit,* wherein the voice becomes the undiluted purveyor of content and intent, and the presence of the body as intermediary is understated. In the ideal notion, one's essence is transcendently transmuted into soundwaves—the epitome of the musical aesthetic of nonmateriality—and large corporeal gesture becomes extraneous and superfluous.

A central point in the discourse about recital movement, therefore, is that physical gesture dilutes the intensity of authentic expression through the musical channel. Robert Schumann, a primary catalyst of the German Art Song form (*Lieder*) in the 19th century, proposed a sensibility so interior that even the popular Salon environment was deemed too public a performative space. Lieder, as suggested in his *Neue Zeitschrift für Musik,* were ideally to be sung alone in a private space or to a small circle of close friends (Ferris 2000). Internationally renowned vocal pianist Julius Drake recently asserted the view that the singer must 'fully internalize each song so that the performer does not have to act it out, but present it with voice enhanced solely with facial expressions' (Globe and Mail, J. Terrauds, June 23, 2013).

In attempting to enhance communicative connection, does gesture-rich performance re-distribute the sources of expression, diluting the sound and forfeiting the essence that it seeks to convey? For the contemporary audience, the acknowledged predilection for visual stimuli is greatly tasked in an art form founded upon a notion of disembodied sound. And yet, how marvelous for an art form to aspire to a state in which the invisible is made manifest solely through the phenomenon of poetic song exhaled upon the air. In that idealized state, achievable by great performers, 'sound as essence' moves from philosophy to presence.

A similar aspiration might stand in the realm of dance, as leaps and lifts emblemize the liberation from gravity's imposition upon the soul's longing for flight and freedom. Yet, physical laws remain intact for flesh-bound artists and their audiences. Just as the dancer must fall to earth, the singer is biologically hard-wired to merge speech with gesture, and audiences are hard-wired to read gesture as supplementary information in cognizing language and meaning. One might argue, therefore, that to decouple gesture and movement from sung speech interrupts fundamental neurophysical processing on both sides of the stage.

### 3.2.3 Use of Facial Cueing

A paradox of Art Song performance is that while its poetic texts may have been conceived as reflective contemplations, singing in a recital hall is a public declamation. The diverse and often intense emotional content of some texts might be expected to generate a spectrum of natural movement if expressed in one's unregarded private space. In the context of the recital, these are tempered by sensibilities and protocols both trained and sensed.

The conundrum of how an Art Song singer conveys extremes of emotion without commensurate embodiment is therefore further layered by the consideration of sensibilities specific to poetic readings. Western poetry is often read aloud with facial and tonal understatement within its professional constituency. Melodicized reading would reasonably align to that practice.

The singer's face and gaze are physical adjuncts to vocal expression. However, the physiological exigencies that operatic vocalization imposes upon speech require substantial modifications to normative usage of the facial muscles. The operatic singer's face functions as more than a communication interface between thinker and receiver; it is also a resonating chamber, part of a veritable musical instrument which is played with no less precision of placement than a violinist requires in placing bow on string and digits upon fingerboard. The technical demands upon processes of jaw, tongue, palate, nasal passages, and even forehead alter the production of words and countermand the commonalities of word-generated facial expressivities. Since beautiful tone is a priority of the professional performer, acuity of facial information-transfer generally accedes to the necessities of vocal production. While this is an accepted inevitability for audiences familiar with operatic singing, noncoherence with the implied nuances of the poetic text does register as a visual dissonance when new listeners are queried.

## 4 The Relation between Movement and Meaning in Art Song

The embodiment of the richly intertwined meaning of text and music that makes up Art Song in a living, breathing human performer carries with it a host of questions surrounding the conveyance of that meaning from both the audience's and the performers' perspectives. We have focused on the role of gesture in how performers enact the meaning of Art Song and how audiences receive it.

### 4.1 Do Audiences Lose Comprehension when Gesture is not Available as Ancillary Content?

The extensive literature on gesture/speech interaction indicates that humans express and process supplementary information through associative movements in the speakers across all cultures (Feyereisen and De Lannoy 1991; Goldin-Meadow 2005); action and language processes share a neural integration system with overlap in Broca's area (Goldin-Meadow 2005; Willems, Özyürek, and Hagoort 2007). It may be that diversities of expressive movement parameters in Art Song must be considered along two axes: 1) the traditions of the era and culture of the composer, and 2) current gestural styles of the country in which the song is being performed, acknowledging that in circumstances where language comprehension is challenged, meaning-making is further compromised when culturally normative interaction of gesture and speech are diminished or extracted.

For example, the German poem *Wanderer's Nachtlied* (Wanderer's Night-song; J. W. v. Goethe) is fused to the early 19$^{th}$ century music of Viennese composer F. Schubert to invoke a sound/state of profound interiority within deep physical quietude. The chordal piano sounds move in tandem with a melodic line that murmurs a hymn to nature at rest—a sonar extrusion of one's inmost philosophical contemplation. The singer's motionless stance would here be a congruency with which an audience could resonate. But how will the same audience then engage *Ne poj, krasavica, pri mne*—a poem by 19$^{th}$ century Russian poet A. Pushkin set by S. Rachmaninoff in 1902 with highly dramatic extremes of vocal range, declaiming great longing for one's lost homeland—if the same static physical stance is enacted? The two songs belong to different historical eras, cultures, languages, worldviews, speech patterns, communication styles, and speech-gesture characteristics. Thus, one would expect some degree of dissonance to arise from a uniformity of gestural spectrum.

The singer's visual focus is highly regulated in the discipline of Art Song. The intimacy of the warmly lit 19$^{th}$ century Salon in which the Art Song was originally performed is significantly altered in the present-day concert hall, as the singer incants words of deep personal revelation into the semi-darkness. Singers are often trained to gaze over the heads of the audience at a point on the back wall, ostensibly communicating with an imagined other, or as if in abstract self-reflection, to prevent uncomfortably intrusive eye contact with individual listeners. When this approach is enacted, the audience becomes a *collective immanence*—present, but indirectly connected to the performers. But humans attune to minute facial gesture in processing meaning; this is confounded when the performer withholds eye contact.

### 4.2 Do Singers Lose Expressive Capacities, Both Eidetic and Technical, when Movement is Decoupled from Speech?

Since gesture carries meaning that is coexpressive but not necessarily redundant to its synchronous speech (McNeil 2005), the obstruction of natural gestural impulse may interfere with an artist's ability to embody poetic intent and emotion, and may even interrupt the flow of creative thought and action (Goldin-Meadow 1998; Streeck 2009).

The trained vocal processes for operatic and Art Song singing involve essentially the same physical processes and mechanisms. However, the integration of movement and speech-action and the entrained neurophysical coordination developed for operatic performance are greatly altered in the recital genre. For singers trained in the expansiveness of operatic gesture, the suppression of expressive movement parameters may negatively influence the technical outcomes. Great vocal production requires temporal and spatial coordination of many internal motor subsystems: the head, face, vocal tract, larynx, and respiratory system. The coupling among subsystems is complex and may entail multiple associations. For example, head motion correlates with vocal pitch and loudness, which is tightly coupled to respiration (Yehia, Kuratate, and Vatikiotis-Bateson 2002). But, the head is also part of the spinal postural control system, which is also heavily influenced by respiration through the expansion and contraction of the chest cavity. Therefore anything that inhibits body and facial gesture is intricately linked to vocal and breathing issues. In young singers, especially, this can affect a host of performance outcomes, including tone control, articulation of diction, range of nuances, phrase length, speech flow, and expressive intensity.

Constraint of any of these elements individually can create technical and/or expressive deficits. In confluence, the systemic impact can lead to a compromised creative state, with reciprocal consequences for the audience. Students learning Art Song performance protocols often cite the 'incapacity to feel the emotional matrix'. It may be that, for many singers, physical disconnection from natural storytelling gesture challenges the ability to form an intrinsic emotional alignment, to describe lived and felt experience in real time. A major aim of our empirical efforts (described below) is to demonstrate that technical and musical puzzles are often resolved autonomically and spontaneously when embodied emotive capacities are re-entitled through simple connections to very basic theatrical contextualization.

# 5 The Collaboration between Performance and Science

## 5.1 The Effects of the Theatricalization of Art Song

The many inherent challenges of the recital stage are reconciled with sudden fluency by the introduction of theatrical frameworks. Beginning with the subtle introduction of staged movement to suggest a character and environment, approaches include two or more characters singing relationally, cabaret-style monologues or monodramas, staged singing, and full-scale, scripted narrative theatre with multiple characters, sets, props, and costumes. Theatricalization contextualizes the poetry within the stage dramatic environment—the commonplace of opera—while retaining the distinctive intensities of poetic singing. Through the narrative thread, each song text acquires a frame and motivation within the character's circumstances, greatly lessening the cognitive task of meaning-making.

As demonstrated in the classroom and professional experiments described below, Art Song Theatre formats help to remedy disconnections both within the singer and between the singer and audience. By inhabiting the character, the singer readily accesses a reservoir of gestural entitlements that might feel inappropriate to recital protocols. Natural movement and relationality appear to trigger spontaneous and instantaneous meaning-making, reciprocally demonstrating changes to the artists' performance capacities and listener receptivity. The shift of audience perception is evidenced through comments such as: *'Lieder Lovers Learn to Listen at Extraordinary Experience'* (Winnipeg Free Press, Sept. 25, 2005). Audience response form: 'Tonight's wonderful presentation opened the doors of comprehension. What a revelation'.

To explore the array of questions and to seek innovative solutions that preserve crucial integrities in Art Song and Art Song performance, a realm of experimental training, data capture, and creative production in Art Song Theatre was initiated at the University of British Columbia School of Music in the context of undergraduate and graduate courses in Song Interpretation commencing in 1993. Through exploratory work with students, a repeated phenomenon emerged demonstrating connections between natural expressive gesture, technical capacities, and theatrical context. In response to those early experiential experiments, a larger set of research and creative initiatives has followed, resulting in the establishment of the Vancouver International Song Institute (VISI), a nexus for groundbreaking experimentation in Song performance practice and creation, arts/humanities scholarship, performance cognition research, and the SONGFIRE Theatre Alliance, a creation/production initiative for professional theatre and student venues. Below we describe three pilot experiments situated within the performance and pedagogical spaces afforded by these developments.

### 5.1.1 Contextualizing Art Song Performance: Measured Responses

The aim of the first study was to examine the diverse outcomes of introducing a relational component to a singer's Art Song performance domain. High definition video recordings were made of trained student singers performing a song previously practiced for several weeks without instructor input or any information regarding the specific purpose of the recording. Students were asked to perform in two consecutive conditions, with instructions given only immediately prior to each version: first, to sing as if they were 'presenting a recital', and then to sing to an introduced actor in a relational mode. We compared segments of the performances under each condition for duration, vibrato rate and amplitude, pitch, breathing choices, volume fluctuations, and diction. Figure 1 demonstrates the spontaneous self-selected changes between recital mode and relational mode, indicating conscious and autonomic choices that overrode the rehearsed version (i.e., the version practiced repeatedly for reliable technical and expressive results). The complex cognitive decisions required to make such real time adjustments are systemic in impact. Most dramatically, the duration of the long note on the final word of the phrase examined ('song') is almost one full second longer in the relational mode than in the recital mode, requiring

Recital mode (no actor) | Relational mode (with actor)

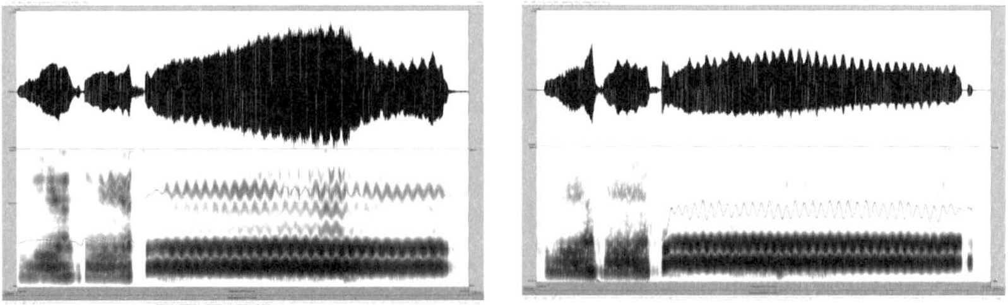

| Recital mode | Measure | Relational mode |
|---|---|---|
| 695 Hz | Mean frequency (pitch) during vibrato | 702 Hz |
| 754 Hz | Max frequency (pitch) of vibrato | 773 Hz |
| 643 Hz | Min frequency (pitch) of vibrato | 647 Hz |
| 5.1 seconds | Duration of 'song' | 6 seconds |

FIGURE 1. (Top) Spectrogram of the phrase 'was the song' as sung in recital mode (left) and relational mode (right). (Middle) Measures taken for each mode. (Bottom) Sample images of each performance mode.

prolongation on a high note with no new air intake. The singer has altered the traditional rules of practice with evident changes to musical choices and technical outcomes.

### 5.1.2 Contextualizing Art Song Performance: Felt Responses

More informally, an experimental performance scenario was presented at the Conceptual Structure, Discourse, and Language Conference in Vancouver, May 2012. A song setting of Elizabeth Barrett-Browning's '*How Do I Love Thee?*' by Vancouver composer David MacIntyre was performed for delegates by soprano Robyn Driedger-Klassen with pianist Rena Sharon in three modalities:

(1) Traditional: singer placed at the piano with minimal stage space parameters.

(2) Expanded traditional: movement and stage space parameters increased.

(3) Theatrical contextualization: a volunteer spontaneously drawn from the audience of delegates served as the relational character to whom the song was performed. The volunteer was instructed to respond to gestural and text cues, while the singer was instructed to imagine performing within the context of a musical theatre work.

The question posed to the audience was: Does your text comprehension and emotional connection vary in the different gestural versions?

The spontaneously offered feedback was consistent with audience-response surveys in other experimental performances, for both men and women:

> Traditional: vocally captivating, beautiful, and impressive acoustically; however, audience described feeling somewhat uninvolved.
>
> Expanded traditional: a sense of increased engagement from singer, with more direct connection to audience, generating stronger emotional impact.
>
> Theatrical contextualization: a large shift in emotional reception: 'ecstatic', 'thrilling', 'fascinating', 'fabulous'.

Comments included, 'I felt little during the first version of the song, but had goose bumps during the second and third versions'. A woman who described herself as an unemotional person said she couldn't understand how it was possible that she had actually wept during both the second and third versions of the song. Her colleague concurred that she had also wept and said, 'I mean, who weeps at an academic conference?' A frequently expressed perception was that in processing the changes from the traditional to the expanded traditional to the relational-theatrical, they didn't just observe the changes; they lived them.

A third investigation took place in the pedagogical space of UBC's School of Music. Student singers and pianists in a 2012 course in Song Interpretation were asked to create short theatrical scripts into which were embedded the texts of selected songs prelearned in traditional practice by their classmates at an earlier point in the course. Scripted monologue or inter-song dialogue was cocreated by participants to generate the motivation for the song texts. Following a short discussion to position the theatrical scenario, performers were asked to use the performance area as though it were a theatrical space set within that constructed story, and to behave as characters within a dramatic scenario. The script-writers directed their classmates to perform an impromptu staging of the songs *in situ*.

Each of the performers was first asked to sing the songs in recital mode —which they had done several times previously during the year—as a baseline for comparison with the theatricalized performance. No technical vocal instruction or musical suggestions were given to the student between the two performance versions (recital and staged). The staged version was performed immediately after a recital performance, with no opportunity for a separate rehearsal session. The student 'directors' provided only minimal instruction about storyline and placements on stage. The continual instantaneous shifts in *aesthetic* choice-making that occurred were engaged by the performers without instruction or guidance. From a pedagogical standpoint this was like handing the key to a turbo-charged race car to someone with no instruction about how to drive the vehicle, and watching them drive it at 150 mph without a learning curve—except in this case, instead of a monumental crash-and-burn, we observed a smooth, effortless transition to new levels of entirely self-sourced technical and expressive capacity, with immediately observable consequences. In numerous iterations, the outcomes generated similar comments from the students and their colleagues in the class, a sample of which is presented in Table 1.

The experiment—undertaken with some skepticism by the students—was later described as profoundly transformative. Comments referenced the impact of embodied characterization on their capacities to comprehend the poetry directly, and how that shift catalyzed spontaneous change to their performances at levels that were autonomically generated. The encompassing performative changes to songs that had been repeated in the nongestured modality over a course of months demonstrated how permission to allow character-driven gesture triggered by relational placement of the text generates immediate systemic overhauls of thought, emotional context, gesture, and musical parameters. Many singers and pianists reported that despite extensive discussion of the poetic meaning in prior interpretive work, the meaning of the texts remained elusive until they engaged the theatrically embodied performance. Students reported reconciling previous confusions about textual content through an immediate interior creative processing sparked by the narrative and the feedback from the dramatic characters.

TABLE 1. Sample comments of singers, audience, and pianist comparing recital mode to theatrical mode.

| **Singer** | **Audience** |
|---|---|
| I wasn't thinking about the singing. I was just thinking about what the character was thinking. Usually I just think about making it sound nice. | I know how she feels about this song, but I was shocked to hear how well she was singing, best I ever heard. |
| The less I think about singing and the more I think about what the words mean, the better I sing. | They were singing as though they were thinking about what they were saying without even noticing what they were choosing. |
| Since the poetry is so difficult, having someone to whom I'm singing made me much more comfortable. How do you share your entirety? | It suspends the audience's barriers. |
| It just helps to enter into the whole thing. | We all hear the phrasing so much more easily. |
| The poetry itself becomes more natural. When you have the context I felt the words and I was connected to saying it to someone I really cared about and would want to see again. The words themselves had so much meaning, they became so present and profound. | (pianist) I had rehearsed a bunch of directions before, but when she started her song I threw everything away. |

Student commentary from the class experiments identified a series of commonalities:

(1) profound, holistic interior comprehension and connection with text.

(2) surprise at the vocal ease that emerged organically with no conscious attention to technical craft.

(3) a shift of the performative attention from technical craft to meaning-making.

(4) intense engagement with deeper emotional layers of the text, linked to new recognition of the fusion with musical sound.

(5) changes to musical phrasing selected without conscious consideration, catalyzed by the impetus of story immersion and the gestural reaction cues from the other 'characters'.

While the students reported heightened levels of awareness during the performances, they had no ability to catalogue the emergent alterations in terms of quantifiable measures—durations of notes, dynamic variables such as pitch and loudness, phrasing, etc.—although as we saw above, there is no doubt that these changes occurred. They were also not able to explain the causes of enhanced technical ease in terms of body alignments; they all reported not being consciously aware of their range of movements.

One might propose that in the move from the recital mode to the theatrical mode, *attention* is supplanted by *intention*, and in the latter state choices are selected by a mind utilizing an array of integrated components—gesture, relational communication, and facial response processing, for example—within a dynamically creative and fluid synthesis. We suggest that these choices result from a complexity of neural network syntheses that may be different in nature from the recital modality. As well, the acute self-consciousness of a student's recital performance mode, in which the audience is often experienced as a judgmental 'other', is transmuted into a hyper awareness wherein self, other, and audience cohabit a charged environment.

## 5.2 Art Song is Multimodal and Multisensory

In order to characterize the factors that underlie the profound differences between musical expression in recital and in relational or theatrical modes, we have begun to examine the linkage between the audible and visible components of Art Song. We have tested both the signal correspondence between intentionally differentiated performance styles and their impressionistic effects on audiences, using *in situ* resources from UBC/VISI classes and performances as experimental environments, as well as more traditional and rigorously controlled experimentation conducted in collaboration with the UBC Communication Dynamics Laboratory.

Beginning in 2007, we set out to address several seemingly simple questions:

(1) To what extent is the audience's experience of Art Song affected by its audio-visual presentation? More particularly, does it matter

whether or not the audience can see the performers during an art song recital? Since both orchestral and operatic performance can be richly experienced within the auditory modality alone via an acoustic recording, we wanted to test the extent to which Art Song can be appreciated the same way.

(2) Are audiences sensitive to the specific combination of vocalization and body motion employed by a singer? Extensive experimentation previously with auditory-visual speech processing has shown that motions of the head and face are highly correlated with certain components of the acoustics of speech and with the motions of the primary vocal tract articulators, i.e., jaw, lips, and tongue (Munhall and Vatikiotis-Bateson 1998; Vatikiotis-Bateson and Munhall 2012; Yehia et al. 2002; Yehia, Rubin, and Vatikiotis-Bateson 1998). In short, the nature of the correspondence between audible and visible components in speech production is highly redundant, is predominantly integrated within the same neuromotor control structures (head and neck) as singing, and serves to make speech perception more robust under nonideal listening conditions (Sumby and Pollack 1954; Summerfield 1979). Exploiting multiple modalities also increases the bandwidth for concurrent linguistic and emotional expression (Cassell, Sullivan, Prevost, and Churchill 2000). Insofar as Art Song has at least one foot in linguistic communication, it therefore stands to reason that either suppressing or exaggerating orofacial and head motion should be detectable in the vocal acoustics.

Both of these questions were addressed in an online manner in the context of a master class during the first iteration of VISI in 2007. The VISI audience consisted of instructors and students who had no previous experience with these questions or the research methods for addressing them. Specifically, we explored the first question by asking a sequence of performance pairs (singer and pianist) to present their rehearsed pieces first in plain view and then behind an opaque screen. The audience was then asked whether or not being able to see the performers affected their experience of the song. For each performance pair the answer was 'yes', accompanied by a wide range of florid descriptions of the perceived difference. Some audience members found the acoustic-only performance 'muddy' and had more difficulty parsing the sung text. Others noted a perceived reduction in loudness during the acoustic-only performance. Both of these observations are characteristic of the large body of research on audiovisual speech showing that intelligibility, perceived loudness, etc., are enhanced in the multisensory audiovisual context (for review, see Munhall and Vatikiotis-Bateson 2004).

The second question, concerning the effect of the (in)congruence of auditory and visual behavior, was addressed by asking the same performance pairs to perform their songs in three ways: normally as would be expected by the audience and as they had rehearsed, with 'greater than usual' expressiveness, and with 'ridiculous expressiveness'. The two new styles of performance were performed both while visible to the audience and invisible. The results were revealing on two counts: First, when asked to increase their level of expressivity to a higher than normal level, singers were adamant that they had complied with the instruction, but shocked by the video record, which showed very little and only intermittent increases in hand, body, and/or head motion. Second, the audience was extremely accurate at describing what the singer was doing behind the screen in the ridiculous expressiveness condition. For example, 'the singer was twirling around while rapidly bending and straightening at the waist'. We interpret this second finding as strong evidence that how, and the extent to which, a singer moves during performance are readily perceptible to the audience. The former finding that singers overestimate the amount of motion they have introduced to their performance suggests that trained singers' calibrations of their own body movements differ widely from that of an observer.

## 5.3 The Role of Motion in Musical Expression

Concurrent with these experiments, we embarked on a series of more rigorous studies that were not specifically focused on Art Song, but whose results speak directly to the issues raised in this chapter. Of particular interest to us has been to quantify 1) the connection between visible motion and the sound produced by a singer across a range of output levels (loudness) and 2) the degree to which an audience physically coordinates with the performer.

### 5.3.1 Motion and Vocal Effort

Loudness, or *vocal effort,* is a dimension exploited in both speech and singing. In spoken communication, loudness is modulated automatically and rapidly in variable acoustic settings such as cocktail parties. The context effect, also known as the *Lombard Effect* (Lombard 1911), influences both the volume (amplitude) and the qualitative properties of the acoustics (Summers, Pisoni, Bernacki, Pedlow, and Stokes 1988), so it is no surprise to find visible correlates to these acoustic parameters in the motion of the head and face, respectively (Vatikiotis-Bateson, Barbosa, Chow, Tan, and Yehia 2007). Of course, loudness is also under volitional control. We vary our loudness intentionally to achieve specific communication goals. Such goals may be practical—for example, in getting someone's attention at a distance or when trying not to disturb others in a quiet environment; and they may be stylistic—for example, emphatic speech is always louder than casual conversation. Both manipulations of loudness—online adaptive and intentional—have analogs in music. For example, the reverberation characteristics and other effects of hall size, not to mention the degree of interference from background noise, force a singer to adjust the voice to achieve a desired output. That 'desired outcome' is also affected by style; some songs are more appropriately sung softly, while others need to be belted out.

The need for the singer to adapt her performance, whether voluntary or not, raises issues for Art Song as the performance venue has evolved from the relatively intimate parlor of the 19$^{th}$ century to the much larger recital hall of the 21$^{st}$ century. In one experiment with singers (Vatikiotis-Bateson et al. 2009), we recorded acoustic, motion (body, face and head), and postural signals as opera students at UBC sang and recited lyrics at different amplitudes. The experiment confirmed that motion amplitude (for all measured components) scales with acoustic amplitude.

### 5.3.2 Motion and Audience Response

We analyzed a recording of the 1985 Queen Live Aid concert, whose audience numbered 72,000, in order to begin exploring the relation between the behavior of a performer and the response of the audience. We extracted two-dimensional motion measures from relatively low-resolution video using *optical flow analysis* (Horn and Schunk 1981). Optical flow analysis provides a noninvasive means for recovering 2D motion measures from video image sequences. Briefly, Horn and Schunk's algorithm infers the direction and magnitude of motion at a pixel location in the image from the changes of intensity of that pixel and its neighbors. By computing optical flow within a region of interest, as depicted by the boxes in Figure 2, and summing the values into a single magnitude time series, we obtain a surprisingly sensitive measure of the motion for the singer or section of audience through time (for details of our implementation of optical flow analysis, see Barbosa, Yehia, and Vatikiotis-Bateson 2008).

FIGURE 2. Sample analysis frames for computing the coordination between singer and audience (above) and within the audience (below). The boxes indicate *regions of interest* (ROI). The total amount of motion within each box was calculated for the video sequence and then used to compute the time-varying coordination between audience and singer, and within the audience itself.

The final step in our analysis was to compute the time-varying correspondence between the movements of the singer (Freddie Mercury) and the audience, as well as between different sections of the audience itself using *correlation map analysis* (Barbosa, Déchaine, Vatikiotis-Bateson and Yehia 2012). Figure 3 provides a graphical depiction of the instant-by-instant correlation between two sections of audience over a 4 second stretch of performance (for details, see Barbosa, Munhall, Yehia, and Vatikiotis-Bateson 2009).

Traditionally, the correlation between two event streams, such as the previously discussed correlations between face, head motion, and speech acoustics, was computed as an average over the time-course of the event stream. Although convenient and informative, computing the global correlation is a static assessment of the relation between amplitudes at corresponding time values that ignores what we now know to be crucial effects of the temporal structure of the event on coordination. Correlation map analysis computes the time-varying instant-by-instant correlation between two signals not only for the time-locked pairs of values traditionally measured (the 1D trace in Figure 3), but for any pairing of values between the two signals, depicted in the two dimensional map shown at the bottom of Figure 3. This 2D examination of the relation between signals provides a much richer account of coordination between event streams that are coordinated, but not necessarily synchronized at a fixed temporal offset. In the sample illustrated in Figure 3, the 1D correlation shows that the two sections of audience are closely synchronized. However, the 2D correlation map shows that, despite the high degree of synchronization, there are still fluctuations in audience behavior that could be due to noise in the video or indicative of more subtle aspects of coordination among individuals.

Without access to the original high quality video, we cannot distinguish between these possibilities in the Queen data, but time series analyses of other musical performance data by us and others (e.g. Hennig et al. 2011) has shown that fluctuations in the timing of supposedly synchronized behavior are both ubiquitous and crucial to the perceived quality of the performance. Although musicians report that they attempt to follow the timing dictated by a musical score as closely as possible, the best musicians, especially in ensemble, demonstrate systematic deviations from the prescribed timing that contribute substantially to perceived artistry of the performance. Just as cardiologists have begun to recognize that a healthy heart is one that beats with a certain degree of complex fluctuations (Huikuri, Mäkikallio, and Perkiömäki 2003) and that too synchronous a beat pattern may spell trouble, musical performances that are too temporally precise may receive praise for their virtuosity, but tend to receive criticism for sounding stiff or 'wooden'.

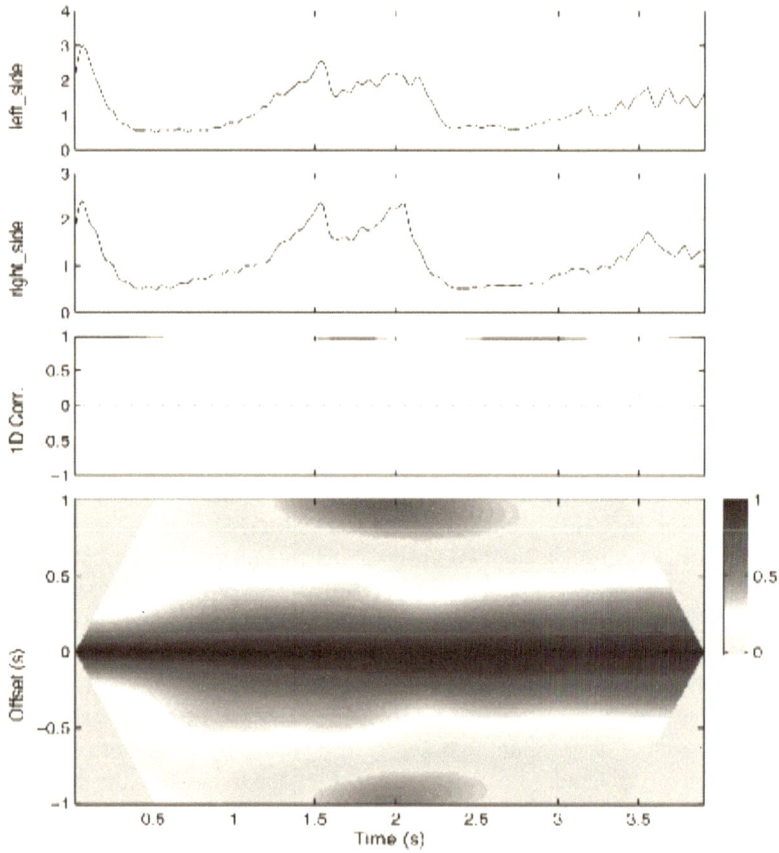


FIGURE 3. The time-varying correlation between two sections of audience for 4 seconds of performance. The top two time series show the total amount of motion for each section of audience as a function of time. The third time-series shows the almost perfect (r > .96) synchronous (1D) correlation between the two amplitude signals. The correlation map at the bottom shows the correlation as both a function of time (x axis) and temporal offset between the two signals (y-axis). The amount of the correlation is indicated by shading: darker ≈ higher correlation, lighter ≈ lower correlation (see gradient bar at right).

## 6 Conclusion

While performative experimentation with Art Song as a theatrical modality has been rich, generating an extensive roster of new produced works, to date our efforts to conduct rigourous studies of the performance phenomena have been hindered by problems of methodology and access. Nevertheless, as we have persistently pursued our goal of creating a dialogue between science and art, we have discovered that enormous strides can be made by letting the expert artist probe data recorded by the scientist using her own sophisticated conceptual vernacular. The challenge still remains of spanning the gulf between such different conceptual vocabularies, but the collaboration underlying this chapter has made it abundantly clear that for any examination of an art form as elaborate as Art Song to be fruitful, both the artistic and the scientific perspectives are essential.

As aesthetic schools have polarized into fronts of action, this project questions the essential elements of expressive authenticity that form Art Song's generative, ineffable essence. Does Art Song lose present-day relevance in rigorous adherence to conventions of another era, or does it lose essential elements if it strays too far from its origin? It is possible that a philosophical framework for recital protocols has formed around some emergent practices that have latterly acquired the mantle of doctrine. Accounts of 19th and early 20th century performances suggest that they accommodated more latitude and diversity than are currently in practice (Elliot 2007). Amidst current evidence regarding the ratio of visual/aural processing for modern audiences, a new paradigm that includes expansive natural movement and stage usage, multimedia content, and theatrical components of narrative and staging, may be key to sustaining the immense global Art Song archive in the 21st century. This new paradigm need not subvert the art form's aesthetic foundation; indeed, it must not. Rather, the added elements integrate and align untapped reservoirs of sensing, meaning-making, and expression. They afford the flexible balance of parameters needed to suit the diversity of emerging global audiences and insure that, whatever mode of performance is chosen, the essential touchstone of artistic practice remains constant: the expressive coalescence of self, community, and cosmos.

## Acknowledgments

Funding support was provided by the Social Science and Humanities Research Council (SSHRC), the Natural Sciences and Engineering Research Council (NSERC), the Canada Foundation for Innovation (CFI), and a UBC Faculty of Arts Undergraduate Research Award (AURA). Special thanks to Adriano Barbosa, Martin Oberg, and Murray Schellenberg for their unstinting support with the recording and analysis of the musical performances, and to Richard Kurth and many others in the UBC School of Music for facilitating our efforts. Support from colleagues through these institutions was also deeply appreciated: CBC/SRC, Festival Vancouver, UBC Department of Theatre & Film, The Peter Wall Institute for Advanced Studies, VISI, UBC Faculty of Arts and VP Research, and University of Manitoba.

Grateful thanks are extended to the large group of great performing/creative artists involved in the exploration and productions of Art Song Theatre at the UBC School of Music Song Circle, and the Vancouver International Song Institute (VISI), especially original pioneers Tyler Duncan, Karen Lee-Morlang, Phoebe MacRae, David Maggs, Professor Erika Switzer (Bard College), and Professor David Walsh (University of Minnesota). Special gratitude to Professor Gayle Shay and Vanderbilt University.

## References

Almén, D., and E. Pearsall. 2006. The Divining Rod—On Imagination, Interpretation, and Analysis. In Byron Almén and Edward Pearsall (eds), *Approaches to Meaning in Music*, 1–10. Bloomington: Indiana University Press.

Barbosa, A. V., R.-M. Dechaine, E. Vatikiotis-Bateson, and H. C. Yehia. 2012. Quantifying Time-Varying Coordination of Multimodal Speech Signals Using Correlation Map Analysis. *The Journal of the Acoustical Society of America* 131(3): 2162–72.

Barbosa, A. V., K. G. Munhall, H. C. Yehia, and E. Vatikiotis-Bateson. 2009, 19 May. *Quantifying the Time-Varying Coordination between Performer and Audience*. Paper presented at the 157th Meeting of the Acoustical Society of America, Portland, OR.

Barbosa, A. V., H. C. Yehia, and E. Vatikiotis-Bateson. 2008. Linguistically Valid Movement Behavior Measured Non-Invasively. In R. Goecke, P. Lucey and S. Lucey (eds), *Auditory and Visual Speech Processing (AVSP08)*, 173–7. Moreton Island, Australia: Causal Productions.

Cassell, J., J. Sullivan, S. Prevost, and E. Churchill, eds. 2000. *Embodied Conversational Agents*. Cambridge, MA: MIT Press.

Cross, I. 2005. Music and Meaning, Ambiguity and Evolution. In D. Mielle, A. R. MacDonald, and D. Hargreaves (eds), *Musical Communication*, 27–44. Oxford: Oxford University Press.

Cross, I. 2003. Music, Cognition, Culture and Evolution. In I. Peretz and R. J. Zatorre (eds), *The Cognitive Neuroscience of Music*, 42–56. Oxford: Oxford University Press.

Davis, W. 2001. *Light at the Edge of the World: A Journey through the Realm of Vanishing Cultures*. Vancouver: Douglas and MacIntyre Ltd.

Elliott, M. 2008. *Singing in Style: A Guide to Vocal Performance Practices*. New Haven: Yale University Press.

Ferris, D. 2000. *Schumann's Eichendorff Liederkreis and the Genre of the Romantic Cycle*. New York: Oxford University Press.

Feyereisen, P. and J.-D. de Lannoy. 1991. *Gestures and Speech: Psychological Investigations—Studies in Emotion and Social Interaction*. Cambridge: Cambridge University Press.

Goldin-Meadow, S. 2005. *Hearing Gesture: How Our Hands Help Us Think*. Boston: Belknap Press of Harvard University Press.

Hennig, H., R. Fleischmann, A. Fredebohm, Y. Hagmayer, J. Nagler, A. Witt, . . . and T. Geisel. 2011. The Nature and Perception of Fluctuations in Human Musical Rhythms. *PLoS ONE*, *6*(10), e26457. doi: 10.1371/journal.pone.0026457

Horn, B. K. P., and B. G. Schunk. 1981. Determining Optical Flow. *Artificial Intelligence* 17: 185–203.

Huikuri, H. V., T. H. Mäkikallio, and J. Perkiömäki. 2003. Measurement of Heart Rate Variability by Methods Based on Nonlinear Dynamics. *Journal of Electrocardiology* 36 (Suppl 1): 95–9.

Johnson, G. 2003. *Britten, Voice and Piano, Lectures on The Vocal Music of Benjamin Britten*. London: The Guildhall School of Music and Drama.

Lombard, E. 1911. Le signe de l'elevation de la voix. *Ann Maladie Oreille Larynx Nez Pharynx* 37: 101–19.

Malin, Y. 2010. *Songs in Motion: Rhythm and Meter in the German Lied*. Oxford; New York: Oxford University Press.

McNeill, D. 2005. *Gesture and Thought*. Chicago: University of Chicago Press.

Munhall, K. G., and E. Vatikiotis-Bateson. 1998. The Moving Face During Speech Communication. In R. Campbell, B. Dodd and D. Burnham (eds), *Hearing by Eye, Part 2: Advances in the Psychology of Speechreading and Auditory-Visual Speech*, 123–39. Sussex: Taylor and Francis—Psychology Press.

Munhall, K. G., and E. Vatikiotis-Bateson. 2004. Spatial and Temporal Constraints on Audiovisual Speech Perception. In G. Calvert, C. Spence, and B. Stein (eds), *The Handbook of Multisensory Processes*, 177–88. Cambridge, MA: MIT Press.

Russo, F. A., L. Chan, and D. Edwards. 2011, August. When Vocal Training Masks Structure: Individual Differences in Visual Aspects of Sung Interval Size. *Proceedings of the International Symposium for Performance Science*. Toronto.

Serinus, J. 2012. Mark Padmore, Transporting Through Song. San Francisco Classical Singer. Webjournal

Sharon, R. and E. Vatikiotis-Bateson. 2011. Breaking Traditions: Art Song Theatre Cognitive Shifts Through Staged Modalities. In A. Williamon, D. Edwards, and L. Bartel (eds), *Proceedings of the International Symposium on Performance Science 2011*, 493–494. Utrecht: Association Européenne des Conservatoires.

Streeck, J. 2009. *Gesturecraft: The Manu-facture of Meaning*. Amsterdam: John Benjamins Publishing.

Sumby, W. H., and I. Pollack. 1954. Visual Contribution to Speech Intelligibility in Noise. *Journal of the Acoustical Society of America* 26: 212–5.

Summerfield, Q. 1979. Use of Visual Information for Phonetic Perception. *Phonetics* 36: 314–31.

Summers, W. V., D. B. Pisoni, R. H. Bernacki, R. I. Pedlow, and M. A. Stokes. 1988. Effects of Noise on Speech Production: Acoustic and Perceptual Analyses. *Journal of the Acoustical Society of America* 84(3): 917–28.

Vatikiotis-Bateson, E., A. V. Barbosa, C. Y. Chow, J. Tan, and H. C. Yehia. 2007. Audiovisual Lombard Speech: Reconciling Production and Perception. In J. Vroomen, M. Swerts and E. Krahmer (eds), *International Conference on Auditory-Visual Speech Processing—AVSP 2007*, 45–50. The Netherlands: ISCA.

Vatikiotis-Bateson, E., and K. G. Munhall. 2012. Empirical Perceptual-Motor Linkage of Multimodal Speech. In G. Bailly, P. Perrier and E. Vatikiotis-Bateson (eds), *Advances in Auditory and Visual Speech Perception*, 346–67. Cambridge: University Press.

Vatikiotis-Bateson, E., M. Oberg, A. V. Barbosa, K. McAllister, N. Hermiston, and R. Kurth. 2009. Postural Entrainment by Vocal Effort in Singing and Speech. In T. E. Jukka Louhivuori, S. Saarikallio, T. Himberg, and P.-S. Eerola (eds), *Proceedings of the 7th Triennial Conference of European Society for the Cognitive Sciences of Music (ESCOM 2009)*, 604–9. Jyväskylä, Finland.

Willem, R.M., A. Özyürek, and P. Hagoort. 2007. When Language Meets Action: The Neural Integration of Gesture and Speech. *Cerebral Cortex* 17(10): 2322–33.

Yehia, H. C., T. Kuratate, and E. Vatikiotis-Bateson. 2002. Linking Facial Animation, Head Motion, and Speech Acoustics. *Journal of Phonetics* 30(3): 555–68.

Yehia, H. C., P. E. Rubin, and E. Vatikiotis-Bateson. 1998. Quantitative Association of Vocal-tract and Facial Behavior. *Speech Communication* 26: 23–44.

22

# Iconic Pitch Expresses Vertical Space

NATHANIEL CLARK, MARCUS PERLMAN, AND MARLENE JOHANSSON FALCK

## 1 Introduction

As bipedal primates, *Homo sapiens* experience the world from a distinctly vertical perspective as they move through and manipulate their environment. Within the first few years of development, human infants grow into mobile, upright toddlers. They learn to balance and walk on two legs, climb up and down, reach for objects high and low, and unfortunately, fall from time to time. Motivated by its prominent role in human experience and development, the conceptual schema of vertical space serves as the basis for making sense of a variety of more abstract concepts (Lakoff and Johnson 1980). Work in cognitive linguistics, for example, has identified a number of conceptual metaphors, so-called orientational metaphors, related to vertical space, including MORE IS UP, LESS IS DOWN; HAPPY IS UP, SAD IS DOWN; and GOOD IS UP, BAD IS DOWN. These metaphors manifest in much of the language we use (Lakoff and Johnson 1980; 1999), in our gestures (Casasanto 2008; Cienki 1998; Cienki and Müller 2008), as well as in non-communicative tasks (Meier and Robinson 2004).

For speakers of many languages, verticality also serves to structure how people talk about, conceptualize, and experience auditory pitch (Pratt 1930; Rusconi et al. 2005; Zbikowski 1998). In English, the use of vertical spatial terms is the standard (and practically sole) convention to talk about the pitch of sounds. Indeed, it is difficult to avoid tautology in describing this relationship: relatively 'high' fundamental frequencies are described with terms referring to high vertical space, and sounds with relatively 'low' fundamental frequencies are described with low terms. English speakers talk

*Language and the Creative Mind*.
Mike Borkent, Barbara Dancygier, and Jennifer Hinnell (eds).

about *high* and *low* musical tones and voices, moving *up* or *down* the scale in music, *rising* and *falling* pitches, and so on. While this mapping is not universal (other languages use *thin/thick* and *small/large*, for example), it is prevalent in most Western European languages, plus many other non-Indo-European languages (Ashley 2004; Shayan, Ozturk, and Sicoli 2011).

The basis for using vertical spatial terminology for pitch is argued to be motivated by embodied experience, specifically the different parts of the body that resonate during the production of high and low pitches (Pratt 1930; Shayan et al. 2011; Zbikowski 1998). As Zbikowski explains, 'When we make *low* sounds, our chest resonates; when we make *high* sounds, our chest no longer resonates in the same way, and the source of the sound seems located near our head.' Additionally, the position of the larynx further motivates this metaphorical association. The larynx is lowered in the production of lower frequencies and raised for higher frequencies, an action that is experienced proprioceptively by speakers and is sometimes visible in movements of the Adam's apple.

Experiments show that the use of spatial terms to talk about pitch is not just a verbal phenomenon, but reflects a deeper metaphorical conceptualization. A number of studies — couched variously in terms of cross-modal associations, synesthesia, and stimulus-response compatibility — demonstrate an interaction between the processing of pitch and spatial position (Eitan and Timmers 2010; Marks 1996). One pioneering study found that English speakers tend to localize high- and low-pitched sounds as emanating from high and low spatial positions, respectively (Pratt 1930). Participants listened to one of five tones varying by octave intervals that were played in random order by hidden speakers at five randomized vertical positions. Their task was to indicate the spatial position of the sound source on a numbered scale running from the floor to the ceiling. The study found that participants were highly consistent in locating higher pitched tones higher in the vertical array than lower pitched tones. As Pratt expresses, 'The results are clear-cut and unequivocal. *High tones are phenomenologically higher in space than low ones*' (1930: 283, italics in original). These results were later confirmed in a more rigorous replication by Trimble (1934), which found the same pattern with nine tones played from a fixed sound source. Roffler and Butler (1968) later expanded this paradigm by manipulating the listener's orientation and distance to the sound source. Additionally, the study found similar results with congenitally blind participants and 4 to 5-year-old children.

Despite the robust findings of these studies, they are subject to the methodological criticism that spatial processing is an explicit part of the task. Thus, people might not normally conflate the perception of pitch and vertical space, but are primed to do so because of the spatial nature of the task. More recently, Rusconi, Kwan, Giordano, Umiltà, and Butterworth (2005) addressed this confound, demonstrating what they called the Spatial-Musical Association of Response Codes effect (the 'SMARC' effect). For example, in one experiment, musically naïve participants performed a pitch comparison task, indicating whether a probe tone was higher or lower in pitch than a reference tone. Compatible responses—higher frequency tones indicated with a button press at the 'top' of the keyboard ('6') and lower tones with a button press at the 'bottom' of the keyboard ('spacebar')—were made significantly faster than incompatible responses with the buttons reversed. Further experiments found that the effect of stimulus-response compatibility was somewhat attenuated in an instrument identification task (wind or percussion) that did not attend explicitly to pitch, but the compatibility effect was generally strengthened by musical expertise.

Further experimental evidence comes from studies investigating cross-modal, synesthetic correspondences between the auditory dimension of pitch and the visual dimension of vertical position (Ben-Artzi and Marks 1995; Melara and O'Brien 1987; also see similar interactions in infants: Wagner, Winner, Cicchetti, and Gardner 1981). In one set of studies, for example, Melara and O'Brien presented participants with compound stimuli consisting of high- or low-pitched tones matched with high or low positioned dots. Participants made speeded classifications of the stimuli along one or the other of these dimensions, with the irrelevant dimension varied orthogonally in one version of the experiment, or held constant in another. The categorization of either dimension was slower when the irrelevant dimension was varied orthogonally, characteristic of Garner interference. Additionally, classification times exhibited Stroop interference, with faster classifications for congruent combinations of stimuli and slower times for incongruent combinations.

### *Vocal Iconic Gesture*

These various studies provide strong converging evidence that speakers of English and numerous other languages may use vertical space as a source domain to conceptualize auditory pitch. Furthermore, phenomena like the SMARC effect, Garner interference, and Stroop interference suggest that people might also incorporate pitch into their conceptualization of vertical space. These phenomena raise the intuitive possibility that people might sometimes modulate the pitch of their voice when talking about meanings related to high or low vertical space. Indeed, evidence for such spatially motivated modulations of vocal pitch can be readily found in popular music, such as in Garth Brook's hit country song *Friends in Low Places* (Perlman 2010). As Brooks sings the line from the chorus, 'I've got friends in low places,' he uses the pitch of his voice to convey a sense of low vertical space, singing the word 'low' at the bottom of his vocal range, a major sixth below the prior note. This vocal effect places an iconic emphasis on the sense of lowness he is expressing, which metaphorically extends to the target domain of social class. Perlman (2010) suggests that these kinds of iconic vocal effects are not restricted to performative contexts like popular music, but instead reflect the common process of conceptualizing different kinds of semantic domains in terms of movements of the vocal tract.

Gesture scholars tout the value of studying manual iconic gestures as a window into the conceptualizations that underlie spoken communication and thought (Cienki and Müller 2008; Kendon 2004; McNeill 1992, 2005), and recent research suggests that conceptualizations are also revealed in iconic modulations of the speech signal (Nygaard, Herold, and Namy 2009; Okrent 2002; Perlman 2010; Perlman, Clark, and Johansson Falck, [under review]; Shintel, Nusbaum, and Okrent 2006). These modulations bear important functional similarity to iconic gestures in the visual-kinesthetic modality. Like manual gestures, vocal iconic gestures manifest as spontaneously formed, conceptually motivated movements that tend to be co-expressive with co-occurring speech (Okrent 2002; Perlman 2010). For example, Perlman demonstrated that people spontaneously modulated their speech rate in iconic correspondence with spontaneous, open-ended descriptions of various fast or slow events presented in video clips. Participants tended to speak faster or slower as they described fast or slow events, and especially as they articulated adverbial phrases related to their speed.

Similar results were found in a more controlled study in which participants used prescribed sentences to describe the direction of motion of an animated dot on a computer screen (Shintel et al. 2006). In one experiment, participants described a dot as moving to the left or right, while it also traveled either quickly or slowly. The results showed that participants spoke the prescribed sentences with a longer duration for the slow moving dot compared to the fast one, even though the dot's speed was incidental to the explicit communicative task. A second experiment in this paradigm provided evidence that people also produce iconic gestures of pitch related to the expression of vertical space. Participants increased or decreased their fundamental frequency as they described the dot moving upward or downward, respectively.

Finally, in another study, participants were recorded as they read short vignettes with physical and metaphorical instantiations of meanings related to speed and size, such as someone racing down a highway or signing an enormous contract (Perlman et al. [under review]). Analysis revealed that participants spoke faster when describing fast physical motion, and used lower pitches when describing both physically and metaphorically large entities. These results not only provide further documentation of the iconic mapping between speech rate and pitch, but also indicate the metaphorical potential of these acoustic features.

## 2 The Current Study

The current study aimed to explore the possibility that people produce vocal gestures of pitch related to spatial vertical meanings. To assess this possibility, we used a similar methodology as in our earlier exploration of the speech rate-speed and pitch-size mappings (Perlman et al. [under review]). Participants read short stories that related to different meanings communicated by terms of verticality: actual vertical space, emotion, and auditory pitch. For each story, they read either a *high* version in one condition or a *low* version in the other condition. We predicted that participants would use a higher pitch when reading stories related to positive emotion, high vertical space, and high auditory pitch, and a lower pitch when reading stories related to negative emotion, low vertical space, and low auditory pitch.

These three target domains represent an array of different mapping types from conceptualizations of verticality to its realization in acoustic pitch. The mapping from emotion to pitch is a link that is generally well-established. Further, prosody is widely acknowledged to convey affective information (Bolinger 1986), and under some views this function of prosody is universal and possibly evolutionarily deep (Cosmides 1983). In reporting a sound, the specific mapping from the pitch of a reported sound to the pitch of the report of the sound is mimetic rather than metaphorical. In contrast, though, the mapping from vertical space to pitch is cross-modal, exploiting grounded elements of the source domain of pitch to express information about the target domain of vertical space.

Additionally, this study introduces a powerful new methodology for the analysis of vocal gestures. This method of Acoustic Contour Analysis, based on the analysis of mouse tracking trajectories, addresses a weakness of previous studies that have examined iconicity in speech prosody. Previous studies have generally focused on the averages of prosodic variables over intervals of speech such as a word, phrase, or entire sentence (e.g., Nygaard et al. 2009; Perlman 2010; Shintel et al. 2006). Consequently, these analyses lose information of the temporal dimension of speech and thus the contour of the acoustic variable. For example, two phrases may have very different pitch contours (starting low and rising vs. starting high and falling), but very similar averages across the contour.

# 3 Methods

## 3.1 Participants

Thirty-four undergraduate participants from the University of California, Santa Cruz received course credit in exchange for their time. All participants were self-reported native speakers of English. Two participants' data were excluded due to excessive disfluencies, leaving a total of 32 participants (20 women) in the analysis.

## 3.2 Materials

Four pairs of short target stories were created, which included two stories related to vertical motion, one story related to emotion, and one story related to a reported sound. (Full texts of the stories appear in the Appendix.) Each story pair contained a high version with terms referring to high spatial position, and a low version with terms referring to low spatial position. Other than this semantic contrast in high or low terminology, the paired stories were identical. The stories followed a general format of containing a short introduction, a plot, and a conclusion, with each section presented slide-by-slide in a PowerPoint presentation. In addition, five filler stories were created, which were similar in structure, but did not focus on vertical space in any way.

The stories were combined together into four counterbalanced lists of four target stories interspersed among the five fillers. The valences of verticality were counterbalanced across the pitch and emotion stories. Participants who read a story about a dog with a high-pitched bark also read a story about a person feeling emotionally low, while those who read about a dog with a low-pitched bark also read about a person feeling emotionally high. The two physical motion stories were also counterbalanced, so that participants who read a story about riding an elevator to the top floor of a building also read a story about bending down for an object on the bottom shelf, and those who read about riding an elevator down to the basement also read about reaching up for an object on the top shelf. The order of story presentation was also counterbalanced across participants.

## 3.3 Procedure

Participants read one of the four lists of stories from a PowerPoint presentations displayed on a laptop computer. In order to make the task more communicative and meaningful, participants were assigned to read the stories to an undergraduate confederate, who played the role of a listener who would afterwards have to answer questions about the stories. Participants were instructed to read clearly and 'be an interesting storyteller' so that their partner would be able to understand and remember what was read to them. The participant first read through each story once silently to ensure familiarity with it, and then read it aloud to the confederate. The readings were recorded at 44.2 kHz using a digital audio recorder with a flat boundary microphone sitting unobtrusively next to the computer. Finally, after reading all nine stories, participants filled out an exit questionnaire. In total, a typical session lasted 15-20 minutes.

### 3.3.1 Analysis of Contrasting and Shared Phrases

The digital recordings were analyzed in Praat (Boersma 2001). For each story, the boundaries of contrasting (the high or low terms contrasted within the story pairs) and shared phrases (the identical portions within the story pairs) were marked in a Praat TextGrid. Disfluencies, such as false starts and repetitions, were marked and later excised from the analysis. The recorded readings and associated TextGrid annotations were fed into a Praat script that computed pitches of each marked interval. Due to the difficulties of accurately measuring F0, each participant's recording was analyzed twice using the autocorrelation pitch tracking algorithm in Praat. The first pass was run with default settings on the raw recordings from each participant. This provided a baseline pitch for each participant, based on their average pitch across the whole task, which was used in the second pass of the pitch tracker to refine the settings for more accurate tracking.

For the second pass, several adjustments were made to the recording and to the default settings of Praat's pitch tracking algorithm. First, each participant's recording was low-pass filtered, with the upper bound of the pass band set at eight semitones (2/3 octave) above the speaker's average pitch across the whole recording. This filter guarantees an absence of doubling for the upper octave of the speakers' constrained vocal range, starting at four semitones below their baseline pitch. The filter also removes formants, reducing the potential influence of supralaryngeal articulation on tracked F0. Further, to ignore amodal (breathy, creaky) voicing and reduce pitch halving, the Silence Threshold of Praat's pitch tracking algorithm was set to 0.075 (from a default of 0.03) and the floor of the pitch tracker window was set to eight semitones below the speaker's previously determined baseline (Boersma 1993).

Pitches for the contrasting intervals of each story were computed as the duration-weighted average pitch of all contrasting phrases; pitch for the shared elements was a duration-weighted average of the pitches of the remaining, shared intervals. In addition, the two stories about physical space both contained the phrase 'all the way,' which allowed for a within-speaker

Acoustic Contour Analysis of phonologically identical material across opposite semantic contexts.

### 3.3.2 Acoustic Contour Analysis of 'all the way'

The phrase 'all the way,' which occurred in both physical space stories, is ideal for a within-speaker Acoustic Contour Analysis because it is composed entirely of voiced continuants, which means that there is an F0 signal throughout the phrase. This phrase thus afforded a second, finer-grained analysis. Here, rather than simply comparing the average pitch across participants' two productions of this identical phrase, we compared the trajectories of speakers' pitches over time. This approach has the advantage of being able to detect differences in the shape of a pitch contour that do not necessarily change its average pitch, as illustrated in Figure 1.

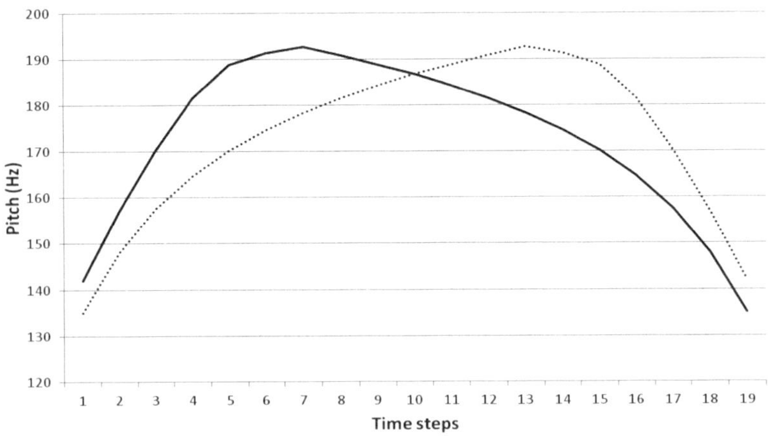


FIGURE 1. Contrasting pitch contours with same mean.

The analysis used a Praat script to slice each phrase into twenty intervals and computed the average pitch in each ventile. Then, within-speaker comparisons were conducted for each of the twenty time steps. Following the mouse tracking paradigm established by Dale, Kehoe, and Spivey (2007), we then conducted a bootstrap simulation to assess the significance of the largest region of consecutive significant differences. If our contours show a region of consecutive significant differences larger than could be expected by chance, we can conclude that the difference is due to the semantic context in which the identical phonological material was uttered.

# 4 Results

An overview of our results is presented in Table 1. To reduce the influence of individual differences in the emotion and reported sound stories (for which the 'up' vs. 'down' contrast was between speakers), participants' pitch measurements were normalized using their average pitch in the filler stories as a baseline.

TABLE 1. Descriptive statistics of pitch (Hz) produced in stories

| | | Shared Phrases | | Contrasting Phrases | |
|---|---|---|---|---|---|
| | | Up | Down | Up | Down |
| Emotion | *M* | 178.3 | 178.2 | 160.1 | 161.0 |
| | *s* | 7.1 | 5.4 | 8.2 | 8.0 |
| Reported Sound | *M* | 173.0 | 171.0 | 160.3 | 156.9 |
| | *s* | 5.7 | 6.8 | 6.6 | 7.9 |
| Physical Space | *M* | 176.4 | 171.6 | 166.7 | 160.7 |
| | *s* | 5.5 | 5.3 | 6.5 | 5.4 |

Note: For emotion and pitch stories, the 'up' vs. 'down' contrast is between-speakers; for physical space stories, the contrast is within-speakers. All statistics are corrected for intra-speaker differences in baseline pitch.

## 4.1 Contrasting and Shared Phrases

For the emotion stories, a mixed two-way ANOVA was conducted on participants' pitch measurements, with contrastiveness ('contrasting' vs. 'shared' phrases) as a within-speaker variable, and semantic valence ('up' vs. 'down') as a between-speaker variable. This analysis revealed only a main effect for contrastiveness, and no main or interaction effect involving semantic valence.

For the reported sound stories, the same two-way ANOVA was conducted on participants' pitch measurements, with contrastiveness ('contrasting' vs. 'shared' phrases) as a within-speaker variable, and semantic valence ('up' vs. 'down') as a between-speaker variable. This analysis revealed also only a main effect for contrastiveness, and no main or interaction effect involving semantic valence.

For the physical space stories, a two-way within-speaker ANOVA targeted participants' pitch measurements with contrastiveness ('contrasting' vs. 'shared' phrases) and semantic valence ('up' vs. 'down' stories). This analysis revealed that the overall model captured a significant portion of the variance in average pitch scores. There were significant main effects for both contrastiveness and semantic valence ($F(1, 30) = 11.43, p = .002$), but the interaction between the two did not reach significance. For the main effect of semantic valence, phrases in stories in the 'up' condition were spoken at a higher pitch ($M$ = 171.5 Hz, $s$ = 4.6 Hz) than those in the 'down' condition ($M$ = 166.2 Hz, $s$ = 5.3 Hz).

## 4. 2 Pitch Contour of 'all the way' in Physical Space Stories

In the analysis of the phrase 'all the way' as produced in the context of 'up' or 'down' stories, a paired $t$-test of the two average pitch across the two conditions revealed a marginal difference, $t(31) = 1.97, p = .058$, with productions in the 'up' condition ($M$ = 186.1 Hz) averaging about 6.6 Hz higher pitch than those in the 'down' condition ($M$ = 179.5 Hz). However, as previously noted, comparing averages across the whole phrase does not take into account the shape of the contours resulting in these averages (recall Figure 1). We also examined the pitch contour of the phrase, and found that, from the $11^{th}$ through the $15^{th}$ ventiles of the duration of this phrase (a region corresponding to the third quartile of the phrase), the average pitch of the phrase when produced in the 'up' condition was significantly higher than the 'down' condition (All $t > 2.25$, all $p < .033$). See Figure 2 for an illustration of this region.

Next, in order to assess the statistical significance of a region of difference totaling 25% of the duration of the phrase, we conducted a bootstrap simulation based on the observed contour data. In each iteration of the simulation, we created a simulated dataset by randomly sampling (with replacement) 32 pairs of productions of the phrase. Then, for each phrase, we randomly reassigned one of the productions to the 'up' condition and the other to the 'down' condition. We then counted the number of consecutive significantly different timesteps in the resampled dataset. For each iteration, this count of consecutive significantly different steps was entered into our Monte Carlo distribution. We ran a simulation of 10,000 iterations, and found that the $95^{th}$ percentile (corresponding to $\alpha = .05$) of the Monte Carlo distribution was 2 consecutive significant differences, the $99^{th}$ percentile (corresponding to $\alpha = .01$) of the distribution was 4 consecutive significant differences, and the $99.9^{th}$ percentile (corresponding to $\alpha = .001$) was 7 consecutive significant differences. Thus, we can conclude that our five-ventile region of difference is significant at $\alpha = .01$. As shown in Figure 2, in both conditions, the shape of the contour was generally a downward-facing parabola, with its highest point in the $3^{rd}$ quartile of the phrase. This analysis revealed that region around the peak pitch, from the $11^{th}$ through the $15^{th}$ ventiles of the phrase's duration, was spoken at a significantly higher pitch in the 'up' condition.

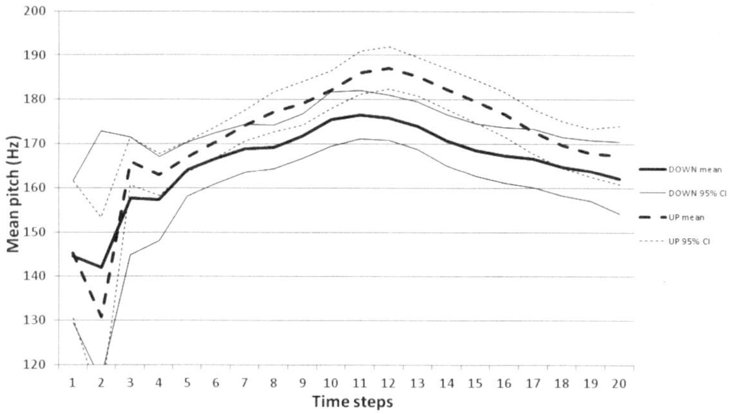


FIGURE 2. Pitch contours of 'all the way' in UP VS. DOWN.

## 5 Discussion

Previous research has documented the close conceptual relationship between vertical space and auditory pitch, particularly in Western, English-speaking cultures. Yet little is known about the intuitive possibility that people use pitch, embodied through movements and tensions of the vocal tract, to understand vertical space. Based on previous work on vocal iconic gesture and related phenomena, we examined this idea by testing whether speakers produced pitch-related vocal gestures as they read aloud stories related to high and low vertical space, high and low emotion, and high and low pitch. Our prediction was that readers would produce higher pitches when reading 'high' events and lower pitches when reading 'low' events.

The main analysis investigated whether there was a difference in average pitch between the up and down versions of stories, and also whether differences in pitch might be more localized to directly contrastive portions of the story compared to the identical, noncontrastive portions. Interestingly, we did not find evidence that people made iconic modulations of pitch when reading the stories related to high and low emotion or to the high or low pitch of a dog's bark, despite the less abstract pitch-meaning mapping of these stories. In these cases, the iconic use of pitch to express positive and negative emotions is acknowledged to be a basic function of prosody (Bolinger 1986), and the use of pitch to convey the high or low pitch of a sound involves a directly imitative mapping. We caution, however, that these exploratory null results are based on the average pitches across just a couple idiosyncratic stories, and do not license generalization. Future research must use a broader range of stimuli to further examine the role of pitch in conceptualizing these and other polysemous senses of vertical terms, and how these meanings are expressed through vocal gesture.

In contrast, we did find a significant main effect for semantic valence in the two stories about high and low vertical space. In these stories, there was no interaction between semantic valence and contrastiveness, suggesting that the pitch difference was not just localized to contrastive sections, but more spread out across the story. These results support previous research on the close conceptual connection between pitch and vertical space, and specifically demonstrate how pitch modulations manifest as conceptually motivated vocal gestures, produced as people talk about vertical space.

While the main analysis compared average pitches across relatively large segments of speech, it is elucidating to examine pitch with a more fine-grained temporal resolution. Towards this goal, we examined the pitch contours of the phrase 'all the way', which appeared in both semantic conditions of the two vertical motion stories. Our novel Acoustic Contour Analysis, derived from mouse tracking studies, compared the pitch contours of speakers' productions of the identical phonological content across the high and low conditions. Over both conditions, the shapes of the pitch contours were generally similar. However, as can be seen in Figure 2, around the peak pitch of the phrase, the pitch contour in the high condition separates upward from the pitch of the low condition. Statistical analysis confirms that the region around the peak pitch, from the $11^{th}$ through the $15^{th}$ ventiles of the phrase's duration, was spoken at a significantly higher pitch in the 'up' condition.

In addition to the theoretical value of demonstrating a vocal iconic gesture in which conceptualized vertical space is expressed through acoustic pitch, we stress the value of this Acoustic Contour Analysis as a method for comparing the shapes of pitch contours, and thereby examining co-speech iconic gestures in the vocal modality. Through this analysis, we were able to describe a pattern of speech production that would not otherwise have been detected by pitch averages measured over whole phrases. Since language production unfolds through time, it is crucial to investigate pitch as a dynamic variable, rising and falling over the time course of an utterance. This treatment of pitch as a dynamic analog signal underscores the similarity between iconic gestures produced by the vocal tract, and their more well-studied counterparts produced by other, more visible bodily effectors. Acoustic Contour Analysis affords empirical investigation of vocal gestures on the same time scale as the preparations, strokes, and holds of manual gestures. This possibility presents a marked contrast to Hockett's (1978: 274) claim that human language is characterized by an arbitrary relationship between forms and meanings, because iconicity is squeezed out when the four dimensions of reality are reduced into the single dimension language. As our figures make clear, pitch (as well as other acoustic variables like intensity) can be rendered visible in two dimensions, serving as proxies for the obscured movements of the vocal tract over time. Thus, spoken language is not in fact unidimensional, but rather affords substantial iconicity in the dynamics of its many acoustic variables changing over time.

There are, of course, differences between vocal iconic gestures and manual iconic gestures. Whereas manual iconic gestures communicate through the visual modality, independent of the speech channel, vocal iconic gestures are typically superimposed on, and thus constrained by, the articulatory business of producing speech. As a consequence, they can be challenging to identify and study, similar to the challenge posed by the co-sign gestures that are produced by users of signed languages (Duncan 2003; Okrent 2002). Our Acoustic Contour Analysis overcomes this challenge by focusing on phonologically identical phrases in different semantic contexts. When the conventional, linguistic content is identical, but analog, non-conventionalized aspects of the signal differ in ways that are predictable from the semantic context, one can conclude that such differences result from vocal iconic gestures.

Previously, researchers interested in vocal iconic gestures have stressed a modality independent notion of iconic gesture to account for their production across the manual/visual and vocal/auditory modalities (Okrent 2002). As McNeill (1992) observes, vocal and bodily iconic gestures and language (both spoken and signed) seem to behave as deeply interlinked parts of the human conceptualization and communication system. However, the affordances of each modality, and the constraints imposed by the need to coordinate linguistic communication, mold characteristic styles of gesture in each modality. For example, the pitch gestures studied here are based on highly schematic correspondences between pitch and verticality, rather than depicting a more detailed image of the scene as with some manual gestures. On the other hand, vocal iconicity is highly suitable to more detailed depictions of auditory images, such as during the quotation of sounds (Blackwell, Perlman, and Fox Tree [under review]), which is difficult to accomplish through manual gesture. But while the pitch-verticality mapping may be abstract and schematic, it is also robust enough to generate the vocal gestures we document, underscoring the prominent role both domains play in everyday human experience.

## 6 Conclusion

Historically speaking, vocal iconicity has typically been viewed as a marginal aspect of language. The received view of Saussurian arbitrariness between form and meaning, though, has been eroding for some time. For example, Perniss, Thompson, and Vigliocco (2010) have recently argued that motivated sound-meaning relationships are in fact a common feature of language, both spoken and signed. In spoken languages, evidence for this claim includes phonological phenomena like sound symbolism and phonaesthemes, as well as lexical phenomena like onomatopoeia. Additionally, the present work contributes to a growing body of research that focuses on iconic uses of prosody, demonstrating various ways that prosody can express semantic meaning in an utterance (Nygaard et al. 2009; Perlman 2010; Perlman et al. [under review]; Shintel et al. 2006; Shintel and Nusbaum 2007; 2008). This avenue of research is well-suited to the language of gesture studies, and specifically addresses the question of how vocal iconic gestures may be superposed on the articulation of speech.

The present study advances research on vocal iconic gesture in two ways. First, our results expand upon previous findings (Nygaard et al. 2009; Shintel et al. 2006), demonstrating that contrasts of 'up' vs. 'down' are encoded in speakers' prosody. These results contribute more broadly to a large body of work showing the tight conceptual relationship between vertical space and pitch. Second, our Acoustic Contour Analysis methodology offers researchers a powerful new analytical tool to study the temporal unfolding of vocal gestures. This method affords two-dimensional visualization and comparison of any prosodic variable, making vocal gestures substantially more amenable to the fine-grained description and temporal analysis that has been so productive for studies of manual gesture.

## Acknowledgments

The study was initiated while the third author, Marlene Johansson Falck, was a postdoctoral fellow in the Department of Psychology, University of California, Santa Cruz, and funded by the Swedish Research Council. Her contribution to writing this manuscript was funded by the Royal Swedish Academy of Letters, History and Antiquities, supported by a grant from the Knut and Alice Wallenberg Foundation (KAW 2009.0295).

# 7 Appendix

## 7.1 Physical Space Stories

Climbing Up High

Melinda is at the store. She is staring up at a box on the very highest shelf. It is high up, and she must climb to get it. Melinda climbs all the way up to the top. She gets the box.

Bending Down Low

Melinda is at the store. She is staring down at a box on the very lowest shelf. It is low down, and she must squat to get it. Melinda bends all the way down to the floor. She gets the box.

Going Up a Skyscraper

Chris is in an elevator with a view. It is going up a skyscraper. He watches out the window as he rises up and up, all the way to the top of the building. He reaches the end of the ride.

Going Down a Skyscraper

Chris is in an elevator with a view. It is going down a skyscraper. He watches out the window as he descends down and down, all the way to the bottom of the building. He reaches the end of the ride.

## 7.2 Emotion Stories

High on Life

Janet is walking to class. She is in high spirits. She looks at the trees surrounding her. They are uplifting. She feels like she is rising into the sky. Janet is high on life. She reaches school.

Low on Life

Janet is walking to class. She is in low spirits. She looks at the trees surrounding her. They are depressing. She feels like she is sinking into the ground. Janet is low on life. She reaches school.

## 7.3 Reported Sound Stories

A Deep Bark

Max is a dog with a low-pitched bark. He just spotted the mailman out the window. He runs to the door and barks his deep bark. Ruff! The mailman is not frightened.

A High Bark

Max is a dog with a high-pitched bark. He just spotted the mailman out the window. He runs to the door and barks his high bark. Ruff! The mailman is not frightened.

## References

Ashley, R. 2004. Musical Pitch Space across Modalities: Spatial and Other Mappings through Language and Culture. In S. D. Lipscomb, R. Ashley, R. O. Gjerdingen, and P. Webster (eds), *Proceedings of the 8th International Conference on Music Perception and Cognition*, 64–71. Adelaide: Causal Productions.

Blackwell, N., M. Perlman, and J. Fox Tree. [Under Review]. Quotation as a Multimodal Construction.

Bolinger, D. 1986. *Intonation and its Parts*. Stanford, CA: Stanford University Press.

Ben-Artzi, E. and L. Marks. 1995. Visual-Auditory Interaction in Speeded Classification: Role of Stimulus Difference. *Perception and Psychophysics* 57: 1151–1162.

Boersma, P. 1993. Accurate analysis of the fundamental frequency and the harmonics-to-noise ratio of a sampled sound. *Institute for Phonetic Science, University of Amsterdam, Proceedings* 17: 97–110.

Boersma, P. 2001. Praat, a system for doing phonetics by computer. *Glot International* 5: 341–345.

Casasanto, D. 2008. Conceptual Affiliates of Metaphorical Gestures. In *Proceedings of the International Conference on Language, Communication, and Cognition*. Brighton, UK.

Cienki, A. 1998. Metaphoric gestures and some of their relations to verbal metaphoric expressions. *Discourse and Cognition: Bridging the Gap,* ed. Jean-Pierre Koenig, 189–204. Stanford, CA: Center for the Study of Language and Information.

Cienki, A. and C. Müller. 2008. Metaphor, Gesture, and Thought. *Cambridge Handbook of Metaphor and Thought*, ed. R. Gibbs, 483–501. Cambridge: Cambridge University Press.

Cosmides, L. 1983. Invariances in the acoustic expression of emotion during speech. *Journal of Experimental Psychology: Human Perception and Performance* 9: 864–881.

Dale, R., C. Kehoe, and M. Spivey. 2007. Graded Motor Responses in the Time Course of Categorizing Atypical Exemplars. *Memory and Cognition* 35: 15–28.

Duncan, S. 2003. Gesture in Language: Issues for Sign Language Research. *Perspectives on Classifier Constructions in Signed Languages*, ed. K. Emmory, 259–268. Mahwah, NJ: Lawrence Erlbaum Associates.

Eitan, Z. and R. Timmers. 2010. Beethoven's Last Piano Sonata and Those Who Follow Crocodiles: Cross-domain Mappings of Auditory Pitch in a Musical Context. *Cognition* 114: 405–422.

Grady, J. 1997. *Foundations of Meaning: Primary Metaphors and Primary Scenes*. Ph.D. dissertation, University of California, Berkeley.

Hockett, C. 1978. In Search of Jove's Brow. *American Speech: A Quarterly of Linguistic Usage* 53(4): 243–313.

Kendon, A. 2004. *Gesture: Visible Action as Utterance*. Cambridge: Cambridge University Press.

Lakoff, G. and M. Johnson. 1980. *Metaphors We Live By*. Chicago: University of Chicago Press.

Lakoff, G. and M. Johnson. 1999. Philosophy in the Flesh: The Embodied Mind and its Challenge to Western Thought. New York: Basic Books

Marks, L. 1996. On Perceptual Metaphors. *Metaphor and Symbolic Activity* 11: 39–66.

McNeill, D. 1992. *Hand and Mind: What Gestures Reveal about Thought*. Chicago: Chicago University Press.

McNeill, D. 2005. *Gesture and Thought*. Chicago: Chicago University Press.

Meier, B. and M. Robinson. 2004. Why the Sunny Side is Up: Associations between Affect and Vertical Position. *Psychological Science* 15: 243–247.

Melara, R. and T. O'Brien. 1987. Interaction between Synaesthetically Corresponding Dimensions. *Journal of Experimental Psychology: General* 116: 323–336.

Nygaard, L., D. Herold, and L. Namy. 2009. The Semantics of Prosody: Acoustic and Perceptual Correlates to Word Meaning. *Cognitive Science* 33: 127–146.

Okrent, A. 2002. A modality-free notion of gesture and how it can help us with the morpheme vs. gesture question in sign linguistics, or at least give us some criteria to work with. *Modality and Structure in Signed and Spoken Languages*, ed. R. Meier, D. Quinto, and K. Cormier, 175–198. Cambridge: Cambridge University Press.

Perlman, M. 2010. Talking Fast: The Use of Speech Rate as Iconic Gesture. In F. Perrill, V. Tobin, and M. Turner (eds), *Meaning, Form, and Body*, 245–262. Stanford, CA: CSLI Publications.

Perlman, M., N. Clark, and M. Johansson Falck. [under review]. Conceptually motivated prosody in story reading.

Perniss, P., R. Thompson, and G. Vigliocco. 2010. Iconicity as a General Property of Language: Evidence from Spoken and Signed Languages. *Frontiers in Psychology* 1: 1–14.

Pratt, C. 1930. The Spatial Character of High and Low Tones. Journal of Experimental Psychology, 13, 278–285.

Roffler, S. and R. Butler. 1968. Localization of Tonal Stimuli in the Vertical Plane. *The Journal of the Acoustical Society of America* 43: 1260–1266.

Rusconi, E., B. Kwan., B. Giordano, C. Umiltá, and B. Butterworth. Spatial Representation of Pitch Height: The SMARC Effect. *Cognition* 1: 1–17.

Shayan, S., O. Ozturk, and M. Sicoli. 2011. The Thickness of Pitch: Crossmodal Metaphors in Farsi, Turkish, and Zapotec. *Senses and Society* 10: 96–105.

Shintel, H., H. Nusbaum, and A. Okrent. 2006. Analog Acoustic Expression in Speech Communication. *Journal of Memory and Language, 5,* 167–177.

Shintel, H. and H. Nusbaum. 2007. The Sound of Motion in Spoken Language: Visual Information Conveyed by Acoustic Properties of Speech. *Cognition* 105: 681–690.

Shinttel, H. and H. Nusbaum. 2008. Moving to the Speed of Sound: Context Modulation of the Effect of Acoustic Properties of Speech. *Cognitive Science* 32: 1063–1074.

Trimble, O. 1934. Localization of Sound in the Anterior, Posterior, and Vertical Dimensions of Auditory Space. *British Journal of Psychology* 24: 320–334.

Wagner, Y., E. Winner, D. Cicchetti, and H. Gardner. 1981. 'Metaphorical' Mapping in Human Infants. *Child Development* 52: 728–731.

Zbikowski, L. 1998. Metaphor and Music Theory: Reflections from Cognitive Science. *Music Theory Online* 4.

# 23

# Convergence in Music and Language Syntactic Representations

CHRISTINA GALEANO

## 1 Introduction

Music and language bear a number of commonalities. They are both endeavors that are unique to humans, have expressive power (though the content of musical and linguistic expressions are arguably very different), and convey emotion. Furthermore, there are acoustic and prosodic processing commonalities between spoken language and music, such as segmentation processes that appear to operate both on speech on nonspeech input (Creel et al. 2004).

The list of commonalities between music and language goes on and on, but one very important link between the two is the fact that both systems employ discrete units that are combined to form (both musical and linguistic) phrase structures. Notes/chords are the discrete units that are used for music, and phonemes and lexemes are the units that are combined to make phrases in language (Patel 2003: 674). The result is that music and language each have a syntax that ensures 'grammaticality' of any unit groupings. As Patel notes:

> the existence of two distinct syntactic systems raises the question of whether the processing of (harmonic) relations has anything in common with the syntactic processing of language. This question addresses the much-debated issue of modularity in language processing: whether or not the neural operations underlying syntactic processing in language are unique to that domain.
>
> (Patel 2003: 675)

*Language and the Creative Mind.*
Mike Borkent, Barbara Dancygier, and Jennifer Hinnell (eds).

Patel (2007) has spearheaded and summarized much of the literature detailing various neural mechanisms that are shared in music- and language-related syntactic processing tasks. Given that music and language both have a syntax, his question on the domain-specificity of the neural operations underlying syntactic processing is intriguing. However, I wish to address certain starting assumptions before attempting to tackle domain-specificity of syntactic processors, specifically, starting assumptions for where the locus of syntactic processing is. What is actually being processed when we process syntactic structure? If music and language both have syntactic structure, the starting assumptions for where the locus of syntax is in general will greatly influence what is interpreted as being shared and processed, and what kinds of formalisms are developed for both music and language syntax.

Given that mental representations are pivotal to comprehension of any syntactic structure in music and language, I argue that a crucial data point for investigating domain-specificity of syntactic processors needs to be at the mental representation level. Specifically, a type of investigation like this should explore the nature of how the mental representations for music and language syntactic structure develop into a grammar for individuals. In order to parse syntactic structure of any kind, individuals have a certain mental representation of it. This representation, and how it is comparable between music and language, can serve as a starting point for investigating commonalities of processing mechanisms in order to answer questions of domain-specificity. If we can consider what type of mental representations we actually have when we can parse syntactic structures in language and music, then we can consider potentially common means by which these representations are rendered, finally leading to Patel's broader question of domain-specificity for the mechanisms that parse music and language syntax.

Patel finds a number of convergence points for the processing of music and language syntax, but we can't develop a formalism for what is stored as any kind of shared syntax if we cannot first define how each of these syntactic systems is represented. Currently, literature on the formal analysis of music/language syntactic convergence is scant, with the most notable attempts coming from Patel (2003), Lerdahl and Jackendoff (1983), and most recently, Katz and Pesetsky (2011). I address the preceding authors' starting assumptions for their formalisms of music and language syntactic convergence, arguing that we cannot begin to set a formalism for music/language syntactic processing convergence unless we first consider a wider variety of possibilities of how syntax is represented in the mind. I begin by briefly explaining how music has syntax, and how this parallels language syntax. I then explain the nature of musical syntax, and highlight the starting theoretical viewpoint toward it taken by the above authors. I explain why it is also necessary to factor in theories of the development of music and language syntax in addition to looking at their surface structure similarities. In looking at how music and language develop into distinct domains, I explain a model of syntactic convergence that is built around the syntactic structures of music and language grammars, where both are considered to involve form-representation construction that results in statistical tracking.

## 2 Music and Language Syntactic Parallels

It is generally known that language has a syntax, and therefore the bulk of the explanation will be on syntactic structures in music. All musical examples used here are based on the Western Tonal harmonic system, the standard by which most US and European music is designed. There are other harmonic structure systems that characterize music of the world though, such as Indian Classical music. The ideas presented here should apply to other systems of music as well. Only melodies of notes played in succession will be considered here. Notes played simultaneously (chords), as well as rhythmic and beat groupings, will not be considered.

Music syntax shares attributes that characterize language syntax, such as nonadjacent dependencies and recursion, both of which are hallmarks for complexity in human language. In music, the capacity for understanding nonadjacent dependencies arises from human perceptions of scales (or keys) within the culture's music system. A scale is a set pattern of notes at particular fixed acoustic intervals from one another (see Figure 1 below). A major scale in the Western Tonal music system, for example, is constructed with this pattern of whole and half steps: WWHWWWH, where W = a whole step and H = a half step. These intervals are consistent across all major scales, regardless of what note the scale starts on.

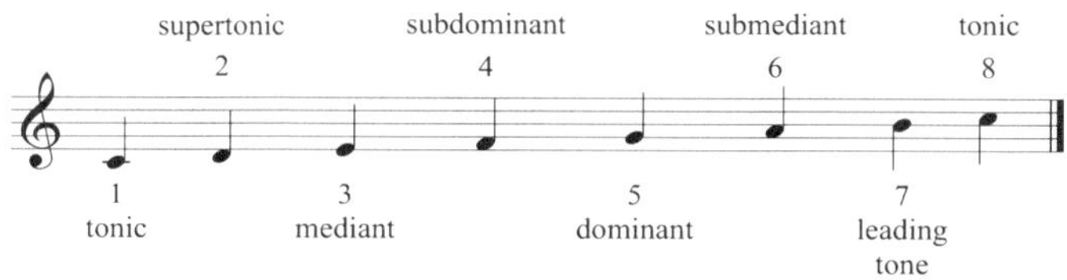


FIGURE 1. Scale Degree Numbers and Names.

Non-tone-deaf individuals who have been exposed to their culture's musical system will develop implicit awareness of scales, as evidenced by their perceptions of 'wrong notes' in melodies that don't conform to the scalar grammar they have acquired (Osterhout 1992: 786). Thus, human perceptions of musical phrase structure are built on implicit understanding of pitches as they relate to one another in a scale.

Awareness of pitch relations manifests as a hierarchy assigned to pitches that expresses melodic tension/resolution and continuity/progression of each pitch relative to the others in the scale (Lerdahl 1983: 8). This hierarchy of tension/resolution is known as Prolongational Reduction (PR). PR phrase hierarchies are perceived and constructed in real time as listeners listen to melodies. Katz' example below shows PR hierarchies of a short melody, with notes labeled by their scale degree name. In this case, each of the phrases TonP (Tonic Phrase), DomP (Dominant Phrase), and SubP (Subdominant Phrase) encode different levels of melodic tension/resolution relative to any previously sounded notes in the musical phrase, with TonP being the most musically stable and DomP having the most perceived tension and inclination to resolve to TonP (Patel 2003: 678).

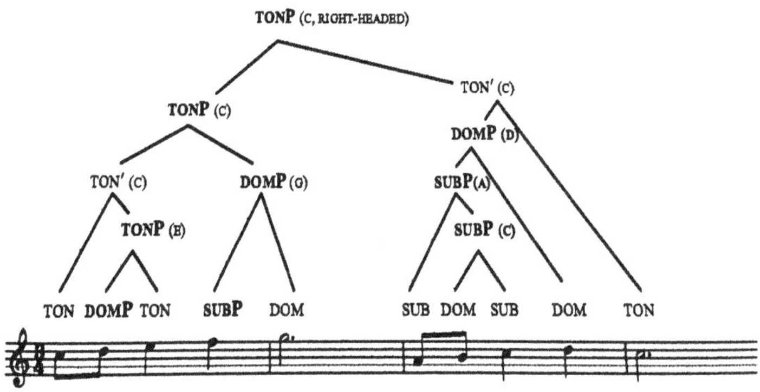


FIGURE 2. Prolongational Reduction Phrase Structure Hierarchies in Music (Katz 2009: 2).

Dominant and Leading-tone phrases, built on the fifth and seventh scale degrees, respectively, demonstrate the maximal amount of perceived tension relative to Tonic Phrases. Furthermore, all other scale degrees have varying levels of tension and resolution relative to one another as notes are sounded successively.

## 2.1 Prolongational Reduction and Nonadjacent Note Groupings

The perception of continuity/progression in Prolongational Reduction allows for nonadjacent notes to be interpreted as part of the same phrase. In the first phrase of Katz' melody (first two measures), the Tonic is followed by a Dominant, another Tonic, a Subdominant and finally a Dominant. As listeners perceive phrase structure, the beginning Tonic and final Dominant note, when played in succession as part of a single (musical) phrase, constitute an overarching Tonic Phrase. Regardless of how many intervening notes of the scale occur between the Tonic and Dominant in the phrase, the concatenation of Tonic and Dominant is still perceived overall as a Tonic Phrase. Thus, perception of nonadjacent notes as constituents of the same phrase does not result from the simple recognition of linear patterns of notes in a melody. Rather, perception of nonadjacent notes in the same phrase is possible when notes (or subphrases) form parts of an abstract, hierarchically-organized category.

In the same way that music involves the grouping of nonadjacent notes under the same category, language can involve nonadjacent items that are grouped under the same category, as in the case of phrasal verbs like *Jonah switched the lamp off,* where the phrasal verb *switch off* is separated by intervening constituents. Similarly, in the simple phrase structure tree below, the determiner *that* and the noun *cat* can be separated by a number of intervening adjectives, but are still understood to be part of the same phrase due to the overarching NP categorization, which can encompass a determiner and any number of embedded NPs, each of which can include an AdjP and another NP or a noun. It is this hierarchical organization that allows for the determiner to be linked with the noun via its inheritance through the intermediate NP nodes, even when the noun and determiner are not adjacent.

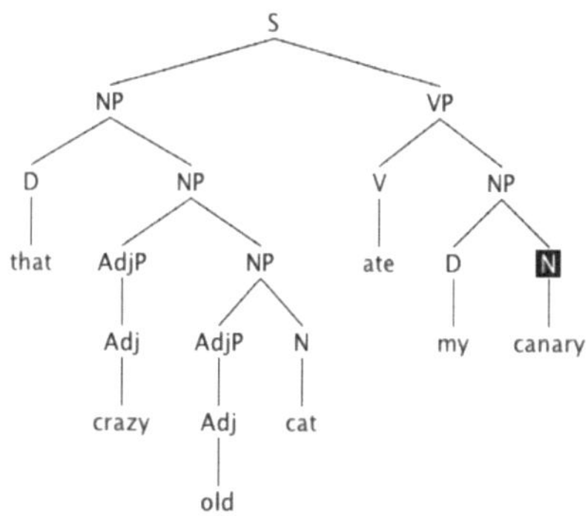


FIGURE 3. Nonadjacent Dependencies in Simple Phrase Structure Grammar.

## 2.2 Head-Driven Phrase Structure in Music

Music and language share analogous properties of head-driven phrase structure. In addition to nonadjacent dependencies, both domains' syntactic structures are defined by a particular element projecting to a more abstract category, which encompasses other elements. In language, a verb is the head of a verb phrase, which signals that both the verb and its object are under the same category together as a single constituent. In music, a similar phenomenon happens where particular notes project to more abstract chord constituent categories. Head-driven phrase structure can be seen in Figure 4 below, where the first note (a C) defines the tonic pitch, and projects to a higher category of a Tonic Phrase, denoted as 1P. The Tonic Phrase encompasses the following D and E as well, along with the C. Nevertheless, C is still considered the defining pitch for that phrase as a constituent, and it is the basis around which the phrase is realized.

If passing tones (D and E) are deleted, and only heads are left, listeners judge the resultant melody to be a simpler version of the one in which passing tones are preserved. However, if heads are deleted, and not passing tones, listeners judge the resultant melody to be a bad simplification of the original melody, not bearing much resemblance to it. Listeners' judgments of 'good' and 'bad' melody reductions based on whether or not heads are preserved is the main idea behind Schenkerian reduction analyses in music theory (Salzer 1952: 28). In Schenkerian reduction analyses, phrase structure is considered to be analyzed via reduction to the notes that define a given chord, regardless of how many other pitches occur within the phrase, and any theme and its variations must minimally preserve the head of the chord in order to bear resemblance to one another for listeners.

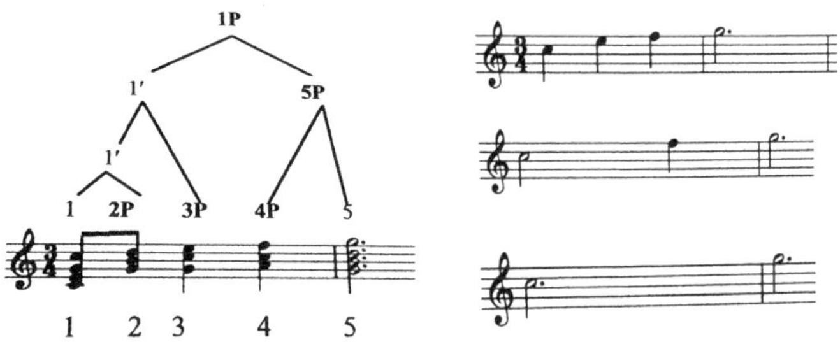


FIGURE 4. Headedness in tonal music: The three Shenkerian reductions to the right are perceived as well-formed reductions of the first melody (top notes) because they only eliminate nonheads in the hierarchical structure.

## 3 Music and Language Syntax: A Formal Divide

Both music and language feature psychologically real syntactic structures involving hierarchical categorization of nonadjacent elements and recursion. A natural next step, then, is to determine how the psychological reality of music structures relates to that of linguistic structures, and then consider whether any relation constitutes evidence that music and language syntax are parsed and processed using some of the same neurocognitive processes.

Determining how the psychological reality of music and language structures relate is confounded by the range of definitions for what is stored as syntax at the mental representation level, especially with regard to acquisition. Traditional approaches involving Universal Grammar posit innate, linguistically-specific rules, principles, and parameters, that become activated over the course of acquisition (Chomsky 1965: 24). Construction-based approaches, on the other hand, indicate that language is learned, and that children acquire constructions, in item-based fashion via statistical tracking and generalization (Tomasello 2006: 14). If we are to consider potential shared underpinnings of music and language syntactic processing, as Patel's question states at the beginning of this paper, we must first consider whether their origins must necessarily be domain-specific in order for them to manifest.

Formalizations of language and music syntax individually often result in theory blindness, masking their potential convergence points. Lerdahl and Jackendoff (1983), for instance, assume a stance toward music syntax based on Generative Linguistics as their starting point for developing a formal music/language comparison. Lerdahl and Jackendoff's model assumes a learned grammar of rules for music that specifies how notes can be combined, allowing for the integration of notes into structure. Despite the commonality of integration of units into structure between music and language, they maintain that the rules for generativity and parsing in music are specific only to music, cautiously claiming that the generative grammar of language and the generative grammar of music do not look anything alike (Jackendoff 1983: 5).

Lerdahl and Jackendoff's theory might not be entirely amiss. Music and language could in fact have separate syntactic systems, such that music-specific rules only are relied upon when interpreting pitch elements and integrating them into hierarchical structure. It is equally possible that language-specific rules alone are relied upon during the interpretation and integration of phonemic units into hierarchical structure for language. However, must the parsing and processing of two syntactically-driven systems for music and language be wholly separate just because of their surface differences? Even if the rules posited to explain syntactic generativity in each domain are specific to that domain, perhaps there are broader syntactic principles that music and language share, which their separate formalisms mask.

The integration of units into structure is common to both music and language, and thus presents a useful point of comparison in addition to Lerdahl and Jackendoff's comparison of generativity in each domain's structure. In comparing unit integration in music and language, the significance of the origins of structural integration is a valuable place to start. If we consider certain avenues by which music and language can develop into separate domains during acquisition, we might see that they are both systems that are wrought by statistical learning and representation of input. Thus, the common properties of music and language structure result from having a common processor on their inputs during acquisition. Surface differences arise due to differences in the building blocks of each domain's input that are subject to statistical learning and representation.

Convergence in music and language syntax will be considered from the hypothesis that they are both 'constructional products' of statistical learning. This idea begins with the notion that music and language both have psychologically real mental representations for syntactic structures/hierarchies (which we know is common to both), and then consider how they got that way. This developmental approach to syntactic convergence emphasizes the importance of understanding a system's development in regard to characterizing its eventual outcome. The goal, then, is to explore *how* syntactic structures come to achieve psychological reality in both music and language, and whether there is any commonality in this respect.

Investigating how syntactic structures come to achieve psychological reality in both music and language (at the mental representation level) will allow us to address what is actually being processed when we process syntactic structure for each domain. If we can address what is actually being processed when we process syntactic structure, it will allow us to address our starting assumptions for where we think the locus of syntactic processing is, thus providing a truer comparison of music and language syntactic processing.

## 4 Statistical Learning Toward Structure Building

One promising way in which music and language could possibly share a syntactic link is in those theories that consider the emergence of syntax to be rooted in statistical learning abilities. Statistical learning (or tracking) is a domain-general cognitive function that involves the tracking of a continuous stream of unparsed input data over time. Statistical tracking is used to determine the distributional/probabilistic frequencies of each unit's occurrences in the data, relative to one another. Those elements that have a high probability of co-occurring are considered good candidates for a higher-level representation. For music, Saffran et al. (1999) and Creel et al. (2001) provide a large amount of evidence for statistical tracking of tone sequences, from which both children and adults can use probabilistic note/chord co-occurrence cues to induce organizational patterns and categories.

Statistical learning is important to many usage-based accounts of language acquisition, in that it can provide a continuous model by which children can bootstrap from the lowest-level representations of language (i.e. phonemic categories) to higher-level tiers like morphology and syntax during the course of acquisition, reducing the reliance on any innate structural representations. Tomasello, for example, notes that children can use statistical learning in both the acquisition of phonemic categories as well as syntactic categories by taking assessments of the input data (2006: 17). Babies are known to be excellent statistical learners for speech and gesture input, tracking phonemic co-occurrence in the language input around them (Saffran 2003: 484).

Saffran, Tomasello, and many others argue that children 'build' a grammar with this tracking mechanism by forming representations of lower levels of language (i.e. phonemic categories), which can bootstrap to higher levels of representation in language (i.e. words) (Tomasello 2006: 8). The process is accomplished when children can induce higher-level categorical representations from patterns in the lower-level ones, taking the representational output of one tracked set of elements, and using it as the tracking input to another tier. For example, statistical abilities can track distributional patterns of speech sounds, such as the occurrences of place, manner, and voicing features, and use this data to form the basis for a categorical representation for particular phonemes, based on which features have a high probability of occurring together (as opposed to random co-occurrences). Having segmented speech sounds, one can then track frequencies of phoneme co-occurrence as an aid to figuring out word boundaries, thus segmenting out words.[1]

Children and infants can use statistical tracking to go even further than word segmentation. Given an artificial language, all groups can acquire word classes by analyzing the consistency of sequences that occur in the auditory input and by using the contrast between highly consistent and less

[1] This brings up a worthwhile question of whether the tiers of phoneme, morpheme, and syntax should really be considered separate from the outset as part of what children track during L1 acquisition, or whether these are just 'constructed realities' that result from statistical learning. That is, we want to know whether these tiers, which are common to the world's languages, exist as a result of the common vehicle by which they are produced (the human body), and the human ability to have discrete elements that can be sequenced at various levels.

consistent sequences to distinguish word categories from accidental co-occurrences (Saffran 2003).

### 4.1 Statistical Learning in Language vs. Music: Absence of Meaning

If infants can acquire artificial word classes from auditory input, then what is to stop statistical learning from continuing in this fashion to parse out/represent phrase structure? By the same token, does it necessarily need to be the case that the representations gleaned from statistical learning are semantically meaningful? In the case of natural language, word classes have a certain broad semantic content, but that is because the constituent elements (words) have a symbolic-semantic value, from which a schematic word-class meaning can be gleaned. Thus, these meaningful representations are formed by induction over form-meaning units.

If, however, the building block units from which higher representations are gleaned have no symbolic content, there is still a psychological reality to the resultant representations from the statistical tracking process. This is the case with music, where the representation of Prolongational Reduction structure has no symbolic content, but it is nonetheless a psychologically real representation to listeners. As Katz points out, though, this is hardly surprising given that the building blocks of language (morphemes/lexemes) are semiotic in nature (having a form-to-meaning mapping), whereas the building blocks of music (notes/chords) do not have semiotic meaning mappings. The differences between the types of phrase structure that arise in each domain, then, are simply due to the difference between the building blocks of language and music, respectively (Katz 2011: 76).

The end result of statistical learning over two different types of input is that language and music come to have very different categories (e.g. there is no musical correlate of a VP). However, in both instances, statistical learning can be a vehicle by which higher-level mental representations of phrase structure are gleaned from lower-level representations of constituents (words/notes).

Statistical learning for musical structure building is most clearly similar to the aforementioned linguistic statistical learning that occurs for phonemic categories. In the formation of phonemic categories, the statistical tracking of place and manner co-occurrence regularities dictates the phonemic representations that will be gleaned for the language system. In this case, statistical tracking can root out perceptual pattern regularities to form an abstract schema for a given phoneme, which is not meaning-symbolic. Linguistic representations are gleaned above the phonemic level in the same manner, except that they *are* meaning-symbolic. Music, however, continues in the same manner as language phonemic construction, rooting out more complex patterns in the musical structure that are *not* meaning-symbolic.

Statistical learning that does not involve meaning-symbolic generalizations plays more heavily into language structure/class building beyond the phonemic level. It can also factor heavily into pattern representations that allow children to bootstrap to the meaning-symbolic content behind statistical regularities. For example, statistical learning can track two different elements that both occur before the same group of elements, and represent these two elements under a make-shift category. The category would simply be one to denote that these two different elements are part of a set that can occur before the same group of second elements, but does not have to entail any meaning. For example, if the string 'little' and 'big' are found to occur before many of the same items (e.g. ball, house, etc.), they can be considered to be part of the same class—a schematic class that encompasses both 'little' and 'big', which designates them as occurring before objects. This type of generalization can occur even before any kind of generalization about the meaning of 'little' and 'big' is incurred (i.e. an adjectival meaning). Overall, this type of quick statistical learning can serve as a guide to help children make faster connections to the meaning-symbolic generalizations of constructions.

Nonsymbolic statistical learning of the type described here can function for both language and music structure representations. Figure 5 below illustrates this process for word class building with X and Y elements occurring before the same elements P, F, R, and Q. If you know a word X, and you know other words P, F, R, and Q, and you find P, F, R, and Q to occur after X on a regular basis, you will begin to form some sort of generalization for P, F, R, and Q as a class, and get a basic word order for where these elements occur in relation to X. Furthermore, if you also see Y occurring before these same elements, you might infer something about X and Y as behaving as a single class, which can precede the class of which P, F, R, and Q are a part. Even devoid of any meaning, we can form some kind of generalization based on statistical learning, however it is actually represented.

| X | < | P | Y | < | P |
|---|---|---|---|---|---|
| | | F | | | F |
| | | R | | | R |
| | | Q | | | Q |

FIGURE 5. Model for class building via statistical learning.

In Figure 5, both X and Y elements occur with statistical frequency before the same elements P, F, R, and Q, designating X and Y as part of the same class that occurs before P, F, R, and Q, even if it is not apparent what the meanings of X and Y are.

The crucial idea here is that statistical learning makes it possible to extract forms and link them to some sort of representation, regardless of whether that representation has meaning-symbolic content or not. What is most important is the link between a particular form and a particular *representation*.

In the case of music, then, we glean forms that correlate to mental representations from the input data via statistical learning. In the case of language, we glean forms that correlate to mental representations with a meaning component. Thus, the same process of statistical learning works to build up what results in language-specific and music-specific mental representation systems. This ability, coupled with an ability to somehow represent these gleaned patterns in the input data, can be all that are needed to build language and music syntactic domains, and do not necessarily need to implicate any innate, specifically-linguistic or specifically-musical syntactic mechanisms for their instantiation.

## 5 Construction Grammar as a Theoretical Model

The above idea subsumes a Construction Grammar theoretical basis of grammar. Construction Grammar (CG), as developed by Goldberg (1995) centers around the idea that grammar inherently consists of form-meaning pairs of varying levels, what she terms as 'constructions all the way down' (Goldberg 2003: 219). In other words, we see examples of constructions (forms) of various levels, and we understand that these forms correspond to some sort of meaning. In other words, a single morpheme, such as the prefix *anti-*, can be a construction: the form *anti* corresponds to the meaning of 'against' or 'opposite'. Similarly, words like *cake* and *cat* are constructions that are linked to a particular meaning. Beyond the word level, partially-filled idioms like *jog (someone's) memory,* and abstract constructions such as Sub [V Obj1 Obj2] co-occur with the meanings of remembrance and ditransitivity, respectively.

The multi-tiered nature of constructions embedded within larger constructions is apparent in Figure 6 below, where the forms [Liza], [buy], [the], [child], [what], [did] are all considered constructions—word constructions. Combining the word constructions [the] and [child] results in yet another construction—the NP construction [the child]. In combining multiple smaller constructions, we end up with the sentence *What did Liza buy the child,* which itself is considered a construction: the question construction.

1. (a) [What did Liza buy the child?]

(b) Constructions (i.e. words): Liza, buy, the, child, what, did

2. Ditransitive construction:
3. Question construction: [ ]
4. Subject–Auxiliary inversion construction:
5. VP construction:
6. NP construction:

FIGURE 6. (a) An expression, or 'construct', that is a combination of the constructions shown in (b), line-coded to the appropriate parts of the expression. (VP, Verb Phrase; NP, Noun Phrase) (Goldberg 2003: 220).

Forms thus can occur as words, morphemes, phrases, etc., in the architecture of grammar. Statistical learning addresses *how* these forms come to achieve form status. They are gleaned from the tracking of patterns in lower levels of input, and linked to some sort of representation.

## 5. 1 Extending CG to Encompass Form-Representation Constructions

While CG centers on linguistic constructions having a form-meaning linkage, an interesting theoretical avenue to pursue is to extend the form-meaning attribute of CG to also encompass form-representation pairs. As noted before, statistical learning can occur for language to build up phonemic representations and aid word class building by pure statistical frequency tracking, even when there is no meaning encoded at these levels. Music structure building could likely proceed in this same manner too, with generalizations about statistical regularities in tone patterns dictating the musical grammar that results.

In extending the CG model to encompass form-representation pairs, it is important to clarify the distinction between meaning and representation as it is used here. Linguistic units at multiple levels are forms linked to meaning in human-construed reality. The linguistic form /duck/, for example, links to the meaning of the aquatic bird as humans construe it, and the form V NP NP links to an abstract meaning of ditransitivity that humans construe in multiple situations. Meaning can also be derived from the linguistic system itself, as in the concept of the phoneme /a/ as a classifiable sound in one's language.

In contrast to meaning linked to forms, representation is a stored rendering of forms, sometimes at multiple levels, without linkage to any construed meaning. This process of representing is most notable in those individuals who can mimic syllabic and prosodic features of foreign languages they do not know, sometimes for extended phrases, without understanding what they are saying. Apart from those with exceptional phonological memory, average adult nonnative speakers of (a language) show preference for correct word order sentences in (the language) over incorrect word order following only one hour of passive exposure to (the language), indicating a means of representing patterns in articulatory and stress/prosodic co-occurrences. Like adults, infants frequently produce words or phrases for which there is no demonstrable semantic linkage, such as the word 'duck' in a variety of contexts, while neither requesting a duck nor seeing a duck (Golinkoff 1994: 126). In this case, they have latched onto the phonological co-occurrences of the word, and have simply recognized that the separate sounds of 'duck' can (and do) co-occur frequently. Thus, children can represent patterns in their language even before they represent these patterns as symbolic constituents of the linguistic system (i.e. as phonemes, morphemes, etc.).

The focus of CG on form-meaning/form-function pairings for language obscures the broader process of form-representation pairings that happen with this system, which is utilized in music as well. I argue that linkage of form to meaning and form to representation are both necessary for the acquisition of language, and that they are actually the same process. For language acquisition, children can rely on form-representation pairings while simultaneously noting regularities in forms' regular co-occurrence with construed meaning, thus enabling the use of forms as constructions that can function symbolically. The symbolic nature of constructions, however, is rendered by the same process of form-representation mapping, which contains an additional layer of meaning due to its forms having consistent co-occurrence with construed meaning in the world.

Like language, music involves form-representation mappings at multiple levels, as seen in the Prolongational Reduction hierarchies shown in Figure 2. However, forms in music do not occur regularly with construed meaning, and therefore do not acquire the same symbolic import simultaneously as language does. This idea supports Katz' original statement that surface distinctions between music and language are due to differences in their respective building blocks, with the building blocks of language having symbolic linkage.

## 6 Conclusions

As explained in the previous section, the same process of statistical learning works to build up what results in language-specific and music-specific mental representation systems. With this model, syntactic development is integrated into a theory of shared processing mechanisms for music and language syntax. A developmentally-based theory of the origin of music and language syntactic domains can tell us the properties of the syntactic processor(s) that must parse incoming music and language structure, addressing what, if anything, is shared for both domains.

Despite surface differences between both music and language, they could both originate by the same statistical learning/representation process. Thus, a processor that recognizes hierarchical structure in music and language could have a common property for music and language parsing insofar as it is concerned with recognizing constituent units in each domain as form-representation pairs, products of statistical learning/representation, with or without additional music- and language-specific syntactic processors.

## References

Chomsky, N. 1965. *Aspects of the Theory of Syntax*. Boston: MIT Press.

Creel, S. C., E. Newport, and R. Aslin. 2004. Distant melodies: Statistical Learning of Nonadjacent Dependencies in Tone Sequences. *Journal of Experimental Psychology: Learning, Memory, and Cognition* 30: 1119–1130.

Goldberg, A. 2003. Constructions: a New Theoretical Approach to Language. *TRENDS in Cognitive Sciences* 7(5): 219–224.

Goldberg, A. 1995. *Constructions: a Construction Grammar Approach to Argument Structure*. Chicago: University of Chicago Press.

Golinkoff, R., C. Mervis, and K. Hirsch-Pasek. 1994. Early Object Labels: The Case for a Developmental Lexical Principles Framework. *Journal of Child Language* 21(1): 125–155.

Katz, J. & D. Pesetsky. 2011. The Identity Thesis for Music and Language. Doctoral Dissertation, MIT.

Katz, J. & D. Pesetsky. 2009. The Recursive Syntax and Prosody of Tonal Music. Presented at *Recursion: Structural Complexity in Language and Cognition*. University of Massachusetts, Amherst. May 26–28, 2009.

Langacker, R. 2008. *Cognitive Grammar: A Basic Introduction*. Oxford: Oxford University Press.

Lerdahl, F., and R. Jackendoff. 1983. *A Generative Theory of Tonal Music*. Boston: MIT Press.

Osterhout, L., and P. Holcomb. 1992. Event-Related Potentials Elicited by Syntactic Anomaly. *Journal of Memory and Language* 31: 785–806.

Patel, A. 2007. *Music, Language, and the Brain*. NY: Oxford University Press.

Patel, A. 2003. 'Language, Music, Syntax, and the Brain.' *Nature Neuroscience* 6(7): 674–81.

Saffran, J., and E. Theissen. 2003. Pattern Induction by Infant Language Learners. Developmental Psychology 39 (3): 484–494.

Saffran, J., E. Johnson, and R. Aslin, Newport, E. 1999. Statistical Learning of Tone Sequences by Human Infants and Adults. *Cognition* 70: 27–52.

Salzer, F. *Structural Hearing: Tonal Coherence in Music.* Dover: Mineola Publications.

Tomasello, M. 2006. Acquiring Linguistic Constructions. *Handbook of Child Psychology: Cognitive Development*, R. Siegler and D. Kuhn (eds). Hoboken: John Wiley & Sons.

24

# Elastic Anchors for Imaginative Conceptual Blends: A Framework for Analyzing Animated Computer Interfaces

KENNY K. N. CHOW AND D. FOX HARRELL

## 1 Introduction

In today's digital media environments people not only view, but also interact with, animated graphics in user interfaces, websites, video games, and computer-based artworks. Human experience of interactive animated interfaces relies upon both sensory and motor apparatuses, constituting a type of embodied cognitive process (Chow and Harrell 2009; Chow and Harrell 2012). We call such processes 'material-based imagination'. Through sensorimotor experience of interactive animation, users can recall previously experienced scenarios and infer associated visceral sensations. Furthermore, people can conceptually elaborate upon animated visuals, for example an animator imagining an animated stick figure's walk cycle used for early planning as the specific swaggering character it will become in a feature film. Drawing upon the concepts of material anchors and conceptual blending along with neuroscience results regarding mirror neurons, we present our concept of 'elastic anchors' to help explicate imaginative meaning-making processes involving animated interfaces. Toward this end, we analyze a range of digital media interfaces including graphical user interfaces (GUIs) for computer operating systems, viral websites, and mobile devices.

*Language and the Creative Mind.*
Mike Borkent, Barbara Dancygier, and Jennifer Hinnell (eds).

With recent interactive multimedia technologies, users now frequently interact with interfaces designed to convey a sense of liveliness. For instance, when clicking on an application icon in the Macintosh OS X environment, that icon then responds with restless bouncing before launching. A user witnessing this might recall or imagine the common experience of receiving enthusiastic response from a motivated child eager to be called upon. In this manner, since the perceived liveliness in the interface is often reminiscent of everyday life experience, users readily (even prereflectively) compare the animation to a past experience or familiar scenario. This comparison is a kind of conceptual blend that connects the experience or scenario (e.g. the enthusiastic bodily movement) to the animated phenomenon (e.g. the computer icon's restless bouncing), and compresses the mappings of sensorimotor experiences (e.g. the point-and-click mouse action and the bouncing icon animation in the interface environment) into an embodied concept of an 'enthusiastic' icon. This kind of imagination relies upon users' embodied understandings of material images triggered by interactive animation. This kind of imagination is not purely a mental activity located in the head, but is an embodied cognition process.

## 2 From Image Interpretation to Imagination

Imagination based on material images can take place at the automatic, perceptual level. To argue this here, we primarily build upon approaches suggesting a close relationship between meaning and perception such as those of Ludwig Wittgenstein as described by Mitchell (1986), Arnheim (1969), Stafford (2007), and Johnson (2008). Once viewers perceive a material artifact as associated with some meaning, whether a screen displaying a digital image or a shadow cast by a puppet in a shadow play, the perceived image becomes a mental image. This mental image may lose some detail from the original image, but it preserves the original's structural characteristics, the 'shape' of the concept (Arnheim 1969: 116).

Observing this connection between material images and mental images is a result of our adherence to an embodied cognition perspective holding that human conceptualization is largely built upon a foundation of sensorimotor experience (image schemas; Lakoff and Johnson 2003). Embodied cognition theories are particularly useful here for articulating the forms of material-based imagination involved in interactive animated interfaces in which people make meaning of interactive dynamic images through both sensory perception and motor action.

### 2.1 Material Anchors

While the notion of image schemas suggests that many concepts are built upon experiences with spatial structures of perceptual images, Edwin Hutchins's influential concept of material anchors reciprocally theorizes the distribution of concepts onto the physical structures of images. Hutchins (2005) has introduced the concept of 'material anchors', whose structures or patterns 'hold' information in place or incorporate constraints for mental manipulation. For example, consider the case of an analog stopwatch. The position of the stopwatch's minute hand and the target time marking on its face form a circular sector that, when considered relative to a complete circle, informs the user of the time left. Such a material image in the physical world can carry information for, or impose constraints upon, direct input to cognitive processes. That is, structural images in the world, such as a sector in a circle, physically represent information and people do not need to hold these representations in their heads. This is one sense in which images span from the material to the conceptual.

### 2.2 Anchors for Conceptual Blends

Building upon the earlier concepts of mental spaces (Fauconnier 1985) and conceptual metaphors (Lakoff and Johnson 2003), Gilles Fauconnier and Mark Turner argue that conceptual blending is a basic mental operation that generates new meanings by integrating concepts, forming emergent networks (Fauconnier and Turner 2002). Blending is pervasive in common sense meaning making, as well as in other creative feats like rhetoric, gameplay, and even in interface design (Fauconnier 2001: 279). Fauconnier and Turner have explored the role of material anchors in blending, examining how material images of everyday objects like watches and money can serve as inputs into conceptual blending networks (2002: 210–16). For Fauconnier and Turner, a material anchor can be a perceived structural constant representing a concept, for example the distinct images of different forms of money such as coins. In contrast to Fauconnier and Turner's account of the role of material anchors in conceptual blending, Hutchins demands that more information is loaded into the structures of material anchors. For example, he argues that the compass rose, with all of its marks used for calculation, has incorporated much more information and many more constraints (such as angular distance) than a coin (Hutchins 2005). Here, we emphasize this entire span from 'weak' material anchors in blends such as proposed by Fauconnier and Turner to Hutchins's highly structured material anchors, again providing examples of the tight relationship between perception and conceptualization in images.

### 2.3 Toward Material Imagination in Animation

For the purposes here, the important aspects of the brief accounts above are summarized as follows:

(1) Structural features in images can be perceived as concepts, and

(2) Structured images can be inputs to blends.

Such structured images blur previously assumed boundaries between mind and matter, mental and material, and conception and perception.

Yet 'structure' here is not limited to only static or stable images. For computer interface animation, images are interactive and dynamically generated, appearing different from moment to moment. As we will show in the following sections, understandings of interactive animation results from bodily experience that triggers imaginative concept construction and elaboration.

## 3 Embodied Understanding of Animated Images

Hutchins's examples of material anchors mainly focus on their roles in human-performed instrumental and operational tasks such as maritime navigation. Due to this focus, his viewpoint requires that material anchors be stable and faithful representations. However, this stability and faithfulness does not necessarily apply to cases in which the outcome is not a priori clear and task specific, such as process-driven creative activities. For example, in filmmaking a storyboard is not strictly a faithful representation of the mental image inside the director's mind, but is also a device used for reflection upon a creative work-in-progress. While engaging in such reflection, the director projects evocative sensation onto the work that goes beyond the physically represented information. In that process, the director allows the storyboard to trigger generation of subsequent imaginative images.

Animated images cross the boundary between the original and the imaginative even more strongly, drawing upon viewers' motor-sensory experiences. At early stages in making films, directors often use animated visual images (technically called 'animatics' or 'rough cuts') when aiming to judge whether the work elicits the correct visceral sensations such as suspense or sadness. There are many nuances to these 'gut feelings' that are conveyed differently than static images can. For example, an animation viewer is able to distinguish a character's giggling from shuddering because the viewer perceives and understands it as exhibiting movement qualities previously experienced in everyday life. This is quite different than the use of culturally specific symbolic conventions such as trembling lines around a comic strip character without which a still image could not convey these distinctions.

Neuroscience results regarding activation of the peculiar brain structures known as mirror neurons have been able to shed some light on such visceral feelings engendered by animated images. Studies on both monkeys and humans show that some neurons fire both when a subject performs an action and when the subject merely *sees* another doing the same action (Rizzolatti and Craighero 2004; Rizzolatti et al. 1996). While overlapping of neuron activation patterns in brain areas certainly does not mean that perception and action are equivalent, it does imply that some degree of immediate understanding of action occurs through perception by pattern recognition. These findings have been posited as suggesting that, when perceiving a performed action, such as in moving images, the viewer's immediate interpretation relies upon evocation of the corresponding sensorimotor knowledge from a repertoire of his or her own bodily experience (Rizzolatti and Sinigaglia 2008: 94–98, 124–25). Furthermore, this coupling of perception and action may enable the viewer to recall the associated sensation. Neurons have been found that respond to both the perception of others receiving painful stimuli and to direct experience of pain (Rizzolatti and Sinigaglia 2008: 187). Neurons have also been found that activate both when seeing others' facial expressions of disgust and when directly smelling an unpleasant odor (Rizzolatti and Sinigaglia 2008: 191). This all suggests that when we see, for example, someone jumping restlessly, we readily understand that person's excitement via our own experiences. By the same token, a movie director can 'feel' whether an actor's performance matches his or her mental image. An animator can 'feel' if an animated object is moving the right way. In short, 'feeling' animated images constitutes an embodied cognitive process. This kind of visceral understanding largely takes place at the immediate and pre-reflective level—requiring minimal cognitive effort.

As philosopher Mark Johnson puts it, 'mirror-neuron phenomena suggest that understanding is a form of simulation' (Johnson 2008: 161). Yet at present we do not have enough neuroscientific evidence to account for bodily understanding of every kind of sensation. Cognitive semantics research helps by providing us with convincing accounts of how we understand sensation through perception. When discussing animacy, Turner states that we cannot perceive others' sensations, so we can only infer their sensations by comparing their actions to our own reactions in similar situations (1996: 21). He refers to this analogical inference as a type of projection of parable, a kind of elaborate metaphor in which partial structure from a source story of the perceiver (which primarily comes from one's own experiences, actions, and emotions) is projected onto the target story of the perceived scenario. Hence, a viewer of an animated movie can infer the sensation at hand by cognitively projecting his or her own experience onto the perceived motion. The director or animator of the movie can even 'sense' the gap between the inferred sensation and what he or she actually looks for, subsequently making necessary amendments.

In processes of projecting onto animated scenarios, the act of 'inference' seems to suggest that the projection of a source story onto a scenario takes place at a higher cognitive level, requiring conscious mental operations. However, such mental projections can seem to be cognitively effortless. This point can be illustrated in terms of conceptual blending theory. The matches between two input mental spaces, what Fauconnier and Turner call 'vital relations' (2002: 92), in some blends can be so tightly compressed that they become automatic and unnoticed. Fauconnier has cited the computer interface phenomenon as an example of this kind of immediate blend (Fauconnier 2001: 264–65). For instance, a user dragging a window on a computer desktop slides the mouse on a real horizontal desk. Meanwhile, the user's eyes track the vertically-oriented movement of the graphics on the screen. There are a set of mappings between the physical space and the screen space, including from the mouse to the window, from the mouse-click to the act of 'picking-up' the window, from forward to up, from backward to down, and so on. Most users, however, are unaware of the blend. They just feel that they are directly manipulating the window.

In this regard, we add that for directors or animators there are also blends of experiences with perceived actions that yield inferred visceral sensations. The compression can be so tight that the animated images are immediately associated with the right sensation. The images become an immediate and embodied input to the integration network.

## 4 The Material-Based Reflective Process

So far we have discussed the understanding of animated images based on single-level blends. In fact, conceptual blending enables further imagination because it yields emergent structure that allows for imaginative elaboration. Together with material anchors, conceptual blends provide a good model for describing successive integrations of perceptual images and mental images, which we believe supports accounting for the embodied forms of imagination involved in interactive animated interfaces. However, since Hutchins's material anchors largely address stable images additional theory is needed in order to account for animated phenomena.

We argue that animated images can be 'elastic' material anchors. Such animated images hold sensation in place while also being flexible and adaptable. They are elastic enough for one to match partial similarities between sensations (e.g. matches in motion or shape) and mental images in order to elaborate blends. We introduce the term 'elastic anchor' to describe these imagination-provoking artifacts. Elastic anchors engender nuanced forms of imagination though conveying the subtle differences and partial similarities between the bodily understood, immediately inferred sensations represented by animated images and associated mental images.

Such nuanced interplay may go unnoticed when the reflective process becomes instantaneous and continuous. This can be illustrated by a particular type of animated image, namely those resulting from shadow play. Consider the difference between natural moving images (e.g. incidental shadows) and author-intended animated images (see Figure 1). The two images could be considered to be materially and perceptually caused by the same phenomenon. Neither representation may be valuable as a material anchor because their structural features do not seem to hold information; they are simply silhouettes. However, the shadow on the right in Figure 1 can be an elastic anchor for conceptual blends in which the silhouette in motion is integrated with the viewer's mental image of a figure moving in a similar fashion (i.e. the silhouette of a barking dog), thus enabling the shadow to be imaginatively interpreted as that of an animated dog. On the audience's side, this blended image is the meaning of the puppet show. On the puppeteer's side, this might be an interim image that the puppeteer can fine-tune in order to create another animated shadow. In both cases, the material image blends with the mental image to give rise to the next imaginative image.

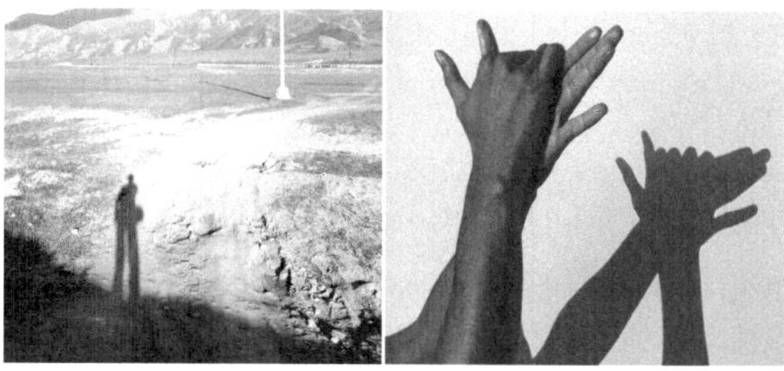

FIGURE 1. An incidental shadow vs. an intended shadow of a barking dog.

It follows that material images and mental images have a very intricate relationship. In goal-specific computational operations, they can be regarded as largely equivalent. In creative activities, to give an illustrative analogy, they may seem like dancing or boxing partners irregularly approaching each other, whether collaboratively or combatively. Moving images like hand shadows, with their distilled visual forms, evocative movements, and material-based reflective processes, serve as excellent elastic inputs to conceptual blends. This is because their flexibility and adaptability facilitates partial structural projection between the material and the mental that gives rise to new blends and imaginative images.

## 5 Coupling of Animated Feedback and Motor Input in Interfaces

If animated images are instantaneously reactive, as in shadow play, the elastic anchors involved include not only sensory perception, but also motor action. In computer interfaces, elastic anchors are even more adaptable and elaborative because a user might interpret his or her motor input quite variably according to perceived dynamic feedback. In other words, dynamic feedback defines, or re-defines, the meaning of motor input action. For example, when a user of OS X (the default Tiger or Leopard versions) scrolls within a window using two fingers on the touchpad, the scrolling effect defines the action as moving the viewpoint because the scrolling direction is the same as the finger motion. When a user runs a finger across an iPhone screen, the contrasting scrolling effect (in the opposite direction) redefines the action as moving the panel instead. A few other examples follow. Turning a new page on an iPhone's screen by tilting the device defines the action as flipping the page. Leaving marks on a touch screen using a finger defines the touch-and-move action as drawing. A swarm of dancing particles following a pointing finger defines the action of moving the finger as conducting choreography. Furthermore, in the OS X dock (a user-interface element of the system holding a list of application icons for quick launching) the mouse-over action results in magnification of icons so as to feel as if the user is considering selecting them. Similarly, in the cases of some interactive advertisements we have analyzed, the mouse-over action causes human figures to giggle, resulting in the feeling that the user is tickling the figure.

In other words, motor action embodies our intentions toward something. An illustrative example related to machine operation is the jog dial of a video tape recorder (see Figure 2). When a user spins the dial, the motion, including speed and direction, conveys the user's intentions of going forward or backward at variable speed. Likewise, in digital interactive media, motor input embodies users' consciousness 'moving' to enable animated feedback. Since the animated feedback is dynamic, programmable, and variable, the embodied meaning of motor action becomes adaptable and emergent. It follows that a coupling of animated visual images and motor input may yield adaptive, evocative blends. This coupling enables the motor-sensory feedback loop that we have been describing. Motor action triggers animation that, in turn, incites further bodily engagement. This loop is sometimes delayed, such as in a hand-drawn animation test or computer animation preview that needs rendering. Occasionally, the loop is instantaneous and continuous, such as in shadow play or interface animation. This loop, which relies on the materiality of images that one perceives and acts upon, is the core of elastic anchors. Elastic anchors are elastic in the sense that the meaning at hand is flexibly dependent on the dynamic nature of the animation and bodily interaction.

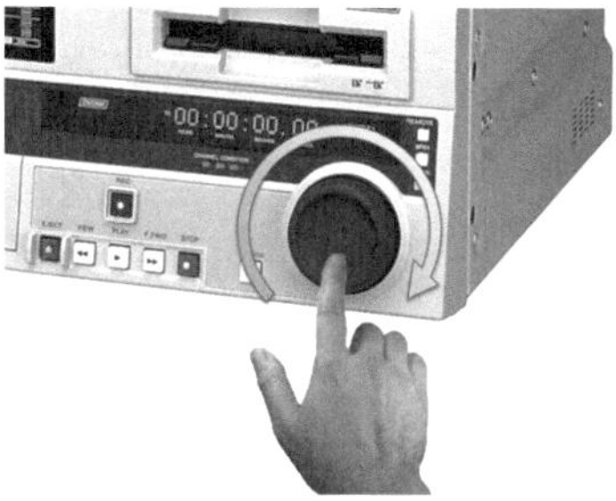

FIGURE 2. Use of the jog dial of a video tape recorder.

## 6 Analyses of Animated Interfaces

This section introduces a few examples to illustrate the imaginative conceptual blending process that takes place in animated computer interfaces. They include the GUIs of prevalent operating systems, the interface of a unique artistic viral website, and a peculiar and intriguing mobile phone interface.

### 6.1 The GUIs of OS X and iOS

Pixar's animated short film *Luxo Jr*. (1986) famously anthropomorphized a desk lamp. The GUIs of OS X (on Macintosh computers) and iOS (on iPhone or iPad devices) similarly anthropomorphize software interfaces. When the mouse pointer moves across the dock in OS X, the docked icons are magnified successively as described earlier. We saw that if the user clicks on one of them, the icon responds by bouncing. Through conceptual blending at the immediate level, the user understands that the application icon is taking responsive action. The user spontaneously and effortlessly blends the interactive animation, anchoring the sensorimotor experience of moving across icons, clicking, and seeing bouncing feedback, with socially recognized forms of body language for anticipation. These are gestures that most people have experienced in everyday life. For example, the precocious child jumping up and down with excitement when called upon from in a classroom. The blend includes, among other elements, a compression of *moving the mouse pointer across icons* and *moving a pointing finger across candidates* into *selecting from a list of 'competing' icons*, as well as a compression of *bouncing icon* and *jumping student* into 'excited' launching icons. The output of the blend is an anthropomorphizing concept of selecting from a list of 'attentive, enthusiastic' candidate icons.

More blends take place after an application has been launched. If the user clicks to minimize the application window, the animated window 'enacts' a playful genie, stretching and twisting into the dock. When clicked again, the minimized window icon reveals itself with another twist as if a genie emerging from a bottle. The user acquires the connotative meaning (genie) when blending the click and twisting animation with the concept of a genie from the cinema or television. In the blend, the motor-sensory feedback loop of user click and window twist has a counterpart in our sensory experience of seeing a cartoon film (e.g. Disney's *Aladdin*), in which rubbing an oil lamp causes a genie to come out. The link between the user click and rubbing is compressed into an analogy relation: an imaginative act of summoning in the GUI environment. The links between the window's twist and the genie's twist, as well as the desktop and the film background, are also compressed into a virtual and magical spectacle. The new blended concept is a genie window in the GUI.

There are other similar blends in the iOS GUI. When an iOS device user tries to reconfigure the home screen layout, he or she starts with moving one of the many jiggling icons across a grid of others; the others automatically move around to make way. The user can blend the jiggling and shuffling motions with common experiences such as rearranging seating plans. The mapping between jiggling icons and slightly nervous workers preparing for relocation is compressed into nervous, but prepared, icons awaiting reconfiguration by the user. The mapping between quick shuffling of an arrangement and smooth relocation of elements is compressed into a sense of a field of icons well-prepared for action. The blend results in a concept of icons responsive to rearrangement.

The blends just discussed mostly take place at an immediate level of understanding. Users usually apprehend their meanings spontaneously and effortlessly. However, users can further elaborate these blends at a metaphorical level. The icons in the dock or in windows, and the tiled icons on a handheld device, can be clicked to launch applications. They can be regarded as various 'incarnations' of the same set of applications in different visual forms. In a metaphorical blend, the incarnation frame can be invoked (Fillmore 1985). Attentive docked icons, magically helpful genie windows, and cooperatively prepared tiled icons all can be mapped onto the creations of a determined design spirit, which is compressed into 'personified' representatives of the applications serving at your wish like an intimate companion.

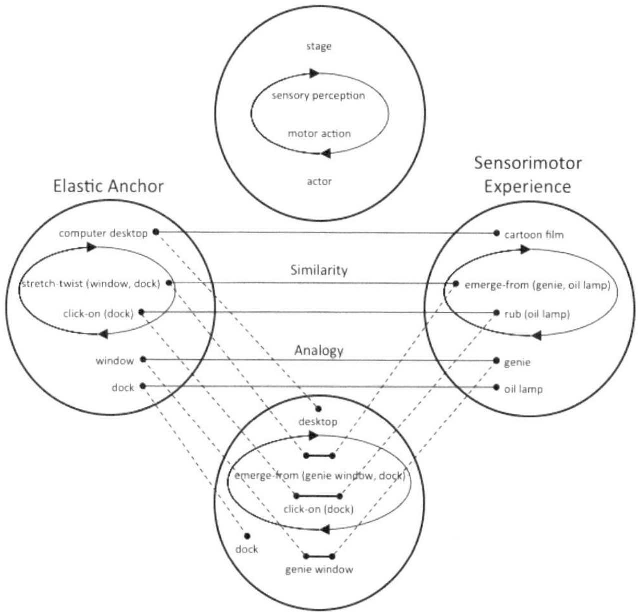


FIGURE 3a. An immediate blend in the OS X environment.

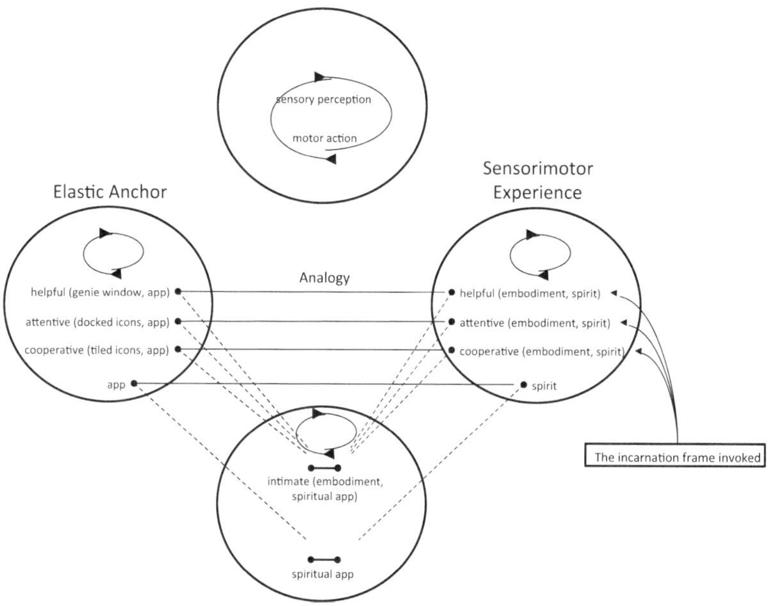


FIGURE 3b. A metaphorical (second level) blend in the OS X environment.

These multiple levels of GUI blends are illustrated using conceptual integration diagrams in Figures 3a and 3b. Based on Fauconnier and Turner's (2002) graphical notation for blends, an integration diagram depicts the input spaces as two circles on the same horizontal axis, with the output of the blend in the bottom circle. The lines between these spaces are mappings, selective projections, or compressions of vital relations. The top circle is the generic space, which describes elements shared by the input spaces. Within this structure, we add a circular loop to represent a motor-sensory feedback loop. Moreover, motor actions and perceptions are represented using mathematical relations. For example, 'stretch-twist (window, dock)' means that the window stretches and twists into and out of the dock, while 'rub (oil lamp)' denotes rubbing the oil lamp.

### 6.2 The Mobile Interface of NEC FOMA N702iS

Let us now consider the 'water-level' battery meter interface of the mobile phone FOMA N702iS manufactured by NEC Corporation in 2006 (see Figure 4). The phone's interface displays an image visually resembling water. The subtle movement of water in the interface invites the user to tilt the cell phone a bit, resulting in animation of reactive water graphics. This motor-sensory feedback loop runs continuously, building a material-based mental space and holding in place the embodied meaning that this artifact affords the tilt action and interactive animated visuals resembling naturalistic movement of water in a container. The interactive image anchors this meaning as a direct input to the blend with the user's sensorimotor experience of tilting a bottle of water, yielding an imaginative construct of a water-filled cell phone, in which elements, including animation (flowing), action (tilting), and artifacts (the cell phone and the water container) are selectively projected into, and compressed within, the blend. These compressions rely on a match between motor and sensory patterns in the immediate situation and from memory. The patterns encode not only spatial information (where to grip, which direction to tilt, etc.), but also temporal data (how fast to move, when to pause, etc.).

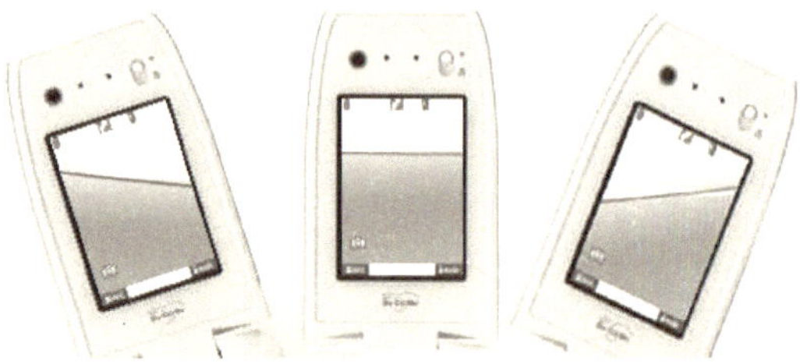

FIGURE 4. The water-level interface of NEC N702iS

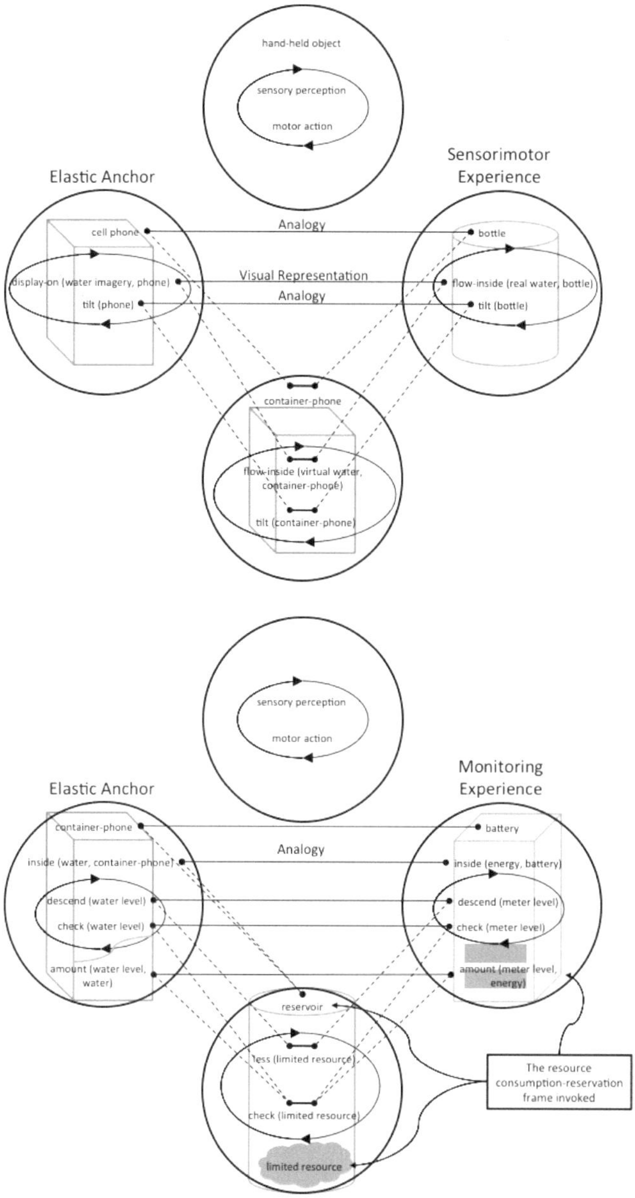


FIGURE 5. Two levels of blending taking place in the water-level interface.

What makes the artifact even more intriguing is that the computer-generated water level is synchronized with the battery level of the phone. When checking the water level intermittently (just like checking the battery level of an ordinary cell phone), the user notices that the water level descends gradually, reflecting the ongoing energy consumption in the container-phone. This articulation further incites the secondary blend of water with energy in the battery. The generic space now includes a concept of a level indicator, which reflects the amount of a particular resource left. In the blend, the outer-space analogy link between the water level and the battery meter level is compressed tightly into an inner-space category relation: the water level is a battery meter. The blend might then be elaborated into an imaginative narrative about someone in some harsh environment checking how much water is left in a bottle or similar tales of water-conservation. The monitoring of water consumption invokes a common frame nowadays: conservation of energy or other scarce natural resources. The elaboration of such a blend could leave the user a strong message: 'save the juice!' Figure 5 illustrates the two levels of blends in the water level interface. In the first level, the generic space consists of a concept of the motor-sensory loop, together with a handheld artifact. In the blend, there are compressions of outer-space representation links (a type of vital relation; here representation of virtual water imagery displayed on the phone is linked with actual liquid water flowing inside the bottle), and compressions of outer-space analogies (e.g. tilting the cell phone is linked with tilting the bottle), forming a new concept (the cell phone contains virtual water). The output is an imaginative blend of a water-filled container-phone. The second meaning, coupling the water level and energy consumption, supports the imagination of a metaphorical narrative in the secondary blend (in the sense of Turner (1996), the narrative is a small spatial story).

### 6.3 The Web Interface of SnowDays

SnowDays (http://snowdays.me) is a website incorporating textual messaging into animated imagery. The site depicts a snowy scene in which each falling snowflake has been previously crafted by a web visitor. Visitors may leave messages 'inside' flakes; recipients are notified by the site. Any site visitor may also go to the page and respond. The website projects an illusion of messaging through snowflakes in an animated world (see Figure 6).

The animated snowfall on the website is able to constitute multiple levels of understanding. When a visitor gazes at the graphical scene and moves the mouse pointer over a particular falling flake, a close-up view of the snowflake pops up and an immediate blend arises. The link between the falling graphic (technically called a sprite) and an actual falling flake in the

FIGURE 6. Cutout snowflakes tailor-made by individual users carry their greeting messages evocative of personal memories.

two input spaces is compressed into a representation relation in the blended space: a virtual flake in delicate sixfold symmetry. The motor action of moving a mouse or a finger across the touchpad relates to the act of catching a digital snowflake to examining a real snowflake in one's past experience. Similarly, the perception of zooming in the interface relates to the act of looking closely at something in past experience. These links are compressed into an imaginative act of pointing in order to examine a virtual flake in a GUI window reminiscent of a real window overlooking a snowy scene.

The other features of SnowDays virtual snowflakes are even more intriguing. Since each flake carries a message from its creator to a particular receiver, this messaging function makes the flake comparable to airmail or a note from the sky. The website narrows the distance between the sender and the receiver. Second, since the sender tailor-makes a snowflake for the receiver, with the web tool provided by SnowDays, the tool simulates the technique many people learn for constructing snowflake-like cutouts in elementary school. The memory of such experiences can be integrated with the sensorimotor experience of using the website, and then compressed into an imaginative act of constructing a tailor-made handcrafted paper snowflake together with a written greeting and then letting the sky send it to someone special (see Figure 7). In this blend, the season's greetings frame is invoked, including tailor-made greeting cards, greeting messages, air mailings, and possibly replies. This metaphorical blend elaborates an imaginative narrative of exchanging heartfelt blessings and handcrafted gifts with someone from a distance in a lonely winter day. When the attendant visceral and nostalgic association is triggered, the hidden meaning can be evocative and affective: 'you are not alone!'

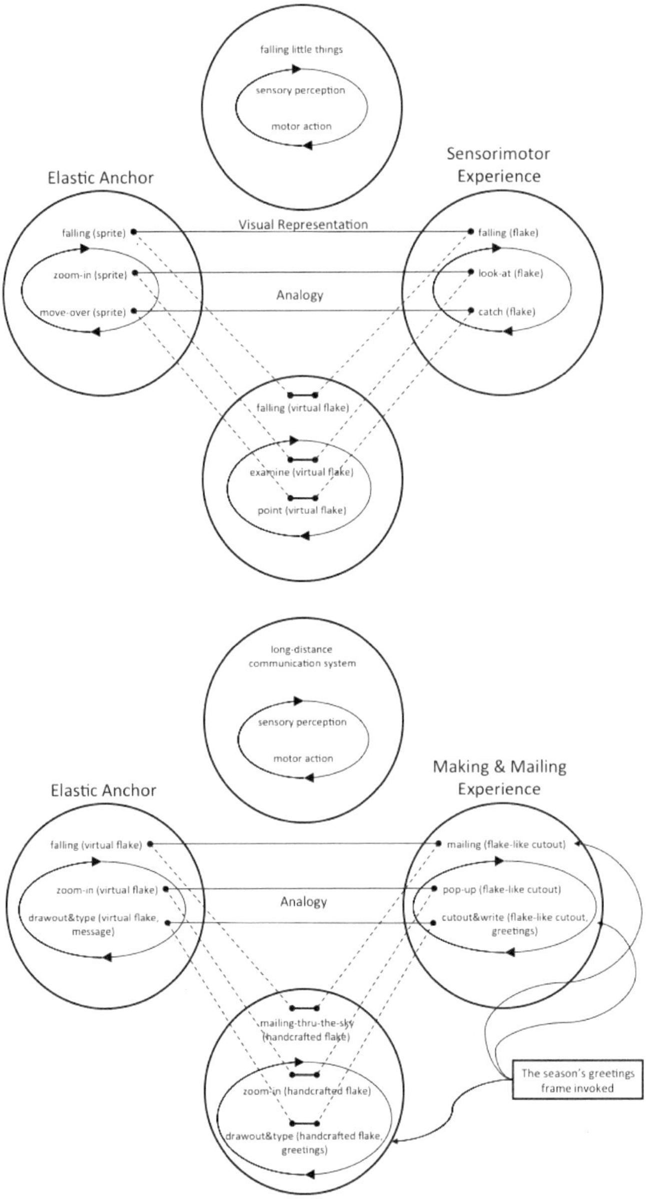


FIGURE 7. Two levels of blends taking place in SnowDays.

# 7 Conclusion and Implications

Elastic anchors embody sensation and meaning in flexible forms. The concept of the elastic anchor is grounded in terms of previously theorized cognitive processes such as material anchors along with conceptual metaphors and blends along with results from neuroscience. Elastic anchors render dynamic imaginative elaboration of blends possible. The analyses above show that elastic anchors in imaginative blends of concepts are the key to understanding animated interfaces at both immediate and metaphorical levels.

Our account provides an embodied cognition approach to understanding animated phenomena in digital media. More specifically, our analyses, spanning diverse kinds of animated computer interfaces, provide evidence for the tight relationship and unstable border between material and conceptual images. More broadly and more importantly, the argument here provides an embodied cognition approach to understanding production of expressive and artistic meanings, an underexplored area in cognitive science necessary for better understanding the nature of humanistic interpretation of artworks and creative artifacts at large.

# References


Arnheim, Rudolf. 1969. *Visual Thinking*. Berkeley: University of California Press.

Chow, Kenny K. N. and D. Fox Harrell. 2009. Material-Based Imagination: Embodied Cognition in Animated Images. Paper presented to the Digital Art and Culture 2009, Univeristy of California, Irvine USA, 2009.

_____. 2012. Understanding Material-Based Imagination: Cognitive Coupling of Animation and User Action in Interactive Digital Artworks. *Leonardo Electronic Almanac* 17:50–65.

Fauconnier, Gilles. 1985. *Mental Spaces: Aspects of Meaning Construction in Natural Language*. Cambridge, Mass.: MIT Press.

_____. 2001. Conceptual Blending and Analogy. *The Analogical Mind : Perspectives from Cognitive Science*, ed. by D. Gentner, K. J. Holyoak and B. N. Kokinov, 255–85. Cambridge, Mass.: MIT Press.

Fauconnier, Gilles and Mark Turner. 2002. *The Way We Think : Conceptual Blending and the Mind's Hidden Complexities*. New York: Basic Books.

Fillmore, C. 1985. Frames and the Semantics of Understanding. *Quaderni di Semantica* 1:222–54.

Hutchins, Edwin. 2005. Material Anchors for Conceptual Blends. *Journal of Pragmatics* 37:1555-77.

Johnson, Mark. 2008. *The Meaning of the Body: Aesthetics of Human Understanding*. Chicago, Ill.: University of Chicago Press.

Lakoff, George and Mark Johnson. 2003. *Metaphors We Live By*. Chicago: University of Chicago Press.

Mitchell, W. J. Thomas. 1986. *Iconology: Image, Text, Ideology*. Chicago: University of Chicago Press.

Rizzolatti, Giacomo and Laila Craighero. 2004. The Mirror-Neuron System. *Annual Review of Neuroscience* 27:169–92.

Rizzolatti, Giacomo, Luciano Fadiga, Vittorio Gallese and Leonardo Fogassi. 1996. Premotor cortex and the recognition of motor actions. *Cognitive Brain Research* 3:131–41.

Rizzolatti, Giacomo and Corrado Sinigaglia. 2008. *Mirrors in the Brain: How Our Minds Share Actions and Emotions*. Oxford: Oxford University Press.

Stafford, Barbara Maria. 2007. *Echo Objects: The Cognitive Work of Images*. Chicago: University of Chicago Press.

Turner, Mark. 1996. *The Literary Mind*. New York: Oxford University Press.